GREEK COINS
AND THEIR VALUES

By

DAVID R. SEAR

Volume II

ASIA AND NORTH AFRICA

London

A CATALOGUE OF GREEK COINS by G. ASKEW, 1951
GREEK COINS AND THEIR VALUES by H. A. SEABY and J. KOZOLUBSKI
First Edition 1959
Second Edition (by H. A. SEABY) 1966
Second Edition (*revised prices*) 1975

GREEK COINS AND THEIR VALUES (Volume I: Europe) by David R. Sear, 1978

Volume II: Asia and North Africa by David R. Sear 1979

Photographs by P. Frank Purvey

© SEABY PUBLICATIONS LTD., 1979

Distributed by
B. A. SEABY LTD.
AUDLEY HOUSE
11 MARGARET STREET, LONDON, W1N 8AT

also

Numismatic Fine Arts, Inc.,
POB 3788, 342 North Rodeo Drive,
Beverly Hills, California 90210, U.S.A.

Whitman Publishing Co.,
1220 Mound Avenue,
Racine, Wisconsin 53404, U.S.A.

M. R. Roberts,
Wynyard Coin Centre,
7, Hunter Arcade,
Sydney, N.S.W. 2000,
Australia.

All rights reserved. No part of this publication may be reproduced, stored in a retrieval system, or transmitted, in any form or by any means, electronic, mechanical, photocopying, recording or otherwise, without the prior permission of Seaby Publications Ltd.

ISBN 0 900652 50 0

Printed in England by ROBERT STOCKWELL LTD., LONDON, SE1 IYP

CONTENTS

CONTENTS

PREFACE

Two decades have now elapsed since the last major revision of Seaby's Greek coin catalogue was undertaken by H. A. Seaby and J. Kozolubski in 1959. This work, which I myself assisted in compiling, proved immensely popular with collectors in the U.K. and overseas, and went through several editions. I am glad to have had the opportunity of preparing the successor to this catalogue and hope that it will be equally well received by classical numismatists everywhere.

The precise chronology of much of the ancient Greek coinage remains controversial, even after a century of intense study. Recently, argument has centred on the date of the famous "Demareteion" dekadrachm of Syracuse, with all its implications for the subsequent chronology of the 5th Century Sicilian coinage. Similarly, there is dispute over the Athens dekadrachm. Even in the late Hellenistic period there are problems with the exact dating of the vast "new style" issues of the Athenian mint, despite the masterly treatment of the subject by Miss Margaret Thompson.

The evidence of coin hoards, which is now being interpreted with great skill by the leading scholars of Greek numismatics, is forcing us to make many adjustments to the traditionally accepted dates for the introduction and spread of coinage in the ancient world. The message of every archaic hoard analysed would seem to be the same—the first Greek coins are not as early as we used to think. Little, if any, coinage was produced before the last quarter of the 7th Century B.C.; and the first European issues—those of Aigina—are probably no earlier than *circa* 550 B.C., a century and a half later than the traditional date for their introduction. This down-dating has had a significant effect on our view of the archaic period of Greek coinage. We now see it as little more than a century of exciting expansion and development, most of it, indeed, compressed into just seven decades (550-480 B.C.). This is very different from the view held by previous generations of numismatists, who saw the archaic Greek coinage as something which evolved quite gradually over more than two hundred years.

In preparing this new catalogue I have tried to incorporate most of the current views on chronology, attribution, and interpretation of types which are the result of the immense amount of research undertaken over the past few decades by scholars in Europe and America. The scope of the listing has also been enlarged to include representative examples of each period of issue for every mint. Bronze coins have received particular attention, as so many collectors these days have to specialize in coins at the lower end of the price scale. For this reason, and also because they are generally more difficult to date with precision than the silver issues, I have listed the bronze coins separately under each mint heading. In the cases of Italy and Sicily the lists of bronzes are entirely separate from the precious-metal issues. Once again this is for the convenience of collectors, many of whom specialize in the bronze coins of the western mints, where token money originated.

Another new feature of this work is the incorporation of photographs in the text. The advantages of having description and illustration printed together on the same page are obvious, and the popularity of *Byzantine Coins and Their Values*, published five years ago, has encouraged us to adopt the same arrangement in the case of the present catalogue. The illustrations are exceedingly numerous and should add greatly to the value of the book as an aid to identifying Greek coins.

In order to carry out these improvements the size of the work had to be increased to the point where it was no longer feasible to publish it in a single volume. Accordingly, the decision was taken to divide it into two volumes—EUROPE, and ASIA & NORTH AFRICA. Volume One includes Greek coins of Spain and Gaul, Italy, Sicily, the Balkans, Greece, the Cyclades and Crete, together with Celtic issues of western Europe (including Britain) and the Danubian area. Volume Two deals with the coins of the Asiatic Greeks (the earliest coin-issuing states), the Persian Empire, the Hellenistic Kingdoms and subsequent autonomous issues, North Africa and Carthage. This two-volume work should prove to be an invaluable aid to the collector, in identifying and valuing the coins in his collection, and to the student of Greek art and coinage, to whom it presents a fully illustrated documentation of the development of numismatic art in every state of the Greek world.

The various forms of spelling for many ancient Greek names have occasioned a certain amount of confusion amongst collectors. The standard practice in the past, for most popular publications, has been the adoption of the later, Roman, form rather than the original Greek name. Thus, Thourioi is more often referred to as Thurium, Akragas as Agrigentum and Taras as Tarentum. Recently, the trend has been to revert to the original spellings in books dealing specifically with Greek coins, and collectors who have read G. K. Jenkins' excellent

Ancient Greek Coins, published in 1972, will already be aware of this. I have followed this practice in the present publication and feel sure that collectors will soon familiarize themselves with the different spellings. In many cases I have also given the later form, in parentheses, following the mint-heading. Inevitably, of course, I have not been able to achieve total uniformity in this. Athens, for example, is so well known to English-speaking people under this modern version of its name that it would have been foolish to start calling it "Athenai" in this catalogue. And there are other lesser known instances where the precise original form of the name would be unacceptable for one reason or another. Nevertheless, I feel that I have followed the right path in endeavouring to get back to the original Greek names in a catalogue which is devoted to Greek coinage.

A considerable amount of research has gone into the estimation of values as quoted in this catalogue, and my thanks are due to Gavin Manton, of Seaby's Ancient Department, with whom I collaborated in this task. However, in the present situation of uncertain currencies and considerable market fluctuations it must be borne in mind that the valuations here expressed can only be taken as an approximate guide, especially those quoted for rarities, in which the Greek series abounds. The prices given are for specimens in an average state of preservation—*VF* in the case of gold, electrum and silver, *F* in the case of billon and bronze. Poorly preserved examples are, of course, worth much less than the values quoted; unusually well-preserved coins and those of better than average style are worth substantially more.

Almost all the coins illustrated in this catalogue are from the National Collection, and I should like to express my deep gratitude to the Keeper and staff of the Department of Coins and Medals, British Museum, for the facilities which they so readily granted to Frank Purvey and myself. With one of the finest collections of Greek coins in the world at our disposal we were able, with the minimum of difficulty, to assemble and photograph a superb selection of pieces, adding immeasurably to the value of the catalogue as a work of reference. Frank Purvey's photographs are of his usual matchless standard, and I should also like to thank him for all the help and encouragement which he has given me in the preparation of this work. My thanks are also due to Terry Hardaker, of Oxford, for the superb maps which he has produced for both volumes of this catalogue; and to David Sellwood for advance information on his reattributions of certain types within the Parthian series. My wife, Margaret, assisted in the laborious tasks of proof-reading and compiling the index. The four tables of ancient alphabets are reproduced by kind permission of Oxford University Press.

Little Melton, Norfolk.
August, 1979

DAVID R. SEAR

TO THE MEMORY
OF MY FATHER

JOSEPH
JULIUS
SEAR

ON COLLECTING GREEK COINS

Many potential collectors of this series might hesitate these days to embark on a hobby which, on the face of it, appears to be beyond their financial resources. Greek coins have so much to offer the collector that I feel it would be a pity for him to dismiss them, in favour of something less interesting but less costly, without going a little further into the subject.

Greek numismatics spans a period of no less than nine centuries, though for the last three hundred years Greek coins were merely a secondary 'local currency' in the eastern half of the Roman Empire. And for several centuries before this Rome had exerted a strong political influence over most of the Greek world. From their origins, then, shortly before 600 B.C. to the time of the establishment of the Roman Empire, Greek coins underwent six centuries of development and change, and this is the period covered by *Greek Coins and Their Values*. These six centuries have bequeathed to us a truly remarkable array of coins, issues of a multitude of independent city-states as well as of the great kingdoms of the Hellenistic age. The rise and fall of tyrants and of whole communities are faithfully chronicled in the numismatic record which has come down to us, providing fertile ground for the growth of a collection which can be a source of endless interest and satisfaction to its owner. Such a collection need not be large, as long as the coins are carefully selected, and need not be very costly; though, of course, those fortunate few with large sums to invest will, by specializing in Greek coins, have the opportunity of possessing some of the most beautiful numismatic creations which mankind has ever produced.

It must be stated that many of the silver issues will be beyond the price range of the majority of collectors. The products of tiny city states of limited resources, and only circulating within a small area, these coins are often of great beauty and command prices commensurate with their rarity. Of course there are many exceptions to this—cities like Athens and powerful kingdoms such as Macedon, Syria and Egypt—which were prosperous enough to issue vast quantities of silver money. Examples of these, even the collector of quite modest means should be able to acquire. But a really exciting field is opened up by the masses of token bronze currency put into circulation by the Greeks. Originating in Sicily in the mid-5th Century B.C., bronze coins were not widely adopted until the first half of the 4th Century, but thereafter quickly replaced the inconveniently small fractional denominations in silver. Greek bronze coins can be costly in the highest grades of preservation, but they are seldom seen in this state and if the collector does not set himself an unrealistically high standard he should be able to assemble a really worthwhile collection at quite modest cost. The problem of counterfeit coins is also largely avoided by the collector who specializes in bronzes, which brings us to another important topic.

Forgery of Greek coins, particularly of the most spectacular types in gold and silver, has been going on for hundreds of years, but the most dangerous copies have been produced in the 19th and 20th Centuries. It is not possible, in a brief introduction such as this, to go deeply into the question of recognition of forgeries. The most obvious things to look for are indications of casting (air-bubbles on the surface, filing on the edge) and signs that the piece may be a modern electrotype copy (traces of the joining together of the two halves of the coin round the edge). The exact weight is also of importance, as Greek gold and silver coins conform to quite strict standards and many forgeries do not fall within the correct range of weights. The recognition of die-struck forgeries, however, requires a degree of experience and expertise which few collectors possess, and for this reason it cannot be too strongly emphasized that one should never purchase expensive Greek gold and silver coins from a dubious source. Some forgeries are so good that they have been known to pass undetected through the hands even of experienced numismatists. But if coins are purchased from a reputable dealer one will always have the assurance that if a piece is proved to be false it will be taken back and your money refunded without question.

Before commencing the formation of a collection one would be well advised to read an authoritative book covering all aspects of ancient Greek coinage. Having obtained a good grounding in the subject it will be easier to plan the development of a collection, and one may be saved the costly error of purchasing pieces not really required. The books recommended in the previous *Greek Coins and Their Values* have been somewhat outdated by recent developments in the study of Greek coins, so works published within the past decade are to be preferred. My recommendation would be G. K. Jenkins' *Ancient Greek Coins* published in 1972 by Barrie and Jenkins in the series *The World of Numismatics*. Scholarship of the highest calibre combined with superb illustrations, many in full colour, make this an invaluable volume to anyone with an interest in Greek numismatics, and the beginner will find the text easy to follow.

A BRIEF ACCOUNT OF GREEK HISTORY AND THE DEVELOPMENT OF COINAGE

For several centuries prior to the invention of coined money the Greeks, then emerging from the dark ages following the destruction of Mycenaean civilization, had been engaged in colonization. The pressures created by an expanding population, together with the desire to foster trade led to the establishment of settlements far from the mother cities. Southern Italy and Sicily, and the northern coastline of the Aegean were areas particularly popular with the settlers, but colonies were also established in Spain, southern Gaul, north Africa and along the Black Sea coastline.

Prior to the advent of coinage, then, the Greeks were already widely scattered throughout much of the Mediterranean world, so it is hardly surprising that the new invention, once established, spread so rapidly over a large area. It is doubtful if we shall ever know the precise origin of the first coins but we can feel reasonably sure that this remarkable development occurred in the latter part of the 7th Century B.C., in western Asia Minor (modern Turkey). Whether it was the Ionian Greeks or their eastern neighbours, the Lydians, who made the first crude attempts at coinage it is impossible to say. But examples of these primitive pieces—globules of electrum without obverse or reverse design—have been found at the Ionian city of Ephesos; whilst the metal of which they are composed occurs as a natural alloy in the silt of the river which passes through the Lydian capital of Sardis.

Electrum sixth-stater of Ionia, late 7th Cent. B.C.   *Silver stater of Aigina, circa 530 B.C.*

In 560 B.C. Kroisos (Croesus) came to the Lydian throne. His reign was significant for the development of coinage, as he was responsible for the introduction of the first bimetallic currency—coins struck in both gold and silver, instead of the alloy electrum alone. This provided a much greater range of denominations and is evidence of the important part coinage was already playing in the economic life of the Lydian kingdom. In 546 B.C. Kroisos was defeated by Cyrus, King of the Medes and Persians. The Lydian kingdom ceased to exist and the Greek cities of Asia Minor were obliged to acknowledge Persian suzerainty. This was the beginning of the long struggle between Greeks and Persians which culminated in Alexander's epic eastern campaign more than two centuries later.

The second half of the 6th Century witnessed the westward expansion of coinage from its origins in Asia Minor. Probably the first European city to issue coins was Aigina, situated on an island between Attica and eastern Peloponnese. Soon after followed the earliest coins of mints such as Athens, Corinth and the Euboian cities of Chalkis and Eretria. All of these mints were active from the middle of the century, or within the following decade. From these beginnings originated two of the important weight-standards to which many later Greek coinages adhered. The Aiginetic standard, based on a silver didrachm-stater of about 12 grams, became very widespread in central Greece, Peloponnesos and the Aegean islands, including Crete. The Attic weight, with a didrachm of about 8.5 grams and, later, a tetradrachm of 17 grams, was to become the principal standard of a later period, following Athens' domination of the Aegean world throughout the latter part of the 5th Century. In the west the closing decades of the 6th Century also saw much activity in coin production at the colonies in southern Italy and in Sicily. A unique type of coin production was used at some of the Italian mints, in which the obverse type was 'mirrored' on the reverse, though incuse instead of in relief. This peculiar technique was abandoned in the early part of the 5th Century.

Silver stater of Poseidonia in Italy,
circa 530 B.C.

Silver siglos of Darius I of Persia,
circa 500 B.C.

The conflict between Greeks and Persians which had been threatening in the closing decades of the 6th Century, suddenly erupted in 499 B.C. with the revolt of the Ionian cities of Asia Minor against Persian domination.   Despite Athenian help the rebellion collapsed in 494 B.C., but there was only a short respite before hostilities recommenced.   This time (490 B.C.) Darius of Persia sent a naval expedition against Athens, but after initial successes the Persian forces were decisively beaten at the battle of Marathon and were later obliged to return home. Darius died five years later and his son and successor, Xerxes, resolved to avenge the Persian humiliation by a full-scale invasion of Greece.   This eventually took place in 480 B.C., after much preparation, when an immense Persian army crossed the Hellespont and advanced through Thrace and Macedon into Greece, supported by a large fleet.   Against all the odds the Greeks first checked the enemy at Thermopylai, then destroyed the Persian fleet at the battle of Salamis and, finally (in 479 B.C.), defeated the invading army at Plataia.   This brought the conflict to an end and the Persians never again intervened directly in the affairs of mainland Greece.

These momentous events were to have far-reaching effects on the subsequent history of Greece.   Athens emerged as the 'saviour of the Greeks' and capitalized on this to extend her influence throughout the Aegean world.   The Confederacy of Delos, constituted soon after the victory over the Persians, was ostensibly an Athenian-led alliance of independent maritime states, dedicated to freeing the Ionian cities of Asia Minor from the Persian yoke.   In reality, it quickly developed into an Athenian maritime empire, the annual contributions of the member-states being paid to Athens, making her the richest and most powerful state in mainland Greece.

Silver tetradrachm of Athens,
circa 485 B.C.

Electrum stater of Kyzikos,
circa 430 B.C.

In the decades following the Persian wars Greek coinage was entering a transitional stage which was to see the stiff and unrealistic style of the early (archaic) period gradually give way to the more elegant representations of the classical era.   Proper reverse types were now being employed by most mints in preference to the simple incuse squares which had typified most archaic issues.   Silver was the primary metal used for coin production, right down to the tiniest denominations which were inconveniently small to use.   These were not generally replaced by token bronze coinage until the first half of the following century (after 400 B.C.). In Asia Minor, however, electrum—the metal of the earliest coins—was still extensively employed by important mints such as Kyzikos, Phokaia and Mytilene (the chief city of the island of Lesbos).   As the power of Athens grew she attempted to place restrictions on the freedom of other states to issue silver coins, culminating in the enigmatic 'Coinage Decree' of *circa* 449 B.C. promulgated by Perikles, the author of Athenian imperialism.   This measure brought about the severe curtailment of issues from many mints during the sixth and seventh decades of the century.   But with the outbreak of the Peloponnesian War, in 431 B.C., Athens' iron grip was relaxed.

Silver tetradrachm of Syracuse by the artist Kimon, circa 410 B.C.

The West (south Italy and Sicily) was relatively unaffected by these events and developments in Greece. Here, at about the same time as the Persian defeat, another great enemy of the Greeks—the Carthaginians—suffered humiliation at the hands of Gelon, tyrant of Syracuse, when they attacked the Sicilian colonies. Thereafter Syracuse became the dominant Greek state in the West, and the artists producing the dies for her coinage were in the forefront of a remarkable advance in numismatic art. The Greek coinage of Sicily in the closing decades of the 5th Century was to reach heights of artistic brilliance which were unmatched elsewhere and which served as an inspiration to the die-engravers of later periods. Notable amongst the beautiful creations of this period are the noble dekadrachms by the engravers Euainetos and Kimon, and also the latter's superb rendering of the facing female head in his masterpiece—the Arethusa head—on a Syracusan tetradrachm. Many of the Greek mints in Sicily participated in this blossoming of numismatic art, but the whole movement was brought to an abrupt end by the Carthaginian invasions at the end of the century (commencing 409 B.C.).

Silver tetradrachm of Athens,
circa 430 B.C.

Athenian domination of the Aegean world was not destined to last beyond the closing years of this century. The Athenian mint, with its plentiful supplies of silver from the mines of Laurion, had produced prodigious quantities of tetradrachms from *circa* 449 B.C. Much of this wealth was used to finance grandiose building schemes in the city, such as the Parthenon, but after 431 B.C. ever-increasing sums were required to defray the costs of war. The great Peloponnesian War was sparked-off by an incident at the Boeotian city of Plataia. It dragged on, intermittently, for the next twenty-seven years and was, in essence, a struggle for supremacy between the old arch-enemies, Athens and Sparta. Finally, in 404 B.C., Athens capitulated. She was financially and politically ruined, and although she made a remarkable recovery from this disaster in the first half of the following century, she never again achieved the pre-eminence which she had enjoyed during the age of Perikles. Her mantle now passed to the Spartans who soon showed themselves to be too insular to establish and maintain a position of leadership amongst the Greek states. The first half of the 4th Century was a period of seemingly interminable strife, but despite the political confusion, these years saw the production of some of the most beautiful coins in the Greek series. Classical art had now reached a peak from which it was gradually to decline.

Silver tetradrachm of the Chalkidian League
circa 385 B.C.

These were also troubled years in the West. The Carthaginians had invaded Sicily and attacked many of the Greek cities at the end of the 5th Century. Dionysios, the powerful ruler of Syracuse, conducted a long and inconclusive war against the invaders which resulted in a division of the island between Greeks and Carthaginians. Dionysios also adopted an aggressive policy in southern Italy in order to extend the influence of Syracuse. But two great powers were beginning to arise on the fringes of the Greek world. In the north, the Kingdom of Macedon was emerging from a period of confusion, led by its brilliant young ruler Philip II (359-336 B.C.). Philip's ambitions knew no bounds, and he and his son, Alexander the Great, transformed the political face of the ancient world in less than three decades. In the west, however, another power was stirring; one which was destined, ultimately, to engulf the whole of the Mediterranean basin and reduce all the Greek lands to provincial status. That power was Rome.

Gold stater of Philip II of Macedon
(359-336 B.C.)

Silver tetradrachm of Amphipolis,
circa 380 B.C.

In 357 B.C. Philip captured Amphipolis, an Athenian colony near the rich silver-mining area of Mt. Pangaion in eastern Macedon. Nine years later he destroyed Olynthos, the capital city of the Greek colonies forming the Chalkidian League. In 338 B.C., at the battle of Chaeronea, the combined forces of Athens and Thebes were defeated by Philip, who was now acknowledged as the master of Greece. At a congress of Greek states, held at Corinth, Philip was chosen to lead an attack on the Persian Empire, in order to liberate the Greek cities of Asia Minor. Preparations for this expedition were already far advanced when, in 336 B.C., Philip was assassinated and was succeeded on the Macedonian throne by his son, Alexander, known to posterity as 'the Great.' The remarkable series of military campaigns, by which Alexander destroyed the Persian power and established a Greek empire in its place, need not be described in detail here. Suffice it to say that his thirteen-year reign was a turning-point in Greek history. The age of the city-states was over; its place being taken by an era marked by the dominance of great Kingdoms, such as the Ptolemaic in Egypt and the Seleukid in Syria and the east. With the eventual weakening and disintegration of these kingdoms came the spread of Roman power in the eastern Mediterranean.

Silver stater of Olympia, circa 360 B.C.

These great political changes were reflected in the coinage. As already mentioned, the first half of the 4th Century B.C., during which many of the city-states enjoyed their final period of autonomy, produced some of the artistic masterpieces of the Greek coinage. Noteworthy are the magnificent tetradrachms of Amphipolis with facing head of Apollo; those of Olynthos, in the name of the Chalkidians, with reverse type lyre; some of the staters issued at Olympia by the Eleans, with noble heads of Zeus and his consort Hera; and the fine staters of the Arkadians depicting, on the reverse, Pan seated upon a rock. Some of the earlier issues of Philip II of Macedon are also of a high artistic standard; but as the territorial extent of Philip's realm was extended and the coinage was produced in ever-increasing quantities, so the quality of the workmanship declined. This is particularly noticeable in the coins issued after his death, though still in the name of Philip. Alexander's money was an imperial coinage in every sense, unlike anything which the Greek world had seen before, with the possible exception of the Athenian tetradrachms of the Periklean age. But it set the pattern for centuries to come— mass produced regal issues largely replacing autonomous coins of individual cities. Inevitably this brought about a decline in artistic standards. When many of the cities regained a degree of independence, in the 2nd Century B.C., the process had gone too far to be reversed. Some individual pieces amongst the autonomous coins of the late Hellenistic age might be called attractive rather than beautiful.

Silver tetradrachm of Alexander the Great   *Gold stater of Philip III Arrhidaeus*
(336-323 B.C.)   *(323-317 B.C.)*

On the death of Alexander at Babylon (June, 323 B.C.) his vast realm, stretching from Macedon to India, became the object of endless disputes between his generals. These 'wars of the Diadochi' ultimately led to the formation of a number of independent kingdoms, though in the early years the appearance of unity was maintained. Officially, Alexander was succeeded by his infant son, Alexander IV, and by an idiot-brother of the great king, called Arrhidaeus, now named Philip (III). During the minority of the boy-kings the responsibility for administering the huge empire rested with men such as Perdikkas, Antipater, Antigonos the One-eyed, Ptolemy, Seleukos and Lysimachos. These were the true successors of Alexander and some of them went on to found dynasties which endured for many generations. The unfortunate Alexander IV and Philip III met violent ends; both were dead within twelve years of Alexander the Great's decease.

Silver tetradrachm of Ptolemy I of Egypt, circa 310-305 B.C.

Other than the original Kingdom of Macedon, the two great realms to emerge from these struggles were the Kingdom of Egypt, founded by Ptolemy, and the dominions of Seleukos, commonly known as the Seleukid Empire, comprising the greater part of Alexander's conquests. About the middle of the 3rd Century B.C. the Seleukid Empire was further divided when the eastern provinces of Baktria and Parthia each achieved independence; the latter destined to survive for nearly five centuries and to become the troublesome eastern neighbour of the Roman Empire.   Meanwhile, in the west the power of Rome was rapidly growing.   Following her victory over Carthage in the First Punic War (241 B.C.) Rome acquired her first province—Sicily—and to this was added Spain in the closing years of the century.   At about the same time came the first conflict with the Macedonian Kingdom, now ruled by the energetic Philip V

Silver tetradrachm of Philip V of Macedon (221-179 B.C.)

(221-179 B.C.).   In 197 B.C., at the battle of Kynoskephalai, the Romans inflicted a heavy defeat on Philip.   The following year the Roman general Flamininus made his celebrated proclamation of the 'Freedom of Greece' at the Isthmian Games.   But in reality Greece had merely become subject to a new and more powerful master.   The once proud Macedonian Kingdom lingered on for three decades more, under Philip V and his son Perseus, but was finally destroyed by the Romans in 168 B.C.   Macedonia was divided into four republics and in 146 B.C. was reduced to provincial status.

Silver tetradrachm of Antiochos the Great (223-187 B.C.)

Roman conflict with another of the great Hellenistic monarchies, the Seleukid, came soon after the Macedonian defeat at Kynoskephalai.   Antiochos III, the Great (223-187 B.C.), a bitter opponent of Rome, invaded Greece in 192 B.C. at the invitation of the Aitolians.   Defeated at Thermopylai, Antiochos fled back to Asia Minor.   The Romans relentlessly followed him there and in 190 B.C., at the battle of Magnesia (Caria), the power of the Seleukids was broken. Most of their possessions in Asia Minor were given to King Eumenes of Pergamon, Rome's ally during the campaign.   The Seleukid Kingdom, now restricted to Syria and the surrounding area, maintained a precarious existence for more than a century.   It finally succumbed to Pompey the Great in 64 B.C.   The other great Hellenistic Kingdom, that of Egypt, was the furthest removed, geographically, from Rome's eastward advance.   But Roman supremacy in the eastern Mediterranean from the early part of the 2nd Century necessitated the maintenance of friendly relations on the part of the Greek rulers of Egypt.   This policy succeeded in maintaining the existence of the Ptolemaic Kingdom longer than that of any of the other

Silver tetradrachm of Cleopatra VII of Egypt, Askalon mint, 30 B.C.

Hellenistic states.   Rome did not intervene directly in Egyptian affairs until 48 B.C., when Caesar, in pursuit of Pompey, came to Alexandria and found himself involved in a dynastic squabble between Queen Cleopatra and her brother Ptolemy.   The story of Cleopatra, Caesar and Mark Antony is well known, and need not be recounted here.   The upshot of the whole affair was the termination of the three hundred year-old Greek dynasty in Egypt. Henceforth the country became part of the Roman Empire and was administered as a private estate of the emperor.

"New style" silver tetradrachm of Athens, circa 157/6 B.C.

The coinage in this final phase of Greek history is varied, interesting, but mostly lacking in artistic merit.   The Kingdoms of Macedon, Pergamon, Syria and Egypt produced a considerable volume of currency, mostly silver tetradrachms, in continuation of the traditions established by Alexander the Great and his successors.   Side by side with these, and in ever increasing numbers as the power of the Kingdoms declined, came the autonomous issues of individual city-states and groups of cities which banded together for reasons of trade and defence.   The large, spread flans, which had typified the tetradrachm coinage of the later Macedonian Kings, were adopted as the norm by many of the newly-liberated states in the 2nd Century B.C.   Athens led the way with her vast and complex 'new style' coinage; whilst in Asia Minor mints such as Kyzikos, Lampsakos, Tenedos, Kyme, Myrina, Kolophon, Herakleia, Magnesia and Smyrna produced extensive issues of large and impressive tetradrachms.   Also much in evidence were the coinages of the various confederacies and leagues, notably that of Thessaly in the north, with its handsome double victoriati, and the Achaean League in Peloponnesos, with its prodigious output of little hemidrachms issued by more than twenty mints.   As Rome's grip on Greece and the eastern Mediterranean area gradually tightened, so this last flowering of Greek coinage withered.   In the final stages of this process most of the Greek cities were deprived of the right to issue silver coinage and many ceased issuing altogether.

Silver double victoriatus of the Thessalian   Silver hemidrachm of the Achaean League,
League, 196-146 B.C.   Patrai mint, 196-146 B.C.

However, under the Roman Empire there was a revival of coinage at many of the Greek mints in the East, particularly in Asia Minor.   This 'Greek Imperial' coinage survived well into the 3rd Century A.D. until the political and economic collapse of the Roman Empire put an end to it.   Most, though not all, Greek Imperial issues bore an imperial portrait as the obverse type, whilst the reverse often featured an inscription or type of purely local interest—names of games and festivals, names of magistrates and provincial administrators, types picturing local architecture and statuary.   This final phase of Greek coinage, providing a wealth of detailed information on the eastern provinces of the Roman Empire, is not included in this present work.   Chronologically, the Greek Imperial series belongs to Roman times and will be given full treatment in a new catalogue to be published at some future date.

GREEK COIN TYPES

The designs appearing on ancient Greek coins are remarkably varied. Even the issues of one mint can exhibit a surprising diversity of types, but the underlying theme is nearly always religious.

Silver tetradrachm of Athens,
circa 510-505 B.C.

In the archaic period a design is normally found only on the obverse of the coin, produced by the lower (anvil) die. The reverse die, consisting merely of a square or oblong punch, was employed simply to hold the blank firmly in position during striking and to ensure that sufficient pressure was exerted to obtain a clear impression of the obverse die. Towards the end of the archaic period, as minting techniques improved, designs began appearing on the reverse dies too, though still within the incuse square, which now formed a frame for the type. Good examples of early 'double-sided' types are to be found at Athens (head of Athena/owl) and at Corinth (Pegasos/head of Athena), both types introduced at the end of the 6th Century.

Silver stater of Corinth, circa
500 B.C.

The choice of types in this formative period of Greek numismatics is of special interest. Traditions were being established which were to have a lasting influence on all subsequent coinage, right down to the present day. It was recognized, almost from the start, that here was a completely new medium for artistic expression, whilst the issuing authorities saw the opportunity of advertising the special characteristics of their states. The great diversity of deities in the Greek pantheon and the different interpretations of the roles played by each god and goddess provided scope for much local variation in religious beliefs. It is hardly surprising, therefore, that religious subjects were dominant in the earliest phases of coinage. In this way the individuality of each city could be proclaimed whilst the artist was given the greatest scope for his talents in representing the grandeur and mystery of the Olympians and their minions.

Gold third-stater of Metapontion,
late 4th Cent. B.C.

Silver tetradrachm of Ephesos,
mid-4th Cent. B.C.

Although religious types dominated the obverses and reverses of the Greek coinage down to the age of Alexander the Great, nevertheless there are many issues which do not fall within this category. The corn-ear of Metapontion, the crab of Akragas, the shield of Boeotia, the bee of Ephesos and the silphium plant of Kyrene are all emblematic types, being the official 'badges' of their states. Even here, however, there are religious connotations: the ear of corn is associated with Demeter and Persephone, whilst the bee was sacred to Artemis who was especially revered by the Ephesians. Other 'badges', such as the amphora, triskelis, knuckle-bone, wheel, etc., found on the 'Wappenmunzen' coinage of Athens, could be heraldic devices associated with the Athenian nobility of the 6th Century B.C. But, here again, a religious interpretation of the types seems more likely, with the various aspects of the cult of Athena providing the inspiration. Punning allusions to the names of cities are also not infrequently encountered. At Selinus, in Sicily, the leaf of the wild celery plant (*selinon*) is the constant obverse type of the city's archaic coinage, whilst the Aegean island of Melos similarly features the apple (*melon*). There are many such examples from mints in all parts of the Greek world.

Silver didrachm of Selinus, late 6th Cent. B.C.

With the establishment of the great Hellenistic Kingdoms in the period following the death of Alexander came a most important development in the evolution of Greek coin types—the beginnings of royal portraiture. The names of the Macedonian Kings had appeared regularly on the coinage from the first half of the 5th Century B.C., but no effigy had ever been produced by the die-engravers, not even of the great Alexander himself. Several of Alexander's successors, however, placed their portraits on their coins and once the tradition was established

Silver tetradrachm of Antiochos I of Syria (280-261 B.C.)

the heads of kings and queens became a regular feature of much of the Greek coinage from the 3rd to the 1st Century B.C. Why it was that none of the powerful tyrants of the 5th and 4th Centuries ever seized this opportunity to proclaim their position and immortalize their features must remain something of a mystery.

The main series of portrait coins were produced by the Ptolemaic dynasty in Egypt, the Seleukids of Syria and the Antigonids of Macedon. The Ptolemies, unfortunately, adopted the practice of reproducing the head of their founder, Ptolemy Soter, on most of their regular silver issues right down to the end of the dynasty. This detracts greatly from the interest of the series (and also complicates the attributions of coins to particular reigns). The Seleukid coinage, on the other hand, presents us with a portrait gallery of kings and queens spanning

Silver tetradrachm of Antimachos of Baktria (circa 171-160 B.C.)

more than two centuries. Mention should also be made here of the splendid coinage produced by the Greek rulers of Baktria and India—once the easternmost part of the Seleukid realm, but independent from the mid-3rd Century B.C. The remarkable series of portraits featured on these coins have the additional interest of being, in many cases, the only evidence for the very existence of these rulers. The Antigonids of Macedon produced some fine portrait coins in

Silver tetradrachm of Demetrios Poliorketes of Macedon (294-287 B.C.)

the 3rd and 2nd Centuries, notably tetradrachms of Demetrios Poliorketes, Philip V and Perseus; whilst the Kingdoms of Pergamon, Bithynia and Pontus all made notable contributions to numismatic portraiture in the Hellenistic age. On these regal issues religious symbolism was now mostly relegated to the reverses of the coins and each dynasty tended to adopt a tutelary deity. The earlier Seleukids favoured Apollo, who is depicted seated on the omphalos of Delphi on many of the 3rd Century silver and bronze coins. An eagle standing upon a thunderbolt, both symbolic of Zeus, is the constant reverse design for the Ptolemaic coinage in Egypt, and the bearded head of the god himself regularly occupies the obverse of the bronze denominations.

Silver tetradrachm of Mithradates III of Pontos (circa 220-185 B.C.)

In conclusion, there follows a list of some of the principal deities appearing as Greek coin types, with explanatory notes relating to their origins and functions. This list is largely the work of Lieut.-Col. J. Kozolubski and first appeared in the 1959 edition of this catalogue. The names in parentheses are the equivalent Roman deities.

Zeus Ammon on a silver tetradrachm of Kyrene, circa 360 B.C.

Ammon. Originally a Libyan divinity, probably protecting and leading the flocks, Ammon was later introduced into Egypt and Greece, where he was identified with Zeus. The head of Zeus Ammon is represented on Egyptian coins as a bearded man, diademed and with a ram's horn at the temple (Ammon's horn), the ram being sacred to him.

Aphrodite on a silver stater of Aphrodisias, circa 380 B.C.

Aphrodite (Venus). One of the twelve great Olympian divinities, Aphrodite was goddess of love and beauty. She was believed to have been created from the foam of the sea, hence she sometimes appears on coins with a sea-horse or dolphin. Others of her attributes are the myrtle, rose, apple, poppy; and doves, swans and sparrows were sacred to her. She is represented on coins nude, semi-nude or dressed and crowned, often accompanied by Eros, her child attendant. The apple she sometimes holds in her hand is the prize awarded her by Paris in the contest with Hera and Athena on Mount Ida.

Apollo with tripod on a silver tetradrachm of Seleukos II (246-226 B.C.)

Apollo. He was the sun-god, one of the great gods of the Greeks, and was the son of Zeus and Leto; he was also the god of prophecy, of song, music and the arts, and protector of flocks and herds. He punished and destroyed the wicked and overbearing, but afforded help to men in distress by warding off evil. He exercised his power of prophecy through various oracles, of which that at Delphi was the most important. The head of Apollo and his attribute the lyre are common types on early Greek coinage.

Ares (Mars). God of war and another of the great Olympian deities, Ares was the son of Zeus and Hera. He loved war for its own sake and often changed sides in assisting one or the other combatant parties, but he could be worsted in battle and even be wounded by mortals. His helmeted head, beardless or bearded, appears on many coins and his full-length figure is sometimes depicted helmeted but naked, or wearing a cuirass, and holding shield, spear or trophy. He is sometimes shown in the company of Aphrodite, whose lover he was.

Artemis and stag on a silver octobol of Ephesos, circa 270 B.C.

Artemis (Diana). One of the great divinities and sister of Apollo, Artemis was the deity of the chase, goddess of the Moon, and protectress of the young. In Ionia, and in particular as goddess of the famous temple of Ephesos, she took over the fructifying and all-nourishing powers of nature from an older Asiatic divinity whom the Greeks, who settled in that area, renamed Artemis. The coin types representing Artemis are very varied for she is represented as a huntress with bow and arrow, running with a hound or killing a stag. As Artemis Tauropolos she is portrayed riding a bull holding a veil over her head. Yet another type is the cultus-statue of the Ephesian Artemis, standing facing, and she is also shown carrying one or two torches.

Asklepios (Aesculapius). God of medicine and healing, he is shown as a man of mature years, leaning on a staff about which a serpent is entwined. Sometimes the boy Telesphoros, the personification of the genius of recovery, stands by his side. Serpents, symbols of prudence and renovation, were sacred to Asklepios for they were believed to have the power of guarding wells and discovering healing herbs.

Athena with Nike on a silver stater of Aphrodisias, circa 380 B.C.

Athena (Minerva). Surnamed Pallas, and sometimes known by this name alone, Athena was goddess of wisdom, patroness of agriculture, industry and the arts. She guided men through the dangers of war, where victory was gained by prudence, courage and perseverance. Her full-length image, or bust or head only, are amongst the commonest of Greek coin types. She is usually wearing the Spartan sleeveless chiton, peplos, and helmet, and holds spear and shield. She is sometimes shown hurling a thunderbolt, covering her left arm with an aegis, or holding Nike. Sacred to her were the owl, serpent, cock and olive, and these attributes often appear with her on coins. She had many additional titles, such as Areia (at Pergamon), Ilia (at Ilion), Argeia (at Alexandria), Itonia (in Thessaly), etc.

Baal. A Semitic god, lord (deity) of a locality, Baal was usually identified by the Greeks with Zeus.

Bakchos. *See* Dionysos.

Head of Demeter on a silver stater of Delphi, 336 B.C.

Demeter (Ceres). Goddess of fertility, agriculture and marriage, Demeter was sister to Zeus. When her daughter Persephone was carried off to the underworld by Hades, Demeter, by her mourning, withheld fertility from the earth until, through the mediation of Zeus, it was arranged that Persephone should spend half the year (winter) with Hades and the other half with her mother. The myth of Demeter and her daughter embodies the idea that the productive powers of nature are rested and concealed during the winter season. The head of Demeter on coins is wreathed with corn or veiled. She sometimes carries a sceptre or ears of corn, or searches for her daughter with a torch. She is also represented holding two torches and standing in a chariot drawn by two winged and crested serpents.

Dione. The consort of Zeus at Dodona, Dione was probably a sky-goddess. She appears on coins of Epeiros together with Zeus, with a laureate stephanos and veil, or alone, laureate and veiled.

Dionysos on a silver tetradrachm of Maroneia, circa 145 B.C.

Dionysos (Liber). Sometimes known as Bakchos (Bacchus), Dionysos was god of vegetation and the fruits of the trees, particularly the vine. Represented on coins as a youth holding a bunch of grapes, or with his head crowned with ivy or vine leaves, or riding or accompanied by a panther. Vine branches, kantharos and thyrsos are symbols of Dionysos.

The Dioskouroi on horseback: gold stater of Taras, circa 315 B.C.

Dioskouroi (Dioscuri). Kastor (Castor) and Polydeukes (Pollux), sons of Zeus and Leda and brothers of Helen of Troy, were protectors of travellers, particularly sailors, and helpers of those in distress. They received divine honours at Sparta and their worship spread from the Peloponnesos over the whole of Greece, Sicily and Italy. On coins the two brothers are represented on horseback or standing by their horses, carrying lances and wearing egg-shaped helmets surmounted by stars. They are sometimes confused with the Kabeiroi.

Eros (Cupid). The god of love, and later connected with Aphrodite, Eros is represented as a youth or boy, naked, winged, and holding a bow and arrows or a torch. Sometimes he is depicted riding on a dolphin (coins of Carteia) or driving the chariot of Hades who is carrying off Persephone. Occasionally, two Erotes are shown.

Head of Gorgo on a silver stater of Neapolis, circa 500 B.C.

Gorgo or **Medusa.** A monster with a round, ugly face, snakes instead of hair, teeth of a boar and huge wings, Gorgo was said to have eyes that could transform people into stone. Killed by the hero Perseus, she gave birth to Pegasos and Chrysaor in the moment of her death. Her head is shown as a main type on some coins and also as an adornment of shields.

Helios (Sol). The sun-god, who crosses the sky from east to west in his chariot each day, sees and hears everything. He was later identified with Apollo. He is usually depicted nude or with chlamys, with radiate head and holding a globe, whip or torch. On some coins he rides in a quadriga of horses.

Hera (Juno). The sister and consort of Zeus, and the queen of heaven, Hera was the great goddess of nature, worshipped from the earliest times. She was considered to be the mother of many other gods and goddesses, and is usually represented as a majestic woman of mature age, her hair adorned with a crown or diadem, often with a veil hanging down her back. One of her chief attributes was the peacock, her favourite bird.

Herakles fighting the Hydra: silver stater of Phaistos, circa 300 B.C.

Herakles (Hercules). The son of Zeus and Alkmene, Herakles was the most famous of all the heroes of antiquity; his strength, courage and wonderful exploits being the subject of numerous stories and poems all over the ancient world. His head, bust or full-length figure are amongst the most common of Greek coin types. He is often represented as a young beardless man with his head covered by the skin of the Nemean lion whom he strangled with his hands. He is also shown as a bearded, bull-necked man, usually naked, holding his club, lion's skin or bow. A club, bow, and also a bow-case, are also types referring to Herakles.

Head of Hermes on a silver stater of Lycia, late 5th Cent. B.C.

Hermes (Mercury). A son of Zeus and Maia, Hermes was the messenger of the gods, hence his herald's staff, the ribbons of which were later changed into the serpents of the caduceus. Other attributes of Hermes are the broad-brimmed travelling hat (petasos) adorned with wings, the golden sandals, the winged ankles, and a purse, for Hermes was patron not only of merchants but also of thieves, as well as artists, orators and travellers. He was regarded as the inventor of the lyre and plectrum, and of the syrinx. The palm-tree and tortoise were sacred to Hermes, so too were the number 4 and several kinds of fish. The caduceus adorned with a pair of wings to indicate the speed of the messenger is occasionally used as a coin type.

Isis. The wife of Osiris and mother of Horus, Isis was a national deity in Egypt, and during Hellenistic times became a leading goddess in the Mediterranean lands. She is portrayed on coins in a long garment with a characteristic knot of drapery on the breast (the *nodus Isiacus*) and with the ancient Egyptian head-dress which is one of her symbols. The sistrum, a musical instrument, is another attribute.

Kabeiroi. These non-Hellenic, probably Phrygian deities—from four to eight in number—promoted fertility and protected sailors. On coins they are represented with hammer and snake (coins of the Balearic Islands) or with rhyton (drinking horn ending in animal's head). Often confused with the Dioskouroi.

Kore. *See* Persephone.

Medusa. *See* Gorgo.

Melqarth riding hippocamp: silver double shekel of Tyre, circa 360 B.C.

Melqarth or **Melkart.** "Lord" of Tyre (Baal-Tsur), worshipped in Phoenicia, seems to have been originally a marine deity, as he is represented riding a sea-horse. Later he was identified with Herakles.

Nike with wreath and trophy: gold stater of Pyrrhos, 278-276 B.C.

Nike (Victoria). Greek goddess of victory, Nike was depicted as a woman in a long chiton, sometimes wingless (as on the coins of Terina) but more usually winged, holding wreath and palm and crowning the horses of a victorious charioteer or decorating a trophy.

Pan (Faunus). God of shepherds and flocks, Pan had horns, beard, puck nose, tail, goat's feet, was covered with hair and dwelt in grottoes. He is said to have had a terrific voice that struck terror into those who heard it. He was fond of music and is regarded, besides Hermes, as inventor of the syrinx or shepherd's pipes with which he is sometimes represented on coins (of Arkadia).

Persephone or **Kore.** Daughter of Demeter and wife of Hades (Plouton), Persephone is associated with the cult of her mother. She is usually represented with a wreath of corn on her head. *See* Demeter.

Poseidon brandishing trident: silver tetradrachm of Demetrios Poliorketes.

Poseidon (Neptune).   A brother of Zeus, Poseidon was god of earthquakes and ruler of the sea.   He is usually represented holding a dolphin and a trident, or the prow ornament of a galley, and standing with one foot on a rock.   A trident ornamented or entwined with dolphins appears on coins as the symbol of Poseidon.

Sarapis.   The name is derived from the Egyptian *Hesar-Hapi*, the deified sacred bull Apis.   The cult of Sarapis arose at Memphis under the Ptolemies and the deity combined the attributes of many Hellenic gods with some characteristics of Osiris.   He was represented bearded with a modius on his head.   Sarapis was a healer of the sick, worker of miracles, superior to fate, ruler of the visible world and underworld, and god of the sun.

Head of Zeus on a silver tetradrachm of Philip II.

Zeus (Jupiter).   The greatest of the Olympian gods, Zeus was considered to be the father of both gods and men.   He was a son of Kronos and Rhea and brother of Poseidon, Hades, Hestia, Demeter, and Hera; and he was also married to his sister Hera.   He was worshipped throughout the Greek world, and in the later Hellenic age was frequently identified with local supreme gods like Ammon, Sarapis, etc.   He had an immense number of epithets and surnames which were derived partly from the localities where he was worshipped and partly from his functions and powers.   The eagle and oak-tree were sacred to him.   His usual attributes are the sceptre, eagle, thunderbolt, and also a small figure of Nike which he holds in his hand.   The Olympian Zeus sometimes wears a wreath of olive and the Dodonaean Zeus a wreath of oak leaves.   He is usually represented bearded, nude or semi-nude, hurling a thunderbolt or sitting on a throne.

WEIGHT STANDARDS AND DENOMINATIONS

The earliest coins, issued by the Ionians or the Lydians in western Asia Minor in the latter part of the 7th Century B.C., were produced in only one metal, electrum, a naturally-occurring alloy of gold and silver. They were based on a stater weighing a little over 14 grammes, and although various fractional denominations were struck from an early date (half, third, sixth, etc.) the relatively high intrinsic value of the metal precludes the possibility that these coins enjoyed a wide everyday circulation. The truth of the matter would seem to be that the earliest coins provided a convenient means of paying quite large sums (possibly to mercenary soldiers) rather than to facilitate the day-to-day commerce of the ordinary citizens. The electrum stater, in fact, probably represented a month's pay for a soldier.

Silver half-stater of Kroisos of Lydia
(561-546 B.C.)

Gold daric of the Persian Empire,
5th-4th Cent. B.C.

This state of affairs continued until the Lydian King Kroisos (Croesus), who reigned 561-546 B.C., introduced a new monetary system based on coins of gold and silver instead of electrum. The gold stater, although still of the same value as its electrum predecessor was necessarily of lighter weight (a little over 8 grammes) and fractional denominations down to one-twelfth (hemihekton) were produced in the same metal. Silver denominations, now issued for the first time, bore the same design as the gold and provided a much greater range of values at the lower end of the scale. In these times the ratio of silver to gold was $13\frac{1}{3}:1$ and the weight of the silver stater was fixed so as to make it the equivalent of one-tenth of the gold stater (almost 11 grammes). The smallest coin in this series, the silver hemihekton, was 1/120th of the gold stater, which gives some idea of the wide range of values obtainable under this new bimetallic system. The main disadvantage was the inconvenience of handling such tiny coins in everyday transactions—the silver hemihekton was less than half the diameter of our modern $\frac{1}{2}$ New Penny. This was a problem which was not finally solved until the 4th Century B.C., when token bronze coinage largely replaced the smallest silver denominations. The Lydian Kingdom ceased to exist in 546 B.C. when Kroisos was defeated by the Persians under King Cyrus. But coinage, on the same standard and with the same types, continued to be issued from Sardis under the new regime. Towards the end of the 6th Century the old Lydian type (foreparts of lion and bull) was replaced by a Persian type showing an archer (sometimes described as the King) in a kneeling-running pose. The gold stater, now called a 'daric' (after Darius), was initially the same weight as Kroisos' coin, whilst the silver 'siglos' was the equivalent of the old half-stater and worth one-twentieth of the 'daric'. Subsequently, slight adjustments had to be made in their weights to maintain the correct ratio when there were changes in the relative values of the precious metals. These coins continued in issue, with only minor modifications, for almost two centuries, until the Persian Empire was overthrown by Alexander.

Electrum stater of Chios, circa 550 B.C.

When the Lydian Kingdom fell in 546 B.C. the Greek cities of Ionia were obliged to acknowledge Persian overlordship, though this seems to have had no effect on their output of coinage. Unlike the Lydians, the Greeks had continued using electrum for the majority of their coins, issued as staters and fractions right down to ninety-sixths. Silver was introduced in the closing decades of the 6th Century, though it seems to have played only a subsidiary role to the more important electrum issues. Quite a large number of mints would seem to have been at work—Ephesos, Phokaia, Miletos, and others—though it is difficult for us now to attribute most types to their cities of origin. The picture is further complicated by the existence of several different weight-standards for the electrum coinage, and we find staters weighing 17.2 grammes ('Euboic' standard), 16.1 gm. (Phokaic) and 14.1 gm. (Milesian). Of these, the Phokaic standard was ultimately adopted for the extensive electrum coinages which the Asiatic Greeks produced in the 5th and 4th Centuries B.C., down to the time of Alexander. Three mints were principally involved in the production of this fascinating and beautiful coinage. Kyzikos, a Milesian colony on the sea of Marmara, issued a series of staters (weight 16.1 gm.) of which more than two hundred different types are known. The Ionian mint of Phokaia, and Mytilene, the chief city of the island of Lesbos, produced long series of hektai (sixth-staters, 2.6 gm.), possibly striking in alternate years. The products of the two mints are easily distinguished—those of Phokaia are without reverse type, whilst the examples from Lesbos always have a reverse design, sometimes in intaglio.

Electrum sixth-stater of Phokaia,
4th Cent. B.C.

Electrum sixth-stater of Lesbos,
4th Cent. B.C.

Around the middle of the 6th Century the practice of issuing coined money spread to Greece itself and a number of mints commenced operations in the decade following 550 B.C. Electrum was foreign to the European Greeks who never adopted this metal for their coinage. In its place silver was employed right from the start. The first issues of Aigina, Athens, Corinth, and the Euboian cities of Chalkis, Eretria and Karystos all belong to this time. Important weight standards, which were destined to play a leading role in the development of Greek coinage, now appeared for the first time. The Attic standard, based initially on a didrachm of 8.6 gm. but later on a tetradrachm of 17.2 gm., was adopted at Athens and later spread to Sicily and the northern Aegean area. The great prosperity and political importance of Athens in the 5th Century contributed to the widespread popularity of this weight standard and it was later adopted by Alexander the Great for his vast imperial coinage.

Silver stater of Corinth, circa 525 B.C.

The Corinthian standard was closely linked to the Attic in that it was based on a stater of 8.6 gm., the same weight as the Attic didrachm. However, the Corinthian stater was divided into *three* drachms of 2.9 gm. Coins on this standard were produced over a long period at Corinth, with smaller and mostly late issues coming from her numerous colonies in north-west Greece, Italy and Sicily.

Silver Aiginetic stater of Naxos, late
6th Cent. B.C.

The Aiginetic standard received its name from the maritime state, situated between the coastlines of Attica and Argolis, which was in all probability the earliest mint in European Greece. The Aiginetic stater, normally weighing about 12.3 gm., was widely adopted in the Peloponnese, in Central Greece, and especially in the southern Aegean area (the Cyclades group of islands, Crete and south-west Asia Minor). Politically and economically Aigina was eclipsed by Athens in the mid-5th Century B.C. though her weight standard remained in use in many places.

Other important standards in use from early times include the Achaean (silver stater of 8 gm.), used by the Greek colonies in southern Italy; and the Euboic (stater of 17.2 gm.), employed by colonies from Euboia situated in the northern Aegean area and in Sicily. In the East, the Persian standard, derived from the bimetallic coinage of Kroisos, was adhered to by many of the mints of Asia Minor under Achaemenid domination, including those of Cyprus. After *circa* 400 B.C. the Chian (or Rhodian) standard achieved considerable popularity in Asia Minor, and was also adopted at Ainos in Thrace. It was based on a tetradrachm of 15.6 gm.

Phoenician 4-shekel piece of Sidon, circa 375 B.C.

In the Levant, the Phoenician standard (silver shekel of 7 gm.) was used by Sidon, Tyre and Byblos. A not dissimilar standard is found in parts of northern Greece, though there can hardly have been any connection between the two. In fact, the whole question of weight standards in northern Greece is fraught with difficulties. Different standards appear to have been in use contemporaneously, sometimes at the same mint, and there were certainly three series of weights with no simple inter-relationship. The whole group is termed "Thraco-Macedonian".

Within each weight standard there was normally a wide range of denominations, serving the requirements of major transactions down to everyday purchases in the market-place. Some denominations were struck more regularly than others, such as the tetradrachm at Athens, the tridrachm-stater at Corinth and the didrachm-stater at Aigina. Some areas had a preference for small denominations: most Peloponnesian mints, for example, seldom issued anything larger than a triobol (hemidrachm) during the 5th Century B.C. Other areas preferred larger coins: the Thraco-Macedonian tribes of the north regularly produced silver octadrachms (*c.* 29 gm.), dodekadrachms (*c.* 40.5 gm.) and even a double octadrachm, the heaviest of all Greek silver coins.

Thraco-Macedonian dodekadrachm of the Derrones, circa 475 B.C.

The table below shows the large number of denominations which were produced under the Attic weight system. Not all of these denominations would have been in regular issue—the dekadrachm, for example, was only struck on special occasions—and some mints never produced the tiny fractions of the obol. The weights given are approximate, and reflect the figures actually achieved rather than the ideal.

Dekadrachm	=10	drachms :	43 gm.
Tetradrachm	= 4	drachms :	17.2 gm.
Didrachm	= 2	drachms :	8.6] gm.
Drachm	= 6	obols :	4.3 gm.
Tetrobol	= 4	obols :	2.85 gm.
Triobol (hemidrachm)	= 3	obols :	2.15 gm.
Diobol	= 2	obols :	1.43 gm.
Trihemiobol	= 1½	obols :	1.07 gm.
Obol		:	0.72 gm.
Tritartemorion	= ¾	obol :	0.54 gm.
Hemiobol	= ½	obol :	0.36 gm.
Trihemitartemorion	= ⅜	obol :	0.27 gm.
Tetartemorion	= ¼	obol :	0.18 gm.
Hemitartemorion	= ⅛	obol :	0.09 gm.

The smallest coin in this system, the hemitartemorion represents 1/480th of the largest piece, the dekadrachm. Similar tables can be constructed for other weight standards, but it should be borne in mind that in some systems the stater is divided into thirds, sixths, twelfths, etc., instead of halves and quarters.

Silver litra of Kamarina, circa
460 B.C.

Bronze hemilitron of Himera, circa 450 B.C.

One weight standard which we have not so far mentioned is that based on the Sicilian *bronze* litra. Indigenous to the island, the litra was at first represented by a small silver coin (wt. 0.86 gm.) which was only slightly heavier than the obol and had to be distinguished by the use of different types. The Sicilian Greeks must have found this a troublesome arrangement, for as early as the mid-5th Century B.C. they hit on the idea of producing a bronze litra.   Such a coin would not be so inconveniently small to handle and there would no longer be any danger of confusing it with the silver obol.   Which city was the first to take this step we cannot be certain but Himera, on the north coast of the island, was certainly amongst the earliest of the bronze-issuing mints.   Although some of the original bronze litrai were somewhat cumbersome, the weight was soon reduced to a more acceptable level for everyday circulation.   So from their earliest stages bronze coins came to be accepted as a token currency, the intrinsic value of which was considerably below the circulating value which had been placed upon them by the issuing authority.   By the latter part of the 5th Century many of the Greek cities in Sicily had adopted this base-metal currency and were finding it very useful indeed for the small daily transactions of urban life—the purchase of food and drink, clothing, etc.   In fact the modern concept of currency, as a convenient means of payment for all goods and services from the largest transactions down to the most trifling, is a direct result of this important development in Greek Sicily 2,400 years ago.

Bronze litra of Syracuse, circa 340 B.C.

The bronze litra was divided into twelve onkiai—hence the Roman uncia (1/12th of a pound), the troy ounce (1/12th of a pound) and the inch (1/12th of a linear foot).   The hemilitron (=6 onkiai, mark of value six pellets) was also struck, together with the pentonkion (5 onkiai, five pellets), the tetras (4 onkiai, four pellets), the trias (3 onkiai, three pellets), the hexas (2 onkiai, two pellets), and the onkia itself (mark of value one pellet).   In the earliest stages of bronze coinage in Sicily the denomination produced in greatest quantities was the trias or quarter-litra.

Bronze trias of Syracuse, early 4th Cent. B.C.

From its beginnings in Sicily the idea of base-metal token coinage eventually spread to all parts of the Greek world.   In the half century after *circa* 400 B.C. most mints produced their first issues of bronze though some, such as Athens, seemed reluctant to adopt the innovation. Athens, from the early years of the 5th Century, had possessed plentiful supplies of silver from her rich mines at Laurion, and well on into the 4th Century was still producing quantities of the absurdly small fractions of the obol.   Eventually she, too, acknowledged the obvious advantages of having token bronze denominations to represent the lowest values, and the Athenian mint began striking them in the latter part of the 4th Century.

One of the problems of Greek bronze coins is trying to relate them to the silver denominations is the absence, in most cases, of marks of value.   Unfortunately, few Greek mints followed the practice of the Sicilian innovators of bronze coinage by clearly marking the denomination in terms of some basic unit representing a known fraction of the smallest silver coin in common

Bronze obol of Metapontion, inscribed "οβολος"

use.   A remarkable late 4th Century bronze of the south Italian mint of Metapontion bears the inscription 'οβολος' clearly proclaiming its value as the equivalent of one obol, and it would seem a fair surmise that the majority of Greek bronzes represent fractions or, in rarer cases, multiples of the silver obol.   It is known that at Athens the obol was divided into eight chalkoi, and in all probability the tiniest Athenian bronze piece represents the chalkos.   Larger pieces would be multiples, such as the dichalkon (two chalkoi), tetrachalkon (four chalkoi=hemiobol), etc.   It may be hoped that one day we shall have acquired sufficient knowledge of the Greek bronze coinage to give precise names to most pieces.   The present system of merely measuring the diameter in millimetres or inches is most unsatisfactory.

THE DATING OF GREEK COINS

Tetradrachm of Alexander I of Syria: Seleukid date 162=151/150 B.C.

In general, Greek coins were not marked with their year of issue until a very late period (2nd Century B.C.), when the Hellenistic Kingdoms of Syria and Egypt commenced the practice. The Seleukids dated their coins according to an era commencing in 312 B.C., when Seleukos I regained possession of Babylon. The Ptolemies, on the other hand, used the less satisfactory method of indicating only the regnal year; and as every Greek King of Egypt bore the name 'Ptolemy' the dates appearing on their coins provide only limited assistance in our efforts to establish the precise chronology of the Ptolemaic series. But even in the case of these late regal issues many of the coins are not dated and the practice only spread to a limited number of autonomous city mints. In attempting to establish the approximate period of issue for the majority of Greek coins, then, the numismatist must have recourse to other criteria, such as style and fabric.

Archaic winged figure on a tetradrachm of Peparethos, circa 500 B.C.   *Archaic eagle on a stater of Elis, early 5th Cent. B.C.*

Broadly speaking, the six centuries of Greek coinage, prior to the establishment of the Roman Empire, divide up into three periods, each characterized by artistic style and, to a lesser extent, by the method of production. In the Archaic period (from the invention of coinage down to the time of the Persian defeat in 479 B.C.) representations of the human form have a stiff, almost stylized look. In profile heads the eye tends to be represented full face, whilst in showing the full-length figure to left or to right there is a tendency to depict the head and legs correctly in profile, whilst the torso has a more frontal aspect. Similarly, with flying birds the body is in profile whilst the wings are depicted as if viewed from below. Although lacking the artistic finesse and sculptural qualities of later periods much of the work produced by the early die-engravers is pleasing to the eye and fascinating in its symbolization of a most exciting period in the history of civilization. To begin with, coins bore no reverse types and simply had an incuse square sometimes roughly divided into segments. In the later archaic period the divisions of the incuse square became more formalized and finally, in the closing years of the 6th Century, the first true reverse types began to appear. However, some mints, such as Aigina, never abandoned the use of the incuse square reverse. In the Aegean area the flans of the earliest coins are often very thick, almost globular, whilst subsequent issues gradually become thinner and larger. In the West the opposite is often the case; the very thin, spread flans of the earliest issues giving way to thicker, more compact coins. A curious feature of the first issues of many of the Magna Graecian mints was the mirroring of the obverse type on the reverse, in incuse form.

Tetradrachm of Segesta in Sicily, circa 410 B.C.

The period 479-336 B.C., from the Persian Wars to the time of Alexander, is termed the Classical period of Greek coinage. Its first few decades witness a progressive transition from the unlifelike representations of archaic art to a more natural style, though still retaining something of the old severity in the earlier phases. Towards the latter part of the 5th Century, and especially in Sicily, numismatic art reaches a level of realism combined with nobility of style which makes many of the coins masterpieces in miniature. Nothing comparable has been produced in the twenty-four centuries which have since elapsed. Although the Sicilian coinage was cut short by the Carthaginian invasions at the end of the century, mints in other parts of the Greek world were also producing coins of fine style, and these issues continued until the beginning of the Macedonian domination of Greece. This despite the political turmoil which the Greek world found itself in as the aftermath of the great Peloponnesian War.

Hellenistic tetradrachm of Myrina, circa 150 B.C.

The eastern conquests of Alexander and the subsequent establishment of great kingdoms brought about fundamental changes in the coinage. The Hellenistic period, which lasted three centuries until the suicide of Cleopatra of Egypt (30 B.C.), saw the first mass-production of Greek coinage, with the possible exception of the Athenian 'owls' produced in the age of Perikles. The vast realms over which the Hellenistic monarchs ruled required coinage on a scale unknown in the days of the city-states. Working under such pressure even experienced die-engravers could hardly be expected to produce notable work, and as time went by there was a steady decline in the artistic standard of the coinage. Although there was something of a revival in the 2nd Century B.C., when many cities were temporarily liberated from regal control by Rome's intervention in eastern affairs, still the general impression conveyed by most of the later Hellenistic coins is one of artistic decadence and hurried, careless production.
     In the foregoing notes I have tried to make clear the principal characteristics of each major period—Archaic, Classical and Hellenistic. In order to arrive at a more precise dating for an individual piece a close study of the history of the mint can sometimes provide valuable clues. Many Greek cities were destroyed by their neighbours, or by foreign invaders, to be rebuilt at a later date and sometimes even to suffer a second destruction. The names of cities could be changed, sometimes more than once: the Italian city of Sybaris was renamed Thourioi in

425 B.C., the name which it bore until the Romans changed it to Copia in 194 B.C.   Such events enable us to construct a chronological framework for the coinages of certain cities; and as the majority of mints were active only sporadically we are able, sometimes, to fix the precise occasion for some special issue.   This knowledge can then be used to date the coins of other mints in the same vicinity, and so the picture is gradually built up like a giant jigsaw puzzle.

There is much still to be learnt about the chronology of Greek coins, and our views often have to be modified in the light of evidence provided by hoards.   But in this brief survey of a most complex and controversial subject I hope I have not only made the reader aware of the difficulties involved in the dating of Greek coins but also have conveyed something of the fascination and the challenge which this subject affords.

The table below explains the Greek letter-numerals by which dates are expressed on certain issues of the 2nd and 1st Centuries B.C.

1	A	9	Θ	80	Π
2	B	10	I	90	Ϙ
3	Γ	20	K	100	P
4	Δ	30	Λ	200	Σ
5	Є	40	M	300	T
6	S	50	N	400	Y
7	Z	60	Ξ	500	Φ
8	H	70	O	600	X

BOOKS OF REFERENCE AND OTHER SOURCES QUOTED IN THIS CATALOGUE

Babelon, E.   Traité des Monnaies grecques et romaines.   Paris, 1901-1933.

Babelon, E.   Catalogue des Monnaies grecques, Bibliothèque Nationale, Paris:
      (i) Les Rois de Syrie, d'Arménie et de Commagène, 1890.
      (ii) Les Perses Achéménides, les Satrapes et les Dynastes tributaires de
      leur Empire, Cypre et Phénicie, 1893.

Babelon, J.   Catalogue de la collection de Luynes.   Paris, 1924-1936.

Barron, J. P.   The Silver Coins of Samos.   London, 1966.

Bedoukian, Paul Z.   Coinage of the Artaxiads of Armenia.   London, 1978.

Boston Museum Catalogue=Museum of Fine Arts: Catalogue of Greek Coins, by A. Baldwin Brett.   Boston, 1955.

British Museum Catalogue of Greek Coins, various authors, London, 1873-1927.   Twenty out of the twenty-nine volumes are quoted in this catalogue, numbered in order of publication as follows:

B.M.C. 3.	Thrace, etc.: published 1877.
B.M.C. 4.	Seleucid Kings of Syria: published 1878.
B.M.C. 6.	Ptolemaic Kings of Egypt: published 1883.
B.M.C. 11.	Attica, etc.: published 1888.
B.M.C. 13.	Pontus, Paphlagonia, Bithynia: published 1889.
B.M.C. 14.	Ionia: published 1892.
B.M.C. 15.	Mysia: published 1892.
B.M.C. 17.	Troas, Aeolis and Lesbos: published 1894.
B.M.C. 18.	Caria and the Islands: published 1897.
B.M.C. 19.	Lycia, Pamphylia, Pisidia: published 1897.
B.M.C. 20.	Galatia, Cappadocia, Syria: published 1899.
B.M.C. 21.	Lycaonia, Isauria, Cilicia: published 1900.
B.M.C. 22.	Lydia: published 1902.
B.M.C. 23.	Parthia: published 1903.
B.M.C. 24.	Cyprus: published 1904.
B.M.C. 25.	Phrygia: published 1906.
B.M.C. 26.	Phoenicia: published 1910.
B.M.C. 27.	Palestine: published 1914.
B.M.C. 28.	Arabia, Mesopotamia, Persia: published 1922.
B.M.C. 29.	Cyrenaica: published 1927.

(B.M.C. references in this catalogue provide the volume number, the page and the listing number.   The reference B.M.C. 15. 123, 87 is to no. 87, in the listing of Pergamene issues, on page 123 of the volume "Mysia".)

British Museum Catalogue of Indian Coins (B.M.C. India), Greek and Scythic Kings of Bactria and India, by Percy Gardner, London, 1886.

Davis, N. and Kraay, C. M.   The Hellenistic Kingdoms.   London, 1973.

De Morgan, J.   Ancient Persian Numismatics, Elymais.   New York, 1976 (English translation of the original French publication, Paris, 1930).

Forrer, L.   Descriptive catalogue of the collection of Greek coins formed by Sir Hermann Weber.   London, 1922-9.

Franke, P. R.   Kleinasien zur Römerzeit.   Munich, 1968.

Grose, S. W.   Catalogue of the McClean Collection of Greek Coins.   Cambridge, 1923-9.

Head, B. V.   Historia Numorum.   Oxford, 1911.

Head, B. V.   History of the Coinage of Ephesus.   London, 1880.

Head, B. V.   The Coinage of Lydia and Persia.   London, 1877.

Head, B. V.   A Guide to the Principal Coins of the Greeks.   Revised edition, London, 1959.

Hunterian Catalogue=Catalogue of Greek Coins in the Hunterian Collection, by G. Macdonald.   Glasgow, 1899-1905.

Jenkins, G. K.   Ancient Greek Coins.   London, 1972.

Jenkins, G. K. and Lewis, R. B.   Carthaginian Gold and Electrum Coins.   London, 1963.

Kraay, C. M.   Archaic and Classical Greek Coins.   London, 1976.

Le Rider, G.   Le Monnayage d'Argent et d'Or de Philippe II.   Paris, 1977.

Meshorer, Y.   Jewish Coins of the Second Temple Period.   Tel-Aviv, 1967.

Mitchiner, M.   Indo-Greek and Indo-Scythian Coinage.   Sanderstead, 1975.

Müller, L.   Die Münzen des thrakischen Königs Lysimachos.   Copenhagen, 1858.

Müller, L.   Numismatique d'Alexandre le Grand.   Copenhagen, 1855.

Müller, L.   Numismatique de l'ancienne Afrique.   Copenhagen, 1860-63.

Naville, L.   Les Monnaies d'Or de la Cyrénaïque.   Geneva, 1951.

Newell, E. T.   Alexander Hoards, Demanhur, 1905.   New York, 1923.

Newell, E. T.   The Coinages of Demetrius Poliorcetes.   Oxford, 1926.

Newell, E. T.   The Coinage of the Eastern Seleucid Mints.   New York, 1938.

Newell, E. T.   The Coinage of the Western Seleucid Mints.   New York, 1941.

Newell, E. T.   The Seleucid Mint of Antioch.   1918.

Newell, E. T.   The Seleucid Coinages of Tyre.   New York, 1936.

Newell, E. T.   Late Seleucid Mints in Ake-Ptolemais and Damascus.   New York, 1939.

Newell, E. T.   The Pergamene Mint under Philetaerus.   New York, 1936.

Numismatic Chronicle = the annual publication of the Royal Numismatic Society, London.

Price, M.   Coins of the Macedonians.   London, 1974.

Price, M. and Waggoner, N.   Archaic Greek Silver Coinage: the "Asyut" Hoard.   London, 1975.

Robinson, E. S. G.   Punic Coins of Spain, in Essays in Roman Coinage presented to Harold Mattingly.   Oxford, 1956.

Sellwood, D.   An Introduction to the Coinage of Parthia.   London, 1971.

Svoronos, J.   Ta nomismata tou kratous ton Ptolemaion.   Athens, 1904-8.

Sylloge Nummorum Graecorum, H. von Aulock Collection.   Berlin, 1957-68.

Waddington, W. H.   Recueil général des monnaies grecques d'Asie Mineure.   Paris, 1904-12.

Westermark, U.   Das Bildnis des Philetairos von Pergamon.   Stockholm, 1961.

	Greek earlier	Greek later	Lycian
α	ΑΑΑΑΛ	Α Α	ΡΑΑ = α ↑ = ä
β	ΒΒ<СΨSΥ Ѵ	Β Β	Βb = β
γ	<СΛΓ	Γ	Υ V = γ
δ	⊅DΔ	Δ	Δ = δ
ε	ⱹⱹEEⱹEE	Ε Є	Ε Ɛ = ι
ϝ	⊂ΓFFΥΛ		FϜ = v
ζ	ⱶΙ	IΖ	Ι = z
η,h	ⱶΗⱶΗΘΗⱶ	Η	+ ✝ = h
θ	⊞⊠◈◊⊕⊗▢◊⊙	⊙ΘⴵΘ	⊃C = θ (?)
ι	⸑⸑ⱾⱾSΙ	Ι	Ι = ι conson.
κ	Κ	Κ	Κⱪ = κ
λ	ⱡⱡΛΓΛ	Λ	Λ = λ
μ	∿ΜΜΜ	ΜΜ	ΜΜ = μ
ν	∿ΝΝΛΛ	Ν	∿Ν = ν
ξ	+ΧΗⱶ ΞⱶΞⱶ	ΞⱶΞΞ	Χ = m̃ Ξ = ñ
ο	▢◊⊙ΟΩC	Ο	Ο⊙ = υ
π	ΓΡC	ΓΠΠ	ΓΓ = π
ϙ	ϙϙϙΥ		
ρ	RRⱠⱠΡΡ	Ρ	ΡⱠⱠ = ρ
σ	SSⱾⱾ M	ΣⱢC	SS = σ Χ = σ(?)
σσ	Τ Ψ		
τ	ⱦΤ	Τ	Τ = τ
υ	ΥVΥ	Υ	
φ	⊟◫◍◐⊕Φ⊙ⁿᴮ	ΦⴲΨ	
χ	↓ΥΥↆↆΧ	Χ	ѴѴΥΨΥ = kh
ψ	↓Υ	Ψ	Ψ⅄⅄↓↓Ѵ = ẹ
ω	⊙ΟΩ	ΩΩωⱲ	⅄ⱲⱮⱯ⅄Υ⅄Υ = ạ

TABLE I. GREEK AND LYCIAN

	A	E	I	O	U
	a	e	i	o	u
K	ka	ke	ki	ko	ku
T	ta	te	ti	to	tu
P	pa	pe	pi	po	pu
L	la	le	li	lo	lu
R	ra	re	ri	ro	ru
N	na	ne	ni	no	nu
M	ma	me	mi	mo	mu
Y	ya	ye			
F	fa,va	fe,ve	fi,vi	fo,vo	
S	sa	se	si	so	su
Z	za			zo	
X		xe			
	A	E	I	O	U

TABLE II. CYPRIOTE

Hebrew Square	Phoenician earlier	Phoenician later	Punic earlier	Punic later	Israelite earlier	Israelite later	Aramaic Satrap coins
א							
ב							
ג							
ד							
ה							
ו							
ז							
ח							
ט							
י							
כ ך							
ל							
מ ם							
נ ן							
ס							
ע							
פ ף							
צ ץ							
ק							
ר							
ש							
ת							

TABLE III. SEMITIC

a	go	tra	psa	yu	ṣa
aṃ	gha	tha	pha	ye	ṣi
ā medial	cha	thi	phi	ra	spa
i	chha	the	phthi	raṃ	ṣva
iṃ	ja	da	phre	ri	sha
u	ji	di	ba	ru	shka
e	ju	du	bi	rkhe	sa
o	jha	de	bu	rte	saṃ
ka	jho	dra	bra	rna	si
ki	ṭa	dha	bha	rma	su
ku	ṭha	dhra	bhe	rva	sta
ke	ḍa	na	bhra	la	stra
kra	ḍi	ni	ma	li	sya
kri	ṇa	no	maṃ	lu	ssa
kre	ṇi	pa	mi	lo	ha
kha	ta	pi	me	va	haṃ
khu	ti	pu	mo	vi	hi
ga	tu	pe	ya	vu	he
gaṃ	te	pra	yaṃ	ve	ho
gu	to	pri	yi	vra	ṃ

TABLE IV. KHAROṢṬHĪ LETTERS ON GRAECO-INDIAN COINS

GLOSSARY

Akrostolion:	the gunwale of a ship.
Amphora:	a jar for storing wine.
Ampyx:	a head-band, visible above the forehead.
Aphlaston (=Aplustre):	the curved stern of a ship, with its ornaments.
Astragalos:	the knuckle-bone of an animal, used as a die in games of chance.
Biga:	a chariot drawn by a team of two animals, usually horses.
Billon:	an alloy of silver with a predominating amount of some base metal.
Bipennis:	an axe with a double edge or blade.
Bucranium:	the head or skull of a cow.
Caduceus:	(see Kerykeion).
Carnyx:	a Gallic war-trumpet.
Cestus:	a glove worn by boxers.
Chlamys:	a short mantle, or military cloak.
Cippus:	a short round pillar, often used as a boundary marker.
Cista Mystica:	a sacred basket used in Dionysiac rites, usually containing a serpent.
Cornucopiae:	the horn of plenty.
Distaff:	a cleft stick on which wool or flax was wound for spinning by hand.
Electrum:	an alloy of silver and gold, either manufactured or of natural occurrence.
Exergue:	the small space on the reverse of a coin, below the principal device.
Flan:	the prepared blank on which the types of the coin are struck with the obverse and reverse dies.
Harpa or Harpe:	a sword or dagger with a hook projecting from the blade. It is particularly associated with the hero Perseus.
Hippocamp:	a fabulous animal, having the forepart and body of a horse and the tail of a fish.
Hydria:	a water-pail for holding clean water.
Kalathos:	a vase-shaped basket.
Kantharos:	a wine cup with handles, particularly associated with Dionysos.
Kausia:	a Macedonian flat-topped hat.
Kerykeion (=Caduceus):	a herald's wand, especially that of Hermes which is ornamented with snakes and wings.
Kithara:	a kind of lyre or lute, of triangular shape and with seven strings.
Korymbos:	a distinctive form of female coiffure, in which the hair is drawn up to the top of the head and tied to resemble a cluster of ivy berries.
Krater:	a large bowl, in which wine was mixed with water, and from which cups were filled.
Krobylos:	an archaic form of coiffure, in which the hair is drawn back from the roots all round the head, and fastened in a knot at the top.
Lagobolon (=Pedum):	a shepherd's staff, usually associated with Pan.

Lebes:	a copper cauldron, normally depicted on a three-legged stand (see Tripod).
Obverse:	the side of the coin which bears the head or principal design. It is struck from the anvil (lower) die and has a slightly convex field.
Oikistes:	the founder of a city.
Oinochoe:	a can for ladling wine from the mixing bowl into the cups.
Omphalos:	the sacred stone of Apollo at Delphi. It was believed to mark the middle point of Earth, hence its name meaning "navel".
Overstriking:	the use of an older coin as the blank for striking with new types. Traces of the original types often survive helping to establish the sequence of issues.
Palladion:	an ancient sacred image of Athena, said to have been sent down from heaven by Zeus to Dardanos, the founder of Troy.
Pedum:	(see Lagobolon.)
Peplos:	a robe, worn by women over the common dress, and falling in folds about the person.
Petasos:	a broad-brimmed felt hat.
Phiale (=Patera):	a broad, flat bowl for drinking or pouring libations.
Pilos:	a felt skullcap.
Pistrix:	a sea-monster with dragon's head.
Prochous:	an ewer for pouring water on the hands of guests.
Quadriga:	a chariot drawn by a team of four animals, usually horses.
Reverse:	the side of the coin which bears the secondary design, and usually the date and mint mark where present. It is struck from the punch (upper) die and has a more or less concave field.
Sakkos:	a coarse hair-cloth.
Sepia:	cuttle-fish.
Sphendone:	the decorated back part of a hair-band. The literal meaning is a "sling".
Stephane:	part of a woman's head-dress, a diadem or coronal.
Syrinx:	a shepherd's pipe: the musical instrument invented by Pan, and formed of reeds or canes of several unequal lengths joined together.
Tainia:	a flat band worn round the head to keep the hair in a set form of arrangement.
Thymiaterion:	a vessel for burning incense, a censer.
Thyrsos:	a long pole, with an ornamented head formed by a fir cone, or by ivy or vine leaves. It is associated with Dionysos by whom it is normally carried.
Tripod:	a bronze three-legged stand supporting a bowl or cauldron (see Lebes). It is usually symbolic of Apollo.
Volute:	a spiral scroll decoration.
Wappenmünzen:	meaning "heraldic coins", it is a name applied to the Sixth-century Athenian silver issues prior to the introduction of the first "owls".

GRAMMES-GRAINS CONVERSION TABLE

GRAMMES	GRAINS	GRAMMES	GRAINS	GRAMMES	GRAINS
·06	1	2·00	31	7	108
·13	2	2·25	35	8	123
·19	3	2·50	39	9	139
·26	4	2·75	42	10	154
·32	5	3·00	46	12	185
·39	6	3·25	50	15	231
·45	7	3·50	54	20	309
·52	8	3·75	58	25	386
·58	9	4·00	62	30	463
·65	10	4·25	66	40	617
·78	12	4·50	70	50	772
·90	14	4·75	73	60	926
1·00	15	5·00	77	70	1081
1·25	19	5·25	81	80	1234
1·50	23	5·50	85	90	1388
1·75	27	5·75	89	100	1543
		6·00	93		

INCHES-MILLIMETRES CONVERSION TABLE

INCHES	MM.	INCHES	MM.	INCHES	MM.
0·3	8	0·85	22	1·4	36
0·35	9	0·9	23	1·45	37
0·4	10	0·95	24	1·5	38
0·45	11	1·0	26	1·55	40
0·5	13	1·05	27	1·6	41
0·55	14	1·1	28	1·65	42
0·6	15	1·15	29	1·7	43
0·65	17	1·2	31	1·75	44
0·7	18	1·25	32	1·8	46
0·75	19	1·3	33	1·85	47
0·8	20	1·35	34	1·9	48

ABBREVIATIONS

A̸	gold	r.	right	rad.	radiate
Ꞧ	silver	l.	left	diad.	diademed
Æ	copper or bronze	hd.	head	dr.	draped
obv.	obverse	var.	variety	cuir.	cuirassed
Ꞧ or *rev.*	reverse	laur.	laureate	stg.	standing

STATES OF PRESERVATION IN ORDER OF MERIT

Abbreviation	English	French.	German.	Italian.
FDC	mint state.	fleur-de-coin.	Stempelglanz.	fior di conio
EF	extremely fine.	superbe.	vorzüglich.	splendido.
VF	very fine.	très beau.	sehr schön.	bellisimo.
F	fine.	beau.	schön.	multo bello.
Fair	fair.	très bien conservé.	sehr gut erhalten.	bello.
M	mediocre.	bien conservé.	gut erhalten.	discreto.
P	poor.			

VALUES

The prices given are for specimens in an average state of preservation—'VF' in the case of gold, electrum and silver, 'F' in the case of billon and bronze. Poorly preserved examples are, of course, worth *much* less than the values quoted; unusually well-preserved coins and those of better than average style are worth substantially more.

KEY TO MAPS

Mints which commenced issuing coins during the archaic period are denoted by a dot surrounded by a circle and other mints by a plain dot.

ASIA MINOR

Archaic Period

Western Asia Minor was the birthplace of coinage in the Mediterranean World. Whether it was the Lydians or their western neighbours the Ionian Greeks who produced the first coins, in electrum, we shall probably never know. But the former may have the stronger claim being the possessors of rich deposits of electrum, an alloy of silver and gold, which was the only metal used for coin production in its earliest stages. The Lydians later demonstrated their inventiveness in monetary matters by being the first to introduce a bimetallic currency consisting of coins struck in pure gold and silver instead of electrum, which was of uncertain intrinsic value. The Asiatic Greeks were slow in advancing to a silver-based currency, a circumstance which, perhaps, militates against them as being the inventors of coinage.

No precise date can be given for the first electrum coins. Recent interpretation of the rather meagre evidence available would seem to indicate that the earliest developments took place some time in the third quarter of the seventh century B.C. The first coins bore no distinguishing types, but by *circa* 600 B.C. production techniques had improved with experience and neatly engraved obverse types had already appeared. Reverses, on the other hand, simply bore one or more square or oblong punches. The first true double-sided coins, with a proper design on each face, were still nearly a century away.

Mints are not easy to identify in this earliest phase of coinage. Inscriptions are rarely encountered and the few that are known give personal names rather than those of cities. Attempts have been made to interpret the obverse designs in terms of mint emblems. Undoubtedly some, like the tunny-fish of Kyzikos, were intended to represent their city of origin. But others, perhaps the majority, were simply personal badges of rulers or mint-officials. One celebrated electrum stater, now thought to be a product of the Halikarnassos mint, actually bears the inscription 'I am the badge of Phanes' above the type of a grazing stag.

The coinage identified as that of the Lydian kings is mostly of third-staters and was evidently produced in quite large quantities. It features the head of a lion, with a distinctive nose-wart, and was based on the Milesian (or Lydian) weight standard. The same standard, which produced a stater of about 14·2 grams, was employed by the mints of southern Ionia; whilst further north the Phokaic standard (stater of 16·5 grams) prevailed. King Kroisos (Croesus) of Lydia, who reigned 560-546 B.C., abandoned electrum in favour of a bimetallic currency based on pure silver and gold. When the Persians, under Cyrus, conquered the Lydian Kingdom they continued issuing coins of the type introduced by Kroisos. Towards the end of the sixth century new designs were introduced for this coinage featuring a Persian archer. The gold coin now came to be known as a *daric*, after Darius I, and the silver piece a *siglos* (worth one-twentieth of the *daric*). This Persian coinage of western Asia Minor continued, with little alteration to the main design, until the time of Alexander.

The Greek cities of Ionia also came under the sway of the Persians, in 545 B.C., though their output of coinage, now mainly in silver, was not seriously affected. Mints are more easily identified than with the earlier electrum issues, and the products of Chios, Teos, Samos, Knidos, Kameiros in Rhodes and many other cities can be firmly attributed. In the south silver staters were struck in Lycia towards the end of the sixth century, whilst coinage in Cyprus began even earlier.

In 499 B.C. a revolt against Persian rule broke out in Ionia and lasted for six years. Although the Ionian Revolt was a failure it proved to be the first skirmish of an epic struggle between Greeks and Persians which was not finally resolved until Alexander's conquest of the Persian Empire in 331 B.C. The Ionian revolt provides a convenient point at which to terminate the archaic period of coinage in Asia Minor.

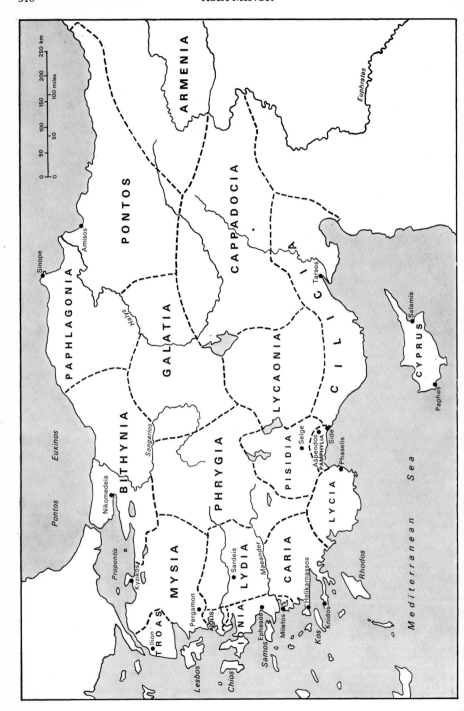

KINGDOM OF LYDIA

3396 **Before Kroisos,** 650-561 B.C. (reigns of Ardys, Sadyattes and Alyattes). Electrum
stater (*c.* 14·2 gm.). Two lions' heads face to face; uncertain objects in field above and
below. ℞. Three punches; the central one oblong, the other two square. *Jenkins*
(*Ancient Greek Coins*) 20 .. .. £10,000

3397   3398

3397 — Forepart of lion r., with protuberance on forehead (nose-wart). ℞. As last. *B.M.C.*
22. 1, 1 .. .. £8,000

3398 Electrum *third* (*c.* 4·72 gm.). Lion's hd. r., with rad. globule on forehead (nose-wart).
℞. Oblong punch, divided into two squares. *B.M.C.22.* 2, 7 .. .. .. £900

3399 — Two lions' heads face to face; between them, ϜΑΛϜΕΙ retrograde (= *walwei*). ℞.
Oblong punch. *Jenkins* (*Ancient Greek Coins*) 10 and 11 .. .. .. £2,500

*This inscription was once thought to represent the name of King Alyattes. Similar coins
with inscription* kali *. . . have since come to light and it now seems more likely that the names are
those of mint-masters. The dies were probably engraved for a larger denomination, now
unknown, and most specimens only show one of the lion's heads. See also no. 3401.*

3400 Electrum *sixth* (*c.* 2·36 gm.). Similar to 3398. *Boston Museum Catalogue* 1769 £600

3401   3403

3401 — Similar to 3399. *B.M.C.* 22. 3, 16 .. .. £1,500

3402 Electrum *twelfth* (*c.* 1·18 gm.). Lion's hd. r., with globule on forehead (nose-wart).
℞. Square punch. *B.M.C.* 22. 3, 17 .. .. £300

3403 Electrum *twenty-fourth* (*c.* 0·59 gm.). Similar. *B.M.C.* 22. 4, 21 .. .. £150

3404 Electrum *forty-eighth* (*c.* 0·3 gm.). Similar. *B.M.C.* 22. 4, 24 .. .. £125

3405 Electrum *ninety-sixth* (*c.* 0·15 gm.). Similar. *B.M.C.* 22. 4, 26 .. .. £100

3406   3411

3406 **Barbarous imitations,** struck by the Cimmerians (?), second half of 7th cent. B.C.
Electrum *third*. Lion's hd. r., represented only in outline without relief. ℞. Square
punch. *Forrer/Weber* 6769 .. .. £750

3407 Electrum *twelfth*. Lion's hd. r., in outline as last. ℞. Square punch. *B.M.C.* 22.
5, 28 .. .. £250

3408 Electrum *twenty-fourth*. Similar. *B.M.C.* 22. 5, 29 .. .. £125

3409 **Time of Kroisos,** 560-546 B.C.   Electrum *stater* (*c.* 14 gm.).   Joined foreparts of lion l. and bull r. back to back.   ℞. Three punches; the central one oblong, the other two square. *Kraay* (*Archaic and Classical Greek Coins*) *pl.* 3, 65   ..   .. £10,000

3410 — Similar, but the lion faces r. and the bull l.   *Head* (*The Coinage of Lydia and Persia*) *pl.* I, 6   ..   .. £10,000

3411 N *heavy stater* (*c.* 10·89 gm.).   Foreparts of lion r. and bull l., face to face.   ℞. Oblong punch, divided into two squares.   *B.M.C. 22.* 5, 30   ..   .. £3,500
   This new denomination was equivalent in value to the heavier electrum stater which it superseded.

3412 N *heavy third* (*c.* 3·63 gm.).   Similar.   *Historia Numorum, p.* 646   ..   .. £1,250

3413 N *heavy sixth* (*c.* 1·82 gm.).   Similar.   *Historia Numorum, p.* 646   ..   .. £800

3414 N *heavy twelfth* (*c.* 0·91 gm.).   Similar.   *Historia Numorum, p.* 646 ..   .. £400

3415   3416

3415 N *light stater* (*c.* 8·17 gm.).   Similar.   *B.M.C. 22.* 6, 31   ..   ..   .. £2,750
   This denomination was equivalent to ten silver staters.   See also no. 3423.

3416 N *light third* (*c.* 2·72 gm.).   Similar.   *B.M.C. 22.* 6, 36   ..   ..   .. £1,000

3417 N *light sixth* (*c.* 1·36 gm.).   Similar.   *Historia Numorum, p.* 647   ..   .. £700

3418 N *light twelfth* (*c.* 0·68 gm.).   Similar.   *Historia Numorum, p.* 647   ..   .. £350

3419   3420

3419 R *stater* (*c.* 10·89 gm.).   Similar.   *B.M.C. 22.* 7, 37 ..   .. £1,250

3420 R *half-stater* (*c.* 5·45 gm.).   Similar.   *B.M.C. 22.* 7, 41   ..   ..   .. £450
   This replaced the previous coin and was equivalent to one-twentieth of the light gold stater. See also no. 3424.

3421 R *third* (*c.* 3·63 gm.).   Similar.   *Historia Numorum, p.* 646 ..   ..   .. £400

3422 R *twelfth* (*c.* 0·91 gm.).   Similar.   *B.M.C. 22.* 8, 53 ..   .. £140

3423   3424

3423 **Under Persian Rule,** 546-510 B.C. (reigns of Cyrus, Cambyses and Darius I).   N *stater* (*c.* 8·17 gm.).   Foreparts of lion and bull/two incuse squares, similar to 3415, but of more formal style.   *Babelon* (*Traité des Monnaies Grecques et Romaines*) *pl.* X, 3   £2,250
   This and the next are not easy to distinguish from their Lydian prototypes (nos. 3415 *and* 3420).   *There was a steady deterioration in style and only those specimens exhibiting the most realistic design and neatest workmanship can be safely attributed to the time of Kroisos.*

3424 — R *half-stater* or *siglos* (*c.* 5·4 gm.).   As last.   *B.M.C. 22.* 7, 45   ..   .. £400

3425   3426   3427

3425 510-486 B.C. (reign of Darius I). *N̄ stater* or *daric* (*c.* 8·35 gm.). Archer (the Great King) kneeling r., shooting with bow. ℞. Oblong punch. *Kraay (Archaic and Classical Greek Coins) p.* 32 ..   ..   £3,000
3426 — *N̄* ¹⁄₁₂ *daric (c.* 0·69 gm.). As last. *B.M.C. 28.* 173, 184 ..   ..   ..   £400
3427 — *R̄ siglos (c.* 5·35 gm.). Half-length figure of archer (the Great King) r., holding two arrows and strung bow. ℞. Oblong punch. *B.M.C. 28.* 175, 197   ..   £300
3428 — —As 3425. *B.M.C. 28.* 173, 185 ..   ..   £250
3429 — *R̄* ⅓ *siglos (c.* 1·78 gm.). As 3425. *Babelon (Catalogue des Monnaies Grecques de la Bibliothèque Nationale) pl.* II, 11 ..   ..   £150
N.B. *For the later Achaemenid coinage, down to the time of Alexander, see below under Classical and Hellenistic periods: Lydia (nos. 4677-83).*

GREEK CITIES OF WESTERN ASIA MINOR

The Early Electrum Coinage

All mint attributions in this earliest phase of coinage must be regarded as conjectural.
3430 **IONIA. Ephesos.** 650-625 B.C. Electrum *eighth* (*c.* 1·77 gm.). Unmarked lump, without *rev.* punch. *Kraay (Archaic and Classical Greek Coins) p.* 21 — *from the Artemision find, Ephesos* £300
3431 — Electrum *stater* (*c.* 14·1 gm.). *Obv.* Blank; irregular rough surface. ℞. Three punches; the central one oblong, the other two square. *Boston Museum Catalogue* 1747 £2,500
3432 — Electrum *forty-eighth* (*c.* 0·3 gm.). *Obv.* Blank; smooth surface. ℞. Square punch. *Kraay (op. cit.) pl.* 3, 50 ..   ..   £100
3433 — Electrum *sixth* (*c.* 2·36 gm.). *Obv.* No type, but the field is striated with roughly parallel lines. ℞. Square punch. *Kraay (op. cit.) pl.* 3, 51 ..   ..   ..   £450

3434   3435   3437

3434 — — Similar, but with oblong punch on *rev.*, divided into two squares. *B.M.C. 14.* 3, 9 ..   ..   £450
3435 — Electrum *twenty-fourth* (*c.* 0·59 gm.). As 3433. *B.M.C. 14.* 5, 19   ..   £150
3436 625-600 B.C. Electrum *third* (*c.* 4·72 gm.). Hd. and neck of goat r., engraved on striated background. ℞. As 3434. *Kraay (op. cit.) pl.* 3, 52 ..   ..   ..   £1,250
3437 — — Cock l., behind hen l. looking back. ℞. Double square punch. *B.M.C. 14.* 3, 8 ..   ..   £1,750
3438 600-550 B.C. Electrum *third* (*c.* 4·3-4·6 gm.). Bee, within rectangular border. ℞. Two square punches side by side. *B.M.C. 14.* 47, 2 ..   ..   ..   £1,500

3439   3442

3439 **Miletos.** 600-550 B.C. Electrum *stater* (*c.* 14·1 gm.). Lion lying l., looking back; all within double rectangular frame divided into segments. ℞. Oblong punch, containing fox, between two square punches containing stag's hd. and star-shaped ornament. *Principal Coins of the Greeks* I.A.7 .. .. £10,000

3440 — — Forepart of rearing horse l. ℞. Similar to last, but designs within punches are indistinct. *Kraay* (*op. cit.*) *pl.* 3, 56 .. .. £9,000

3441 — — Double Gorgoneion. ℞. Three punches; the central one oblong, the other two square — each containing linear pattern. *Kraay* (*op. cit.*) *pl.* 3, 59 .. .. £9,000

3442 — Electrum *half* (*c.* 7·05 gm.). Upper part of winged daimon, his bearded hd. turned to r. ℞. As 3440. *Jenkins* (*Ancient Greek Coins*) 14 .. .. £4,000

3443 — Electrum *sixth* (*c.* 2·59 gm.). Lion advancing r., looking back. ℞. Square punch, divided into two halves. *B.M.C. 14.* 184, 5 .. .. £750

3444 **Samos** (island and city of the same name). 600-550 B.C. Electrum *stater* (*c.* 17·4 gm.). *Obv.* No type; the field filled with various irregular markings. ℞. Two oblong punches, placed side by side. *Kraay* (*op. cit.*) *pl.* 3, 66 .. .. £3,500

3445   3446

3445 — Electrum *half* (*c.* 8·7 gm.). Lion's hd. facing. ℞. Two punches; one oblong, the other triangular; uncertain markings within each. *B.M.C. 14.* 348, 1 .. £3,500

3446 — Electrum *quarter* (*c.* 4·35 gm.). Lion's hd. facing. ℞. Square punch. *B.M.C. 14.* 348, 2 .. .. £1,500

3447 — Electrum *sixth* (*c.* 2·9 gm.). Lion's hd. facing, on background of dashes. ℞. Square punch containing uncertain markings. *Kraay* (*op. cit.*) *pl.* 3, 67 .. £900

3448 **Phokaia.** 600-550 B.C. Electrum *stater* (*c.* 16·5 gm.). Seal r.; O below. ℞. Two square punches, of different sizes. *P.C.G.* I.A.10 .. .. £7,500

3449 — Electrum *sixth* (*c.* 2·75 gm.). Seal's hd. l. ℞. Square punch. *B.M.C. 14.* 204, 7 £1,000

3450 — Electrum *twenty-fourth* (*c.* 0·69 gm.). Similar. *B.M.C. 14.* 204, 9 .. £200

3451 — Electrum *ninety-sixth* (*c.* 0·17 gm.). Similar. *B.M.C. 14.* 205, 11A .. £125

3452 **Teos.** 600-550 B.C. Electrum *stater* (*c.* 16·6 gm.). Griffin's hd. l.; uncertain legend behind. ℞. Square punch, small and deep. *Babelon* (*Traité*) *pl.* V, 2 .. £12,000

3453 — Electrum *twenty-fourth* (*c.* 0·69 gm.). Griffin's hd. r. ℞. Square punch, divided into quarters. *B.M.C. 14.* 205, 14 .. .. £200

3454 **Smyrna.** 600-550 B.C. Electrum *stater* (*c.* 16·1 gm.). Lion's hd. l., with protruding tongue. ℞. Square punch, with irregular surface. *P.C.G.* I.A.17 .. .. £8,500

3454   3455

3455 **Chios** (island and city of the same name). *Circa* 550 B.C. Electrum *stater* (*c.* 14·05 gm.). Sphinx seated r. ℞. Square punch. *P.C.G.* I.A.11 .. .. .. £6,500

3456 **Unidentified Ionian mints.** 600-550 B.C. Electrum *stater* (*c.* 14·3 gm.). Forepart of ibex seated r. ℞. Three punches; the central one oblong, the other two square — each containing uncertain symbol or pattern. *P.C.G.* I.A.8 .. .. .. £7,500

3457   3458   3462   3465

3457 — Electrum *half* (*c.* 7·1 gm.). Floral device consisting of three flowers arranged to form a raised circular boss. ℞. Square punch, with irregular surface. *B.M.C. 14.* 2, 2 £3,500

3458 — — Round shield (?), in high relief, divided by broad bands into four triangular segments. ℞. Square punch, containing large X with globule at each extremity. *P.C.G.* I.A.2.. .. .. £3,500

3459 — — Raised square, with uneven surface. ℞. Square punch, containing wedge-shaped strokes. *B.M.C. 14.* 2, 4 .. .. £3,500

3460 — Electrum *third* (*c.* 4·72 gm.). Quadripartite linear square, each quarter containing irregular raised area. ℞. Oblong punch divided into two squares. *B.M.C. 14.* 3, 7 £1,500

3461 — Electrum *sixth* (*c.* 2·36 gm.). Forepart of Pegasos l. ℞. Square punch, ornamented with symmetrical pattern composed of pellets and dashes with star at centre. *B.M.C. 14.* 3, 10 .. .. £800

3462 Electrum *eighth* (*c.* 1·77 gm.). Circular shield, in relief, ornamented with three crescent-shaped ornaments, containing pellets, placed back to back. ℞. Square punch. *B.M.C. 14.* 4, 11 .. .. £650

3463 Electrum *twelfth* (*c.* 1·18 gm.). Swastika pattern within linear square. ℞. Square punch. *B.M.C. 14.* 4, 13 .. .. £250

3464 Electrum *twenty-fourth* (*c.* 0·59 gm.). Ram's hd. r. ℞. Square punch. *B.M.C. 14.* 5, 17 .. .. £175

3465 Electrum *forty-eighth* (*c.* 0·3 gm.). Swastika. ℞. Square punch. *B.M.C. 14.* 5, 21 £125

3466 Electrum *ninety-sixth* (*c.* 0·15 gm.). Human eye. ℞. Square punch. *B.M.C. 14.* 6, 27 £125

3467 **MYSIA. Kyzikos.** 600-550 B.C. Electrum *stater* (*c.* 16·4 gm.). Tunny fish, upright, between two fillets. ℞. Oblong punch and smaller square punch placed side by side; the former contains irregular markings, the latter a scorpion. *B.M.C. 15.* 18, 1 .. £5,000

3458   3469   3470

3468 — Electrum *sixth* (*c.* 2·7 gm.). Fish's hd. l. with spike; tunny r. above, pellet behind. ℞. Square punch, roughly quartered. *B.M.C. 15.* 18, 2 .. .. .. £600

3469 — Electrum *twelfth* (*c.* 1·35 gm.). Dolphin l.; beneath, tunny l. ℞. Similar to last. *B.M.C. 15.* 19, 13 .. .. £275

3470 — —Pecten-shell; beneath, tunny l. ℞. Similar to last. *B.M.C. 15.* 20, 15 £275

3471 — Electrum *forty-eighth* (*c.* 0·34 gm.). Fish's hd. l.; tunny (?) beneath. ℞. Similar to last. *B.M.C. 15.* 19, 8 .. .. £140

3472 **CARIA. Halikarnassos.** *Circa* 600 B.C. Electrum *stater* (*c.* 14·02 gm.). Stag walking r., hd. lowered; above, retrograde Greek inscription in archaic letters (= 'I am the badge of Phanes'). ℞. Three punches; the central one oblong, the other two square — each containing irregular markings. *P.C.G.* I.A.9 .. .. (*Unique*)

3473 — Electrum *third* (*c.* 4·72 gm.). *Obv.* Similar, but the legend reads 'Of Phanes'. ℞. Two square punches side by side, each containing irregular markings. *Kraay (Archaic and Classical Greek Coins)* pl. 3, 54 .. .. £15,000

A certain Phanes of Halikarnassos is mentioned by Herodotos as having been in the service of Amasis, King of Egypt. Although this was some seventy years later than the probable date of these coins, the earlier Phanes could have been the grandfather of Herodotos' mercenary (see Kraay, op. cit., p. 23).

3474 — Electrum *twelfth* (*c.* 1·18 gm.). Forepart of stag kneeling r., looking back. ℞. Square punch containing irregular markings. *Boston Museum Catalogue* 1816 £400

Archaic Silver Coinage and Late Sixth Century Electrum

3475   3476

3475 **MYSIA. Kyzikos.** *Circa* 520 B.C. Billon (base silver) *stater* (*c.* 14·7 gm.). Hd. of tunny fish l.; above, fish's tail r. ℞. Square punch containing irregular markings. *B.M.C. 15.* 20, 16-17 .. .. £1,000

3476 Late 6th cent. B.C. Electrum *stater* (*c.* 16·4 gm.). Ram kneeling l., looking back; beneath, tunny l. ℞. Square punch roughly divided into four square segments. *B.M.C. 15.* 24, 48 .. .. £2,500

3477 — —Forepart of cock l.; beneath, tunny l. ℞. As last. *B.M.C. 15.* 24, 49 £2,750

3478   3480

3478 — — Archaic hd. of Athena l., wearing crested helmet with cheek-pieces; beneath, tunny l. R. As last. *B.M.C. 15.* 20, 19   ..   ..   £5,000

3479 — Electrum *sixth* (c. 2·7 gm.). As last. *B.M.C. 15.* 20, 20   ..   ..   £1,250

3480 — — Naked figure, bearded, kneeling l., holding tunny fish by tail. R. As last. *B.M.C. 15.* 22, 29 ..   ..   £650

N.B. *This series of electrum coins, mostly staters, extends in an unbroken sequence down to the time of Alexander the Great. For the fifth and fourth century issues see below under Classical and Hellenistic periods.*

3481   3484

3481 **TROAS. Tenedos** (island and city of the same name). Late 6th cent. B.C. Æ *didrachm* (c. 8·94 gm.). Janiform hds. of Tenes l. and Philonome r. R. TE/NE (retrograde) above and below double-axe, within dotted square; all within incuse square. *B.M.C. 17.* 91, 2   ..   ..   £900

3482 — Æ *hemidrachm* ? (c. 1·9 gm.). Similar, but the legend is in two lines either side of axe shaft — TE – NE/ΛΙ–ΟΝ (retrograde). *B.M.C. 17.* 91, 4   ..   ..   £200

3483 **LESBOS.** Mid-6th cent. B.C. Billon (base silver) *stater* (c. 15·3 gm.). Lion's hd. r., jaws open. R. Small square punch, of rough form. *B.M.C. 17.* 150, 2   ..   £750

3484 — — (c. 14·4 gm.). Gorgoneion. R. As last. *B.M.C. 17.* 151, 6 ..   ..   £650

3485 — Billon *half-stater* (c. 6·7 gm.). Forepart of boar r. R. Similar to 3483, but the square is roughly divided into four segments. *B.M.C. 17.* 151, 9   ..   ..   £500

3486   3487

3486 Late 6th cent. B.C. Billon *stater* (c. 11 gm.). Two calves' heads face to face; olive-tree between them. R. Small square punch, of rough form. *B.M.C. 17.* 154, 46   £550

3487 — Billon *half-stater* (c. 5·4 gm.). Calf's hd. l. R. As last. *B.M.C. 17.* 154, 50   £450

3488 — Billon *tenth* ? (c. 1·15 gm.). Two boars' heads face to face. R. Incuse square, of rough form. *B.M.C. 17.* 151, 15 ..   ..   £140

3489 — Billon *twelfth* ? (c. 0·93 gm.). Boar's hd. r.; eye above. R. As last. *B.M.C. 17.* 152, 23   ..   ..   £110

Lesbos *continued*

3490 — Billon *fifteenth*? (*c.* 0·74 gm.). Calf's hd. l. ℞. As last. *B.M.C. 17.* 154, 52 £100

3491 — Billon *twenty-fourth*? (*c.* 0·47 gm.). Two eyes. ℞. Quadripartite incuse square. *B.M.C. 17.* 152, 27 .. .. £90

3492 — — Calf's hd. l. ℞. Lion's hd. l., within incuse square. *B.M.C. 17.* 154, 54 £90

3493 — Billon *forty-eighth*? (*c.* 0·24 gm.). Eye. ℞. Incuse square of rough form. *B.M.C. 17.* 153, 37 .. .. £75

3494 — Billon *ninety-sixth*? (*c.* 0·12 gm.). Similar. *B.M.C. 17.* 153, 39 .. .. £60

| 3495 | 3497 | 3499 | 3500 |

3495 **IONIA. Phokaia.** Mid-6th cent. B.C. Æ *drachm* (*c.* 3·8 gm.). Seal r. ℞. Incuse square, roughly quartered. *B.M.C. 14.* 214, 78 .. .. £350

3496 — Æ *trihemiobol* ? (*c.* 0·97 gm.). Hd. of seal l. ℞. As last. *Forrer (Weber collection)* 6089 .. .. £150

3497 — Æ *tritartemorion* ? (*c.* 0·42 gm.). Similar. *B.M.C. 14.* 214, 79 .. .. £125

3498 Late 6th cent. B.C. Electrum *sixth* (*c.* 2·6 gm.). Ram's hd. l; beneath, small seal. ℞. As 3495. *B.M.C. 14.* 207, 28 .. .. £600

3499 — — Bull's hd. l.; beneath, small seal. ℞. As 3495. *B.M.C. 14.* 206, 25 .. £600

3500 — Electrum *twenty-fourth* (*c.* 0·65 gm.). As 3498. *B.M.C. 14.* 207, 29A .. £200

N.B. *This series of electrum coins, mostly hektai (sixth-staters), extends down to the time of Alexander, like the staters of Kyzikos. Another long series of hektai was produced on Lesbos, but this appears to have commenced at a slightly later date.*

3500A — Æ *hemidrachm* (*c.* 1·6 gm.). Hd. of griffin l. ℞. Incuse square, roughly quartered. *B.M.C. 14.* 215, 82 .. .. £200

3500B — — Hd. of griffin r. ℞. Square segmented frame containing star, set diagonally within incuse square. *B.M.C. 14.* 215, 80 .. .. £90

3500C — Æ *trihemiobol* (*c.* 0·75 gm.). Similar to 3500A. *S.N.G. Von Aulock* 2118 £150

3500D — Æ *tritartemorion* (*c.* 0·4 gm.). Similar, but hd. of griffin r. *B.M.C. 14.* 215, 85 £95

500E — Æ *tetartemorion* (*c.* 0·14 gm.). Similar to 3500A. *B.M.C. 14.* 216, 88 .. £65

| 3501 | 3504 |

3501 **Klazomenai.** Late 6th cent. B.C. Æ *didrachm* (*c.* 7 gm.). Forepart of winged boar r. ℞. Incuse square, roughly quartered. *B.M.C. 14.* 18, 6 .. .. .. £550

3502 — Æ *drachm* (*c.* 3·5 gm.). Similar, but *obv.* type to l. *B.M.C. 14.* 18, 10 .. £300

3503 — Æ *diobol* (*c.* 1·15 gm.). Similar to 3501, but with K in one quarter of incuse square. *B.M.C. 14.* 18, 14 .. .. £150

3504 **Erythrai.** Late 6th cent. B.C. Æ *didrachm* (c. 7 gm.). Naked rider on horse cantering r. ℞. Incuse square, roughly quartered. *B.M.C. 14.* 119, 15 .. .. £750

3505 — Æ *tetrobol* (*c.* 2·3 gm.). Similar. *B.M.C. 14.* 119, 17 .. .. .. £300

3506 — Æ *diobol* (*c.* 1·15 gm.). Similar. *Boston Museum Catalogue* 1834 .. £200

3507	3508	3509

3507 Chios. Mid-6th cent. B.C. Æ *didrachm* (*c.* 7·5 gm.). Archaic Sphinx seated l., hair in uniform mass like an Egyptian wig. R. Square punch. *Forrer/Weber* 6245   £800

3508 Late 6th cent. B.C. Æ *didrachm* (*c.* 7·5 gm.). Archaic Sphinx seated l., r. foreleg raised, hair long. R. Incuse square, roughly quartered. *Forrer/Weber* 6247   £650

3509 Teos. Mid-6th cent. B.C. Æ *drachm* (*c.* 5·95 gm.). Griffin seated r., l. foreleg raised. R. Incuse square, of rough form. *B.M.C. 14.* 309, 1 .. ..   £750

3510 — Æ *hemidrachm* (*c.* 2·97 gm.). Similar. *Forrer/Weber* 6198   .. ..   £300

3511 — Æ *trihemiobol* (*c.* 1·48 gm.). Similar. *Forrer/Weber* 6199   .. ..   £200

3512	3514	3517

3512 Late 6th cent. B.C. Æ *didrachm* (*c.* 11·9 gm.). *Obv.* Similar. R. Quadripartite incuse square. *B.M.C. 14.* 309, 3 .. ..   £1,250

3513 Ephesos. Mid-6th cent. B.C. Æ *drachm* (*c.* 3·5 gm.). Bee crawling r. R. Square punch. *Head (Coinage of Ephesus) pl.* I, 5 .. ..   £400

3514 — — Bee crawling l. R. Incuse square, roughly quartered. *B.M.C. 14.* 48, 5   £375

3515 — — Bee. R. As last. *Head (op. cit.) pl.* I, 8 .. ..   £275

3516 — Æ *hemidrachm.* Bee flying. R. As last. *Head (op. cit.) pl.* I, 7 .. ..   £250

3517 Late 6th cent. B.C. Æ *drachm.* Bee; volute in upper field to l. R. Quadripartite incuse square. *B.M.C. 14.* 48, 6 .. ..   £250

3518	3519	3520

3518 Samos. 530-526 B.C. Æ *tetrobol* (*c.* 2·8 gm.). Lion's scalp facing. R. Square punch of rough form. *B.M.C. 14.* 350, 10. *Barron (The Silver Coins of Samos) pl.* I, 2a   £300

3519 526-522 B.C. Æ *drachm* (*c.* 3·55 gm.). Forepart of winged boar r. R. Lion's scalp facing, within dotted square; all within incuse square. *B.M.C. 14.* 354, 46. *Barron, pl.* I, 10a £225
See also no. 3525, of lighter weight.

3520 — — Similar, but *obv.* type to l., and the lion's scalp within a *triple* square border — dots between double lines. *B.M.C. 14.* 354, 42. *Barron, pl.* II, 34b £250

3521 — Æ *diobol* (*c.* 1·2 gm.). Hd. of panther r., within circular border of dots. R. Hd. of ram r., within dotted square; all within incuse square. *B.M.C. 14.* 356, 65. *Barron, pl.* XV, 2 .. ..   £175

Samos *continued*

3522 *Circa* 525 B.C. Counterfeit *stater*, in lead, originally plated with electrum. Naked Herakles (?) kneeling l. ℞. Two oblong punches, placed side by side. *Kraay (Archaic and Classical Greek Coins)* 68 .. .. £2,500

    Herodotos recounts the story that Polykrates, tyrant of Samos, bribed a besieging force of Spartans with leaden coins plated with gold (525/4 B.C.).

3523   3526

3523 522-520 B.C. Æ *didrachm* (*c.* 6·65 gm.). Forepart of ox r., with dotted truncation. ℞. Lion's hd. r., within triple square border — dots between double lines; all within incuse square. *B.M.C. 14.* 352, 23. *Barron, p.* 174, 1b £700

3524 — Æ *trihemiobol* (*c.* 0·8 gm.). Hd. of ox r., with dotted truncation. ℞. Lion's hd. r., within linear square; all within incuse square. *B.M.C. 14.* 352, 27. *Barron, p.* 174, 1d £150

3525 510-500 B.C. Æ *drachm* (*c.* 3·2 gm.). Forepart of winged boar r. ℞. Lion's scalp facing, within dotted square; all within incuse square. *B.M.C. 14.* 354, 47. *Barron, pl.* V, 106 .. .. £275

    See also no. 3519, *of heavier weight.*

3526 — Æ *hemidrachm* (*c.* 1·6 gm.). Forepart of winged boar l. ℞. Lion's hd. l., within dotted square; all within incuse square. *B.M.C. 14.* 355, 55. *Barron, pl.* XV, 4 £200

3527 499-495 B.C. Æ *tetradrachm* (*c.* 13 gm.). Lion's scalp within border of dots. ℞. Hd. of ox r., within dotted square; all within incuse square. *B.M.C. 14.* 351, 19. *Barron, pl.* VI, 1a £1,750

3528   3532

3528 — Æ *diobol* (*c.* 1·1 gm.). Similar, but without the dotted square on *rev.* *B.M.C. 14.* 352, 26. *Barron, pl.* VI, 4 .. .. £150

3529 — Æ *obol* (*c.* 0·55 gm.). Lion's scalp. ℞. Hd. of ox l., within dotted square; all within incuse square. *Barron, pl.* VI, 1 .. .. £110

3530 — Æ *hemiobol* (*c.* 0·27 gm.). Similar, but *rev.* type to r., and without dotted square. *B.M.C. 14.* 357, 81. *Barron, pl.* VI, 3 .. .. £75

3531 **Miletos.** Mid-6th cent. B.C. Æ *twenty-fourth stater* (*c.* 0·6 gm.). Lion's hd. l. ℞. Square punch, of rough form. *Forrer/Weber* 6039 .. .. £120

3532 Late 6th cent. B.C. Æ *twelfth* (*c.* 1·2 gm.). Forepart of lion r., hd. turned back. ℞. Star ornament within incuse square. *B.M.C. 14.* 185, 14, *etc.* £65

3533 — — Similar, but lion forepart to l., hd. turned back. *B.M.C. 14.* 186, 34 .. £75

    N.B. *See below, under 'Ionian Revolt', for a series of electrum staters sometimes attributed to the Miletos mint.*

3534   3538

3534 **CARIA. Uncertain mints.** *Circa* 530 B.C. Æ *stater* (*c.* 12·2 gm.). Forepart of horse l. ℞. Two square punches, of different sizes; the larger containing floral device, the smaller containing star. *B.M.C. 17.* 105, 7 (*attributed to Kyme*) £2,500

3535 — — Crab. ℞. Similar to last, but the two squares are roughly divided into compartments. *B.M.C. 18.* 193, 1 (*attributed to Kos*) £2,250

3536 — — Archaic Sphinx crouching l., uncertain object before. ℞. As last. *Forrer/Weber* 6243 (*attributed to Chios*) £2,250

3537 — Æ *hemidrachm* (*c.* 3 gm.). Similar to 3534, but without the smaller square punch on rev. *B.M.C. 17.* 105, 9 (*attributed to Kyme*) £450

3538 Late 6th cent. B.C. Æ *stater* (*c.* 12 gm.). Forepart of lion l., looking back; o.\. in field to r. ℞. Incuse square, roughly quartered. *B.M.C. 14.* 184, 6 (*attributed to Miletos*) £1,400

3539 — — *Obv.* Similar, but without legend. ℞. Star ornament within incuse square. *B.M.C. 14.* 184, 10 (*attributed to Miletos*) £1,250

3540   3541

3540 ~~Termera.~~ Tymnes, ruler of Termera, *c.* 510 B.C. Æ *third-stater* (*c.* 4·72 gm.). TVMNO. Herakles kneeling r., r. hand raised and holding club, strung bow in l. ℞. TEPMEPIKON. Lion's hd. l.; all within incuse square. *B.M.C. 18.* 176, 2 .. .. .. (*Unique*)

3541 **Kalymna** (island and mint of the same name). Late 6th cent. B.C. Æ *stater* (*c.* 10·5 gm.). Archaic hd. of bearded warrior l., wearing crested helmet with vizor, cheek-piece and neck-piece. ℞. Seven-stringed lyre, within incuse area which follows the shape of the instrument. *B.M.C. 18.* 188, 1 *and* 2 .. .. £12,500

3542 **Knidos.** 530-520 B.C. Æ *trihemiobol* (*c.* 1·77 gm.). Lion's hd. r. ℞. Archaic hd. of Aphrodite r., hair bound with tainia and falling in formal curls down neck; all within incuse square. *B.M.C. 18.* 85, 8 .. .. £175

3543   3545   3547

3543 520-500 B.C. Æ *drachm* (*c.* 6·25 gm.). Lion's hd. r. ℞. Archaic hd. of Aphrodite r., wearing sakkos bound with riband; all within incuse square. *B.M.C. 18.* 84, 2 £450

3544 — — Forepart of lion r. ℞. Similar to last, but with KИ before hd. of Aphrodite. *B.M.C. 18.* 84, 4 .. .. £500

3545 **Knidian Chersonesos** (a community on the peninsula of Loryma, south-east of Knidos). 530-520 B.C. Æ *tritartemorion* (c. 0·89 gm.). Lion's hd. r. ℞. +EP before hd. and neck of ox r.; all within incuse square. *B.M.C. 18.* 80, 3 .. .. .. £250

3546 520-500 B.C. Æ *stater* (c. 11·9 gm.). Forepart of lion r. ℞. +EP (retrograde) below hd. and neck of ox r.; all within incuse square. *B.M.C. 18.* 80, 1 .. .. £3,000

3547 — Æ *drachm* (c. 5·95 gm.). Forepart of lion r. ℞. +EP to l. of ox's hd. facing; all within incuse square. *B.M.C. 18.* 80, 2 .. .. £1,500

3548   3550

3548 **Kamiros** (on the island of **Rhodos**). Mid-6th cent. B.C. Æ *stater* (c. 12·3 gm). Fig-leaf, with sprouts between the lobes. ℞. Oblong punch divided into two oblong compartments. *B.M.C. 18.* 223, 2 .. .. £450

3549 — Æ *drachm* (c. 6 gm.). Similar. *B.M.C. 18.* 224, 8 .. .. .. £250

3550 *Circa* 520 B.C. Æ *stater* (c. 11·75 gm.). Fig-leaf; K-A either side of stalk. ℞. Similar to 3548, but with irregular lines in each oblong compartment. *B.M.C. 18.* 224, 6 £500

             3551   3554

3551 *Circa* 500 B.C. Æ *stater* (c. 11·35 gm.). *Obv.* Similar to 3548. ℞. KAMI/PEΩN in the two compartments of incuse oblong divided by thin band. *B.M.C. 18.* 224, 12 £600

3552 — Æ *trihemiobol* (c. 1·2 gm.). Fig-leaf. ℞. K-A in the two compartments of incuse oblong, as last. *B.M.C. 18.* 225, 13 .. .. £140

3553 — Æ *obol* (c. 0·9 gm.). Rose. ℞. KA before griffin's hd. l.; all within incuse square. *B.M.C. 18.* 225, 14 .. .. £120

3554 **Lindos** (on the island of **Rhodos**). *Circa* 520 B.C. Æ *stater* (c. 13·8 gm.). Lion's hd. r. ℞. Oblong punch divided into two oblong compartments, each containing irregular lines. *B.M.C. 18.* 228, 1 .. .. £750

3555 — Æ *diobol* (c. 1·1 gm.). Lion's hd. r. ℞. Incuse square, divided into two oblong compartments, the surface of each irregular. *B.M.C. 18.* 228, 3 .. .. £150

3556 *Circa* 500 B.C. Æ *stater* (c. 13·8 gm.). Similar to 3554, but with tuft of hair on lion's forehead, and with ΛΙΝΔΙ on the dividing bar on *rev.* *B.M.C. 18.* 228, 2 .. £1,000

            3557   3559   3560

3557 — Æ *tetrobol* (*c.* 2·2 gm.).   Forepart of horse r.; ΛΙΝΔΙ (usually indistinct) before.   Ɫ.
Lion's hd. r., within dotted square; all within incuse square.   *B.M.C. 18.* 229, 7-11   £225

3558 — Æ *obol* (*c.* 0·55 gm.).   Similar, but lion's hd. l. on *rev.*   *B.M.C. 18.* 229, 12   £120

3559 **Ialysos** (on the island of **Rhodos**).   *Circa* 500 B.C.   Æ *stater* (*c.* 14·8 gm.).   Forepart
of winged boar l.   Ɫ. Eagle's hd. r., floral volute above, ΙΕΛΥΣΙΟΝ beneath; all in dotted
square within incuse square.   *B.M.C. 18.* 226, 1   ..   ..   £4,000

3560 — Æ *third-stater* (*c.* 4·9 gm.).   Similar, but eagle's hd. to l. on *rev.*, and without inscription.   *B.M.C. 18.* 227, 7   ..   ..   £1,250

3561 — Æ *sixth* (*c.* 2·4 gm.).   As last.   *B.M.C. 18.* 227, 8   ..   ..   £400

3562 — Æ *twelfth* (*c.* 1·1 gm.).   Forepart of winged boar l.   Ɫ. Eagle's hd. l., in dotted square;
all within incuse square.   *B.M.C. 18.* 226, 4   ..   ..   £175

3563 — Æ *twenty-fourth* (*c.* 0·5 gm.).   Similar.   *B.M.C. 18.* 226, 6   ..   ..   £110

3564   3566

3564 **Poseidion** (on the island of **Karpathos**).   *Circa* 525 B.C.   Æ *stater* (*c.* 13·9 gm.).   Two
dolphins, one above the other; the upper one to l., the lower to r.; floral ornaments in upper
field to l. and to r., small fish below; ΠΟΣ above upper dolphin; all within dotted square
enclosed by linear square.   Ɫ. Oblong punch, divided by broad band into two compartments, each containing irregular markings.   *B.M.C. 18.* 192, 1   ..   ..   £1,600

3565 — — Two dolphins, one above the other; the upper one to r., the lower to l.; small fish
below; all within square frame consisting of pellets between two lines.   Ɫ. Similar to last;
the dividing band is of three parallel lines.   *B.M.C. 18.* 192, 3 ..   ..   ..   £1,250

3566 **"IONIAN REVOLT"** (these electrum staters, struck on the Milesian weight standard,
appear to date from the late sixth or early fifth century B.C.   From their uniformity of
style and fabric it seems likely that they were produced by one mint, possibly Miletos, and
are associated with the revolt of the Greek cities against Persian domination.   The more
traditional mint attributions are given in parentheses).   499-494 B.C.   Electrum *stater* (*c.*
14·1 gm.).   Forepart of Pegasos l., palmette ornament above.   Ɫ. Quadripartite incuse
square.   *B.M.C. 14.* 7, 32 (Lampsakos) £5,500

3567   3571

3567 — — Eagle stg. l., looking back.   Ɫ. As last.   *B.M.C. 14.* 7, 33 (Abydos) ..   £5,500

3568 — — Cock walking r., palmette ornament above.   Ɫ. As last.   *B.M.C. 14.* 8, 34
(Dardanos) £5,000

3569 — — Sow walking r.   Ɫ. As last.   *B.M.C. 14.* 8, 35 (Methymna) £6,000

3570 — — Horse prancing l., flower beneath.   Ɫ. As last.   *B.M.C. 14.* 8, 36 (Kyme)   £6,500

3571 — — Forepart of winged boar r.   Ɫ. As last.   *B.M.C. 14.* 8, 38 (Klazomenai)   £5,500

3572 — — Sphinx seated r., l. forepaw raised.   Ɫ. As last.   *Boston Museum Catalogue*
1809 (Chios) £6,500

"Ionian Revolt" *continued*

3573 — — Forepart of bull r., looking back. ℞. As last. *B.M.C. 14.* 8, 37 (Samos)　　£5,500

3574 — — Helmeted hd. of Athena r. ℞. As last. *Kraay (Archaic and Classical Greek Coins) pl.* 4, 77 (Priene)　..　　..　　..　　..　　..　　..　　..　　..　　£7,000

3573　　　　　　　　　　　　　　　　3575

SOUTHERN ASIA MINOR AND CYPRUS

3575 **CARIA. Mylasa.** *Circa* 500 B.C. ℛ *stater* (*c.* 11 gm.). Forepart of bounding lion l.; on shoulder, Carian monogram. ℞. Incuse square divided by broad band into two oblong compartments, each with irregular field. *Kraay (Archaic and Classical Greek Coins) pl.* 5, 100　..　　..　　..　　..　　..　　..　　..　　..　　£900

3576　　　　　　　　　　　　　　　　3578

3576 **LYCIA. Uncertain mint.** Late 6th-early 5th cent. B.C. ℛ *stater* (*c.* 9·5 gm.). Forepart of boar r., r. foreleg only visible. ℞. Square punch, roughly divided into two oblong compartments. *B.M.C. 19.* 1, 1 ..　　..　　..　　..　　..　　..　　£350

3577 — — Forepart of boar l., both forelegs visible; monogram on shoulder. ℞. Incuse square, of rough form, with dividing lines in the form of an 'X'. *B.M.C. 19.* 2, 6　　£300

3578 — — Similar, but with KVB (retrograde) on the boar's shoulder. *B.M.C. 19.* 2, 9　　£325

　　Kubernis, son of Kossikas, is mentioned by Herodotos (VII, 98) as the commander of the Lycian contingent in Xerxes' fleet at the time of the expedition to Greece, 490 B.C.

3579　　　　　　　　　　　　　　　　3580

3579 — — Forepart of boar l., both forelegs visible. ℞. Similar to 3577, but the design more formalized, and with ϴ — M in two of the divisions. *B.M.C. 19.* 3, 13 ..　　£300

3580 — — *Obv.* Similar, but with T on boar's shoulder. ℞. Incuse square, containing conical-shaped object surmounted by globe (?); network of lines on either side. *B.M.C. 19.* 3, 14　..　　..　　..　　..　　..　　..　　..　　..　　..　　£275

3581   3585

3581 — Æ *third-stater* (*c.* 3·15 gm.). Boar's hd. l. Ŗ. Similar to 3579, but without letters.
B.M.C. 19. 2, 11 .. .. £175

3582 — Æ *sixth* (*c.* 1·5 gm.). Forepart of boar r., r. foreleg only visible. Ŗ. Similar to 3577.
B.M.C. 19. 1, 2 .. .. £125

3583 **Phaselis.** Late 6th-early 5th cent. B.C. Æ *stater* = *double siglos* (*c.* 11 gm.). Prow
of galley r., resembling the forepart of a boar; three circular shields are visible along the
gunwale. Ŗ. Quadripartite incuse square. *Price & Waggoner (Archaic Greek Silver
Coinage: the Asyut Hoard)* 732 .. .. £650

3584 — — Similar, but the incuse square, on *rev.*, is divided into two oblong compartments,
each containing irregular linear pattern. *Kraay (Archaic and Classical Greek Coins) pl.*
57, 991 .. .. £650

3585 — — *Obv.* Similar, but prow to l. Ŗ. Incuse square divided by double line into two
oblong compartments, the lower of which contains two lines forming 'Λ'. *Price &
Waggoner* 736-8 .. .. £650

3586 — — As last, but with dolphin l. beneath prow on *obv.* *Price & Waggoner* 739 £650

3587   3590

3587 **CYPRUS** (most of the mint attributions in this earliest phase of Cypriot coinage are
only conjectural). **Salamis.** 520-500 B.C. Æ *stater* = *double siglos* (*c.* 11·1 gm.).
Ram lying l.; above and below, inscription in Cypriot characters (= Euelthon). Ŗ.
Smooth. B.M.C. 24. 46, 2 .. .. £650
    *King Euelthon was ruler of Salamis 560-525 B.C., but it seems unlikely that any coins were
struck during his reign. The name 'Euelthon' continues to appear on coins of Salamis well
into the following century.*

3588 — Æ *third-stater* (*c.* 3·7 gm.). Similar. B.M.C. 24. 47, 5 .. .. .. £225

3589 — Æ *sixth* (*c.* 1·8 gm.). Similar. B.M.C. 24. 47, 7 .. .. £150

3590 — Æ *twelfth* (*c.* 0·9 gm.). Ram's hd. l. Ŗ. Smooth. B.M.C. 24. 47, 8-9 .. £120

3591 — Æ *forty-eighth* (*c.* 0·23 gm.). Similar. B.M.C. 24. 47, 10-11 .. .. £85

3592 *Circa* 500 B.C. Æ *stater* (*c.* 11 gm.). Ram lying l. Ŗ. Ram's hd. l., *ankh* symbol and
branch before; all in dotted square within incuse square. B.M.C. 24. 52, 33 .. £1,250

3593 **Paphos** (or, more probably, **Amathos** or **Soloi**). Late 6th-early 5th cent. B.C. Æ
stater = *double siglos* (*c.* 11·1 gm.). Bull walking l.; Cypriot legend *Pa A* in field. R.
Eagle's hd. l., palmette above, guilloche pattern below; all in dotted square within incuse
square. *Larnaka hoard*, 1933, no. 186. *Cf. Price & Waggoner 783-4.. ..* £3,000

3594 — — Bull stg. l.; Cypriot legend *Ba* (above), *Ba Si* (below). R. As last. *Price &*
Waggoner 785 .. .. *Unique*

3595 — — Bull stg. l.; Cypriot legend *Pu-nu* above. R. Similar to 3593, but the eagle's hd.
has flaring neck-feathers. *B.M.C. 24.* 36, 5 .. .. £750

3596 — — Similar, but with Cypriot legend *Pu* only above bull on *obv.* *B.M.C. 24.* 36, 6
£750

3597 — — Similar, but without legend. *B.M.C. 24.* 37, 13 .. .. .. £700

3598 — Æ *third-stater* (*c.* 3·5 gm.). As last. *Price & Waggoner 786* £350

3599 **Lapethos.** Late 6th-early 5th cent. B.C. Æ *stater* = *double siglos* (*c.* 11·2 gm.). Hd.
of Athena r., in close-fitting Athenian helmet. R. Hd. of Athena r., in Corinthian
helmet; all within incuse square. *B.M.C. 24.* 29, 1 .. .. £2,000

3600 — — Similar, but with Phoenician legend *Demonikos* behind Athena's hd. on *rev.*
Kraay (*Archaic and Classical Greek Coins*) *pl.* 63, 1091 .. .. £2,500

3601   3603

3601 — — Hd. of Aphrodite r., wearing diadem and circular earring; hair waved on hd.,
hanging in curls on neck. R. Small hd. of Athena r., wearing Corinthian helmet; all
within incuse square. *B.M.C. 24.* 29, 3 .. .. £900

3602 — — *Obv.* As 3599. R. Hd. of bearded Herakles r., clad in lion's skin; all in dotted
square within incuse square. *Price & Waggoner 781* £3,000

3603 **Idalion.** *Circa* 500 B.C. Æ *stater* = *double siglos* (*c.* 11 gm.). Sphinx seated r., l.
foreleg raised; behind, circle of dots with pellet at centre. R. Incuse square, of irregular
form. *B.M.C. 24.* 24, 2 .. .. £1,600

3604   3607

3604 Uncertain mints. Late 6th-early 5th cent. B.C. Æ *stater* = *double siglos* (*c.* 11·2 gm.).
Hd. of roaring lion r. ℞. Incuse square, roughly divided into four quarters. *Kraay*
(*Archaic and Classical Greek Coins*) *pl.* 64, 1099 .. .. £1,000

3605 — — *Obv.* Similar. ℞. Goat's hd. l.; Cypriot letter *E* in lower field behind; all in dotted
square within incuse square. *Price & Waggoner* 813 .. .. .. £1,600

3606 — — Hd. of roaring lion l. ℞. Bull's hd. r.; Cypriot legend *Ba Phi* above; all within
incuse square. *B.M.C. 24.* 69, 3 .. .. £1,400

3607 — — *Obv.* Similar. ℞. Octopus; Cypriot letter *Ka* in lower field to l.; all within
incuse square. *Kraay* (*Archaic and Classical Greek Coins*) *pl.* 64, 1101 .. £1,500

3608 — — *Obv.* Similar. ℞. *Ankh* symbol between two branches; Cypriot legend *Ba E* in
field; all in linear square within incuse square. *B.M.C. 24.* 68, 2 .. .. £1,400

3609 — — *Obv.* As 3604. ℞. Gorgoneion; Cypriot legend *Ba A* beneath; all within incuse
square. *B.M.C. 24.* 68, 1 .. .. £1,500

ASIA MINOR

Classical and Hellenistic Periods

During the first half of the fifth century B.C. Greek coinage in western Asia Minor followed
the patterns already established in the archaic period. The growing influence of Athens
tended to restrict the development of coinage in this area and from *circa* 450 B.C. most silver
issues ceased altogether — no doubt as a result of the Athenian Coinage Decree. However,
the great electrum coinages of Kyzikos, Lesbos and Phokaia continued without interruption.

With the weakening of Athenian power towards the end of the fifth century a number of
cities resumed issuing their own types. This trickle of new coinage became a torrent following
Athens' fall in 404 B.C. The Attic weight standard of the Athenian imperial coinage, based
on a tetradrachm of 17·2 gm., was now rejected by the newly-liberated cities in favour of the
Chian (Rhodian) standard, with a tetradrachm weighing 15·6 gm.

The fourth century, down to the time of Alexander the Great, was a period of considerable
numismatic development in Asia Minor, though it also witnessed the strengthening of Persian
authority in the area. Many of the Greek cities produced issues of fine style, whilst even
those areas with Achaemenid allegiances had a substantial output of varied and interesting
types, including the earliest developments in numismatic portraiture. The Persian coinage of
gold darics and silver sigloi continued in abundant production, no doubt from the Lydian mint
of Sardeis.

Alexander's conquest of the Persian Empire, 334-331 B.C., was one of the great turning
points in history. In Asia Minor it brought to an end the autonomous coinages of most of the
cities — Rhodes being a major exception. Instead of issuing purely local types many of the
important mints were now commissioned to strike the new imperial coinage of Alexander on
the Attic weight standard. The third century was the heyday of the great Hellenistic monarchies, and whilst the powerful Greek kings vied with each other for control of various parts of
Asia Minor, there was little opportunity for individual cities to assert their independence for
any length of time. On the rare occasions when they were able to do so they usually minted
tetradrachms reviving the types of Alexander the Great with the addition of the name or symbol
of the city.

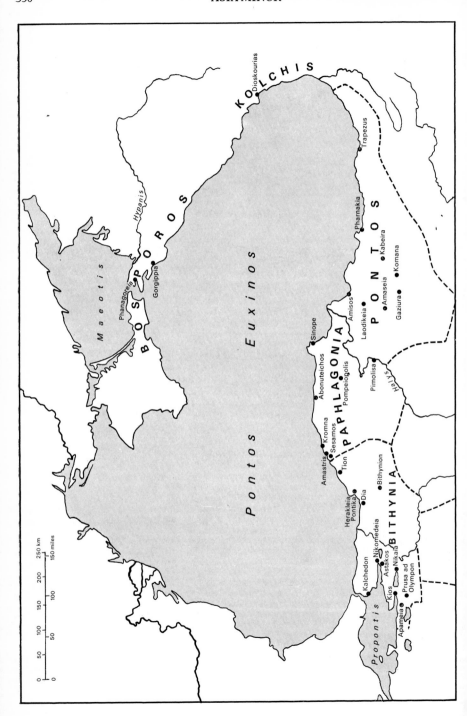

The collapse of the power of the kingdoms before the might of Rome, early in the second century B.C., brought about a dramatic revival of local coinage in Asia Minor as well as in Greece itself. Splendid tetradrachms on large flans, often of remarkably fine style for this late period, were struck by many of the famous cities of the western coastal region, as if to celebrate their new-found freedom. But that freedom was illusory. As Rome's iron grip tightened on the territories of the former Hellenistic Kingdoms so the privilege of issuing gold and silver coin was gradually withdrawn from the cities. In their final phase of semi-autonomous coinage the cities of Asia Minor were mostly restricted to the production of bronze coins — the forerunners of the 'Greek Imperial' coinage of the Roman Empire.

BLACK SEA AREA

Comprising the districts of Asiatic Bosporos, Kolchis, Pontos, Paphlagonia and Bithynia.

3610 **BOSPOROS. Phanagoreia** (a Greek city, founded by a colony of Teians under Phanagoras, Phanagoreia was the chief city of Asiatic Bosporos). 4th cent. B.C. Æ *trihemidrachm?* (c. 4·45 gm.). Young male hd. l., wearing conical cap. R. ΦΑΝΑ above bull butting l.; corn-grain in ex. *B.M.C. 13.* 3, 1 ..   ..   £450

| 3611 | 3612 | 3614 |

3611 — Æ *hemidrachm?* (c. 1·3 gm.). Similar, but with forepart of bull on *rev.*, with ΦΑ above and corn-grain behind. *Historia Numorum, p.* 494   ..   ..   £200

3612 1st cent. B.C. Æ *didrachm* (c. 8·6 gm.). Hd. of young Dionysos r., wreathed with ivy. R. ΦΑΝΑ/ΓΟΡΙ/ΤΩΝ in three lines, bunch of grapes above; all within ivy-wreath. *Historia Numorum, p.* 495 ..   ..   £250

3613 — Æ *drachm* (c. 4·1 gm.). Laur. hd. of Apollo r. R. ΦΑΝΑΓΟ/ΡΙΤΩΝ above and below thyrsos. *Grose (McClean collection)* 7336   ..   ..   £200

3614 — Æ *hemidrachm?* (c. 1·6 gm.). Hd. of Artemis Agrotera r., quiver at neck. R. ΦΑΝΑΓΟ / ΡΙΤΩΝ above and below rose. *B.M.C. 13.* 3, 4   ..   ..   ..   £150

3615 *Bronze Coinage.* 3rd-2nd cent. B.C. Æ 15. Hd. of Pan r. R. ΦΑ beneath bow and arrow r. *B.M.C. 13.* 3, 2 ..   ..   £18

| 3616 | 3619 |

3616 1st cent. B.C. Æ 21. Hd. of Artemis r., hair tied in bunch behind. R. ΦΑΝΑΓ beneath stag seated l. *Forrer (Weber collection)* 4745 ..   ..   £25

3617 — — Laur. hd. of Apollo r. R. Tripod, against which rests thyrsos; ΦΑΝΑ — ΓΟΡΙ / ΤΩΝ across field; monograms in field, to l. and to r. *B.M.C. 13.* 3, 7 ..   ..   £20

3618 — Æ 19. *Obv.* Similar. R. ΦΑΝΑΓΟ / ΡΙΤΩΝ above and below prow l. *B.M.C. 13.* 3, 5   £22

3619 **Gorgippia** (situated south-east of Phanagoreia). 1st cent. B.C. Æ *drachm* (c. 4 gm.). Laur. hd. of Apollo r. R. ΓΟΡΓΙΠ / ΠΕΩΝ above and below stag galloping r.; thyrsos in background. *B.M.C. 13.* 2, 1 ..   ..   £225

3620 — Æ *hemidrachm* (c. 2·2 gm.). *Obv.* Similar. R. ΓΟΡΓΙ. Bow in case, and club. *Historia Numorum, p.* 494 ..   ..   £200

3621   3622

Gorgippia *continued*

3621 — Æ 20. Laur. hd. of Apollo r. ℞. Tripod, against which rests club; ΓΟΡ — ΓΙΠ / ΠΕ
— ΩΝ across field; monogram in lower field to r. *Forrer/Weber* 4744 .. £25

3622 **The Sindi** (a Scythian tribe occupying territory bordering on the east coast of the Black
Sea). 4th cent. B.C. Æ *hemidrachm*? (*c.* 1·6 gm.). Hd. of young Herakles r., clad in
lion's skin. ℞. ΣΙΝΔΩΝ above horse's hd. r.; all within incuse square. *B.M.C. 13*, 4, 1
£200

3623 — Æ *diobol* (*c.* 1·2 gm.). Griffin seated r., corn-grain before. ℞. As last. *Historia
Numorum, p.* 495 .. .. £200

3624 — — Herakles kneeling r., stringing bow. ℞. ΣΙΝΔΩ. Owl stg. facing; all within
incuse square. *Historia Numorum, p.* 495 .. .. £225

3625 — Æ *hemiobol* (*c.* 0·3 gm.). As 3622. *Historia Numorum, p.* 495 .. .. £90

3626 — Æ *tetartemorion* (*c.* 0·15 gm.). Ox's hd. r. ℞. ΣΙΝΔΩ. Horse's hd. r. *Historia
Numorum, p.* 495 .. .. £80

3627   3628   3629

3627 **KOLCHIS** (the region bordering on the south-eastern coastline of the Black Sea, in
legend Kolchis was the goal of Jason's expedition). 5th cent. B.C. Æ (base) *stater* (*c.*
8·6 gm.). Lion seated l., looking back. ℞. Minotaur, with bull's hd. and forelegs and
human body, kneeling r.; all within oblong incuse. *Boston Museum Catalogue* 1352
£5,000

3628 5th-4th cent. B.C. Æ (base) *hemidrachm* (*c.* 2·3 gm.). Female hd. r., of archaistic style.
℞. Bull's hd. r., within linear circle. *B.M.C. 13.* 4, 1-5 .. .. .. £90

3629 **Dioskourias** (in the north of Kolchis, Dioskourias was a Milesian foundation, and provided a great market-place for the peoples of the surrounding area). Late 2nd — early 1st
cent. B.C. (time of Mithradates VI of Pontos). Æ 17. Caps of the Dioskouroi, each surmounted by star. ℞. Thyrsos; ΔΙ — ΟΣ / ΚΟΥ — ΡΙΑ / Δ — ΟΣ across field. *B.M.C.
13.* 5, 1 .. .. £25

3630 **PONTOS. Amaseia** (the capital of the Pontic kings until early in the 2nd cent. B.C.,
Amaseia was a strongly fortified city on the river Iris. It was the birthplace of Mithradates
the Great). Late 2nd-early 1st cent. B.C. (time of Mithradates). Æ 19. Hd. of young
Ares r., wearing crested helmet. ℞. Sword in sheath; ΑΜΑΣ — ΣΕΙΑΣ across field. *B.M.C.
13.* 6, 1 .. .. £12

3631   3633

3631 — Æ 18.   Bare-headed and dr. bust of Perseus r., winged.   R. Cornucopiae between
caps of the Dioskouroi; ΑΜΑΣ — ΣΕΙΑΣ across field.   *B.M.C. 13.* 6, 2 ..   ..   £15

3632 — Æ 15.   Rad. hd. of Helios r.   R. Wolf at bay to r., ΑΜΑΣΣΕΙΑΣ below.   *Forrer / Weber*
4753 ..   ..   £12

3633 **Amisos** (a flourishing Greek city on the Black Sea coast commanding an important
trade route to the south, Amisos was founded in the 6th cent. B.C.   It was re-settled by
Athenians in the following century and they renamed the place **Peiraeeus**).   400-350
B.C.   Æ *drachm* (*c.* 5·7 gm.).   Hd. of Tyche of the city l., wearing turreted stephanos,
hair rolled.   R. Owl stg. facing on shield, wings spread; ΗΓΗ — ΣΑΓ across field; ΠΕΙΡΑ in
ex.   *B.M.C. 13.* 13, 1   ..   ..   £160

3634   3635

3634 — — Similar, but with ΔΙ — ΟΓ across *rev.* field, and with sword in sheath to r. of owl,
club (?) to l.   *B.M.C. 13.* 14, 7 ..   ..   £140

3635 300-250 B.C.   Æ *hemidrachm* (*c.* 1·75 gm.).   Hd. of Tyche of the city r., hair tightly
rolled and wearing low, turreted stephanos.   R. Owl stg. facing on shield, wings spread;
Α in field to l., ΑΣΚΛΕΟΥΣ below shield.   *B.M.C. 13.* 14, 14-15 ..   ..   ..   £75

3636 Late 2nd — early 1st cent. B.C. (time of Mithradates).   Æ 31.   Laur. hd. of Zeus r.
R. ΑΜΙΣΟΥ.   Eagle stg. l. on thunderbolt, hd. r.; monogram to l.   *B.M.C. 13.* 15, 22
£24

3637   3638

3637 — Æ 29.   Hd. of Athena r., wearing triple-crested helmet ornamented with Pegasos.
R. Perseus stg. facing, holding harpa and hd. of Medusa, whose decapitated body lies at
his feet; ΑΜΙ — ΣΟΥ across field; monograms to l. and to r.   *B.M.C. 13.* 16, 32-3   £18

3638 — Æ 26.   Youthful bust of Mithras (?) r., wearing Persian head-dress.   R. Quiver,
with strap; ΑΜΙ — ΣΟΥ across field.   *B.M.C. 13.* 20, 80-82 ..   ..   ..   £20

3639   3640

3639 — Æ 23.   Hd. of Perseus r., wearing Phrygian helmet.   R. Pegasos stg. l., drinking;
in ex., ΑΜΙΣΟΥ and two monograms.   *B.M.C. 13.* 18, 61 ..   ..   ..   £12

3640 — Æ 22.   Hd. of young Dionysos r., wreathed with ivy.   R. Cista mystica, behind
which, thyrsos placed diagonally; monogram to l., ΑΜΙΣΟΥ below.   *B.M.C. 13.* 18, 53-4
£9

3641   3644

Amisos *continued*

3641 — — Bust of Amazon Lykastia (?) r., clad in wolf's skin. R. Nike advancing r., holding
wreath and palm; AMI — ΣΟΥ across field. *B.M.C. 13.* 20, 79 ..   ..   ..   £24

3642 — Æ 21. Aegis, with Gorgon's hd. at centre. R. Nike advancing r , carrying palm-
branch; AMI — ΣΟΥ across field; monograms to l. and to r. *B.M.C. 13.* 20, 74   £6

3643 — Æ 20. Hd. of young Ares r., wearing crested helmet. R. Sword in sheath; AMI —
ΣΟΥ across field. *B.M.C. 13.* 17, 40-41 ..   ..   £8

3644 — — Similar to 3636. *B.M.C. 13.* 15, 24-5 ..   ..   £7

3645   3648

3645 — Æ 18. Diad. hd. of Artemis r., quiver at neck. R. AMI — ΣΟΥ either side of tripod-
lebes. *B.M.C. 13.* 16, 38   ..   ..   £7

3646 — — *Obv.* As 3640. R. AMI — ΣΟΥ either side of thyrsos with fillet and bell; monogram in lower field to r. *B.M.C. 13.* 18, 58   ..   ..   £8

3647 — — Bust of Perseus / cornucopiae between caps, as 3631, but with legend AMI — ΣΟΥ
across *rev.* field. *B.M.C. 13.* 19, 65-7 ..   ..   £10

3648 — — AMIΣΟΥ. Cista mystica, behind which, thyrsos; monogram in field to l. R.
Panther r., stag's hd. between forepaws. *B.M.C. 13.* 18, 59 ..   ..   ..   £12

3649 — Æ 17. Diad. hd. of Artemis r. R. AMI — ΣΟΥ either side of quiver with strap.
B.M.C. 13. 16, 39 ..   ..   £7

3650   3651

3650 — Æ 14. Hd. of Perseus r., wearing winged helmet with apex in form of vulture's hd.
R. AMI — ΣΟΥ either side of winged harpa; monogram in lower field to r. *B.M.C. 13.* 19,
68 ..   ..   £9

3651 56 B.C. Æ 20. Bust of Roma r., wearing crested Corinthian helmet; AMI — ΣΟΥ across
field. R. Roma seated l. on shields, holding Nike; ΕΠΙ ΓΑΙΟΥ to r., ΚΑΙΚΙΛΙΟΥ / ΚΟΡΝΟΥΤΟΥ
to l., ΡΩΜΗ in ex. *B.M.C. 13.* 21, 83   ..   ..   £25
    C. Caecilius Cornutus was Proconsul of Bithynia in 56 B.C.

3652 **Kabeira** (situated in the valley of the Lykos, Kabeira was a favourite residence of
Mithradates, and it was in the vicinity of this place that the Pontic King was defeated by
Lucullus in 71 B.C.). Late 2nd-early 1st cent. B.C. (time of Mithradates). Æ 28. Hd. of
Athena / Perseus with body of Medusa, as 3637, but with *rev.* legend ΚΑΒΗ — ΡΩΝ and
without monograms in field. *B.M.C. 13.* 25, 1   ..   ..   £20

3653   3654

3653 — Æ 23. Aegis, with Gorgon's hd. at centre. ℞. Nike advancing r., carrying palm-branch; ΚΑΒΗ — ΡΩΝ across field. *B.M.C. 13.* 25, 2-3 .. .. .. £10

3654 **Chabakta.** Late 2nd-early 1st cent. B.C. (time of Mithradates). Æ 21. Hd. of young Ares r., wearing crested helmet. ℞. Sword in sheath; ΧΑΒΑ — ΚΤΩ across field; star within crescent and monogram in field to l. *B.M.C. 13.* 27, 1-2 .. .. .. £14

3655 — — Aegis, with Gorgon's hd. at centre. ℞. Nike advancing r., carrying palm-branch; ΧΑΒΑ — ΚΤΩΝ across field; monogram to r. *B.M.C. 13.* 27, 3-4 .. .. .. £12

3656   3658

3656 **Komana** (situated on the river Iris, Komana possessed a famous temple of Artemis, the high-priests of which wielded great power). Late 2nd-early 1st cent. B.C. (time of Mithradates). Æ 28. Hd. of Athena / Perseus with body of Medusa, as 3637, but with *rev.* legend ΚΟΜΑ — ΝΩΝ, and with monogram in field to l. only. *B.M.C. 13.* 28, 1 £20

3657 — Æ 20. Aegis, with Gorgon's hd. at centre. ℞. Nike advancing r., carrying palm-branch; ΚΟΜΑ — ΝΩΝ across field; monograms to l. and to r. *B.M.C. 13.* 28, 2 £9

3658 **Gaziura** (on the river Iris, between Komana and Amaseia, Gaziura was once a residence of the Pontic Kings but later lost its importance and fell into decay). 330-322 B.C. (under Ariarathes I of Cappadocia). Æ *drachm* (*c.* 5·65 gm.). Baal of Gaziura seated l., hd. facing, holding eagle, corn-ear and vine-branch in r. hand, sceptre in l.; Aramaic legend *Baal-Gazur* to r., Greek monogram to l. ℞. Griffin l., attacking stag kneeling l.; below, Aramaic legend *Ariorath*. *B.M.C. 20.* 29, 1 .. .. £250

3659 Late 2nd-early 1st cent. B.C. (time of Mithradates). Æ 29. Laur. hd. of Zeus r. ℞. ΓΑΖΙΟΥΡΩΝ. Eagle stg. l. on thunderbolt, looking back. *B.M.C. 13.* 30, 1 .. £30

3660 — Æ 22. Hd. of young Ares r., wearing crested helmet. ℞. ΓΑΖΙ — ΟΥΡΩΝ either side of sword in sheath. *B.M.C. 13.* 30, 2 .. .. £18

3661 **Laodikeia** (situated on the road between Amisos and Amaseia). Late 2nd — early 1st cent. B.C. (time of Mithradates). Æ 20. Aegis, with Gorgon's hd. at centre. ℞. Nike advancing r., carrying palm-branch; ΛΑΟΔΙ — ΚΕΩΝ across field; monogram to r. *B.M.C. 13*. 31, 1   ..   ..   £15

3662   3664

3662 **Pharnakia** (a strongly fortified coastal town, Pharnakia was founded by the grandfather of Mithradates the Great on the site of the former Kerasus). 2nd cent. B.C. Æ 19. Laur. hd. of Zeus r. ℞. ΦΑΡΝΑ / ΚΕΩΝ above and below humped bull r., hd. facing. *B.M.C. 13*. 36, 1   ..   ..   £17

3663 Late 2nd — early 1st cent. B.C. (time of Mithradates). Æ 22. Laur. hd. of Zeus r. ℞. Eagle stg. l. on thunderbolt, looking back; ΦΑΡΝΑΚΕΙΑΣ below, monogram in field to l. *B.M.C. 13*. 36, 2   ..   ..   £11

3664 **Taulara.** Late 2nd-early 1st cent. B.C. (time of Mithradates). Æ 28. Similar to last, but with *rev.* legend ΤΑΥΛΑΡΩΝ. *Grose/McClean* 7388 ..   ..   £30

3665 —- Æ22. Hd. of young Ares r., wearing crested helmet. ℞. ΤΑΥΛΑ — ΡΩΝ either side of sword in sheath. *B.M.C. 13*. 39, 1   ..   ..   £18

3666   3667

3666 **Trapezus** (a colony of Sinope, Trapezus was a coastal city of eastern Pontos not far distant from the Armenian border). 400-350 B.C. Æ *drachm* (*c.* 5·7 gm.). Young hd. of Hermes (?) l., with close beard. ℞. Table surmounted by bunch of grapes; ΤΡΑ below. *B.M.C. 13*. 40, 1   ..   ..   £750

3667 — Æ *trihemiobol* ? (*c.* 1·43 gm.). Similar, but without grapes on *rev.*, and the ΤΡΑ above the table. *B.M.C. 13*. 40, 2   ..   ..   £200

 The reverse type (table = trapeza) is a pun on the name of the city.

3668 **PAPHLAGONIA. Abonuteichos** (on the Black Sea coast). Late 2nd-early 1st cent. B.C. (time of Mithradates). Æ 20. Laur. hd. of Zeus r. ℞. ΑΒΩΝΟΥΤΕΙΧΟΥ. Eagle stg. l. on thunderbolt, looking back. *Historia Numorum, p.* 505   ..   £30

3669   3670

3669 **Amastris** (founded *circa* 300 B.C. on the site of the former Sesamos, Amastris became an
important city and Black Sea port). 300-288 B.C. Æ *stater* (*c.* 9·6 gm.). Hd. of
Amastris r., wearing mitra wreathed with laurel; behind, bow and quiver. ℞. Amastris,
as Aphrodite, enthroned l., holding small Eros; sceptre rests against throne; ΑΜΑΣΤΡΙΟΣ
to r., ΒΑΣΙΛΙΣΣΗΣ to l.   *Forrer/Weber* 4796   ..   ..   £750

> The lady depicted on both sides of this coin is Amastris, formerly wife of Lysimachos of
> Thrace, and foundress of the city.   She was a niece of Darius III, the last King of Persia, and
> was the wife of Dionysios, tyrant of Herakleia, before her marriage to Lysimachos.

3670 After 288 B.C. Æ *stater* (*c.* 9·6 gm.). Hd. of Mithras r., wearing mitra wreathed with
laurel and ornamented with star. ℞. Female figure (Anaitis ?) enthroned l., holding
Nike and sceptre; ΑΜΑΣΤΡΙΕΩΝ to r., myrtle-bud to l. *B.M.C. 13.* 84, 2-3 ..   £250

3671 *Bronze Coinage.* 300-288 B.C. Æ 17. *Obv.* As 3669. ℞. ΑΜΑΣΤΡΙΟΣ ΒΑΣΙΛΙΣΣΗΣ.
Bow in case. *Historia Numorum, p.* 506 ..   ..   £22

3672   3674

3672 After 288 B.C. Æ 22. Hd. of Athena r., in crested Athenian helmet. ℞. Thunderbolt
surmounted by owl stg. l.; ΑΜΑΣΤΡΙΕΩΝ below, monogram above. *B.M.C. 13.* 84, 4   £17

3673 Late 2nd-early 1st cent. B.C. (time of Mithradates). Æ 31. Laur. hd. of Zeus r. ℞.
Eagle stg. l. on thunderbolt, looking back; ΑΜΑΣΤΡΕΩΝ below. *B.M.C. 13.* 84, 5   £24

3674 — — Hd. of Athena r., wearing triple-crested helmet ornamented with Pegasos. ℞.
Perseus stg. facing, holding harpa and hd. of Medusa, whose decapitated body lies at his
feet; ΑΜΑΣ — ΤΡΕΩΝ across field; monograms to l. and to r. *B.M.C. 13.* 85, 8   £18

3675 — Æ 23. Aegis, with Gorgon's hd. at centre. ℞. Nike advancing r., carrying palm-
branch; ΑΜΑΣ — ΤΡΕΩΝ across field; monograms to l. and to r. *B.M.C. 13.* 85, 9   £7

3676 — Æ 14. Turreted bust of the Tyche (or Hera) l., hair rolled. ℞. ΚΡ / ΩΜ either side of
84, 6 ..   ..   £8

3677 After 64 B.C. Æ 20. Bust of the Tyche r., wearing turreted head-dress. ℞. ΑΜΑΣ /
ΤΡΕΩΣ in two lines, date numerals above; all within laurel-wreath. *Forrer/Weber* 4799
£14

3678　　　　　　　　　　　　　　　3679

3678 **Kromna** (a coastal town, to the east of Sesamos, Kromna was abandoned *circa* 300 B.C. when its inhabitants were moved to the newly-founded Amastris). 340-300 B.C. Æ *tetrobol* (*c.* 3·55 gm.). Laur. hd. of Zeus l. ℞. Turreted bust of the Tyche (or Hera) l., hair rolled; ΚΡΩΜΝΑ to r., swastika symbol above, И below chin, Κ behind neck. *B.M.C. 13*. 90, 4 　.. 　　.. 　　.. 　　　.. 　　.. 　　.. 　　.. 　　.. 　　£130

3679 — Æ 14. Turreted bust of the Tyche (or Hera) l., hair rolled. ℞. ΚΡ / ΩΜ either side of amphora surmounted by bunch of grapes. *B.M.C. 13*. 91, 9 　.. 　　.. 　　£15

3680 **Pimolisa** (about 60 miles south of the Black Sea coastline, Pimolisa was situated on the river Halys). Late 2nd-early 1st cent. B.C. (time of Mithradates). Æ 25. Laur. hd. of Zeus r. ℞. Eagle stg. l. on thunderbolt, looking back; ΠΙΜΩΛΙΣΩΝ below. *Forrer/ Weber* 4806 　.. 　　.. 　　.. 　　.. 　　.. 　　.. 　　.. 　　.. 　　£24

3681　　　　　　　　　　　　　　　3685

3681 — Æ 19. Hd. of young Ares r., wearing crested helmet. ℞. ΠΙΜΩ — ΛΙΣΩΝ either side of sword in sheath. *B.M.C. 13*. 37, 1 　.. 　　.. 　　.. 　　.. 　　.. 　　£14

3682 **Pompeiopolis** (situated south-west of Sinope). 1st cent. B.C. Æ 20. Laur. hd. of Zeus r. ℞. ΠΟΜΠΗΙΟΠΟΛΙΤΩΝ. Torch; all within wreath. *Historia Numorum, p.* 507
　　　　　　　　　　　　　　　　　　　　　　　　　　　　　　　　　£20

3683 **Sesamos** (a coastal town close to the Bithynian border, Sesamos was refounded *circa* 300 B.C. under the name of Amastris). 340-300 B.C. Æ *tetrobol* (*c.* 3·55 gm.). Laur. hd. of Zeus l. ℞. Hd. of Demeter l., wreathed with corn; ΣΗΣΑΜ behind, anchor above. *Babelon* (*Traité*) *pl.* 183, 22 　.. 　　.. 　　.. 　　.. 　　.. 　　.. 　　£250

3684 — Æ *diobol* (*c.* 1·75 gm.). Similar. *Babelon* (*Traité*) *pl.* 183, 23 　.. 　　.. 　　£150

3685 — Æ 15. Laur. hd. of Zeus l. ℞. Hd. of Demeter (?) l., hair rolled; ΣΗ/ΣΑ either side of neck. *B.M.C. 13*. 94, 1 .. 　.. 　　.. 　　.. 　　.. 　　.. 　　.. 　　£15

3686 — Æ 13. Laur. hd. of Apollo l. ℞. ΣΗ / ΣΑ either side of kantharos. *Babelon* (*Traité*) *pl.* 183, 26 　.. 　　.. 　　.. 　　.. 　　.. 　　.. 　　.. 　　£13

3687　　　　　　　　　　　　　　　3688

3687 **Sinope** (a colony of Miletos, founded in the 7th cent. B.C., Sinope rose to become the most important city on the southern coastline of the Black Sea). 480-450 B.C. Æ *drachm* (*c.* 6 gm.). Hd. of eagle l.; dolphin below. ℞. Quadripartite incuse square; the alternate depressions deeper, with granulated surfaces, and each containing pellet. *B.M.C. 13*. 95, 1 　.. 　　.. 　　.. 　　.. 　　.. 　　.. 　　.. 　　.. 　　£225

3688 — — Similar, but the *obv.* type is of very crude style and is barely recognizable as an eagle's hd. *B.M.C. 13*. 95, 3 　.. 　　.. 　　.. 　　.. 　　.. 　　.. 　　£150

3689   3690

3689 — — Similar, but eagle's hd. larger and of much better style; on *rev.* the surfaces of the deeper depressions are not granulated. *B.M.C. 13.* 95, 4   ..   ..   ..   £325

3690 415-365 B.C. *Æ drachm* (*c.* 6 gm.). Hd. of nymph Sinope l., hair in sphendone. R. Sea-eagle l., wings spread, stg. on the back of dolphin l.; ΣΙΝΩ below; all within incuse square. *B.M.C. 13.* 95, 6 ..   ..   £175

3691 — — Similar, but without incuse square on *rev.*, and with ΠΡ between eagle's wing and tail. *B.M.C. 13.* 95, 7   ..   ..   £140

3692   3693

3692 — — Hd. of nymph Sinope l., hair in sphendone, wearing necklace and earring. R. Sea-eagle l., wings spread, stg. on the back of dolphin l.; ΣΙΝΩ below; ΠΟΣ between eagle's wing and tail. *B.M.C. 13.* 96, 11-12, *var.* £140

3693 — — *Obv.* Similar. R. Sea-eagle on dolphin, as last; ΔΑΤΑΜΑ below; ΑΠΟ between eagle's wing and tail; ΗΡ monogram beneath tail. *B.M.C. 13.* 96, 8   ..   ..   £200

   This was issued circa 365 B.C. *when the Persian satrap Datames attacked and occupied Sinope.*

3694 — *Æ hemidrachm* (*c.* 2·9 gm.). *Obv.* Similar. R. ΣΙ — ΝΩ either side of conventional representation of eagle facing, hd. l., wings spread; Π in field to r. *B.M.C. 13.* 97, 21

£65

3695   3696

3695 — *Æ trihemiobol* (*c.* 1·5 gm.). Hd. of nymph Sinope three-quarter face to l., wearing necklace and earrings. R. As last, but without Π in field. *B.M.C. 13.* 97, 23-5   £85

3696 365-322 B.C. *Æ drachm* (*c.* 6 gm.). Hd. of nymph Sinope l., hair in sphendone, wearing necklace and earring; before, aplustre. R. Sea-eagle l., wings spread, stg. on the back of dolphin l.; ΣΙΝΩ below; ΚΡΗΘ between eagle's wing and tail. *B.M.C. 13.* 97, 18   £125

3697 — — Similar, but with magistrate's name ΠΟΛΥ instead of ΚΡΗΘ on *rev.* *B.M.C. 13.* 97, 19   ..   ..   £125

3698   3700

Sinope *continued*

3698 — — *Obv.* Similar. R. Sea-eagle l., wings spread, stg. on the back of dolphin l.; below, Aramaic legend *Abd Sisin*. *Forrer/Weber* 4815 ..   £275

     The name on this coin is possibly that of Sysinas, son of Datames.

3699 — — *Obv.* Similar, but with Aramaic letters behind nymph's hd. R. Sea-eagle on dolphin, as last, but with the name *Ariarathes* in Aramaic script below dolphin. *B.M.C.* *13*. 96, 9 ..   £250

     This type, issued circa 330 B.C., bears the name of Ariarathes I, King of Cappadocia.

3700 306-290 B.C. Æ *tetrobol?* (*c.* 2·5 gm.). Hd. of nymph Sinope l., hair rolled, wearing turreted head-dress. R. ΣΙΝΩ above prow l.; before, aplustre and monogram. *B.M.C.* *13*. 98, 26-8 ..   £75

3701   3702

3701 3rd cent. B.C. Æ *tetradrachm* (*c.* 16·9 gm.). Turreted hd. of the Tyche r. R. Naked Apollo seated r. on omphalos, holding plectrum and lyre; ΣΙΝΩΠΕΩΝ behind, Α/Μ/Τ before. *Waddington* (*Recueil général*) *pl.* 25, 36 ..   £1,500

3702 — Æ *didrachm* (*c.* 8·2 gm.). Turreted hd. of the Tyche l. R. ΣΙ — ΝΩ either side of Poseidon seated l., holding dolphin and trident; monogram behind seat. *B.M.C. 13*. 98, 34-5 ..   £250

     These are often countermarked on both sides—obv. rad. bust of Helios facing, ΣΙΝΩΠΕΩΝ *between rays; rev. hd. of Zeus or Poseidon l.*

3703 — Æ *drachm* (*c.* 3·9 gm.). Laur. hd. of Apollo l. R. ΣΙΝΩ above prow l.; before, lyre and monogram. *B.M.C. 13*. 99, 36 ..   £110

     These are sometimes countermarked, on obv., with hd. of Hermes r., in petasos.

3704   3707

3704 — Æ *hemidrachm* (*c.* 1·9 gm.). Turreted hd. of the Tyche l. R. Conventional representation of eagle facing, hd. l., wings spread; ΣΙ — ΝΩ in lower field, bunch of grapes to l., monogram to r. *B.M.C. 13*. 98, 30-32 ..   £55

     These sometimes bear the same countermark as the drachmas.

3705 — Æ *diobol* (*c.* 1·1 gm.).   Hd. of Hermes l., wearing petasos.   ℞. ΣΙ — ΝΩ either side of conventional representation of eagle, as last.   *Forrer/Weber* 4829   ..   ..   £75

3706 — Æ *trihemiobol* (*c.* 0·8 gm.).   Laur. hd. of Apollo l.   ℞. ΣΙ — ΝΩ either side of tripod; bunch of grapes to l., A to r.   *B.M.C. 13.* 98, 33 ..   ..   £60

3707 Late 2nd-early 1st cent. B.C. (time of Mithradates).   Æ 31.   Hd. of Athena r., wearing triple-crested helmet ornamented with Pegasos.   ℞. Perseus stg. facing, holding harpa and hd. of Medusa, whose decapitated body lies at his feet; ΣΙΝΩ — ΠΗΣ across field, monogram to l.   *B.M.C. 13.* 99, 44, *var.* £18

3708 — Æ 27.   Laur. hd. of Zeus r.   ℞. Eagle stg. l. on thunderbolt, looking back; ΣΙΝΩΠΗΣ below.   *B.M.C. 13.* 99, 37   ..   ..   £20

3709   3711

3709 — Æ 20.   Aegis, with Gorgon's hd. at centre.   ℞. Nike advancing r., carrying palm-branch; ΣΙΝ — ΩΠΗΣ across field; Μ in field to r.   *B.M.C. 13.* 100, 47 ..   ..   £7

3710 — — Hd. of young Ares r., wearing crested helmet.   ℞. ΣΙΝΩ — ΠΗΣ either side of sword in sheath.   *B.M.C. 13.* 100, 50   ..   ..   £9

3711 — — Similar to 3708, but also with monogram in *rev.* field to l., star to r.   *B.M.C. 13.* 99, 38-9   ..   ..   £8

3712 — Æ 18.   Diad. hd. of Artemis r., quiver at neck.   ℞. ΣΙΝΩ — ΠΗΣ either side of tripod-lebes.   *B.M.C. 13.* 100, 51   ..   ..   £8

3713 — — Bare-headed and dr. bust of Perseus r., winged.   ℞. Cornucopiae between caps of the Dioskouroi; ΣΙΝΩ — ΠΗΣ across field.   *B.M.C. 13.* 100, 45-6   ..   £11

3714   3717

3714 **PAPHLAGONIAN KINGS.   Pylaimenes.**   Late 2nd cent. B.C.   Æ 20.   Bare hd. of young Herakles r., lion's skin round neck, club over shoulder.   ℞. Nike stg. l., holding wreath and palm; ΒΑΣΙΛΕΩΣ to r., ΠΥΛΑΙΜΕΝΟΥ/ΕΥΕΡΓΕΤΟΥ to l.   *B.M.C. 13.* 103, 1   £25

3715 Æ 17.   Bull's hd. facing.   ℞. Winged caduceus; ΒΑΣΙΛΕΩΣ to r., ΠΥΛΑΙΜΕΝΟΥ/ΕΥΕΡΓΕΤΟΥ to l.   *B.M.C. 13.* 103, 2-3 ..   ..   £22

3716 **Deiotaros.**   *Circa* 35-31 B.C.   Æ *drachm* (*c.* 3·8 gm.).   ΒΑΣΙΛΕΩΣ ΔΗΙΟΤΑΡΟΥ ΦΙΛΑΔΕΛΦΟΥ.   Hd. of Deiotaros r., ΖΚΥ in field.   ℞. ΒΑΣΙΛΙΣΣΗΣ ΑΔΟΒΟΓΙΩΝΑΣ.   Bust of Queen Adobogiona r.   *Historia Numorum, p.* 509   ..   ..   £450

3717 Æ 24.   ΒΑΣΙΛΕΩΣ ΔΗΙΟΤΑΡΟΥ ΦΙΛΑΔΕΛΦΟΥ.   Diad. hd. of Deiotaros r.   ℞. ΒΑΣΙΛΕΩΣ ΔΗΙΟΤΑΡΟΥ ΦΙΛΟΠΑΤΟΡΟΣ.   Caps of the Dioskouroi, monogram between.   *Historia Numorum, p.* 509   ..   ..   £55

3718 **BITHYNIA.** **Apameia** (originally named **Myrleia,** the town was a colony of Kolophon. Prusias I of Bithynia renamed it in honour of his wife, *c.* 202 B.C.). Before 202 B.C. Æ 23. Laur. hd. of Apollo r. ℞. ΜΥΡΛΕΑΝΩΝ. Athena seated l., holding Nike and resting l. arm on shield at her side; bunch of grapes in field to l. *B.M.C. 13.* 110, 8
£16

3719   3722

3719 — Æ 20. Hd. of Athena l., in crested Corinthian helmet. ℞. Humped bull butting r., ΜΥΡΛΕΑ in ex. *B.M.C. 13.* 109, 5   ..   .. £15

3720 — Æ 17. Rad. hd. of Helios facing. ℞. Horseman prancing r., his r. hand raised; ΜΥΡΛΕΑ below. *B.M.C. 13.* 109, 6   ..   .. £14

3721 — Æ 14. Veiled hd. of Demeter r. ℞. ΜΥΡ/ΛΕΑ either side of lyre. *B.M.C. 13.* 110, 12-13   ..   .. £10

3722 — Æ 13. Helmeted hd. of Athena r. ℞. Wheel, with Μ — Υ — Ρ — Λ between the spokes. *B.M.C. 13.* 109, 1-2   ..   .. £9

3723   3725

3723 47/46 B.C. Æ 24. Laur. hd. of Apollo r., ΑΠΑΜΕΩΝ behind. ℞. ΤΩΝ ΜΥΡ/ΛΕΑΝΩΝ either side of lyre; ΕΛΣ (= year 236) below. *B.M.C. 13.* 111, 17   ..   .. £12

3724 — — ΑΠΑΜΕΩΝ ΤΩΝ ΜΥΡΛΕΑΝΩΝ. Laur. hd. of Apollo r. ℞. ΕΠΙ ΓΑΙΟΥ/ΟΥΙΒΙΟΥ/ΠΑΝΣΑ. Lyre; ΕΛΣ (= year 236) below. *B.M.C. 13.* 110, 15   ..   .. £24
    C. Vibius Pansa was Roman Proconsul of the province of Bithynia et Pontus.

3725 After *circa* 47 B.C. Æ 17. Hd. of Hermes r., wearing close-fitting winged petasus. ℞. C.I.C.A.D.D. Winged caduceus. *B.M.C. 13.* 111, 18   ..   ..   .. £9
    The letters on rev. stand for Colonia Julia Concordia Apamea, Decurionum Decreto.

3726 — — Similar, but with *rev.* type three Roman standards. *B.M.C. 13.* 111, 19   £9

3727 **Astakos** (a colony of Megara, Astakos was an important city situated south-east of a large gulf on the eastern shores of the Propontis. The place was destroyed by Lysimachos in 281 B.C.). *Circa* 470 B.C. Æ *drachm* (*c.* 5 gm.). Lobster. ℞. Diad. female hd. r., of archaic style, wearing necklace; ΑΣ (retrograde) before, swastika behind; all within incuse square. *Babelon* (*Traité*) *pl.* 181, 1   ..   .. £1,750
    The obv. type represents a pun on the name of the city.

3728 — Æ *hemidrachm* (*c.* 2·5 gm.). Similar. *Babelon, pl.* 181, 2 ..   ..   .. £750

3729 — Æ *diobol* (*c.* 1·65 gm.). Similar, but without swastika on *rev. Babelon, pl.* 181, 3
£500

3730 *Circa* 435 B.C. Æ *drachm* (*c.* 5 gm.). Lobster; ΑΣ to r. ℞. Female hd. l., hair confined in sakkos; all within incuse square. *Babelon, pl.* 181, 5   ..   ..   .. £1,750

3731 — — Similar, but without legend on *obv.*, and lobster holds shell in claws. *Babelon, pl.* 181, 4   ..   .. £1,750

3732 — Æ *hemidrachm* (*c.* 2·5 gm.). As last. *Babelon, pl.* 181, 6 ..   ..   .. £750

3733   3734

3733 **Bithynion** (an inland town, about 40 miles south of Herakleia Pontika). 59 B.C. Æ 23. Hd. of young Dionysos r., wreathed with ivy; ΒΙΘΥΝΙΕꞶΝ behind, ΔΚΣ (= year 224) before. ℞. Roma seated l. on shields, holding Nike and sceptre; ΕΠΙ ΓΑΙΟΥ to r., ΠΑΠΙΡΙΟΥ/ΚΑΡΒꞶΝΟΣ to l., ΡꞶΜΗ in ex. *B.M.C. 13.* 117, 1   ..   ..   ..   £35
       C. Papirius Carbo was Roman Proconsul of the province of Bithynia et Pontus.

3734 **Kalchedon** (a colony of Megara, founded early in the 7th cent. B.C., Kalchedon was situated on the Asiatic side of the Bosporus, almost opposite Byzantion. Its history and coinage were closely linked with its more important European neighbour). Mid-5th cent. B.C. Æ *drachm* (*c.* 4·2 gm.). Male hd. (Kalchas ?) l., bearded, hair plaited behind. ℞. Κ — Α — Λ — Χ between the spokes of radiate wheel; all within circular incuse. *B.M.C. 13.* 124, 1   ..   ..   £1,750

3735 — Æ *hemidrachm* (*c.* 2·1 gm.). Hd. of Apollo (?) l. ℞. As last. *B.M.C. 13.* 124, 2   £750

           3736   3738   3739

3736 Late 5th cent. B.C. Æ *hemidrachm* (*c.* 2·1 gm.). Hd. of Apollo (?) r. ℞. Κ — Α — Λ and ivy-leaf between the spokes of a wheel; all within circular incuse. *B.M.C. 13.* 124, 3   ..   ..   £750

3737 — Æ *trihemiobol* (*c.* 1·05 gm.). Circular shield, with dotted edge and uncertain decoration (Gorgoneion ?). ℞. Κ — Α — Λ — Χ between the spokes of a wheel. *Babelon (Traité) pl.* 181, 13   ..   ..   £375

3738 Early 4th cent. B.C. Æ *drachm* or *siglos* (*c.* 5·3 gm.). Bull stg. l. on ear of corn; ΚΑΛΧ above. ℞. Incuse square of "mill-sail" pattern. *B.M.C. 13.* 124, 4-7   ..   £110

3739 — Æ *hemidrachm* (*c.* 2·6 gm.). Similar, but with legend ΚΑΛ on *obv*. *B.M.C. 13.* 125, 10   ..   ..   £55

3740 — Æ *trihemiobol* (*c.* 1·3 gm.). Similar, but with legend ΚΑ on *obv*. *B.M.C. 13.* 125, 12   ..   ..   £35

3741 Mid-4th cent. B.C. Æ *tetradrachm* (*c.* 15 gm.). Bull stg. l. on ear of corn; ΚΑΛΧ above, monogram before. ℞. Quadripartite incuse square of "mill-sail" pattern; the surfaces granulated. *Forrer/Weber* 4848   ..   ..   £500

Kalchedon *continued*

3742 — Æ *drachm* (*c.* 3·65 gm.).   Similar, but with caduceus instead of monogram on *obv.*
B.M.C. 13. 125, 14 ..   ..   £80

3743 — Æ *hemidrachm* (*c.* 1·8 gm.).   Forepart of bull l. stg. on ear of corn; ΚΑΛ above, monogram before.   ℞. Three ears of corn bound together.   *Forrer/Weber* 4850 ..   £45
*The half-animal on obv. designates the coin as a hemidrachm, the three corn-ears on rev.
indicating three obols. A similar interpretation can be placed on the contemporary hemidrachms
of Byzantion—forepart of cow/trident.*

3744   3746

3744 Second half of 4th cent. B.C.   Æ *tetradrachm* (*c.* 15 gm.).   Bull stg. l. on ear of corn;
ΚΑΛΧ above, monogram before.   ℞. Small quadripartite incuse square, with granulated
field; all within circular depression.   *Babelon* (*Traité*) *pl.* 181, 26 ..   ..   £750

3745 — Æ *drachm* (*c.* 3·75 gm.).   Similar, but with caduceus as well as monogram before bull
on *obv.* *Forrer/Weber* 4849 ..   ..   £125

3746 Mid-3rd cent. B.C.   Æ *tetradrachm* (*c.* 14 gm.).   Veiled hd. of Demeter r., wreathed
with corn.   ℞. Naked Apollo seated r. on omphalos, holding arrow and bow; monogram
in field to l., ΔΙ to r., ΚΑΛΧ below.   *B.M.C. 13.* 126, 19 ..   ..   ..   £1,000

             3747   3751

3747 — Æ *octobol* (*c.* 5·3 gm.).   Similar; on *rev.*, Ε in field to l., nothing to r., ΚΑΛΧ below.
B.M.C. 13. 126, 20 ..   ..   £400

3748 3rd-2nd cent. B.C.   Æ *tetradrachm* (*c.* 16·8 gm.), restoring the type of King Lysimachos
of Thrace.   Hd. of deified Alexander the Great r., with horn of Ammon.   ℞. ΒΑΣΙΛΕΩΣ/
ΛΥΣΙΜΑΧΟΥ either side of Athena seated l., holding Nike; ΜΗΝΙ in field to l.; corn-ear and
ΚΑΛΧΑ in ex.   *Müller* (*Die Münzen des thrakischen Königs Lysimachos*) 379 ..   £175

3749 *Bronze Coinage.* 4th cent. B.C.   Æ 16.   Bull stg. l. on ear of corn; ΚΑΛΧ above.   ℞.
Two ears of corn.   *Babelon* (*Traité*) *pl.* 182, 9 ..   ..   £15

3750 — Æ 11.   Astragalos.   ℞. ΚΑ/ΛΧ either side of ear of corn.   *Forrer/Weber* 4851   £12

3751 3rd-2nd cent. B.C.   Æ 27.   Conjoined heads of Apollo and Artemis l.   ℞. ΚΑΛΧΑ/
ΔΟΝΙΩΝ either side of lyre.   *B.M.C. 13.* 126, 22 ..   ..   £25

3752 — Æ 20.   Laur. hd. of Apollo l.   ℞. ΚΑΛΧΑ/ΔΟΝΙΩΝ either side of tripod.   *B.M.C. 13.*
127, 23-4 ..   ..   £10

3753   3754

3753 **Kalchedon** and **Byzantion,** in alliance. 3rd cent. B.C. Æ 26. Veiled hd. of Demeter r., wreathed with corn. R. ΒΥΙΑΝ/ΚΑΛΧΑ either side of Poseidon seated r. on rock, holding aplustre and trident; monogram in field to r. *B.M.C. 3.* 107, 2   ..   ..   £24

3754 — Æ 23. Laur. hd. of Apollo r. R. ΒΥΙΑΝΤ/ΚΑΛΧΑ either side of tripod surmounted by holmos. *B.M.C. 3.* 107, 1   ..   ..   £20

3755   3757   3759

3755 **Kios** (at the head of a large bay on the eastern coastline of the Propontis, Kios was a place of commercial importance as the port of entry to the interior of Phrygia. It was destroyed *c.* 202 B.C. by Philip V of Macedon, but later rebuilt under the name of **Prusias**). 350-300 B.C. *N* stater (*c.* 8·6 gm.). Laur. hd. of Apollo r. R. ΑΓΝΩ/ΝΙΔΗΣ above and below prow of galley l.; before, eagle stg. l., wings closed; above prow, club l. *B.M.C. 13.* 130, 1   £10,000

The gold staters of Kios were issued between 345 and 330 B.C.

3756 — Æ drachm (*c.* 5·2 gm.). Laur. hd. of Apollo r. R. ΗΓΕΣ/ΤΡΑΤΟΣ above and below prow of galley l. *Grose/McClean* 7459   ..   ..   £250

3757 — Æ hemidrachm (*c.* 2·6 gm.). Laur. hd. of Apollo r., ΚΙΑ beneath. R. ΠΡΟΣ/ΕΝΟΣ above and below prow of galley l. *B.M.C. 13.* 130, 11   ..   ..   £100

3758 — Æ trihemiobol (*c.* 1·3 gm.). *Obv.* Similar. R. ΑΘΗΝΟ/ΔΩΡΟΣ above and below prow of galley l.; behind, ear of corn. *B.M.C. 13.* 131, 15   ..   ..   £65

3759 3rd cent. B.C. Æ 20. Hd. of young Herakles r., clad in lion's skin. R. ΚΙΑΝΩΝ. Club and bow in case. *B.M.C. 13.* 132, 26   ..   ..   ..   £14

3760 — Æ 18. Laur. hd. of Apollo r. R. ΚΙΑΝΩΝ. Club r.; monograms beneath. *B.M.C. 13.* 132, 24 ..   ..   £13

3761 — — Youthful hd. of Mithras (?) r., wearing Persian head-dress wreathed with laurel; M beneath. R. As last. *B.M.C. 13.* 131, 17   ..   ..   ..   £16

3762   3763

3762 — Æ 14. *Obv.* Similar. R. Kantharos between two bunches of grapes and two ears of corn; Κ — Ι across field, Α above. *B.M.C. 13.* 131, 22 ..   ..   £10

3763 2nd-1st cent. B.C. Æ 26. Diad. hd. of bearded Herakles r. R. ΠΡΟΥΣΙΕΩΝ/ΤΩΝ ΠΡΟΣ/ΘΑΛΑΣΣΗΙ. Club and bow in case. *B.M.C. 13.* 132, 28-30   ..   ..   £18

Kios *continued*

3764 — Æ 20. Laur. hd. of Apollo r. ℞. Tripod; ΠΡΟΥCΙΕΩΝ to r., ΤΩΝ ΠΡΟC/ΘΑΛΑCCΗΙ to
 l. *B.M.C. 13.* 132, 31 .. .. £14

3765   3766

3765 **Dia** (situated on the Black Sea coast, about 25 miles west of Herakleia). Late 2nd-early
 1st cent. B.C. (time of Mithradates). Æ 20. Laur. head of Zeus r. ℞. Eagle stg. l. on
 thunderbolt, looking back; ΔΙΑΣ below, monogram in field to l. *B.M.C. 13.* 138, 1-3 £12

3766 **Herakleia Pontika** (an important city on the Black Sea coast, Herakleia was founded
 by colonists from Megara and Tanagra in the mid-6th cent. B.C. It achieved its period of
 greatest prosperity in the latter part of the 4th cent., under the rule of a succession of
 tyrants). 394-364 B.C. Æ *drachm* (*c.* 4·9 gm.). Hd. of bearded Herakles l., clad in
 lion's skin; club beneath. ℞. ΗΡΑΚ/ΛΕΙΑ above and below bull butting l. *B.M.C. 13.*
 139, 4-5 .. .. £450

3767 — Æ *hemidrachm* (*c.* 2·4 gm.). *Obv.* Similar, but without club. ℞. ΗΡΑΚ/ΛΕΙΑ above
 and below club and bow in case. *Grose/McClean* 7462 .. .. .. £200

3768 — Æ *trihemiobol* (*c.* 1·2 gm.). *Obv.* As last. ℞. ΗΡΑΚ. Forepart of butting bull l.
 B.M.C. 13. 139, 6 .. .. £120

3769   3770

3769 — — — ℞. ΗΡΑΚ/ΛΕΙΑ above and below club r. *B.M.C. 13.* 139, 7 .. £75

3770 364-352 B.C. (time of Klearchos I, tyrant). Æ *drachm* (*c.* 4 gm.). Similar to 3766, but
 also with Κ (retrograde) above bull on *rev.* *B.M.C. 13.* 140, 10 .. .. £450

3771 — Æ *hemidrachm* ? (*c.* 1·6 gm.). ΗΡΑΚ. Dr. bust of the Tyche l., wearing turreted
 stephanos. ℞. Bow in case, club and Κ. *Forrer/Weber* 4880 .. .. .. £225

3772 — Æ *obol* (*c.* 0·65 gm.). Similar. *Forrer/Weber* 4881 .. .. .. £110

3773   3774

3773 352-345 B.C. (time of Satyros, tyrant). Æ *stater* (*c.* 12 gm.). Hd. of young Herakles l.,
 clad in lion's skin; club beneath. ℞. ΗΡΑΚΛΕΙΑ behind dr. bust of the Tyche l., wearing
 turreted stephanos adorned with floral devices. *B.M.C. 13.* 141, 16 .. .. £500

3774 — Æ *drachm* (*c.* 4 gm.). Similar. *B.M.C. 13.* 141, 18 .. .. .. £250

3775 — Æ *hemidrachm* (*c.* 2 gm.). *Obv.* Similar, but without club. ℞. ΗΡΑΚ above hd. of the
 Tyche l., wearing turreted stephanos, as last. *B.M.C. 13.* 141, 19 .. .. £140

3776 — — ΗΡΑΚ behind dr. bust of the Tyche l., as *rev.* of 3773. ℞. Trophy of arms; Σ in
 field to l. *Babelon (Traité) pl.* 182, 30 .. .. £175

3778   3780

3778 Timotheos and Dionysios, tyrants 345-337 B.C. Æ *stater* (*c.* 9·7 gm.). Hd. of young Dionysos l., wreathed with ivy; thyrsos over r. shoulder. ℞. Naked Herakles stg. l., erecting trophy against which rests club; ΤΙΜΟΘΕΟΥ to r., ΔΙΟΝΥΣΙΟΥ to l. *B.M.C. 13.* 142, 22   ..   ..   £225

3779 — Æ *hemidrachm* (*c.* 2·4 gm.). Similar. *B.M.C. 13.* 142, 24   ..   ..   £125

3780 Dionysios alone, tyrant 337-305 B.C. Æ *stater* (*c.* 9·7 gm.). Similar to 3778, but with *rev.* legend ΔΙΟΝΥΣΙΟΥ only, behind Herakles; ram's hd. l. on ground between Herakles' legs. *B.M.C. 13.* 142, 25   ..   ..   £250

3781 — Æ *drachm* (*c.* 4·85 gm.). As last, but without ram's hd. on *rev.* *B.M.C. 13.* 142, 27   £175

3782   3783

3782 305-302 B.C. (time of Klearchos II and Oxathres, tyrants). Æ *stater* (*c.* 9·7 gm.). Obv. Similar to 3778. ℞. ΗΡΑΚΛΕΩΤΑΝ. Herakles stg. facing, resting on club set on rock, crowned by Nike stg. on column; monogram in field to r. *Historia Numorum, p.* 515 £1,000

3783 302-281 B.C. (time of Lysimachos). Æ *stater* (*c.* 9·7 gm.). Hd. of young Herakles r., clad in lion's skin. ℞. ΗΡΑΚΛΕΩ behind young Dionysos seated l., holding kantharos and thyrsos; monogram beneath seat. *B.M.C. 13.* 143, 30   ..   ..   ..   £200

3784 — Æ *tetradrachm* (*c.* 16·5 gm.). Similar, but without monogram beneath seat on *rev.* *B.M.C. 13.* 143, 33 ..   ..   £750

3785   3787

3785 *Bronze Coinage.* Mid-4th cent. B.C. Æ 17. Hd. of bearded Herakles r., clad in lion's skin. ℞. Bow, club and quiver; ΗΡΑ below. *B.M.C. 13.* 140, 14   ..   ..   £14

3786 Dionysios, tyrant 337-305 B.C. Æ 16. Hd. of young Herakles l., clad in lion's skin. ℞. Bow in case; ΔΙΟΝΥΣΙΟΥ to l. *Forrer/Weber* 4885   ..   ..   £16

3787 3rd-2nd cent. B.C. Æ 15. Laur. hd. of young Herakles r., lion's skin knotted round neck. ℞. ΗΡΑΚΛΕΩ/ΤΑΝ above and below table surmounted by bow in case; club l. in front of table; ΑΙ in field to l. *B.M.C. 13.* 142, 28   ..   ..   £12

3788   3792

Herakleia Pontika *continued*

3788 — — Hd. of young Herakles r., clad in lion's skin. R. ΗΡΑΚΛΕ/ΩΤΑΝ above and below
lion leaping r.; monogram above, club beneath. *B.M.C. 13.* 144, 38 ..   £9

3789 — Æ 11. *Obv.* Similar. R. ΗΡΑΚΛΕ/ΩΤΑΝ above and below forepart of leaping lion r.;
monogram above. *B.M.C. 13.* 144, 40 ..   ..   £7

3790 — Æ 22. *Obv.* Similar. R. ΗΡΑΚΛΕΩΤΑΝ between bow in case and club. *B.M.C. 13.*
144, 41 ..   ..   £12

3791 **Nikaia** (an ancient city, renamed by Lysimachos in honour of his wife, Nikaia became a
place of great importance in the Hellenistic period). C. Papirius Carbo, Roman Proconsul 62-59 B.C. Æ 23. ΝΙΚΑΙΕΩΝ behind hd. of young Dionysos r., wreathed with
ivy; beneath, ΒΚΣ (= year 222 = 61/60 B.C.); monogram beneath chin. R. Roma seated l.
on shields, holding Nike and spear; ΕΠΙ ΓΑΙΟΥ to r., ΠΑΠΙΡΙΟΥ/ΚΑΡΒΩΝΟΣ to l., ΡΩΜΗ in
ex. *B.M.C. 13.* 152, 2 ..   ..   £16

3792 — Æ 20. ΝΙΚΑΙΕΩΝ behind laur. hd. of Apollo r.; beneath, ΔΚΣ (= year 224 = 59 B.C.);
monogram beneath chin. R. Thyrsos; ΕΠΙ ΓΑΙΟΥ to r., ΠΑΠΙΡΙΟΥ/ΚΑΡΒΩΝΟΣ to l.
B.M.C. 13. 152, 7   ..   ..   £15

3793 — Æ 19. Kantharos; to r., ΝΙΚΑΙΕΩΝ; to l., monogram and ΒΚΣ (= year 222 = 61/60
B.C.). R. Club-handled caduceus; ΕΠΙ ΓΑΙΟΥ to l., ΠΑΠΙΡΙΟΥ/ΚΑΡΒΩΝΟΣ to r. *B.M.C.*
13. 152, 1 ..   ..   £16

3794   3795

3794 C. Vibius Pansa, Roman Proconsul 47-46 B.C. Æ 26. ΝΙΚΑΙΕΩΝ behind bare hd. of
Julius Caesar r. R. Nike advancing r., holding wreath and palm; ΕΠΙ ΓΑΙΟΥ and mono-
gram to r., ΟΥΙΒΙΟΥ/ΠΑΝΣΑ and monogram to l.; below, ϹΛΣ (= year 236 = 47/6 B.C.).
B.M.C. 13. 153, 8 ..   ..   £75

3795 **Nikomedeia** (an important city founded by King Nikomedes I of Bithynia, Nikomedeia
was close to the site of the ruined Astakos). C. Papirius Carbo, Roman Proconsul 62-59
B.C. Æ 24. ΝΙΚΟΜΗΔΕΩΝ. Laur. hd. of Zeus r. R. Roma seated l. on shields, holding
Nike and spear; ΕΠΙ ΓΑΙΟΥ to r., ΠΑΠΙΡΙΟΥ/ΚΑΡΒΩΝΟΣ to l., ΡΩΜΗ in ex., monogram in
field to l.; beneath shields, ΔΚΣ (= year 224 = 59 B.C.). *B.M.C. 13.* 179, 1-3   £16

3796 — Æ 18. ΝΙΚΟΜΗΔΕΩΝ. Helmeted hd. of Roma r. R. Nike advancing l., holding
wreath and palm; ΕΠΙ ΓΑΙΟΥ to r., ΠΑΠΙΡΙΟΥ/ΚΑΡΒΩΝΟΣ to l.; in field to l., monogram and
ΔΚΣ (= year 224 = 59 B.C.). *B.M.C. 13.* 179, 4 ..   ..   £15

3797 **Tion** (a Milesian colony on the Black Sea coast north-east of Herakleia). *Circa* 282 B.C.
Æ 18. ΤΙΑΝΟΝ. Female hd. l., wearing stephane, hair in sakkos. R. ΕΛΕΥΘΕΡΙΑ.
Eleutheria seated l., leaning forward, her r. hand raised. *B.M.C. 13.* 203, 1-2   £18

WESTERN ASIA MINOR

Comprising the areas of Mysia, Troas, Aiolis, Ionia, Lydia and Caria.

3800   3801

3800 **MYSIA. Adramytteion** (a coastal town situated north-west of Pergamon, Adramytteion is said to have been founded by Adramys, brother of King Kroisos of Lydia). Mid-2nd cent. B.C. *Æ cistophoric tetradrachm* (*c.* 11·8 gm.). Cista mystica containing serpent; all within ivy-wreath. R. Bow in case between two coiled serpents; AΔP monogram to l., another monogram above, cornucopiae to r. *B.M.C. 15.* 3, 6   ..   £125

> *In common with many other cistophori, this dates from the period of the Pergamene Kingdom's greatest prosperity, under Eumenes II and Attalos II.*

3801 After 133 B.C. *Æ drachm* (*c.* 2·9 gm.). Laur. hd. of Zeus l. R. AΔPAMY/THNΩN above and below eagle stg. l. on thunderbolt; monogram in field to l. *B.M.C. 15.* 2, 1   £100

3802 *Bronze Coinage.* Mid-4th cent. B.C. Æ 15. Laur. hd. of Zeus r. R. AΔPA above forepart of winged horse r. *Babelon (Traité) pl.* 170, 13   ..   ..   ..   £16

3803 — Æ 11. Hd. of Zeus three-quarter face to r. R. AΔPA above eagle stg. l. on altar, wings closed. *Babelon, pl.* 170, 15   ..   ..   £14

3804 3rd-2nd cent. B.C. Æ 17. Laur. hd. of Apollo r., hair long. R. AΔPAMYTHNΩN. Cup, with long stem. *Historia Numorum, p.* 520   ..   ..   £12

3805   3808

3805 — Æ 18. Laur. hd. of Zeus l. R. AΔPAMY/TH — NΩN above and below horseman prancing r., r. hand raised. *B.M.C. 15.* 2, 2   ..   ..   £12

3806 — Æ 10. Diad. male hd. r. R. AΔPA. Owl stg. r. *B.M.C. 15.* 2, 4   ..   £9

3807 Late 2nd-early 1st cent. B.C. (time of Mithradates). Æ 20. Laur. hd. of Apollo l., quiver at shoulder. R. Cornucopiae between caps of the Dioskouroi; AΔPA — MY/TH — NΩN across field. *B.M.C. 15.* 3, 7-8   ..   ..   ..   £12

3808 **Apollonia ad Rhyndakon** (situated west of Prusa ad Olympon, on a lake through which the Rhyndakos flows on its way to the Propontis). 2nd-1st cent. B.C. Æ 24. Laur. hd. of Apollo r. R. ΑΠΟΛΛΩΝΙΑΤΩΝ PYN. Lyre; all within wreath. *Historia Numorum, p.* 521   ..   ..   £14

3809 — Æ 10. Hd. of Hermes r., wearing winged diadem. R. ΑΠΟΛΛΩΝΙΑΤΩΝ PYNΔA. Winged caduceus. *Historia Numorum, p.* 521   ..   ..   £11

MAP 16. NORTH-WESTERN ASIA MINOR

3810   3813

3810 **Atarneus** (a colony of Chios, Atarneus was situated on the coast, opposite Lesbos, and a few miles west of Pergamon). Mid-4th cent. B.C. *Æ drachm* ? (*c.* 2·9 gm.). Laur. hd. of Apollo r., of fine style. ℞. ATAP below coiled serpent r. *Forrer/Weber* 4956   £750

3811 — Æ 8. Female hd. r., hair rolled. ℞. Similar to last, but legend ATAPN. *Historia Numorum, p.* 521 .. .. £18

3812 3rd cent. B.C. Æ 18. Laur. hd of Apollo r. ℞. Forepart of prancing horse r.; ATAP below, coiled serpent above, monogram before. *B.M.C. 15.* 14, 1 .. .. £14

3813 Cn. Asinius, Roman Proconsul of Asia *circa* 79-76 B.C. Æ 19. Forepart of prancing horse r.; behind, coiled serpent and monogram. ℞. Caduceus; ΑΣΙΝΙΟΥ to r., ΑΝΘΥΠΑΤΟΥ/ΡΩΜΑΙΩΝ to l. *B.M.C. 15.* 14, 7 .. .. £16

3814 **Kisthene** (a coastal town, south-west of Adramytteion). 3rd-2nd cent. B.C. Æ 18. Veiled hd. of Demeter r., wreathed with corn. ℞. ΚΙΣ. Horseman prancing r., r. hand raised; below, dolphin r. *B.M.C. 15.* 17, 1-2 .. .. £17

3815 — — Similar, but with legend ΚΙΣΘΗ, and bee instead of dolphin on *rev.* *B.M.C. 15.* 17, 3 .. .. £17

3816 **Kyzikos** (a colony of Miletos, founded mid-8th cent. B.C., Kyzikos was situated on the island of Arktonnesos, just off the southern coastline of the Propontis. It occupied a position of great commercial importance and its electrum staters, called 'Kyzikenes', circulated widely in international trade throughout the 5th and most of the 4th cent. B.C. In Hellenistic times Kyzikos preserved its prosperity by maintaining friendly relations with the Pergamene kings and, later, with Rome). 500-450 B.C. Electrum *stater* (*c.* 16·2 gm.). Winged female figure (Nike ?), of archaic style, running l., looking back; she holds tunny in her r. hand. ℞. Quadripartite incuse square; the surface of each quarter slopes downward from the inner to the outer edge. *B.M.C. 15.* 21, 25 .. .. .. £3,500

3817   3821   3822

3817 — — Youthful warrior, naked, kneeling l., holding crested helmet and sword; tunny beneath. ℞. As last. *B.M.C. 15.* 22, 33 .. .. £2,750

3818 — — Sphinx stg. l., r. foreleg raised; tunny beneath. ℞. As last. *B.M.C. 15.* 23, 36   £3,000

3819 — — Roaring lion seated l., r. foreleg raised; tunny beneath. ℞. As last. *B.M.C. 15.* 23, 41 .. .. £2,750

3820 — — Chimaera seated l.; tunny beneath. ℞. As last. *B.M.C. 15.* 24, 50 .. £3,250

3821 — Electrum *sixth* (*c.* 2·7 gm.). Similar to 3816. *B.M.C. 15.* 21, 26 .. £750

3822 — — Naked youth kneeling r., holding knife downwards in r. hand, and tunny on extended l. ℞. Quadripartite incuse square, as 3816. *B.M.C. 15.* 22, 31-2 .. £650

3823 — — Hd. of lioness facing; tunny, downwards, in field to r. ℞. As last. *B.M C. 15.* 23, 40 .. .. £550

3824   3826   3829

Kyzikos *continued*

3824 — Electrum *twelfth* (*c.* 1·35 gm.).   Similar to 3819.   *B.M.C. 15.* 23, 44   ..   £350

3825 450-400 B.C.   Electrum *stater* (*c.* 16·2 gm.).   Laur. hd. of Apollo three-quarter face to r.; tunny beneath.   ℞. Quadripartite incuse square; the surface of each quarter angled, as 3816, and sometimes exhibiting a coarse stippling. *B.M.C. 15.* 25, 56   ..   £5,000

3826 — — Poseidon kneeling r., holding dolphin and trident; tunny beneath.   ℞. As last. *B.M.C. 15.* 26, 62   ..   ..   £3,000

3827 — — Upper part of female figure (Gaia) r., holding naked boy (Erichthonios) in her outstretched arms; tunny beneath.   ℞. As last.   *B.M.C. 15.* 27, 65   ..   ..   £6,500

3828 — — Bearded male figure (Kekrops) l., with serpent's tail, holding branch in r. hand, l. on side; tunny beneath.   ℞. As last.   *B.M.C. 15.* 27, 66   ..   ..   ..   £4,500

3829 — — Naked boy seated astride dolphin l., holding tunny by the tail; another tunny beneath.   ℞. As last.   *B.M.C. 15.* 29, 76   ..   ..   £3,000

3830 — — Forepart of man-headed bull swimming r.; behind, tunny upwards.   ℞. As last. *B.M.C. 15.* 30, 82   ..   ..   £3,000

3831 — Electrum *sixth* (*c.* 2·7 gm.).   Orestes kneeling l. beside Delphic omphalos, holding drawn sword; tunny beneath.   ℞. As last.   *B.M.C. 15.* 28, 74   ..   ..   £850

3832   3835

3832 — — Similar to 3830.   *B.M.C. 15.* 30, 83   ..   ..   £600

3833 — — Bull kneeling l.; tunny beneath.   ℞. Quadripartite incuse square, as 3825. *B.M.C. 15.* 30, 87   ..   ..   £600

3834 — — Sow stg. l.; tunny beneath.   ℞. As last.   *B.M.C. 15.* 31, 90   ..   ..   £600

3835 — — Dog l., at bay; tunny beneath.   ℞. As last.   *B.M.C. 15.* 31, 91-2   ..   £600

3836 — Electrum *twelfth* (*c.* 1·35 gm.).   Fox l.; tunny beneath.   ℞. As last.   *B.M.C. 15.* 31, 93   ..   ..   £350

3837 — — Forepart of deer l., with curled wing; tunny behind.   ℞. As last.   *B.M.C. 15.* 32, 99   ..   ..   £350

3838 400-330 B.C.   Electrum *stater* (*c.* 16·2 gm.).   Two eagles seated face to face on netted omphalos of Delphi; tunny beneath.   ℞. Quadripartite incuse square; the surface of each quarter angled, as 3816, and decorated with coarse stippling.   *B.M.C. 15.* 32, 100

£4,000

3839   3841   3844

3839 — — Male portrait hd. r.; bald, bearded and laur.; tunny beneath.   ℞. As last.   *B.M.C. 15.* 33, 103   ..   ..   £4,500

The head on this type is so realistic that it may well be a portrait of a living ruler, perhaps one of the princes in the Black Sea area with whom the Kyzikenes conducted trade.

3840 — — Diad. hd. of Aphrodite l., hair rolled; tunny beneath. ℞. As last. *B.M.C. 15.* 33, 102 .. .. £4,000

3841 — — Eagle stg. l. on tunny, wings closed. ℞. As last. *Kraay (Archaic and Classical Greek Coins) pl.* 56, 963 .. .. £3,500

3842 — — Nike kneeling l. on ram which she is about to sacrifice; tunny beneath. ℞. As last. *Kraay, pl.* 56, 961 .. .. £5,500

3843 — — Hd. of young Herakles l., clad in lion's skin; tunny beneath. ℞. As last. *Kraay, pl.* 56, 964 .. .. £4,500

> *This type, perhaps one of the latest in the series, may be inspired by the coinage of Alexander the Great.*

3844 — Electrum *sixth* (c. 2·7 gm.). Naked Helios kneeling r., holding by the bridles two horses prancing in opposite directions; tunny beneath. ℞. As last. *B.M.C. 15.* 33, 106 £850

3845 — — Perseus kneeling r., looking back, holding harpa and head of Medusa; tunny beneath. ℞. As last. *Boston Museum Catalogue* 1549 .. .. £850

3846   3849

3846 *Silver Coinage.* 480-450 B.C. Æ *trihemiobol* (c. 1·3 gm.). Forepart of running boar l.; behind, tunny upwards. ℞. Hd. of roaring lion l., within incuse square. *B.M.C. 15.* 34-5, 108-13 .. .. £40

3847 — — Similar, but with H on boar's shoulder. *B.M.C. 15.* 35, 117 .. .. £50

3848 — Æ *obol* (c. 0·85 gm.). Similar to 3846, but with K (retrograde) above lion's hd. *B.M.C. 15.* 35, 121 .. .. £45

3849 — Æ *tritartemorion* (c. 0·63 gm.). Similar to 3846. *B.M.C. 15.* 35, 116 .. £45

3850 — Æ *hemiobol* (c. 0·42 gm.). Forepart of running boar l. K (retrograde) on shoulder; behind, tunny upwards. ℞. Hd. of roaring lion l.; small hd. of lioness facing above; all within incuse square. *B.M.C. 15.* 35, 119 .. .. £55

3851 — — Forepart of running boar r.; behind, tunny upwards. ℞. Hd. of roaring lion l., K (retrograde) above; all within incuse square. *B.M.C. 15.* 35, 123 .. .. £50

3852   3854

3852 *Circa* 395/4 B.C. Æ *tetradrachm* (c. 15·1 gm.). ΦΑΡΝΑΒΑ. Bearded hd. of Pharnabazos r., wearing low Persian tiara. ℞. Prow of war-galley l., the superstructure ornamented with griffin; before and behind, dolphin downwards; tunny beneath. *B.M.C. 14 (Ionia)* 325, 12 .. .. £17,500

> *The precise occasion for this exceptional issue is not certainly known, but it may be connected with the assistance given by the Persian satrap to the Athenian admiral Konon who was blockaded in Kaunos by the Spartans (cf. Kraay 'Archaic and Classical Greek Coins' p. 258).*

3853 390-330 B.C. Æ *tetradrachm* (c. 15·1 gm.) ΣΩΤΕΙΡΑ. Hd. of Persephone l., wreathed with corn and wearing veil wound round head. ℞. ΚΥΖΙ. Lion's hd. l.; tunny l. beneath. *B.M.C. 15.* 36, 128-30 .. .. £800

3854 — — Similar, but with star behind lion's hd. *B.M.C. 15.* 36, 127 .. .. £850

3855 — — Similar, but with oinochoë instead of star behind lion's hd. *Forrer/Weber* 5035 .. .. £850

3856   3859

Kyzikos *continued*

3856 — — *Obv.* Similar. ℞. ΚΥΙΙΚΗΝΩΝ. Lion's hd. l.; tunny l. beneath; kantharos behind. *B.M.C. 15.* 36, 135 .. .. £900

3857 — Æ *octobol* (*c.* 5 gm.). Similar to 3853. *Forrer/Weber* 5037 .. .. £500

3858 — Æ *drachm* (*c.* 3·75 gm.). Similar, but with Λ behind lion's hd. *B.M.C. 15.* 36, 131 £250

3859 3rd cent. B.C. Æ *tetradrachm* (*c.* 13·3 gm.). ΣΩΤΕΙΡΑ. Hd. of Persephone l., similar to 3853; beneath, tunny l. ℞. ΚΥΙΙ. Apollo seated l. on omphalos, holding patera and resting l. elbow on lyre at side; cock l. before; monogram behind. *B.M.C. 15.* 36, 132 £1,400

3860   3861

3860 2nd cent. B.C. Æ *tetradrachm* (*c.* 16·8 gm.). Female hd. (Apollonis ?) r., wearing diadem and oak-wreath. ℞. ΚΥΙΙ/ΚΗΝΩΝ above and below flaming torch l.; monograms in upper and lower field; all within oak-wreath. *B.M.C. 15.* 38, 146 .. .. £1,000

3861 *Bronze Coinage.* 4th-3rd cent. B.C. Æ 18. Hd. of Persephone r., wreathed with corn and wearing sphendone. ℞. Κ—Υ/Ι—Ι either side of tripod; tunny beneath, plectrum in field to r. *B.M.C. 15.* 37, 136 .. .. £10

3862 — Æ 11. *Obv.* Similar. ℞. ΚΥ/ΙΙ either side of tripod; tunny beneath. *B.M.C. 15.* 37, 141-2 .. .. £6

3863   3866

3863 — Æ 15. Hd. of Persephone l., wreathed with corn and wearing veil wound round head. ℞. ⋈Æ monogram within wreath; ΚΥ beneath. *B.M.C. 15.* 37, 144 .. £8

3864 2nd-1st cent. B.C. Æ 20. Hd. of Persephone r., wreathed with corn. ℞. ΚΥ/ΙΙ above and below monogram; all within oak-wreath. *B.M.C. 15.* 38, 147 .. .. £6

3865 — Æ 14. Hd. and neck of bull r. ℞. As last. *B.M.C. 15.* 39, 155 .. .. £8

3866 — Æ 26. Bull butting r. ℞. ΚΥΙΙ/ΚΗΝΩΝ above and below flaming torch l.; monogram in upper field to r. *B.M.C. 15.* 39, 162 .. .. £12

3867 — Æ 29. Laur. hd. of Apollo r. ℞. ΚΥΙΙ/ΚΗΝΩΝ either side of tripod; wreath above, torch beneath, monograms in field to l. and to r. *B.M.C. 15.* 40, 165 .. .. £12

3868   3871   3875

3868 **Gambrion** (an inland town situated east of Pergamon). *Circa* 350 B.C. Æ *diobol*? (*c.* 1·7 gm.). Laur. hd. of Apollo r. ℞. ΓΑΜ above forepart of butting bull r. *B.M.C. 15.* 62, 1 .. .. £140

3869 4th-3rd cent. B.C. Æ 10. Laur. hd. of Apollo r. ℞. Bull butting l. *B.M.C. 15.* 63, 14-16 .. .. £8

3870 — Æ 8. Laur. hd. of Apollo l. ℞. ΓΑΜ above Gorgon's hd. facing. *Babelon (Traité) pl.* 170, 6 .. .. £9

3871 — Æ 17. Laur. hd. of Apollo r. ℞. Large star; Γ — A — M between four of the rays. *B.M.C. 15.* 62, 2-3 .. .. £10

3872 — — Laur. hd. of Apollo l. ℞. Bull butting l.; star above, ΓΑΜ in ex. *B.M.C. 15.* 63, 12-13 .. .. £12

3873 — — Laur. hd. of Apollo r. ℞. Tripod; ΓΑΜ to l. *B.M.C. 15.* 63, 18-19 .. £11

3874 **Iolla** (site uncertain, though probably in the vicinity of Adramytteion). Mid-4th cent. B.C. Æ 19. Hd. of Athena r., in close-fitting crested helmet. ℞. Forepart of winged horse r.; ΙΟΛΛΕΩΝ below. *Babelon (Traité) pl.* 170, 24 .. .. £16

3875 — Æ 17. Laur. hd. of Zeus r. ℞. Forepart of winged horse r.; ΙΟΛΛΑ above, ear of corn below. *B.M.C. 15.* 77, 1 .. .. £15

3876   3881

3876 **Lampsakos** (a colony of Phokaia, Lampsakos was stretegically placed at the eastern entrance to the Hellespont and rose to be a city of great importance. Although under Persian and Athenian control for much of the sixth and fifth centuries, Lampsakos managed to preserve its prosperity into the Hellenistic age). 480-450 B.C. Æ *drachm* (*c.* 5·35 gm.). Janiform female hd., of fine late archaic style, wearing tainia, earring and necklace. ℞. Hd. of Athena l., wearing Corinthian helmet; all within incuse square. *B.M.C. 15.* 79, 10 .. .. £350

3877 — — Similar, but of slightly later style, and with caduceus behind hd. of Athena on *rev.* *B.M.C. 15.* 80, 17 .. .. £250

3878 — Æ ¾ *drachm* (*c.* 4 gm.). Similar to 3876. *B.M.C. 15.* 79, 15 .. .. £250

3879 — Æ *trihemiobol* (*c.* 1·33 gm.). Similar. *Forrer/Weber* 5092 .. .. £110

3880 — Æ *obol* (*c.* 0·89 gm.). Similar, but with wheel ornament on Athena's helmet. *Forrer/Weber* 5093 .. .. £90

3881 *Circa* 450 B.C. Electrum *stater* (*c.* 15·35 gm.). Forepart of winged horse l., Ξ beneath; all within vine-wreath. ℞. Quadripartite incuse square, the alternate compartments deeper. *B.M.C. 15.* 79, 8 .. .. £2,500

Lampsakos *continued*

3882 390-330 B.C. *N stater* (*c.* 8·48 gm.). Child Herakles kneeling r., wrestling with serpents. R. Forepart of winged horse l., within incuse square. *Kraay* (*Archaic and
Classical Greek Coins*) *pl.* 54, 918 ..   ..   £12,500
   *This would seem to be associated with a series of silver staters issued circa 390 B.C. by a
number of cities belonging to a political alliance. The coins all share a common obverse type,
similar to the above, but have reverses appropriate to the mint of issue—see below under
Ephesos, Samos, Knidos, Iasos and Rhodos.*

3883   3884

3883 — — Nike kneeling r., holding hammer and nail, about to attach helmet to trophy
before her. R. Forepart of winged horse r., within incuse square. *B.M.C. 15.* 82, 31
                                                                        £10,000

3884 — — Bearded male hd. (Odysseos ?) l., wearing conical pilos wreathed with laurel.
R. As last. *B.M.C. 15.* 81, 25 ..   ..   £9,000

3885 — — Laur. hd. of Zeus l., thunderbolt behind. R. As last. *B.M.C. 15.* 81, 28 £7,500

3886 — — Hd. of Athena l., wearing crested helmet ornamented with olive-leaves and floral
scroll. R. As last. *Kraay* (*Archaic and Classical Greek Coins*) *pl.* 54, 924 .. £7,500
   This obverse type is a close copy of the contemporary Athenian coinage.

3887 — — Bearded hd. of the Persian satrap Orontas l., wearing satrapal tiara. R. As last.
Kraay, pl. 54, 922 ..   ..   £15,000
   *This may have been struck on the occasion of Orontas' revolt against Artaxerxes II,
circa 362 B.C. See also nos. 3889, 3899 and 3900.*

3888 — — Hd. of Helios l., on rad. solar disk. R. As last. *Babelon* (*Traité*) *pl.* 171, 18 £10,000

3889   3890

3889 — Æ *hemidrachm* (*c.* 2·55 gm.). Hd. of Athena l., in close-fitting crested helmet. R.
ΟΡΟΝΤΑ below forepart of winged horse r. *B.M.C. 14.* (*Ionia*) 326, 15 ..   £350
   An issue of the satrap Orontas—see also nos. 3887, 3899 and 3900.

3890 — — Janiform female hd., wearing tainia and earring. R. ΛΑΜ. Hd. of Athena r.,
wearing Corinthian helmet ornamented with forepart of winged horse. *B.M.C. 15.*
82, 32-3 ..   ..   £75

3891   3893   3894

3891 — — Hd. of Athena r., in Corinthian helmet. R. ΛΑΜ. Forepart of winged horse r.,
ear of corn below. *B.M.C. 15.* 83, 49 ..   ..   £90

3892 — Æ *diobol* (*c.* 1·6 gm.). Similar to 3890, but with *rev.* legend ΛΑΜΨΑ, and Athena's
helmet is undecorated. *Grose/McClean* 7633-4 ..   ..   £55

3893 — Æ *trihemiobol* (*c.* 1·27 gm.).   As last, but with ivy-leaf beneath Athena's hd. on *rev.*
   B.M.C. 15. 83, 43 ..   ..   £45

3894 — — Laur. hd. of Apollo r.   Ʀ. ΛΑΜ.   Forepart of winged horse r.; dolphin r. beneath.
   B.M.C. 15. 83, 46-7 ..   ..   £60

3895 3rd cent. B.C.   Æ *tetradrachm* (*c.* 16·8 gm.), restoring the types of Alexander the Great:
   large, spread flan.   Hd. of young Herakles r., clad in lion's skin.   Ʀ. Zeus enthroned l.,
   holding eagle and sceptre; ΑΛΕΞΑΝΔΡΟΥ behind, forepart of winged horse and monogram
   to l., another monogram beneath throne.   *Müller* (*Numismatique d'Alexandre le Grand*)
   915-17 ..   ..   £200

3896 — Æ *drachm.*   Similar, but with forepart of winged horse in *rev.* field to l., and ΛΑ
   beneath throne.   *Müller* 913 ..   ..   £85

3897 2nd cent. B.C.   Æ *tetradrachm* (*c.* 16·8 gm.).   Bearded hd. of Priapos r., horned and
   wreathed with ivy.   Ʀ. ΛΑΜΨΑ — ΚΗΝΩΝ either side of Apollo Kitharoidos stg. r., holding
   plectrum and lyre; ϹΩΚΡΑΤΟΥΤΟΥ/ΞΕΝΟΦΑΝΟΥ in ex.; monogram in field to l., palm-branch
   to r.   *B.M.C. 15.* 86, 68 ..   ..   £1,400

3898 — Æ *hemidrachm* (*c.* 2·1 gm.).   Laur. hd. of Apollo r.   Ʀ. ΛΑΜ above forepart of winged
   horse r.; monogram below.   *Grose/McClean* 7636 ..   ..   £95

3899 *Bronze Coinage.*   4th cent. B.C.   Æ 11.   Laur. hd. of Zeus r.   Ʀ. ΟΡΟΝΤΑ below forepart
   of winged horse r.   *B.M.C. 14 (Ionia)* 326, 16 ..   ..   £20
      This, and the next, belong to the time of Orontas' revolt against Artaxerxes II, circa 362
   B.C.   *See also nos.* 3887 *and* 3889.

3900 — Æ 10.   Bearded hd. of the Persian satrap Orontas r., wearing satrapal tiara.   Ʀ. As
   last.   *Grose/McClean* 7635 ..   ..   £30

3901 — Æ 17.   ΛΑΜ.   Janiform female hd.   Ʀ. Forepart of winged horse r.; harpa r. below.
   B.M.C. 15. 84, 50 ..   ..   £10

3902 — Æ 9.   Janiform female hd.   Ʀ. ΛΑΜ.   Hd. of Athena r., wearing crested helmet.
   Babelon (*Traité*) *pl.* 172, 21 ..   ..   £8

Lampsakos *continued*

3903 3rd cent. B.C. Æ 22. ΛΑΜ. Laur. female hd. r., hair rolled. ℞. ΨΑ. Forepart of winged horse r.; rad. hd. of Helios facing below. *B.M.C. 15.* 84, 53 .. .. £10

3904 — Æ 15. Hd. of Poseidon (?) r., bearded. ℞. ΛΑΜ. Forepart of winged horse r.; dolphin r. beneath. *B.M.C. 15.* 85, 65 .. .. £8

3905 3906

3905 — Æ 13. Caduceus within wreath. ℞. ΛΑΜΨΑ. Forepart of winged horse r. *B.M.C. 15.* 85, 62 .. .. £8

3906 — Æ 11. ΛΑΜ. Crested Corinthian helmet r. ℞. ΨΑ. Forepart of winged horse r.; pellet beneath. *B.M.C. 15.* 85, 60 .. .. £7

3907 — Æ 9. Helmeted hd. of Athena l.; pellets before and behind. ℞. ΛΑ/ΜΨ either side of amphora. *B.M.C. 15.* 85, 61 .. .. £6

3908 3912

3908 2nd-1st cent. B.C. Æ 22. Hd. of Priapos r., similar to 3897. ℞. ΛΑΜΨΑ/ΚΗΝΩΝ above and below forepart of winged horse r. *B.M.C. 15.* 86, 69 .. .. .. £12

3909 — Æ 19. *Obv.* Similar. ℞. ΛΑΜΨΑ. Kantharos. *B.M.C. 15.* 86, 70 .. £11

3910 — Æ 17. *Obv.* Similar. ℞. ΛΑ/ΜΨ/Α within ivy-wreath. *B.M.C. 15.* 86, 71 £10

3911 — Æ 23. Laur. hd. of Apollo r. ℞. Lyre; ΛΑΜ to r., forepart of winged horse to l. *B.M.C. 15.* 87, 75 .. .. £9

3912 — Æ 20. Similar. ℞. ΛΑΜΨΑΚΗ/ΝΩΝ either side of Athena stg. l., holding Nike and resting on shield. *B.M.C. 15.* 86, 73 .. .. £8

3913 — Æ 15. Veiled hd. of Demeter r. ℞. Thunderbolt; ΛΑΜ above, forepart of winged horse r. below. *B.M.C. 15.* 87, 74 .. .. £7

3914 **Miletopolis** (situated in the north of the country at the confluence of the Rhyndakos and Makestos). 3rd-2nd cent. B.C. Æ 19. Hd. of Athena r., in crested helmet. ℞. ΜΙΛΗΤΟ. Double-bodied owl, hd. facing. *B.M.C. 15.* 91, 1 .. .. .. £13

3915 — — Similar, but hd. of Athena smaller, and with *rev.* legend ΜΙΛΗΤΟΠΟΛΙΤΩΝ. *B.M.C. 15.* 91, 7 .. .. £12

3916 3917

3916 — Æ 11. Young male hd. r., hair long. ℞. ΜΙΛΗ/Τ — ο above and below bull stg. l. *B.M.C. 15.* 91, 3 *variety* £9

3917 **Parion** (on the shores of the Propontis, Parion was founded *c.* 710 B.C. and became a flourishing port through the excellence of its harbour). *Circa* 480 B.C. Æ ¾ *drachm* (*c.* 4 gm.). Gorgoneion. ℞. Incuse square containing cruciform pattern with pellet at centre. *B.M.C. 15.* 94, 1 .. .. £200

The attribution to Parion of this and the following coin is not certain.

3918 — Æ *hemidrachm* (*c.* 2·6 gm.). Similar. *B.M.C. 15.* 95, 10 .. .. £120

3919   3922

3919 350-300 B.C. Æ *hemidrachm* (*c.* 2·45 gm.). ΠΑ/ΡΙ above and below bull stg. l., looking
back. Ɍ. Gorgoneion. *B.M.C. 15.* 95, 14-16 ..   ..   £85

3920 — — Similar, but with club beneath bull on *obv.* *B.M.C. 15.* 95, 20   ..   £85

3921 — — Similar, but with bunch of grapes beneath bull. *B.M.C. 15.* 96, 24-5   £85

3922 — — Similar, but with star beneath bull. *B.M.C. 15.* 96-7, 35-7 ..   ..   £85

3923 2nd cent. B.C. Æ *tetradrachm* (*c.* 13·6 gm.). Gorgoneion. Ɍ. ΠΑΡΙΑΝΩΝ. Nike stg.
l., holding wreath and palm; cornucopiae and monogram in field to l., ear of corn to r.
Hunter Catalogue, pl. 48, 10   ..   ..   £7,500

3924 — Æ *tetradrachm* (*c.* 16·8 gm.). Hd. of Demeter r. Ɍ. ΑΠΟΛΛΩΝΟΣ/ΑΚΤΑΙΟΥ —
ΠΑΡΙΑΝΩΝ/ΠΟΛΥΚΛΗΣ. Apollo Aktaios stg. l., between altar and omphalos, holding
patera and lyre. *B.M.C. 15.* 99, *ii* £3,500

3925   3928

3925 *Bronze Coinage.* 350-300 B.C. Æ 19. Bull butting r., wreath above. Ɍ. The great
altar of Parion, showing the front, with amphora before, and r. side; Π — Α/Ρ — Ι in
field. *B.M.C. 15.* 97, 42 ..   ..   £20

3926 — Æ 11. Bull stg. r. Ɍ. As last. *B.M.C. 15.* 98, 48-9   ..   ..   ..   £10

3927 — Æ 15. Bull butting l. Ɍ. Torch; Π — Α/Ρ — Ι in field; all within corn-wreath.
B.M.C. 15. 98, 51-2   ..   ..   £12

3928 2nd-1st cent. B.C. Æ 18. Hd. of Athena r., in crested helmet. Ɍ. Thunderbolt;
Π — Α/Ρ — Ι in field. *B.M.C. 15.* 100, 64   ..   ..   £9

3929 — Æ 15. Bust of Zeus r. Ɍ. Artemis stg. r., holding bow and spear; Π — Α/Ρ — Ι in
field. *B.M.C. 15.* 100, 62   ..   ..   £8

3930 — Æ 13. Hd. of Medusa. Ɍ. Owl stg. on palm-branch; Π — Α/Ρ — Ι in field. *B.M.C.
15.* 100, 66   ..   ..   £8

3931   3933

3931 — Æ 23. Hd. of Medusa. Ɍ. ΠΑ — ΡΙ/ΑΝΩΝ above and below eagle stg. r., monogram
before; all within wreath. *B.M.C. 15.* 100, 69 ..   ..   £14

3932 — Æ 19. Dr. bust of Hermes r., wearing petasos, caduceus at shoulder. Ɍ. Lyre;
Π — Α/Ρ — Ι in field. *B.M.C. 15.* 101, 71   ..   ..   £11

3933 — — Dr. bust of Artemis r., bow and quiver at shoulder. Ɍ. ΠΑΡΙΑΝΩΝ ΑΣΚΛΗΠΙΑΔΗΣ.
Eagle stg. r.; all within wreath. *B.M.C. 15.* 101, 72   ..   ..   ..   £11

Parion *continued*

3934 — Æ 14.　*Obv.* Similar.　℞. Stag stg. r.; ΠΑ/P — I in field.　*B.M.C. 15.* 101, 73　　£9

3935 — Æ 11.　Female hd. r.　℞. Lighted altar; Π — A / P — I in field.　*B.M.C. 15.* 101, 75　..　..　..　..　..　..　..　..　..　..　£8

3936 — Æ 10.　Female hd. r.　℞. Sistrum; Π — A / P — I in field.　*B.M.C. 15.* 101, 76　£8

3937　　　　　　　　　3940　　　　　　　　　3942

3937 **Pergamon** (situated in the Kaikos valley, about 15 miles from the coast, Pergamon was a city of uncertain origin and of no great importance before the time of Alexander. In the 3rd cent. B.C. it became the centre of an independent kingdom ruled by the Attalid dynasty founded by Philetairos.　The city was extended and beautified as the prosperity of the kingdom increased, and by late Hellenistic times Pergamon ranked as one of the great cultural centres of the Greek world.　After the end of the kingdom, 133 B.C., Pergamon became capital of the Roman province of Asia).　400-350 B.C.　Æ *diobol* (*c.* 1·6 gm.).　Laur. hd. of Apollo r.　℞. ΠΕΡΓΑ.　Bearded hd. r., wearing Persian head-dress (the satrap Eurysthenes ?); crescent above; all within incuse square.　*B.M.C. 15.* 110, 1　　£500

3938 — Æ *hemiobol* (*c.* 0·4 gm.).　*Obv.* Similar.　℞. ΠΕΡΓ.　Hd. and neck of bull r.; all within shallow incuse square.　*Forrer/Weber* 5155 　..　..　..　..　..　£90

3939 330-284 B.C.　N *stater* (*c.* 8·6 gm.).　Hd. of young Herakles r., clad in lion's skin.　℞. Cultus-statue of Athena facing, brandishing spear and holding shield, from which hangs fillet; crested helmet in field to l.　*P.C.G.* IV. A.25　..　..　..　..　£5,000

3940 — N *third-stater* (*c.* 2·87 gm.).　Hd. of Athena r., wearing crested helmet, necklace and earring.　℞. As last, but without helmet in field.　*B.M.C. 15.* 110, 4　..　£1,750

3941 — Æ *diobol* (*c.* 1·33 gm.).　Similar to 3939, but with inscription ΠΕΡΓΑ instead of helmet in *rev.* field to l.　*B.M.C. 15.* 111, 5-7　..　..　..　..　..　£75

3942 — — Similar, but with inscription ΠΕΡΓΑΜΗ.　*B.M.C. 15.* 111, 9-10　..　£75

3942A Early 2nd cent. B.C.　Æ *tetradrachm* (*c.* 16·08 gm.).　Circular shield, ornamented with Gorgoneion three-quarter face to l.　℞. ΑΘΗΝΑΣ — ΝΙΚΗΦΟΡΟΥ either side of cultus-statue of Athena Nikephoros facing, shield at side.　*Leu Auction, May 1973, lot* 207　..　..　..　..　..　..　..　..　..　£10,000

3943 — Æ *diobol* (*c.* 1·5 gm.).　Hd. of Athena r., in crested helmet.　℞. ΑΘΗΝΑΣ / ΝΙΚΗΦΟΡ above and below owl stg. facing on palm-branch, wings spread; ΝΙ in field to l., mint-monogram of Pergamon (ΠΕΡΓ) to r.　*Grose/McClean* 7677　..　..　..　£250

3944 190-133 B.C. (time of Eumenes II, Attalos II and Attalos III).　Æ *cistophoric tetradrachm* (*c.* 12·6 gm.).　Cista mystica containing serpent; all within ivy-wreath.　℞. Bow in case between two coiled serpents; mint-monogram of Pergamon (ΠΕΡΓ) to l., eagle to r.　*B.M.C. 15.* 123, 87 ..　..　..　..　..　..　..　..　£75

3945 — — Similar, but with race-torch instead of eagle in *rev.* field to r.　*B.M.C. 15.* 123, 90　　£75

3946 — — Similar, but with vase instead of torch on *rev.*　*B.M.C. 15.* 123, 91　..　£75

3947 After 133 B.C. (Roman Province of Asia). Æ *cistophoric tetradrachm* (*c.* 12·6 gm.). Cista mystica, as 3944. ℞. Bow-case between serpents, as 3944; mint-monogram of Pergamon (ΠΕΡΓ) to l., snake-entwined Asklepian staff to r., AM above. *B.M.C. 15.* 123-4, 94-5 .. .. £85

3948　　　3951

3948 — — Similar, but with ΠΡΥ monogram, star and ΑΠ above bow-case on *rev.* (instead of AM). *B.M.C. 15.* 124, 98-100 .. .. £85

3949 — — Similar, but with ΠΡΥ monogram and ΔΙ above bow-case. *B.M.C. 15.* 124, 106-7 £85

3950 — — Similar, but with ΠΡΥ monogram, within wreath, and ΜΟΣ above bow-case. *B.M.C. 15.* 125, 118-19 .. .. £85

3951 — Æ *quarter-cistophorus* or *drachm* (*c.* 3·15 gm.). Club draped with lion's skin; all within oak-wreath. ℞. Bunch of grapes on vine-leaf; mint-monogram of Pergamon (ΠΕΡΓ) to l., snake-entwined Asklepian staff to r., ΠΡΥ monogram and ΔΗ above. *B.M.C. 15.* 126, 126 .. .. £125

3952 C. Fabius, Roman Proconsul of Asia, 57-56 B.C. Æ *cistophoric tetradrachm.* Cista mystica, as 3944. ℞. Bow-case between serpents, as 3944; mint-monogram of Pergamon (ΠΕΡΓ) to l., snake-entwined Asklepian staff to r., C.FABI. M.F. / PRO. COS. above, ΜΗΝΟΦΙΛΟΣ below. *Franke (Kleinasien zur Römerzeit)* 470 .. .. £150

3953 Q. Caecilius Metellus Pius Scipio, Imperator, 49-48 B.C. Æ *cistophoric tetradrachm.* Cista mystica, as 3944. ℞. Legionary eagle between two coiled serpents; mint-monogram of Pergamon (ΠΕΡΓ) to l., Q.METELLVS PIVS above, SCIPIO IMPER. below. *B.M.C. 15.* 126, 127-8 .. .. £300

Pergamon *continued*

3954 *Bronze Coinage. Circa* 350 B.C. Æ 9. Laur. hd. of Apollo r. ℞. ΠΕΡΓΑ below two bulls' heads face to face; between them, club. *B.M.C. 15.* 110, 3   ..   ..   £12

3955 — — Hd. of Aphrodite (?) r. ℞. ΠΕΡΓ below boar's hd. r.; snail (?) above. *Forrer/ Weber* 5158   ..   ..   £13

3956 *Circa* 300 B.C. Æ 18. Hd. of Athena l., wearing crested helmet wreathed with olive. ℞. ΠΕΡΓΑ below two bulls' heads face to face; bee in field above. *B.M.C. 15,* 111, 13 £14

3957 — Æ 17. Hd. of Athena l., wearing crested Corinthian helmet. ℞. ΠΕΡΓΑ below hd. and neck of bull l.; owl in field to r. *B.M.C. 15.* 112, 20-21 ..   ..   ..   £14

3958	3959	3960

3958 — Æ 10. Hd. of young Herakles r., clad in lion's skin. ℞. ΠΕΡ below hd. of Athena r., in crested helmet. *B.M.C. 15.* 112, 22-3 ..   ..   £10

3959 — — Hd. of Athena r., in crested helmet. ℞. ΠΕΡΓ below two stars; Θ above. *B.M.C. 15.* 112, 24-5 ..   ..   £10

3960 2nd-1st cent. B.C. Æ 20. Hd. of Athena r., in crested Corinthian helmet. ℞. ΑΘΗΝΑΣ / ΝΙΚΗΦΟΡΟΥ either side of trophy; mint-monogram of Pergamon (ΠΕΡΓ) in lower field to r. *B.M.C. 15.* 130, 172-5 ..   ..   £9

3961 — Æ 23. Similar, but with ΕΦ in *rev.* field to r. instead of mint-monogram. *B.M.C. 15.* 131, 178 ..   ..   £10

3962 — Æ 18. Hd. of Athena r., in close-fitting crested helmet ornamented with star. ℞. ΑΘΗ-ΝΑΣ / ΝΙΚΗΦΟΡΟΥ above and below owl stg. facing on palm-branch, wings spread. *B.M.C. 15.* 132, 190-91 ..   ..   £8

3963	3965

3963 — — Similar, but with Π — Δ in *rev.* field either side of owl. *B.M.C. 15.* 133, 201 £8

3964 — Æ 17. *Obv.* Similar. ℞. ΑΘΗ — ΝΑΣ / ΝΙΚΗΦΟΡΟΥ above and below owl stg. facing on thunderbolt, wings closed. *B.M.C. 15.* 132, 187 ..   ..   £8

3965 — Æ 14. *Obv.* Similar. ℞. ΑΘΗΝΑΣ/ΝΙΚΗΦΟΡΟΥ either side of owl stg. facing, wings closed; all within olive-wreath. *B.M.C. 15.* 131, 185 ..   ..   ..   £7

3966 — Æ 17. Dr. bust of Athena r., wearing crested Corinthian helmet. ℞. As last, but with mint-monogram of Pergamon (ΠΕΡΓ) below owl. *B.M.C. 15.* 131, 183   £9

3967 3970

3967 — Æ 18. Laur. hd. of Asklepios r. R. ΑΣΚΛΗΠΙΟΥ / ΣΩΤΗΡΟΣ either side of Asklepian snake coiled r. round omphalos. *B.M.C. 15.* 129, 158 .. .. £10

3968 — Æ 17. *Obv.* Similar, but with ΔΙΟΔΩΡΟΥ beneath hd. R. ΑΣΚΛΗΠΙΟΥ / ΣΩΤΗΡΟΣ either side of snake-entwined Asklepian staff. *B.M.C. 15.* 129, 151-2.. .. £12

3969 — Æ 18. Laur. hd. of Apollo r. R. ΑΣΚΛΗΠΙΟΥ / ΣΩΤΗΡΟΣ either side of tripod. *B.M.C. 15.* 130, 171 .. .. £9

3970 — Æ 15. ΑΣΚΛΗΠΙΑΔΟΥ beneath hd. of Hygieia r., snake before. R. ΑΣΚΛΗΠΙΟΥ / ΚΑΙ ΥΓΙΕΙΑΣ either side of Asklepian snake coiled r. round omphalos. *B.M.C. 15.* 129, 163 .. .. £13

3971 — — Bust of Asklepios r. R. Asklepian snake coiled round crooked staff. *B.M.C. 15.* 130, 164 .. .. £11

3972 — Æ 14. Similar, but *obv.* type to l., and with Γ in *rev.* field to r. *B.M.C. 15.* 130, 169 £12

3973 3976

3973 — Æ 26. Bust of Athena l., wearing crested Corinthian helmet and clad in aegis; ΜΙΘΡΑΔΑΤΟΥ beneath. R. Asklepios stg. facing, holding snake-entwined staff; ΠΕΡΓΑΜΗΝΩΝ to r. *B.M.C. 15.* 127, 129-30 .. .. £14

3974 — Æ 19. Hd. of Athena r., wearing close-fitting crested helmet ornamented with star. R. Nike stg. r., holding palm and crowning legend, ΠΕΡΓΑΜΗ, before. *B.M.C. 15.* 127, 135-6 .. .. £9

3975 — — Similar, but with ΔΗΜΗΤΡΙΟΥ beneath hd. of Athena on *obv*, and with legend ΠΕΡΓΑΜΗΝΩΝ on *rev.* *B.M.C. 15.* 128, 140 .. .. £10

3976 — Æ 22. Laur. hd. of Asklepios r., ΣΕΛΕΥΚΟΥ beneath. R. Eagle stg. l. on thunderbolt, looking back; Π — ΕΡ / Γ — Α / ΜΗΝΩΝ in field. *B.M.C. 15.* 128, 149 .. .. £12

N.B. *For coins of the Pergamene kings, see below under 'Hellenistic Monarchies'.*

3977 **Perperene** (a small town, possessing celebrated vineyards, situated north-west of Pergamon). 2nd cent. B.C. Æ 9. Laur. hd. of Apollo r. R. Bunch of grapes; Π — ΕΡ across field. *B.M.C. 15.* 168, 1 .. .. £14

3978 **Pitane** (situated south-west of Pergamon, Pitane was a coastal town on the Elaitic gulf). Late 5th cent. B.C. Æ *hemiobol* (c. 0·4 gm.). Hd. r. R. ΠΙΤΑΝΑ. Pentagram. *Historia Numorum*, p. 537 .. .. £110

3979 4th-3rd cent. B.C. Æ 17. Bearded hd. of Zeus Ammon r., horned. R. ΠΙΤΑΝ. Pentagram; pellet at centre. *B.M.C. 15.* 171, 5 .. .. £14

3980   3981

Pitane *continued*

3980 — Æ 10.   Similar, but with inscription ΠI on *rev.*   *B.M.C. 15.* 171, 2   ..   £12

3981 — Æ 18.   Bearded hd. of Zeus Ammon, horned, three-quarter face to r.   ℞. ΠITANAIΩN.
Pentagram; serpent in field to l.   *B.M.C. 15.* 172, 11 ..   ..   £17

3982 2nd-1st cent. B.C.   Æ 15.   Laur. hd. of Zeus r.   ℞. ΠITANAIΩN.   Bearded hd. of Zeus
Ammon, horned, three quarter face to l.; all within ivy-wreath. *B.M.C. 15.* 172, 14   £14

3983 **Plakia** (situated on the shores of the Propontis, east of Kyzikos). *Circa* 350 B.C.   Æ 11.
Hd. of Kybele r., wearing turreted headdress, hair rolled.   ℞. ΠΛAKIA above lion r.,
devouring prey; ear of corn beneath.   *B.M.C. 15.* 174, 5   ..   ..   ..   £14

3984 — Æ 10.   *Obv.* Similar.   ℞. ΠΛAKI.   Lion's hd. r.   *B.M.C. 15.* 174, 4   ..   £13

3985   3987   3990

3985 — Æ 12. Diad. hd. of Kybele r., hair rolled.   ℞. ΠΛA above bull walking r.   *B.M.C. 15.*
174, 1-3   ..   ..   £14

3986 **Poimanenon** (situated south of Kyzikos, on the road to Adramytteion, Poimanenon
possessed a famous temple of Asklepios).   2nd-1st cent. B.C.   Æ 22.   Laur. hd. of Zeus r.
℞. ΠOIMA / NHNΩN above and below thunderbolt; BI beneath.   *B.M.C. 15.* 175, 1-3   £20

3987 **Priapos** (on the coast of the Propontis, east of Parion, Priapos was a Kyzikene colony
and a centre for the worship of the god of the same name).   3rd cent. B.C.   Æ 10.   Laur.
hd. of Apollo r.   ℞. ΠPI below cray-fish l.; caduceus above.   *B.M.C. 15.* 176, 1   £15

3988 — Æ 18.   *Obv.* Similar.   ℞. ΠPIAΠHNΩN above shrimp r.; bunch of grapes beneath.
B.M.C. 15. 176, 3   ..   ..   £18

3989 2nd-1st cent. B.C.   Æ 24.   Veiled hd. of Demeter r., wreathed with corn.   ℞. ΠPIA /
ΠHNωN in two lines, facing bull's hd. beneath; all within corn-wreath.   *B.M.C. 15.*
177, 14   ..   ..   £17

3990 — Æ 20.   *Obv.* Similar, but within corn-wreath.   ℞. Stag stg. r.; before, cista, containing serpent, and thyrsos; ΠPI / AΠH / NΩN in field.   *B.M.C. 15.* 177, 12   ..   £16

3991 — Æ 18.   Hd. of Dionysos r., wreathed with ivy.   ℞. ΠPI / AΠH in two lines within
ivy-wreath.   *B.M.C. 15.* 176-7, 7-9   ..   ..   £14

*This type is often countermarked, usually with half-stag r. on obv., and ΠPI / AΠH with
amphora on rev.*

3992   3994   3997

3992 Prokonnesos (an island at the western end of the Propontis, mid-way between the coast-lines of Mysia and Thrace, Prokonnesos was celebrated for the quality of its marble). 400-350 B.C. Æ ¾ drachm (c. 3·6 gm.). ΑΝΑΞΙΓΕΝΗΣ above laur. hd. of Aphrodite r., hair in sakkos. Ŗ. ΠΡΟ / ΚΟΝ above stag lying r., looking back; oinochoë before, astragalos beneath. *B.M.C. 15.* 178, 1   ..   ..   £500

3993 — Æ hemidrachm (c. 2·5 gm.). *Obv.* Similar, but without magistrate's name. Ŗ. ΠΡΟ / ΚΟΝ above forepart of stag lying r., looking back; oinochoë behind. *B.M.C. 15.* 178, 2   £350

3994 — — Hd. of Aphrodite l., hair in sphendone. Ŗ. ΠΡΟ / ΚΟΝ either side of oinochoë l. *B.M.C. 15.* 178, 3 ..   ..   £275

3995 — Æ hemiobol (c. 0·45 gm.). Forepart of horse l., inscribed Α. Ŗ. Oinochoë; ivy-leaf and Π to r.; all within incuse square. *Forrer/Weber* 5250   ..   ..   £85

3996 *Circa* 350 B.C. Æ 18. *Obv.* Similar to 3992, but with magistrate's name ΔΗΜΗΤΡΙΟΥ. Ŗ. Oinochoë r.; ΠΡΟ to r. *B.M.C. 15.* 178, 4 ..   ..   £16

3997 — Æ 14. *Obv.* Similar, but without magistrate's name. Ŗ. ΠΡΟ / ΚΟΝ above dove stg. r.; oinochoë before, dolphin behind. *B.M.C. 15.* 179, 6   ..   £14

3998 — Æ 10. *Obv.* As last. Ŗ. ΠΡΟ / ΚΟΝ either side of oinochoë r. *Babelon (Traité) pl.* 179, 26   ..   ..   £11

3999 Teuthrania (situated south-west of Pergamon). Prokles I, dynast *circa* 399 B.C. Æ diobol (c. 1·6 gm.). Laur. hd. of Apollo l. Ŗ. ΤΕΥ behind young male hd. r., beardless, wearing Persian head-dress. *Babelon (Catalogue des Monnaies Grecques de la Bibliothèque Nationale) p. lxx, fig. 31* £500

4000   4001B

4000 Thebe (situated north-east of Adramytteion, Thebe was a town of considerable antiquity, built on the slopes of Mt. Plakios). *Circa* 350 B.C. Æ 10. Laur. female hd. r., hair in sakkos. Ŗ. Θ — Η — Β between three crescents joined at central point. *B.M.C. 15.* 179. 1   £18

4001 — Æ 9. *Obv.* Similar. Ŗ. ΘΗΒ below forepart of winged horse r. *Babelon (Traité) pl.* 170, 17 ..   ..   £18

4001A Zeleia (situated on the river Aisepos, in Kyzikene territory, Zeleia was the head-quarters of the Persian army at the time of Alexander's invasion of Asia Minor, 334 B.C.). *Circa* 334 B.C. Æ 19. Hd. of Artemis r., wearing stephanos. Ŗ. Stag stg. r.; I — E / Λ — E in field. *B.M.C. 17.* 90, 1 ..   ..   £16

4001B — Æ 14. Similar. *B.M.C. 17.* 90, 2   ..   ..   ..   £13

4001C — Æ 11. *Obv.* Similar. Ŗ. I — E / Я — Λ around monogram; all within corn-wreath. *Babelon (Traité) pl.* 172, 32   ..   ..   £11

4002   4004   4006

4002 **TROAS. Abydos** (a Milesian colony on the shores of the Hellespont, opposite Sestos).
  Circa 450 B.C. Æ *drachm* (*c.* 5·3 gm.). ΑΒΥΔΗΝΩΝ. Eagle stg. l., wings closed. ℞.
  Gorgoneion, within incuse square. *B.M.C. 17.* 1, 1-2 .. .. £400

4003 — Æ ¾ *drachm* (*c.* 4 gm.). Similar, but with *obv.* legend ΑΒΥ, and with large star above
  eagle. *Grose/McClean* 7753 .. .. £350

4004 — Æ *obol* (*c.* 0·9 gm.). Similar to 4002, but without legend on *obv.* *B.M.C. 17.* 1, 1
                                                                          £125

4005 — Æ *hemiobol* ? (*c.* 0·5 gm.). Similar to 4002, but with *obv.* legend ΑΒΥ, and with monogram behind eagle. *B.M.C. 17.* 1, 7 .. .. £90

4006 — Æ *hemitartemorion* = ⅛ *obol* (*c.* 0·11 gm.). As last, but without monogram. *B.M.C.*
  17. 1, 8 .. .. £65

4007 Late 5th cent. B.C. *N stater* (*c.* 8·6 gm.). Artemis seated on stag walking l. ℞. Eagle
  stg. r., wings closed; bunch of grapes before; all within incuse square. *Babelon* (*Traité*)
  pl. 168, 2 .. .. £10,000

4008   4009

4008 Early 4th cent. B.C. *N stater* (*c.* 8·4 gm.). Nike kneeling l. on ram, holding sword in
  raised r. hand, with which she is about to sacrifice the animal. ℞. As last, but with
  aplustre instead of bunch of grapes. *B.M.C. 17.* 2, 9 .. .. £10,000

4009 — Æ *tetradrachm* (*c.* 15 gm.). Laur. hd. of Apollo l. ℞. Eagle, wings closed, stg. r.
  on aplustre; before, ΑΒΥ and triskelis within circle; behind, ΜΗΤΡΟΔΩΡΟΣ. *B.M.C. 17.* 2,
  10 .. .. £3,500

4010 Mid-4th cent. B.C. Æ *stater* (*c.* 10·6 gm.). Laur. hd. of Apollo r. ℞. Eagle stg. l.,
  wings closed; before, ΑΒΥ and bee; behind, ΥΛΛΙΠΠΟΣ. *B.M.C. 17.* 2, 11 .. £1,500

4011   4013

4011 — Æ *hemidrachm* (*c.* 2·65 gm.). Similar, but with magistrate's name ΓΟΡΓΙΑΣ on *rev.*,
  and with dolphin instead of bee. *B.M.C. 17.* 2, 15 .. .. £125

4012 — — Laur. hd. of Apollo l.   ℞. Eagle stg. l., wings closed; before, ABY and trident; behind, ΠΡΩΤΑΓΟΡΑΣ and aplustre.   *B.M.C. 17.* 4, 31-2   ..   ..   ..   £140

4013 2nd cent. B.C.   Æ *tetradrachm* (*c.* 16·75 gm.).   Diad. and dr. bust of Artemis r., bow and quiver over l. shoulder.   ℞. Eagle stg. r., wings spread; ABYΔHNΩN above, palm-branch before, ΑΠΟΛΛΟΦΑ / NOV below; all within laurel-wreath.   *B.M.C. 17.* 6, 52   £500

4014 — — Similar, but with bee instead of palm-branch in *rev.* field to r., and magistrate's name ΦΕΡΕΝΙ / ΚΟΥ below.   *B.M.C. 17.* 6, 57   ..   ..   £500

4015   4016

4015 *Bronze Coinage.*   Mid-4th cent. B.C.   Æ 19.   Laur. hd. of Apollo l.   ℞. Eagle stg. r., wings closed; ABY behind, crescent before.   *B.M.C. 17.* 4, 35 ..   ..   ..   £14

4016 3rd-2nd cent. B.C.   Æ 22.   Hd. of Artemis three-quarter face to r., laur. and wearing stephanos.   ℞. Eagle stg. r., wings spread; ABY and aplustre before.   *B.M.C. 17.* 4, 36   £15

4017 — — Turreted hd. of Artemis r.   ℞. Eagle, wings closed, stg. r., looking back; ABY behind, corn-ear before.   *B.M.C. 17.* 4, 38   ..   ..   £14

4018 — — Turreted hd. of Artemis three-quarter face to r.   ℞. Stag stg. r., ABY above; all within wreath.   *B.M.C. 17.* 5, 42-3   ..   ..   £15

4019   4024

4019 — Æ 18.   Laur. bust of Artemis three-quarter face to l.   ℞. Lyre; A — B — Y / Δ — H in field.   *B.M.C. 17.* 5, 48   ..   ..   £13

4020 — Æ 13.   Turreted bust of Artemis facing.   ℞. ABY.   Eagle, wings closed, stg. r., looking back.   *B.M.C. 17.* 5, 40 ..   ..   £11

4021 — — Hd. of Artemis r., bow and quiver at shoulder.   ℞. Two torches, crossed; A — BY across field; star above, bunch of grapes beneath.   *B.M.C. 17.* 5, 44 ..   ..   £9

4022 — — Hd. of Artemis r., hair tied in bunch behind.   ℞. Torch and quiver, crossed; A — B / Y / Δ — H in field.   *B.M.C. 17.* 5, 45   ..   ..   £9

4023 **Achilleion** (situated near Sigeion, close to the entrance of the Hellespont, Achilleion was reputed to be the burial-place of Achilles).   350-300 B.C.   Æ 10.   Helmet.   ℞. ΑΧ monogram.   *Historia Numorum, p.* 540 ..   ..   £25

4024 **Alexandreia Troas** (a coastal city situated south-west of Ilion, it was founded *c.* 310 B.C. by Antigonos and originally bore the name Antigoneia.   A decade later Lysimachos re-named the place Alexandreia).   3rd cent. B.C.   Æ *tetradrachm* (*c.* 16·75 gm.), restoring the types of Alexander the Great.   Hd. of young Herakles r., clad in lion's skin.   ℞. Zeus enthroned l., holding eagle and sceptre; ΑΛΕΞΑΝΔΡΟΥ behind, two monograms before, horse grazing l. in ex.   *Müller* (*Numismatique d'Alexandre le Grand*) 923-4   £200

4025   4027

Alexandreia Troas *continued*

4025 2nd-1st cent. B.C.   Æ *tetradrachm* (*c.* 16·75 gm.).   Laur. hd. of Apollo l.   ℞. Apollo
Smintheos stg. r., holding phiale in r. hand, bow and arrow in l.; ΑΠΟΛΛΩΝΟΣ / ΙΜΙΘΕΩΣ
before and behind, ΑΛΕΞΑΝΔΡΕΩΝ / ΛΥΣΑΓΟΡΟΥ in ex.; in field to r., ΡΠΓ (= year 183); to l.,
monogram.   *B.M.C. 17.* 11, 22   ..   ..   £1,000
*The date on reverse, if reckoned according to the Seleukid era, is equivalent to 130/129
B.C.   Earlier and later dates are also known.*

4026 *Bronze Coinage.   Circa* 300 B.C.   Æ 20.   Laur. hd. of Apollo r.   ℞. ΑΛΕΞ / ΔΡΕΩΝ
above and below horse grazing r.; two palm-branches before, ΚΑ monogram beneath,
ear of corn in ex.   *B.M.C. 17.* 9, 4   ..   ..   £11

4027 — Æ 14.   *Obv.* Similar.   ℞. ΑΛΕΞ behind Apollo Smintheos stg. r., holding phiale and
bow, mouse at feet.   *B.M.C. 17.* 9, 1   ..   ..   £11

4028 3rd-2nd cent. B.C.   Æ 17.   *Obv.* Similar.   ℞. ΑΛΕΞΑΝ above horse grazing l.; monogram beneath, thunderbolt in ex.   *B.M.C. 17.* 10, 16   ..   ..   £10

4029 — Æ 11.   *Obv.* Similar.   ℞. ΑΛΕ above horse grazing r.; wreath beneath, thunderbolt in
ex.   *B.M.C. 17.* 10, 11   ..   ..   £8

4030 — Æ 7.   Similar, but with star instead of wreath on *rev.*   *B.M.C. 17.* 10, 13   £7

4031   4034   4037

4031 2nd-1st cent. B.C.   Æ 22.   Laur. bust of Apollo three-quarter face to r.   ℞. ΑΛΕ / ΞΑΝ
either side of lyre, caduceus beneath; all within laurel-wreath.   *B.M.C. 17.* 12, 35-6   £13

4032 — Æ 18.   Laur. hd. of Apollo l., within laurel-wreath.   ℞. ΑΛΕΞ.   Tripod.   *B.M.C. 17*
12, 28   ..   ..   £9

4033 — Æ 9.   Lyre.   ℞. Tripod; A — Λ / E — Ξ across field.   *B.M.C. 17.* 11, 25-7   £8

4034 **Antandros** (on the northern shores of the Gulf of Adramytteion, Antandros was an
Aiolian colony).   *Circa* 400 B.C.   Æ *drachm* (*c.* 3·9 gm.).   Hd. of Artemis Astyrene r.,
hair rolled and bound with crossed cord.   ℞. ΑΝΤΑ / Ν.   Goat stg. r.; all within incuse
square.   *Boston Museum Catalogue* 1623 ..   ..   £750

4035 — Æ *tetrobol* (*c.* 2·6 gm.).   *Obv.* Similar.   ℞. ΑΝΤ / Α / Ν.   Goat stg. r., r. foreleg raised;
fir-tree before; all within incuse square.   *B.M.C. 17.* 33, 1   ..   ..   ..   £600

4036 — Æ *hemidrachm* (*c.* 1·95 gm.).   Similar to 4034.   *S.N.G. Von Aulock* 1492   £350

4037 — Æ *diobol* (*c.* 1·3 gm.).   *Obv.* Similar.   ℞. ΑΝΤΑΝ above goat stg. r.; bunch of grapes
in upper field; all within incuse square.   *B.M.C. 17.* 33, 2   ..   ..   ..   £200

4038 — Æ *obol* (*c.* 0·65 gm.). Similar to 4034. *Boston Museum Catalogue* 1625 .. £120

4039 — — *Obv.* Similar. R. Lion's hd. facing, A — N in lower field; all within incuse square. *Babelon* (*Traité*) *pl.* 163, 2 .. .. £140

4040 *Circa* 350 B.C. Æ 19. Laur. hd. of Apollo r. R. ANTAN. Lion's hd. r.; bunch of grapes beneath. *B.M.C. 17.* 33, 3-5 .. .. £16

4041   4042   4046

4041 — Æ 14. Similar, but with ivy-leaf instead of bunch of grapes on *rev.* *B.M.C. 17.* 33, 6 .. .. £15

4042 **Assos** (situated on the Gulf of Adramytteion, west of Antandros, Assos was opposite the northern coastline of Lesbos). *Circa* 450 B.C. Æ *tetrobol* (*c.* 3·6 gm.). Griffin recumbent l., r. forepaw raised. R. Lion's hd. r., within incuse square. *B.M.C. 17.* 36, 1 .. .. £900

4043 — Æ *diobol* (*c.* 1·55 gm.). Similar, but with griffin to r., l. forepaw raised. *B.M.C. 17.* 36, 2 .. .. £400

4044 — Æ *obol* (*c.* 0·85 gm.). As last. *B.M.C. 17.* 36, 3 .. .. .. £140

4045 *Circa* 400 B.C. Æ *tetradrachm* (*c.* 15 gm.). Hd. of Athena l., wearing crested helmet ornamented with griffin. R. ΑΣΣΙΟΝ behind archaic statue of Athena Polias r., holding spear and fillets; all within incuse square. *Babelon* (*Traité*) *pl.* 163, 28 .. £4,500

4046 — Æ *drachm* (*c.* 3·1 gm.). Hd. of Athena l., wearing crested helmet wreathed with olive. R. ΑΣΣΟΟΝ (*sic*). Lion's hd. l.; all within incuse square. *Forrer/Weber* 5320 £650

4047 *Circa* 350 B.C. Æ *tetrobol* (*c.* 3·1 gm.). *Obv.* Similar. R. ΑΣ — ΣΙ — ΟΝ to l., above and to r. of bull's hd. facing; crescent below. *Boston Museum Catalogue* 1627 £550

4048 — Æ *hemidrachm* (*c.* 2·3 gm.). As last, but with ear of corn in *rev.* field to l., and without crescent below bull's hd. *B.M.C. 17.* 36, 4 .. .. £300

4049   4053   4055

4049 — Æ *diobol* (*c.* 1·55 gm.). *Obv.* Similar. R. ΑΣ — ΣΙ to l. and above bull's hd. facing; ear of corn to r. *B.M.C. 17.* 37, 7 .. .. £200

4050 Mid-3rd cent. B.C. Æ *tetradrachm* (*c.* 16·75 gm.), restoring the types of Alexander the Great. Hd. of young Herakles r., clad in lion's skin. R. Zeus enthroned l., holding eagle and sceptre; ΑΛΕΞΑΝΔΡΟΥ behind, griffin l. and monogram before, leaf beneath throne. *Müller* (*Numismatique d' Alexandre le Grand*) 929 .. .. .. £200

4051 *Bronze Coinage.* *Circa* 350 B.C. Æ 10. Hd. of Athena r., in close-fitting crested helmet. R. Bull's hd. facing; ΑΣ — ΣΙ in lower field, lion's hd. r. above. *B.M.C. 17.* 37, 9 £12

4052 4th-3rd cent. B.C. Æ 22. *Obv.* Similar, but helmet is wreathed with olive. R Griffin recumbent l.; ΑΣΣΙ above, bee in ex. *B.M.C. 17.* 37, 10 .. .. .. £15

4053 — Æ 14. As last, but with corn-ear instead of bee on *rev.* *B.M.C. 17.* 38, 18-20 £13

4054 2nd-1st cent. B.C. Æ 19. Hd. of Athena three-quarter face to r., wearing crested helmet wreathed with olive. R. Griffin stg. l.; ΑΣΣΙ above, star before, helmeted hd. l. beneath. *B.M.C. 17.* 38, 23 .. .. £14

4055 — Æ 13. Diad. female hd. r. R. Thunderbolt; ΑΣΣΙ above, monogram beneath. *Forrer/Weber* 5331 .. .. £10

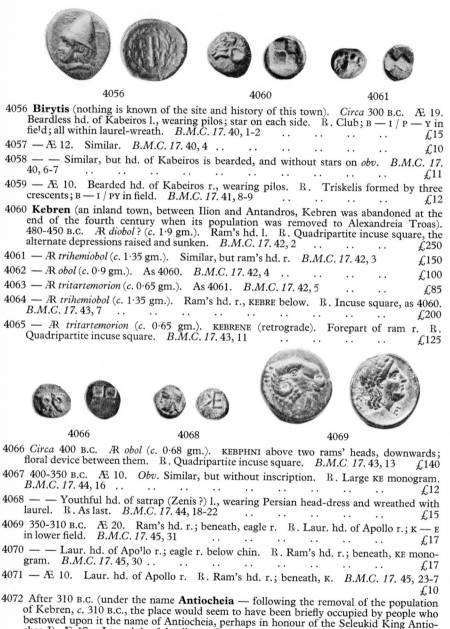

4056   4060   4061

4056 Birytis (nothing is known of the site and history of this town). *Circa* 300 B.C. Æ 19.
Beardless hd. of Kabeiros l., wearing pilos; star on each side. R. Club; B — I / P — Y in
field; all within laurel-wreath. *B.M.C.* 17. 40, 1-2   ..   ..   £15

4057 — Æ 12. Similar. *B.M.C.* 17. 40, 4 ..   ..   £10

4058 — — Similar, but hd. of Kabeiros is bearded, and without stars on *obv.* *B.M.C.* 17.
40, 6-7   ..   ..   £11

4059 — Æ 10. Bearded hd. of Kabeiros r., wearing pilos. R. Triskelis formed by three
crescents; B — I / PY in field. *B.M.C.* 17. 41, 8-9   ..   ..   ..   £12

4060 Kebren (an inland town, between Ilion and Antandros, Kebren was abandoned at the
end of the fourth century when its population was removed to Alexandreia Troas).
480-450 B.C. Æ *diobol* ? (*c.* 1·9 gm.). Ram's hd. l. R. Quadripartite incuse square, the
alternate depressions raised and sunken. *B.M.C.* 17. 42, 2   ..   ..   £250

4061 — Æ *trihemiobol* (*c.* 1·35 gm.). Similar, but ram's hd. r. *B.M.C.* 17. 42, 3   £150

4062 — Æ *obol* (*c.* 0·9 gm.). As 4060. *B.M.C.* 17. 42, 4 ..   ..   ..   £100

4063 — Æ *tritartemorion* (*c.* 0·65 gm.). As 4061. *B.M.C.* 17. 42, 5   ..   £85

4064 — Æ *trihemiobol* (*c.* 1·35 gm.). Ram's hd. r., KEBRE below. R. Incuse square, as 4060.
B.M.C. 17. 43, 7   ..   ..   £200

4065 — Æ *tritartemorion* (*c.* 0·65 gm.). KEBRENE (retrograde). Forepart of ram r. R.
Quadripartite incuse square. *B.M.C.* 17. 43, 11   ..   ..   £125

4066   4068   4069

4066 *Circa* 400 B.C. Æ *obol* (*c.* 0·68 gm.). KEBPHNI above two rams' heads, downwards;
floral device between them. R. Quadripartite incuse square. *B.M.C.* 17. 43, 13   £140

4067 400-350 B.C. Æ 10. *Obv.* Similar, but without inscription. R. Large KE monogram.
B.M.C. 17. 44, 16 ..   ..   £12

4068 — — Youthful hd. of satrap (Zenis ?) l., wearing Persian head-dress and wreathed with
laurel. R. As last. *B.M.C.* 17. 44, 18-22   ..   ..   £15

4069 350-310 B.C. Æ 20. Ram's hd. r.; beneath, eagle r. R. Laur. hd. of Apollo r.; K — E
in lower field. *B.M.C.* 17. 45, 31   ..   ..   £17

4070 — — Laur. hd. of Apollo r.; eagle r. below chin. R. Ram's hd. r.; beneath, KE monogram. *B.M.C.* 17. 45, 30 ..   ..   £17

4071 — Æ 10. Laur. hd. of Apollo r. R. Ram's hd. r.; beneath, K. *B.M.C.* 17. 45, 23-7
£10

4072 After 310 B.C. (under the name **Antiocheia** — following the removal of the population
of Kebren, *c.* 310 B.C., the place would seem to have been briefly occupied by people who
bestowed upon it the name of Antiocheia, perhaps in honour of the Seleukid King Antiochos I). Æ 17. Laur. hd. of Apollo r. R. ANTIOXEΩN. Ram's hd. r.; beneath, eagle r.
B.M.C. 17. 46, 37   ..   ..   £20

4073 — Æ 10. *Obv.* Similar. R. ANTIO / XEΩN above and below ram's hd. r. *B.M.C.* 17.
46, 39   ..   ..   £14

4074 Kolone (the inhabitants of Kolone were, like those of several other towns of the Troad, removed to Antigoneia/Alexandreia *c.* 310 B.C.). 350-310 B.C. Æ 17. Hd. of Athena r., wearing close-fitting crested helmet. ℞. K — O — Λ — Ω — N — A — Ω — N between the eight rays of a large star. *B.M.C. 17.* 47, 2 .. .. £18

4075   4076   4078

4075 — Æ 10. Similar, but *obv.* type to l. *B.M.C. 17.* 47, 5-6 .. .. .. £13

4076 Dardanos (situated on the Hellespont, south of Abydos, Dardanos was an Aiolian colony. The modern name of the Hellespont (Dardanelles) is derived from this city). *Circa* 450 B.C. Æ *drachm* (*c.* 4·7 gm.). Naked male rider on horse pacing l. ℞. Cock stg. l., ΔAP before, IH monogram above; all within incuse square. *B.M.C. 17.* 48, 1 £750

4077 — Æ *trihemiobol* (*c.* 1·05 gm.). Similar, but with two cocks confronted, on *rev.;* IH monogram to l., ΔAP to r. *Babelon (Traité) pl.* 167, 18 .. .. £200

4078 *Circa* 375 B.C. Æ *hemidrachm* (*c.* 2·5 gm.). Male rider, his cloak floating behind, on horse prancing r. ℞. Cock stg. r.; ΔAP behind, ΓΛΑΥΚΕΤΑΣ and ear of corn before. *B.M.C. 17.* 48, 2 .. .. £300

4079 *Circa* 350 B.C. Æ 22. *Obv.* Similar. ℞. Cock stg. r.; ΔAP behind, small figure of Athena r. before. *B.M.C. 17.* 48, 4 .. .. £18

4080   4083   4084

4080 — Æ 15. *Obv.* Similar; thunderbolt beneath. ℞. ΔAPΔA above cock r., in fighting attitude; ear of corn beneath. *B.M.C. 17.* 50, 20 .. .. .. £14

4081 — Æ 13. *Obv.* As 4078. ℞. Cock stg. r., looking back; ΔAP behind. *B.M.C. 17.* 49, 15 .. .. £14

4082 — Æ 9. Cock stg. l. ℞. ΔAP arranged concentrically within linear border. *B.M.C. 17.* 49, 17 .. .. £11

4083 2nd cent. B.C. Æ 17. Bearded hd. of Zeus (?) r. ℞. Male rider on horse prancing r.; ΔAP below. *B.M.C. 17.* 50, 23-4 .. .. £10

4084 Gargara (on the Gulf of Adramytteion, between Antandros and Assos, the territory of Gargara was famed for the fertility of its soil). *Circa* 400 B.C. Æ *tetrobol* (*c.* 3·2 gm.). Young male hd. r., bare. ℞. ΓAΡΓ above bull stg. l., feeding; all within incuse square. *B.M.C. 17.* 52, 1 .. .. £450

4085 — Æ *diobol* (*c.* 1·45 gm.). *Obv.* Similar. ℞. ΓAP above horse galloping r.; all within incuse square. *B.M.C. 17.* 52, 2 .. .. £250

4086 — Æ *tritartemorion* ? (*c.* 0·6 gm.). *Obv.* Similar. ℞. ΓAP above ram's hd. r.; all within incuse square. *Babelon (Traité) pl.* 163, 10 .. .. £110

4087 — Æ *hemiobol* ? (*c.* 0·45 gm.). *Obv.* Similar. ℞. Γ — A — P — Γ between the spokes of a wheel; all within circular incuse. *Babelon (Traité) pl.* 163, 11 .. .. £85

4088   4090   4094

Gargara *continued*

4088 *Circa* 350 B.C.   Æ *tetrobol* (*c.* 3·2 gm.).   Laur. hd. of Apollo r.   ℞. ΓΑΡΓ above bull stg. l.,
feeding. *B.M.C. 17.* 52, 3   ..   ..   £350

4089 — Æ 18.   Laur. hd. of Apollo r.   ℞. ΓΑΡ above horse galloping r.; thunderbolt beneath.
B.M.C. 17. 52, 5   ..   ..   £15

4090 — Æ 9.   Similar, but bunch of grapes instead of thunderbolt on *rev.* *B.M.C. 17.* 53,
14 ..   ..   £11

4091 2nd-1st cent. B.C.   Æ 19.   Laur. hd. of Zeus r.   ℞. ΓΑΡΓΑ / ΡΕ above and below bull
butting r.; star above, monogram beneath. *S.N.G. Von Aulock* 1512   ..   £10

4092 — Æ 17.   Laur. hd. of Apollo r.   ℞. ΓΑΡ.   Horse stg. l., r. foreleg raised; above, bunch
of grapes. *B.M.C. 17.* 53, 15   ..   ..   £10

4093 — Æ 12.   Turreted female hd. r.   ℞. ΓΑΡ.   Lion stg. r., looking back. *Forrer/Weber*
5373   ..   ..   £9

4094 **Gentinos** (mentioned by only one ancient author, the history and precise location of
Gentinos are unknown to us).   350-300 B.C.   Æ 16.   Laur. hd. of Apollo r.   ℞. Bee;
Γ — Ε / Ν — Τ in field; all within laurel-wreath. *B.M.C. 17.* 54, 3   ..   £17

4095 — Æ 15.   Hd. of Artemis (?) r., hair rolled.   ℞. Bee; Γ — Ε / Ν in field, palm-tree to l.
B.M.C. 17. 54, 1   ..   ..   £16

4096 — Æ 10.   Hd. of Artemis (?) r., in mural crown.   ℞. Bee; Γ — Ε / Ν — Τ / Ι — Ν in
field; all within linear square. *Babelon (Traité) pl.* 169, 13   ..   ..   ..   £13

4097 **Gergis** (the site of this town is not certainly known, but was probably on the rocky
heights of Bali-Dagh, a few miles south of Ilion).   Mid-4th cent. B.C.   Æ *hemiobol* (*c.*
0·45 gm.).   Laur. hd. of the Sibyl Herophile three-quarter face to r.   ℞. ΓΕΡ before
Sphinx seated r. *B.M.C. 17.* 55, 1   ..   ..   £120

4098   4102

4098 — Æ 9.   Similar. *B.M.C. 17.* 55, 2-3 ..   ..   £12

4099 Mid-4th — mid-3rd cent. B.C.   Æ 17.   Similar, but the Sibyl also wears necklace, and
with ear of corn in ex. on *rev.* *B.M.C. 17.* 55, 5-8   ..   ..   £17

4100 **Hamaxitos** (a coastal town situated south of Alexandreia Troas, Hamaxitos possessed
the temple of Apollo Smintheos within its territory.   The population were removed to
Alexandreia at the end of the fourth century).   350-310 B.C.   Æ 17.   Laur. hd. of Apollo
l.   ℞. ΑΜΑ / ΞΙ either side of lyre. *B.M.C. 17.* 56, 1   ..   ..   ..   £17

4101 — Æ 14.   Laur. hd. of Apollo r.   ℞. ΑΜΑΞΙ behind Apollo Smintheos stg. r., holding
phiale and bow; monogram before. *B.M.C. 17.* 56, 3 ..   ..   £15

4102 **Ilion** (a city founded by the Aiolians in the seventh century B.C. on the site of ancient
Troy, Ilion boasted a famous temple of Athena visited by both Xerxes and Alexander the
Great.   The city was honoured by Alexander and, later, by the Romans who regarded
Troy as their ancestral home).   *Circa* 250 B.C.   Æ *hemidrachm* (*c.* 2·1 gm.).   Hd. of
Athena l., in crested Corinthian helmet.   ℞. ΙΛΙ behind Athena Ilias stg. l., holding
spear and distaff; in field to l., monogram and owl. *B.M.C. 17.* 57, 1 ..   ..   £350

4103   4106

4103 2nd-1st cent. B.C. Æ *tetradrachm* (*c.* 16·6 gm.), of thin, spread fabric. Hd. of Athena r., wearing triple-crested Athenian helmet wreathed with laurel. ℞. ΑΘΗΝΑΣ / ΙΛΙΑΔΟΣ either side of Athena Ilias stg. r., holding spear and distaff; owl before, caduceus behind; ΚΛΕ — ΩΝΟΣ across central field, ΙΩΙΛΟΥ in ex. *B.M.C. 17.* 58, 10   ..   ..   £1,400

4104 — — of thicker fabric. *Obv.* Similar, but Athena also wears necklace. ℞. ΑΘΗΝΑΣ / ΙΛΙΑΔΟΣ either side of Athena Ilias, as last; monogram behind, fly before; in ex., ΜΕΝΕΦ-ΡΟΝΟΣΤΟΥ / ΜΕΝΕΦΡΟΝΟΣ. *B.M.C. 17.* 58, 13 ..   ..   £1,400

4105 *Bronze Coinage.* 3rd cent. B.C. Æ 22. Hd. of Athena r., wearing crested Corin.hian helmet. ℞. ΙΛΙ behind Athena Ilias stg. l., holding spear and distaff. *B.M.C. 17.* 57, 6   ..   ..   £15

4106 — Æ 13. Similar, but with owl in *rev.* field to l. *B.M.C. 17.* 57, 3 ..   ..   £10

4107 — Æ 18. Similar, but Athena, on *obv.*, wears crested Athenian helmet; and with olive-branch instead of owl in *rev.* field to l. *B.M.C. 17.* 57, 7 ..   ..   ..   £13

4108 2nd-1st cent. B.C. Æ 16. Hd. of Athena r., in crested Athenian helmet. ℞. ΙΛΙ behind Athena Ilias stg. r., holding spear and distaff; ear of corn before; all within olive-wreath. *Forrer/Weber* 5383   ..   ..   £10

4109 — Æ 14. Helmeted hd. of Athena three-quarter face to r. ℞. ΙΛΙ behind Athena Ilias stg. r., holding spear and distaff; monogram before. *B.M.C. 17.* 59, 18   ..   £14

4110   4113   4114

4110 **Lamponeia** (the exact site of this city is not known, but it was probably in the vicinity of Gargara). *Circa* 400 B.C. Æ *drachm* (*c.* 3·8 gm.). Hd. of bearded Dionysos r. ℞. Bull's hd. facing, Λ — Α — Μ around; all within incuse square. *B.M.C. 17.* 72, 1   £750

4111 — Æ *hemidrachm* (*c.* 1·9 gm.). Similar. *B.M.C. 17.* 72, 2 ..   ..   ..   £350

4112 — Æ *obol* (*c.* 0·6 gm.). Similar. *Historia Numorum, p.* 547   ..   ..   £120

4113 *Circa* 350 B.C. Æ 12. Hd. of bearded Dionysos r., wreathed with ivy. ℞. Bull's hd. facing; ΛΑ — Μ across lower field, kantharos above. *B.M.C. 17.* 72, 3..   ..   £18

4114 **Neandreia** (in common with several other towns of the Troad, Neandreia's population was removed, at the end of the fourth century, to Alexandreia Troas which was situated a short distance to the north-west). *Circa* 400 B.C. Æ *drachm* (*c.* 3·8 gm.). Laur. hd. of Apollo r. ℞. ΝΕΑΝ above horse grazing r.; all within incuse square. *Forrer/Weber* 5415   £650

Neandreia *continued*

4115 — Æ *hemidrachm* (*c.* 1·9 gm.). Similar. *B.M.C. 17.* 73, 1 .. .. .. £300

4116 — — *Obv.* Similar. ℞. NEAN. Laurel-bush behind altar; all within incuse square. *Historia Numorum, p.* 547 .. .. £350

4117   4120

4117 — Æ *obol* (*c.* 0·6 gm.). *Obv.* Similar. ℞. NEAN. Ram stg. l.; all within incuse square. *B.M.C. 17.* 73, 2 .. .. £110

4118 — Æ *hemiobol*? (*c.* 0·35 gm.). Crested helmet (?) r. ℞. NE/AN either side of corn-grain; all within circular incuse. *B.M.C. 17.* 73, 3 .. .. £85

4119 350-310 B.C. Æ 20. Laur. hd. of Apollo r. ℞. NEAN above horse grazing r.; corn-grain in ex. *B.M.C. 17.* 74, 8-10 .. .. £17

4120 — Æ 11. *Obv.* Similar. ℞. NEAN. Corn-grain and bunch of grapes. *B.M.C. 17.* 73, 4 .. .. £13

4121 **Ophrynion** (situated south of Dardanos, close to the shores of the Hellespont, Ophrynion possessed a grove consecrated to Hektor). *Circa* 350 B.C. Æ *hemidrachm* (*c.* 2·7 gm.). Bearded hd. of Hektor facing, wearing triple-crested helmet. ℞. ΟΦΡΥΝΕΩΝ. Naked youth riding on horse pacing r., holding branch. *Babelon* (*Traité*) *pl.* 167, 10 £1,000

4122   4124

4122 — Æ *trihemiobol* (*c.* 1·35 gm.). Similar. *B.M.C. 17.* 75, 1 .. .. .. £600

4123 350-300 B.C. Æ 19. *Obv.* Similar, but hd. three-quarter face to l. ℞. ΟΦΡΥ behind infant Dionysos, naked, kneeling r., holding bunch of grapes; ivy-spray beneath. *B.M.C. 17.* 75, 2-3 .. .. £24

4124 — Æ 13. As last, but hd. of Hektor three-quarter face to r., and without ivy-spray on rev. *B.M.C. 17.* 75, 4-7 .. .. £18

4125 — Æ 10. Bearded hd. of Zeus (?) r. ℞. ΟΦΡΥ behind Hektor advancing l., holding spear and large oval shield. *B.M.C. 17.* 76, 8 .. .. £16

4126 **Rhoeteion** (situated a short distance south-west of Ophrynion). Circa 350 B.C. Æ *tetrobol*? (*c.* 3·1 gm.). Laur. hd. of Apollo l. ℞. PO — IT — EI between triquetra of crescents. *Babelon* (*Traité*) *pl.* 167, 9 .. .. (*Unique*?)

4127   4129

4127 **Skamandria** (the precise location of this small town is not known, but it was situated on the river Skamander, possibly about 20 miles west of Skepsis. Skamandrios was the son of Hektor). 350-300 B.C. Æ 20. Hd. of mountain-nymph Ide r., wreathed with fir. ℞. Fir-tree; ΣΚ — A across field, boar's hd. r. to r. *B.M.C. 17.* 79, 1 .. £24

4128 — Æ 10. Hd. of mountain-nymph Ide r., ΙΔΗ behind. ℞. ΣΚΑ. Pine-cone. *Babelon* (*Traité*) *pl.* 165, 31 .. .. £16

4129 **Skepsis** (a town in the interior of the Troad, on the Skamander, Skepsis was abandoned at the end of the fourth century when its inhabitants were removed to Antigoneia/Alexandreia. Soon afterwards, however, Lysimachos allowed them to return to their former homes). *Circa* 400 B.C. Æ *drachm* (*c*. 3·8 gm.). ΣΚΗΨΙΟΝ. Forepart of winged horse r. R. Fir-tree between two bunches of grapes ,in lower field; all in linear square surrounded by dots, contained within incuse square. *B.M.C. 17.* 80, 5 .. .. £450

4130 — Æ *hemidrachm* (*c*. 2 gm.). *Obv.* Similar, but with legend ΣΚΑΨΙΟΝ. R. As last, but with N — E (retrograde) in field, instead of bunches of grapes. *B.M.C. 17.* 80, 3 £250

4131 — Æ *trihemiobol* (*c*. 0·85 gm.). ΣΚΑΨΙΟΝ. Forepart of prancing horse r. R. As last. *B.M.C. 17.* 80, 2 .. .. £150

  4132   4134   4136

4132 *Circa* 350 B.C. Æ *tetrobol* (*c*. 3·2 gm.). Forepart of winged horse r., body terminating in horn. R. ΣΚΗ — ΨΙ — Ω — N around linear square containing fir-tree between crab and ΑΚ monogram; all within incuse square. *B.M.C. 17.* 81, 8 .. .. £350

4133 — Æ *trihemiobol* (*c*. 1·2 gm.). Similar, but with Α — Κ either side of fir-tree on *rev.* (no crab). *Babelon* (*Traité*) *pl*. 165, 10 .. .. £200

4134 *Bronze Coinage. Circa* 400 B.C. Æ 10. Forepart of winged horse r. R. Fir-tree within linear square; all in incuse square. *B.M.C. 17.* 81, 7 .. .. .. £18

4135 350-310 B.C. Æ 20. Forepart of winged horse l., body terminating in horn. R. Fir-tree within linear square; Σ — Κ — Η across lower field. *B.M.C. 17.* 81, 10 .. £18

4136 — Æ 16. *Obv.* Similar. R. Σ — Κ either side of fir-tree; all within linear square. *B.M.C. 17.* 82, 14-15 .. .. £15

4137 — — Similar to 4135, but with cornucopiae to l. of linear square on *rev.* B.M.C. 17. 82, 19 .. .. £15

4138 — Æ 13. *Obv.* As 4135. R. Fir-tree dividing Σ — ΚΗ; kantharos in field to r. B.M.C. 17. 82, 22 .. .. £13

4139 — Æ 10. Hd. of bearded Dionysos r., wreathed with ivy. R. Thyrsos; Σ — Κ across upper field, bunch of grapes to l. *B.M.C. 17.* 83, 24 .. .. .. £11

4140 2nd cent. B.C. Æ 18. Hd. of bearded Dionysos facing, horned and wearing kalathos and ivy-wreath. R. Eagle stg. r., Σ — ΚΗ across lower field; all within oak-wreath. *B.M.C. 17.* 83, 25 .. .. £16

4141 **Sigeion** (situated close to the entrance of the Hellespont, Sigeion was an Athenian colony and possessed a temple of Athena). *Circa* 350 B.C. (time of the despot Chares). Æ *hemidrachm* (*c*. 2·77 gm.). Hd. of Athena three-quarter face to r., wearing triple-crested helmet. R. Owl stg. r., hd. facing; ΣΙΓΕ before, crescent behind. *B.M.C. 17.* 86, 1 £850

4142 3rd cent. B.C. Æ *tetradrachm* (*c*. 16·75 gm.), restoring the types of Alexander the Great· Hd. of young Herakles r., clad in lion's skin. R. Zeus enthroned l., holding eagle and sceptre; ΑΛΕΞΑΝΔΡΟΥ behind, crescent and ΣΙ monogram before, ΜΑ monogram beneath throne. *Müller* (*Numismatique d'Alexandre le Grand*) 918 .. .. .. £200

Sigeion *continued*

4143 *Bronze Coinage. Circa* 350 B.C. Æ 22. Hd. of Athena, as 4141. R. ΣΙΓΕ below double-bodied owl; crescent to r. *B.M.C. 17.* 87, 14   ..   ..   £22

4144   4147

4144 — Æ 19. As 4141. *B.M.C. 17.* 86, 2   ..   ..   £17

4145 — Æ 13. Hd. of Athena r., in crested Athenian helmet. R. Owl stg. r., hd. facing; ΣΙΓΕ before. *B.M.C. 17.* 87, 19-20   ..   ..   £12

4146 — Æ 10. *Obv.* Similar. R. Crescent; Σ — Ι / Γ — E in field. *B.M.C. 17.* 88, 21-2   £10

4147 **Thymbra** (a small town, south-east of Ilion, possessing a temple dedicated to Apollo Thymbraios). *Circa* 350 B.C. Æ 18. Bearded and horned hd. of Zeus Ammon l., laur. R. Θ — Υ between three rays of an eight-rayed star. *B.M.C. 17.* 89, 1   ..   £15

4148 — Æ 14. Hd. of Athena l., in crested helmet. R. Θ — Υ either side of race-torch; all within olive-wreath. *Forrer/Weber* 5443   ..   ..   £13

4149 **Tenedos** (an island and town off the coast of the Troad, situated south-west of Ilion, Tenedos was one of the earliest mints in the area and remained a place of importance down to late Hellenistic times. The island was renowned for the exceptional beauty of its women). 480-450 B.C. Æ *tetradrachm* (*c.* 15·5 gm.). Janiform hds. of Tenes l., bearded, and Philonome r. R. Double-axe, to r. of which amphora attached to it by fillet; ΤΕ / ΝΕ / ΔΕΟΝ to l.; all in linear square contained within incuse square. *Forrer/Weber* 5446   ..   ..   £1,750

4150   4152

4150 — Æ *didrachm* (*c.* 8·1 gm.). *Obv.* Similar, but both hds. are beardless, possibly both female. R. Hd. of Athena (?) l., wearing Corinthian helmet; ΤΕΝΕ (retrograde) before; all in dotted square contained within incuse square. *B.M.C. 17.* 92, 8   ..   £750

4151 — Æ *obol* (*c.* 0·53 gm.). *Obv.* Similar to 4149, but the heads reversed. R. Double-axe, Τ — E either side of shaft; all in linear square contained within incuse square. *Forrer/Weber* 5448   ..   ..   £90

4152 *Circa* 400 B.C. Æ *tetradrachm* (*c.* 14·2 gm.). Janiform hds. of bearded Zeus, laur., l., and Hera r., diad. R. ΤΕΝΕ — ΔΙ — ΟΝ above and on either side of double-axe; bunch of grapes to l. of shaft, lyre to r.; all within incuse square. *B.M.C. 17.* 92, 11   ..   £1,500

4153   4156

4153 — Æ *drachm* (*c.* 3·55 gm.).   Similar, but the heads on *obv.* are reversed, and with
kantharos instead of lyre on *rev.*   *B.M.C. 17.* 93, 14   ..   ..   £275

4154 — Æ *hemidrachm* (*c.* 1·7 gm.).   Janiform hds. of bearded Zeus (?) r. and Hera (?) l.
R. Double-axe; T — E / N — E either side of shaft; all within incuse square. *B.M.C.*
17. 92, 9-10 ..   ..   £175

4155 *Circa* 350 B.C. Æ *tetradrachm* (*c.* 13 gm.).   Janiform hds. of Zeus and Hera, as 4152.
R. TENEΔION above double-axe; bunch of grapes and bee either side of shaft; A — N in
lower field. *B.M.C. 17.* 92, 12 ..   ..   £1,250

4156 — Æ *drachm* (*c.* 3·5 gm.).   *Obv.* Similar. R. TENE — ΔI — ON above and on either side
of double-axe; bunch of grapes to l. of shaft, Nike stg. l. to r. *B.M.C. 17.* 92, 13   £250

4157 2nd cent. B.C. Æ *tetradrachm* (*c.* 16·7 gm.).   Janiform hds. of Zeus and Hera, as 4152,
but of late style. R. TENEΔIΩN above double-axe; bunch of grapes and caps of the Dioskouroi either side of shaft; ΓAY monogram in lower field to l.; all within laurel-wreath.
B.M.C. 17. 94, 29 ..   ..   £750

4158 — Æ *drachm* (*c.* 4 gm.).   Similar, but with Hermes stg. l. instead of caps of the Dioskouroi on *rev.*, and with ΔY monogram in field to l. *B.M.C. 17.* 94, 33   ..   £250

4159   4163

4159 *Bronze Coinage.* *Circa* 350 B.C. Æ 9. Hd. of Artemis (?) r., wearing stephanos. R.
Double-axe; T — E either side of shaft. *B.M.C. 17.* 93, 32 ..   ..   ..   £13

4160 — Æ 8. Double-axe; T — E above, caps of the Dioskouroi either side of shaft. R.
Double-axe; T — E above. *Babelon* (*Traité*) *pl.* 166, 37   ..   ..   ..   £12

4161 2nd-1st cent. B.C. Æ 14. Hd. of Artemis r. R. Double-axe; T — E / NI — A in field;
all within laurel-wreath. *S.N.G. Von Aulock* 1591 ..   ..   £10

4162 — — Hd. of Athena r., in crested helmet. R. Double-axe; T — E above, monograms (?)
either side of shaft. *Grose*/*McClean* 7873   ..   ..   £10

4163 **AIOLIS.**   **Aigai** (an inland town on the river Pythikos, south-east of Myrina). 3rd
cent. B.C. Æ *hemidrachm* (*c.* 2·1 gm.).   Hd. of Athena r., wearing crested helmet ornamented with griffin. R. AIΓAE behind goat's hd. r. *B.M.C. 17.* 95, 1   ..   £350

Aigai *continued*

4164 2nd cent. B.C. Æ *tetradrachm* (*c.* 16·7 gm.). Laur. hd. of Apollo r., bow and quiver at neck. Ŗ. Naked Zeus stg. l., holding eagle and sceptre; ΑΙΓΑΙΕΩΝ behind, monogram before; all within oak-wreath. *B.M.C. 17.* 96, 9 .. .. £1,000

4165 *Bronze Coinage.* 3rd cent. B.C. Æ 18. Laur. hd. of Apollo r. Ŗ. As 4163. *B.M.C. 17.* 95, 2-4 .. .. £15

4166 — Æ 10. Similar. *B.M.C. 17.* 95, 6-8 .. .. £11

4167 2nd-1st cent. B.C. Æ 19. Helmeted hd. of Athena r. Ŗ. Naked Zeus stg. facing, holding eagle and sceptre; ΑΙΓΑΕΩΝ to r., three monograms to l. *B.M.C. 17.* 96, 12-13
£12

4168   4173   4174

4168 — Æ 17. Laur. hd. of Apollo r. Ŗ. Goat stg. r., ΑΙΓΑΕΩΝ in ex. *B.M.C. 17.* 96, 10-11 .. .. £14

4169 — Æ 16. Helmeted hd. of Athena r. Ŗ. Nike stg. l., holding wreath and palm; ΑΙΓΑΕΩΝ before, monograms in field to l. and to r. *S.N.G. Von Aulock* 1598 .. £12

4170 — Æ 13. *Obv.* Similar. Ŗ. ΑΙΓΑ. Lyre. *B.M.C. 17.* 96, 15 .. .. £10

4171 **Autokane** (site uncertain; possibly west of Pitane). *Circa* 300 B.C. Æ 15. Laur. hd. of Zeus r. Ŗ. ΑVΤΟΚΑΝ. Hd. of Athena r., in crested helmet wreathed with olive. *Forrer/Weber* 5473 .. .. £20

4172 — Æ 9. *Obv.* Similar. Ŗ. ΑVΤΟΚ. Female hd. r., hair rolled. *Forrer/Weber* 5472
£15

4173 **Boione** (site uncertain; possibly in the vicinity of Larissa Phrikonis). *Circa* 300 B.C. Æ 11. Female hd. l., wearing earring and necklace. Ŗ. ΒΟΙΩΝΙΤΙ/ΝΟΝ above and below bull stg. r. *B.M.C. 17.* 101, 1-3 .. .. £14

4174 **Kyme** (by far the most important of the Aiolian coastal cities, Kyme was situated south-west of Myrina. For much of its history it was dominated by the great powers — Persia, Athens, the Hellenistic Kingdoms and, finally, Rome). *Circa* 450 B.C. Æ *hemiobol* (*c.* 0·5 gm.). ΚΥ. Eagle's hd. l. Ŗ. Incuse square of "mill-sail" pattern. *B.M.C. 17.* 105, 11 .. .. £110

4175   4179

4175 *Circa* 350 B.C. Æ *drachm* (*c.* 6·1 gm.). KY. Eagle stg. r., looking back, wings closed.
R. ΘΕΥΓΕΝΗΣ. Forepart of prancing horse r. *B.M.C. 17.* 106, 14 .. .. £450

4176 — Æ *obol* (*c.* 0·9 gm.). KY. Horse's hd. r. R. Rosette. *Historia Numorum*, p. 553
£140

4177 — Æ *trihemitartemorion*? (*c.* 0·32 gm.). Similar, but forepart of prancing horse r.
on *obv.* *B.M.C. 17.* 106, 15 .. .. £85

4178 *Circa* 300 B.C. Æ *hemidrachm* (*c.* 1·8 gm.). KY. Eagle stg. r., looking back, wings
closed. R. Forepart of prancing horse r.; above, one-handled vase. *B.M.C. 17.* 106,
21-2 .. .. £100

4179 300-250 B.C. Æ 2½ *drachm* (*c.* 10·5 gm.). Hd. of the Amazon Kyme r., hair rolled and
bound with ribbon. R. Horse pacing r.; KY above, two monograms below. *B.M.C. 17.*
109, 58 .. .. £650

4180   4182

4180 — Æ *hemidrachm* (*c.* 2·1 gm.). Eagle stg. r., looking back, wings closed; ΞΕΝΩΝ behind.
R. Forepart of prancing horse r.; KY above, one-handled vase below. *B.M.C. 17.* 107,
25 .. .. £100

4181 3rd cent. B.C. Æ *tetradrachm* (*c.* 16·75 gm.), restoring the types of Alexander the Great.
Hd. of young Herakles r., clad in lion's skin. R. Zeus enthroned l., holding eagle and
sceptre; ΑΛΕΞΑΝΔΡΟΥ behind, one-handled vase and monogram before. *Müller* (*Numismatique d'Alexandre le Grand*) 943-7 .. .. £175

4182 — — Similar, but before Zeus, on *rev.*, one-handled vase and circular shield ornamented
with forepart of horse; in ex., ΔΙΟΓΕΝΗΣ. *Müller* 949 .. .. £225

4183   4186

4183 2nd cent. B.C. Æ *tetradrachm* (*c.* 16·75 gm.). Hd. of the Amazon Kyme r., hair bound
with ribbon. R. Horse pacing r., one-handled vase at feet; ΚΥΜΑΙΩΝ before, ΚΑΛΛΙΑΣ in
ex.; all within laurel-wreath. *B.M.C. 17.* 111, 73 .. .. £375

4184 — — Similar, but the one-handled vase is beneath horse on *rev.*, and with magistrate's
name ΔΙΟΓΕΝΗΣ in ex. *B.M.C. 17.* 112, 84 .. .. £375

4185 *Bronze Coinage.* Mid-4th cent. B.C. Æ 11. Eagle's hd. r. R. Rosette. *Babelon*
(*Traité*) *pl.* 157, 12 .. .. £15

4186 — — Eagle stg. r., wings closed. R. K — Y either side of one-handled vase. *B.M.C.*
17. 106, 20 .. .. £12

Kyme *continued*

4187 3rd cent. B.C. Æ 18. Eagle stg. r., wings closed; APICT — ANΔPOC behind. ℞. As last.
B.M.C. 17. 107, 29 .. .. £11

4188 4191

4188 — — Forepart of prancing horse r., KY above, APIΣTOΦΩN below. ℞. One-handled
vase; monogram to l. *B.M.C. 17.* 108, 40 .. .. £10

4189 — — Hd. of the Amazon Kyme r. ℞. Forepart of prancing horse r., one-handled
vase behind, HPAKΛEIΔHΣ below. *B.M.C. 17.* 109, 56 .. .. £13

4190 — Æ 11. *Obv.* Similar. ℞. K — Y either side of one-handled vase, HPAIOΣ below.
B.M.C. 17. 109, 53 .. .. £9

4191 — Æ 23. *Obv.* Similar. ℞. Horse pacing r.; KY above, monogram before, APIΣTOΦANHΣ
in ex. *B.M.C. 17.* 110, 59 .. .. £12

4192 — Æ 20. Similar, but on *rev.* KYMAI / ΩN above horse, one-handled vase before,
ΠYΘAΣ in ex. *B.M.C. 17.* 110, 67-8 .. .. £12

4193 4196

4193 2nd-1st cent. B.C. Æ 17. Dr. bust of Artemis r., bow and quiver at shoulder. ℞.
One-handled vase between two laurel-branches; KY above, I — Ω / I — Λ / O — Σ in field.
B.M.C. 17. 113, 87-9 .. .. £12

4194 — Æ 13. Forepart of prancing horse r., KY above. ℞. Bow and quiver, large monogram above. *B.M.C. 17.* 112, 85 .. .. £10

4195 — Æ 18. Artemis stg. r., holding long torch and clasping hands with Amazon Kyme (?)
stg. l., holding spear; K — Y in field. ℞. Two figures in slow quadriga r., one of them
holding long sceptre. *B.M.C. 17.* 113, 96 .. .. £13

4196 **Elaia** (a coastal town situated south-west of Pergamon, Elaia served as a port for its
more important neighbour during the time of the Pergamene Kingdom). Late 5th cent.
B.C. Æ *diobol* (*c.* 1·25 gm.). Hd. of Athena l., wearing crested helmet. ℞. Ǝ — Λ — A —I
around olive-wreath; all within incuse square. *B.M.C. 17.* 125, 1 .. .. £200

4197 — Æ *hemiobol* (*c.* 0·35 gm.). Similar, but the E on *rev.* not retrograde. *Forrer/Weber*
5542 .. .. £90

4198 Early 4th cent. B.C. Æ *diobol* (*c.* 1·35 gm.). Hd. of Athena r., wearing crested helmet.
℞. Olive-wreath; pellet at centre. *B.M.C. 17.* 125, 3 .. .. .. £200

4199 Mid-4th cent. B.C. Æ *drachm* (*c.* 3·2 gm.). Hd. of Athena l., wearing crested helmet.
℞. Corn-grain within olive-wreath; E below. *S.N.G. Von Aulock* 1602 .. £350

4200 — Æ *diobol* (*c.* 1 gm.). Similar, but without E on *rev. S.N.G. Von Aulock* 1603 £150

4201 4203

4201 4th-3rd cent. B.C. Æ 19. Hd. of Athena l., wearing crested Corinthian helmet. R.
  E — Λ either side of corn-grain; all within olive-wreath. *B.M.C. 17.* 125, 6-7   £12

4202 — Æ 18. Prow of galley to r. R. EΛAI within laurel-wreath. *Forrer /Weber* 5548   £14

4203 — Æ 16. Hd. of Athena r., wearing crested Corinthian helmeᵗ. R. EΛAI below horseman galloping r., r. hand raised; all within olive-wreath. *B.M.C. 17.* 126, 15   £11

4204 — Æ 10. Hd. of Athena l., wearing crested Athenian helmet. R. Corn-grain between
  two olive-branches. *B.M.C. 17.* 125, 4 ..   ..   £9

4205 — Æ 9. *Obv.* Similar. R. Olive-branch between two corn-grains. *B.M.C. 17.* 125,
  5   ..   ..   £9

4206 2nd-1st cent. B.C. Æ 18. Hd. of Demeter r., wreathed with corn. R. Torch; EΛ —
  AI / T — ΩN in field; all within corn-wreath. *B.M.C. 17.* 127, 20   ..   ..   £10

4207 — Æ 14. Prow r.; bow (?) above. R. EΛAI below olive-wreath. *Grose/McClean*
  7937 ..   ..   £10

4208   4210

4208 **Grynion** (a coastal town of early foundation, situated a short distance north-east of
  Myrina, Grynion possessed a famous temple and oracle of Apollo. The town was destroyed by Parmenion towards the close of the 4th century). Before 306 B.C. Æ 17.
  Laur. hd. of Apollo three-quarter face to l. R. ΓΥΡΝΗΩΝ above mussel-shell. *B.M.C. 17.*
  133, 1   ..   ..   £20

4209 — Æ 11. Similar, but with inscription ΓΥΡ / N — H above and below the mussel-shell.
  B.M.C. 17. 133, 3 ..   ..   £15

4210 **Larissa Phrikonis** (a strongly fortified town situated south-east of Kyme, Larissa
  appears to have declined in importance after *circa* 300 B.C.). *Circa* 350 B.C. Æ *diobol* ? (*c.*
  1·1 gm.). Female hd. r., wearing sphendone. R. ΛΑΡΙΣΑΙ. Amphora. *Historia
  Numorum, p.* 555 ..   ..   £250

4211   4214

4211 350-300 B.C. Æ 22. Bare male hd. r., bearded. R. Amphora between ΛΑΡΙΣΑΙ and
  corn-grain. *B.M.C. 17.* 134, 1 ..   ..   £20

4212 — Æ 18. *Obv.* Similar to 4210. R. Amphora between club and caduceus, bunch of
  grapes above; Λ — A / P — I in field. *B.M.C. 17.* 134, 2   ..   ..   ..   £18

4213 — Æ 11. Female hd.. l. R. Similar to last, but amphora is between caduceus and
  ear of corn. *B.M.C. 17.* 134, 4 ..   ..   £14

4214 **Myrina** (situated north-east of Kyme, Myrina was overshadowed by its powerful
  neighbour, though it appears to have been a place of some importance in Hellenistic
  times). *Circa* 300 B.C. Æ *hemidrachm* ? (*c.* 1·8 gm.). Hd. of Athena r., in crested
  helmet. R. M — Y either side of bust of Artemis three-quarter face to left. *Historia
  Numorum, p.* 555   ..   ..   £450

Myrina *continued*

4215 3rd cent. B.C. Æ *tetradrachm* (*c.* 16·75 gm.), restoring the types of Alexander the Great. Hd. of young Herakles r., clad in lion's skin. ℞. Zeus enthroned l., holding eagle and sceptre; ΑΛΕΞΑΝΔΡΟΥ behind, amphora and MYP monogram before. *Müller (Numismatique d'Alexandre le Grand)* 934 .. .. £200

4216   4217

4216 2nd cent. B.C. Æ *tetradrachm* (*c.* 16·75 gm.). Laur. hd. of Apollo of Grynion r. ℞. MYPINAIΩN behind Apollo of Grynion stg. r., holding phiale and laurel-branch with fillets; omphalos and amphora at feet, monogram behind; all within laurel-wreath. *B.M.C.* 17. 135, 1 .. .. £350

4217 — Æ *drachm* (*c.* 3·8 gm.). Similar; different monogram in *rev.* field. *B.M.C.* 17. 135, 4 .. .. £250

4218 *Bronze Coinage.* *Circa* 300 B.C. Æ 10. Hd. of Athena l., in crested helmet. ℞. M — Y either side of amphora. *S.N.G. Von Aulock* 1659 .. .. £12

4219   4222   4224

4219 2nd cent B.C. Æ 17. Hd. of Athena r., in crested helmet ornamented with griffin. ℞. MY — PI either side of amphora. *B.M.C. 17.* 137, 20 .. .. .. £10

4220 — — Laur. hd. of Apollo r. ℞. As last, but with lyre in field ro r. *B.M.C. 17.* 137, 27 .. .. £10

4221 — Æ 13. Rad. hd. of Helios r. ℞. As 4219. *B.M.C. 17.* 137, 32 .. .. £9

4222 **Neonteichos** (situated a short distance south-east of Larissa Phrikonis). 2nd cent. B.C. Æ 17. Hd. of Athena r., in crested helmet. ℞. Owl stg. r., hd. facing; NE monogram below. *B.M.C. 17.* 141, 3 .. .. £18

4223 — Æ 11. *Obv.* Similar. ℞. NE monogram. *B.M.C. 17.* 141, 1 .. .. £14

4224 **Temnos** (situated a short distance east of Neonteichos, on the hill-side above the right bank of the river Hermos). *Circa* 350 B.C. Æ *trihemiobol* (*c.* 0·9 gm.). Laur. hd. of Apollo l. ℞. TA. Kantharos. *Historia Numorum, p.* 556 .. .. .. £200

4225

4225 3rd cent. B.C. Æ *tetradrachm* (*c.* 16·75 gm.), restoring the types of Alexander the Great. Hd. of young Herakles r., clad in lion's skin. R. Zeus enthroned l., holding eagle and sceptre, ΑΛΕΞΑΝΔΡΟΥ behind; before, tall one-handled vase, framed by vine-branch, and ΠΑ Ε. *Müller* (*Numismatique d'Alexandre le Grand*) 956   ..   ..   ..   £150

4226 — — Similar, but instead of ΠΑΕ on *rev.*, ΕΧΕΝΙΚΟΣ in field to l. and ΓΕΙΤΑΣ beneath throne. *Müller* 966   ..   ..   £200

4227 2nd cent. B.C. Æ *hemidrachm* (*c.* 1·75 gm.). Laur. hd. of Apollo r. R. ΤΑ. Tall one-handled vase dividing Α — Μ; above, vine-branch with four bunches of grapes. *B.M.C. 17.* 143, 8   ..   ..   £225

4228   4230   4233

4228 *Bronze Coinage.* 350-300 B.C. Æ 11. Hd. of bearded Dionysos l., wreathed with ivy. R. Bunch of grapes dividing Τ — Α. *B.M.C. 17.* 142, 1   ..   ..   ..   £14

4229 3rd cent. B.C. Æ 19. Hd. of young Dionysos r., wreathed with ivy. R. As last; all within vine-wreath. *B.M.C. 17.* 142, 4 ..   ..   £14

4230 — —*Obv.* Similar. R. As 4228. *B.M.C. 17.* 142, 5   ..   ..   ..   £14

4231 2nd-1st cent. B.C. Æ 19. *Obv.* Similar. R. ΤΑ. Athena stg. l., holding Nike and bunch of grapes in r. hand, resting l. on shield; Δ — Η in field. *B.M.C. 17.* 143, 10 ..   £12

4232 — Æ 14. Hd. of Athena r., in crested Corinthian helmet. R. Trophy dividing Α — Θ and Τ — Α. *S.N.G. Von Aulock* 1674   ..   ..   £11

4233 **Tisna** (exact site uncertain, but probably on the river Pythikos, east of Kyme and in the vicinity of Aigai). 350-300 B.C. Æ 17. Beardless hd. of horned river-god l. R. ΤΙΣ / ΝΑΙΟΝ either side of one-handled vase. *Babelon* (*Traité*) *pl.* 157, 24   ..   £24

4234 — Æ 11. Young male hd. r., hair short. R. ΤΙΣ / ΝΑΙΟΣ either side of sword in sheath. *Babelon* (*Traité*) *pl.* 157, 27   ..   ..   £17

4235 — —As 4233. *B.M.C. 17.* 149, 1   ..   ..   £16

4236 — Æ 10. *Obv.* As 4233. R. ΤΙΣΝΑ / ΙΟΝ either side of sword in sheath. *S.N.G. Von Aulock* 1681   ..   ..   £17

4237   4239

4237 **LESBOS** (the largest of the islands off the coast of western Asia Minor, Lesbos lay at the entrance to the gulf of Adramytteion. It was a great cultural centre, and its mild climate and fertile soil supported no less than five cities, the most important of which was Mytilene).
Mytilene (the chief city of Lesbos, Mytilene was situated in the south-east of the island, opposite the mainland. There can be little doubt that Mytilene was the mint of the important electrum coinage of Lesbos in the 5th and 4th centuries).
ELECTRUM COINAGE. 480-450 B.C. *Sixth stater* (*c.* 2·55 gm.). Forepart of winged boar l. R. Incuse lion's hd. l.; behind, oblong punch. *B.M.C. 17.* 156, 4   £600

4238 — — Ram's hd. r.; beneath, cock l. R. Incuse lion's hd. r.; behind, oblong punch. *B.M.C. 17.* 156, 7-9   ..   ..   £600

4239 — — Forepart of prancing horse r., ΛΕ beneath. R. Incuse hd. of bearded Herakles r., clad in lion's skin. *B.M.C. 17.* 157, 15-16   ..   ..   £700

4240 — — Lion's hd. r. R. Incuse calf's hd. r.; behind, oblong punch. *B.M.C. 17.* 157, 19-22   ..   ..   £600

Mytilene *continued*

4241 — — Hd. of Athena r., wearing crested helmet. ℞. Incuse lion's hd. facing. *B.M.C.*
17. 158, 27 .. .. £750

4242 450-330 B.C. *Stater* (*c.* 15·45 gm.). Laur. hd. of Apollo r., hair short; MVTI above.
℞. Quadripartite incuse square. *B.M.C.* 17. 158, 28 .. .. (*Unique*)
   The occasion for this exceptional issue of electrum staters may have been the Lesbian
   revolt from Athens, 428/7 B.C.

4243   4245   4247

4243 — *Sixth-stater* (*c.* 2·55 gm.). Forepart of goat r., looking back. ℞. Owl stg. facing,
wings spread; all within incuse square. *B.M.C.* 17. 158, 29-30 .. .. £850

4244 — — Hd. of bearded Satyr r., with pointed ear. ℞. Two rams' heads confronted; all
within incuse square. *B.M.C.* 17. 160, 41-2 .. .. £900

4245 — — Female hd. three-quarter face to r., hair bound with cord. ℞. Bull's hd. l., M
above; all within incuse square. *B.M.C.* 17. 160, 50 .. .. £1,000

4246 — — Hd. of Pan (?) r., horned. ℞. Gorgoneion, within incuse square. *B.M.C. 17.*
161, 52-4 .. .. £850

4247 — — Hd. of Aphrodite (?) r., hair in sakkos. ℞. Lyre, framed by linear square; all
within incuse square. *B.M.C.* 17. 162, 62-4 .. .. £650

4248   4250   4252

4248 — — Hd. of Kybele (?) r., wearing turreted head-dress. ℞. Hd. of Hermes r., wearing
petasos, framed by linear square; all within incuse square. *B.M.C.* 17. 163, 69-70
£750

4249 — — Hd. of young Dionysos r., wreathed with ivy. ℞. Hd. of bearded Seilenos facing,
framed by linear square; all within incuse square. *B.M.C.* 17. 164, 77 .. £900

4250 — — Laur. hd. of Apollo r., serpent behind. ℞. Female hd. r., hair in sphendone,
framed by linear square; all within incuse square. *B.M.C.* 17. 165, 87-9 .. £550

4251 — — Hd. of Athena r., wearing crested helmet. ℞. Bearded hd. of satrap (?) r.,
wearing Persian head-dress, framed by linear square; all within incuse square. *B.M.C.*
17. 166, 105 .. .. £1,250

4252 — — Beardless hd. of Zeus Ammon r., horned. ℞. Eagle stg. r., looking back, wings
closed; framed by linear square within incuse square. *B.M.C.* 17. 167, 110-12 £600
   The head on this type has been identified as portraying the features of Alexander the
   Great.

4253 — — Veiled hd. of Demeter r., wreathed with corn. ℞. Tripod, framed by linear
square; all within incuse square. *B.M.C.* 17. 168, 118-21 .. .. .. £600

4254   4259   4261

4254 BILLON AND SILVER COINAGE. 480-450 B.C. Billon *third-stater* (*c.* 3·85 gm.). youthful male hd. l., wearing Thracian (?) head-dress. ℞. Lion's hd. l., within incuse square. *B.M.C. 17.* 155, 58   ..   ..   £650

4255 — Billon *sixth-stater* (*c.* 1·95 gm.). Female hd. l., hair bound with cord. ℞. MY. Lion's hd. r.; all within incuse square. *B.M.C. 17.* 155, 59   ..   ..   ..   £250

4256 — Billon *twelfth-stater* (*c.* 0·9 gm.). Hd. of Apollo (?) l., bound with tainia. ℞. Quadripartite incuse square. *B.M.C. 17.* 155, 56   ..   ..   ..   £125

4257 — — Similar to 4255, but without inscription on *rev.* *B.M.C. 17.* 155, 60-61   £150

4258 — Billon *twenty-fourth* (*c.* 0·55 gm.). As 4256. *B.M.C. 17.* 155, 57   ..   £75

4259 Late 5th cent. B.C. Æ *drachm* (*c.* 4 gm.). Laur. hd. of Apollo r., hair short. ℞. MVTIΛHNAON around hd. of nymph Mytilene l., wearing sphendone; all within incuse square. *Babelon* (*Traité*) *pl.* 162, 8   ..   ..   £500

4260 — Æ *trihemiobol* ? (*c.* 0·87 gm.). Hd. of nymph Mytilene three-quarter face to l., hair bound with ribbon. ℞. MVTI. Lion's hd. l.; all within incuse square. *B.M.C. 17.* 184, 1-2   ..   ..   £150

4261 — Æ *obol* (*c.* 0·66 gm.). Hd. of Apollo (?) r., hair short, bound with tainia. ℞. MVTI. Calf's hd. r.; all within incuse square. *B.M.C. 17.* 184, 5   ..   ..   £110

4262   4264

4262 400-350 B.C. Æ *diobol* (*c.* 1·4 gm.). Laur. hd. of Apollo r. ℞. Hd. of Aphrodite (?) r., hair rolled; behind, cicada. *B.M.C. 17.* 185, 8 ..   ..   £90

4263 — Æ *obol* (*c.* 0·58 gm.). Lyre; M / Y — T in field. ℞. Lyre. *B.M.C. 17.* 186, 16   £75

4264 Mid-4th cent. B.C. Æ *stater* (*c.* 11·4 gm.) . Laur. hd. of Apollo r. ℞. Lyre; MY / T — I in field, thunderbolt to l.; all within linear square. *B.M.C. 17.* 187, 28   ..   £750

4265 — Æ *hemidrachm* (*c.* 2·85 gm.). Similar, but with thyrsos instead of thunderbolt in *rev.* field. *B.M.C. 17.* 187, 32 ..   ..   £120

4266　　　　　　　　　　　　　4270

Mytilene *continued*

4266 3rd cent. B.C. Æ *tetradrachm* (*c.* 16·75 gm.), restoring the types of Alexander the Great. Hd. of young Herakles r., clad in lion's skin. Ŗ. Zeus enthroned l., holding eagle and sceptre, ΑΛΕΞΑΝΔΡΟΥ behind; before, lyre and monogram. *Müller* (*Numismatique d'Alexandre le Grand*) 975 .. 　.. 　.. 　.. 　.. 　.. 　.. 　£175

4267 — — Similar, but without the monogram on *rev.*, and with caduceus beneath throne and ΠΕΙΣΙΣΤΡΑΤΟΣ in ex. *Müller* 970 .. 　.. 　.. 　.. 　.. 　.. 　.. 　£225

4267A 2nd cent. B.C. Æ *tetradrachm* (*c.* 16·75 gm.). Diad. hd. of Zeus Ammon r. Ŗ. ΜΥΤΙΛΗ / ΝΑΩΝ either side of terminal figure of bearded Dionysos facing, on pedestal; monograms in lower field, to l. and to r.; all within ivy-wreath. *Leu auction, May 1979, lot* 129 .. 　.. 　.. 　.. 　.. 　.. 　.. 　.. 　£7,500

4268 BRONZE COINAGE. 400-350 B.C. Æ 10. Laur. hd. of Apollo r., hair short. Ŗ. ΜΥΤ. Calf's hd. r. *B.M.C. 17.* 184, 7 .. 　.. 　.. 　.. 　£13

4269 — — Laur. hd. of Apollo r. Ŗ. Calf's hd. r.; oinochoe behind. *B.M.C. 17.* 186, 17
　　　　　　　　　　　　　　　　　　　　　　　　　　　　£12

4270 — — *Obv.* Similar. Ŗ. ΜΥ. Bull's hd. r.; caduceus behind. *B.M.C. 17.* 186, 20
　　　　　　　　　　　　　　　　　　　　　　　　　　　　£12

4271 4th-3rd cent. B.C. Æ 13. Hd. of Aphrodite (?) r., hair in sphendone. Ŗ. Lyre; Μ — Υ / Τ — Ι in field, serpent to r. *B.M.C. 17.* 188, 37-8 .. 　.. 　.. 　£11

4272 — — Similar, but with tripod in *rev.* field to l., monogram to r. *B.M.C. 17.* 189, 55-7
　　　　　　　　　　　　　　　　　　　　　　　　　　　　£11

4273　　　　　　　　　　　　　4274

4273 3rd-2nd cent. B.C. Æ 19. Laur. hd. of Apollo r. Ŗ. Lyre, between two monograms; ΜΥ / Τ — Ι in field. *B.M.C. 17.* 192-3, 96-105 .. 　.. 　.. 　.. 　£12
　　These are often countermarked, on obv., with a bust of Artemis and/or an owl.

4274 2nd-1st cent. B.C. Æ 18. Beardless hd. of Zeus Ammon r., horned and bound with tainia. Ŗ. Terminal figure of bearded Dionysos facing, on pedestal; Μ — Υ / Τ — Ι in field, monogram to l., ivy-leaf to r. *B.M.C. 17.* 194, 115 .. 　.. 　.. 　£10

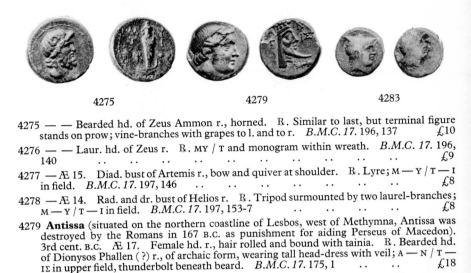

4275   4279   4283

4275 — — Bearded hd. of Zeus Ammon r., horned. R. Similar to last, but terminal figure stands on prow; vine-branches with grapes to l. and to r. *B.M.C. 17.* 196, 137   £10

4276 — — Laur. hd. of Zeus r. R. MY / T and monogram within wreath. *B.M.C. 17.* 196, 140   £9

4277 — Æ 15. Diad. bust of Artemis r., bow and quiver at shoulder. R. Lyre; M — Y / T — I in field. *B.M.C. 17.* 197, 146   £8

4278 — Æ 14. Rad. and dr. bust of Helios r. R. Tripod surmounted by two laurel-branches; M — Y / T — I in field. *B.M.C. 17.* 197, 153-7   £8

4279 **Antissa** (situated on the northern coastline of Lesbos, west of Methymna, Antissa was destroyed by the Romans in 167 B.C. as punishment for aiding Perseus of Macedon). 3rd cent. B.C. Æ 17. Female hd. r., hair rolled and bound with tainia. R. Bearded hd. of Dionysos Phallen (?) r., of archaic form, wearing tall head-dress with veil; A — N / T — IΣ in upper field, thunderbolt beneath beard. *B.M.C. 17.* 175, 1   £18

4280 — Æ 15. Bull stg. l.; club above. R. Apollo stg. l., holding plectrum and lyre; A — N in field. *B.M.C. 17.* 175, 9   £14

4281 — Æ 13. *Obv.* Similar. R. As 4279, but with bunch of grapes instead of thunderbolt. *B.M.C. 17.* 175, 8   £14

4282 **Eresos** (on the west coast of the island, Eresos was famed in antiquity for the quality of its wheat. Archestratos of Gela wrote "if the gods eat bread they send Hermes to buy it at Eresos"). 3rd-2nd cent. B.C. Æ 18. Hd. of Hermes r., wearing petasos. R. EPEΣI. Ear of corn. *B.M.C. 17.* 176, 2   £20

4283 — Æ 14. *Obv.* Similar. R. EPEΣI. Hd. of Apollo (?) r. *B.M.C. 17.* 176, 1   £14

4284 — Æ 11. Hd. of Artemis (?) r., hair in bunch behind. R. Ear of corn between EPEΣI and star. *B.M.C. 17.* 176, 7   £13

4285 — Æ 10. Hd. of Hermes l., wearing petasos. R. Ear of corn; pentagon and crescent to l., EPEΣI to r. *B.M.C. 17.* 176, 3   £13

4286 2nd-1st cent. B.C. Æ 14. Gorgoneion. R. EPECIΩN. Caduceus. *S.N.G. Von Aulock* 1736   £12

4287   4288

4287 **Methymna** (the second city of Lesbos, after Mytilene, Methymna was situated on the north coast, and was the birthplace of the musician and poet Arion). 480-450 B.C. Æ *didrachm* (c. 8·55 gm.). MAΘVMNAIOΣ above boar stg. r., hd. lowered. R. Hd. of Athena r., wearing crested helmet with projecting spike; all in dotted square frame within incuse square. *B.M.C. 17.* 177, 1   £1,500

4288 — Æ *tetrobol* (c. 2·8 gm.). Warrior kneeling l., holding spear and large circular shield. R. Horseman on forepart of galloping horse r.; all in dotted square frame within incuse square. *B.M.C. 17.* 178, 7-8   £350

Methymna *continued*

4289 — Æ *diobol* (c. 1·4 gm.). Gorgoneion. ℞. Hd. of Athena l., wearing Corinthian helmet; all in dotted square frame within incuse square. *B.M.C. 17.* 177, 5-6 .. £175

4290 4294

4290 *Circa* 400 B.C. Æ *didrachm* (c. 6·4 gm.). Hd. of Athena l., wearing crested helmet ornamented with vine-tendrils. ℞. Lyre, placed on raised square tablet around which, MAΘVMNAION; all within incuse square. *B.M.C. 17.* 178, 10 .. .. .. £1,000

4291 — Æ *drachm* (c. 3·15 gm.). *Obv.* Similar. ℞. Kantharos; M / Θ — A in field; all in dotted square frame within incuse square. *Babelon (Traité) pl.* 162, 31 .. £450

4292 — Æ *triobol* ? (c. 1·25 gm.). *Obv.* Similar. ℞. Lion's hd. facing, M — A in lower field; all in dotted square frame within incuse square. *B.M.C. 17.* 178, 9 .. .. £175

4293 — Æ *obol* ? (c. 0·35 gm.). Hd. of Athena r., wearing crested helmet. ℞. Kantharos; M / Θ — A in field; all in dotted circular frame within incuse circle. *Babelon (Traité) pl.* 162, 32 .. .. £90

4294 *Circa* 330 B.C. Æ *hemidrachm* (c. 2·7 gm.). Hd. of Athena r., in crested Corinthian helmet. ℞. Lyre; MA / Θ — Y in upper field, kantharos to l.; all within square frame of bead and reel pattern. *B.M.C. 17.* 178, 12 .. .. £140

4295 — Æ *trihemiobol* (c. 1·35 gm.). Hd. of young Herakles r., clad in lion's skin. ℞. Arion seated facing on dolphin r., r. hand outstretched, holding lyre in l.; M — A / Θ — Y in field. *B.M.C. 17.* 179, 16 .. .. £250

4296 3rd cent. B.C. Æ *tetradrachm* (c. 16·75 gm.), restoring the types of Alexander the Great. Hd. of young Herakles r., clad in lion's skin. ℞. Zeus enthroned l., holding eagle and sceptre, ΑΛΕΞΑΝΔΡΟΥ behind; before, Arion seated on dolphin, similar to *rev.* type of last. *Müller (Numismatique d'Alexandre le Grand)* 981 .. .. £250

4297 4298

4297 — Æ 17. Hd. of Athena r., in crested Corinthian helmet. ℞. Kantharos; M — A / Θ — Y in lower field, wreath to r. *B.M.C. 17.* 179, 17 .. .. £10
These are sometimes countermarked with a bee on obverse.

4298 2nd-1st cent. B.C. Æ 23. Laur. hd. of Apollo r. ℞. Arion seated facing on dolphin r., r. hand outstretched, holding lyre in l.; M — A / Θ — Y in field. *B.M.C. 17.* 181, 35 £14

4299 — Æ 18. Similar to 4297, but of later style and with border of dots on both sides; no symbol in *rev.* field. *B.M.C. 17.* 180, 28 .. .. £9
These are sometimes countermarked with a lyre on obverse.

4300 — Æ 14. Bull stg. l., club above. ℞. Similar to 4298, but Arion's hd. is turned to l. *B.M.C. 17.* 180, 27 .. .. £12

4301   4302   4306

4301 **Pyrrha** (situated on the shores of a deep bay on the western coastline of Lesbos). Mid-4th cent. B.C. Æ 11. Hd. of nymph Pyrrha l., wearing sphendone. ℞. ΠΥΡ above goat stg. l. *B.M.C. 17.* 216, 1 .. .. £20

4302 **Nesos** (the largest island of the Hekatonnesoi group, lying between Lesbos and the Mysian coast. The town bore the same name as the island). *Circa* 350 B.C. Æ *hemidrachm* (*c.* 2·53 gm.). Laur. hd. of Apollo l. ℞. Panther r., looking back, l. forepaw raised; ΝΑΣΙ above, ram's hd. r. before. *B.M.C. 17.* 217, 1 .. .. .. £250

4303 — Æ 9. Laur. hd. of Apollo r. ℞. ΝΑΣ. Panther running l., star (?) beneath. *B.M.C. 17.* 217, 3 .. .. £18

4304 3rd cent. B.C. Æ 19. Laur. hd. of Apollo r. ℞. Dolphin r., ΝΑΣΙ above, palm-branch below. *B.M.C. 17.* 217, 5 .. .. £16

4305 — — *Obv.* Similar. ℞. Lyre between ΝΑΣΙ and branch. *B.M.C. 17.* 218, 9 £16

4306 — — Horseman prancing r., A beneath. ℞. ΝΑ / ΣΙ within laurel-wreath. *B.M.C. 17.* 218, 11 .. .. £16

4307   4309   4313

4307 **Pordosilene** (another island and town of the Hekatonnesoi group, lying to the west of its larger neighbour, Nesos). Late 5th cent. B.C. Æ *drachm* (*c.* 3·95 gm.). Hd. of Apollo (?) r., hair short and bound with tainia. ℞. ΠΟΡΔ / ΟΣΙΛ either side of lyre; all within incuse square. *B.M.C. 17.* 219, 1 .. .. £750

4308 *Circa* 350 B.C. Æ 8. Bearded hd. of Seilenos (?) r. ℞. Dolphin r., ΠΟΡ below. *B.M.C. 17.* 219, 2 .. .. £20

4309 **IONIA. Klazomenai** (situated on the southern shores of the Gulf of Smyrna, Klazomenai was the birthplace of the philosopher Anaxagoras). 480-450 B.C. Æ *drachm* ? (*c.* 3·55 gm.). Forepart of winged boar r., ΚΛΑ above. ℞. Ram's hd. r., within incuse square. *Forrer/Weber* 5745 .. .. £300

4310 — Æ *hemidrachm* (*c.* 1·95 gm.). Forepart of winged boar l. ℞. Gorgoneion, within incuse square. *B.M.C. 14.* 18, 15 .. .. £165

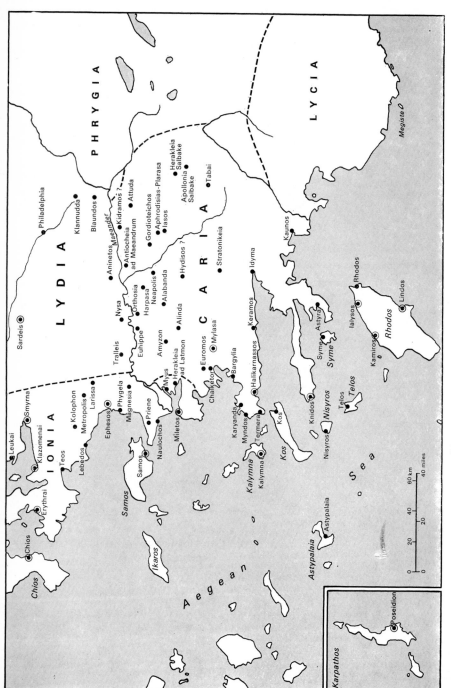

MAP 17   SOUTH WESTERN ASIA MINOR

Klazomenai *continued*

4311 — Æ *diobol* (*c.* 1·2 gm.).   Similar, but *obv.* type to r.   *B.M.C. 14.* 18, 16   ..   £130

4312 — Æ *obol* (*c.* 0·7 gm.).   Ram's hd. l.   Ŗ. As 4310.   *Grose/McClean* 8035   ..   £100

4313 380-350 B.C.   *N stater* (*c.* 5·7 gm.).   Laur. hd. of Apollo three-quarter face to r.   Ŗ. Swan stg. r., wings spread; KΛAIO behind, AΘHN — AΓOPAΣ above and before; beneath, forepart of winged boar r.   *B.M.C. 14.* 19, 17   ..   ..   £20,000

4314 — Æ *tetradrachm* (*c.* 16·9 gm.).   Laur. hd. of Apollo three-quarter face to l.   Ŗ. Swan stg. l., looking back, wings spread; KΛAIO above, HP — AKΛEIΔ below.   *B.M.C. 14.* 19, 18
£8,000

4315   4318   4319

4315 — — *Obv.* Similar, but with engraver's signature ΘEOΔOTOΣ / EΠOEI in field to l.   Ŗ. Swan stg. l., wings spread; KΛAIO behind, MANΔP — ΩNAΞ before and above.   *B.M.C. 14.* 19, 19   ..   ..   £10,000

4316 — Æ *didrachm* (*c.* 7·55 gm.).   Laur. hd. of Apollo three-quarter face to l.   Ŗ. Swan stg. l., wings spread; KΛA—IO below, ΔHMEAΣ above.   *Boston Museum Catalogue* 1859 £4,500

4317 — Æ *drachm* (*c.* 4·1 gm.).   *Obv.* Similar.   Ŗ. Swan stg. l., wings spread, pluming his breast; KΛ — A below, ANTIΦAN—H — Σ above and behind.   *Grose/McClean* 8036 £1,750

4318 — Æ *hemidrachm* (*c.* 2 gm.).   *Obv.* Similar.   Ŗ. Swan stg. l., wings spread; KΛ — A below, AΠOΛΛAΣ above; ram's hd. in field to l.   *B.M.C. 14.* 20, 23   ..   ..   £500

4319 — — Similar, but magistrate's name EYΘYΔAMAΣ on *rev.*, and the swan plumes his back (no ram's hd. in field).   *B.M.C. 14.* 20, 25   ..   ..   £600

4320 3rd cent. B.C.   *N stater* (*c.* 8·6 gm.), restoring the types of Philip II of Macedon.   Laur. hd. of Apollo r.   Ŗ. Biga driven r. by charioteer; forepart of winged boar r. beneath horses, ΦIΛIΠΠOY and spear-head in ex.   *Müller* (*Numismatique d'Alexandre le Grand*) 309
£1,500

4321 — Æ *tetradrachm* (*c.* 16·75 gm.), restoring the types of Alexander the Great.   Hd. of young Herakles r., clad in lion's skin.   Ŗ. Zeus enthroned l., holding eagle and sceptre, AΛEΞANΔPOY behind; before, forepart of winged boar l. and ΦI; EYΘYΔAMAΣ in ex.   *Müller* 996   ..   ..   £225

4322   4324

4322 *Bronze Coinage.* Early 4th cent. B.C.   Æ 10.   Hd. of Athena r., wearing crested helmet.   Ŗ. KΛA.   Ram's hd. r.   *B.M.C. 14.* 21, 32-3   ..   ..   £12

4323 380-300 B.C.   Æ 18.   Hd. of Athena three-quarter face to r., wearing triple-crested helmet.   Ŗ. KΛAIOME / NIΩN above ram walking r., thunderbolt before.   *B.M.C. 14.* 24, 59   ..   ..   £14

4324 — — *Obv.* Similar.   Ŗ. Ram walking r.; BIΩN above, pellet before.   *B.M.C. 14.* 25, 64   ..   ..   £14

Klazomenai *continued*

4325 — — Hd. of Athena r., wearing crested Corinthian helmet. ℞. ΚΛΑΖΟΜΕ / ΝΙΩΝ above ram recumbent r., star before. *B.M.C. 14.* 26, 82 .. .. £12

4326 — Æ 17. *Obv.* Similar. ℞. ΚΛΑ. Ram's hd. r. *B.M.C. 14.* 22, 43 .. £12

4327 4331

4327 — — *Obv.* Similar. ℞. Ram walking r., ΠΥΘΕΟΣ above, monogram before. *B.M.C. 14.* 23, 49 .. .. £11

4328 — Æ 14. Laur. hd. of Apollo r. ℞. ΚΛΑ. Forepart of ram r., pedum beneath. *B.M.C. 14.* 23, 47 .. .. £10

4329 — — Hd. of Athena r., wearing crested helmet ornamented with griffin. ℞. ΞΑΝΘΗΣ above ram's hd. r. *B.M.C. 14.* 21, 37 .. .. £10

4330 — Æ 13. As 4324. *B.M.C. 14.* 25, 65 .. .. £12

4331 — Æ 11. Laur. hd. of Apollo l. ℞. ΗΡΑΚΛΕΙΔΗΣ. Swan stg. l., wings spread; before, forepart of winged boar l. *B.M.C. 14.* 23, 46 .. .. £14

4332 — — Hd. of Athena r., wearing crested helmet. ℞. ΗΓΗΣΑΝΔΡ. Ram walking l. *B.M.C. 14.* 23, 51 .. .. £10

4333 2nd-1st cent. B.C. Æ 22. Laur. hd. of Zeus r. ℞. ΚΛΑΖΟΜΕ / ΝΙΩΝ above swan stg. l., wings spread; ΣΙ — ΜΩΝ across lower field. *B.M.C. 14.* 27, 88 .. .. £12

4334 — — Bust of Athena r., wearing aegis and crested Corinthian helmet. ℞. ΚΛΑ Ζ Ο / ΜΕΝΙΩΝ above and below ram recumbent r., hd. facing. *B.M.C. 14.* 29, 108 .. £13

4335 4336 4340

4335 — Æ 20. Young male hd. r., diad. ℞. ΚΛΑΖΟ / ΜΕΝΙΩΝ either side of Anaxagoras seated l. on globe, r. hand raised, holding scroll in l. *B.M.C. 14.* 28, 104 .. £15

4336 — Æ 19. Forepart of winged boar r. ℞. Caduceus; ΚΛΑ — Ζ Ο / ΜΕΝΙ — ΩΝ in field; all within olive-wreath. *B.M.C. 14.* 28, 100-01 .. .. £13

4337 — — Laur. hd. of Zeus r. ℞. ΚΛΑΖΟΜΕ / ΝΙΩΝ above and below club r. *B.M.C. 14.* 29, 105 .. .. £10

4338 — Æ 18. Forepart of winged boar r., ΕΡΜΗΣΙΛΟΧΟΣ below. ℞. ΚΛΑ — ΙΟ / ΜΕΝΙ — ΩΝ in the quarters of quadripartite incuse square; monogram also in lower l. hand quarter. *B.M.C. 14.* 28, 97 .. .. £14

4339 — — Gorgoneion. ℞. Swan stg. r. on caduceus, wings spread; ΚΛΑΖΟΜΕ / ΝΙ — ΩΝ in field. *B.M.C. 14.* 27, 92 .. .. £13

4340 — Æ 11. Forepart of winged boar r. ℞. Quadripartite incuse square; Κ — Λ in lower quarters. *B.M.C. 14.* 28, 99 .. .. £11

4341   4344   4346

4341 **Kolophon** (situated several miles inland, on the river Halesos, Kolophon was an important city and claimed to be the birthplace of Homer.   The famous oracle of Apollo Klarios
was within its territory).   480-450 B.C.   Æ *drachm* (*c.* 5·45 gm.).   ΚΟΛΟΦΩΝΙΩΝ (retrograde).   Laur. hd. of Apollo r., of archaic style.   ℞. Lyre, within incuse square.   *B.M.C*
14. 36, 1   ..   ..   £750

4342 — Æ *hemiobol* (*c.* 0·45 gm.).   Laur. hd. of Apollo facing.   ℞. ΗΜ monogram within
incuse square.   *Forrer/Weber* 5807   ..   ..   £65

4343 — Æ *tetartemorion* (*c.* 0·23 gm.).   Similar, but with ΤΕ monogram on *rev.*   *Forrer/*
Weber 5808 ..   ..   £55

4344 430-400 B.C.   Æ *drachm* (*c.* 5·5 gm.).   Laur. hd. of Apollo r., hair short.   ℞. Lyre.
ΚΟΛΟΦ — Ω — ΝΙΩΝ around; all within incuse square.   *Forrer/Weber* 5810   ..   £450

4345 — Æ *tetartemorion* (*c.* 0·27 gm.).   *Obv.* Similar.   ℞. ΤΕ monogram, bucranium (?) to
l.; all within incuse square.   *Forrer/Weber* 5809 ..   ..   £60

4345A 390-350 B.C.   Æ *tetradrachm* (*c.* 15 gm.).   Laur. hd. of Apollo l., hair rolled.   ℞. Lyre;
ΚΟΛΟ — Φ — ΩΝΙΟΝ to l., above and to r.; ΤΙΜΟΣ beneath; all within incuse square.
Babelon (*Traité*) *pl.* 153, 15   ..   ..   £10,000

4346 — Æ *drachm* (*c.* 3·55 gm.).   *Obv.* Similar.   ℞. Lyre; ΚΟΛΟΦΩ to l., ΙΗΝΗΣ to r.
B.M.C. 44. 36, 5   ..   ..   £250

4347   4351   4353

4347 — Æ *hemidrachm* (*c.* 1·55 gm.).   *Obv.* Similar.   ℞. Tripod; ΚΟΛΟΦ to l., ΚΟΝΝΙΩΝ to r.
B.M.C. 14. 37, 9   ..   ..   £120

4348 — Æ *diobol* (*c.* 1·05 gm.).   *Obv.* Similar.   ℞. Lyre; ΚΟΛΟΦΩ to l., ΑΙΓΥΠΤΟΣ to r.   *Forrer/*
Weber 5814 ..   ..   £100

4349 3rd cent. B.C.   Æ *tetradrachm* (*c.* 16·75 gm.), restoring the types of Alexander the Great.
Hd. of young Herakles r., clad in lion's skin.   ℞. Zeus enthroned l., holding eagle and
sceptre, ΑΛΕΞΑΝΔΡΟΥ behind; before, lyre and ΚΟΛΟ; monogram beneath throne.   *Müller*
(*Numismatique d'Alexandre le Grand*) 1007   ..   ..   £200

4350 — — Similar, but with lyre and ΗΓΗΣΙΜΑΧΟΣ before Zeus on *rev.*, and with monogram
in ex. *Müller* 1013 ..   ..   £225

4351 *Bronze Coinage.*   Mid-4th cent. B.C.   Æ 10.   Hd. of Apollo r., wearing tainia.   ℞.
Lyre; ΚΟΛΟ — Φ — ΩΝΙΩΝ around, Ι beneath.   *B.M.C.* 14. 38, 16   ..   ..   £12

4352 330-285 B.C.   Æ 18.   *Obv.* Similar.   ℞. Κ — Ο either side of lyre; ΜΟΙΡΑΣ below,
tripod in field to r.   *B.M.C.* 14. 38, 17-18   ..   ..   £12

4353 — Æ 14.   Laur. hd. of Apollo r.   ℞. Forepart of galloping horse r.; ΚΟ below,
ΕΡΜΟΘΕΣ behind.   *B.M.C.* 14. 39, 24   ..   ..   £10

4354 — Æ 20.   Laur. hd. of Apollo r.   ℞. Horseman prancing r., armoured and holding
spear couched; Κ — Ο — Λ in field, ΗΛΙΑΝΑΞ below.   *B.M.C.* 14. 39, 32   ..   £12

4355 3rd cent B.C.   Æ 11.   Laur. hd. of Apollo r.   ℞. Horse trotting r., ΚΟΛ above.   *S.N.G.*
Von Aulock 2015   ..   ..   £9

4356   4357

Kolophon *continued*

4356 2nd-1st cent B.C. Æ 20. Horseman, similar to *rev.* of 4354; beneath, hound running
r. ℞. Apollo Kitharoidos stg. r., altar at feet; ΚΟΛΟΦΩΝΙΩΝ behind, ΕΠΙΓΟΝΟΣ before.
B.M.C. 14. 40, 38   ..   ..   £10

4357 — Æ 18. Homer seated l., holding scroll, hd. resting on r. hand; ΑΠΟΛΛΑΣ before. ℞.
Apollo Kitharoidos advancing r., ΚΟΛΟΦΩΝΙΩΝ behind. *B.M.C. 14.* 41, 42 ..   £14

4358 — Æ 15. Diad. bust of Artemis r., bow and quiver at shoulder. ℞. Caps of the
Dioskouroi; ΚΟΛΟΦΩΝΙΩΝ / ΜΗΤΡΟΔΩΡΟΣ below. *B.M.C. 14.* 40, 41 ..   ..   £10

4359   4363

4359 **Ephesos** (situated at the mouth of the river Kaÿster, Ephesos was founded by Ionian
colonists under Androklos. It rose to be a place of great importance in Classical and
Hellenistic times, due in the main to the illustrious sanctuary of the Ephesian Artemis
dating from the time of Kroisos of Lydia. After the end of the Pergamene Kingdom in
133 B.C. Ephesos passed under the rule of the Romans). 480-450 B.C. Æ *tetradrachm*
(*c.* 13·3 gm.). ΕΦΕΣΙΟΝ. Bee, with curved wings. ℞. Quadripartite incuse square.
B.M.C. 14. 49, 11   ..   ..   £1,000

4360 — Æ *drachm* (*c.* 3·32 gm.). Bee, with curved wings, dividing Ε — Φ; volute in upper
field on either side. ℞. As last. *B.M.C. 14.* 48, 7-9 ..   ..   £225

4361 — — Similar to 4359. *B.M.C. 14.* 49, 12-13 ..   ..   £250

4362 — Æ *hemidrachm* (*c.* 1·85 gm.). Similar to 4360. *Head (Coinage of Ephesus)* p. 19, *no.*
3 ..   ..   £150

4363 — Æ *diobol* (*c.* 1·1 gm.). As last. *B.M.C. 14.* 48, 10 ..   ..   £120

4364 Late 5th cent. B.C. Æ *didrachm* (*c.* 7·55 gm.). Bee, with curved wings, dividing Ε — Φ.
℞. Incuse square, quartered by broad bands. *B.M.C. 14.* 49, 14-15 ..   ..   £350

4365   4366

4365 — — Similar, but with magistrate's name ΤΙΜΑΡΧ beneath bee on *obv.* *B.M.C. 14.*
49, 16   ..   ..   £400

4366 — Æ *drachm* (*c.* 3·1 gm.). Similar to 4364, but bee has straight wings. *B.M.C. 14.* 49,
17   ..   ..   £225

4367 — — Similar to 4364, but with magistrate's name ΤΙΜΗΣΙΑΝΑΞ across dividing band on
rev. *B.M.C. 14.* 50, 20   ..   ..   £275

4368 — Æ *hemidrachm* (c. 1·85 gm.).   As 4364.   *B.M.C. 14.* 50, 18-19   ..   ..   £140

4369 — — Bee, with straight wings, dividing E — Φ.   R. Similar to 4364, but with magistrate's name ΠΟΛΥΚΡΑΤΗΣ across dividing band.   *B.M.C. 14.* 50, 22 ..   ..   ..   £165

4370   4372

4370 394-387 B.C. (Alliance coinage).   Æ *tridrachm* (c. 11·45 gm.).   ΣΥΝ.   Infant Herakles kneeling r., grappling with two snakes.   R. Bee, with curved wings, dividing E — Φ; Π — E in lower field.   *B.M.C. 14.* 51, 25 ..   ..   £3,500

Coins with similar obverse type were issued by a number of cities — Byzantion, Kyzikos, Samos, Knidos, Rhodos and Iasos — as members of an alliance dedicated to their liberation from oppression; though who the oppressor was is not certain.

4371 390-330 B.C.   Æ *tetradrachm* (c. 15·3 gm.).   Bee, with curved wings, dividing E — Φ. R. Forepart of kneeling stag r., looking back; palm tree behind, ΑΡΙΣΤΟΛΕΩΣ before. *B.M.C. 14.* 51, 27 ..   ..   £550

4372 — — Similar, but bee has straight wings, and with magistrate's name ΔΙΝΕΑΣ on *rev.* *B.M.C. 14.* 52, 38 ..   ..   £500

4373 — — As last, but with magistrate's name ΙΠΠΟΚΡΙΤΟΣ on *rev.*   *B.M.C. 14.* 53, 47   £500

Nearly two hundred magistrates' names have been recorded for this extensive series.

4374 — Æ *drachm* (c. 3·43 gm.).   As last, but with knucklebone in *obv.* field to r., and with magistrate's name ΠΡΥΤΑΝΙΣ on *rev.*   *Boston Museum Catalogue* 1826 ..   ..   £250

4375 — Æ *diobol* (c. 1 gm.).   *Obv.* As 4372.   R. ΕΦ above two stags' heads confronted. *B.M.C. 14.* 53, 53 ..   ..   £110

4376   4378

4376 — Æ *trihemiobol* (c. 0·8 gm.).   *Obv.* Similar.   R.   Forepart of kneeling stag r., looking back; E — Φ in field.   *B.M.C. 14.* 53, 54 ..   ..   £85

4377 *Circa* 300 B.C.   Æ *octobol* (c. 5·7 gm.).   Bee, with straight wings, dividing E — Φ.   R. As 4371, but with magistrate's name ΕΚΑΤΟΚΛΗΣ.   *Head (Coinage of Ephesus) pl.* II, 10 £450

4378 295-288 B.C.   Æ *octobol* (c. 5·7 gm.).   Diad. hd. of Artemis r.   R. Bow and quiver; ΕΦΕ and bee below, ΕΧΕΑΝΑΣ above.   *B.M.C. 14.* 53, 55 ..   ..   ..   £400

4379 288-280 B.C. (under the name **Arsinoeia**, bestowed upon the city by Lysimachos in honour of his wife).   Æ *octobol* (c. 5·6 gm.).   Veiled hd. of Arsinoe r.   R. Bow and quiver; ΑΡΣΙ and bee below, ΓΟΝΕΥΣ and monogram above.   *B.M.C. 14.* 55, 71 ..   £550

4380 — Æ *tetrobol* (c. 2·72 gm.).   Similar.   *Head (Coinage of Ephesus) pl.* III, 6 ..   £350

4381   4383

Ephesos *continued*

4381 280-258 B.C.   Æ *octobol* (*c.* 4·87 gm.).   Diad. hd. of Artemis r., bow and quiver at shoulder. R. Forepart of kneeling stag r., looking back; palm tree behind, ΕΟΕΛΘΩΝ before; in field, Ε — Φ. and bee to r.   *B.M.C. 14.* 57, 79   ..   ..   ..   £350

4382 258-202 B.C.   Æ *didrachm* (*c.* 6·6 gm.).   Diad. and dr. bust of Artemis r., bow and quiver at shoulder. R. Forepart of kneeling stag r., looking back; ΑΡΤΕΜΙΔΩΡΟΣ behind; in field, Ε — Φ, and bee to r.   *B.M.C. 14.* 58, 92 ..   ..   £300

4383 — — Similar, but with magistrate's name ΣΩΣΙΣ on *rev.* *B.M.C. 14.* 60, 113-14   £300
    More than forty magistrates' names have been recorded for this series.

4384 Late 3rd-early 2nd cent. B.C.   Æ *tetradrachm* (*c.* 16·75 gm.), restoring the types of Alexander the Great. Hd. of young Herakles r., clad in lion's skin. R. Zeus enthroned l., holding eagle and sceptre, ΑΛΕΞΑΝΔΡΟΥ behind; bee and ΕΦΕ before.   *Müller (Numismatique d'Alexandre le Grand)* 1015   ..   ..   £200

4385 — — — Similar, but with magistrate's monogram instead of ΕΦΕ on *rev.* *Müller* 1019 ..   ..   £175

4386 — Æ *drachm* (*c.* 4·2 gm.), restoring the types of Alexander the Great. As 4384.   *Müller* 1016 ..   ..   £95

4387   4389

4387 202-133 B.C.   Æ *drachm* (*c.* 4·15 gm.).   Bee; Ε — Φ in upper field. R. Stag stg. r., palm tree in background; before, ΑΙΧΜΟΚΛΗΣ.   *B.M.C. 14.* 61, 123   ..   ..   £85

4388 — — Similar, but with magistrate's name ΧΑΛΚΙΔΕΥΣ on ̄rev.   *B.M.C. 14.* 61, 133 £85
    More than sixty magistrates' names have been recorded for this series. A similar issue from the Phoenician mint of Arados (see nos. 5989-90) would seem to indicate some form of monetary alliance between the two cities.

4389 189-133 B.C. (under the rule of the Pergamene kings Eumenes II, Attalos II and Attalos III). Æ *cistophoric tetradrachm* (*c.* 12·6 gm.).   Cista mystica containing serpent; all within ivy-wreath. R. Bow in case between two coiled serpents; ΕΦΕ to l., Artemis and stag to r.   *B.M.C. 14.* 63, 150   ..   ..   £150

4390 — — Similar, but bee in wreath instead of Artemis and stag on *rev.*   *B.M.C. 14.* 64, 152 ..   ..   £150

4391 — Æ *didrachm* (*c.* 5·93 gm.).   Club of Herakles draped with lion's skin; all within laurel-wreath. R. Bunch of grapes upon vine-leaf; ΕΦΕ to r., bow and quiver to l.   *B.M.C. 14.* 64, 154   ..   ..   £175

4392   4394

4392 — Æ *drachm* (*c.* 3·07 gm.). *Obv.* Similar, but vine- instead of laurel-wreath. ℞. Bunch of grapes upon vine-leaf; ЕΦЕ to l., bee in wreath to r. *B.M.C. 14.* 64, 155 ..   £120

4393 133-67 B.C. (under Roman rule). Æ *cistophoric tetradrachm* (*c.* 12·6 gm.). Cista mystica, as 4389. ℞. Bow in case between two coiled serpents; to r., long torch; to l., ЕΦЕ and Γ (=year 3=131 B.C.). *B.M.C. 14.* 64, 156 ..   ..   ..   £125

4394 — — Similar, but on *rev.* date numeral M (=year 40=94 B.C.) instead of Γ, and also with candelabrum above bow-case. *B.M.C. 14.* 65, 160 ..   ..   £125

     Many dates have been recorded for this series, ranging from A (=133 B.C.) *to* ΞZ (=67 B.C.).

4395 — Æ *didrachm* (*c.* 6 gm.). Club of Herakles draped with lion's skin; all within vine-wreath. ℞. Bunch of grapes upon vine-leaf; to l., torch; above, bee; to r., ЕΦЕ and A (=year 1=133 B.C.). *Head (Coinage of Ephesus), p.* 65 ..   ..   £175

4396 — Æ *drachm* (*c.* 3 gm.). Similar, but on *rev.* the torch is to r., the ЕΦЕ and A to l. *S.N.G. Von Aulock* 1859 ..   ..   £120

4397 87-85 B.C. (revolt against Rome—time of Mithradates Eupator). Ν *stater* (*c.* 8·55 gm.). Diad. and dr. bust of Artemis r., bow and quiver at shoulder. ℞. Cultus-statue of Ephesian Artemis facing; ЕΦ — Е across upper field; bee to l. of statue, cornucopiae to r. *S.N.G. Von Aulock* 1869 ..   ..   £3,000

4398   4400

4398 T. Ampius Balbus, Roman Proconsul of Asia, 58-57 B.C. Æ *cistophoric tetradrachm* (*c.* 12·4 gm.). Cista mystica containing serpent; all within ivy-wreath. ℞. Two coiled serpents either side of tripod surmounted by naked Apollo stg. l., holding branch and resting on column; to l., OZ / ЕΦЕ; to r., long torch; above, T. A — MPI. T.F. / PRO — COS.; below, ЄΡΜΙΑC / ΚΑΙΥCΤΡΙΟC. *B.M.C. 14.* 67, 174 ..   ..   ..   £300

4399 C. Fabius, Roman Proconsul of Asia, 57-56 B.C. Æ *cistophoric tetradrachm. Obv.* Similar. ℞. Two coiled serpents either side of aplustre surmounted by Artemis stg. r., holding arrow and bow; to l., OZ / ЕΦЕ; to r., long torch; above, C.FA — BI.M.F. / PRO — COS.; below, ΚΝΩΣΟΣ. *B.M.C. 14.* 67, 175 ..   ..   £300

4400 C. Fannius, Pontifex and Praetor, 49-48 B.C. Æ *cistophoric tetradrachm. Obv.* Similar. ℞. Two coiled serpents either side of tetrastyle shrine surmounted by statue of Athena (?); to l., ΠΙΣ / ЕΦЕ and figure of Nemesis (?) stg. l.; to r., long torch; above, C.FAN. — PONT.PR.; below, ΑΡΧΙΔΗΜΟC. *B.M.C. 14.* 68, 177-8 ..   ..   ..   £300

4401   4404

Ephesos *continued*

4401 *Bronze Coinage.* 350-288 B.C. Æ 19. Bee; E — Φ in upper field. R. Stag kneeling l.,
looking back; astragalos above, ΑΝΤΙΑΛΚΙΔΑΣ before. *B.M.C. 14.* 54, 58 .. £14

4402 — Æ 14. Similar, but with magistrate's name ΜΟΡΙΜΟΣ on *rev.* *B.M.C. 14.* 55, 65
£12

4403 — Æ 10. Similar, but with magistrate's name ΣΩΣΙΚΡΑΤΗΣ. *B.M.C. 14.* 55, 66
£10

4404 288-280 B.C. (under the name **Arsinoeia**). Æ 15. Veiled hd. of Arsinoe r. R. Stag
kneeling l., looking back, astragalos above; ΑΡ — ΣΙ either side of neck, ΑΡΙСΤΑΙОС before.
B.M.C. 14. 56, 72 .. .. £20

4405   4409

4405 280-258 B.C. Æ 18. *Obv.* Similar to 4401, but with border of dots. R. Stag stg. r.,
quiver above; ΑΠΟΛΛΟΔΩΡΟΣ before. *B.M.C. 14.* 57, 80-81 .. .. .. £11

4406 — — *Obv.* Similar, but all within laurel-wreath. R. Stag grazing r., quiver above;
ΣΟΛΩΝ in ex. *B.M.C. 14.* 58, 84 .. .. £12

4407 — Æ 17. *Obv.* As 4405. R. Stag kneeling l., looking back; quiver above. *B.M.C. 14.*
57, 82 .. .. £12

4408 — Æ 13. Female hd. l., laur. and turreted; astragalos behind. R. ΟΙΩ — ΝΟΣ. Bee.
Head (Coinage of Ephesus) pl. III, 15 .. .. £14

4409 — Æ 10. Turreted female hd. l. R. Bee; E — Φ in upper field. *B.M.C. 14.* 55, 68-
70 .. .. £9

4410 258-202 B.C. Æ 17. Diad. and dr. bust of Artemis r., bow and quiver at shoulder.
R. Forepart of kneeling stag r., looking back, bee before; E — Φ in field, ΔΙΟΣΚΟΥΡΙΔΗΣ
behind. *B.M.C. 14.* 60, 118 .. .. £12

4411 202-133 B.C. Æ 19. Bee; E — Φ in upper field; all within laurel-wreath. R. Stag
stg. r., palm tree in background; Δ behind, monogram before, ΔΗΜΗΤΡΙΟΣ in ex. *B.M.C.
14.* 62, 138 .. .. £11

4411   4412

4412 48-27 B.C. Æ 24. Artemis advancing r., drawing arrow from quiver and holding bow,
hound at feet; E — Φ in field. R. Cock stg. r., palm-branch in background; ΙΑΣΩΝ in
ex.; all within laurel-wreath. *B.M.C. 14.* 69, 185 .. .. £20

4413 — Æ 23. Diad. and dr. bust of Artemis r., bow and quiver at shoulder. R. Forepart of kneeling stag r., looking back; E — Φ in field, long torch behind, MHNOΦI / ΛOC below. *B.M.C. 14.* 69, 180 .. .. £14

4414 — Æ 19. *Obv.* Similar. R. Long torch between two stags, face to face; E — Φ beneath stags, ΔHMH — TPIOΣ above, KΩ — KOΣ in field, ΣΩΠATPOΣ in ex. *B.M.C. 14.* 69, 182-4 .. .. £12

4415 — Æ 13. *Obv.* As 4411. R. Stag stg. r., looking back, long torch in background; ΠYΘΩN below. *S.N.G. Von Aulock* 1873 .. .. £10

4416 **Erythrai** (situated on the coast opposite the island of Chios, Erythrai was a prosperous city and boasted a temple of great antiquity dedicated to Herakles and Athena Polias). 480-450 B.C. Æ *drachm* (c. 4·65 gm.). Naked male figure stg. l., restraining cantering horse l.; bee in field to r. R. E — P / Θ — Y in the corners of incuse square containing stellate flower. *B.M.C. 14.* 120, 22-3 .. .. £350

4417   4420   4421

4417 — — Similar, but with ornamented entablature beneath *obv.* type, and without symbol in field. *B.M.C. 14.* 120, 29 .. .. £375

4418 — Æ *diobol* (c. 1·45 gm.). Pegasos flying r.; pilos to l., A beneath. R. Similar to 4416. *B.M.C. 14.* 121, 31 .. .. £140

4419 — Æ *trihemiobol* (c. 1·1 gm.). Similar to 4416, but without symbol in *obv.* field, and no inscription on *rev.* *B.M.C. 14.* 121, 35 .. .. £140

4420 — Æ *obol* (c. 0·9 gm.). As 4418, but without A on *obv.* *B.M.C. 14.* 121, 33 .. £120

4421 — Æ *tetartemorion* (c. 0·2 gm.). Bull's hd. r. R. Stellate flower within incuse square. *B.M.C. 14.* 121, 37 .. .. £85

4422 330-300 B.C. Æ *tetradrachm* (c. 15 gm.). Hd. of young Herakles r., clad in lion's skin. R. Club and bow in case; EPY and owl to l., MOΛIΩN between, monogram to r. *B.M.C. 14.* 122, 42 .. .. £750

4423 — Æ *drachm* (c. 3·75 gm.). Similar, but with magistrate's name ΔIONYΣIOΣ on *rev.*, and with kantharos beneath bow-case instead of monogram to r. *B.M.C. 14.* 123, 48-50 £120

4424   4427   4429

4424 — — Similar to 4422, but with magistrate's name ΦANNOΘEMIΣ on *rev.* *B.M.C. 14.* 123, 57-8 .. .. £120

4425 — Æ *hemidrachm* (c. 1·57 gm.). Hd. of young Herakles l., clad in lion's skin. R. EPY. Club and bow in case. *B.M.C. 14.* 128, 101 .. .. £140

4426 3rd cent. B.C. Æ *tetradrachm* (c. 16·75 gm.), restoring the types of Alexander the Great. Hd. of young Herakles r., clad in lion's skin. R. Zeus enthroned l., holding eagle and sceptre, AΛEΞANΔPOY behind; before, bow in case, club and EPY; in ex., ΔIOΔOTOΣ. *Müller (Numismatique d'Alexandre le Grand)* 999 .. .. £225

4427 200-133 B.C. Æ *drachm* (c. 4·2 gm.). *Obv.* Similar. R. Club and bow in case; EPY above, HPOΔΩPOΣ / ΔIONYΣIOY between; all within vine-wreath. *B.M.C. 14.* 134, 146-7 .. .. £160

4428 — Æ *diobol* (c. 1·4 gm.). Hd. of young Herakles l., clad in lion's skin. R. Club and bow in case; EPY above, MOΛIΩN and caduceus between, ear of corn to l. *B.M.C. 14.* 134, 151 .. .. £120

4429 2nd-1st cent. B.C. Æ *trihemiobol* (c. 1 gm.). Hd. of Athena r., in crested Corinthian helmet. R. EPY above monogram. *B.M.C. 14.* 139, 198-9 .. .. .. £95

Erythrai *continued*

4430 — Æ *obol* (*c.* 0·65 gm.).   Club.   ℞. As last.   *B.M.C. 14.* 139, 200   ..   ..   £75

4431   4434   4439

4431   87-85 B.C. (revolt against Rome — time of Mithradates Eupator).   *N third-stater* (*c.* 2·82 gm.).   *Obv.* As 4428.   ℞. Female divinity, wearing kalathos, stg. facing, holding spear and globe (?); EPY to l., ΠΟΣΕΙΔΩΝΙΟΣ to r.   *B.M.C. 14.* 139, 197   ..   £1,750

4432   *Bronze Coinage.* 350-330 B.C.   Æ 13.   Hd. of bearded Herakles r., clad in lion's skin.   ℞. EPY.   Bow in case and club in saltire; all within wreath.   *S.N.G. Von Aulock* 1949   £14

4433 — Æ 10.   *Obv.* Similar.   ℞. EPYΘ.   Fluted vase.   *Forrer/Weber* 5918   ..   £13

4434 — — *Obv.* Similar.   ℞. Bull's hd. r., EPY above, club behind.   *B.M.C. 14.* 122, 38-40   ..   ..   £12

4435   330-300 B.C.   Æ 22.   Hd. of young Herakles r., clad in lion's skin.   ℞. Bow in case and club; EPY beneath, ΜΗΤΡΟΔΩΡΟΣ and monogram between.   *B.M.C. 14.* 127, 93-4   £14

4436 — Æ 17.   *Obv.* Similar.   ℞. Club and bow in case; EPY above, ΚΑΛΛΙΣ between.   *Forrer/Weber* 5936   ..   ..   £13

4437 — Æ 13.   Similar, but with magistrate's name ΜΙΝΝΙΩΝ on *rev.*   *Forrer/Weber* 5938   £12

4438 — — *Obv.* Similar.   ℞. EPY.   Club, bow in case and cloven hoof.   *B.M.C. 14.* 124, 63-5   ..   ..   £12

4439 — — Hd. of young Herakles three-quarter face to r., clad in lion's skin.   ℞. Club and bow in case; EPY above, ΜΗΤΡΟΔΩΡΟΣ between, monogram beneath.   *B.M.C. 14.* 127, 95   ..   ..   £14

4440 — Æ 11.   Bow in case.   ℞. EPY, club, and ΠΥΘΗΣ.   *B.M.C. 14.* 127, 97   ..   £10

4441   4442

4441   3rd cent. B.C.   Æ 15.   Hd. of young Herakles r., clad in lion's skin.   ℞. EPY above ΑΓΑΣΙΚΛΗΣ / ΑΝΤΙΠΑ / ΤΡΟΥ.   *B.M.C. 14.* 129, 104-5   ..   ..   ..   £10

4442 — — Hd. of young Dionysos r., wreathed with ivy.   ℞. EPY and bunch of grapes beneath ΒΑΤΑΚΟΣ / ΠΑΡΑΜΟ / ΝΟΥ.   *B.M.C. 14.* 130, 121   ..   ..   £10

4443 — Æ 13.   Hd. of Athena r., in crested helmet.   ℞. EPY above ΑΠΟΛΛΩ / ΝΙΟΣ / ΑΠΟΛΛΟ / ΔΟΤΟΥ.   *B.M.C. 14.* 131, 127   ..   ..   £9

4444 — Æ 10.   Rad. hd. of Helios facing.   ℞. EPY above ΗΡΟΤΙ / ΜΟΣ.   *B.M.C. 14.* 132, 138   ..   ..   £9

4445 — — Club.   ℞. EPY above ΦΙΛΩΝ.   *B.M.C. 14.* 133, 143   ..   ..   £8

4446   200-133 B.C.   Æ 20.   Hd. of young Herakles r., clad in lion's skin.   ℞. ΗΡΟΘΕΜΙΣ / ΗΡΑΚΛΕΙΤΟΥ in two lines; above, bow in case; beneath, EPY, bust of Herakles three-quarter face to r., and club.   *Forrer/Weber* 5966   ..   ..   ..   £11

4447   4448

4447 — — Similar, but with magistrate's name ΞΕΙΝΑΣ / ΟΙΝΟΠΙΛΟΥ on *rev.* *B.M.C. 14.* 138, 189 .. ..   £11

4448 2nd-1st cent. B.C. Æ 17. Hd. of bearded Herakles r., clad in lion's skin. ℞. ΔΗΜΗΤΡΙΟΣ / ΑΠΕΛΛΟΥ in two lines; above, bow in case; beneath, club and ΕΡΥ. *B.M.C. 14.* 140, 202 .. ..   £10

These are sometimes countermarked with bees on obv. and rev.

4449 — — *Obv.* Similar. ℞. ΗΡΑΚΛΕΟΣ / ΕΠΙΚΟΥΡΟΥ in two lines; above, bow in case; beneath, bee, club and ΕΡΥ. *B.M.C. 14.* 140, 211-13 .. ..   £10

4450 — — Bare hd. of bearded Herakles l. ℞. ΕΡΥ above ΑΡΙΩΝ / ΑΠΟΛ / ΛΩΝΙ / ΟΥ. *B.M.C. 14.* 141, 215 .. ..   £12

4451 — Æ 13. Hd. of bearded Herakles three-quarter face to r., clad in lion's skin. ℞. ΔΙΟΠΕΙΘΗΣ / ΕΡΜΙΠΠΟΥ in two lines; above, bow in case; beneath, club and ΕΡΥ. *B.M.C. 14.* 141, 217-19 .. ..   £13

4452 **Herakleia ad Latmon** (situated on the Latmic gulf, at the foot of Mt. Latmos, Herakleia produced no coinage until Hellenistic times). 3rd cent. B.C. Æ *tetradrachm* (*c.* 16·75 gm.), restoring the types of Alexander the Great. Hd. of young Herakles r., clad in lion's skin. ℞. Zeus enthroned l., holding eagle and sceptre, ΑΛΕΞΑΝΔΡΟΥ behind; before, club and monogram of Herakleia. *Müller (Numismatique d'Alexandre le Grand)* 1058   £200

4453 2nd cent. B.C. Æ *tetradrachm* (*c.* 16·5 gm.). Hd. of Athena r., wearing crested Athenian helmet, richly ornamented. ℞. ΗΡΑΚΛΕΩΤΩΝ above club r.; beneath, Nike stg. l. between two monograms; all within oak-wreath. *B.M.C. 14.* 151, 1-2 ..   £550

4454 — Æ *octobol* (*c.* 5·15 gm.). Hd. of Athena r., in crested Corinthian helmet. ℞. ΗΡΑΚΛΕ / ΩΤΩΝ above and below club r.; all within laurel-wreath. *Historia Numorum,* p. 579 .. ..   £750

4455 — Æ *tetrobol* (*c.* 2·5 gm.). Similar. *B.M.C. 14.* 151, 3 .. .. ..   £350

Herakleia ad Latmon *continued*

4456 2nd-1st cent. B.C.   Æ 19.   Hd. of Athena r., in crested Corinthian helmet.   R. ΗΡΑΚΛΕ / ΩΤΩΝ in two lines, bow in case above, club below; all within laurel-wreath.   *B.M.C. 14.* 151, 4   ..   ..   £12

4457 — Æ 14.   Hd. of bearded Herakles r., bound with tainia.   R. ΗΡΑ / ΚΛΕ above and below club r.; all within laurel-wreath.   *B.M.C. 14.* 152, 8   ..   ..   £11

4458 — — Bust of Artemis r., quiver at shoulder.   R. ΗΡΑΚΛΕ / ΩΤΩΝ either side of naked Herakles stg. facing, holding club and lion's skin.   *Forrer/Weber* 5987   ..   £12

4459 — Æ 10.   Lyre.   R. ΗΡΑ / ΚΛΕ either side of club.   *B.M.C. 14.* 152, 10   ..   £10

4460 — — Owl stg. r., hd. facing.   R. ΗΡΑΚΛΕ / ΩΤΩΝ above and below crest of helmet.   *B.M.C. 14.* 152, 13 ..   ..   £10

4459

4461   4462

4461 **Larissa** (situated in the Kaÿster valley, 25 miles north-east of Ephesos).   Early 3rd cent. B.C.   Æ 18.   Laur. hd. of Apollo r.   R. Horseman prancing r., holding spear couched; ΛΑ below, ΗΡ monogram above.   *B.M.C. 14.* 153, 1-2   ..   ..   £15

4462 **Lebedos** (a coastal town of early foundation, situated 25 miles north-west of Ephesos).   2nd cent. B.C.   R *tetradrachm* (*c.* 16·55 gm.).   Hd. of Athena r., wearing triple-crested helmet wreathed with olive.   R. Owl stg. r. on club between two cornuacopiae; ΛΕΒΕΔΙΩΝ above, ΑΠΟΛΛΟΔΟΤΟΣ beneath; all within olive-wreath.   *B.M.C. 14.* 154, 1   ..   £1,000

4463 — R *diobol?* (*c.* 1·5 gm.).   Hd. of Athena l., in Corinthian helmet.   R. Owl stg. r.; before, ΛΕ and prow r.; behind, ΗΓΙΑΣ.   *B.M.C. 14.* 154, 3-4   ..   ..   ..   £140

4464 — R *trihemiobol* (*c.* 0·9 gm.).   *Obv.* Similar, but hd. r.   R. Prow l.; above, ΛΕ and owl; below, ΔΟΡΚΩΝ.   *S.N.G. Von Aulock* 2029   ..   ..   £120

4465 *Bronze Coinage.*   Mid-3rd cent. B.C. (under the name **Ptolemaïs**).   Æ 13.   Laur. hd. of Apollo r.   R. ΠΤΟΛΕΜΑΙΕΩΝ.   Amphora.   *S.N.G. Von Aulock* 2026   ..   £18

4466   4468

4466 2nd-1st cent. B.C.   Æ 18.   Hd. of Athena three-quarter face to l., wearing triple-crested helmet.   R. Owl stg. r.; ΛΕ before, ΑΛΚΙΜΑΧΟΣ behind.   *B.M.C. 14.* 155, 9   ..   £15

4467 — — *Obv.* Similar.   R. Dionysos stg. l., holding kantharos and thyrsos; ΛΕ before, ΑΝΤΙΓΕΝΗΣ behind.   *Forrer/Weber* 5992 ..   ..   £16

4468 — — ΛΕ.   Prow r., surmounted by Athena r., brandishing spear and holding trophy.   R. ΕΡΜΙΠΠΟΣ / ΑΡΤΕΜΩΝ either side of owl stg. r.   *B.M.C. 14.* 155, 13-14   ..   £14

4469 — Æ 11.   Hd. of Athena three-quarter face to l., wearing crested helmet.   R. ΛΕ.   Prow l.   *B.M.C. 14.* 154, 6-7   ..   ..   £12

4470 Leukai (founded in 352 B.C. by the Persian general Tachos, Leukai was situated on the northern shores of the gulf of Smyrna). Mid-4th cent. B.C. Æ *obol* (*c.* 0·9 gm.). Female hd. (Aphrodite or Artemis) l., Λ before, crescent behind. R. Swan stg. r., wings spread; Λ before, crescent above. *Babelon* (*Traité*) *pl.* 156, 24 .. .. £160

4471   4472

4471 — Æ *hemiobol* (*c.* 0·5 gm.). Boar's hd. r. R. Laur. hd. of Zeus r., ΛΕΥ behind. *B.M.C. 14.* 157, 1 .. .. £120

4472 350-300 B.C. Æ 17. Laur. hd. of Apollo l. R. Swan stg. l., hd. turned back, wings spread; ΛΕΟ below, ΓΟΡΓΙΑΣ before. *B.M.C. 14.* 157, 5.. .. .. .. £17

4474 Magnesia (situated south-east of Ephesos, on a tributary of the Maeander, Magnesia was originally founded from Thessaly but was re-established by colonists from Miletos in the 7th cent. B.C.). 464-462 B.C. Æ *didrachm* (*c.* 8·55 gm.). ΘΕΜΙΣΤΟΚΛΕΟΣ. Apollo stg. r., holding long staff from which laurel-branch springs. R. Eagle upright, wings spread, hd. l.; Μ — Α either side of tail; all in dotted border within incuse square. *Kraay* (*Archaic and Classical Greek Coins*) 906 .. .. £25,000

This remarkable type belongs to the time of Themistokles' exile in Asia Minor. The Athenian statesman was made governor of Magnesia by the Persian king Artaxerxes I.

4475   4477

4475 Mid-4th cent. B.C. Æ *tridrachm* ? (*c.* 14·65 gm.). Armed horseman prancing r., holding couched spear. R. Humped bull butting l., ΜΑΓΝ above, ΔΙΟΠΕΙΘ below; all within circular Maeander pattern. *B.M.C. 14.* 158, 2 .. .. £2,250

4476 — Æ *didrachm* (*c.* 11 gm.). Similar, but with magistrate's name ΚΑΛΛΙΑΝΑΣ / ΚΑΛΛΙΚ-ΡΑΤΟΥ in ex. on *rev.* *S.N.G. Von Aulock* 2033 .. .. £1,000

4477 — Æ *drachm* (*c.* 5·5 gm.). Similar, but with magistrate's name ΕΡΜΟΚΡΑΤΗΣ and ΚΡ monogram in ex. on *rev.*, and with corn-ear behind bull. *B.M.C. 14.* 158, 5 .. £450

4478 — Æ *tetrobol* (*c.* 3·5 gm.). Similar, but with magistrate's name ΜΙΚΥΘΟΣ on *rev.* (no symbol behind bull). *Forrer/Weber* 5995 .. .. £350

4479 — Æ *hemidrachm* (*c.* 2·5 gm.). Similar, but with Β beneath horse on *obv.*, and with magistrate's name ΑΝΑΞΑΓΟΡΑΣ / ΔΗΜΗΤΡΙΟΥ on *rev.*; also, ΜΑΓΝΗΤΩΝ instead of ΜΑΓΝ above bull. *B.M.C. 14.* 159, 7 .. .. £200

4480 — Æ *diobol* (*c.* 1·75 gm.). *Obv.* As 4475. R. Humped bull butting l.; Maeander pattern and ΜΑΓΝ beneath, ΝΕΑΝΔΡΟΣ above, corn-ear behind. *B.M.C. 14.* 159, 13 £125

4481 — Æ *trihemiobol* (*c.* 1 gm.). Laur. hd. of Apollo l. R. Forepart of butting bull l.; ΜΑΓΝ above, Maeander pattern behind, ΑΝΑΞΙΜΒΡΟΤΟΣ beneath. *B.M.C. 14.* 159, 14 £120

Magnesia *continued*

4482 — Æ *obol* (*c.* 0·75 gm.).   *Obv.* As 4475.   ℞. Humped bull butting l.; ΜΑΓΝ above,
Maeander pattern and ΛΥΚΟΜΗΔ beneath.   *Forrer/Weber* 5998   ..   ..   £100

4483 — — Hd. of Athena r., in crested helmet wreathed with olive.   ℞. Trident, Μ — Α in
lower field; all within circular Maeander pattern.   *B.M.C. 14.* 160, 15-16   ..   £110

4484 3rd cent. B.C.   Æ *tetradrachm* (*c.* 16·75 gm.), restoring the types of Alexander the Great.
Hd. of young Herakles r., clad in lion's skin.   ℞. Zeus enthroned l., holding eagle and
sceptre, ΑΛΕΞΑΝΔΡΟΥ behind; before, humped bull butting r. and monogram; in ex.,
Maeander pattern.   *Müller (Numismatique d'Alexandre le Grand)* 1069   ..   £225

4483   4485

4485 2nd cent. B.C.   Æ *tetradrachm* (*c.* 16·75 gm.).   Diad. bust of Artemis r., bow and quiver
at shoulder.   ℞. ΜΑΓΝΗΤΩΝ — ΕΡΑΣΙΠΠΟΣ / ΑΡΙΣΤΕΟΥ either side of naked Apollo stg. l.
on Maeander pattern, holding branch and resting l. elbow on tripod surmounted by quiver;
all within laurel-wreath.   *B.M.C. 14.* 162, 37   ..   ..   £450

4486 — Æ *drachm* (*c.* 3·5 gm.).   Similar, but with magistrate's name ΕΥΦΗΜΟΣ / ΠΑΥΣΑΝΙΟΥ
on *rev.*   *Forrer/Weber* 6004   ..   ..   £275

4487   4491

4487 *Bronze Coinage.* 4th-3rd cent. B.C.   Æ 17.   Armed horseman prancing r., holding
couched spear.   ℞. Humped bull butting l., ΜΑΓΝ above, ΚΥΔΙΑΣ / ΙΣΑΓΟ in ex.; all within
circular Maeander pattern.   *B.M.C. 14.* 161, 25   ..   ..   £12

4488 — — Similar, but with ΣΩ beneath horse on *obv.*, and with magistrate's name ΝΙΚΗΡΑΤΟΣ
on *rev.*   *B.M.C. 14.* 161, 29   ..   ..   £12

4489 — Æ 14.   Laur. hd. of Apollo l., hair rolled.   ℞. Forepart of rushing bull r.; ΜΑΓ
above, Maeander pattern behind, ΑΠΟΛΛΟΔ beneath.   *Grose /McClean* 8180   ..   £13

4490 — Æ 9.   Horseman r., as 4487.   ℞. Humped bull butting l., ΜΑΓΝ in ex.   *B.M.C. 14.*
161, 35   ..   ..   £10

4491 2nd-1st cent. B.C.   Æ 23.   Bust of Artemis r., as 4485, but all within laurel-wreath.
℞. ΜΑΓΝΗΤΩΝ — ΠΥΡΡΑΣ / ΠΑΜΦΙΛΟΥ either side of cultus-statue of Artemis Leukophryene
facing.   *B.M.C. 14.* 163, 42   ..   ..   £15

4492 — — Hd. of Athena r., in crested helmet.   ℞. Armed horseman galloping r., holding
couched spear; ΜΑΓΝΗΤΩΝ above, ΕΥΚΛΗΣ / ΚΡΑΤΙΝΟΣ beneath.   *B.M.C. 14.* 163, 44-5
£14

4493 — Æ 18.   Armed horseman trotting r., holding spear.   ℞. Humped bull stg. r. on
Maeander pattern; ΜΑΓΝ above, ΔΙΑΓΟΡΑΣ beneath.   *B.M.C. 14.* 163, 40   ..   £12

4494   4495   4499

4494 — — Laur. hd. of Apollo r. ℞. Horse pacing r.; ΝΙ before, ΜΑΓΝΗΤΩΝ in ex. *B.M.C. 14*. 163, 41 ..   ..   £13

4495 — Æ 17. ΜΑΓΝΗΤΩΝ. Rad. hd. of Helios r., bow and quiver at shoulder. ℞. ΕΥΚΛΗΣ / ΑΙΣΧΡΙΩΝΟΣ either side of cultus-statue of Artemis Leukophryene facing. *B.M.C. 14*. 164, 48 ..   ..   £13

4496 — — Stag stg. r.; star above, ΜΑΓΝΗΤ in ex. ℞. As last, but with magistrate's name ΚΡΑΤΙΝΟΣ instead of ΑΙΣΧΡΙΩΝΟΣ. *B.M.C. 14*. 164, 47 ..   ..   ..   £13

4497 **Metropolis** (an inland town, situated north of Ephesos and east of Kolophon). 1st cent. B.C. Æ 17. Hd. of Athena r., in crested helmet. ℞. ΜΗΤΡΟΠΟ / ΛΙΤΩΝ above and below winged thunderbolt. *B.M.C. 14*. 175, 1 ..   ..   £15

4498 — — Turreted bust of Kybele r. ℞. M̄HTPO / ΠΟΛΙ / ΤΩΝ in three lines across field. *B.M.C. 14*. 175, 4 ..   ..   £16

4499 — Æ 11. *Obv.* Similar. ℞. Pine-cone; ΔΙΟΓΕ to r., monogram (of ΜΗΤΡΟΠΟΛΙΤΩΝ) to l. *S.N.G. Von Aulock* 2065 ..   ..   £15

4500   4502   4503

4500 **Miletos** (a settlement of great antiquity, Miletos was the southernmost of the twelve cities of the Ionian confederacy. It was also one of the earliest mints, though its prosperity was greatly curtailed following the defeat of the Ionian revolt against Persia, early in the 5th cent. B.C. It was the mother-city of many famous colonies, including Abydos, Kyzikos, Sinope and Pantikapaion). 480-450 B.C. Æ *hemidrachm* (*c.* 2·1 gm.). Lion crouching r. ℞. Star ornament within incuse square. *B.M.C. 14*. 185, 12-13   £150

4501 Mid-4th cent. B.C. Æ *tetradrachm* (*c.* 15·3 gm.). Laur. hd. of Apollo l. ℞. Lion stg. l., looking back at star in upper field; ΜΙ monogram before, ΣΤΡΑΤΙΔΗΣ below. *S.N.G. Von Aulock* 2089 ..   ..   £1,000

4502 — Æ *drachm* (*c.* 3·7 gm.). Similar, but with magistrate's name ΚΑΛΛΑΙΣΧΡΟΣ on *rev.* *B.M.C. 14*. 189, 58 ..   ..   £130

4503 — Æ *hemidrachm* (*c.* 1·8 gm.). Similar, but with magistrate's name ΡΟΔΙΟΣ on *rev.* *B.M.C. 14*. 190, 72 ..   ..   £100

4504 — — Laur. hd. of Apollo Didymaios three-quarter face to l. ℞. ΕΓ ΔΙΔΥΜΩΝ ΙΕΡΗ. Lion stg. l., looking back at star in upper field. *B.M.C. 14*. 189, 51-2 ..   £500

    This interesting type was minted at the famous shrine of the Didymaian Apollo situated within the territory of Miletos.

Miletos *continued*

4505 300-250 B.C.   Æ *didrachm* (*c.* 6·6 gm.).   Similar to 4501, but with magistrate's name ΛΥΚΟΣ below exergual line on *rev.   B.M.C. 14.* 192, 84 ..   ..   £225

4506 250-200 B.C.   Æ *didrachm* (*c.* 10·5 gm.).   As last, but with magistrate's name ΜΑΙΑΝΔΡΙΟΣ on *rev.   B.M.C. 14.* 192, 92   ..   ..   £350

4507 — Æ *drachm* (*c.* 5·2 gm.).   As last, but with magistrate's name ΑΛΚΩΝ, and also with T in *rev.* field to l.   *B.M.C. 14.* 193, 94   ..   ..   £175

4508 — Æ *hemidrachm* (*c.* 2·5 gm.).   As last, but with magistrate's name ΔΕΙΝΟΣΤΡ / ΑΤΟΣ, and with monogram in *rev.* field to l.   *B.M.C. 14.* 193, 99   ..   ..   £90

4509 3rd cent. B.C.   Æ *tetradrachm* (*c.* 16·75 gm.), restoring the types of Alexander the Great. Hd. of young Herakles r., clad in lion's skin.   ℞. Zeus enthroned l., holding eagle and sceptre, ΑΛΕΞΑΝΔΡΟΥ behind; before, ΜΙ monogram and lion stg. l., looking back at star; monogram beneath throne.   *Müller* (*Numismatique d'Alexandre le Grand*) 1038
£175

4510   4514

4510 2nd cent. B.C.   N *stater* (*c.* 8·44 gm.).   Laur. hd. of Apollo r., bow and quiver at shoulder. ℞. Lion stg. r., looking back at star in upper field; ΜΟΙ and ΜΙ monogram before, ΒΙΩΝ in ex.   *B.M.C. 14.* 194, 113   ..   ..   £5,000

4511 — Æ *tetradrachm* (*c.* 16·9 gm.).   Laur. hd. of Apollo r., within circular border of pellets. ℞. Lion stg. r., looking back at star in upper field; ΜΙΛΗΣΙΩΝ above, ΑΡΤΕΜΙΔΩΡΟΣ before, ΕΠΙΚΟΥΡΟΣ in ex.   *S.N.G. Von Aulock* 2099   ..   ..   £1,250

4512 — Æ *octobol* (*c.* 4·9 gm.).   Laur. hd. of Apollo r.   ℞. Lion stg. r., as last; before, ΜΙ monogram and magistrate's monogram; in ex., ΜΟΛΟΣΣΟΣ.   *B.M.C. 14.* 195, 117   £130

4513 — Æ *tetrobol* (*c.* 2·6 gm.).   Similar to 4510, but without bow and quiver on *obv.*   *B.M.C. 14.* 195, 119 ..   ..   £75

4514 *Bronze Coinage.*   375-350 B.C.   Æ 14.   Lion stg. l., looking back at star in upper field; ΜΙ monogram before.   ℞. Star ornament; Α — Λ — Κ around.   *B.M.C. 14.* 188, 45
£14

4515   4520

4515 350-300 B.C.   Æ 18.   Laur. hd. of Apollo r.   R. Lion stg. r., looking back at star in upper field; ΕΠΙΣΘΕΝΗΣ before. *B.M.C. 14.* 191, 74 ..   ..   £14

4516 — Æ 11.   Similar, but with magistrate's name ΛΑΜΠΡΟΜΑΧΟΥ on *rev.* *B.M.C. 14.* 191, 76 ..   ..   £11

4517 3rd cent. B.C.   Æ 18.   Laur. hd. of Apollo three-quarter face to l.   R. Lion stg. r., looking back at star in upper field; ΔΑΜΑΣ in ex., Τ before. *B.M.C. 14.* 193, 104   £14

4518 — Æ 10.   Similar, but with magistrate's name ΠΡΩΤΩ on *rev.*, and without Τ in field. *Forrer/Weber* 6053 ..   ..   £11

4519 2nd-1st cent. B.C.   Æ 19.   Laur. hd. of Apollo r., within border of pellets.   R. Lion stg. r., looking back at star in upper field; ΜΙ monogram before, ΑΡΤΕΜΙΔΩΡΟΣ in ex.; all within laurel-wreath. *B.M.C. 14.* 196, 124 ..   ..   £10

4520 — — Cultus-statue of Apollo Didymaios, naked, stg. r., holding stag and bow; ΜΙ monogram in lower field to r.   R. Lion seated r., looking back at star in upper field; ΜΙ monogram before, ΑΙΣΧΥΛΙΝΟΣ in ex. *B.M.C. 14.* 197, 134-5 ..   ..   ..   £12

4521 — Æ 18.   Similar, but without ΜΙ monogram on *obv.* and *rev.*, and with ΜΙΛΗϹΙωΝ in ex. instead of magistrate's name. *B.M.C. 14.* 197, 138-40 ..   ..   ..   £11

4523   4525   4526

4522 **Myus** (situated on the south bank of the Maeander, north-east of Miletos).   350-300 B.C. Æ 15.   Laur. hd. of Apollo r.   R. Goose stg. r., ΜΥΗ above; all within circular Maeander pattern. *Babelon (Traité) pl.* 149, 30 ..   ..   £22

4523 — Æ 11.   *Obv.* Similar.   R. Dolphin r.; ΜΥ above, trident below. *Forrer/Weber* 6065   £18

4524 — — Similar, but with *obv.* type laur. hd. of Poseidon r.   *S.N.G. Von Aulock* 2114-5   £18

4525 **Naulochos** (a small coastal town situated south of Priene).   Mid-4th cent. B.C.   Æ 11. Hd. of Athena r., in crested helmet.   R. Dolphin r., ΝΑΥ below; all within circular Maeander pattern. *B.M.C. 14.* 202, 1-2 ..   ..   £18

4526 **Phokaia** (a coastal city of considerable importance, situated forty miles north-west of Smyrna, Phokaia was one of the first mints, producing electrum coinage from early in the 6th cent. B.C.   Electrum hektai (sixth-staters) were issued in great quantity at Phokaia from the late 6th cent. until the time of Alexander, a series that was produced in conjunction with the Lesbian mint of Mytilene).   480-400 B.C.   Electrum *sixth-stater* (*c.* 2·55 gm.).   Bearded hd. of the elder Kabeiros l., in conical pilos; behind, seal.   R. Quadripartite incuse square, of rough form. *B.M.C. 14.* 207, 32 ..   ..   £750

Phokaia *continued*

4527 — — Hd. of Hermes l., in petasos; behind, seal. ℞. As last. *B.M.C. 14.* 208, 35
£500

4528 — — Female hd. l., hair in sakkos; seal above (?). ℞. As last. *B.M.C. 14.* 212, 66
£450

4529   4531   4533

4529 — — Corinthian helmet l., ornamented with floral scroll; beneath, seal. ℞. As last.
   B.M.C. 14. 214, 76-7   ..   ..   £600

4530 400-330 B.C.   Electrum *sixth-stater* (*c.* 2·55 gm.).   Hd. of Athena l., wearing crested
   Corinthian helmet; beneath, seal.   ℞. Quadripartite incuse square, of more regular form.
   B.M.C. 14. 210, 48 ..   ..   £550

4531 — — Hd. of Demeter l., hair rolled and wreathed with corn; beneath, seal. ℞. As last.
   B.M.C. 14. 210, 49 ..   ..   £500

4532 — — Horned female hd. l., fillet across forehead and hanging from each horn; beneath,
   seal. ℞. As last. *B.M.C. 14.* 211, 57   ..   ..   £550

4533 — — Hd. of young Dionysos l., wreathed with ivy; beneath, seal. ℞. As last. *B.M.C.
   14.* 208, 36   ..   ..   £500

4534 350-300 B.C.   Æ *hemidrachm* (*c.* 1·88 gm.).   Hd. of Athena l., wearing crested helmet;
   beneath, seal.   ℞. Hd. of griffin l., ΦΩ monogram before.   *Babelon* (*Traité*) *pl.* 157, 1
£350

4535 3rd cent. B.C.   Æ *tetradrachm* (*c.* 16·75 gm.), restoring the types of Alexander the Great.
   Hd. of young Herakles r., clad in lion's skin. ℞. Zeus enthroned l., holding eagle and
   sceptre, ΑΛΕΞΑΝΔΡΟΥ behind; before, seal r. and ΦΩ monogram.   *Müller* (*Numismatique
   d'Alexandre le Grand*) 983   ..   ..   £225

4536 *Bronze Coinage.* 350-300 B.C.   Æ 16.   Similar to 4534.   *Babelon* (*Traité*) *pl.* 157, 3
£15

4537   4539   4543

4537 — Æ 14.   Hd. of nymph Phokaia l., hair in sphendone. ℞. Hd. of griffin l. *B.M.C. 14.*
   216, 92   ..   ..   £14

4538 3rd-2nd cent. B.C.   Æ 17.   Hd. of Athena r., in crested Corinthian helmet. ℞. Griffin
   walking r., one of the caps of the Dioskouroi in upper field to l.; in ex., ΦΩΚΑΙΕ / ΩΝ.
   B.M.C. 14. 218, 109   ..   ..   £11

4539 — Æ 15.   Dr. bust of Hermes r., wearing petasos. ℞. Forepart of griffin r.; Φ — Ω in
   field, ΤΙΜΟΘΕΟΣ below. *B.M.C. 14.* 217, 107-8 ..   ..   £11

4540 — Æ 11.   Hd. of Hermes l., wearing petasos tied under chin. ℞. Large ΦΩ monogram.
   B.M.C. 14. 217, 98 ..   ..   £10

4541 **Phygela** (a small coastal town situated south-west of Ephesos). *Circa* 350 B.C. Æ
tetradrachm (*c.* 14 gm.). Hd. of Artemis Munychia three-quarter face to l. Ŗ. Bull
butting r., palm tree behind; ΦΥΓΕΛΕΩΝ above, magistrate's name in ex. *Babelon* (*Traité*)
pl. 152, 1 .. .. (*Unique ?*)

4542 — Æ 14. Hd. of Artemis Munychia three-quarter face to l., wearing stephanos. Ŗ.
Bull butting l., palm tree before; ΦΥΓ above, ΣΩΚΡΑΤΗΣ in ex. *B.M.C. 14.* 228, 5-8
£16

4543 — Æ 11. Diad. hd. of Artemis Munychia r. Ŗ. Bull butting r.; ΦΥ above, astragalos
and A beneath. *B.M.C. 14.* 228, 1 .. .. £15

4544   4545

4544 **Priene** (south of Ephesos, on the southern slopes of Mt. Mykale, Priene possessed a
celebrated temple of Athena Polias, dedicated by Alexander the Great in 334 B.C.).
290-270 B.C. Æ *octobol* (*c.* 4·9 gm.). Hd. of Athena Polias l., wearing triple-crested
helmet. Ŗ. Trident-head between ΠΡΙΗ and ΚΛΕΟΜ; all within circular Maeander
pattern. *B.M.C. 14.* 229, 3 .. .. £350

4545 — Æ *drachm* (*c.* 3·65 gm.). Similar, but with magistrate's name ΛΥΣΑΓΟ instead of
ΚΛΕΟΜ on *rev. B.M.C. 14.* 229, 5 .. .. £300

4546 — Æ *tetrobol* (*c.* 2·35 gm.). Similar, but with magistrate's name ΙΩΙΛΟ on *rev. B.M.C. 14.*
229, 6 .. .. £200

4547 — Æ *hemidrachm* (*c.* 1·75 gm.). As 4545. *B.M.C. 14.* 229, 7 .. .. £150

4548 Late 3rd cent. B.C. Æ *tetradrachm* (*c.* 16·75 gm.), restoring the types of Alexander the
Great. Hd. of young Herakles r., clad in lion's skin. Ŗ. Zeus enthroned l., holding
eagle and sceptre, ΑΛΕΞΑΝΔΡΟΥ behind; before, trident-head and ΠΡΙ; beneath throne,
ΒΙ. *Müller* (*Numismatique d'Alexandre le Grand*) 1026 .. .. £200

4549 — — Similar, but with trident-head, ΠΡΙ and ΠΕΛΩ monogram in *rev.* field to l., and
Maeander pattern in ex. *Müller* 1030 .. .. £225

4549A 2nd cent. B.C. Æ *drachm* (*c.* 4·2 gm.). Hd. of Athena r., in crested helmet. Ŗ.
ΠΡΙΗΝΕΩΝ / ΑΝΑΞΙΛΑΣ either side of amphora. *S.N.G. Von Aulock* 7965 .. £400

4550   4553

4550 *Bronze Coinage.* 3rd cent. B.C. Æ 19. Hd. of Athena r., in crested helmet. Ŗ.
ΠΡΙΗ / ΑΙΑΝΤΙ in two lines, within circular Maeander pattern. *B.M.C. 14.* 230, 13
£12

4551 — Æ 17. Laur. hd. of Poseidon Helikonios r., trident behind neck. Ŗ. ΠΡΙΗΝΕΩΝ.
Owl stg. r. on olive-branch. *B.M.C. 14.* 230, 12 .. .. £14

4552 — — *Obv.* As 4550. Ŗ. ΠΡΙΗ / ΝΕΩΝ either side of tripod. *B.M.C. 14.* 230, 9
£12

4553 — Æ 14. Bust of Athena facing, in triple-crested helmet. Ŗ. ΠΡΙΗ / ΑΠΟΛΛΟΔΩ / ΡΟΥ
in three lines, within circular Maeander pattern. *B.M.C. 14.* 232, 34 .. .. £14

4554 2nd cent. B.C. Æ 20. *Obv.* As 4550. Ŗ. Owl stg. r. on amphora; star and ivy-leaf in
upper field to l. and to r.; ΠΡΙ — Η across central field; ΑΧΙΛΛΕΙ / ΔΗΣ beneath; all within
olive-wreath. *B.M.C. 14.* 233, 44 .. .. £11

4555 **Smyrna** (an important city at the head of the gulf of Smyrna, it was refounded by
Antigonos late in the 4th cent. B.C., nearly three centuries after the destruction of the
original settlement by Alyattes of Lydia.   It rose to be one of the great cultural centres
of the East in Roman times.   Smyrna claimed to be the birthplace of Homer).   Mid-4th
cent. B.C.   *Æ tetradrachm* (*c.* 15·06 gm.).   Laur. hd. of Apollo l.   ℞. ΣΜΥΡΝΑΙΩΝ around
lyre.   *Forrer/Weber* 6114 ..   .. (*Unique*)
   *This unique coin provides evidence of the existence of a prosperous community at Smyrna
almost half a century before the refounding by Antigonos.*

4556 2nd cent. B.C.   *Æ tetradrachm* (*c.* 16·85 gm.).   Turreted hd. of Kybele r.   ℞. ΙΜΥΡ /
NAIΩN in two lines, monogram beneath; all within oak-wreath.   *B.M.C. 14.* 237, 3
£650

4557 — — *Obv.* Similar.   ℞. Lion stg. r., ΙΜΥΡΝΑΙΩΝ above, ΗΡΑΚΛΕΙΔΗΣ beneath; all within
oak-wreath.   *B.M.C. 14.* 238, 6 ..   .. £850
4558 — *Æ drachm* (*c.* 4·05 gm.).   Laur. hd. of Apollo r.   ℞. Homer seated l., holding scroll on
knees and resting chin on r. hand, staff behind; ΙΜΥΡΝΑΙΩΝ behind, ΣΑΡΑΠΙΩΝ before.
B.M.C. 14. 238, 7 ..   .. £550

4559 189-133 B.C. (under the rule of the Pergamene kings Eumenes II, Attalos II and Attalos III). Æ *cistophoric tetradrachm* (*c.* 12·4 gm.). Cista mystica containing serpent; all within ivy-wreath. ℞. Bow in case between two coiled serpents; ΖΜΥΡ to l., monogram above, B and turreted hd. of Kybele r. to r. *B.M.C. 14.* 237, 2 .. .. £500

| 4560 | 4562 |

4560 *Bronze Coinage.* 288-280 B.C. (under the name **Eurydikeia**). Æ 17. Veiled hd. of Eurydike r. ℞. Tripod, surmounted by laurel-wreath; ΕΥΡΥΔΙΚΕΩΝ to l. *B.M.C. 14.* 56, 75-6 .. .. £25

  Lysimachos renamed Smyrna in honour of his daughter, Eurydike. The city reverted to its original name after Lysimachos' death.

4561 3rd cent., after 280 B.C. Æ 15. Laur. hd. of Apollo r. ℞. ΣΜΥΡ / ΝΑΙΩΝ either side of tripod. *B.M.C. 14.* 238, 9 .. .. £9

4562 — Æ 14. *Obv.* Similar. ℞. Lyre; ΣΜΥΡΝΑΙΩΝ to r., monogram within circle to l.; shrimp beneath. *B.M.C. 14.* 239, 13 .. .. £10

4563 — Æ 13. Turreted hd. of Kybele r. ℞. Krater surmounted by flaming vessel; ΣΜΥΡ and shrimp to l., ΣΥΜΜΑΧΟΣ to r. *B.M.C. 14.* 239, 15 .. .. £10

4564 2nd-1st cent. B.C. Æ 13. Laur. hd. of Apollo r. ℞. ΙΜΥΡΝΑΙΩΝ / ΠΑΡΑΜΟΝΟΣ either side of tripod. *B.M.C. 14.* 239, 17-18 .. .. £8

4565 — Æ 18. Turreted hd. of Kybele r. ℞. Statue of Aphrodite Stratonikis stg. r., l. arm resting on column and supporting Nike, sceptre at side; ΙΜΥΡΝΑΙΩΝ and Δ to r., ΜΗΤΡΟΔ-ΩΡΟΣ to l. *B.M.C. 14.* 240, 27 .. .. £10

| 4566 | 4568 |

4566 — — *Obv.* Similar, but within oak-wreath. ℞. Statue of Aphrodite Stratonikis stg. facing, holding sceptre in r. hand, l. resting on column and supporting Nike; ΙΜΥΡΝΑΙΩΝ and bird to r., ΠΡΩΤΟΓΕΝΗΣ to l. *B.M.C. 14.* 241, 46 .. .. £11

4567 — Æ 15. Laur. hd. of Apollo r. ℞. Hand in caestus; ΙΜΥΡΝΑΙΩΝ and palm to r., ΜΗΤΡΟΔΩΡΟΣ to l. *B.M.C. 14.* 242, 56 .. .. £10

4568 — Æ 13. *Obv.* Similar. ℞. Two hands in caestus, palm on either side; ΖΜΥΡΝΑΙΩΝ to l., ΑΡΤΕΜΩΝ to r. *B.M.C. 14.* 243, 61 .. .. £12

Smyrna *continued*

4569 — Æ 11.   Turreted hd. of Kybele r.   ℞. Portable altar, with conical cover; ΙΜΥΡ to r.,
ΔΗΜΗ to l.   *B.M.C. 14*. 243, 67   ..   ..   £9
4570 — — Laur. hd. of Apollo r.   ℞. Lyre; ΙΜΥΡ to r., ΑΠΟΛ to l.   *B.M.C. 14*. 244, 71   £8

4571   4575

4571 — Æ 21.   *Obv.* Similar.   ℞. Homer seated l., holding scroll on knees, r. hand raised
to chin, staff behind; ΙΜΥΡΝΑΙΩΝ to r., ΣΗΜΑΓΟΡΑΣ and monogram to l.   *B.M.C. 14*. 245,
98   ..   ..   £12
4572 — — Similar, but with magistrate's name ΕΡΜΟΚΛΗΣ / ΠΥΘΕΟΥ in *rev.* field to l., and
without monogram.   *B.M.C. 14*. 246, 103   ..   ..   £12
4573 — Æ 24.   Similar, but with magistrate's name ΜΗΤΡΟΔΩΡΟΣ and star in *rev.* field to l.
B.M.C. 14. 246, 111   ..   ..   £13
4574 — Æ 20.   Similar, but *obv.* type is within laurel-wreath, and without magistrate's name
or symbol on *rev.*   *B.M.C. 14*. 247, 116 ..   ..   £14
4575 87-85 B.C. (revolt against Rome — time of Mithradates Eupator).   Æ 24.   Diad. hd. of
Mithradates r.   ℞.   Nike advancing r., holding wreath and palm; ΖΜΥΡΝΑΙΩΝ before,
ΕΡΜΟΓΕΝΗΣ / ΦΡΙΞΟΣ behind.   *B.M.C. 14*. 247, 118   ..   ..   £30

4576   4579

4576 **Teos** (a coastal city north-west of Ephesos, Teos was abandoned *c.* 544 B.C. when the
Persians became masters of Ionia and the Teians migrated to Thrace, where they founded
Abdera.   After several years many of the settlers returned to the mother-city and Teos
remained a place of some importance through to Roman times.   The city boasted a
splendid temple of Dionysos, in the Ionic style, by Hermogenes).   470-450 B.C.   Æ *stater*
(*c.* 11·9 gm.).   Griffin, with curled wings, seated r., l. foreleg raised; before, forepart of
Pegasos r.   ℞. Quadripartite incuse square.   *B.M.C. 14*. 310, 6   ..   ..   £1,250
4577 — — Similar, but with legend ΤΗΙΟΝ on *obv.*, and with symbol panther's hd. facing
instead of Pegasos.   *B.M.C. 14*. 311, 19 ..   ..   £1,350
4578 — Æ *trihemiobol* (*c.* 1·48 gm.).   ΤΗ.   Griffin, with curled wings, seated r., l. foreleg
raised.   ℞. Quadripartite incuse square.   *B.M.C. 14*. 310, 12 ..   ..   ..   £125
4579 Late 5th cent. B.C.   Æ *stater* (*c.* 11·9 gm.).   ΤΗΙΟΝ.   Griffin, with pointed wings,
seated r., l. forepaw raised; above, bee.   ℞. Quadripartite incuse square.   *B.M.C. 14*.
312, 20   ..   ..   £1,400
4580 — Æ *obol* (*c.* 1 gm.).   Τ.   Griffin, as last; no symbol.   ℞. Δ — Ι / Ω — Ν in the four
quarters of 'mill-sail' incuse square.   *B.M.C. 14*. 312, 22   ..   ..   ..   £110

4581   4583

4581 Mid-4th cent. B.C. Æ *drachm* (c. 3·6 gm.). Griffin, with pointed wing, seated r., l. forepaw raised. ℞. ΘΙΩΝ and ΑΓ — ΝΩΝ on the cruciform divisions of quadripartite incuse square, the surface of each quarter granulated. *B.M.C. 14.* 312, 24-5   £250

4582 3rd cent. B.C. Æ *tetradrachm* (c. 16·75 gm.), restoring the types of Alexander the Great. Hd. of young Herakles r., clad in lion's skin. ℞. Zeus enthroned l., holding eagle and sceptre, ΑΛΕΞΑΝΔΡΟΥ behind; before, kantharos and ΘΗΙ; beneath throne, Π. *Müller (Numismatique d'Alexandre le Grand)* 1005   ..   ..   £250

4583 2nd cent. B.C. N *third-stater* (c. 2·85 gm.). Griffin springing r. ℞. Lyre; ΘΗΙ above, ΠΟΛΥΘΡΟΥΣ to r. *Jenkins (Ancient Greek Coins)* 690/91   ..   ..   ..   £1,750

4584   4588   4591

4584 — Æ *drachm* (c. 3·05 gm.). Griffin seated r., l. forepaw raised. ℞. Kantharos; ΘΗΙ above, ΑΡΙΣ — ΤΩΝΑΞ across lower field, beneath which monogram (to l.). *B.M.C. 14.* 313, 29   ..   ..   £200

4585 — Æ *hemidrachm* (c. 1·65 gm.). *Obv.* As 4583. ℞. As last, but with magistrate's name ΗΡΟΔ — ΟΤΟΣ across lower field, and without monogram; Ν in field to l., between kantharos and handle. *B.M.C. 14.* 313, 31   ..   ..   £140

4586 — — *Obv.* As 4584. ℞. Kantharos; ΘΗΙ above, ΔΙΟΓΕ — ΝΗΣ around, below. *B.M.C. 14.* 313, 27   ..   ..   £125

4587 — — Hd. of young Dionysos r., wreathed with ivy; thyrsos behind. ℞. Lyre; ΘΗΙ — ΩΝ across lower field. *B.M.C. 14.* 313, 26   ..   ..   £110

4588 *Bronze Coinage.* 3rd cent. B.C. Æ 18. Griffin seated r., l. foreleg raised. ℞. Kantharos, bunch of grapes above; Τ — Η in upper field, ΚΛΕ — ΩΝ across lower field. *B.M.C. 14.* 314, 34   ..   ..   £15

4589 — Æ 16. *Obv.* Similar. ℞. Monogram within ivy-wreath; beneath, ΘΗΙΩΝ. *S.N.G. Von Aulock* 2263   ..   ..   £14

4590 2nd-1st cent. B.C. Æ 15. Griffin springing r. ℞. Lyre; ΘΗΙΩΝ above, ΒΙ — ΩΝ across lower field. *B.M.C. 14.* 315, 40   ..   ..   £11

4591 — — Griffin seated r., l. forepaw raised. ℞. ΤΗ / ΙΩΝ in two lines within ivy-wreath. *B.M.C. 14.* 45-8   ..   ..   £10

4592 — Æ 12. *Obv.* As 4590. ℞. ΘΗΙ within ivy-wreath, ΔΗΜΗΤΡΙ above. *Forrer/Weber* 6225   ..   ..   £9

4593   4594

4593 **Chios** (the city of Chios, the chief settlement on the large and important island of the
same name, started producing coinage in the middle of the 6th century B.C. It had a
fine harbour and achieved great prosperity, as well as being a cultural centre. In 86 B.C.
the city was sacked by Mithradates' forces, but Sulla restored the place and thereafter
the Chians enjoyed special privileges under Roman rule). 480-460 B.C. Æ *didrachm*
(*c.* 7·9 gm.). Sphinx seated l., amphora before. Ŗ. Quadripartite incuse square.
B.M.C. 14. 328, 2-4   ..   ..   £300

4594 460-450 B.C. Æ *didrachm* (*c.* 7·9 gm.). Sphinx seated l., amphora surmounted by
bunch of grapes before; all on circular raised shield. Ŗ. As last. *B.M.C. 14.* 329,
6-11   ..   ..   £250

4595 — — Similar, but *obv.* type is enclosed by vine-wreath. *B.M.C. 14.* 329, 12   £350

4596 — Æ *tetrobol* (*c.* 2·62 gm.). As 4594. *B.M.C. 14.* 329, 13-16   ..   ..   £140

4597 *Circa* 440 B.C. Electrum *stater* (*c.* 15·34 gm.). Sphinx seated l., r. forepaw raised to
pluck bunch of grapes from encircling vine-wreath; amphora before. Ŗ. Quadripartite
incuse square, the surface of each quarter angled. *Kraay (Archaic and Classical Greek
Coins) pl.* 52, 889 ..   ..   (*Unique*)

     *This remarkable issue may represent a Chian attempt to circumvent the Athenian Coinage
Decree.*

                    4598   4599

4598 430-420 B.C. Æ *tetradrachm* (*c.* 15·25 gm.). As 4594. *B.M.C. 14.* 329, 5 ..   £2,500

4599 420-350 B.C. Æ *tetradrachm* (*c.* 15·25 gm.). Sphinx seated l., amphora surmounted by
bunch of grapes before; traces of raised shield, as on coins of preceding issue. Ŗ. Quadripartite incuse square, ΗΡΑΓΟΡΗΣ across one of the broad bands of division; striations
within each quarter. *B.M.C. 14.* 331, 30   ..   ..   £2,000

                    4600   4603

4600 — Æ *drachm* (*c.* 3·7 gm.). As 4594. *B.M.C. 14.* 330, 17-18 ..   ..   ..   £200

4601 — — Similar, but with ΗΓ monogram behind Sphinx on *obv.* *B.M.C. 14.* 330, 20-21
   £200

4602 — — Similar to 4594, but on *rev.* the surface of each quarter of incuse square is granulated. *B.M.C. 14.* 330, 24-6   ..   ..   £200

4603 — — *Obv.* As 4594. Ŗ. Quadripartite incuse square, ΣΩΣΤΡΑ across one of the broad
bands of division; granulation within each quarter. *B.M.C. 14.* 331, 38   ..   £240

4604 — — Similar to 4599, but with magistrate's name ΣΚΥΜΝΟΣ (retrograde) on *rev.* *B.M.C.*
   14. 331, 35 ..   ..   £240

4605   4609

4605 — Æ *hemidrachm* (*c.* 1·87 gm.). *Obv.* Similar to 4594, but with ΓΑ monogram behind
   Sphinx. ℞. Quadripartite incuse square, the surface of each quarter granulated. *B.M.C.*
   14. 330, 27 ..   ..   £140

4606 3rd-2nd cent. B.C. Æ *tetradrachm* (*c.* 16·75 gm.), restoring the types of Alexander the
   Great. Hd. of young Herakles r., clad in lion's skin. ℞. Zeus enthroned l., holding eagle
   and sceptre, ΑΛΕΞΑΝΔΡΟΥ behind; before, Sphinx seated l., and monogram. *Müller*
   (*Numismatique d'Alexandre le Grand*) 1080-90 ..   ..   £175

4607 — — Similar, but with Sphinx seated l. on amphora in *rev.* field to l., and ΕΥΚΛΕΩΝ in
   ex. *Müller* 1112 ..   ..   £200

4608 2nd cent. B.C. Æ *drachm* (*c.* 3·9 gm.). Sphinx seated l., bunch of grapes before.
   ℞. ΖΗΝΟΔΩΡΟΣ / ΧΙΟΣ either side of amphora, palm to l.; all within vine-wreath. *B.M.C.*
   14. 333, 50 ..   ..   £175

4609 — — Similar, but with magistrate's name ΔΕΡΚΥΛΟΣ instead of ΖΗΝΟΔΩΡΟΣ, cornucopiae
   instead of palm, and without vine-wreath encircling *rev.* *B.M.C. 14.* 334, 54-5   £150

4610   4613   4617

4610 *Bronze Coinage.* 4th cent. B.C. Æ 10. Sphinx seated l. ℞. Amphora between
   ΙΗΝΩΝ and ΧΙΟΣ. (*British Museum*) £13

4611 3rd cent. B.C. Æ 17. *Obv.* Similar. ℞. Vine-wreath encircling two bands placed
   crosswise, one inscribed ΧΙΟΣ, the other with magistrate's name. *B.M.C. 14.* 332,
   41-2 ..   ..   £15

4612 — Æ 10. *Obv.* Similar. ℞. Ivy-wreath encircling ΑΘΗ / ΧΙΟC above and below thyrsos
   l. *B.M.C. 14.* 332, 44 ..   ..   £14

4613 2nd-1st cent. B.C. Æ 18. Sphinx seated r., ear of corn before. ℞. Amphora between
   ΗΓΕΜΩΝ and ΧΙΟΣ; bunch of grapes in field to l. *B.M.C. 14.* 335, 60-61   ..   £12

4614 — — *Obv.* Similar, but bunch of grapes before. ℞. As last, but with magistrate's
   name ΚΗΦΙΣΙΑ instead of ΗΓΕΜΩΝ, and race-torch instead of grapes. *B.M.C. 14.* 335,
   69-70 ..   ..   £12

4615 — — Similar, but star before Sphinx on *obv.*, magistrate's name ΓΝΩΣΙΣ and symbol
   caduceus on *rev.* *B.M.C. 14.* 336, 75-6 ..   ..   £12

4616 — — Similar, but club before Sphinx on *obv.*, magistrate's name ΚΑΥΚΑΣ and symbol
   rudder on *rev.* *B.M.C. 14.* 336, 81 ..   ..   £12

4617 — Æ 14. Sphinx seated r., l. forepaw raised over bunch of grapes; beneath, caduceus.
   ℞. Amphora between ΑΙΣΧΙΝΗΣ and ΧΙΟΣ; all within vine-wreath. *B.M.C. 14.* 337,
   85 ..   ..   £10

4618 — — Sphinx seated r., club beneath. ℞. Amphora between ΤΡΥΦΩΝ and ΧΙΟΣ. *B.M.C.*
   14. 338, 97 ..   ..   £10

4619 — Æ 10. Sphinx seated r. ℞. Amphora between ΘΕΟΔΩ and ΧΙΟΣ; bunch of **grapes in**
   field. *B.M.C. 14.* 338, 98 ..   ..   £9

4620   4622

4620 **Oinoe** (the principal town of the island of Ikaria or Ikaros, situated west of Samos).
Circa 300 B.C.   Æ *drachm* (*c.* 3·34 gm.).   Bust of Artemis three-quarter face to r., quiver
at shoulder.   Ṛ. OINAI.   Bull butting r.   *Historia Numorum, p.* 602 ..   ..   £750

4621 — Æ 18.   Bust of Artemis r., bow and quiver at shoulder.   Ṛ. Bull butting r., OINAIΩN
in ex.   *B.M.C. 14.* 347, 1 ..   ..   £20

4622 — — Hd. of young Dionysos r., wreathed with ivy.   Ṛ. Bunch of grapes, OINAIΩN
beneath.   *B.M.C. 14.* 347, 2   ..   ..   £20

4623 — Æ 15.   Bull butting r.   Ṛ. Ram stg. r., OI above.   *S.N.G. Von Aulock* 2286   £16

4624   4626

4624 **Samos** (situated south-east of Chios, Samos was an island of great importance with a
long history of civilization stretching back to Mycenaean times.   Its principal settlement,
in the south-east of the island, bore the same name.   An ally of Athens in the earlier years
of the Delian League, the island revolted *c.* 440 B.C. but was captured and reduced by
Perikles after a long siege.   In 365 B.C. the Samians were expelled from their homes and
replaced by an Athenian kleruchy, after which the island never regained its former
importance.   Pythagoras was, perhaps, the most celebrated son of Samos).   480-470 B.C.
Æ *tetradrachm* (*c.* 13 gm.).   Lion's scalp facing.   Ṛ. Hd. of ox l., ΣA (retrograde) above;
all within incuse square.   *Barron* (*The Silver Coins of Samos*) *pl. VIII,* 8.   *B.M.C. 14.*
351, 22   ..   ..   £1,250

4625 — — Similar, but *rev.* type to r., and legend not retrograde.   *Barron, pl. VIII,* 13
£1,250

4626 470-460 B.C.   Æ *tetradrachm* (*c.* 13 gm.).   Lion's scalp facing.   Ṛ. Hd. of ox r., ΣA
above, amphora behind; all within incuse circle.   *Barron, pl. X,* 39.   *B.M.C. 14.* 353,
29 ..   ..   £1,250

4627 — Æ *hemidrachm* (*c.* 1·5 gm.).   Forepart of winged boar r.   Ṛ. Lion's hd. r., within
incuse square.   *Barron, pl. XV,* 12.   *B.M.C. 14.* 355, 62   ..   ..   ..   £100

4628 — Æ *diobol* (*c.* 1 gm.).   Hd. of panther l.   Ṛ. Ram's hd. r., within incuse square.   *Barron, pl. XVI,* 13.   *B.M.C. 14.* 356, 68   ..   ..   £120

4629   4630

4629 460-453 B.C. Æ *tetradrachm* (*c.* 13 gm.). Lion's scalp facing. Ʀ. Forepart of ox r., ΣΑ above, olive-branch behind; all within incuse square. *Barron, pl. XI,* 57. *B.M.C. 14.* 358, 91 .. .. £1,500

4630 — Æ *hemidrachm* (*c.* 1·3 gm.). Forepart of winged boar r. Ʀ. Lion's hd. r., ΣΑ behind, olive-branch beneath; all within incuse square. *Barron, pl. XV,* 26. *B.M.C. 14.* 359, 104 .. .. £90

4631 — Æ *diobol* (*c.* 0·9 gm.). Hd. of panther l. Ʀ. Ram's hd. r., ΣΑ above, olive-branch beneath; all within incuse square. *Barron, pl. XVI,* 15. *B.M.C. 14.* 360, 119 £120

4632 — Æ *obol* (*c.* 0·4 gm.). Diad. hd. of Hera r., hair confined by net. Ʀ. Lion's hd. r., ΣΑΜ behind; all within incuse square. *Barron, pl. XVI,* 1 .. .. .. (*Unique*)

4633 4636

4633 453-439 B.C. (dated series, years 2-15). Æ *tetradrachm* (*c.* 13 gm.). Lion's scalp facing. Ʀ. Forepart of ox r., ΣΑ above, olive-branch behind, Θ (= year 9 = 446/5 B.C.) before; all within incuse square. *Barron, pl. XIV,* 85. *B.M.C. 14.* 359, 95 .. .. £1,500

4634 — Æ *hemidrachm* (*c.* 1·3 gm.). Forepart of winged boar r. Ʀ. Lion's hd. r., ΣΑ (retrograde) above; all within incuse circle. *Barron, pl. XV,* 32. *B.M.C. 14.* 360, 109 £90

4635 — Æ *diobol* (*c.* 0·9 gm.). Hd. of panther l. Ʀ. Ram's hd. r., within incuse circle. *Barron, pl. XVI,* 19. *B.M.C. 14.* 356, 70-72 .. .. £120

4636 — Æ *trihemiobol* (*c.* 0·65 gm.). Prow of Samian galley r. Ʀ. Amphora; ΣΑ to l., olive-branch to r.; all within incuse circle. *Barron, pl. XVI,* 3. *B.M.C. 14.* 361, 120 £85

4637 — Æ *obol* (*c.* 0·45 gm.). Lion's scalp facing. Ʀ. Hd. of ox r., within incuse circle. *Barron, pl. XVI,* 4. *B.M.C. 14.* 357, 80 .. .. £75

4638 *Circa* 420 B.C. Æ *tetradrachm* (*c.* 13 gm.). Lion's scalp facing. Ʀ. Forepart of ox r., olive-branch behind, ΕΠΙΒΑΤΙ / ΟΣ above and beneath ox's hd.; all within incuse circle. *Barron, pl. XIV,* 97 .. .. £3,000

This rare issue, which lacks the name of Samos, may have been struck on the Ionian mainland by the Samian oligarchs in exile.

4639 4640

4639 412-404 B.C. (period of the Athenian Alliance). Æ *tetradrachm* (*c.* 17 gm.). Lion's scalp facing. Ʀ. Forepart of ox r., ΣΑΜΙ above, olive-branch behind, ΑΡ monogram before; all within incuse square. *Barron, pl. XVII,* 99. *B.M.C. 14.* 361, 126 £2,500

4640 — Æ *drachm* (*c.* 4·25 gm.). *Obv.* Similar. Ʀ. Forepart of ox r., ΣΑΜΙ above, olive-spray before; all within incuse square. *Barron, pl. XVII,* 1. *B.M.C. 14.* 361, 127 £350

Samos *continued*

4641 — Æ *hemidrachm* (*c.* 2·1 gm.). *Obv.* Similar. ℞. Hd. of ox r., ΣΑ above; encircled by olive-wreath, and all within incuse circle. *Barron, pl. XVII, 2* £200

4642 — Æ *obol* (*c.* 0·7 gm.). *Obv.* Similar. ℞. Hd. of ox r., ΣΑ above, A beneath; all within incuse square. *Barron, pl. XVII, 1* £100

4643   4645

4643 400-365 B.C. Æ *tetradrachm* (*c.* 15·25 gm.). Lion's scalp facing. ℞. Forepart of ox r., ΗΓΗΣΙΑΝΑΞ above, olive-branch behind, monogram within circle beneath, ΣΑ before; all within shallow incuse square. *Barron, pl. XIX, 129. B.M.C. 14. 362, 134* .. £1,750

4644 — — Similar, but on *rev.*, ΠΡΩ above ox, olive-branch behind, and ΣΑ before. *Barron, pl. XVIII, 106. B.M.C. 14. 362, 130* £1,800

4645 — Æ *tridrachm* (*c.* 11·45 gm.). ΣΥΝ. Infant Herakles kneeling r., grappling with two snakes. ℞. Lion's scalp facing, ΣΑ beneath; all within incuse circle. *Barron, pl. XXII, 1. B.M.C. 14. 362, 1* £4,000
    Coins with similar obverse type were issued between 394 and 387 B.C. by a number of cities—Byzantion, Kyzikos, Ephesos, Knidos, Rhodos and Iasos—as members of an alliance dedicated to their liberation from oppression; though who the oppressor was is not certain.

4646 — Æ *drachm* (*c.* 3·8 gm.). Lion's scalp facing. ℞. Forepart of ox r., ΗΓΗΣΙΑ above, ΣΑ before beneath which, A within circle; all within incuse square. *Barron, pl. XXII, 3. B.M.C. 14. 363, 136* £300

4647 — Æ *hemidrachm* (*c.* 1·8 gm.). Lion's scalp facing. ℞. Forepart of ox r., ΛΟΧ above, ΣΑ before; all within incuse square. *Barron, pl. XXII, 4. B.M.C. 14. 363, 139* £140

4648   4649

4648 — Æ *diobol* (*c.* 1·1 gm.). Lion's scalp facing. ℞. Prow of Samian galley r., ΣΑ beneath; all within incuse circle. *Barron, pl. XXII, 4. B.M.C. 14. 363, 141* £125

4649 — Æ *trihemiobol* (*c.* 0·8 gm.). Diad. hd. of Hera r. ℞. Lion's scalp facing, ΣΑ beneath. *Barron, pl. XXII, 2. Forrer/Weber 6309* £120

4650 — Æ *obol* (*c.* 0·55 gm.). Lion's scalp facing. ℞. Hd. of ox r., ΣΑ before; all within incuse square. *Barron, pl. XXII, 1-2* £85

4651 — — — ℞. Forepart of ox r., ΣΑ above; all within incuse circle. *Barron, pl. XXII, 4-5* £85

4652   4655

4652 *Circa* 300 B.C. Æ *didrachm* (*c.* 6·5 gm.). Lion's scalp facing. R. Forepart of ox r.; ΛΕΟΝΤΙΣΚΟΣ above, ΣΑ beneath, olive-branch before. *Barron, pl. XXIII*, 3. *B.M.C. 14.* 365, 164 .. .. £400

4653 — — Similar, but with magistrate's name ΜΕΛΑΝΤΗΣ on *rev.* *Barron, pl. XXIII*, 14. *B.M.C. 14.* 365, 165 .. .. £400

4654 — Æ *drachm* (*c.* 3·5 gm.). *Obv.* Similar. R. Forepart of ox r.; ΑΙΓΥΠΤΟΣ above, ΣΑ before. *Barron, pl. XXIV*, 2 .. .. £225

4655 — Æ *hemidrachm* (*c.* 1·65 gm.). Similar, but with magistrate's name ΔΗΜΑΓΗΤΟΣ on *rev.* *Barron, pl. XXV*, 5. *B.M.C. 14.* 363, 138 .. .. £120

4656 — Æ *trihemiobol* (*c.* 0·8 gm.). Diad. hd. of Hera l. R. Prow of Samian galley r., ΑΛΕΞΑΝΔΡΟΣ beneath. *Barron, pl. XXV*, 1 .. .. £120

4657   4659

4657 270-240 B.C. Æ *octobol* (*c.* 4·65 gm.). Lion's scalp facing, within border of dots. R. Forepart of ox r.; ΣΑΜΙΩΝ above, olive-spray before, trident and prow beneath. *Barron, pl. XXV*, 2. *B.M.C. 14.* 366, 174 .. .. £300

4658 — — Similar, but with krater beneath ox on *rev.* *Barron, pl. XXVI*, 25 .. £300

4659 — Æ *tetrobol* (*c.* 2·3 gm.). Diad. hd. of Hera l. R. Prow of Samian galley r.; trident above, ΣΑΜΙΩΝ beneath. *Barron, pl. XXVII*, 1 .. .. £200

4660 — Æ *diobol* (*c.* 1 gm.). *Obv.* As 4657. R. Forepart of ox r.; ΣΑΜΙΩΝ above, trident behind, olive-spray before. *Barron, pl. XXVII*, 1-2 .. .. £90

4661 *Circa* 200 B.C. Æ *tetradrachm* (*c.* 16·75 gm.), restoring the types of Alexander the Great. Hd. of young Herakles r., clad in lion's skin. R. Zeus enthroned l., holding eagle and sceptre, ΑΛΕΞΑΝΔΡΟΥ behind; before, prow of Samian galley l. surmounted by krater, and ΣΑ. *Barron, pl. XXVII*, 1 .. .. £275

4662 — — — Similar, but before seated Zeus, prow of Samian galley l. and B. *Barron, pl. XXVIII*, 11. Müller (*Numismatique d'Alexandre le Grand*) 1126 .. .. £250

4663   4664A

4663 — Æ *tetrobol* (*c.* 2·9 gm.). Lion's scalp facing, within border of dots. R. Forepart of ox r.; ΣΑΜΙΩΝ above, ear of corn before, peacock r. and krater beneath; all within border of dots. *Barron, pl. XXVIII*, 11. *B.M.C. 14.* 367, 177 .. .. .. £120

4664 — Æ *diobol* (*c.* 1·45 gm.). Diad. hd. of Hera r., within border of dots. R. Prow of Samian galley l.; ΣΑΜΙΩΝ beneath, peacock l. before, trident above; all within border of dots. *Barron, pl. XXX*, 1. *B.M.C. 14.* 367, 184 .. .. £130

4664A 2nd cent. B.C. Æ *tetradrachm* (*c.* 16·75 gm.). Laur. hd. of Zeus r. R. Cultus-statue of Samian Hera facing; to r., ΣΑΜΙΩΝ; to l., monogram and prow of Samian galley l. (*British Museum*) .. .. (*Unique ?*)

Samos *continued*

4665 *Bronze Coinage.* Late 5th cent. B.C. Æ 8. Prow of Samian galley r. R. Σ — A either side of amphora; all within olive-wreath. *Barron, p.* 99 *and pl. XVII.* B.M.C. 14. 361, 125 .. .. £15

4666   4669

4666 4th cent., before 365 B.C. Æ 14. Diad. hd. of Hera l. R. Lion's scalp facing, ΣΑ beneath. *Barron, p.* 115. B.M.C. 14. 364, 147-9 .. .. £14

4667 Early 3rd cent. B.C. Æ 18. Diad. hd. of Hera r. R. Lion's scalp facing, MIKIΩN beneath. *Barron, p.* 134 *and pl. XXXI,* 2. B.M.C. 14. 365, 166 .. .. £14

4668 — Æ 15. Circular shield. R. As last, but with magistrate's name ΠΑΡΙΣ. *Barron, p.* 134 *and pl. XXXI,* 3 .. .. £20

4669 — — Diad. hd. of Hera l. R. Lion's scalp facing, ΠΕΛΥΣΙΟΣ beneath. *Barron, p.* 134 *and pl. XXXI,* 4. B.M.C. 14. 365, 170 .. .. £12

4670 — Æ 11. Diad. hd. of Hera facing. R. As last, but with magistrate's name ΣΙΜΟΣ. *Barron, p.* 134. B.M.C. 14. 366, 172 .. .. £12

4671 — Æ 14. Diad. hd. of Hera r. R. Prow of Samian galley r., ΣΑ above, ΙΕΡΩΝ beneath. *Barron, p.* 135 *and pl. XXXI,* 6. B.M.C. 14. 366, 173 .. .. £11

4672 — — Diad. hd. of Hera three-quarter face to r. R. Prow of Samian galley l., ΣΑ above, ΠΑΓΡΩΝ beneath. *Barron, p.* 135 *and pl. XXXI,* 7 .. .. £13

4673   4676

4673 Mid-3rd cent. B.C. Æ 11. Diad. hd. of Hera r. R. Lion's scalp facing, ΣΑΜΙΩΝ beneath. *Barron, p.* 142 *and pl. XXXI,* 9. B.M.C. 14. 368, 190 .. .. £10

4674 Late 3rd-early 2nd cent. B.C. Æ 13. Diad. hd. of Hera facing. R. Prow of Samian galley r., ΣΑΜΙΩΝ beneath. *Barron, p.* 149 *and pl. XXXI,* 10. B.M.C. 14. 368, 193 £11

4675 — Æ 9. Prow r. R. Prow l., upon which peacock stg. on krater; beneath, ΣΑΜΙΩΝ. *Barron, p.* 149 *and pl. XXXI,* 11. B.M.C. 14. 368, 197 .. .. £9

4676 2nd-1st cent. B.C. Æ 18. Laur. and diad. hd. of Hera r. R. Peacock stg. r. on caduceus, transverse sceptre in background; ΣΑΜΙΩΝ beneath, monograms behind, above and before. B.M.C. 14. 369, 203 .. .. £14

4677 **LYDIA** (the later kings of Persia, successors of Darius I, continued in the traditions established by that monarch, issuing gold darics and silver sigloi for circulation in western Anatolia. The Lydian capital of Sardeis, the centre of Persian power in the area, was undoubtedly the principal mint, though other cities may have assisted in the production of this enormous coinage. The kneeling archer, with oblong punch on reverse, remained the sole type for this Persian imperial coinage down to Alexander's conquest in 330 B.C.). PERSIAN IMPERIAL COINAGE. *Circa* 486-450 B.C. (period of Xerxes-Artaxerxes I). N *daric* (*c.* 8·35 gm.). Bearded archer (the Great King) kneeling r., holding spear and bow; two small pellets appear behind the beard. R. Oblong punch. *Babelon (Traité)* pl. 86, 10 .. .. £1,250

[For earlier darics and sigloi see page 321]

4678   4679

4678 — Æ *siglos* (*c.* 5·35 gm.). Similar. *Babelon* , *pl.* 86, 11 .. .. .. £100

4679 *Circa* 450-330 B.C. (period of Artaxerxes I-Darius III). N *daric* (*c.* 8·35 gm.). Similar, but without the two pellets on *obv. Babelon, pl.* 86, 19-21 .. .. .. £900

4680 — — Bearded archer (the Great King) kneeling r., holding dagger and bow. ℞. Oblong punch. *Babelon, pl.* 87, 17 .. .. £1,100

4681   4683   4685

4681 — — *Beardless* archer (the Great King) kneeling r., holding spear and bow. ℞. Oblong punch, beside which mask of bearded and horned Pan l., incuse. *Babelon, pl.* 86, 16-17. *B.M.C. 28.* 156, 61 .. .. £3,000

4682 — Æ *siglos* (*c.* 5·55 gm.). As 4679. *Babelon, pl.* 86, 13-15 .. .. .. £75

4683 — — As 4680. *Babelon, pl.* 87, 18-19 .. .. £85

N.B. *Many sigloi bear small countermarks, possibly the signets of money changers. A large number of emblems have been recorded, and as many as five may sometimes appear on a single specimen. The darics and sigloi with the archer holding a dagger (nos. 4680 and 4683) may have been produced by a secondary mint in southern or south-western Asia Minor.*

4684 **Aninetos** (situated east of Mastaura, on the southern slope of the Messogis). 2nd-1st cent. B.C. Æ 18. Laur. hd. of Apollo r. ℞. ΑΝΙΝΗΣΙΩΝ. Horse stg. l., palm in background; ΔΙΟ — ΔΟ in lower field. *B.M.C. 22.* 17, 1 .. .. £18

4685 — Æ 17. Turreted hd. of Tyche r. ℞. ΑΝΙΝΗΣΙΩΝ. Horse prancing r., ΑΡΚΑ beneath. *S.N.G. Von Aulock* 2894 .. .. £16

4686   4688

4686 **Apollonis** (situated north-west of Sardeis, mid-way between that city and Pergamon). 130 B.C. Æ *cistophoric tetradrachm* (*c.* 12·6 gm.), in the name of the Pergamene pretender Eumenes III (Aristonikos). Cista mystica containing serpent; all within ivy-wreath. ℞. Bow in case between two coiled serpents, thunderbolt between their heads; to l., bearded hd. of Zeus l.; to r., hd. of Apollo (?) r.; within coils of serpents, ΒΑ — ΕΥ, with Δ (=year 4) between; beneath, ΑΠ — ΟΛ. *B.M.C. 22.* 18, 1 .. .. £450

4687 2nd-1st cent. B.C. Æ 20. Turreted hd. of Tyche r. ℞. Zeus enthroned l., holding eagle and sceptre; ΑΠΟΛΛΩΝΙΔΕΩΝ behind. *S.N.G. Von Aulock* 2898 .. .. £17

4688 — Æ 15. Hd. of young Herakles r., clad in lion's skin. ℞. ΑΠΟΛΛΩ / ΝΙΔΕΩΝ above and below winged thunderbolt. *B.M.C. 22.* 19, 4 .. .. £15

4689   4692

4689 **Blaundos** (originally a Macedonian fortress, Blaundos was built on a rocky promontory commanding two narrow ravines, close to the Phrygian border). 2nd-1st cent. B.C. Æ 20. Laur. hd. of Zeus r. ℞. ΜΛΑΥΝΔΕΩΝ / ΘΕΟΤΙΜΙΔΟ above and below eagle stg. l. between caduceus and corn-ear. *B.M.C. 22.* 42, 1-2 ..   ..   £12

4690 — Æ 18.   Hd. of young Dionysos r., wreathed with ivy. ℞. ΜΛΑΥΝΔΕΩΝ — ΑΠΟΛΛΩΝ / ΘΕΟΓΕΝ either side of thyrsos. *B.M.C. 22.* 43, 11   ..   ..   ..   £10

4691 — Æ 17.   Laur. hd. of Apollo l.; fillet border. ℞. ΜΛΑΥΝΔ / ΑΠΟΛΛΩ either side of quiver, bow and laurel-branch. *B.M.C. 22.* 44, 15   ..   ..   ..   £11

4692 — — Laur. hd. of Zeus r. ℞. Hermes stg. l., holding purse and caduceus; ΜΛΑΥΝΔΕΩΝ behind, two monograms before; all within laurel-wreath. *B.M.C. 22.* 44, 20..   £11

4693 — Æ 15.   *Obv.* Similar. ℞. ΜΛΑΥΝ / ΔΕΩΝ either side of female figure stg. facing, feeding serpent from phiale and holding cornucopiae. *B.M.C. 22.* 45, 28   ..   £9

4694 — Æ 14.   Bearded hd. of Herakles r. ℞. ΜΛΑΥΝΔΕΩΝ / ΘΕΟΤΙΜΙΔΟ either side of club. *B.M.C. 22.* 42, 5   ..   ..   £9

4695   4698

4695 **The Kaÿstrianoi** (coins issued in the name of the inhabitants of the plain of the lower Kaÿster). 2nd-1st cent. B.C. Æ 19. ΣΩΣΙΚΡΑΤΟΥ behind laur. hd. of Apollo r. ℞. ΚΑΥΣΤΡΙΑ / ΝΩΝ either side of winged caduceus; monogram in upper field to r. *B.M.C. 22.* 60, 1   ..   ..   £16

4696 — Æ 18.   Turreted hd. of Tyche r. ℞. ΚΑΥΣΤΡΙΑΝΩΝ. Lyre, formed from bucranium; monogram to r. *B.M.C. 22.* 60, 5   ..   ..   £15

4697 — Æ 14.   Hd. of young Dionysos r., wreathed with ivy. ℞. As last, but with monograms in field to l. and to r. *B.M.C. 22.* 61, 7   ..   ..   £14

4698 **Klannudda** (originally a Seleukid stronghold, Klannudda was close to the Phrygian border, about fifteen miles north of Blaundos). 2nd-1st cent. B.C. Æ 20. Laur. hd. of Zeus r. ℞. Eagle stg. r. on thunderbolt, ΚΛΑ — Ν / ΝΟΥΔ — ΔΕ / ΩΝ in field; all within laurel-wreath. *B.M.C. 22.* 68, 2 ..   ..   £20

4699 — Æ 16.   Laur. hd. of Apollo r. ℞. ΚΛΑΝΝΟΥΔ / ΔΕΩΝ either side of cultus-statue of Artemis Anaitis facing; all within laurel-wreath. *S.N.G. Von Aulock* 2996   ..   £17

4700 — Æ 14.   Dr. bust of Hermes r., wearing petasos. ℞. Humped bull butting l., eagle (?) stg. on hump; ΚΛΑΝΝΟΥΔ / ΔΕΩΝ beneath. *B.M.C. 22.* 68, 1   ..   £15

4701 **Magnesia ad Sipylum** (on the northern slopes of Mt. Sipylus, north-east of Smyrna, Magnesia was the scene of the famous defeat of Antiochos the Great by the Romans in 190 B.C.). 2nd cent. B.C. Æ 20. Laur. hd. of bearded Herakles r. ℞. ΜΑΓΝΗΤΩΝ / ΣΙΠΥΛΟΥ either side of Athena stg. l., holding Nike and resting on shield; monogram in upper field to l. *B.M.C. 22.* 138, 9   ..   ..   £12

4702   4703

4702 — Æ 19.   Turreted hd. of Kybele (or Tyche) r.   ℞. ΜΑΓΝΗΤΩΝ / ΣΙΠΥ either side of
Zeus Lydios stg. l., holding eagle and sceptre; monogram in lower field to l.   *B.M.C. 22.*
137, 4 . .   . .   £13

4703 — Æ 17.   Diad. hd. of Artemis r., bow and quiver behind neck.   ℞. Zeus and Hermes
stg. facing, holding sceptre between them; ΣΙΠΥΛΟΥ above, ΜΑΓΝΗΤΩΝ in ex., monogram
to l.   *B.M.C. 22.* 138, 6 . .   . .   £13

4704 — — Laur. hd. of Zeus r.   ℞. ΜΑΓΝΗΤΩΝ — ΤΩΝ ΠΡΟΣ / ΣΙΠΥΛΩΙ either side of Demeter
stg. l., holding corn-ears and sceptre; monogram in upper field to l.   *B.M.C. 22.* 139,
12 . .   . .   £11

4705 — Æ 14.   *Obv.* Similar.   ℞. ΜΑΓΝΗΤΩΝ / ΣΙΠΥΛΟΥ either side of omphalos, around which
serpent twines; monogram beneath.   *B.M.C. 22.* 137, 1 . .   . .   . .   £11

4706 — Æ 12.   *Obv.* Similar.   ℞. ΜΑ / ΣΙΠΥ either side of bunch of grapes; monogram
beneath.   *B.M.C. 22.* 137, 3 . .   . .   £9

4707 **Mostene** (the site of this town has not been located with certainty, but it may have been
in the valley cf the Hermos, north-west of Sardeis).   2nd-1st cent. B.C.   Æ 20.   Laur.
hd. of Zeus r.   ℞. Male rider on horse pacing r., double-axe over shoulder; ΛΥΔΩΝ above,
ΜΟΣΤΗΝΩΝ in ex.; monograms in field to l. and to r.   *B.M.C. 22.* 161, 1 . .   £18

4708 — Æ 15.   Veiled hd. of Demeter r., wreathed with corn; behind, ear of corn.   ℞.
ΛΥΔΩΝ ΜΟΣΤΗΝΩΝ.   Ear of corn, dividing Μ — Ε; all within wreath.   *B.M.C. 22.* 161,
3-4 . .   . .   £16

4709 **Nysa** (originally named Athymbra, after its Spartan founder, Nysa was situated east of
Tralleis and was one of the principal cities of the Maeander valley.   It was re-named
under Antiochos I in honour of one of the wives of that King).   After 133 B.C.   Æ
cistophoric tetradrachm (c. 12·6 gm.).   Cista mystica containing serpent; all within ivy-
wreath.   ℞. Bow in case between two coiled serpents; to l., ΝΥ; above, ΑΝ / ΝΕΩΤΕ / ΡΟΣ;
to r., ΚΓ (= year 23 = 112/111 B.C.) and figure of Kore stg. r.   *B.M.C. 22.* 170, 1-2
£350

4710 — Æ *drachm* (c. 3·15 gm.).   Club draped in lion's skin; all within vine-wreath.   ℞.
Bunch of grapes upon vine-leaf; ΝΥΣΑ to l.   *B.M.C. 22.* 170, 3 . .   . .   £250

4711   4713

Nysa *continued*

4711 2nd-1st cent. B.C. Æ 23. ΝΥΣΑΕΩΝ. Laur. hd. of Hades r. R. ΠΑΙΩΝΙΟΣ / ΑΘΗΝΑΓ-
ΟΡΑΣ — ΦΙΛΟΚΡΑΤΗΣ either side of Kore stg. l., holding sceptre. *B.M.C. 22.* 171, 4
£18

4712 — Æ 22. Veiled bust of Kore r., wreathed with corn. R. ΝΥΣΑΕΩΝ / ΒΑΚΧΙΟΣ either
side of naked slinger stg. r., r. hand raised adjusting sling. *B.M.C. 22.* 172, 13-14
£17

4713 — Æ 18. Jugate hds. r. of Hades, laur., and Kore, veiled. R. ΝΥΣΑΕΩΝ / ΣΙΜΩΝ either
side of Dionysos advancing r., holding kantharos and thyrsos. *B.M.C. 22.* 172, 10
£15

4714 — — Hd. of young Dionysos r., wreathed with ivy. R. ΝΥΣΑΕΩΝ. Hades in galloping
quadriga r., carrying off struggling Persephone, who drops her flower-basket (the rape of
Persephone); ΣΙΜΩΝ in ex. *B.M.C. 22.* 173, 16 ..   ..   £15

4715 — Æ 11. Laur. hd. of Hades r. R. N — Y. Bunch of grapes upon vine-leaf. *B.M.C.
22.* 171, 8   ..   ..   £10

4716 — — Humped bull walking r. R. ΝΥϹΑ / ΕΩΝ. Kalathos, containing flowers. *B.M.C.
22.* 173, 19   ..   ..   £11

4717   4720   4723

4717 **Philadelpheia** (founded by Attalos II Philadelphos, King of Pergamon 159-138 B.C.,
Philadelpheia was situated south-east of Sardeis and commanded the important valley of
the Kogamis). 2nd-1st cent. B.C. Æ 23. Diad. and dr. bust of Artemis r., bow and
quiver at shoulder. R. Apollo stg. r., holding plectrum and lyre; ΦΙΛΑΔΕΛΦΕΩΝ before,
ΕΡΜΙΠΠΟΣ / ΑΡΧΙΕΡΕΥΣ behind. *B.M.C. 22.* 188, 13 ..   ..   ..   £14

4718 — — *Obv.* Similar. R. Apollo enthroned l., holding phiale and resting l. elbow on
lyre, owl perched on back of throne; ΦΙΛΑΔΕΛΦΕΩΝ behind, ΕΡΜΙΠΠΟΣ / ΕΡΜΟΓΕΝΟΥΣ
before, ΑΡΧΙΕΡΕΥΣ in ex. *B.M.C. 22.* 188, 11 ..   ..   £14

4719 — Æ 17. Hd. of Zeus r., bound with tainia. R. ΦΙΛΑΔΕΛ / ΦΕΩΝ either side of lyre,
monogram above, plectrum beneath; all within laurel-wreath. *B.M.C. 22.* 187, 5-7
£12

4720 — — ΦΙΛΑΔΕΛΦΕΩΝ. Hd. of young Dionysos r., wreathed with ivy. R. Pantheress l.,
looking back, thyrsos in background; ΑΡΧΙΕΡΕΥΣ around, ΕΡΜΙΠΠΟΣ in ex. *B.M.C. 22.*
189, 16   ..   ..   £13

4721 — — *Obv.* Similar, but without legend. R. ΦΙΛΑΔΕΛ / ΦΕΩΝ either side of thyrsos;
monogram in upper field to l. *B.M.C. 22.* 189, 17-18 ..   ..   ..   £12

4722 — — Jugate hds. of the Dioskouroi r., laur. R. Caps of the Dioskouroi, surmounted by
stars; monogram between, ΦΙΛΑΔΕΛΦΕΩΝ beneath. *B.M.C. 22.* 189, 19-22 ..   £13

4723 — Æ 15. Circular shield, of 'Macedonian' design. R. ΦΙΛΑΔΕΛ / ΦΕΩΝ above and
beneath thunderbolt, monogram in upper field; all within olive-wreath. *B.M.C. 22.* 187,
1   ..   ..   £14

4724 **Sardeis** (the ancient capital of the Lydian Kings, Sardeis lay under a fortified hill in the Hermos valley, at an important road junction. In the pre-Alexandrine age it was the centre of the principal Persian satrapy, and in all probability the mint-place of much of the Persian imperial coinage of darics and sigloi. In 189 B.C. it came under the rule of the Attalids of Pergamon, and fifty-six years later it passed to the Romans). 3rd cent. B.C. Æ *tetradrachm* (c. 16·75 gm.), restoring the types of Alexander the Great. Hd. of young Herakles r., clad in lion's skin. ℞. Zeus enthroned l., holding eagle and sceptre, ΑΛΕΞΑΝΔ-ΡΟΥ behind; before, turreted and veiled bust of Tyche l. *Jenkins* (*Ancient Greek Coins*) 581/2 .. .. £250

4725   4727

4725 189-133 B.C. Æ *cistophoric tetradrachm* (c. 12·6 gm.). Cista mystica containing serpent; all within ivy-wreath. ℞. Bow in case between two coiled serpents; monogram of Sardeis to l., spear-head to r. *B.M.C. 22.* 236, 1 .. .. £150

4726 — — Similar, but with ΣΑΡ in *rev.* field to l., scallop (?) to r. *B.M.C. 22.* 237, 5
£140

4727 — Æ *didrachm* (c. 6·3 gm.). Club draped in lion's skin; all within laurel-wreath. ℞. Bunch of grapes upon vine-leaf; thyrsos in lower field to l., monogram of Sardeis to r. *B.M.C. 22.* 236, 3 .. .. £225

4728   4729

4728 After 133 B.C. Æ *cistophoric tetradrachm* (c. 12·6 gm.). Cista mystica containing serpent; all within ivy-wreath. ℞. Bow in case between two coiled serpents; to l., Κ (=year 20 =115/14 B.C.) above ΣΑΡ; above, caduceus and ΔΗ; to r., horned panther r., holding spear in jaws. *B.M.C. 22.* 238, 8 .. .. £140

4729 2nd-1st cent. B.C. Æ 23. Diad. hd. of Artemis r., hair in knot above, bow and quiver behind neck. ℞. Athena stg. l., holding Nike, spear and shield; ΣΑΡΔΙΑΝΩΝ behind, ΗΡΑΙΟΣ / ΙΠΠΙΟΥ / ΝΕΩΤ before. *B.M.C. 22.* 242, 53 .. .. £14

4730 — — Hd. of young Dionysos r., wreathed with ivy. ℞. Demeter stg. l., holding corn-ears and long torch; ΣΑΡΔΙΑΝΩΝ behind, ΠΑΠΥΛΟΣ / ΦΑΙΝΙΟΥ before. *B.M.C. 22.* 243, 61 .. .. £14

4731   4736

Sardeis *continued*

4731 — Æ 20. Turreted, laur. and veiled bust of Tyche r. R. Zeus Lydios stg. l., holding eagle and sceptre; ΣΑΡΔΙΑΝΩΝ behind, two monograms before. *B.M.C. 22.* 242, 51

£12

4732 — Æ 18. Hd. of young Herakles r., clad in lion's skin. R. Lion walking r.; ΣΑΡΔΙΑΝΩΝ and bee above, magistrate's name in ex. *B.M.C. 22.* 240, 37 .. .. .. £13

4733 — — Laur. hd. of young Herakles r., lion's skin knotted round neck. R. ΣΑΡΔΙΑΝΩΝ across field; bow in case above, club and bee beneath. *B.M.C. 22.* 240, 38 .. £12

4734 — Æ 17. *Obv.* Similar. R. Naked Apollo stg. l., holding raven and laurel-branch; ΣΑΡΔΙΑΝΩΝ behind, ΗΡΑΚΛΙΔΗΣ before; all within laurel-wreath. *B.M.C. 22.* 240, 33

£9

4735 — — *Obv.* As 4730. R. Horned panther stg. l., holding broken spear in forepaw and jaws; ΣΑΡΔΙ / ΑΝΩΝ above, monograms before and beneath. *B.M.C. 22.* 241, 42

£11

4736 — Æ 15. Laur. hd. of Apollo r. R. ΣΑΡΔΙ / ΑΝΩΝ either side of club, monogram beneath; all within oak-wreath. *B.M.C. 22.* 239, 18 .. .. £9

4737 — — *Obv.* As 4730. R. Forepart of lion r.; ΣΑΡΔΙΑΝΩΝ above, monogram behind. *B.M.C. 22.* 241, 47 .. .. £10

4738 — Æ 14. Hd. of bearded Herakles r., clad in lion's skin. R. ΣΑΡΔΙ / ΑΝΩΝ either side of kantharos; monogram in lower field to r. *B.M.C. 22.* 241, 45 .. .. £10

4739 **Stratonikeia** (situated east of Pergamon, in the valley of the Kaikos, Stratonikeia was the place of Aristonikos' capture by the Romans in 130 B.C.). 130 B.C. Æ *cistophoric tetradrachm* (*c.* 12·6 gm.), in the name of the Pergamene pretender Eumenes III (Aristonikos). Cista mystica containing serpent; all within ivy-wreath. R. Bow in case between two coiled serpents, thunderbolt between their heads; to l., female hd. l.; to r., bearded hd. r.; within coils of serpents, BA — EY, with Δ (= year 4) beneath; ΣΤ — PA across lower field. *B.M.C. 22.* 284, 1 .. .. £450

4740   4742

4740 Thyateira (an early Lydian foundation, Thyateira was situated on the upper Lykos, east of Apollonis). 132/131 B.C. Æ *cistophoric tetradrachm* (*c.* 12·6 gm.), in the name of the Pergamene pretender Eumenes III (Aristonikos). Cista mystica containing serpent; all within ivy-wreath. R. Bow in case between two coiled serpents, thunderbolt between their heads; to l., ΘYA; to r., male hd. r.; within coils of serpents, BA — EY, with B (= year 2) between. *S.N.G. Von Aulock* 3198 .. .. £450

4741 2nd cent. B.C. Æ 22. Diad. and dr. bust of Artemis r., bow and quiver at shoulder. R. ΘYATEIPH / NΩN either side of naked Apollo stg. l., holding arrow and resting on bow; monogram in lower field to l. *B.M.C. 22.* 292, 1 .. .. £16

4742 — — Laur. hd. of Apollo r. R. ΘYATEI / PHNΩN either side of tripod with fillets, monogram above; all within laurel-wreath. *B.M.C. 22.* 292, 3 .. .. .. £16

4743 — Æ 17. *Obv.* Similar. R. Double-axe; ΘYATEI / PHN — ΩN in field. *B.M.C. 22.* 292, 7 .. .. £14

4744 — Æ 15. *Obv.* As 4741. R. ΘYATEI / PHNΩN. Bow and quiver; monogram in field. *B.M.C. 22.* 292, 2 .. .. £12

4745 Tralleis (an important city, set in rich and fertile country on the north side of the lower Maeander valley, Tralleis passed under the rule of the Pergamene kings in 189 B.C. and became one of the principal mints for the cistophoric coinage). 189-133 B.C. Æ *cistophoric tetradrachm* (*c.* 12·6 gm.). Cista mystica containing serpent; all within ivy-wreath. R. Bow in case between two coiled serpents; to l., TPAΛ; to r., helmet and half-thunderbolt. *B.M.C. 22.* 327, 8 .. .. £110

4746   4748

4746 — — Similar, but on *rev.* TPAΛ in field to l., rad. hd. of Helios to r., star above (between serpents' heads) and monogram beneath. *B.M.C. 22.* 329, 26 .. .. .. £110

4747 — — Similar, but on *rev.* TPAΛ in field to l., cultus-statue of goddess to r., and TIME above (between serpents' heads). *B.M.C. 22.* 330, 31-2 .. .. .. £110

4748 — Æ *didrachm* (*c.* 6·2 gm.). Club, draped in lion's skin; all within vine-wreath. R. Bunch of grapes upon vine-leaf; TPAΛ to l., ΠPYT above, cornucopiae to r. *B.M.C. 22.* 330, 30 .. .. £200

4749 — Æ *drachm* (*c.* 3 gm.). Similar, but on *rev.* TPAΛ in lower field to l., corn-grain to r. *B.M.C. 22.* 332, 42 .. .. £150

4750 133-126 B.C. Æ *cistophoric tetradrachm* (*c.* 12·6 gm.). Similar to 4745, but in *rev.* field to l., Γ (=year 3=131 B.C.) above TPAΛ; between serpents' heads, ΠTOΛ; to r., Dionysos stg. r. on pedestal, holding thyrsos and ivy-blossoms. *B.M.C. 22.* 333, 46 £110

4751 C. Fabius, Roman Proconsul of Asia, 57-56 B.C. Æ *cistophoric tetradrachm*. Cista mystica containing serpent; all within ivy-wreath. R. Two coiled serpents either side of bow-case surmounted by eagle; above, C. FA — BI. M. F. / PRO — COS.; to l., TPAΛ and humped bull stg. r. on Maeander pattern; to r., naked Apollo stg. l., holding bow; beneath, ΠAMMENHΣ. *B.M.C. 22.* 333, 50 .. .. £350

4752   4753

Tralleis *continued*

4752 C. Septimius, Roman Proconsul of Asia, 56-55 B.C. *R cistophoric tetradrachm. Obv.* Similar. R. Two coiled serpents either side of bow-case; above, C. SEPTVMIVS / T.F. PROCOS.; to l., TPAΛ; to r., cap of Polydeukes surmounted by star; beneath, ΠΟΛΥΔΕΥΚΗΣ. *B.M.C. 22.* 334, 52 .. .. £350

4753 C. Fannius, Praetor, 48 B.C. *R cistophoric tetradrachm. Obv.* Similar. R. Two coiled serpents either side of circular shrine surmounted by female figure stg. l., holding phiale and sceptre; above, C. FAN. P — ONT . PR.; to l., TPA; to r., hand holding olive-branch; beneath, ΑΡΙCΤΟΚΛΗC. *B.M.C. 22.* 334, 54 .. .. £400

4754   4760

4754 *Bronze Coinage.* 2nd-1st cent. B.C. Æ 20. Laur. hd. of Apollo r. R. TPAΛΛI / ANΩN either side of Delphic tripod; all within laurel-wreath. *B.M.C. 22.* 335, 56 £14

4755 — — Laur. hd. of Zeus r. R. TPAΛΛIANΩN. Eagle stg. r. on thunderbolt, wings open; magistrate's name beneath. *B.M.C. 22.* 336, 69 .. .. £14

4756 — — Laur. hd. of Apollo r. R. Helios in quadriga r.; TPAΛΛIANΩN above, lyre before, ΑΣΚΛΑΠΟΣ in ex. *B.M.C. 22.* 337, 71 .. .. £15

4757 — Æ 19. Veiled hd. of Demeter r. R. TPAΛΛI / ANΩN above and beneath eagle flying to front, between wreath and caduceus. *B.M.C. 22.* 337, 73 .. .. .. £13

4758 — Æ 18. Rad. hd. of Helios r. R. TPAΛ / ΛIANΩN above and beneath Selene in biga r., crescent behind her hd. *B.M.C. 22.* 337, 72 .. .. £14

4759 — Æ 17. Zeus stg. facing, holding Nike and sceptre; all within laurel-wreath. R. TPAΛΛI / ANΩN above and beneath humped bull walking r. *B.M.C. 22.* 336, 61-2 £13

4760 — Æ 14. Laur. hd. of Zeus r. R. Similar to last, but bull to l., and monogram before. *B.M.C. 22.* 336, 63 .. .. £11

4761 — Æ 13. TPAΛΛI / ANΩN above and beneath humped bull butting r. R. Similar to obv., but bull to l., and MI in ex. *B.M.C. 22.* 336, 68 .. .. £12

4762

4762 **CARIA. Alabanda** (an ancient Carian town on the river Marsyas, Alabanda was a prosperous place, with a population reputed to be one of the most dissolute in the whole of Asia Minor). Before 197 B.C. Æ *tetradrachm* (*c.* 15·95 gm.). Laur. hd. of Apollo l. ℞. ΑΛΑΒΑΝΔΕΩΝ. Pegasos flying r.; beneath, quiver and ΔΗΜΗΤΡΙΟΣ. *B.M.C. 18.* 271, 1
£850

4763 197-190 B.C. (under the name **Antiocheia**, in honour of Antiochos III). Æ *tetradrachm* (*c.* 16·6 gm.). *Obv.* Similar. ℞. Pegasos flying r., ΑΝΤΙΟΧΕΩΝ above, ΤΙΜΟΚΛΗΣ beneath. *B.M.C. 18.* 1, 1-2 .. .. £750

4764 — Æ *drachm* (*c.* 4·15 gm.). Laur. hd. of Apollo r. ℞. As last, but with magistrate's name ΔΙΟΝΥΣΙΟΣ beneath Pegasos. *B.M.C. 18.* 1, 3 .. .. £250

4765 After 189 B.C. Æ *tetradrachm* (*c.* 16·75 gm.), restoring the types of Alexander the Great. Hd. of young Herakles r., clad in lion's skin. ℞. Zeus enthroned l., holding eagle and sceptre, ΑΛΕΞΑΝΔΡΟΥ behind; before, Pegasos l.; beneath throne, Α. *Müller (Numismatique d'Alexandre le Grand)* 1144 .. .. £200

4766 — Æ *tridrachm* (*c.* 12 gm.). Laur. hd. of Apollo r. ℞. Pegasos flying r.; ΑΛΑ — ΒΑΝ / ΔΕΩΝ in field, ΙΑ (= year 11) beneath; all within laurel-wreath. *B.M.C. 18.* 2, 10
£450

4767   4772   4773

4767 — Æ *didrachm* (*c.* 7·3 gm.). *Obv.* Similar. ℞. ΑΛΑΒΑΝ / ΔΕΩΝ either side of tripod; helmet and ϡΙ (= year 15) in lower field to l.; all within laurel-wreath. *B.M.C. 18.* 3, 11 .. .. £350

4768 — Æ *octobol* (*c.* 5·2 gm.). *Obv.* Similar. ℞. ΑΛΑΒΑ / ΝΔΕΩΝ either side of tripod; all within laurel-wreath. *B.M.C. 18.* 3, 12 .. .. £250

4769 *Bronze Coinage.* 197-190 B.C. (under the name **Antiocheia**). Æ 17. Laur. hd. of Apollo l. ℞. ΑΝΤΙΟ / ΧΕΩΝ above and beneath humped bull butting r., below which Μ. *B.M.C. 18.* 2, 8 .. .. £14

4770 After 189 B.C. Æ 18. Laur. hd. of Apollo r. ℞. ΑΛΑΒΑΝ / ΔΕΩΝ either side of lyre. *B.M.C. 18.* 3, 15 .. .. £14

4771 — Æ 17. *Obv.* Similar. ℞. ΑΛΑΒΑΝ / ΔΕѠΝ either side of tripod. *B.M.C. 18.* 3, 13
£12

4772 — Æ 15. *Obv.* Similar. ℞. ΑΛΑΒ — ΑΝ / ΔΕ — ΩΝ either side of cultus-statue of goddess facing; all within laurel-wreath. *B.M.C. 18.* 3, 14 .. .. £12

4773 — Æ 9. *Obv.* Similar. ℞. ΑΛΑΒΑΝ. Raven (?) stg. r. *B.M.C. 18.* 4, 17 .. £10

4774 **Alinda** (about twelve miles south-west of Alabanda, and the capital of a district known as Hidrias, Alinda was built on a rocky height). 2nd cent. B.C. Æ *tetrobol* (*c.* 2·24 gm.). Hd. of young Herakles r., clad in lion's skin. ℞. ΑΛΙΝ / ΔΕΩΝ either side of club; all within oak-wreath. *S.N.G. Von Aulock* 2402 .. .. £350

Alinda *continued*

4775 — Æ 19. Similar, but the club, on *rev.*, is draped in lion's skin. *B.M.C. 18.* 10, 1
£14

4776 — Æ 18. Young male hd. r., laur. ℞. ΑΛ — IN / ΔE — ΩN either side of thunderbolt;
all within laurel-wreath. *B.M.C. 18.* 10, 8 .. .. £13

4777 — — *Obv.* Similar. ℞. ΑΛΙΝΔΕΩΝ / ΔΙΟΝΥ either side of club; all within oak-wreath.
B.M.C. 18. 10, 4 .. .. £13

4778 — Æ 14. *Obv.* Similar. ℞. ΑΛΙΝΔΕΩΝ. Pegasos springing r. *B.M.C. 18.* 11, 11
£12

4779 — Æ 13. *Obv.* Similar. ℞. ΑΛΙΝ / ΔΕΩΝ either side of bow in case; all within oak-
wreath. *B.M.C. 18.* 11, 9 .. .. £11

4780 — Æ 9. *Obv.* Similar. ℞. ΑΛΙΝ / ΔΕΩΝ either side of bipennis. *B.M.C. 18.* 11, 10
£10

4781 **Amyzon** (a small town, situated about ten miles north-west of Alinda). 2nd-1st cent.
B.C. Æ 17. Hd. of Artemis r., quiver behind neck. ℞. ΑΜΥΖΟΝΕΩΝ / ΑΠΟΛΛΩΝΙ either
side of tripod. *S.N.G. Von Aulock* 2416 .. .. £20

4782 — Æ 11. *Obv.* Similar. ℞. ΑΜΥΣΟ / ΝΕΩΝ either side of flaming torch. *B.M.C. 18.*
13, 2 .. .. £15

4783 **Antiocheia ad Maeandrum** (in the north of the country, at the confluence of the
Maeander with the Morsynos, Antiocheia was a Seleukid foundation, named probably in
honour of Antiochos I). After 168 B.C. Æ *tetradrachm* (*c.* 16·75 gm.), restoring the
types of Alexander the Great. Hd. of young Herakles r., clad in lion's skin. ℞. Zeus
enthroned l., holding eagle and sceptre, ΑΛΕΞΑΝΔΡΟΥ behind; before, humped bull butting
l., and ΑΝ monogram. *Müller* (*Numismatique d'Alexandre le Grand*) 1176 .. £225

4784   4785

4784 — — Laur. hd. of Apollo r., bow in case behind neck. ℞. Humped bull stg. l.,
ANTIOXEΩN above, AINEAΣ beneath; all within circular Maeander pattern, interrupted
above by caps of the Dioskouroi. *B.M.C. 18.* 14, 1 .. .. £3,000

4785 — — Laur. hd. of Zeus r. ℞. Eagle stg. l. on thunderbolt, cornucopiae behind;
ANTIOXEΩN MENEΦPΩN around; all within circular Maeander pattern. *S.N.G. Von
Aulock* 2417 .. .. £2,500

4786 4788

4786 — Æ *drachm* (*c.* 4 gm.). Laur. hd. of Apollo r. ℞. Humped bull seated l. on Maeander pattern; ΑΝΤΙΟΧΕΩΝ above, ΜΕΝΕΦΡΩΝ beneath, cornucopiae before; all within laurel-wreath. *B.M.C. 18.* 14, 2 .. .. £400

4787 — Æ 20. Dr. bust of Mên r., wearing Phrygian cap, crescent behind shoulders. ℞. Humped bull stg. r., ΑΝΤΙΟΧ above, ΜΕΝΑΝ in ex. *B.M.C. 18.* 15, 6 .. .. £18

4788 — Æ 19. Laur. hd. of Apollo l. ℞. ΑΝΤΙΟΧΕΩΝ ΤΩΝ ΠΡΟΣ ΜΑΙΑΝΔΡΩ. Eagle stg. l. on Maeander pattern. *B.M.C. 18.* 15, 9 .. .. £16

4789 — Æ 18. Laur. hd. of Zeus r. ℞. ΑΝΤΙΟΧΕΩΝ. Humped bull seated l. on Maeander pattern. *B.M.C. 18.* 14, 4 .. .. £15

4790 **Aphrodisias—Plarasa** (Aphrodisias was situated on high ground about twenty miles south-east of Antiocheia. At some time in the 1st century B.C. it appears to have been united with the neighbouring town of Plarasa). 1st half of 1st cent. B.C. (in the name of Aphrodisias only). Æ 19. Hd. of Aphrodite r., bound with wreath. ℞. Bipennis, with two palms crossed over its handle; ΑΦΡΟΔΙ / ΣΙΕΩΝ in field. *B.M.C. 18.* 28, 20 £15

4791 — Æ 18. Veiled hd. of Aphrodite r. ℞. ΑΦΡΟΔΙΣΙΕΩΝ. Eagle stg. r. on thunderbolt. *B.M.C. 18.* 28, 18 .. .. £15

4792 4793

4792 — Æ 17. Laur. hd. of Zeus r. ℞. ΑΦΡΟΔΙ / ΣΙΕΩΝ either side of cultus-statue of Aphrodite r. *B.M.C. 18.* 28, 19 .. .. £14

4793 — Æ 9. Winged bust of Eros r. ℞. ΑΦΡΟΔΙ / ΣΙΕΩΝ either side of rose. *B.M.C. 18.* 25, 5 .. .. £11

4794 4796

4794 2nd half of 1st cent. B.C. (in the names of both communities). Æ *drachm* or *denarius* (*c.* 3·5 gm.). Dr. bust of Aphrodite r., diad. and veiled. ℞. ΠΛΑΡΑΣΕΩΝ ΚΑΙ ΑΦΡΟΔΕΙΣΙΕΩΝ. Eagle stg. l. on thunderbolt, wreath behind hd.; in field to l., ΑΡΤΕ / ΜΙ / ΔΩ / ΡΟΣ / ΑΡΤΕ / ΜΙΔΩ / ΡΟΥ; to r., ΤΟΥ / ΑΝ / ΔΡΩ / ΝΟΣ. *B.M.C. 18.* 26, 9 .. .. .. £150

These exceptionally late silver issues may belong to the time of Mark Antony, circa 39-35 B.C. See also no. 4807.

4795 — Æ 19. Diad. hd. of Aphrodite r. ℞. ΠΛΑΡΑ / ΑΦΡΟΔΙ either side of eagle stg. r. on thunderbolt. *B.M.C. 18.* 28, 15-17 .. .. £15

4796 — Æ 13. ΠΛΑΡΑ / ΑΦ — ΡΟ above and beneath bipennis. ℞. Cuirass, within incuse square. *B.M.C. 18.* 25, 1 .. .. £13

4797 — Æ 10. Similar to 4793, but with inscription ΠΛΑ / ΑΦΡΟ either side of rose on *rev.* *B.M.C. 18.* 25, 4 .. .. £11

4798 Apollonia Salbake (situated south of the Salbakos mountains, Apollonia was close to
the northern source of the river Harpasos). 2nd-1st cent. B.C. Æ 21. Laur. hd. of
Apollo r. ℞. ΑΠΟΛΛΩΝΙΑΤΩΝ ΜΕΝΑΝΔΡΟϹ. Eagle stg. r. on laurel-branch. *B.M.C. 18.*
54, 4 . .   . .   £18

4799 — Æ 14. *Obv.* Similar. ℞. ΑΠΟΛΛΩ / ΝΙΑΤΩΝ either side of lyre. *B.M.C. 18.* 54, 5
£15

4800

4801

4800 Astyra (described by an ancient source as 'a city in the peninsula of Phoenix opposite
Rhodos', the precise site of Astyra is unknown). 480-450 B.C. *Æ stater* (*c.* 9·7 gm.).
Amphora. ℞. ΑΣΤΥ. Oinochoe r. and lyre, beneath which tendril with bud; all within
incuse square. *B.M.C. 18.* 59, 1 . .   . .   £2,500

4801 — *Æ trihemiobol* (*c.* 1·1 gm.). One-handled vase, A to r. ℞. Oinochoe without base, A
in field; all within double incuse square. *B.M.C. 18.* 59, 3   . .   . .   £140

4802 — *Æ tetartemorion* (*c.* 0·2 gm.). Rose. ℞. A within incuse square. *B.M.C. 18.*
60, 7 . .   . .   £75

4803 Mid-4th cent. B.C. Æ 19. Hd. of Helios three-quarter face to r. ℞. ΑΣΤΥ. Amphora; to r., small oinochoe. *B.M.C. 18.* 60, 9 . .   . .   £20

4804

4807

4804 — Æ 13. *Obv.* Similar. ℞. Amphora, surmounted by bunch of grapes; to r., small
oinochoe; in field, A / Σ — T / Υ. *B.M.C. 18.* 60, 11   . .   . .   . .   £15

4805 — — Hd. of Aphrodite (?) r., hair in sphendone. ℞. Amphora; A / Σ — T / Υ in field,
bunch of grapes to l. *B.M.C. 18.* 61, 12-13   . .   . .   £12

4806 — Æ 10. Diad. hd. of Aphrodite (?) r., hair knotted behind. ℞. Amphora; A — Σ /
T — Υ in field, small oinochoe to r. *B.M.C. 18.* 61, 16-19   . .   . .   £10

4807 Attuda (on the northern slopes of the Salbakos mountains, Attuda lay north of Aphro-
disias-Plarasa). 2nd half of 1st cent. B.C. *Æ drachm or denarius* (*c.* 3·5 gm.). Turreted
hd. of Tyche or Kybele r. ℞. Naked Apollo stg. l., r. hand extended, l. elbow resting on
Corinthian column; to r., ΑΤΤΟΥΔΑΕΩΝ; to l., ΣΩΣ / ΙΠΟ / ΛΙΣ / ΧΑΡ / ΜΙ / ΔΗΣ / ΛΕ / ΩΝ.
B.M.C. 18. 62, 1   . .   . .   £350

*This exceptionally late silver issue may belong to the time of Mark Antony, circa 39-35 B.C.
See also no.* 4794.

4808 Bargylia (situated on the southern shores of the Iasic gulf, opposite Iasos, Bargylia
was said to have been named after Bellerophon's companion who was killed by a kick
from Pegasos). 2nd-1st cent. B.C. *Æ drachm* (*c.* 4·23 gm.). Veiled bust of Artemis
Kindyas r., within laurel-wreath. ℞. ΒΑΡ — ΓΥ / ΛΙΗΤΩΝ above and below Pegasos flying
r., torch beneath. *S.N.G. Von Aulock* 2516   . .   . .   £350

4809 — *Æ tetrobol* (*c.* 2·65 gm.). Stag stg. r. ℞. ΒΑΡΓΥΛΙ / ΗΤΩΝ either side of cultus-
statue of Artemis Kindyas facing. *S.N.G. Von Aulock* 2515 . .   . .   . .   £300

4810

4811

4810 — Æ *hemidrachm* (*c.* 1·95 gm.).   *Obv.* Similar to 4808, but without laurel-wreath.
 ℞. ΒΑΡΓΥ / ΛΙΗΤΩΝ either side of stag stg. r., star beneath.   *Forrer/Weber* 6444   £200

4811 — Æ 19.   *Obv.* As 4808.   ℞. ΒΑ — ΡΓΥ / ΛΙΗΤΩΝ above and beneath Pegasos flying r.
 B.M.C. 18. 71, 2   ..   ..   £16

4812 — — Veiled and diad. bust of Artemis Kindyas facing.   ℞. ΒΑΡΓΥΛΙΗ / ΤΩΝ above and
 beneath Bellerophon riding on flying Pegasos r.   *B.M.C. 18.* 72, 8   ..   ..   £20

4813 — — Pegasos flying r.   ℞. ΒΑΡΓΥΛΙ / ΗΤΩΝ either side of stag stg. r.   *B.M.C. 18.* 72, 11
        £18

4814 — Æ 18.   Similar to 4809, but the legend is divided ΒΑΡΓΥ / ΛΙΗΤΩΝ on *rev.*   *B.M.C.*
 18. 72, 10   ..   ..   £18

4815 — Æ 14.   *Obv.* As 4810.   ℞. ΒΑΡΓΥΛΙ / ΗΤΩΝ either side of bow and quiver.   *B.M.C.*
 18. 71, 5   ..   ..   £14

4816

4817

4816 **Karyanda** (situated north-west of Halikarnassos).   2nd half of 4th cent. B.C.   Æ 11.
 Diad. female hd. r.   ℞. ΚΑΡΥ above forepart of bull swimming r.   *Forrer/Weber* 6447
        £18

4817 **Kaunos** (an important city and naval station on the southern coastline, facing Rhodos,
 Kaunos was originally founded from Crete.   The place was famous for its dried figs).
 3rd cent. B.C. (under Ptolemaic rule).   Æ *trihemiobol* ? (*c.* 0·9 gm.).   Diad. hd. of Alexander the Great r.   ℞. Cornucopiae; Κ — ΑΥ in field, *ankh* symbol to r.   *B.M.C. 18.* 75, 11
        £100

4818

4820

4825

4818 After 167 B.C.   Æ *hemidrachm* (*c.* 1·1–1·35 gm.).   Hd. of Athena r., in crested Corinthian helmet.   ℞. Sword in sheath with strap; Κ — ΑΥ in field, ΦΑ — ΡΟΣ above, bunch
 of grapes in lower field to r.   *B.M.C. 18.* 75, 16 ..   ..   £65

4819 — — Similar, but with magistrate's name ΚΤΗ — ΤΟΣ instead of ΦΑΡΟΣ, and with symbol
 cornucopiae in lower field to l.   *S.N.G. Von Aulock* 2568   ..   ..   ..   £65

4820 *Bronze Coinage.* 2nd half of 4th cent. B.C.   Æ 12.   Forepart of bull r.   ℞. Sphinx
 seated r., Κ — Α in field.   *B.M.C. 18.* 74, 1   ..   ..   £15

4821 — — Bull butting r., wreath above.   ℞. Sphinx seated r., Κ — Α / Υ in field.   *B.M.C. 18.*
 74, 7 ..   ..   £15

4822 3rd cent. B.C.   Æ 15.   Hd. of Athena r., in crested Corinthian helmet.   ℞. Cornucopiae; Κ — ΑΥ in field.   *B.M.C. 18.* 75, 13   ..   ..   £13

4823 — Æ 11.   *Obv.* As 4817.   ℞. As last.   *B.M.C. 18.* 75, 12   ..   ..   ..   £13

Kaunos *continued*

4824 After 167 B.C. Æ 15. Laur. hd. of Apollo r. ℞. Naked figure stg. l., holding transverse serpent-staff; κ — A͞Y in field. *Historia Numorum, p.* 613 .. .. £12

4825 — Æ 10. *Obv.* Similar. ℞. Sword in sheath with strap; κ — A͞Y in field. *B.M.C. 18.* 76, 17 .. .. £10

4826 **Keramos** (on the northern coastline of the Keramic gulf, east of Halikarnassos, Keramos was, according to the geographer Strabo, a town of considerable importance). After 167 B.C. Æ *drachm* (*c.* 2·5 gm.). Laur. hd. of Zeus r. ℞. KEPAMIH / ΠΟΛΙΤΗC either side of eagle stg. l., looking back; all within shallow incuse square. *B.M.C. 18.* 77, 1 £100

4827 — Æ *hemidrachm* (*c.* 1·2 gm.). Hd. of Apollo (?) r., hair in formal curls. ℞. KEPA / ΠΟΛΙ either side of bull's hd. facing; all within shallow incuse square. *S.N.G. Von Aulock* 2579.. .. .. £125

4828   4830   4831

4828 2nd-1st cent. B.C. Æ 23. Laur. hd. of Zeus r., hair in formal curls. ℞. KEPAMIH. EPMOΦANTOC. Eagle stg. l., looking back. *B.M.C. 18.* 77, 3 .. .. .. £17

4829 — Æ 18. *Obv.* Similar to 4827. ℞. KEPAMIH / ΔEΩN either side of bull's hd. facing. *S.N.G. Von Aulock* 2580 .. .. £16

4830 — Æ 13. Laur. hd. of Zeus r. ℞. KEPAMI / AΠOΛ either side of eagle stg. r.; all within shallow incuse square. *B.M.C. 18.* 77, 2 .. .. £14

4831 **Chalketor** (a small town situated a short distance south of Euromos). 2nd half of 4th cent. B.C. Æ 9. Female hd. r., hair rolled. ℞. Spear-head, dividing x — A. *B.M.C. 18.* 79, 1-4 .. .. £18
This attribution is not certain. The coins could, equally well, belong to the small island of Chalke off the western coast of Rhodos, or to some other place.

4832 **Kidramos** (the precise site of this town is not known, but it seems to have been close to the Lydian border, possibly between Antiocheia and Attuda). 2nd-1st cent. B.C. Æ 22. Laur. hd. of Zeus r. ℞. KI — ΔPA / MH — NΩN above and beneath winged thunderbolt. *S.N.G. Von Aulock* 2583 .. .. £20

4833 **Knidos** (a city of very early foundation, and a great cultural and commercial centre, Knidos was originally sited on the south coast of a long peninsula at the south-west corner of Asia Minor. About the time of Alexander the city was re-founded at the western extremity of the peninsula, where it continued to flourish down to Roman times). 480-450 B.C. Æ *drachm* (*c.* 6·25 gm.). Forepart of lion r. ℞. Hd. of Aphrodite r., of fine archaic style, hair in queue and bound with diadem of beads; all within incuse square. *B.M.C. 18.* 85, 11-12 .. .. £350

4834   4836

4834 — — Similar, but with inscription KN / I before and behind hd. of Aphrodite on *rev.*
B.M.C. 18. 86, 13-14   ..   ..   £350

4835 *Circa* 430 B.C.   Æ *drachm* (*c.* 6·25 gm.).   Similar to 4833, but hd. of Aphrodite larger
and of more advanced style.   *Kraay* (*Archaic and Classical Greek Coins*) *pl.* 55, 946
£500

4836 410-400 B.C.   Æ *drachm* (*c.* 6·25 gm.).   Forepart of lion r.   R. Hd. of Aphrodite r., of
classical style, wearing sphendone; K — N in lower field, I in upper field to l.; all within
incuse square.   *B.M.C. 18.* 86, 20-21   ..   ..   £750

4837 — Æ *obol* (*c.* 0·87 gm.).   Forepart of lion r.   R. Hd. of Aphrodite r., hair in bunch
behind; all within incuse square.   *B.M.C. 18.* 87, 22   ..   ..   ..   £150

4838

4839

4838 394-387 B.C. (Alliance coinage).   Æ *tridrachm* (*c.* 10·7 gm.).   ΣΥΝ. Infant Herakles
kneeling r., grappling with two snakes.   R. ΚΝΙΔΙΩΝ. Hd. of Aphrodite r., hair in
sphendone; behind, prow r.   *B.M.C. 18.* 88, 27   ..   ..   ..   £4,000

    *Coins with similar obverse type were issued by a number of cities—Byzantion, Kyzikos,
Ephesos, Samos, Rhodos and Iasos—as members of an alliance dedicated to their liberation
from oppression; though who the oppressor was is not certain.*

4839 390-330 B.C.   Æ *tetradrachm* (*c.* 15 gm.).   Hd. of Aphrodite l., wearing ampyx, on
which ΣΑ monogram; K — NI in lower field, prow l. behind.   R. Forepart of lion l.,
ΕΟΒΩΛΟΣ beneath; all within incuse square.   *B.M.C. 18.* 87, 24   ..   £2,500

4840 — — *Obv.* Similar, but hair in sphendone.   R. Forepart of lion l., ΚΛΕΟΣΘΕΝΗΣ beneath;
all within incuse square.   *Babelon* (*Traité*) *pl.* 145, 25   ..   ..   ..   £2,500

4841 — Æ *didrachm* (*c.* 7·5 gm.).   Hd. of Aphrodite r., hair in sphendone; K — NI in lower
field, prow r. behind.   R. Forepart of lion r., ΛΑΜΠΩΝ before.   *B.M.C. 18.* 87, 25
£550

4842 — Æ *drachm* (*c.* 3·5 gm.).   Forepart of lion r.   R. Hd. of Aphrodite r., hair in sphendone; behind, prow; all within incuse square.   *B.M.C. 18.* 88, 26   ..   £250

4843

4845

4843 — — Hd. of Aphrodite r., hair rolled and confined in sphendone.   R. Forepart of lion
r.; ΚΝΙ below, ΑΡΧΕΚΡΑΤΗΣ before.   *B.M.C. 18.* 89, 29 ..   ..   ..   £200

4844 — Æ *hemidrachm* (*c.* 1·8 gm.).   Similar, but with magistrate's name ΚΛΕΙΝΙΠΠΟΣ on *rev.*
B.M.C. 18. 89, 35   ..   ..   £125

4845 — — *Obv.* Similar.   R. Bull's hd. facing; ΚΝΙ to l., ΠΑΝΘΑΛΗΣ to r.   *B.M.C. 18.* 90,
38   ..   ..   £140

4846 1st half of 3rd cent. B.C.   Æ *tetradrachm* (*c.* 15 gm.).   Hd. of Aphrodite r., hair tied in
knot behind; ΤΕ monogram to l.   R. Forepart of lion r.; ΚΝΙ below, ΤΕΛΕΣΙΦΡΩΝ before.
Forrer/Weber 6475   ..   ..   £1,750

4847   4848

Knidos *continued*

4847 — Æ *drachm* (*c.* 3·4 gm.).   Similar, but with magistrate's name ΤΕΛΕΑΣ on *rev.*   *B.M.C.*
18. 91, 46-7 ..   ..   £175

4848 — Æ *tetrobol* (*c.* 2·45 gm.).   Diad. hd. of Artemis r., quiver at shoulder.   ℞. ΚΝΙΔΙΩΝ /
ΚΑΛΛΙΠΠΟΣ either side of tripod.   *B.M.C. 18.* 91, 49   ..   ..   £75

4849 — Æ *hemidrachm* (*c.* 1·7 gm.).   Diad. and dr. bust of Artemis r., quiver at shoulder.   ℞.
ΚΝΙΔΙΩΝ / ΕΥΦΡΩΝ (both retrograde) either side of tripod.   *B.M.C. 18.* 91, 50. .   £65

4850 Latter part of 3rd cent. B.C.   Æ *tetradrachm* (*c.* 16·75 gm.), restoring the types of Alexander the Great.   Hd. of young Herakles r., clad in lion's skin.   ℞. Zeus enthroned l.,
holding eagle and sceptre, ΑΛΕΞΑΝΔΡΟΥ behind; before, prow l. and ΕΥ monogram.   *Olcay
and Seyrig* (*Le Trésor de Mektepini en Phrygie*) *pl.* 19, 419   ..   ..   ..   £225

4851   4853

4851 189-167 B.C.   Æ *didrachm* (*c.* 5 gm.).   Hd. of Rhodian Helios three-quarter face to r.
℞. ΚΝΙ.   Forepart of lion r.; rose behind, ΔΙΟΚΛΗΣ beneath.   *B.M.C. 18.* 94, 74-5
£400

4852 — — Similar, but hd. of Helios is three-quarter face to l., and with magistrate's name
ΕΥΒΟΥΛΟΣ on *rev.*   *S.N.G. Von Aulock* 2614   ..   ..   £400

4853 *Bronze Coinage.*   3rd cent. B.C.   Æ 17.   Turreted hd. of Tyche l.   ℞. Forepart of lion
l., ΚΝΙΔΙΩΝ beneath.   *B.M.C. 18.* 92, 52-4   ..   ..   £15

4854 — Æ 15.   ΔΑΜΟΚΡΑΤΙΑΣ.   Hd. of Democracy r., hair in sphendone; ΤΕ monogram
behind.   ℞. ΚΝΙ.   Prow r.; ΑΡΙΣΤΑΓΟΡ / ΑΣ above, club beneath.   *B.M.C. 18.* 92, 56
£16

4855 — Æ 13.   Diad. hd. of Aphrodite (?) r.   ℞. Prow r.; ΚΝΙ above, caduceus behind, club
and ΜΟΙΡΙΧΟΣ beneath.   *B.M.C. 18.* 93, 63   ..   ..   £10

4856   4857

4856 — Æ 10.   Laur. hd. of Apollo l.   ℞. Prow r.; ΚΝΙ above, ΛΑΧΑΡΤΟΣ beneath.   *B.M.C.*
18. 93, 65   ..   ..   £9

4857 — Æ 20.   Diad. hd. of Artemis r., quiver at shoulder.   ℞. Tripod; ΚΝΙΔΙΩΝ to l.,
ΦΙΛΟΚΡΑΤΙΔΑC below and to r.   *B.M.C. 18.* 94, 72   ..   ..   £14

4858 — Æ 13.   *Obv.* Similar.   ℞. Bull's hd. facing; ΚΝΙ above, ΑΡΙΣΤΑΓΟΡΑΣ below.   *B.M.C.*
18. 94, 73   ..   ..   £11

4859 2nd-1st cent. B.C.   Æ 23.   Diad. hd. of Artemis r., bow and quiver at shoulder.   ℞.
ΚΝΙΔΙΩΝ / ΠΑΝΤΑΛΕ either side of tripod.   *S.N.G. Von Aulock* 2615   ..   ..   £16

4860   4864   4865

4860 — Æ 19. Laur. hd. of Apollo r. ℞. ΠΑΝΤΑΛΕ ΚΝΙΔΙΩ. Hd. and neck of bull l., hd. facing. *B.M.C. 18.* 95, 82   ..   ..   £14

4861 — — — ℞. Bunch of grapes; ΚΝΙΔΙΩΝ to r., ΑΡΙΣΤΟΠΟ / ΛΙΣ to l. *B.M.C. 18.* 95, 85 ..   ..   £13

4862 — Æ 29. Hd. of the Aphrodite of Praxiteles r. ℞. ΚΝΙΔΙΩΝ. Dionysos stg. l., holding kantharos and thyrsos. *B.M.C. 18.* 96, 93   ..   ..   £35

4863 — Æ 28. Hd. of young Dionysos l., wreathed with ivy. ℞. Two bunches of grapes on branch; ΚΝΙΔΙΩΝ below, ΕΠΑ / ΓΑΘΟΣ above. *B.M.C. 18.* 96, 87-8   ..   ..   £25

4864 — Æ 19. Hd. of Athena r., in crested helmet. ℞. ΚΝΙΔΙΩΝ ΤΕΛΕΣΙΠΠΟΣ. Nike advancing l., holding wreath and palm. *B.M.C. 18.* 96, 91   ..   ..   ..   £15

4865 **Euhippe** (a small town situated north of Alabanda). 2nd-1st cent. B.C. Æ 11. Bust of Artemis r., bow and quiver at shoulder. ℞. ΕΥΙΠΠΕΩΝ (and magistrate's name). Quiver. *B.M.C. 18.* 98, 1 ..   ..   £22

4866 **Euromos** (a small town situated north-west of Mylasa). Late 5th cent. B.C. Æ *tritartemorion*? (*c.* 0·47 gm.). Laur. hd. of Zeus r., ΥΡΩ before. ℞. Forepart of boar r. *S.N.G. Von Aulock* 2521   ..   ..   £250

4867 2nd-1st cent. B.C. Æ 17. Laur. hd. of Zeus r. ℞. ΕΥΡΩ / ΜΕΩΝ either side of double-axe; all within laurel-wreath. *B.M.C. 18.* 99, 1   ..   ..   £16

4868 — Æ 16. Zeus Labraundos stg. r., holding double-axe and sceptre. ℞. As last, but without wreath. *S.N.G. Von Aulock* 2523   ..   ..   £17

4869 — Æ 19. Hd. of young Dionysos r., wreathed with ivy. ℞. ΕΥΡΩ / ΜΕΩΝ either side of Zeus Labraundos stg. facing between caps of the Dioskouroi. *B.M.C. 18.* 99, 3   £15

4870   4871

4870 — Æ 18. Stag stg. r.; ΕΥΡΩΜ / ΕΩΝ above, ΠΟΛΕ beneath, double-axe before. ℞. As last, but without legend. *B.M.C. 18.* 99, 4   ..   ..   £16

4871 **Gordioteichos** (a small town on the left bank of the Morsynos, north-west of Aphrodisias). 2nd cent. B.C. Æ 16. Laur. hd. of Zeus r. ℞. ΓΟ — ΡΔΙΟ / ΤΕΙΧΙΤΩΝ either side of cultus-statue of Aphrodite stg. r., both hands extended. *B.M.C. 18.* 101, 1-2   £22

4872 **Halikarnassos** (a coastal city north-east of the island of Kos, Halikarnassos was a Greek settlement of very early foundation, and the birthplace of the historian Herodotos. About 367 B.C. it became the residence of Maussollos, Satrap of Caria, and he and his successors enlarged and beautified the city. It was besieged and captured by Alexander in 334 B.C. after which it lost much of its importance). Before 450 B.C. Æ *obol* (*c.* 0·68 gm.). Forepart of Pegasos r. ℞. Goat's hd. and foreleg r., within incuse square. *B.M.C. 18.* 102, 1-2 ..   ..   £150

Halikarnassos *continued*

4872A Late 5th-early 4th cent. B.C. Æ *tetradrachm* (*c.* 14 gm.). Laur. hd. of Apollo three-quarter face to r. ℞. ΑΛΙΚΑΡΝΑΣΣΕΩΝ. Eagle stg. r.; bow in field to r.; all within incuse square. *Leu auction, April* 1978, *lot* 131 .. .. £15,000

4873   4875

4873 — Æ *drachm* (*c.* 3·42 gm.). *Obv.* Similar. ℞. Eagle stg. r.; ΑΛΙ behind, olive-spray before; all within incuse square. *B.M.C. 18.* 102, 3-4 .. .. £300

4874 — Æ *obol* (*c.* 0·66 gm.). Forepart of Pegasos r. ℞. ΑΛΙ. Forepart of leaping goat r.; all within incuse circle. *B.M.C. 18.* 102, 6 .. .. £125

4875 2nd-1st cent. B.C. Æ *drachm* (*c.* 4·2 gm.). Hd. of the Rhodian Helios three-quarter face to r. ℞. Bust of Athena r., in crested helmet; ΑΛΙΚΑΡΝΑΣ behind, ΜΟΣΧΟΣ before. *B.M.C. 18.* 106, 46 .. .. £200

4876 — Æ *hemidrachm* (*c.* 2·1 gm.). Laur. hd. of Apollo r. ℞. ΑΛΙΚΑΡ / ΝΑΣΣΕΩΝ either side of lyre. *B.M.C. 18.* 107, 48 .. .. £140

4877 — Æ *trihemiobol* (*c.* 1·05 gm.). Bust of Athena r., in crested helmet. ℞. ΑΛΙ / ΟΙΔ (= ΔΙΟ) either side of owl stg. r., hd. facing. *B.M.C. 18.* 107, 49 .. .. £90

4878   4881

4878 *Bronze Coinage.* 1st half of 4th cent. B.C. Æ 9. Forepart of Pegasos l., ΑΛΙ beneath. ℞. Lyre, between two laurel-branches. *B.M.C. 18.* 103, 7-11 .. .. .. £14

4879 3rd cent. B.C. Æ 16. Bearded hd. of Poseidon (?) r. ℞. ΑΛΙΚΑΡ / ΝΑΣΣΕΩΝ either side of tripod. *B.M.C. 18.* 103, 16 .. .. £12

4880 — Æ 13. Laur. hd. of Apollo l. ℞. Eagle stg. l.; ΑΛΙ above, lyre before. *B.M.C. 18.* 104, 18 .. .. £12

4881 2nd-1st cent. B.C. Æ 17. Bearded hd. of Poseidon r. ℞. ΑΛΙΚΑ / ΕΣΤΙ either side of ornamented trident-head, with dolphins between prongs. *B.M.C. 18.* 104, 21-2 £8

4882 — Æ 11. Hd. of young Herakles r., clad in lion's skin. ℞. ΑΛΙ / ΚΛΕΙ either side of bow in case and club. *B.M.C. 18.* 106, 38 .. .. £8

4883 — Æ 20. Hd. of the Rhodian Helios facing. ℞. ΑΛΙΚΑΡΝ. ΑΙΘΩΝ. Bust of Athena r., in crested helmet. *B.M.C. 18.* 107, 54-5 .. .. £14

4884   4888

4884 — Æ 19. Diad. hd. of Poseidon r. ℞. Veiled goddess stg. facing, holding phiale and cornucopiae (?); ΑΛΙΚΑΡ to l., ΑΠΟΛΛΟ to r. *B.M.C. 18.* 109, 75 .. .. £12

4885 — Æ 18. Rad. hd. of Helios r. ℞. Lyre; ΑΛΙΚΑ to r., ΑΝΔΡΟΜΕ to l. *B.M.C. 18.*
108, 58   ..   ..   £11

4886 — Æ 15. Laur. hd. of Zeus r. ℞. ΑΛΙΚ / ΑΡΝΑ either side of head-dress of Isis. *B.M.C.*
18. 109, 73 ..   ..   £12

4887 — Æ 13. Laur. hd. of Apollo r. ℞. ΑΛΙΚΑΡ / ΝΑΣΣΕΩΝ either side of lyre. *B.M.C.*
18. 108, 64 ..   ..   £10

4888 — Æ 11. Hd. of Athena r., in crested helmet. ℞. ΑΛΙ. Owl stg. r., hd. facing.
B.M.C. 18. 109, 68-70   ..   ..   £9

4889 — Æ 10. *Obv.* Similar. ℞. Α — ΛΙ. Ornamented trident-head. *B.M.C. 18.* 108,
66   ..   ..   £9

N.B. *For coins struck at Halikarnassos in the names of Maussollos and his successors
(367-334 B.C.) see below under Satraps of Caria, nos. 4954-69.*

4890   4892

4890 **Harpasa** (situated on the right bank of the Harpasos, about twelve miles upstream of
that river's junction with the Maeander). 2nd-1st cent. B.C. Æ 19. Laur. hd. of
Zeus r. ℞. ΑΡΠΑΣΗ / ΝΩΝ either side of Apollo Kitharoedos stg. r., holding plectrum and
lyre; laurel-branch before. *B.M.C. 18.* 113, 1 ..   ..   £20

4891 **Herakleia Salbake** (situated to the south of the Salbakos mountains, east of Aphrodisias). 1st cent. B.C. Æ 17. Hd. of Artemis r., quiver at shoulder. ℞. ΗΡΑΚΛΕ /
ΩΤΩΝ either side of naked Herakles stg. facing, holding club and lion's skin. *B.M.C. 18.*
116, 1 ..   ..   £17

4892 **Hydisos** (a small town situated between Mylasa and the coastline of the Keramic gulf).
2nd-1st cent. B.C. Æ 19. Bust of Athena r., in crested helmet. ℞. ΥΔΙ / ΣΕΩΝ either
side of Zeus Areios (?) stg. facing, hd. r., holding spear and shield. *B.M.C. 18.* 122,
1-2 ..   ..   £20

4893 — Æ 16. Helmeted hd. of bearded Zeus Areios (?) r. ℞. ΥΔΙΣΕΩΝ. Pegasos flying r.
S.N.G. Von Aulock 2553 ..   ..   £18

4894   4898

4894 **Iasos** (a coastal city west of Mylasa, Iasos was an Argive colony of early foundation).
Circa 400 B.C. Æℛ *hemidrachm* (*c.* 1·8 gm.). Laur. hd. of Apollo r. ℞. ΙΑΣΕ / ΩΝ either
side of lyre; all within incuse square. *Forrer/Weber* 6521 ..   ..   ..   £300

4895 394-387 B.C. (Alliance coinage). Æℛ *tridrachm* (*c.* 10·75 gm.). ΣΥΝ. Infant Herakles
kneeling r., grappling with two snakes. ℞. Laur. hd. of Apollo r., Ι — Α in lower field.
Babelon (Traité) pl. 146, 25   ..   ..   £4 500

   *Coins with similar obverse type were issued by a number of cities—Byzantion, Kyzikos,
Ephesos, Samos, Knidos and Rhodos—as members of an alliance dedicated to their liberation
from oppression; though who the oppressor was was not certain.*

4896 Mid-3rd cent. B.C. Æℛ *drachm* (*c.* 5·3 gm.). Laur. hd. of Apollo r. ℞. The youth
Hermias swimming r., his l. arm over the back of dolphin r. beside him; ΙΑ above,
ΛΑΜΠΙΤΟΣ beneath. *B.M.C. 18.* 124, 1-2   ..   ..   £450

Iasos *continued*

4897 — Æ *hemidrachm* (*c.* 2·75 gm.). Similar, but with magistrate's name ΠANTAI / NOΣ on *rev.* *B.M.C. 18.* 124, 4 .. .. £250

4898 — — Similar, but without magistrate's name on *rev.*, and with IAΣEΩN beneath Hermias. *B.M.C. 18.* 124, 5 .. .. £250

4899 3rd-2nd cent. B.C. Æ 18. Similar to 4896, but with magistrate's name ANAΞIΠΠOΣ on *rev.* *B.M.C. 18.* 125, 6 .. .. £17

4900 — — Conjoined hds. of Apollo and Artemis r. Ṛ. IAΣE / ΩN above and beneath the youth Hermias swimming r., his l. arm over the back of dolphin r. beside him. *S.N.G. Von Aulock* 2556 .. .. £20

4901 — Æ 17. Naked Apollo stg. facing, hd. r., holding arrow. Ṛ. IAΣEΩN. Artemis stg. facing, holding bow and drawing arrow from quiver; to r., star; all within laurel-wreath. *B.M.C. 18.* 126, 14 .. .. £18

4902 4904

4902 — Æ 13. Lyre, within laurel-wreath. Ṛ. As 4900, but with legend IACEωN and magistrate's name beneath. *B.M.C. 18.* 125, 13 .. .. £14

4903 — Æ 11. Laur. hd. of Apollo r. Ṛ. IAΣ / EΩN within ivy-wreath. *B.M.C. 18.* 125, 12 £12

4904 **Idyma** (situated near the head of the Keramic gulf). Late 5th-early 4th cent. B.C. Æ *drachm* (*c.* 3·75 gm.). Hd. of horned Pan facing. Ṛ. IΔVMION around fig-leaf; all within incuse square. *B.M.C. 18.* 127, 1-5 .. .. £550

4905 — Æ *hemidrachm*? (*c.* 2·07 gm.). Similar. *S.N.G. Von Aulock* 2562 .. £350

4906 — Æ *trihemiobol* (*c.* 0·9 gm.). Similar. *Historia Numorum, p.* 621 .. .. £175

4907 *Circa* 350 B.C. Æ 9. Female hd. r., hair confined by net behind. Ṛ. IΔVMION (retrograde) around fig-leaf. *Babelon (Traité) pl.* 146, 12-13 .. .. £18

4908 **Mylasa** (the principal non-Greek city of Caria, Mylasa was situated west of Stratonikeia and not far from the head of the Bargylian gulf. It became the capital of the country under the satrap Hekatomnos, 395-377 B.C., but his successor, Maussollos, removed the seat of government to Halikarnassos, *circa* 367 B.C.). 3rd cent. B.C. Æ *tetradrachm* (*c.* 16·75 gm.), restoring the types of Alexander the Great. Hd. of young Herakles r., clad in lion's skin. Ṛ. Zeus enthroned l., holding eagle and sceptre, AΛEΞANΔPOY behind; before, MY monogram beneath trident and labrys combined. *Müller (Numismatique d'Alexandre le Grand)* 1141 .. .. £200

4909

4911

4909 *Bronze Coinage.* *Circa* 314 B.C. Æ 17. Three Macedonian shields, piled on top of one another. ℞. ΕΥΠΟ / ΛΕΜΟΥ either side of sword in sheath; labrys in field to l. *B.M.C. 18.* 128, 2-3 .. .. £18

> *Eupolemos, general of Kassander, campaigned in Caria, 314 B.C., and Mylasa seems the likely mint for his coinage.*

4910 3rd-2nd cent. B.C. Æ 18. ΜΥΛΑΣΕΩΝ. Horse trotting r. ℞. Trident and labrys combined. *B.M.C. 18.* 128, 7 .. .. £12

4911 — Æ 11. Horse trotting r. ℞. Ornamented trident-head; Μ — Υ in upper field. *B.M.C. 18.* 129, 11 .. .. £10

4912 — — Forepart of galloping horse r. ℞. ΜΥΛΑ / ΣΕΩΝ either side of ornamented trident-head. *B.M.C. 18.* 129, 13.. .. .. £11

4913 — Æ 9. Labrys (double-axe). ℞. As last. *B.M.C. 18.* 129, 16 .. .. £9

N.B. *For coins struck at Mylasa in the name of Hekatomnos, see no. 4952 below.*

4914 **Myndos** (a coastal town situated west of Halikarnassos, Myndos was a Dorian colony founded from Troizen). 2nd cent. B.C. Æ *tetradrachm* (*c.* 17·04 gm.). Laur. hd. of Apollo r. ℞. Winged thunderbolt; ΜΥΝΔΙΩΝ above, two monograms beneath; all within olive-wreath. *B.M.C. 18, pl. XLV,* 9 .. .. (*Unique* ?)

4915

4918

4915 2nd-1st cent. B.C. Æ *drachm* (*c.* 4·3 gm.). Laur. hd. of Zeus r., with head-dress of Osiris. ℞. ΜΥΝΔΙΩΝ / ΘΕΟΔΩΡΟΣ either side of head-dress of Isis; thunderbolt beneath. *B.M.C. 18.* 134, 6 .. .. £150

4916 — Æ *tetrobol* (*c.* 2·72 gm.). Similar, but with magistrate's name ΕΠΙΓΟΝΟΣ instead of ΘΕΟΔΩΡΟΣ, and with star as well as thunderbolt beneath Isis head-dress. *Forrer/Weber* 6534 .. .. £175

4917 — Æ *hemidrachm* (*c.* 2·15 gm.). Hd. of young Dionysos r., wreathed with ivy, thyrsos behind neck. ℞. ΜΥΝΔΙΩΝ / ΙΕΡΟΚΛΗΣ either side of winged thunderbolt. *B.M.C. 18.* 135, 9 .. .. £120

4918 — Æ *trihemiobol* (*c.* 1·05 gm.). Hd. of young Dionysos r., wreathed with ivy. ℞. ΜΥΝΔΙ / ΕΞΗΚΕΣ either side of bunch of grapes. *B.M.C. 18.* 135, 13 .. .. £90

4919 — Æ 26. Laur. hd. of Zeus r. ℞. Eagle stg. r. on thunderbolt; ΜΥΝΔΙΩΝ beneath, ΙΣΙΔΩΡΟΣ before. *B.M.C. 18.* 136, 17 .. .. £22

4920   4923

Myndos *continued*

4920 — Æ 18. Laur. hd. of Apollo r. ℞. Owl perched r. on filleted olive-branch; MYNΔIΩN above, ЄPMIAΣ beneath. *B.M.C. 18.* 136, 24 ..   ..   £14

4921 — Æ 15. Laur. hd. of Zeus r. ℞. Winged thunderbolt; MYNΔIΩN above, MHNOΔO / TOC beneath. *B.M.C. 18.* 136, 19-20 ..   ..   £9

4922 — Æ 11. Laur. hd. of Apollo (?) r. ℞. MYN / ΔIΩN either side of portable fire-altar, with conical top. *B.M.C. 18.* 137, 37 ..   ..   £10

4923 — — Hd. of Artemis r., bow and quiver at shoulder. ℞. MYNΔIΩN. Two dolphins swimming r., one above the other. *B.M.C. 18.* 138, 38   ..   ..   ..   £10

4924 — Æ 10. *Obv.* Similar to 4922. ℞. MYN / ΔIΩN either side of tripod. *B.M.C. 18.* 138, 42-4 ..   ..   £8

4925   4928

4925 **Neapolis** (in the valley of Harpasos, south of Harpasa). 1st cent. B.C. Æ 19. Laur. hd. of Zeus r., with formal curls. ℞. NЄAПOΛITΩN. Eagle stg. r. on thunderbolt, wings spread. *Historia Numorum, p.* 623 ..   ..   £20

4926 **Orthosia** (situated north-west of Harpasa, Orthosia occupied on elevated site overlooking the valley of the Maeander). 2nd-1st cent. B.C. Æ 20. Dr. bust of Artemis r., bow and quiver at shoulder. ℞. Zeus seated l., holding Nike and sceptre; OPΘΩΣIEΩN behind. *S.N.G. Von Aulock* 2644 ..   ..   £20

4927 — Æ 18. Laur. hd. of Zeus r. ℞. Athena stg. r., brandishing spear and holding shield, helmet (?) in field to r.; OPΘΩΣIEΩN before, APTEMIΔ / IAΣ behind. *B.M.C. 18.* 143, 1   £18

4928 — Æ 14. OPΘΩΣIEΩN. Hd. of young Dionysos r., wreathed with ivy. ℞. APIΣTEAΣ / OΠΛEITOY either side of thyrsos. *B.M.C. 18.* 143, 2-3 ..   ..   £18

4929 **Stratonikeia** (an important town in the upper valley of the Marsyas, east of Mylasa, Stratonikeia was named in honour of the wife of Antiochos I). 3rd cent. B.C. Æ *tetra-drachm* (*c.* 16·75 gm.), restoring the types of Alexander the Great. Hd. of young Herakles r., clad in lion's skin. ℞. Zeus enthroned l., holding eagle and sceptre, AΛEΞANΔPOY behind; before, ΣTPA monogram; beneath throne, labrys (double-axe). *Müller (Numismatique d'Alexandre le Grand)* 1136 ..   ..   £225

4930   4933

4930 2nd cent. B.C. (after 166). Æ *hemidrachm* (c. 1·4 gm.). Laur. hd. of Zeus r. R. Eagle stg. l., wings spread, coiled serpent before; Σ — T in field, ΛΕΩΝ above; all within shallow incuse square. *B.M.C. 18.* 147, 1 .. .. £50

4931 — — Similar, but eagle to r. on *rev.*, torch and quiver before, C — T in field, and ΜΕΝΟΙΤΙΟC above. *B.M.C. 18.* 147, 5 .. .. £50

4932 1st cent. B.C. Æ *tetradrachm* (c. 10·75 gm.). Laur. hd. of Zeus r. R. ΣΤΡΑΤΟΝΙΚΕΩΝ / ΜΕΛΑΝΘΙΟΣ. Hekate stg. facing, holding phiale and torch. *Historia Numorum, p.* 625 .. .. £3,000

4933 — Æ *octobol* (c. 3·75 gm.). Similar, but with *rev.* legend ΣΤ — ΡΑ / ΛΕ — ΩΝ across field, and with altar at Hekate's feet to r. *B.M.C. 18.* 150, 23 .. .. .. £300

4934 4938

4934 — Æ *tetrobol* (c. 1·8 gm.). Laur. hd. of Hekate r., wearing crescent. R. Nike advancing r., holding wreath and palm, torch before; C — T in field, ΔΙΟΝΥCΙΟC above; all within shallow incuse square. *B.M.C. 18.* 148, 8 .. .. £100

4935 — Æ *triobol* (c. 1·4 gm.). *Obv.* Similar, but with legend ΕΚΑΤΑΙΟC CωCΑΝΔΡΟΥ around. R. CΤΡΑΤΟ / ΝΙΚΕωΝ either side of Nike stg. r.; all within shallow incuse square. *B.M.C. 18.* 148, 6 .. .. £120

4936 *Bronze Coinage.* 2nd-1st cent. B.C. Æ 15. Laur. hd. of Zeus r. R. Eagle stg. r. on torch, ΣΤΡΑΤΟ above. *B.M.C. 18.* 148, 9 .. .. £10

4937 — Æ 13. Similar, but the *rev.* type is enclosed within shallow incuse square, with the legend C — T / P — A in the four corners. *B.M.C. 18.* 149, 13-14 .. .. £9

4938 — Æ 11. *Obv.* Similar to 4934. R. ΣΤΡΑΤΟ / ΝΙΚΕωΝ either side of torch; all within shallow incuse square. *B.M.C. 18.* 149, 15-17 .. .. £10

4939 — Æ 9. Torch. R. As last, but with border of dots instead of incuse square. *B.M.C. 18.* 149, 19-21 .. .. £8

4940 — Æ 17. Laur. hd. of Zeus r. R. ΣΤΡΑΤΟ / ΝΙΚΕΩΝ above and beneath Pegasos flying r. *B.M.C. 18.* 150, 24 .. .. £12

4941 — — Laur. hd. of Hekate r., wearing crescent. R. Similar to last, but Pegasos l., and with B in field to r. *B.M.C. 18.* 150, 29 .. .. £13

4942 — Æ 19. *Obv.* Similar. R. ΣΤΡΑΤΟ / ΝΙΚΕωΝ either side of Nike advancing r., holding wreath and palm. *B.M.C. 18.* 151, 31-2 .. .. £12

4943 4947 4949

4943 **Tabai** (situated in the interior of the country, near the Phrygian border, Tabai derived its name from the Carian or Lydian word *Taba*, meaning rock). 1st cent. B.C. Æ *drachm* (c. 3·8 gm.). Hd. of young Dionysos r., wreathed with ivy. R. Female figure stg. l., holding phiale and cornucopiae; ΤΑΒΗΝΩΝ behind; ΚΕΤ — ΤΑ before. *B.M.C. 18.* 160, 1 £250

Tabai *continued*

4944 — Æ *hemidrachm* (*c.* 1·9 gm.). Bust of Athena r., in crested Corinthian helmet. ℞. Nike advancing r., holding wreath and trophy; ΤΑΒΗΝΩΝ behind, ΚΑΛ before; all within laurel-wreath. *S.N.G. Von Aulock* 2701   ..   ..   £140

4945 — Æ *trihemiobol* (*c.* 0·95 gm.). Veiled female hd. r. ℞. Forepart of humped bull butting r., hd. facing; ΤΑΒ monogram above. *Grose/McClean* 8508   ..   ..   £110

4946 — Æ 18. Laur. hd. of Zeus r. ℞. Caps of the Dioskouroi; Γ — Ο — Ρ in field, ΤΑΒΗΝΩ / Ν beneath. *B.M.C. 18.* 161, 7-8 ..   ..   £10

4947 — Æ 15. Beardless male bust r., in crested helmet, spear over l. shoulder. ℞. Humped bull butting r., ΤΑΒΗΝΩΝ above, ΦΙΜ in ex. *B.M.C. 18.* 161, 14   ..   £13

4948 — Æ 14. Laur. hd. of Zeus r. ℞. Caduceus between caps of the Dioskouroi; ΤΑΒ — ΗΝ in field. *B.M.C. 18.* 160, 2 ..   ..   £11

4949 — Æ 10. Similar to 4945, but with ΤΑ above bull on *rev.* *B.M.C. 18.* 161, 16
         £12

4950 **SATRAPS OF CARIA. Hekatomnos,** 395-377 B.C. (a native of Mylasa, Heka-tomnos was the son and successor of Hyssaldomos, satrap of Caria. He commanded the Persian fleet in the operations against Cyprus in 390 B.C.). Æ *tridrachm-stater* (*c.* 12·25 gm.). Lion's hd. l., with open jaws, its foreleg r. beneath; above, ΕΚΑ. ℞. Ornamented star within incuse circle. *S.N.G. Von Aulock* 2355   ..   ..   ..   £1,250
     This, and the following, would seem to have been minted at Miletos. The types are a revival of the archaic Milesian silver issues.

       4951   4952

4951 — Æ *drachm* (*c.* 4·25 gm.). Similar. *B.M.C. 14.* 187, 37-41   ..   ..   £200

4952 — Æ *tetradrachm* (*c.* 15·2 gm.). Zeus Labraundos stg. r., holding labrys (double-axe) and spear. ℞. Lion r., at bay; above, ΕΚΑΤΟΜΝΩ; all within incuse circle. *S.N.G. Von Aulock* 2354   ..   ..   £1,750
     This type was minted at Mylasa, Hekatomnos' native city and the seat of government during his reign.

4953 **Maussollos,** 377-353 B.C. (son of Hekatomnos, Maussollos succeeded to the satrapy in 377 B.C., and about a decade later transferred the seat of government to the Greek city of Halikarnassos. His famous tomb, the Mausoleum, one of the seven wonders of the ancient world, was completed by his widow, Artemisia). Æ *tridrachm-stater* (*c.* 12·7 gm.). Similar to 4950, but with ΜΑ instead of ΕΚΑ on *obv.* *B.M.C. 14.* 188, 43 ..   £1,250
     This, like the similar issues of Maussollos' father, was probably minted in Miletos.

4954 — Æ *tetradrachm* (*c.* 15·25 gm.).   Laur. hd. of Apollo three-quarter face to r.   Ꞧ. Zeus Labraundos stg. r., holding labrys and spear; to r., ΜΑΥΣΣΩΛΛΟ.   *B.M.C. 18.* 181, 1-2
£1,500
This, and all subsequent issues of the Carian satraps, was minted at the new capital city of Halikarnassos.

4955 — — Similar, but with A in *rev.* field to r., between Zeus and his spear.   *B.M.C. 18.* 181, 3   ..   ..   £1,500
4956 — Æ *drachm* (*c.* 3·75 gm.).   As 4954.   *B.M.C. 18.* 182, 9-12 ..   ..   ..   £160
4957 — — Similar, but with wreath in *rev.* field to l.   *B.M.C. 18.* 182, 14..   ..   £160
See also no. 4988, of Kos.

4958 **Hidrieus,** 351-344 B.C. (second son of Hekatomnos and brother of Maussollos whose widow, Artemisia, he succeeded).   Æ *tetradrachm* (*c.* 15·1 gm.).   Similar to 4955, but with E instead of A in *rev.* field, and with legend ΙΔΡΙΕΩΣ instead of ΜΑΥΣΣΩΛΛΟ.   *B.M.C. 18.* 183, 1   ..   ..   £1,600

4959   4964

4959 — Æ *didrachm* (*c.* 7·1 gm.).   As last, but with Ꝫ instead of E in *rev.* field, between Zeus and his spear.   *B.M.C. 18.* 183, 2-3   ..   ..   £500
4960 — Æ *drachm* (*c.* 3·75 gm.).   As last, but with M in *rev.* field, to l. of Zeus.   *B.M.C. 18.* 183, 5   ..   ..   £175
4961 — Æ *hemidrachm* (*c.* 1·85 gm.).   As last, but without letter in *rev.* field.   *S.N.G. Von Aulock* 2369   ..   ..   £110
4962 — Æ *trihemiobol* (*c.* 0·95 gm.).   Laur. hd. of Apollo three-quarter face to r.   Ꞧ. Ornamented star, with Ι — Δ — Ρ — Ι between the rays.   *B.M.C. 18.* 183, 7   ..   £125

4963 **Pixodaros,** 340-334 B.C. (the youngest of Hekatomnos' sons, Pixodaros succeeded to the Carian Satrapy on the retirement of Hidrieus' widow, Ada.   His coinage is exceptional in that several denominations were issued in gold, a prerogative of the Persian king which was never formally delegated to any of his satraps).   *N hekte* (*sixth-stater, c.* 1·4 gm.).   Laur. hd. of Apollo r.   Ꞧ. Zeus Labraundos stg. r., holding labrys and spear; to r., ΠΙΞΩΛ.   *B.M.C. 18.* 184, 2   ..   ..   £1,250
4964 — *N hemihekton* (*twelfth-stater, c.* 0·7 gm.).   Similar, but *obv.* type to l., and legend ΠΙΞΩΛΑ on *rev.*   *B.M.C. 18.* 184, 3   ..   ..   £650
4965 — *N twenty-fourth stater* (*c.* 0·35 gm.).   *Obv.* As last.   Ꞧ. Labrys (double-axe); Π — Ι either side of shaft.   *B.M.C. 18.* 184, 4 ..   ..   £350
4966 — Æ *didrachm* (*c.* 7 gm.).   Laur. hd. of Apollo three-quarter face to r.   Ꞧ. Similar to 4963, but with legend ΠΙΞΩΛΑΡΟΥ.   *B.M.C. 18.* 185, 5-10   ..   ..   ..   £450

4967   4968

Pixodaros *continued*

4967 — Æ *drachm* (*c.* 3·6 gm.). As last. *B.M.C. 18.* 185, 11-13 ..   ..   ..   £165

4968 — Æ *trihemiobol* (*c.* 0·75 gm.). *Obv.* As 4966. ℞. Ornamented star, with Π — Ι — Ξ —
Ω — Δ — A — P — O (retrograde) between the rays. *B.M.C. 18.* 185, 15   ..   £125

4969 **Rhoontopates,** 334-333 B.C. (Pixodaros was succeeded by his son-in-law, Rhoontopates,
but the dynasty was soon after brought to an end by Alexander's capture of Halikarnassos).
Æ *tetradrachm* (*c.* 14·95 gm.). Laur. hd. of Apollo three-quarter face to r. ℞. Zeus
Labraundos stg. r., holding labrys and sceptre with lotiform head; to r., POONTOΠATO.
Grose/McClean 8526   ..   ..   £4,500

4970   4976

4970 **ISLANDS OFF CARIA. Astypalaia** (this island is situated south-west of Kos, its
settlement being a port on the important trade-route between Phoenicia and European
Greece). 3rd cent. B.C. Æ 11. Hd. of Perseus r., in winged Phrygian helmet. ℞.
Harpa; AΣ (retrograde) above. *B.M.C. 18.* 186, 1   ..   ..   £15

4971 2nd cent. B.C. Æ 14. *Obv.* Similar. ℞. AΣTY. Hd. of Medusa facing. *B.M.C. 18.*
186, 5-8 ..   ..   £14

4972 — Æ 12. Hd. of Medusa facing. ℞. Harpa; AΣTY beneath. *B.M.C. 18.* 187, 9-10
£14

4974 1st cent. B.C. Æ 19. Veiled female hd. r. ℞. AΣTYΠAΛ. Hd. of Athena r., in crested
Corinthian helmet. *B.M.C. 18.* 187, 13 ..   ..   £16

4975 — Æ 17. Hd. of young Dionysos r., wreathed with ivy. ℞. AΣTV / ΠA before and behind
veiled female hd. r. *B.M.C. 18.* 187, 11-12   ..   ..   £15

4976 — Æ 14. Hd. of Asklepios r. ℞. AΣTY / ΠAΛ either side of serpent-staff. *B.M.C. 18.*
187, 14 ..   ..   £14

4977   4981

4977 **Kalymna** (an island about ten miles off the Carian mainland, west of Myndos. The
town was situated on its southern coast). 3rd cent. B.C. Æ *didrachm* (*c.* 6·6 gm.).
Young male hd. r., wearing close-fitting crested helmet. ℞. Lyre, KAΛYMNION beneath;
all within dotted square. *B.M.C. 18.* 188-9, 3-9   ..   ..   £450

4978 — Æ *drachm* (*c.* 3·25 gm.). Similar, but on *rev.* the legend is either side of lyre, KAΛY /
MNION, and without dotted square. *B.M.C. 18.* 189, 10   ..   ..   ..   £250

4979 — Æ *hemidrachm* (*c.* 1·6 gm.). As last. *B.M.C. 18.* 189, 12 ..   ..   ..   £150

4980 — Æ 13. *Obv.* Similar, but hd. l. ℞. Lyre, KAΛY beneath. *B.M.C. 18.* 190, 18-20
£14

4981 — — *Obv.* As 4977. ℞. Veiled female hd. r., ΚΑΛΥ behind. *B.M.C. 18.* 190, 27-9
£15

4982 — — — ℞. ΚΑΛΥ beneath laurel-wreath. *B.M.C. 18.* 191, 31-4 ..   ..   £13

4983 **Kos** (this important island, north-west of Knidos, was colonized by Dorians from
Epidauros, who brought with them the worship of Asklepios. In the fifth century
Hippokrates of Kos laid the foundations of medical science, and the island also became a
literary centre, under the rule of the Ptolemaic kings in the third century).   470-450 B.C.
Æ *triple-siglos* (*c.* 16·5 gm.).   Naked diskobolos stg. facing, legs crossed, body inclined to
l., preparing to hurl diskos, held aloft in r. hand; in background, to l., prize tripod on
stand; to r., ΚΟΣ. ℞. Crab, at centre of incuse square divided diagonally; border of dots
within square. *B.M.C. 18.* 194, 6   ..   ..   £5,000

*The obv. type refers to the games at the festival of Apollo Triopios, celebrated on the
Triopian promontory in the territory of Knidos.*

4984   4986

4984 — — *Obv.* Similar, but with legend ΚΩΙΟΝ. ℞. Crab, framed by dotted square; all
within incuse square. *B.M.C. 18.* 194, 9   ..   ..   £6,000

4985 After 366 B.C. (when a new capital city was built in the north-east of the island).   Æ
tetradrachm (*c.* 15·3 gm.).   Hd. of bearded Herakles l., clad in lion's skin. ℞. Crab;
ΦΙΛΕΩΝΙΔΑΣ above, ΚΩΙΟΝ and club r. beneath; framed by dotted square within incuse
square. *B.M.C. 18.* 194, 10   ..   ..   £750

4986 — — *Obv.* Similar, but hd. r. ℞. Crab; ΚΩΙΟΝ above, club r. and ΔΙΩΝ beneath; all
within dotted square frame. *B.M.C. 18.* 195, 14   ..   ..   ..   £750

4987 — Æ *didrachm* (*c.* 6·8 gm.).   Hd. of young Herakles r., clad in lion's skin. ℞. Crab;
ΚΩΙΟΝ above, club r. and ΑΡΙΣΤΙΩΝ beneath; framed by dotted square within incuse
square. *B.M.C. 18.* 195, 15   ..   ..   £375

4988   4991

4988 — — *Obv.* As 4986. ℞. Veiled female hd. l., ΚΩΙΟΝ beneath, ΦΙΛ behind. *B.M.C. 18.*
195, 20   ..   ..   £600

*It has been suggested that these heads represent portraits of the Satrap Maussollos and his
wife Artemisia.*

4989 — Æ *drachm* (*c.* 3·7 gm.).   *Obv.* As 4986. ℞. Crab; ΚΩΙΟΝ above, club r. and ΜΟΣΧΙΩΝ
beneath; framed by dotted square within incuse square. *S.N.G. Von Aulock* 2750.
B.M.C. 18. 199, 62 ..   ..   £150

4990 300-190 B.C. Æ *tetradrachm* (*c.* 15 gm.).   Hd. of young Herakles r., clad in lion's skin.
℞. Crab; ΚΩΙΟΝ above, ΜΟΣΧΙΩΝ and bow in case beneath; all within dotted square frame.
B.M.C. 18. 197, 43 ..   ..   £750

4991 — Æ *didrachm* (*c.* 6·8 gm.).   Similar, but with club and ΞΩΙΛΟΣ beneath crab on *rev.*
B.M.C. 18. 198, 49 ..   ..   £350

Kos *continued*

4992 — Æ *drachm* (*c.* 3·4 gm.). Hd. of bearded Herakles r., clad in lion's skin. ℞. As last, but with magistrate's name ΠΟΛΥΑΡΧΟΣ instead of ΙΩΙΛΟΣ. *B.M.C. 18.* 199, 63   £150

4993 — Æ *hemidrachm* (*c.* 1·55 gm.). *Obv.* As 4990. ℞. Crab; ΚΩΙΟΝ above, ΔΗΜΗΤΡΙΟΣ beneath. *B.M.C. 18.* 200, 67   ..   ..   £120

4994 190-167 B.C. Æ *tetradrachm* (*c.* 16·75 gm.), restoring the types of Alexander the Great. Hd. of young Herakles r., clad in lion's skin. ℞. Zeus enthroned l., holding eagle and sceptre, ΑΛΕΞΑΝΔΡΟΥ behind; before, monogram and crab surmounted by club. *Olcay and Seyrig* (*Le Trésor de Mektepini en Phrygie*) *pl.* 19, 416   ..   ..   £250

4995   4997

4995 — Æ *didrachm* (*c.* 6·8 gm.). Hd. of young Herakles three-quarter face to r., clad in lion's skin. ℞. Crab; ΚΩΙΟΝ above, club and ΔΑΜΟΞΕΝΟC beneath; all within dotted square frame. *B.M.C. 18.* 200, 71   ..   ..   £350

4996 — Æ *drachm* (*c.* 3·2 gm.). Hd. of bearded Herakles r., clad in lion's skin. ℞. Crab; ΚΩΙΟΝ above, club and ΞΑΙΓΡΕΤΟΣ beneath. *B.M.C. 18.* 201, 80-81   ..   £140

4997 — Æ *hemidrachm* (*c.* 1·5 gm.). Hd. of young Herakles r., clad in lion's skin. ℞. Club above bow in case; ΚΩΙΩΝ above, ΔΙΟΓΕΝΗΣ between, Α beneath. *B.M.C. 18.* 201, 84   £125

4998 — Æ *trihemiobol* (*c.* 0·85 gm.). Similar, but with magistrate's name ΕΚΑΤΟΔΩ on *rev.*, and with coiled serpent instead of Α. *B.M.C. 18.* 201, 85   ..   ..   £110

4999 167-88 B.C. Æ *tetradrachm* (*c.* 16·53 gm.). Hd. of Aphrodite r., wearing myrtle-wreath bound with diadem. ℞. Asklepios stg. facing, hd. r., resting on serpent-staff held in l. hand; ΚΩΙΩΝ to r., ΝΙΚΟΣΤΡΑΤΟΣ to l. *B.M.C. 18. pl. XLV,* 6   ..   (*Unique*)

5000   5004

5000 — Æ *drachm* (*c.* 3 gm.). Hd. of young Herakles r., clad in lion's skin. ℞. Crab; ΚΩΙΩΝ above, club and ΑΡΧΙΑΣ beneath, Δ to l.; all within incuse square. *B.M.C. 18.* 205, 117   ..   ..   £120

5001 — Æ *drachm* (reduced weight, *c.* 2·2 gm.). Laur. hd. of Asklepios r. ℞. ΚΩΙΩΝ / ΑΝΘΕΣΤ either side of coiled serpent; all within incuse square. *B.M.C. 18.* 205, 119   £75

5002 — — Similar, but with ΚΩΝ / ΑΝΔΡΟΣ either side of coiled serpent, star to l., and Α beneath, outside incuse square. *B.M.C. 18.* 205, 122   ..   ..   £75

5003 — — Similar, but with ΠΡΟΣΤ / ΝΙΚΙΑC either side of serpent, ΚΩ beneath, and Δ outside incuse square. *B.M.C. 18.* 206, 129   ..   ..   £75

5004 — — Similar, but with ΤΙΜΟΣ / ΕΚΑΤΑ either side of serpent, ΚΩΙ beneath, star to l., and Δ outside square (another Δ beneath hd. of Asklepios on *obv.*). *B.M.C. 18.* 208, 150-1   £75

5005 — Æ *tetrobol* (*c.* 1·4 gm.). Laur. hd. of Asklepios r., ΑΣ beneath. ℞. As 5002, but ΑΝΔΡΟ for ΑΝΔΡΟΣ, and Δ outside square. *S.N.G. Von Aulock* 2761   ..   £90

5006 88-50 B.C. Æ *drachm* (*c.* 2·5 gm.). Laur. hd. of Asklepios r. ℞. Serpent-staff, placed horizontally; ΚΩΙ above, ΑΓΗΣΙΑΣ / Κ beneath; all within wreath. *B.M.C. 18.* 211, 177   £140

5006   5007

5007 — — *Obv.* Similar. ℞. Coiled serpent, star behind; ΚΩΙ — ΟΝ across field, ΠΥΘΟΚΛΗΣ beneath. *B.M.C. 18.* 212, 193 ..   ..   £100

5008 — Æ *hemidrachm* (*c.* 1·55 gm.). Laur. hd. of Apollo r. ℞. ΚΩΙΩΝ / ΑΡΙΣΤΑΙΟΣ either side of lyre. *B.M.C. 18.* 210, 165-7 ..   ..   £100

5009 — Æ *diobol* (*c.* 1·05 gm.). Similar, but with magistrate's name ΙΕΡΩΝ (partly retrograde) on *rev.* *B.M.C. 18.* 210, 169 ..   ..   £90

5010 *Bronze Coinage.* 350-300 B.C. Æ 10. Bare hd. of bearded Herakles r. ℞. Crab; ΚΩΙ beneath. *B.M.C. 18.* 196, 25..   ..   ..   £11

5011   5013   5015

5011 — Æ 14. Veiled female hd. r. ℞. Crab; ΚΩΙΟΝ above, ΑΝΑΞΑΝΔ beneath. *B.M.C. 18.* 196, 27 ..   ..   £10

5012 3rd cent. B.C. Æ 15. Hd. of young Herakles l., clad in lion's skin. ℞. Crab; ΚΩΙΟΝ above, ΗΡΟΔΟΤΟΣ and club beneath. *B.M.C. 18.* 202, 91-2 ..   ..   ..   £12

5013 — Æ 11. *Obv.* Similar, but hd. r. ℞. Crab; ΚΩΙ above, ΔΑΜΩΝ beneath; all within incuse square. *B.M.C. 18.* 203, 101 ..   ..   £10

5014 190-167 B.C. Æ 18. Hd. of young Herakles three-quarter face to r., clad in lion's skin. ℞. Bow in case and club; ΚΩΙΟΝ above, ΠΑΡΜΕΝΙΣΚΟΣ beneath. *B.M.C. 18.* 203, 108   £14

5015 — Æ 13. Hd. of Helios three-quarter face to r. ℞. Club and bow in case; ΚΩΙΟΝ above, ΜΙΚΥΘΟΣ between. *B.M.C. 18.* 204, 113 ..   ..   £13

5016 167-88 B.C. Æ 17. *Obv.* As 5014. ℞. Club and bow in case; ΚΩΙΩΝ beneath, ΔΙΟΦΑΝ above. *B.M.C. 18.* 209, 160 ..   ..   £14

5017 88-50 B.C. Æ 26. Laur. hd. of Apollo r. ℞. ΚΩΙΩΝ / ΕΥΚΡΑΤ either side of lyre; all within laurel-wreath. *B.M.C. 18.* 211, 174 ..   ..   £16

5018 — Æ 23. Laur. hd. of Asklepios r. ℞. ΚΩΙΩΝ / ΑΓΗΣΙΑΣ either side of serpent-staff. *B.M.C. 18.* 211, 178 ..   ..   £16

5019 — Æ 22. *Obv.* Similar. ℞. ΚΩΙΩΝ ΠΥΘΟΚΛΗΣ. Coiled serpent r. *B.M.C. 18.* 213, 195 ..   ..   £15

5020 50-30 B.C. (reign of the tyrant Nikias). Æ 31. Diad. hd. of Nikias r., ΝΙΚΙΑΣ behind. ℞. Laur. hd. of Asklepios r., ΚΩΙΩΝ before, ΧΑΡΜΥΛΟΣ behind. *B.M.C. 18.* 213, 199-200   £105

5021 Megiste (a small island off the Lycian coast, about eighty miles east of Rhodos). 2nd half of 4th cent. B.C. *Æ drachm* (*c.* 3·1 gm.). Hd. of Helios l., encircled by radiate disk, in background. R. Rose, with bud on either side; in field, M — E. *B.M.C. 18.* 221, 1-3
£250

5022 — Æ 10. Similar, but hd. of Helios to r. *B.M.C. 18.* 221, 4   ..   ..   £20

5021   5026   5027

5023 Nisyros (a small volcanic island situated south of Kos and west of Knidos). 2nd half of 4th cent. B.C. *Æ didrachm* (*c.* 6·54 gm.). Rad. hd. of Helios r., disk in background (?). R. Rose, with bud on r.; to l., star and NI. *S.N.G. Von Aulock* 2770 ..   ..   £900

5024 — *Æ drachm* (*c.* 3·05 gm.). *Obv.* Similar to 5021. R. Rose, with bud on either side; in field, N — I. *Babelon* (*Traité*) *pl.* 148, 8   ..   ..   £400

5025 — *Æ drachm* ? (*c.* 2·26 gm.). Diad. hd. of Artemis (?) r. R. ΝΙΣΥΡΙΟΝ ΙΜΕΡΑΙΟΣ. Poseidon seated facing on rock, body inclined towards l., holding trident. *Historia Numorum, p.* 635   ..   ..   £500

5026 — Æ 12. Hd. of bearded Poseidon r. R. NI. Dolphin r. and trident crossed. *B.M.C. 18.* 222, 1   ..   ..   £18

5027 — — Diad. hd. of Artemis (?) r. R. ΝΙΣΥ. Dolphin r., trident beneath. *B.M.C. 18.* 222, 5-7   ..   ..   £18

5028 — Æ 10. Laur. hd. of Zeus Ammon r. R. Similar to 5026, but dolphin and trident not crossed. *B.M.C. 18.* 222, 3   ..   ..   £18

5029   5032

5029 Rhodos (the large and important island of Rhodos, off the south-west coast of Asia Minor, produced a considerable coinage in the archaic period from its three major cities, Ialysos, Kamiros and Lindos. After the Persian wars no further coinage was issued on the island until the foundation of the new federal capital *circa* 408 B.C. This splendid city, situated on the northern promontory only 12 miles from the mainland, was given the same name as the island. It quickly achieved great prosperity and eventually became one of the principal trading centres of the ancient world. In the third century Rhodos exercised much political influence in the eastern Mediterranean, through the strength of its fleet. But in 167 B.C. the Romans declared Delos a free port, and the Rhodians, their prosperity now greatly diminished, sank into comparative obscurity). 408-394 B.C. *Æ tetradrachm* (*c.* 15·3 gm.). Hd. of Helios three-quarter face to r., hair loose. R. Rose, with bud on r.; to l., Sphinx seated l.; above, ΡΟΔΙΟΝ; all within incuse square. *B.M.C. 18.* 231, 11
£2,500

5030 — *Æ hemidrachm* (*c.* 1·8 gm.). Similar, but without Sphinx in *rev.* field. *S.N.G. Von Aulock* 2784   ..   ..   £140

5031 394-387 B.C. (Alliance coinage). *Æ tridrachm* (*c.* 11·34 gm.). ΣΥΝ. Infant Herakles kneeling r., grappling with two snakes. R. Ρ — Ο either side of rose; all within incuse square. *B.M.C. 18., pl.XLV,* 2   ..   ..   £4,000

Coins with similar obverse types were issued by a number of cities—Byzantion, Kyzikos, Samos, Ephesos, Knidos and Iasos—as members of an alliance dedicated to their liberation from oppression; though who the oppressor was is not certain.

5032 — Æ *triple-siglos?* (*c.* 16·77 gm.).   *Obv.* Similar to 5029.   ℞. Rose, between two bunches of grapes and vine tendrils; POΔION above; all within incuse square.   *B.M.C. 18.* 230, 1   ..   ..   £3,000

5033 — Æ *hemidrachm* (*c.* 2·1 gm.).   Similar.   *B.M.C. 18.* 230, 2 ..   ..   ..   £150

5034   5037

5034 387-304 B.C.   *N stater* (*c.* 8·6 gm.).   Hd. of Helios three-quarter face to r., of exquisite style, hair falling in locks.   ℞. POΔION above rose, with bud on r.; to l., E and bunch of grapes on vine-branch; all within incuse square.   *B.M.C. 18.* 231, 10 ..   ..   £25,000

5035 — Æ *tetradrachm* (*c.* 15·1 gm.).   Hd. of Helios three-quarter face to r., hair loose.   ℞. POΔION above rose, with bud on l.; to r., lyre; to l., I; all within incuse square.   *B.M.C. 18.* 232, 16   ..   ..   £2,000

5036 — — Similar, but with Boeotian shield instead of lyre on *rev.*, and Φ instead of I.   *B.M.C. 18.* 232, 25 ..   ..   £2,000

5037 — Æ *didrachm* (*c.* 6·8 gm.).   *Obv.* Similar.   ℞. POΔION above rose, with bud on r.; to l., E and bunch of grapes; all within incuse square.   *B.M.C. 18.* 233, 27-9 ..   £300

5038 — — — ℞. POΔION above rose, with bud on r.; E — Y in lower field; bunch of grapes to l.   *B.M.C. 18.* 233, 34 ..   ..   £300

5039   5042   5045

5039 — — Rad. hd. of Helios r.   ℞. POΔION above rose, with bud on r.; to l., EY and cornucopiae.   *B.M.C. 18.* 234, 41   ..   ..   £400

5040 — — Hd. of Helios three-quarter face to r., hair loose.   ℞. Rose, with bud on r.; above, ΑΡΙΣΤΟΝΟΜΟΣ; to l., prow; P — o in lower field.   *B.M.C. 18.* 235, 45 ..   £350

5041 — Æ *drachm* (*c.* 3·5 gm.).   *Obv.* Similar.   ℞. POΔION above rose, with bud on r.; to l., Δ and bunch of grapes; all within incuse square.   *B.M.C. 18.* 234, 38   ..   £175

5042 — — Similar, but with star instead of grapes in *rev.* field to l., and without incuse square.   *B.M.C. 18.* 236, 56-7 ..   ..   £150

5043 — Æ *hemidrachm* (*c.* 1·85 gm.).   Hd. of Helios three-quarter face to r., inclined to one side, hair flying loose.   ℞. P — o either side of rose; all within incuse square.   *B.M.C. 18.* 230, 3-7 ..   ..   £120

5044 — — Hd. of Helios three-quarter face to r., hair loose.   ℞. Rose, with bud on r.; to l., Δ and PO.   *B.M.C. 18.* 236, 62   ..   ..   £100

5045 — Æ *diobol* (*c.* 1·12 gm.).   Rad. hd. of Helios r.   ℞. Two rosebuds, E between; P — o in lower field; all within incuse square.   *B.M.C. 18.* 234, 42 ..   ..   ..   £75

5046 304-167 B.C.   Æ *tetradrachm* (*c.* 13·5 gm.).   Rad. hd. of Helios three-quarter face to r.   ℞. POΔION above rose, with bud on r.; to l., prow r.; AMEIN — IAΣ in lower field.   *B.M.C. 18.* 241, 120 ..   ..   £750

5047   5048

Rhodos *continued*

5047 — — *Obv.* Similar. ℞. Rose, with bud on r.; above, ΤΕΙΣΥΛΟΣ; to l., Aphrodite (?) stg.
facing, l. hand raised to her breast; P — O in lower field.   *B.M.C. 18.* 242, 128   £750

5048 — Æ *didrachm* (*c.* 6·75 gm.).   *Obv.* Similar. ℞. Rose, with bud on r.; above, ΑΓΗΣΙΔ —
AMOΣ; to l., Artemis running l., holding torch; P — O in lower field.   *B.M.C. 18.* 242,
130-32   ..   ..   £150

5049 — — — ℞. ΡΟΔΙΟΝ above rose, with bud on r.; to l., anchor; ΕΥΚΡΑ — ΤΗΣ in lower
field.   *B.M.C. 18.* 243, 141   ..   ..   £150

5050 — Æ *drachm* (*c.* 3·25 gm.).   Hd. of Helios three-quarter face to r., hair loose. ℞. Rose,
with bud on r.; above, ΕΡΑΣΙΚΛΗΣ; to l., helmet; P — O in lower field.   *S.N.G. Von
Aulock* 2813   ..   ..   £85

5051   5054

5051 — Æ *drachm* (*c.* 2·75 gm.).   Hd. of Helios three-quarter face to l., hair floating loosely.
℞. P — O either side of rose, with bud on r.; above, ΑΙΝΗΤΩΡ; to l., caduceus.   *B.M.C. 18.*
245, 155-60 ..   ..   £75

5052 — — *Obv.* As 5050. ℞. Rose, with bud on r.; above, ΓΟΡΓΟΣ; to l., bow in case; P — O
in lower field.   *B.M.C. 18.* 245, 164-8   ..   ..   £65

5053 — Æ *hemidrachm* (*c.* 1·62 gm.).   *Obv.* As 5050. ℞. As 5048.   *S.N.G. Von Aulock*
2816 ..   ..   £55

5054 — Æ *hemidrachm* (*c.* 1·32 gm.).   *Obv.* As 5050. ℞. Rose, with bud on r.; above,
ΑΜΕΙΝΙΑΣ; to l., bearded ithyphallic term r.; P — O in lower field.   *B.M.C. 18.* 247,
189-91   ..   ..   £45

5055 — Æ *diobol* (*c.* 0·9 gm.).   Rad. hd. of Helios r. ℞. Two rosebuds; between them,
Artemis running r., holding torch; P — O in lower field.   *B.M.C. 18.* 237, 64 ..   £40

5056 189-167 B.C.   ℕ *stater* (*c.* 8·5 gm.).   Rad. hd. of Helios three-quarter face to r. ℞. P —
O either side of rose, with bud on l.; above, ΑΝΤΑΙΟΣ; to r., bee; all within shallow incuse
square.   *B.M.C. 18.* 251, 229   ..   ..   £5,000

5057   5058

5057 — *N half-stater* (*c.* 4·25 gm.).   Similar, but with caduceus instead of bee in *rev.* field to
   r. *B.M.C. 18.* 272, 230A £2,500

5058 — *N quarter-stater* (*c.* 2·13 gm.).   Rad. hd. of Rhodos r., wearing stephane.   R. Rose,
   with bud on l.; ΤΙΜΟΚΡΑ above, Ρ — O in field, aplustre to r.; all within circle of dots.
   B.M.C. 18. 252, 234 ..   ..   £1,500

5059 — *N stater* (*c.* 8·5 gm.), restoring the types of Lysimachos of Thrace.   Diad. hd. of
   Alexander r., with horn of Ammon.   R. ΒΑΣΙΛΕΩΣ / ΛΥΣΙΜΑΧΟΥ either side of Athena
   seated l., holding Nike and spear; shield at side; to l., rose and ΑΡΙΣΤΟΒΟΥΛΟΣ; in ex.,
   trident.   *Müller (Die Münzen des thrakischen Königs Lysimachos)* 451 ..   ..   £1,500

5060 — — restoring the types of Philip II of Macedon.   Laur. hd. of Apollo r.   R. Galloping
   biga driven r. by charioteer, ΦΙΛΙΠΠΟΥ in ex.; in field, rose, ΡΟ and ΜΝΑΣΙΜΑΧΟΣ.   *Müller*
   (Numismatique d'Alexandre le Grand) 308 ..   ..   £1,500

5061 — Æ *tetradrachm* (*c.* 16·75 gm.), restoring the types of Alexander the Great.   Hd. of
   young Herakles r., clad in lion's skin.   R. Zeus enthroned l., holding eagle and sceptre,
   ΑΛΕΞΑΝΔΡΟΥ behind; before, ΑΙΝΗΤΩΡ and rose; beneath seat, ΡΟ.   *Müller* 1160   £175

5062 — — — Similar, but with monogram instead of ΑΙΝΗΤΩΡ in *rev.* field to l.   *Müller*
   1154 ..   ..   £150

5063 167-88 B.C.   Æ *drachm* (*c.* 3 gm.).   Rad. hd. of Helios r.   R. Ρ — O either side of rose,
   with bud on r.; above, ΑΝΑΞΙΔΟΤΟΣ; to l., serpent coiled round omphalos; all within
   shallow incuse square.   *B.M.C. 18.* 253, 247-8 ..   ..   £45

5064   5065   5066

5064 — — Similar, but on *rev.* magistrate's name ΦΙΛΟΚΡΑΤΗΣ instead of ΑΝΑΞΙΔΟΤΟΣ, an₅
   bucranium instead of serpent.   *B.M.C. 18.* 256, 288 ..   ..   £4

5065 — Æ *hemidrachm* (*c.* 1·4 gm.).   Rad. hd. of Helios three-quarter face to r.   R. Similar
   to 5063, but with magistrate's name ΘΡΑΣΥΜΕΝΗΣ, and symbol rising sun to l.   *B.M.C.*
   18. 257, 304 ..   ..   £40

5066 — Æ *diobol* (*c.* 0·9 gm.).   Rad. hd. of Helios r.   R. Ρ — O either side of rose, with bud
   on l.; to r., ear of corn; all within circle of dots.   *B.M.C. 18.* 258, 311   ..   £35

5067 88-43 B.C.   Æ *trihemidrachm* (*c.* 4·25 gm.).   Hd. of Helios or Medusa three-quarter face
   to r., wearing winged diadem tied beneath chin.   R. Ρ — O either side of rose, with bud
   on r.; above, ΓΟΡΓΟΣ; to l., star.   *Forrer/Weber* 6754 ..   ..   £500

5068

5072

Rhodos *continued*

5068 — — Rad. hd. of Helios three-quarter face to l. ℞. Full-blown rose to front; P — O in field; above, palm-branch; all within circle of dots. *B.M.C. 18*. 260, 334 .. £175

5069 — — Rad. hd. of Helios three-quarter face to r. ℞. Full-blown rose to front; ΚΡΙΤΟ-ΚΛΗΣ above, P — O in field, ear of corn beneath; all within circle of dots. *B.M.C. 18*. 261, 337-8 .. .. £150

5070 — *R drachm (c.* 2·6 gm.). Rad. hd. of Helios facing. ℞. Full-blown rose to front, ΡΟΔΙΩΝ around; all within circle of dots. *S.N.G. Von Aulock* 2840 .. .. £140

5071 *Bronze Coinage.* Before 304 B.C. Æ 11. Diad. hd. of Rhodos r., hair rolled. ℞. Rose, with bud on r.; ivy-leaf to l., P — O in lower field. *B.M.C. 18*. 238, 85 .. £9

5072 — — Similar, but with thunderbolt instead of ivy-leaf in *rev.* field. *B.M.C. 18*. 238, 82-4 .. .. £9

5073 — — Similar, but with M instead of thunderbolt in *rev.* field. *B.M.C. 18*. 240, 112-13 £9

5074

5075

5074 — Æ 10. Rose, with bud on r. ℞. Rose; P — O in lower field, Σ to l. *B.M.C. 18*. 237, 73 .. .. £8

5075 3rd cent. B.C. Æ 19. Laur. hd. of Zeus r. ℞. Rose, with bud on r.; P — O in lower field, ΦI to l. *B.M.C. 18*. 250, 219-21 .. .. £12

5076 — Æ 17. *Obv.* Similar. ℞. Rose, surmounted by rising sun; P — O in field, branch to l., dolphin to r. *B.M.C. 18*. 250, 223 .. .. £15

5077 — — Veiled and diad. female hd. r. ℞. Rose, with bud on r.; P — O in lower field, ΤΕ to l. *B.M.C. 18*. 251, 227 .. .. £12

5078 — Æ 15. *Obv.* Similar. ℞. Prow r.; above, ΡΟ and rosebud. *B.M.C. 18*. 251, 228 £13

5079 167-88 B.C. Æ 28. Rad. hd. of Helios r. ℞. Rose, with bud on l.; P — O in field, fish-hook to l., dolphin and trident to r.; all within circle of dots. *B.M.C. 18*. 258, 312-13 .. .. £30

5080 — Æ 12. *Obv.* Similar. ℞. Rose, with bud on r.; P — O in lower field. *B.M.C. 18.*
259, 326   ..   ..   £10

5081 — — Rad. and diad. hd. of Rhodos r. ℞. Rose, dividing P — O; all within shallow
incuse square. *B.M.C. 18.* 259-60, 327-32   ..   ..   £9

5082 88-43 B.C. Æ 36. Rad. hd. of Helios three-quarter face to l. ℞. Full-blown rose to
front, within oak-wreath; above, ZHNΩN and P — O. *B.M.C. 18.* 261, 342   ..   £125

5083 — — *Obv.* Similar, but hd. three-quarter face to r. ℞. Full-blown rose to front; PO
above, ΣΦAI — POΣ, divided by star, beneath; all within oak-wreath. *B.M.C. 18.* 261,
345 ..   ..   £140

5084 — Æ 18. Rad. hd. of Helios r. ℞. Full-blown rose to front; EΠITYXHΣ around, P — O
above, caduceus beneath; all within circle of dots. *B.M.C. 18.* 262, 346-9   ..   £10

5085 — — — ℞. Full-blown rose to front; POΔIΩN around, dolphin and branch beneath;
all within circle of dots. *B.M.C. 18. 262, 358* £11

5086 **Rhodian Peraia** (the Rhodian possessions on the mainland. Coins were issued there
from time to time, some perhaps from Kaunos, with types resembling the regular Rhodian
coinage but without the name of the mint). 2nd half of 4th cent. B.C. *Æ drachm (c.*
3·7 gm.). Hd. of Helios l., encircled by rad. disk, in background. ℞. Rose, with bud on
either side; in field, E — Y. *S.N.G. Von Aulock* 2862   ..   ..   £350

5087 3rd-2nd cent. B.C. *Æ tetradrachm (c.* 8·57 gm.). Rose, with bud on either side; to l.,
bunch of grapes and M. ℞. Eagle stg. r. on thunderbolt, wings open; IA — A in upper
field; ΠA to r. *S.N.G. Von Aulock* 2863 ..   ..   £2,500

5088   5090

5088 — *Æ drachm (c.* 1·8—2·6 gm.). Hd. of Helios three-quarter face to l., hair loose. ℞.
Rose, with bud on r.; above, BABΩN; to l., MI monogram beneath star; to r., KP monogram.
B.M.C. 18. 248, 198   ..   ..   £110

5089 — — *Obv.* Similar, but hd. three-quarter face to r. ℞. Rose, with two buds on r.;
above, ΣTAΣIΩN; to l., bunch of grapes. *B.M.C. 18.* 249, 207 ..   ..   ..   £100

5090 — — Hd. of Helios facing, with eagle stg. r. before his r. cheek. ℞. Rose, with bud on
r. *B.M.C. 18.* 249, 210 ..   ..   £120

Rhodian Peraia *continued*

5091 — — — ℞. Rose, with bud on either side; in field, Υ — Π / Μ — Ι. *B.M.C. 18.* 250, 218 .. .. £120

5092 2nd cent. B.C. *Æ drachm (c.* 2·6 gm.). Hd. of Helios three-quarter face to r., hair loose. ℞. Rose, with bud on r.; above, ΕΡΜΙΑΣ; in lower field, Ι — Ω £60

Most, if not all, coins of this type come from the Sitichoro hoard of 1968. The majority of specimens are close to 'extremely fine' in condition, and worth about double the value quoted here.

5092A **Syme** (a small island between Rhodos and the Triopian promontory. The settlement, bearing the same name, was on the northern coast). 3rd cent. B.C. Æ 9. Laur. hd. of Zeus r. ℞. Spear-head dividing Σ — Υ; all within olive-wreath. *S.N.G. Von Aulock* 2867 .. .. £20

5093 **Telos** (a small island north-west of Rhodos. Its town lay on the northern coast). 2nd half of 4th cent. B.C. Æ 13. Laur. hd. of Zeus r. ℞. ΤΗΛΙ. Crab. *Historia Numorum, p.* 642 .. .. £24

5094 — — ΔΑΜΟΚΡΑΤΙΑΣ. Helmeted hd. of Athena facing, with aegis outspread in background. ℞. As last, but also with magistrate's name in field. *Historia Numorum, p.* 642 .. .. £25

5095 — Æ 10. Helmeted hd. of Athena r. ℞. As 5093. *Historia Numorum, p.* 642 £22

CENTRAL AND SOUTHERN ASIA MINOR, AND CYPRUS

Comprising the areas of Phrygia, Lycia, Pamphylia, Pisidia, Lycaonia, Cilicia, Galatia, Cappadocia and Cyprus.

5096 5097

5096 **PHRYGIA. Abbaitis** (this district of western Phrygia was occupied by a people of Mysian origin. Their coins were probably struck at the city of **Ankyra**). Mid-2nd cent. B.C. Æ 20. Laur. hd. of Zeus r. ℞. ΜΥΣΩΝ / ΑΒΒΑΙΤΩΝ above and below winged thunderbolt, monogram beneath; all within oak-wreath. *B.M.C. 25.* 1, 4-6 .. £9

5097 — Æ 18. Hd. of young Herakles r., clad in lion's skin. ℞. ΜΥΣΩΝ / ΑΒΒΑ either side of club draped with lion's skin, monogram to r.; all within oak-wreath. *B.M.C. 25.* 2, 8 £10

5098 — Æ 15. Hd. of Apollo Chromios (?) r., hair rolled and bound with wreath. ℞. ΜΥ / ΣΩΝ and ΑΒΒΑ either side of double-axe, monogram beneath; all within laurel-wreath. *B.M.C. 25.* 2, 9-10 .. .. £11

5099 **Akmoneia** (an important city of central Phrygia, Akmoneia was situated on a tributary of the river Senaros). Late 2nd-early 1st cent. B.C. Æ 22. Bust of Athena r., wearing crested helmet and aegis. ℞. Eagle r. on thunderbolt, wings spread, star on either side; above, ΑΚΜΟΝΕΩΝ; beneath, ΤΙΜΟΘΕΟΣ / ΜΗΤΡΟ. *B.M.C. 25.* 4-5, 6-9 .. £13

5100 — Æ 20. Turreted and veiled bust of Tyche r. ℞. Artemis advancing r., drawing arrow from quiver and holding bow, stag r. at her side; before, ΑΚΜΟΝΕΩΝ; behind, ΤΙΜΟΘΕΟ / ΜΕΝΕΛΑ. *B.M.C. 25.* 5, 13 .. .. £12

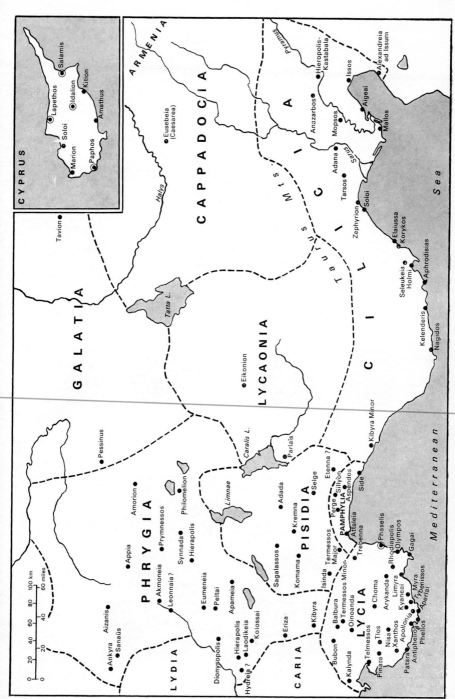

MAP 18 CENTRAL AND SOUTHERN ASIA MINOR AND CYPRUS

5101

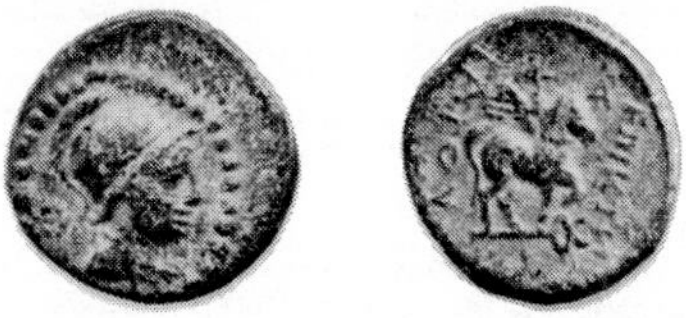

5103

Akmoneia *continued*

5101 — Æ 18. Hd. of Zeus r., wreathed with oak. ℞. Asklepios stg. facing, resting on serpent-staff; to r., ΑΚΜΟΝΕ; to l., ΘΕΟΔΟΤ / ΙΕΡΟΚΛΕ. *B.M.C. 25.* 4, 3-5 .. £12

5102 **Aizanis** (an important city in the north-west of the country, near the source of the river Rhyndakos. It lay in a district known as **Epiktetos** the name of which appears on the earliest coins of Aizanis). Late 2nd-early 1st cent. B.C. Æ 20. Dr. bust of Ares (?) r., in triple-crested helmet. ℞. Free horse pacing r.; above, cap of Dioskouros; before, ΕΠΙΚΤΗΤΕ; behind, ΑΣ; beneath, Ε. *B.M.C. 25.* 200, 2 .. .. £14

5103 — — *Obv.* Similar; behind, Θ. ℞. Free horse pacing r. above caduceus, palm-branch across shoulder; above, cap of Dioskouros; before, ΕΠΙΚΤΗΤ and ΑΡΤ monogram; behind, ΕΤ monogram and ΓΑΙΟΥ. *B.M.C. 25.* 201, 9 .. .. £14

5104 — Æ 17. Laur. and dr. bust of Zeus r. ℞. ΕΠΙΚΤΗ / ΤΕΩΝ either side of eagle stg. r. on thunderbolt, hd. l.; monogram to l., ΙΑ to r. *B.M.C. 25.* 200, 4 .. .. £13

5105 — Æ 14. Crested Macedonian helmet. ℞. ΕΠΙΚΤΗ / ΤΕΩΝ either side of sword in sheath; monogram to l., Δ to r. *B.M.C. 25.* 200, 5 .. .. £12

5106 2nd half of 1st cent. B.C. Æ 18. Laur. hd. of bearded Herakles l., club behind neck. ℞. ΕΖΕΑΝ / ΙΤΩΝ either side of Hermes stg. l., holding purse and caduceus. *B.M.C. 25.* 23, 1 .. .. £12

5107

5109

5107 — — Turreted and laur. hd. of Tyche l. ℞. Dionysos stg. l., holding kantharos and thyrsos; to r., ΕΖΕΑΝΙΤΩΝ. *B.M.C. 25.* 23, 2 .. .. £12

5108 **Amorion** (a city of eastern Phrygia, not far from the Galatian border, Amorion was the reputed birth-place of Aesop, the writer of Fables). 2nd-1st cent. B.C. Æ 20. Hd. of Zeus r., wreathed with oak. ℞. ΑΜΟΡ — ΙΑΝΩΝ beneath and before eagle stg. r. on thunderbolt, caduceus across l. wing; to l., ΣΟΛΕ; to r., ΚΛΕΑΡ. *B.M.C. 25.* 47, 2 £10

5109 — Æ 15. Turreted hd. of Tyche (or Kybele) r. ℞. ΑΜΟΡΙΑΝΩΝ beneath and before lion springing r. from caduceus; ΔΙ above. *B.M.C. 25.* 47, 7 .. .. .. £11

5110

5110 **Apameia** (founded by Antiochos I, and named after that king's mother, Apama, Apameia was situated near the sources of the great river Maeander and was an important road junction for routes in all directions. It grew to become one of the great cities of Asia Minor, and participated in the silver cistophoric coinage under the later Pergamene kings and, after 133 B.C., under the Romans). 189-133 B.C. Æ *cistophoric tetradrachm* (*c.* 12·6 gm.). Cista mystica containing serpent; all within ivy-wreath. ℞. Bow in case between two coiled serpents; to l., AΠA monogram; to r., wreath. *B.M.C. 25.* 69, 1
£125

5111 — — Similar, but with Sphinx seated r. instead of wreath on *rev. B.M.C. 25.* 69, 4
£125

5112 — Æ *didrachm* (*c.* 6·3 gm.). Club draped in lion's skin; all within ivy-wreath. ℞. Bunch of grapes upon vine-leaf; AΠA monogram to l., uncertain symbol to r. *S.N.G. Von Aulock* 3456 .. .. £250

5113 After 133 B.C. Æ *cistophoric tetradrachm* (*c.* 12·6 gm.). Cista mystica containing serpent; all within ivy-wreath. ℞. Bow in case between two coiled serpents; to l., AΠA surmounted by B; above bow-case, KΩKOY; to r., two flutes. *B.M.C. 25.* 70, 11 £110

5114 — — Similar, but without letter above AΠA in *rev.* field to l., and with magistrate's name AΠOΛΛΩ / NIOY instead of KΩKOY. *B.M.C. 25.* 71, 20-21 .. .. .. £110

5115 P. Lentulus Spinther, Roman Proconsul of Cilicia, 56-53 B.C., and Imperator. Æ *cistophoric tetradrachm* (*c.* 12·6 gm.). Cista mystica containing serpent; all within ivy-wreath. ℞. Bow in case between two coiled serpents; to l., AΠA; to r., two flutes; above bow-case, P. LENTVLVS P.F. / IMPERATOR; beneath, MVIΣKOV. *B.M.C. 25.* 73, 27-8
£350

5116 Appius Claudius Pulcher, Roman Proconsul of Cilicia, 53-51 B.C., and Imperator. Æ *cistophoric tetradrachm* (*c.* 12·6 gm.). Similar, but with AP. PVLCHER AP.F. / IMP. above bow-case on *rev.*, and HPA / TIMΩNOΣ beneath. *B.M.C. 25.* 73, 30 .. .. £350

5117 C. Fannius, Pontifex and Praetor, 49-48 B.C. Æ *cistophoric tetradrachm* (*c.* 12·6 gm.). *Obv.* Similar. ℞. Two coiled serpents either side of tetrastyle shrine surmounted by statue of Athena (?); to l., AΠA, and strung bow behind the serpent; to r., two flutes; above, C.FAN. — PONT. PR.; beneath, MANTIΘEOΣ / MANTIΘEOY. *B.M.C. 25.* 73, 31
£400

5118 *Bronze Coinage.* 2nd cent. B.C. Æ 19. Laur. hd. of Zeus r. ℞. AΠAMEΩN between caps of the Dioskouroi; all within laurel-wreath. *B.M.C. 25.* 74, 32 .. .. £16

Apameia *continued*

5119 133-48 B.C. Æ 37. Bust of Athena r., wearing aegis and crested Corinthian helmet ornamented with griffin; all within ornamental frame consisting of plain circle between two circles of pellets. R. Eagle flying r. above Maeander pattern between caps of the Dioskouroi; above, ΑΠΑΜΕΩΝ and star; beneath, ΑΝΤΙΦΩΝ / ΜΕΝΕΚΛΕΟΥΣ. *B.M.C. 25.* 77, 44 .. .. £150

 These large coins, with ornamental border on obv., were probably not current as money, but had some special function, perhaps as presentation pieces.

5120 — Æ 24. Similar, but without the triple-border on *obv.*, and with magistrate's name ΑΤΤΑΛΟΥ / ΒΙΑΝΟΡΟΣ beneath Maeander pattern on *rev.* *B.M.C. 25.* 79, 56-7 .. £14

  5121   5125

5121 — Æ 21. Laur. hd. of Zeus r. R. Cultus-statue of Artemis Anaitis facing; to r., ΑΠΑΜΕ; to l., ΑΛΕΞΑΝ / ΑΡΤΕΜΙ. *B.M.C. 25.* 75, 33-6 .. .. £12

5122 — Æ 17. Turreted bust of Artemis r., bow and quiver at shoulder. R. Naked Marsyas advancing r., playing double flute, Maeander pattern beneath; to r., ΑΠΑΜΕ; to l., ΠΑΝΚΡ / ΖΗΝΟ. *B.M.C. 25.* 85, 91-3 .. .. £13

5123 — Æ 13. Laur. hd. of Zeus r. R. ΑΠΑΜ / ΣΚΑΥ either side of crested helmet r., above Maeander pattern. *B.M.C. 25.* 85, 95 .. .. £11

5124 **Appia** (situated on a tributary of the river Tembris, Appia was midway between Akmoneia and Kotiaeion on an important north-south route). 2nd-1st cent. B.C. Æ 18. Turreted hd. of Kybele r. R. ΑΠΠΙΑΝΩΝ. Zeus seated l., holding eagle and sceptre. *Historia Numorum, p.* 667 .. .. £22

5125 **Kibyra** (an important city in the far south of the country, near the Lycian border, Kibyra retained its independence until 84 B.C. when it was added to the Roman province of Asia. It was celebrated for its iron products). 166-84 B.C. Æ *tetradrachm* (*c.* 12·6 gm.). Young male bust r., dr. and wearing crested helmet. R. Armed horseman galloping r., holding spear couched; behind, bee; beneath, Α — ΚΕΔ / Ο — ΔΙ and ΚΙΒΥΡΑ-ΤΩΝ. *B.M.C. 25.* 131, 4 .. .. £550

5126 — Æ *drachm* (*c.* 3·1 gm.). *Obv.* Similar, but no drapery round neck. Ŗ. As last, but eagle instead of bee behind, and ΚΙΒΥΡΑΤΩΝ only beneath horse. *B.M.C. 25.* 132, 8
£140

5127 — — *Obv.* As 5125. Ŗ. Armed horseman galloping r., holding palm over r. shoulder; beneath, ΙΟ and ΚΙΒΥΡΑΤΩΝ. *B.M.C. 25.* 133, 15 .. .. £150

5128 — Æ 15. Rad. hd. of Helios facing. Ŗ. ΚΙΒΥ / ΡΑΤΩΝ above and beneath humped bull butting r. *S.N.G. Von Aulock* 3720 .. .. £14

5129 — Æ 10. *Obv.* As 5126. Ŗ. Κ — Ι either side of eagle stg. r., wings closed. *B.M.C. 25.* 134, 16 .. .. £12

5130 — — — Ŗ. Incuse square containing humped bull butting r.; beneath, ΚΙΒΥΡΑΤΩΝ. *B.M.C. 25.* 134, 17 .. .. £12

5131 **Kolossai** (situated on the river Lykos, south-east of Laodikeia on the road to Apameia). 2nd-1st cent. B.C. Æ 18. Laur. hd. of Zeus r. Ŗ. ΚΟΛΟΣ / ΣΗΝΩΝ above and beneath winged thunderbolt. *Forrer/Weber* 7070 .. .. £20

5131   5132

5132 **Dionysopolis** (founded in the 2nd cent. B.C. by the Pergamene kings, Dionysopolis was close to the Lydian border and lay in the valley of the upper Maeander). 2nd-1st cent. B.C. Æ 20. Bust of young Dionysos r., wreathed with ivy, thyrsos behind shoulder. Ŗ. Dionysos stg. facing, hd. l., holding bunch of grapes and thyrsos, panther at feet; to r., ΔΙΟΝΥΣΟ; to l., ΜΕΝΕΚΛ / ΒΙΑΝ. *B.M.C. 25.* 182, 4 .. .. .. £14

5133 — Æ 17. Hd. of young Dionysos r., wreathed with ivy. Ŗ. Bunch of grapes; ΔΙΟΝΥΣ to r. *B.M.C. 25.* 182, 1 .. .. £12

5134 — Æ 14. Mask of Silenos r. Ŗ. ΔΙΟΝΥ / ΣΟΠΟ either side of bunch of grapes. *B.M.C. 25.* 182, 2 .. .. £13

5135 **Eriza** (a small town in the south of the country, in the lower Indos valley, north of Kibyra). 2nd-1st cent. B.C. Æ 17. Diad. hd. of Poseidon (?) r. Ŗ. ΕΡΙΖΗ / ΝΩΝ either side of eagle stg. r. on thunderbolt. *Forrer/Weber* 7086 .. .. .. £18

5136 — Æ 15. *Obv.* Similar. Ŗ. ΕΡΙΖΗ / ΝΩΝ either side of Nike advancing r., holding wreath and palm. *S.N.G. Von Aulock* 3572 .. .. £15

5137 — Æ 10. Є — Ρ either side of double-axe. Ŗ. Trident. *B.M.C. 25.* 202, 1 £12

5138 **Eumeneia** (founded in the 2nd cent. B.C. and named after the Pergamene King Eumenes
II, Eumeneia lay in fertile country in the valley of the river Glaukos, and at an important
road junction). Before 133 B.C. Æ 15. Hd. of Zeus r., wreathed with oak. R.
EYME / NEΩN in two lines within oak-wreath. *B.M.C. 25.* 211, 1-2   ..   ..   £12

5139 After 133 B.C. Æ 22. Hd. of young Dionysos r., wreathed with ivy. R. Tripod-lebes,
with stars above and on either side; to r., EYMENEΩN and filleted laurel-branch; to l.,
ΔΙΟΝΥΣΙΟΥ / ΦΙΛΩΝΙΔ and double-axe entwined by serpent. *B.M.C. 25.* 212, 13
£12

5140 — Æ 20. Hd. of Athena r., in crested Corinthian helmet. R. EYME / NEΩN either side of
Nike advancing l., holding wreath and palm; to l., MENEKP. *B.M.C. 25.* 211, 9   £11

5141   5142

5141 44-40 B.C. (under the name of **Fulvia,** bestowed upon Eumeneia by Mark Antony in
honour of his wife). Æ 15. Winged hd. of Nike r., with features of Fulvia (?). R.
Athena advancing l., holding spear and shield; ΦΟΥΛΟΥΙΑΝΩΝ behind, ΣΜΕΡΤΟΡΙΓΟΣ /
ΦΙΛΩΝΙΔΟΥ before. *B.M.C. 25.* 213, 20 ..   ..   £75

5142 **Hierapolis** (situated on high ground east of the junction of the rivers Lykos and
Maeander, Hierapolis was revered as a holy place because of its hot springs and a supposed
entrance to the underworld). 2nd-1st cent. B.C. Æ 21. Laur. hd. of Apollo r. R. ΙΕΡΟ /
ΠΟΛΙΤΩΝ either side of Roma (?) seated l. on shields, holding Nike and sceptre; monograms before and behind. *B.M.C. 25.* 228, 4-5 ..   ..   £14

5143 — Æ 18. Laur. hd. of Zeus r. R. ΙΕΡΟ / ΠΟΛΙΤΩΝ either side of Apollo Kitharoedos
advancing r., holding plectrum and lyre. *B.M.C. 25.* 229, 8 ..   ..   ..   £14

5144 — Æ 14. Laur. hd. of Apollo r. R. ΙΕΡΟ / ΠΟΛΙΤΩΝ either side of tripod; monogram
above. *S.N.G. Von Aulock* 3616   ..   ..   £12

5145 **Hydrela** (the exact site of this town is not certain, but it seems to have stood in the
vicinity of Hierapolis, perhaps on the left bank of the Maeander, opposite Tripolis in
Lydia). 2nd-1st cent. B.C. Æ 20. Diad. bust of Artemis r., bow and quiver at shoulder.
R. Mên seated on horse stg. r.; YΔPH above. *S.N.G. Von Aulock* 3674   ..   £21

5146 — Æ 14. *Obv.* Similar. R. YΔPHΛ / ITΩN either side of Mên stg. l., r. hand extended.
B.M.C. 25. 271, 1 ..   ..   £16

5147 **Laodikeia** (an important city in the valley of the Lykos, north-west of Kolossai, Laodikeia was founded by Antiochos II, on the site of an earlier town, and named after that king's wife, Laodike). 189-133 B.C. Æ *cistophoric tetradrachm* (*c.* 12·6 gm.). Cista mystica containing serpent; all within ivy-wreath. ℞. Bow in case between two coiled serpents; to l., ΛΑΟ; to r., wolf r. above lyre. *B.M.C. 25.* 278, 2   ..   ..   £150

5148   5150

5148 After 133 B.C. Æ *cistophoric tetradrachm* (*c.* 12·6 gm.). *Obv.* Similar. ℞. Bow in case between two coiled serpents; to l., ΛΑΟ; to r., winged caduceus; above bow case, ΞΕΥΞΙΣ / ΑΠΟΛΛΩΝΙΟΥ / ΤΟΥ ΑΜΥΝΤΟΥ. *B.M.C. 25.* 279, 4   ..   ..   ..   £125

5149 — — Similar, but with magistrate's name ΔΙΟΔΩ / ΡΟΥ above bow case on *rev. B.M.C. 25.* 280, 8   ..   ..   £125

5150 — Æ *drachm* (*c.* 3 gm.). Club draped in lion's skin; all within vine-wreath (?). ℞. Bunch of grapes upon vine-leaf; ΛΑ to l., caduceus to r., ΑΘ — ΗΝ above. *B.M.C. 25.* 281, 14   ..   ..   £175

5151 C. Fabius, Roman Proconsul of Asia, 57-56 B.C. Æ *cistophoric tetradrachm.* Cista mystica containing serpent; all within ivy-wreath. ℞. Bow case between two coiled serpents, bow behind the one on l.; to l., ΛΑΟ; to r., caduceus; above bow case, C.FBI (*sic*) M.F. / PRO. COS.; beneath, ΣΙΤΑΛΚΑΣ. *S.N.G. Von Aulock* 3802   ..   ..   £350

5152 P. Lentulus Spinther, Roman Proconsul of Cilicia, 56-53 B.C., and Imperator. Æ *cistophoric tetradrachm.* Similar, but with P. LENTVLVS P.F. / IMP. above bow case on *rev.*, and ΑΡΤΕΜΙΔΩΡΟΣ / ΔΑΜΟΚΡΑΤΟΥ beneath. *B.M.C. 25.* 281, 15   ..   ..   £350

5153 Appius Claudius Pulcher, Roman Proconsul of Cilicia, 53-51 B.C., and Imperator. Æ *cistophoric tetradrachm.* Similar, but with AP. PVLCHER AP. F. / PROCOS. above bow case, and ΑΠΟΛΛΩΝΙΟΣ / ΔΑΜΟΚΡΑΤΟΥ / ΙΩΣΙΜΟΣ beneath. *B.M.C. 25.* 282, 19   ..   £350

5154 — — Similar, but with AP. PVLCHER F. / IMP. above bow case, and ΑΠΟΛΛΩΝΙΟΣ / ΕΥΑΡΧΟΥ beneath; also with Ι above the mint mark in *rev.* field to l. *B.M.C. 25.* 282, 21   £350

5155 *Bronze Coinage.* 2nd cent. B.C. Æ 17. Dr. bust of Aphrodite r., hair bound with cord. ℞. ΛΑΟΔΙ / ΚΕΩΝ either side of Aphrodite seated r., r. hand at side, holding dove in l. *B.M.C. 25.* 283, 26 ..   ..   £14

5156   5158

5156 — — *Obv.* Similar. ℞. ΛΑΟΔΙΚΕΩΝ behind Aphrodite stg. l., holding dove; before, rose on stalk. *B.M.C. 25.* 284, 27   ..   ..   £13

5157 — Æ 13. Turreted hd. of goddess r. ℞. ΛΑΟΔΙ / ΚΕΩΝ either side of lion seated l., r. forepaw raised. *B.M.C. 25.* 283, 22   ..   ..   £11

5158 — — Laur. hd. of Zeus r. ℞. ΛΑΟΔΙΚΕΩΝ. Lotus-flower. *B.M.C. 25.* 283, 24   £12

5159   5161

Laodikeia *continued*

5159 2nd-1st cent. B.C.   Æ 19.   Hd. of Aphrodite (or Queen Laodike) r., wearing stephane and diad.   R. ΛΑΟΔΙ / ΚΕΩΝ either side of double cornucopiae bound together with fillet. *B.M.C. 25.* 284, 32-3   ..   ..   £12

5160 — — Laur. and dr. bust of Queen Laodike (?) r., wearing necklace.   R. ΛΑΟΔΙ / ΚΕΩΝ either side of cornucopiae bound with fillet, caduceus on l.   *B.M.C. 25.* 285, 40   £15

5161 — Æ 17.   Hd. of Apollo (?) r.   R. ΛΑΟΔΙ / ΚΕΩΝ either side of tripod.   *B.M.C. 25.* 286, 44   ..   ..   £11

5162 1st cent. B.C.   Æ 20.   Bearded hd. of Zeus (?) r., bound with tainia.   R. Eagle seated facing, hd. r., on cornucopiae; beneath, ΕΚΑΤ monogram; to l., ΛΑΟΔΙΚΕΩΝ.   *B.M.C. 25.* 286, 48-9   ..   ..   £12

5163 — Æ 17.   Hd. of young Dionysos r., wreathed with ivy; behind neck, ΕΚΑΤ monogram.   R. ΛΑΟΔΙ / ΚΕΩΝ above and beneath cista mystica between caps of the Dioskouroi.   *B.M.C. 25.* 286, 50   ..   ..   £13

5164 — Æ 15.   Wild boar running l., ΕΚΑΤ monogram beneath.   R. ΛΑΟΔΙ / ΚΕΩΝ above and beneath wolf stg. r.   *B.M.C. 25.* 287, 52-3   ..   ..   £14
       The boar and the wolf represent the two rivers, Kapros and Lykos, which bounded the territory of Laodikeia.

5165 **Leonnaia** (the site of this town is not certainly known, but it may have lain in the plain of the river Sindros, south-west of Akmoneia).   2nd cent. B.C.   Æ 16.   Turreted hd. of goddess r.   R. ΛΕΟΝΝΑΙΤΩΝ.   Lion seated on spear-head, holding broken shaft in raised l. forepaw.   *Historia Numorum, p.* 680   ..   ..   £24

5166   5168

5166 **Peltai** (situated south-west of Eumeneia, at an important road junction, Peltai was a Macedonian colony.)   2nd-1st cent. B.C.   Æ 19.   Young male bust r., dr. and wearing crested helmet.   R. ΠΕΛ / ΤΗΝΩΝ either side of lion seated l.; two monograms in ex. *B.M.C. 25.* 347, 1   ..   ..   £16

5167 — — Hd. of Athena r., in crested Corinthian helmet.   R. Similar to last, but with star behind lion, and ΔΙΟΝΥΣ instead of monograms in ex.   *B.M.C. 25.* 347, 3   ..   £16

5168 — Æ 17.   Laur. hd. of Zeus r.   R. Winged thunderbolt; ΠΕΛ — ΤΗ above, ΤΡΩ — ΙΑ beneath.   *B.M.C. 25.* 347, 4   ..   ..   £14

5169 — Æ 10.   Laur. hd. of bearded Herakles r.   Ʀ. ΠΕΛΤΗ / ΝΩΝ either side of club draped with lion's skin.   *B.M.C. 25.* 347, 7   ..   ..   £12

5170 **Philomelion** (a city of eastern Phrygia, close to the Pisidian border, Philomelion lay on the river Gallos.   The place was, doubtless, an outpost of the Pergamene Kingdom). 2nd-1st cent. B.C.   Æ 20.   Dr. bust of Mên r., wearing Phrygian cap and with crescent behind shoulders.   Ʀ. Zeus seated l., holding eagle and sceptre; ΦΙΛΟΜΗ behind, ΣΚΥΘΙΝΟ before.   *B.M.C. 25.* 353, 1-2   ..   ..   £18

5171   5172

5171 — Æ 23.   Winged bust of Nike r., dr., and with palm behind shoulder.   Ʀ. Two cornuacopiae crossed; between, thunderbolt surmounted by star and crescent; ΦΙΛΟΜΗΛΕ above, ΜΕΝΕ — ΚΛΕ beneath.   *B.M.C. 25.* 354, 5-6   ..   ..   £20

5172 **Prymnessos** (situated on a tributary of the river Kaystros, Prymnessos was sited at an important road junction for trade routes in all directions.   It became, therefore, a place of commercial importance).   1st cent. B.C.   Æ 19.   Turreted hd. of Tyche r.   Ʀ. ΠΡΥΜΝΗ / ΣΣΕΩΝ either side of Hermes stg. l., holding caduceus; ΝΕ in field to r., ΕΡ to l.   *B.M.C. 25.* 361, 1   ..   ..   £18

5173 **Sanaüs** (situated midway between Kolossai and Apameia, Sanaüs lay close to the northern shores of the salt lake Anava).   2nd-1st cent. B.C.   Æ 17.   Laur. hd. of Apollo r.   Ʀ. ΣΑΝΑΗΝΩΝ.   Tripod, between laurel-boughs; ΑΠΟΛ in field.   *Historia Numorum, p.* 684   ..   ..   £22

5174 **Synnada** (an important city situated north-east of Apameia and south of Prymnessos, Synnada stood in a fertile plain planted with olives.   Beautiful white marble, known as Synnadic, was quarried in the area).   Before 133 B.C.   Ʀ *cistophoric tetradrachm* (*c.* 12·6 gm.).   Cista mystica containing serpent; all within ivy-wreath.   Ʀ. Bow in case between two coiled serpents; to l., monogram of ΚΥΝΝΑ; to r., flute.   *S.N.G. Von Aulock* 3971 ..   ..   £450

5175 After 133 B.C.   Ʀ *cistophoric tetradrachm* (*c.* 12·6 gm.).   Similar, but in *rev.* field to l., ΣΥΝΝΑ; to r., owl stg. on amphora; and above bow case, Α.   *B.M.C. 25.* 392, 1   £450

5176   5177

5176 — Æ 21.   Turreted hd. of Tyche r.   Ʀ. Zeus stg. l., holding thunderbolt and sceptre; ΣΥΝΝΑΔ to r., ΑΔΜΗΤ to l.   *B.M.C. 25.* 392, 2   ..   ..   £16

5177 — — Laur. hd. of Zeus r., sceptre behind.   Ʀ. Poppy-head and ear of corn side by side between caps of the Dioskouroi; above, ΣΥΝΝ; beneath, ΠΑΠΥΛΟ / ΜΝΗΣ.   *B.M.C. 25.* 393, 6   ..   ..   £16

5178   5180

5178 **LYCIA: DYNASTS** (the various Lycian dynasts of the 5th and 4th centuries, down to the time of Maussollos' invasion *c.* 360 B.C., produced a varied coinage of silver staters and fractions under Persian suzerainty. The earlier issues are anonymous and mint attributions in the main uncertain). **Uncertain Dynasts.** 480-440 B.C. Æ *stater* (*c.* 9·7 gm.). Forepart of boar r. R. Triskeles r., in linear square; all within incuse square. *B.M.C. 19.* 6, 29 ..   ..   £350

5179 — — (*c.* 9·05 gm.). Boar l., at bay. R. Tortoise, in dotted square; all within incuse square. *B.M.C. 19.* 4, 20 ..   ..   £450

5180 — — (*c.* 9·25 gm.). Sphinx seated r., l. foreleg raised. R. Crab, in dotted square; all within incuse square. *B.M.C. 19.* 5, 26 ..   ..   £450

5181   5186

5181 — — (*c.* 9·1 gm.). Boar stg. l., sniffing at ground. R. Male hd. l., bearded, wearing crested Corinthian helmet; all in dotted square within incuse square. *B.M.C. 19.* 5, 28 ..   ..   £650

5182 — — (*c.* 9·15 gm.). Boar stg. r. R. Bull's hd. facing, + — + in lower field; all within incuse square. *B.M.C. 19.* 4, 23 ..   ..   £500

5183 — — (*c.* 9·7 gm.). Naked Herakles advancing l., brandishing club; hound at his feet, between legs. R. Triskeles l., smaller triskeles beneath; all in dotted circle within circular incuse. *S.N.G. Von Aulock* 4096-7   ..   ..   £550

5184 — Æ *third-stater* or *tetrobol* (*c.* 2·7 gm.). Boar walking r. R. Triskeles r., in dotted square; all within incuse square. *B.M.C. 19.* 7, 37   ..   ..   ..   £150

5185 — — (*c.* 2·6 gm.). Conjoined foreparts of two boars, walking in opposite directions; triskeles on flank, at point of juncture. R. As last, but triskeles l. *S.N.G. Von Aulock* 4066 ..   ..   £200

5186 — — (*c.* 2·5 gm.). Boar walking r. R. Forepart of griffin r., r. foreleg raised; all in linear border within incuse square. *B.M.C. 19.* 5, 27 ..   ..   ..   £175

5187 — Æ *sixth-stater* or *diobol* (*c.* 1·23 gm.). Forepart of boar r. R. Triskeles l., in dotted square; all within incuse square. *Forrer/Weber* 7218 ..   ..   ..   £120

5188 — — — Boar walking r. R. As last, but triskeles r. *B.M.C. 19.* 7, 38   ..   £110

5189 — — (*c.* 1·6 gm.). Pegasos, with curled wing, flying r.; all on circular shield. R. Triskeles r., in dotted circle within circular incuse. *S.N.G. Von Aulock* 4091   £140

5190 **Thiban** (mid-5th cent. B.C.). Æ *stater* (*c.* 9·8 gm.). Two dolphins r. and l., one above the other. R. Tetraskeles l., Lycian letters (=*Thiba*) in field; all in dotted square within incuse square. *S.N.G. Von Aulock* 4106   ..   ..   ..   £450

5191 — Æ *tetrobol* (*c.* 2·67 gm.). Boar walking l. R. Triskeles l., composed of three cocks' heads; in field, Lycian letters (=*Thiban*); all in linear square within incuse square. *Forrer/Weber* 7220 ..   ..   £175

5192 — Æ *diobol* (*c.* 1·5 gm.). Horse trotting r. R. Triskeles r., Lycian letters (=*Thi*) in field; all in dotted square within incuse square. *S.N.G. Von Aulock* 4108   ..   £125

5193   5195

5193 **Thap** (dynast of Telmessos (?), mid-5th cent. B.C.). Æ *stater* (*c.* 9·7 gm.). Two
dolphins l. and r., one above the other; astragalos (?) between them, human eye beneath.
R. Triskeles r., Lycian letters (= *Thap*) in field; all in dotted square within incuse square.
B.M.C. 19. 11, 51 ..   ..   £500

5194 **Uvug** (third quarter of 5th cent. B.C.). Æ *tetrobol* (*c.* 2·8 gm.). Forepart of winged
human-headed bull r.   R. Hd. of Sphinx (?) r., hair long; behind, Lycian letters (= *Uvug*);
all in dotted square within incuse square. *B.M.C. 19.* 16, 74 ..   ..   ..   £350

5195 — Æ *trihemiobol* (*c.* 1·05 gm.).   Sphinx seated r., l. foreleg raised.   R. As last.   *B.M.C.
19.* 16, 76 ..   ..   £120

5196 — Æ *obol* (*c.* 0·7 gm.).   Forepart of winged human-headed bull l.   R. Hd. of negro l.,
in dotted square; all within incuse square.   *B.M.C. 19.* 17, 78 ..   ..   ..   £90

5197   5199

5197 **Tenagure** (third quarter of 5th cent. B.C.).   Æ *stater* (*c.* 8·6 gm.).   Winged and horned
lion crouching l., *ankh* symbol behind; in ex., Lycian letters (= *Tenagure*).   R. Triskeles
r., in dotted square; all within incuse square.   *B.M.C. 19.* 18, 82   ..   ..   £550

5198 **Kuprlli** (third quarter of 5th cent. B.C.   A dynast of considerable importance judging
from the extent of his coinage).   Æ *stater* (*c.* 9·55 gm.).   Dolphin r., above two parallel
dotted lines.   R. Triskeles l., the branch on r. terminating in hd. of monster; Lycian
letters (= *Ku*) in lower field to r.; all in dotted square within incuse square.   *B.M.C. 19.*
12, 53   ..   ..   £450

5199 — — (*c.* 8·8 gm.).   Winged and horned lion stg. l.   R. Triskeles r., Lycian letters
(= *Kuprlli*) around; all in dotted square within incuse square.   *B.M.C. 19.* 14, 63
£400

5200   5202

5200 — — (*c.* 8·5 gm.).   Naked Herakles, wearing lion's skin head-dress, striding l., brandishing club.   R. Similar to last, but triskeles l.   *B.M.C. 19.* 13, 58   ..   ..   £500

5201 — — — Bull walking l.; above, Lycian letters (= *Arnn*).   R. As last.   *S.N.G. Von
Aulock* 4155 ..   ..   £600
    The obverse inscription indicates that this type was struck at Xanthos.

5202 — Æ *tetrobol* (*c.* 2·65 gm.).   Hd. of panther facing, Lycian letters (= *Kuprlli*)around.
R. As 5197.   *B.M.C. 19.* 12, 55 ..   ..   £225

Kuprlli *continued*

5203 — — — — Horse kneeling r., looking back; above, triskeles. ℞. Triskeles r., Lycian letters (=*Ku*) in field; all in dotted circle within circular incuse.   *B.M.C. 19.* 15, 70   £175

5204 — Æ *diobol* (*c.* 1·32 gm.).   Forepart of winged human-headed bull l.   ℞. Triskeles l., Lycian letters (=*Kup*) in field; all in dotted square within incuse square.   *Forrer/Weber* 7222 .. .. £125

5205 — Æ *trihemiobol* (*c.* 1·05 gm.).   Sphinx seated r.   ℞. As last, but with Lycian letters (=*Kupr*) in field.   *B.M.C. 19.* 14, 66 .. .. £120

5206   5209

5206 — Æ ¾ *obol* (*c.* 0·53 gm.).   Forepart of winged lion l., l. foot raised.   ℞. Triskeles l., one branch terminating in hd. of monster; Lycian letters (=*Ku*) in field; all in dotted square within incuse square.   *B.M.C. 19.* 14, 65 .. .. £85

5207 **Teththiveibi** (dynast of Antiphellos (?), third quarter of 5th cent. B.C.).   Æ *stater* (*c.* 9·85 gm.).   Hd. of Aphrodite (?) l., hair fastened by band passing three times round head.   ℞. Tetraskeles l., Lycian letters (=*Teththiveibi*) around; all in dotted square within incuse square.   *B.M.C. 19.* 19, 89 .. .. £1,250

5208 — — (*c.* 8·45 gm.).   Two cocks stg. face to face, Lycian monogram (?) between; all on raised circular shield.   ℞. As last, but with Lycian letters (= *Teththivei*) around tetraskeles.   *Forrer/Weber* 7226 .. .. £650

5209 — Æ *tetrobol* (*c.* 2·52 gm.).   Facing hd. of Seilenos, bald and bearded.   ℞. As 5207, but tetraskeles r.   *B.M.C. 19.* 19, 88 .. .. £500

5210 **Sppntaza** (dynast of Antiphellos (?), third quarter of 5th cent. B.C.).   Æ *stater* (*c.* 8·4 gm.).   Cow stg. l., looking back, suckling calf.   ℞. Tetraskeles l., Lycian letters (= *Sppntaza*) around; all within incuse square.   *B.M.C. 19.* 20, 94 .. .. £750

5211 **Kherei** (dynast of Xanthos and other cities, last quarter of 5th cent. B.C.).   Æ *stater* (*c.* 8·37 gm.).   Hd. of Athena r., in crested helmet ornamented with olive-leaves and floral scroll.   ℞. Hd. of bearded satrap (Kherei?) r., wearing Persian tiara; Lycian letters before (=*Kherei*) and behind (=*Arnnahe*); all within incuse square.   *B.M.C. 19.* 22, 101 .. .. £1,500

5212 — Æ *drachm* (*c.* 4·13 gm.).   *Obv.* Similar.   ℞. Hd. of bearded satrap r., as last; Lycian letters (= *Khereh*) before; all in dotted circle within circular incuse.   *S.N.G. Von Aulock* 4176 .. .. £450

5213 — Æ *tetrobol* (*c.* 3·22 gm.).   Hd. of Aphrodite (?) l., flower behind.   ℞. Owl stg. l., hd. facing; behind, Lycian letters (= *Kherei*); before, Lycian monogram (?); all within incuse square.   *S.N.G. Von Aulock* 4170 .. .. £250

5214 — Æ *trihemiobol* (*c.* 1·15 gm.).   Two cocks on circular shield, as 5208.   ℞. Eagle stg. l., Lycian letters (= *Kherei*) in field; all in dotted square within incuse square.   *S.N.G. Von Aulock* 4169 .. .. £130

5215 Hepruma (dynast of Patara (?), last quarter of 5th cent. B.C.). Æ *stater* (*c.* 8·25 gm.). Hd. of Athena l., in crested helmet. R. Hd. of Hermes l., in winged petasos; Lycian letters (= *Hepruma*) around, Lycian monogram (?) behind; all in dotted square within incuse square. *B.M.C. 19.* 25, 113 .. .. £1,400

5216 Vekhssere I (dynast of Patara (?), *circa* 400 B.C.). Æ *stater* (*c.* 8·4 gm.). Hd. of Athena r., in crested helmet. R. Hd. of Hermes r., in winged petasos, chlamys fastened at neck; Lycian letters (= *Vekhssere*) around; all in dotted circle within circular incuse. *B.M.C. 19.* 26, 114 .. .. £1,250

5217 Erbbina (dynast of Telmessos, *circa* 400 B.C.). Æ *stater* (*c.* 8·45 gm.). Hd. of Athena l., in crested helmet. R. Herakles fighting l., brandishing club and holding bow, lion's skin on head and l. arm; behind, Lycian letters (= *Erbbina*); all in dotted circle within circular incuse. *B.M.C. 19.* 30, 132 .. .. £1,600

5218 Vekhssere II (dynast of Antiphellos, early 4th cent. B.C.). Æ *tetrobol* (*c.* 3·05 gm.). Lion's scalp facing. R. Triskeles l., Lycian monogram within central circle; Lycian letters (= *Vakhsse*) around; all in dotted circle within circular incuse. *S.N.G. Von Aulock* 4201 .. .. £140

5219   5221

5219 Zagaba (dynast of Antiphellos, early 4th cent. B.C.). Æ *stater* (*c.* 9·6 gm.). Lion's scalp facing. R. Triskeles l.; Lycian letters (= *Zag*) around, corn-grain in field; all within circular incuse. *B.M.C. 19.* 35, 153 .. .. £350

5220 — — (*c.* 9·3 gm.). Lion's scalp facing. R. Hd. of Athena three-quarter face to l., wearing plumed helmet inscribed *Vahn* in Lycian letters; in field to l., Lycian letters (= *Zakhabaha*); to r., laurel-branch; all within circular incuse. *Kraay* (*Archaic and Classical Greek Coins*) *pl.* 57, 988 .. .. £2,500

    This remarkable reverse type, of fine Greek style, is a very close copy of Eukleidas' master-piece on a Syracusan tetradrachm of the late 5th cent. B.C. (see no. 941 in Vol. I. of this catalogue).

5221 — Æ *tetrobol* (*c.* 3·05 gm.). Similar, but without inscription on Athena's helmet, Lycian letters (= *Zakhabahe*) in *rev.* field to l., and monogram to r. *S.N.G. Von Aulock* 4210, *variety* £500

5222 Aruvatijesi (dynast of Antiphellos, early 4th cent. B.C.). Æ *stater* (*c.* 9·6 gm.). Lion's scalp facing. R. Triskeles l., Lycian letters (= *Aruvatijesi*) around; all within incuse square. *S.N.G. Von Aulock* 4202 .. .. £500

5223 Aruvatijesi and Zagaba. Æ *tetrobol* (*c.* 3 gm.). Similar, but with Lycian inscription *Aruvatij* and *Zag* around triskeles on *rev.* *S.N.G. Von Aulock* 4204 .. .. £165

5224   5226   5229

5224 — Æ *obol*? (*c.* 0·62 gm.). Lion's scalp facing. ℞. Triskeles l., Lycian letters (= *Aru* and *Z*) around; all within circular incuse. *B.M.C. 19.* 31, 133 .. .. £110

5225 Mithrapata (dynast of Antiphellos, *circa* 380 B.C.). Æ *stater* (*c.* 9·9 gm.). Forepart of lion r. ℞. Bearded head of the dynast Mithrapata l.; Lycian letters (= *Mithrapata*) around, small triskeles behind; all within incuse square. *S.N.G. Von Aulock* 4236-7 £2,000

5226 — — Lion's scalp facing, small triskeles below. ℞. As last, but the Lycian inscription reads *Mithrapati*. *Numismatic Chronicle*, 1959, *p.* 34, *no.* 16 .. .. .. £1,750

5227 — — Lion's scalp facing. ℞. Triskeles l., Lycian letters (= *Mithrapata*) above and to r.; to l., hd. of young Herakles in lion's skin three-quarter face to l., club beside it on r.; all within incuse square. *Num. Chron.*, 1959, *p.* 34, *no.* 18 .. .. .. £350

5228 — Æ *diobol* (*c.* 1·4 gm.). Lion's scalp facing. ℞. Triskeles l.; Lycian letters (= *Mithrapata*) around, astragalos in field to l.; all within incuse square. *B.M.C. 19.* 32, 136 .. .. £120

5229 — Æ ¾ *obol* (*c.* 0·5 gm.). Whelk-shell. ℞. Hd. of Apollo facing, chlamys fastened at neck; Lycian letters (= *Mith*) in field; all in dotted circle within circular incuse. *B.M.C. 19.* 32, 139 .. .. £150

5230 Trbbenimi (dynast of Limyra, *circa* 380 B.C.). Æ *stater* (*c.* 9·8 gm.). Lion's scalp facing. ℞. Triskeles l.; Lycian letters (= *Trb*) around, club in field; all within incuse square. *B.M.C. 19.* 34, 145 .. .. £350

5231   5232

5231 — — (*c.* 9·65 gm.). Lion's scalp facing; Lycian letters (= *Trb*) below. ℞. Triskeles l., Lycian letters (= *Zem*) around; all within circular incuse. *B.M.C. 19.* 33, 144 £450

The inscription on rev. indicates the mint-place (Zem = Zemuri = Limyra).

5232 — Æ *tetrobol* (*c.* 2·6—3·2 gm.). Lion's scalp facing. ℞. Triskeles l., Lycian letters (= *Trbbenimi*) around; all within circular incuse. *B.M.C. 19.* 34, 147 .. £100

5233 — — Triskeles l., Lycian letters (= *Zemuhu*) around. ℞. Triskeles l., Lycian letters (= *Trbbenimi*) around; all in dotted circle within circular incuse. *S.N.G. Von Aulock* 4222 .. .. £200

5234 — Æ *diobol* (*c.* 1·45 gm.). Lion's scalp facing. ℞. As last, but with Lycian inscription *Trbben*. *B.M.C. 19.* 34, 150 .. .. £120

5235 — Æ *obol* (*c.* 0·7 gm.). As 5232. *B.M.C. 19.* 35, 151 .. .. .. £110

5236 Vedrei and Trbbenimi (whether Vedrei is the name of a city or of another dynast is unknown at present). Æ *tetrobol* (*c.* 3·15 gm.). Triskeles l., Lycian letters (= *Vedrei*) around. R. As 5233. *S.N.G. Von Aulock* 4230   ..   ..   £200

5237   5240

5237 Vedrei. Æ *stater* (*c.* 9·5 gm.). Lion's scalp facing. R. Triskeles l., Lycian letters (= *Ved*) around; all within circular incuse. *B.M.C. 19.* 35, 152   ..   ..   £350

5238 — Æ *tetrobol* (*c.* 2·75 gm.). Triskeles l., Lycian letters (= *Vedrevi*) around; all in dotted circle within circular incuse. *S.N.G. Von Aulock* 4234   £175

5239 Perikle (dynast of Antiphellos from *circa* 380 B.C., Perikle had extended his rule over most of Lycia by the time of his death, about 362 B.C.). Æ *stater* (*c.* 9·9 gm.). Laur. and dr. bust of the dynast Perikle three-quarter face to l., bearded; dolphin downwards in field to r. R. Warrior, naked but for helmet, advancing r., brandishing sword and holding shield; behind, triskeles and Lycian letters (= *Perikle*); before, Lycian letters (= *Vehnteze*); all within incuse square. *S.N.G. Von Aulock* 4251   ..   ..   ..   £2,250

5240 — — Bearded bust of the dynast Perikle three-quarter face to l. R. Warrior, as last; Lycian letters (= *Perikle*) behind and above; star in field to l., triskeles at warrior's feet to r.; all within incuse square. *S.N.G. Von Aulock* 4253   ..   ..   ..   £2,000

5241 — Æ *tetrobol* (*c.* 2·6—3·2 gm.). Lion's scalp facing. R. Triskeles l., Lycian letters (= *Perikle*) around; all within circular incuse. *B.M.C. 19.* 36, 157   ..   ..   £90

5242 — — Similar, but also with hd. of Hermes facing in *rev.* field. *B.M.C. 19.* 36, 156
£110

5243 — Æ 13. Hd. of young Pan l., horned. R. Triskeles l., Lycian letters (=*Perikl*) around. *B.M.C. 19.* 36, 158   ..   ..   £15

5244 — Æ 11. Forepart of goat l. R. As last. *B.M.C. 19.* 37, 163   ..   ..   £14

5245 Vedevie and Perikle (Vedevie, a name otherwise unknown, was presumably another dynast who reigned jointly with Perikle at some time during the third or fourth decade of the 4th cent.). Æ *trihemiobol* (*c.* 1·2 gm.). Bull kneeling l., attacked by lion r. on its back; Lycian letters (=*Vedevie*) below and in field. R. Bust of Athena three-quarter face to l., wearing crested Corinthian helmet; small triskeles in field to l., Lycian letters (=*Perikle*) around; all within circular incuse. *S.N.G. Von Aulock* 4247-8   ..   £350

5246 LYCIA: CITIES (during the time of the dynasts, down to *circa* 360 B.C., a few of the more important Lycian cities produced coinages in their own names. After the Macedonian conquest, 334/3 B.C., no coins were struck in Lycia until the 2nd cent. B.C.; except at the Greek city of Phaselis which had a plentiful output of silver in the 3rd cent. The Romans freed the Lycians from Rhodian rule in 168 B.C. when the cities united to form a League. Federal coinage, mostly silver drachms, was issued by the member-cities until the dissolution of the League by the Emperor Claudius, A.D. 43). **Antiphellos** (a coastal city, situated between Patara and Aperlai, Antiphellos was originally the port of Phellos). Before 168 B.C. Æ 11. Hd. of Apollo (?) r. R. ANT. Dolphin l. *B.M.C. 19.* 41, 1   ..   ..   £12

5247

5253

Antiphellos *continued*

5247 After 168 B.C. (League coinage). Æ 11. Laur. hd. of Apollo r. R. ΛΥΚΙΩΝ, A — N. Bow and quiver; all within incuse square. *B.M.C. 19.* 41, 3-4   ..   ..   £9

5248 — Æ 10. Similar, but with *rev.* legend ΑΝΤΙ / ΦΕΛ. *B.M.C. 19.* 41, 5   ..   £10

5249 **Aperlai** (a coastal town, between Antiphellos and Myra). Mid-5th cent. B.C. Æ *stater* (*c.* 9·77 gm.). Two dolphins, l. and r., one above the other; beneath, ram's hd. l. R. Triskeles l., Lycian letters (=*Pre*) around; all in dotted square within incuse square. *S.N.G. Von Aulock* 4109 ..   ..   £450

     The attribution of this type, and the next, to Aperlai is not certain.

5250 — Æ *tetrobol* (*c.* 2·9 gm.). Dolphin l.; ram's hd. r. beneath. R. As last, but the Lycian legend reads *Prl*. *S.N.G. Von Aulock* 4110 ..   ..   £200

5251 After 168 B.C. (League coinage). Æ 11. Laur. hd. of Apollo r. R. ΛΥΚΙΩΝ, A — Π. Bow and quiver; all within incuse square. *S.N.G. Von Aulock* 4270 ..   £12

5252 **Apollonia** (the exact site of this town has not been certainly identified, but it is known to have been in the vicinity of Aperlai). After 168 B.C. (League coinage). Æ 11. As last, but with mint name ΑΠΟ instead of ΑΠ on *rev.* *Historia Numorum, p.* 694   £18

5253 **Arykanda** (an inland city, north-west of Limyra). 2nd-1st cent. B.C. Æ 16. Rad. hd. of Sozon (?) r. R. Naked Apollo stg. l., resting on column and holding bow over altar; ΑΡ monogram in field to r. *B.M.C. 19.* 44, 1   ..   ..   ..   £14

5254 — — Laur. hd. of Apollo r. R. Bow and quiver, between ΑΡ monogram and ΙΡ; all within wreath. *S.N.G. Von Aulock* 4275   ..   ..   ..   £15

5255 **Balbura** (close to the northern frontier of Lycia, south-east of Kibyra in Phrygia). 2nd-1st cent. B.C. Æ 16. Veiled hd. of Demeter r., wreathed with corn. R. ΒΑΛΒΟΥ / ΡΕΩΝ either side of ear of corn. *B.M.C. 19.* 46, 1   ..   ..   ..   £14

5256   5260

5256 — — Eagle stg. l., looking back, wings spread. R. ΒΑΛΒΟΥ / ΡΕΩΝ either side of thunderbolt; all within wreath. *B.M.C. 19.* 46, 2   ..   ..   £14

5257 — Æ 15. Helmeted hd. of Athena r. R. ΒΑΛΒΟΥ / ΡΕΩΝ either side of owl perched on helmet; all within wreath. *S.N.G. Von Aulock* 4282 ..   ..   ..   £15

5258 — Æ 9. Caduceus, within double border (linear and dotted). R. ΒΑΛ / ΒΟΥ either side of club; all within wreath. *S.N.G. Von Aulock* 4280   ..   ..   £13

5259 **Bubon** (a few miles west of Balbura). 2nd-1st cent. B.C. Æ 16. Hd. of Artemis r. R. Lighted torch; ΒΟΥ — Β across field. *S.N.G. Von Aulock* 4285   ..   £15

5260 — Æ 10. Hd. of Artemis r., quiver behind neck. R. ΒΟΥ. Bow and quiver, crossed. *B.M.C. 19.* 47, 1   ..   ..   £12

5261 — — — R. Stag stg. r., ΒΟΥ above. *S.N.G. Von Aulock* 4286   ..   £13

5262   5265

5262 Kalynda (in the far west of the country, close to the Carian border). 1st cent. B.C. Æ 14. Bust of Artemis r., wearing stephane. ℞. Lighted torch; κ — Α / Λ — Υ in field. *B.M.C. 19.* 48, 8   ..   ..   £13

5263 — Æ 11. *Obv.* Similar; bow and quiver at shoulder. ℞. Stag stg. r., ΚΑΛΥ in ex. *B.M.C. 19.* 48, 7   ..   ..   £10

5264 — Æ 10. *Obv.* As last. ℞. Forepart of stag r., ΚΑΛΥΝ beneath. *B.M.C. 19.* 48, 3   £11

5265 Choma (site uncertain, but possibly in the area north-west of Podalia in central Lycia). 1st cent. B.C. Æ 18. Laur. hd. of Zeus l. ℞. Horseman riding r., brandishing club; ΧΩ beneath. *B.M.C. 19.* 49, 1   ..   ..   £16

5266 — Æ 13. Laur. hd. of Zeus r. ℞. Χ — Ω either side of club; all within laurel-wreath. *S.N.G. Von Aulock* 4289-90   ..   ..   £14

5267   5269

5267 Kragos (a mountainous region of western Lycia, between the Xanthos river and the coast. The coins were issued by several mints within the Monetary District). After 168 B.C. (League coinage). Æ *drachm* (c. 1·4–2·1 gm.). Laur. hd. of Apollo r., Λ — Υ either side of neck. ℞. Lyre; κ — Ρ across lower field; all within shallow incuse square. *B.M.C. 19.* 51, 1   ..   ..   £65

5268 — — Similar, but also with eagle stg. on helmet in *rev.* field to l. *B.M.C. 19.* 51, 3-4   £65

5269 1st cent. B.C. (League coinage). Æ *drachm* (c. 1·3–2 gm.). Laur. hd. of Apollo r., hair in formal curls, bow and quiver behind neck. ℞. Lyre; ΛΥΚΙΩΝ above, ΚΡ — Α across lower field; all within shallow incuse square. *B.M.C. 19.* 51, 5   ..   ..   £60

5270 — — Laur. hd. of Apollo r., hair in formal curls; Λ — Υ either side of neck. ℞. Κ — Ρ either side of lyre; spray with fillets in lower field to l.; all within shallow incuse square. *B.M.C. 19.* 52, 10   ..   ..   £50

5271 — — Hd. of Apollo r., hair in formal curls and bound with tainia, bow behind neck. ℞. Lyre; ΛΥΚΙΩΝ above, Κ — Ρ / Α — Γ in field; all within shallow incuse square. *B.M.C. 19.* 52, 12-14   ..   ..   £55

5272 — Æ *diobol* ? (c. 0·75 gm.). Hd. of Artemis r., wearing stephane, bow and quiver behind neck. ℞. Quiver; Κ — Ρ / Λ — Υ in field; all within shallow incuse square. *B.M.C. 19.* 52, 15   ..   ..   £110

Kragos *continued*

5273 — Æ 24. Hd. of Apollo r., hair in formal curls and bound with laurel-wreath and tainia. R. Lyre; Λ — Υ / Κ — Ρ in field; all within laurel-wreath. *B.M.C. 19.* 53, 20 .. £18

5274 — Æ 22. Laur. hd. of Apollo r. R. Apollo stg. l., holding branch and bow; Κ — Ρ in lower field. *B.M.C. 19.* 53, 18 .. .. £16

5275 5277

5275 — Æ 18. Hd. of Artemis r., wearing stephane; Λ — Υ in field. R. Κ — Ρ either side of quiver. *B.M.C. 19.* 53, 21 .. .. £14

5276 — Æ 10. Laur. hd. of Apollo r. R. ΛΥΚΙ, Κ — Ρ. Bow and quiver; all within shallow incuse square. *B.M.C. 19.* 53, 17 .. .. £11

5277 — Æ 24 (struck at **Tlos**). Laur. hd. of Apollo r., hair in formal curls; Λ — Υ either side of neck. R. Tripod; Κ — Ρ / ΤΛ — Ω in field. *B.M.C. 19.* 54, 27 .. .. £20

5278 — Æ 17 (struck at **Tlos**). Dr. bust of Artemis r., bow and quiver behind shoulder. R. Stag stg. r.; Κ — Ρ behind and before, ΤΛ above. *S.N.G. Von Aulock* 4470 £16

5279 — Æ 23 (struck at **Xanthos**). Laur. hd. of Apollo r., hair long; Λ — Υ either side of neck. R. Lyre; Κ — Ρ / Ξ / Α — Ν in field; all within laurel-wreath. *B.M.C. 19.* 55, 28

£20

5280 — Æ 17 (struck at **Xanthos**). *Obv.* As 5278. R. Quiver; Κ — Ρ across upper field, Ξ / Α to l., Ν to r. *S.N.G. Von Aulock* 4316-17 .. .. £14

5281 — Æ 18 (struck at **Telmessos**). Similar to 5278, but with Λ — Υ in *obv.* field, and with ΤΕΛ instead of ΤΛ on *rev.* *S.N.G. Von Aulock* 4454 .. .. £16

5282 — Æ 20 (struck at **Dias** ?). Hd. of Artemis r., quiver behind neck; Δ — Ι either side of neck. R. Stag stg. r., Κ — Ρ behind and before, ΛΥ above; in ex., mallet (?). *B.M.C. 19.* 58, 1 .. .. £22

5283 5284

5283 **Kyaneai** (situated in the south, midway between Antiphellos and Myra). After 168 B.C. (League coinage). *R drachm* (c. 1·6–2·8 gm.). Laur. hd. of Apollo r., bow and quiver behind neck. R. Lyre; ΛΥΚΙΩΝ above, Κ — Υ across field, sword and shield to l.; all within shallow incuse square. *B.M.C. 19.* 56, 1 .. .. £120

5284 1st cent. B.C. (League coinage). Æ 19. *Obv.* As 5278. R. Stag stg. r.; Λ — Υ behind and before, ΚΥΑ above. *B.M.C. 19.* 56, 4 .. .. £16

5285   5286

5285 **Gagai** (a coastal town, south-east of Limyra, Gagai was noted for the *Gagates lapis*, or jet, found in the area). After 168 B.C. (League coinage). Æ *drachm* (*c.* 2·8 gm.). Laur. hd. of Apollo r., bow and quiver behind neck. R. Lyre; ΛVKIΩN above, Γ — A across field, crested helmet to l.; all within shallow incuse square. *B.M.C. 19.* 59, 1   ..   £140

5286 **Limyra** (an important city of south-eastern Lycia, a short distance from the southern coast, Limyra was active as a mint from the time of the dynasts — see nos. 5231 and 5233 above). Early 4th cent. B.C. Æ *stater* (*c.* 9·8 gm.). Lion's scalp facing, H on forehead, T beneath. R. Triskeles l., Lycian letters (= *Zem*) around; all within incuse square. *B.M.C. 19.* 33, 142 ..   ..   £400

        The rev. inscription is an abbreviation of the Lycian name for Limyra (Zemuri).

5287 After 168 B.C. (League coinage). Æ *drachm* (*c.* 2–2·9 gm.). Laur. hd. of Apollo r. R. Lyre; ΛVKIΩN above, Λ — I across field; all within shallow incuse square. *B.M.C. 19.* 60, 4   ..   ..   £90

5288 *Bronze Coinage.* Before 168 B.C. Æ 20. Laur. hd. of Apollo r. R. Winged thunderbolt; Λ — I across field. *B.M.C. 19.* 60, 1   ..   ..   ..   £15

5289 — Æ 11. Similar, but with *rev.* legend ΛIMY / PEΩN either side of the thunderbolt. *B.M.C. 19.* 60, 3 ..   ..   £12

                   5290   5292

5290 After 168 B.C. (League coinage). Æ 10. *Obv.* Similar. R. ΛVKI, Λ — I. Bow and quiver; all within shallow incuse square. *B.M.C. 19.* 61, 8   ..   ..   £10

5291 **Masikytes** (a mountainous region of central southern Lycia, east of the Xanthos river. It would seem that **Myra** was the chief town of the Monetary District and the principal mint for the coinage issued in the name of Masikytes). After 168 B.C. (League coinage). Æ *drachm* (*c.* 2·93 gm.). Laur. hd. of Apollo r., hair flowing. R. Lyre; ΛVKIΩN above, M to l.; all within shallow incuse square. *S.N.G. Von Aulock* 4325 ..   ..   £75

5292 — — (*c.* 1·5–2 gm.). Similar, but bow behind neck of Apollo on *obv.*, and MA — Σ in *rev.* field instead of M. *B.M.C. 19.* 63, 1   ..   ..   ..   £65

5293 — — *Obv.* As 5291, but also with Λ — Y either side of neck. R. M — A either side of lyre; in field to l., snake-entwined omphalos; all within shallow incuse square. *B.M.C. 19.* 63, 4   ..   ..   £60

5294 — — — Laur. hd. of Apollo r., hair rolled; Λ — Y either side of neck. R. As last, but with flaming torch instead of omphalos in field to l. *B.M.C. 19.* 63, 5   ..   £55

5295   5298   5300

Masikytes *continued*

5295 1st cent. B.C. (League coinage). Æ *drachm* (*c.* 1·3–1·9 gm.). Laur. hd. of Apollo r., hair in formal curls; Λ — Υ either side of neck. Ṛ. Μ — Α either side of lyre; in field to r., tripod; all within shallow incuse square. *B.M.C. 19.* 64, 14-18   ..   £45

5296 — — Similar, but without Λ — Υ on *obv.*, and with ΛΥΚΙΩΝ above lyre on *rev.;* laurel-branch instead of tripod in *rev.* field to r. *B.M.C. 19.* 64, 10 ..   ..   ..   £50

5297 — — Laur. hd. of Apollo l., hair in formal curls; Υ — Λ either side of neck. Ṛ. Μ — Α either side of lyre; tripod in field to l., caduceus to r.; all within shallow incuse square. *B.M.C. 19.* 65, 19-20   ..   ..   £75

5298 — — Hd. of Apollo r., hair bound with tainia, bow and quiver behind neck. Ṛ. Lyre; ΛΥΚΙΩΝ above, Μ — Α / Σ — Ι in field; all within shallow incuse square. *B.M.C. 19.* 65, 21-3 ..   ..   £55

5299 — Æ *hemidrachm* (*c.* 0·9 gm.). Bust of Artemis r., wearing stephane, bow and quiver behind shoulder. Ṛ. Quiver; Λ — Υ / Μ — Α across upper and lower field, torch to l.; all within shallow incuse square. *S.N.G. Von Aulock* 4336 ..   ..   ..   £125

5300 — Æ *diobol* ? (*c.* 0·75 gm.). Similar, but without symbol in *rev.* field. *B.M.C. 19.* 65, 24   ..   ..   £100

5301 *Bronze Coinage.* 2nd-1st cent. B.C. (League coinage). Æ 14. Hd. of Hermes r., wearing petasos, caduceus behind neck. Ṛ. Winged caduceus; Λ — Υ / Μ — Α in field; all within shallow incuse square. *B.M.C. 19.* 66, 25 ..   ..   ..   £12

5302   5305

5302 — Æ 22. Laur. bust of Apollo r., Λ — Υ either side of neck. Ṛ. Apollo stg. l., holding branch and bow; Μ — Α in field. *B.M.C. 19.* 66, 27   ..   ..   ..   £16

5303 — Æ 20. Hd. of Artemis r., wearing stephane; bow and quiver behind neck; Λ — Υ in field. Ṛ. Stag stg. r.; Μ — Α behind and before, ΙΠΠΟ / ΛΟ above. *B.M.C. 19.* 66, 28   £14

5304 — — Similar, but the ΛΥ before Artemis' neck on *obv.;* and on *rev.* no magistrate's name, ΜΑ above stag, and hem-hem crown before. *B.M.C. 19.* 67, 33   ..   £15

5305 — Æ 19. *Obv.* As 5303. Ṛ. Μ — Α either side of quiver; stag's hd. r. in field to r. *B.M.C. 19.* 67, 34 ..   ..   £14

5306 — Æ 11. Similar, but on *rev.* Ι — Π / Μ — Α either side of quiver, and without symbol in field to r. *S.N.G. Von Aulock* 4344 ..   ..   £11

5307 — Æ 27. Hd. of Apollo r., wearing tainia, hair in formal curls; Λ — Y either side of neck. ℞. м — A either side of tripod-lebes; laurel-branch in field to l.; all within linear border outside which, above, ΛΥΚΙΩΝ. *B.M.C. 19.* 67, 35 .. .. .. £22

5308 — Æ 20. *Obv.* Similar, but wearing laurel-wreath. ℞. м — A either side of lyre; all within laurel-wreath. *B.M.C. 19.* 67, 36 .. .. £16

5309 — Æ 18. Dr. bust of Artemis r., Λ — Y in field. ℞. Dr. bust of Apollo r., hair in formal curls; м — A in field. *S.N.G. Von Aulock* 4346 .. .. .. £14

5310 — Æ 20 (struck at **Myra**). Hd. of Artemis r., wearing stephane, bow behind neck; before, MA. ℞. Stag stg. r.; MY above, hem-hem crown before. *B.M.C. 19.* 70, 9 £15

5311 **Myra** (situated on the river Myros, close to the sea, Myra was an important town and principal mint for the Monetary District of Masikytes). After 168 B.C. (League coinage). Æ *drachm* (c. 2·5—2·9 gm.). Laur. hd. of Apollo r., bow and quiver behind neck. ℞. Lyre; ΛΥΚΙΩΝ above, м — Y in field, hem-hem crown to l.; all within shallow incuse square. *B.M.C. 19.* 69, 3 .. .. £110

5312   5314

5312 — — (c. 1·8—1·9 gm.). *Obv.* Similar, but without bow and quiver, and with Λ — Y either side of neck. ℞. Lyre; м — Y / P — A in field, hem-hem crown to l.; all within shallow incuse square. *B.M.C. 19.* 69, 4 .. .. £90

5313 — Æ 11. Laur. hd. of Apollo r. ℞. ΛΥΚΙ, м — Y. Bow and quiver; all within shallow incuse square. *B.M.C. 19.* 70, 5 .. .. £10

5314 1st cent. B.C. (League coinage). Æ 20. Bust of Artemis r., wearing stephane, bow and quiver behind shoulder; before neck, ΛΥ. ℞. Stag stg. r.; MY above, hem-hem crown behind. *B.M.C. 19.* 70, 8 .. .. £15

See also no. 5310 *above.*

5315 — Æ 18. Laur. bust of Apollo r., hair in formal curls; м — Y either side of neck. ℞. Lyre, within laurel-wreath. *B.M.C. 19.* 70, 7 .. .. £14

5316 — — Veiled bust of Artemis Eleuthera facing, wearing modius; м — Y in field. ℞. Nike stg. r., holding wreath and palm. *B.M.C. 19.* 71, 10 .. .. £18

5317 **Nisa** (a town of central Lycia, north-east of Xanthos). 2nd cent. B.C. Æ 13. Laur. hd. of Zeus r. ℞. Hd. of Artemis l., ΝΙΣΕ before. *S.N.G. Von Aulock* 4373

(*Unique*)

5318 **Oinoanda** (a town of northern Lycia, in the upper valley of the Xanthos). 2nd cent.
B.C. Æ *didrachm* (*c.* 8·15 gm.). Laur. hd. of Zeus r., sceptre behind. ℞. Eagle stg. r.
on thunderbolt; Γ behind, sword and shield before; beneath, OINOANΔE / ωN. *B.M.C.*
19. 73, 1 .. .. *(Unique)*

5319   5321

5319 **Olympos** (on the eastern coast of Lycia, about ten miles south of Phaselis). After 168
B.C. Æ *drachm* (*c.* 1·8—2·5 gm.). Laur. hd. of Apollo r., bow behind neck. ℞. Lyre;
OΛYM above, torch to l., sword and shield to r.; all within shallow incuse square. *B.M.C.*
19. 74, 1 .. .. £120

5320 — Æ 17. Hd. of Athena r., in crested Corinthian helmet. ℞. OΛYMΠHNωN. Winged
thunderbolt. *S.N.G. Von Aulock* 4376 .. .. £16

5321 **Patara** (an important city near the mouth of the Xanthos, Patara possessed a famous
oracle of Apollo). *Circa* 400 B.C. Æ *stater* (*c.* 8·4 gm.). Hd. of Athena r., in crested
helmet. ℞. Bust of Hermes r., in winged petasos, caduceus behind; Lycian letters
(= *Pttaraze*) above and before; all within incuse square. *B.M.C. 19.* 27, 119 £1,250

5322   5325   5328

5322 After 168 B.C. (League coinage). Æ *drachm* (*c.* 2·5—2·9 gm.). Laur. hd. of Apollo r.,
bow and quiver behind neck. ℞. Lyre; ΛYKIΩN above, Π — A in field; all within shallow
incuse square. *S.N.G. Von Aulock* 4380 .. .. £130

5323 — — Similar, but without bow and quiver on *obv.*, and with caduceus in *rev.* field to r.
S.N.G. Von Aulock 4381 .. .. £130

5324 — Æ 17. Apollo stg. facing. ℞. As 5322. *S.N.G. VonAulock* 4382 .. £16

5325 — Æ 10. Laur. hd. of Apollo r. ℞. ΛYKIΩN, Π — A. Bow and quiver; all within shallow incuse square. *B.M.C. 19.* 75, 2-3 .. .. £11

5326 2nd-1st cent. B.C. Æ 13. Laur. hd. of Apollo three-quarter face to r. ℞. ΠATAPEΩN.
Hd. of Artemis three-quarter face to l., wearing stephane. *B.M.C. 19.* 76, 11 £14

5327 — Æ 11. Similar, but hd. of Artemis to l. on *rev.* *B.M.C. 19.* 76, 9-10 .. £13

5328 — Æ 9. As last, but hd. of Apollo to r. on *obv.* *B.M.C. 19.* 76, 6-8.. .. £12

5329   5333

5329 **Phaselis** (the only Lycian city of purely Greek origin, Phaselis was founded from Rhodos *circa*. 690 B.C. Situated on the inhospitable east coast, its fine harbours ensured the development of the place as a great commercial centre. The abundance of its 3rd century silver coinage is evidence of the prosperity of Phaselis in early Hellenistic times, a period of numismatic inactivity at the native Lycian mints). Mid-5th cent. B.C. Æ *stater* (*c.* 11 gm.). Prow of galley r., resembling the forepart of a boar; three circular shields are visible along the gunwale. R. Stern of galley l., ΦΑΣ above; all within incuse square. *B.M.C. 19.* 79, 3 .. .. £550

5330 — Æ *tetrobol* (*c.* 3·4 gm.). Similar. *S.N.G. Von Aulock* 4395 .. .. £250

5331 1st half of 4th cent. B.C. Æ *stater* (*c.* 10·3 gm.). Prow of galley r.; beneath, dolphin r. R. Stern of galley r.; ΦΑΣ above, dolphin r. beneath; all within circular incuse. *S.N.G. Von Aulock* 4397 .. .. £650

5332 3rd cent. B.C. Æ *stater* (*c.* 10·3 gm.). Prow of galley l., with superstructure; HP monogram before. R. Stern of galley r.; above, ΦΑΣΗ and shield surmounted by helmet. *S.N.G. Von Aulock* 4398 .. .. £475

5333 — — Prow of galley r., with superstructure ornamented with club; crab beneath. R. Stern of galley r.; above, ΤΙΜΩΝ / ΦΑΣΗ. (*British Museum*) £450

5334 — — Prow of galley r., with superstructure ornamented with shield; star above. R. Stern of galley l.; above, ΛΙΒΥΚΡΑΤΗΣ / ΦΑΣΗ. *S.N.G. Von Aulock* 4410 .. £450

5335 — — Prow of galley r., with superstructure ornamented with club; hippocamp beneath. R. Stern of galley r.; above, ΠΟΛΙΤΑΣ / ΦΑΣΗ. *S.N.G. Von Aulock* 4420 .. £450

5336   5337

5336 — — Prow of galley r., the superstructure surmounted by figure kneeling r. R. Stern of galley l.; above, ΕΥΣΘΕΝΗΣ / ΦΑΣΗ. *S.N.G. Von Aulock* 4425 .. .. £450

5337 Late 3rd-early 2nd cent. B.C. Æ *stater* (*c.* 11·2 gm.). Laur. hd. of Apollo r. R. Prow of galley r., surmounted by Athena stg. r., brandishing thunderbolt and holding aegis, Φ behind; beneath prow, ΙΗΝΩΝ. *B.M.C. 19.* 81, 14 .. .. £500

5338   5340

Phaselis *continued*

5338 — Æ *drachm* (*c.* 5·55 gm.). Prow of galley r., surmounted by owl stg. r.   Ŗ. Athena stg. r., brandishing thunderbolt and holding aegis; Φ before, ΘΕΟΧΡΗΣΤΟΣ behind.   *B.M.C. 19.* 81, 15 .. .. £300

5339 — Æ *tetradrachm* (*c.* 16·75 gm.), restoring the types of Alexander the Great.   Hd. of young Herakles r., clad in lion's skin.   Ŗ. Zeus enthroned l., holding eagle and sceptre, ΑΛΕΞΑΝΔΡΟΥ behind; before, Φ and ΙΒ (=year 12).   *Müller* (*Numismatique d'Alexandre le Grand*) 1186 .. .. £175
 This dated series runs from year 1 (Α) *to* 31 (ΛΑ), *but the era is uncertain.   See also no.* 5401, *of Aspendos, and* 5412, *of Perge.*

5339A After 168 B.C.   Æ *tetradrachm* (*c.* 16·2 gm.).   Laur. hd. of Apollo l.   Ŗ. Athena stg. l., holding Nike (who bears wreath and ship's mast) and spear; behind, ΕΡΥΜΝΕΥΣ; in field to l., ΦΑ.   *Leu auction, May* 1979, *lot* 144.. .. .. £4,500

5340 — Æ *drachm* (*c.* 2·2—2·8 gm.).   Laur. hd. of Apollo r.   Ŗ. Lyre; ΦΑΣΗΛΙ above, head-dress of Isis to l., torch to r.; all within shallow incuse square.   *B.M.C. 19.* 81, 16
 £125

5341 *Bronze Coinage.* 3rd cent. B.C.   Æ 17.   Prow of galley r.   Ŗ. Stern of galley r., ΦΑΣΗ above.   *B.M.C. 19.* 80, 5, 7 .. .. £14

5342 — Æ 10.   Prow of galley l.   Ŗ. As *obv.*, but with ΦΑ monogram beneath.   *B.M.C. 19.* 80, 13 .. .. £11

5343 2nd-1st cent. B.C.   Æ 19.   Prow of galley r., crowned by Nike flying r. above.   Ŗ. Athena stg. r., brandishing thunderbolt and holding aegis; Φ — Α in field.   *B.M.C. 19.* 82, 18 .. .. £12

5344 — — Similar, but with Φ — Β in *rev.* field.   *B.M.C. 19.* 82, 19 .. .. £12

5344A **Phellos** (a city of some importance in early times, Phellos was situated north-west of Antiphellos which originally served as its port).   After 168 B.C. (League coinage).   Æ *drachm* (*c.* 2·75 gm.).   Laur. hd. of Apollo r., bow and quiver behind neck.   Ŗ. Lyre; ΛΥΚΙΩΝ above, Φ — Ε in field, bow and quiver to l.; all within shallow incuse square. (*British Museum*) £250

5345 — Æ 12.   Laur. hd. of Apollo r.   Ŗ. ΛΥΚΙΩΝ, Φ — Ε.   Bow and quiver; all within shallow incuse square.   *B.M.C. 19.* 83, 1 .. .. £12

5346 **Pinara** (situated on the eastern slopes of the Antikragos mountains, west of the Xanthos river).   After 168 B.C. (League coinage).   Æ *drachm* (*c.* 2·5 gm.).   Laur. hd. of Apollo r., bow behind neck.   Ŗ. Lyre; ΛΥΚΙΩΝ above, Π — Ι in field; all within shallow incuse square.   *Forrer/Weber* 7300 .. .. £130

5347   5351

5347 — — (*c.* 1·9 gm.). Similar, but without bow on *obv.* or ΛΥΚΙΩΝ on *rev.* *B.M.C. 19.*
84, 5 ..   ..   £110

5348 — Æ 11. Laur. hd. of Apollo r. ℞. ΛΥΚΙΩΝ, π — ι. Bow and quiver; all within
shallow incuse square. *Historia Numorum, p.* 697   ..   ..   £13

5349 2nd-1st cent. B.C. Æ 13. Male (?) hd. r., wearing crested helmet. ℞. ΠΙΝΑΡΕΩΝ
around circular shield ornamented with star. *S.N.G. Von Aulock* 4447   ..   £14

5350 — Æ 10. Hd. of Artemis (?) r. ℞. Bucranium; ΠΙΝΑ / PE — ΩN in field. *B.M.C. 19.*
84, 2 ..   ..   £12

5351 **Rhodiapolis** (a town of south-eastern Lycia, between Limyra and Olympos). After
168 B.C. (League coinage). *R drachm* (*c.* 2—2·7 gm.). Laur. hd. of Apollo r., bow behind
neck. ℞. Lyre; ΛΥΚΙΩΝ above, P — O in field, torch (?) to l.; all within shallow incuse
square. *B.M.C. 19.* 85, 1 ..   ..   £130

5352 **Telmessos** (an important city of north-western Lycia, Telmessos was frequently subject
to foreign domination, being close to the Carian border). Late 5th cent. B.C. *R stater*
(*c.* 8·5 gm.). Hd. of Athena r., in crested helmet ornamented with olive-leaves and floral
scroll. ℞. Hd. of bearded Herakles r., clad in lion's skin; before, Lycian letters (=*Tele-
behihe*); all within incuse square. *B.M.C. 19.* 29, 127 ..   ..   £1,400

5353   5355

5353 — *R diobol* (*c.* 1·5 gm.). Hd. of Athena r., in crested Corinthian helmet. ℞. As last,
but without the inscription. *B.M.C. 19.* 29, 129-30 ..   ..   £225

5354 *Circa* 300 B.C. Æ 15. Hd. of Alexander the Great r., with ram's horn. ℞. ΤΕΛΕ-
ΜΗΣΣΕΩΝ (in ex.). Panther l., r. foreleg raised; ΠΤ monogram above. *Historia Numorum,*
p. 698   ..   ..   £20

5355 196-189 B.C. (under Antiochos III). Æ 17. Rad. hd. of Helios three-quarter face to r.
℞. ΤΕΛΜΗ behind Apollo seated l. on omphalos, holding arrow and bow. *B.M.C. 19.*
86, 1 ..   ..   £17

5356 After 133 B.C. Æ 11. Hd. of Hermes r., wearing petasos. ℞. Fly; Τ — E above, Λ
beneath, to r.; all within shallow incuse square. *B.M.C. 19.* 86, 2   ..   ..   £14

5357 After 81 B.C. (League coinage). Æ 18. Hd. of Artemis r., wearing stephane. ℞.
Stag stg. r.; ΤΕΛ above, ΛΥ before. *B.M.C. 19.* 86, 3 ..   ..   £16
See also no. 5281 above.

5358   5360

5358 **Termessos Minor** (a colony of the Pisidian Termessos; the exact site is uncertain, but
is probably to be looked for in the vicinity of Oinoanda in northern Lycia). 1st cent. B.C.
Æ 20. Laur. hd. of Zeus r., sceptre behind. ℞. Winged thunderbolt; ΤΕΡ — ΜΗΣ /
ΣΕ — ΩΝ above and beneath. *B.M.C. 19.* 277, 9-14 .. .. £14

5359 — Æ 18. Laur. hd. of Apollo r. ℞. ΤΕΡΜΗΣ / ΣΕΩΝ either side of lyre. *B.M.C. 19.*
276, 5, 7 .. .. £14

5360 — Æ 13. Dr. bust of Hermes r., wearing petasos, caduceus behind shoulder. ℞.
ΤΕΡΜΗΣ / ΣΕΩΝ either side of eagle stg. r. on caduceus. *B.M.C. 19.* 276, 1 .. £12

5361 **Tlos** (an important city of western Lycia, on the slopes of the Masikytes mountains
east of the Xanthos river). Early 4th cent. B.C. Æ *stater* (c. 8·05 gm.). *Obv.* Similar to
5352. ℞. Two lions seated confronted, their hds. facing and r. forepaws raised; between
them, diskeles; Lycian letters (=*Tlavi*) in ex. and in field; all in dotted circle within
circular incuse. *S.N.G. Von Aulock* 4185 .. .. £2,000

5362 — Æ *tetrobol* (c. 2·77 gm.). Lion's scalp facing. ℞. Two lions confronted, as last;
in ex., diskeles; in field, Lycian letters (=*Tl*); all in dotted circle within circular incuse.
S.N.G. Von Aulock 4187 .. .. £300

5363   5365

5363 — Æ *diobol* (c. 1·2 gm.). Lion's scalp facing. ℞. Hd. of Apollo (?) facing, chlamys
fastened at neck; Lycian letters (=*Tlavi*) on either side; all in dotted circle within circular
incuse. *B.M.C. 19.* 31, 134 .. .. £250

5364 — Æ *obol* (c. 0·62 gm.). Lion's scalp facing. ℞. Hd. of Apollo l., Lycian letters
(=*Tlavi*) before; all in dotted circle within circular incuse. *S.N.G. Von Aulock* 4192
£140

5365 After 168 B.C. (League coinage). Æ *drachm* (c. 2·4—2·9 gm.). Laur. hd. of Apollo r.,
bow and quiver behind neck. ℞. Lyre; ΛΥΚΙΩΝ above, Τ — Λ in field, crested helmet to
r.; all within shallow incuse square. *B.M.C. 19.* 88, 1 .. .. .. £100

5366 — Æ *diobol* (c. 0·66 gm.). Hd. of Artemis r., wearing stephane, bow and quiver behind
neck. ℞. Quiver; Τ — Λ in upper field, caduceus to r.; all within shallow incuse square.
S.N.G. Von Aulock 4464 .. .. £120

5367 — Æ 11. Laur. hd. of Apollo r. ℞. ΛΥΚΙΩΝ, Τ — Λ. Bow and quiver; all within
shallow incuse square. *B.M.C. 19.* 88, 3-5 .. .. £11

5368 1st cent. B.C. (League coinage). Æ 18. Laur. bust of Apollo r., Λ — Υ either side of
neck. ℞. Bust of Artemis r., Τ — Λ either side of neck. *B.M.C. 19.* 89, 7-8 .. £15

See also nos. 5277-8 *above.*

5369 **Trebenna** (a town of north-eastern Lycia, west of Attaleia in Pamphylia). After 168 B.C. (League coinage). Æ 11. Similar to 5367, but with T — P instead of T — Λ on *rev. B.M.C. 19.* 90, 1-2 .. .. £13

5370 **Tybenissos** (a small town close to the southern coast, north-east of Aperlai. The attribution of the following coin to this place is not certain). 1st cent. B.C. (League coinage). Æ 18. Similar to 5368, but with T — Y instead of T — Λ on *rev. B.M.C. 19.* 91, 1 .. .. £17

5371 **Xanthos** (the principal city of Lycia, Xanthos was situated in the south-west of the country, on the river which bore the same name. It possessed many splendid temples foremost amongst which was that of the Lycian Apollo). *Circa* 400 B.C. Æ *stater* (c. 8·15 gm.). Hd. of Athena r., wearing crested helmet. R. Laur. hd. of Apollo r., diskeles behind, Lycian letters (=*Arnnahe*) before; all in dotted circle within circular incuse. *B.M.C. 19.* 23, 106 .. .. £1,250

5372 — Æ *diobol* (c. 1·25 gm.). *Obv.* Similar. R. Eagle stg. l., wings open, diskeles before; all in dotted circle within circular incuse. *B.M.C. 19.* 24, 107 .. .. .. £175

5373 — Æ *obol* (c. 0·65 gm.). *Obv.* Similar. R. Hd. of Athena, as *obv.*, but with diskeles before; all in dotted circle within circular incuse. *B.M.C. 19.* 24, 108 .. £130

5374 After 168 B.C. (League coinage). Æ *drachm* (c. 2·75 gm.). Laur. hd. of Apollo r., bow and quiver behind neck. R. Lyre; ΛΥΚΙΩΝ above, Ξ in field to l.; all within shallow incuse square. *Forrer/Weber* 7308 .. .. £120

5375   5376

5375 — — Laur. hd. of Apollo r. R. Similar to last, but with Ξ — Λ in field. *S.N.G. Von Aulock* 4475-6 .. .. £110

5376 — Æ 13. Laur. hd. of Apollo r. R. Bust of Artemis r., bow and quiver behind shoulder; ΛΥΚΙΩΝ above, Ξ — Λ in field; all within shallow incuse square. *B.M.C. 19.* 92, 3 £12

5377 — Æ 11. *Obv.* Similar. R. ΛΥΚΙΩΝ, Ξ — Λ. Bow and quiver; all within shallow incuse square. *B.M.C. 19.* 92, 4 .. .. £11

5378 — Æ 10. Hd. of Apollo (?) facing. R. ΛΥΚΙΩΝ. Bow and quiver. *B.M.C. 19.* 38, 1 £13

5379 — — Laur. hd. of Apollo three-quarter face to r.; lyre in field to r. R. ΛΥΚΙΩΝ. Beardless hd. three-quarter face to r. *B.M.C. 19.* 38, 4 .. .. £14

5380 1st cent. B.C. Æ 13. Laur. hd. of Apollo r. R. ΞΑΝ / ΘΙΩΝ either side of lyre. *B.M.C. 19.* 92, 1 .. .. £12

See also nos. 5201, 5279 *and* 5280 *above.*

5381   5383

5381 **PAMPHYLIA. Aspendos** (although situated 8 miles from the mouth of the Eurymedon river, Aspendos was an important port and naval base. It seems to have preferred
Persian rule, despite its Greek origins, and even offered resistance to Alexander on his
advance through Asia Minor. It was included within the dominions of the Pergamene
Kings from 189 to 133 B.C.). 460-420 B.C. Æ *stater* (*c.* 11 gm.). Naked warrior advancing r., holding sword and shield. R. Triskeles of human legs r., within incuse square.
B.M.C. 19. 93, 1-2   ..   ..   £750

5382 — — Similar, but with legend ΕΣΤFΕ above triskeles, and sling in *rev.* field to r. *B.M.C.*
19. 93, 6   ..   ..   £750

      The legend represents the Pamphylian form of the name of Aspendos—Estvediys.

5383 — — *Obv.* Similar, but the warrior holds spear instead of sword. R. Lion r., triskeles of
human legs r. in background; above, ΕΣΠ; all within incuse square. *B.M.C. 19.* 94, 9
                                                            £1,250

5384 — Æ *obol* (*c.* 0·75 gm.). Vase, without handles. R. As 5381. *S.N.G. Von Aulock*
4485 ..   ..   £125

         5385   5387

5385 420-375 B.C. Æ *drachm* (*c.* 5·4 gm.). Naked horseman (Mopsos, founder of Aspendos)
galloping l., hurling spear. R. Boar running r., ΕΣΤΕΕ in ex.; all in dotted circle within
circular incuse. *B.M.C. 19.* 94, 10   ..   ..   £275

      These types refer to the legend that Mospos sacrificed a boar to Aphrodite in fulfilment of a
vow.

5386 410-385 B.C. Æ *stater* (*c.* 10·9 gm.). Two naked athletes, wrestling; the one on r.
punches his opponent's stomach with r. hand and grasps with l. his r. wrist; the one on l.
holds his opponent round the neck. R. Slinger advancing r., about to discharge his sling;
triskeles before, ΕΣΤΕΕ behind; all in dotted square within incuse square. *B.M.C. 19.*
95, 16   ..   ..   £275

5387 — — *Obv.* Similar, but the wrestler on l. grasps with r. hand his opponent's l. leg, and
with l. punches his stomach; the one on r. grasps his opponent's arms. R. Similar to last,
but with legend ΕΣΤFΕΔΙΙVΣ behind slinger. *B.M.C. 19.* 95, 15   ..   £275

5388 — — *Obv.* Similar to 5386, but the wrestler on l. punches his opponent's stomach with
l. hand and grasps with r. his l. wrist; whilst the one on r. holds his opponent round the
neck. R. Slinger advancing r., about to discharge his sling; herm before, triskeles and
ΕΣΤFΕΔΙΙVΣ behind; all in dotted square within incuse square. *S.N.G. Von Aulock*
4511 ..   ..   £300

5389 385-370 B.C. Æ *stater* (*c.* 10·9 gm.). Two naked athletes, wrestling; the one on l.
grasps with both hands his opponent's l. arm; the one on r. holds his opponent round the
neck. R. Similar to 5387, but also with sling-stone beneath the triskeles. *S.N.G.*
Von Aulock 4512   ..   ..   £250

5390   5392

5390 — — Two naked athletes, wrestling, grasping each other by the arms. ℞. As 5387.
B.M.C. 19. 96, 20 .. .. £225

5391 — — Two wrestlers, as last; between them, on ground, ivy-leaf. ℞. Similar to 5387,
but also with eagle in lower field to r. S.N.G. Von Aulock 4522 .. .. £250

5392 — — Two naked athletes, wrestling; the one on l. grasps with both hands his opponent's
l. arm; the one on r. holds his opponent's l. shoulder; between them, VMA (retrograde).
℞. Slinger advancing r., about to discharge his sling; before, winged Eros, naked, stg.
facing; behind, triskeles and ΕΣΤFΕΔΙΙVΣ; all in dotted square within incuse square.
B.M.C. 19. 101, 60 .. .. £275

5393 — — Similar to 5390, but the wrestler on r. extends his r. leg behind his opponent in
order to trip him. S.N.G. Von Aulock 4531 .. .. £300

5394 — — Two naked athletes stg. face to face, their hands raised in the attitude of boxers.
℞. As 5387. S.N.G. Von Aulock 4536 .. .. £325

5395 — — Similar to 5390, but both wrestlers stand to front, the one on r. with his r. leg
raised against his opponent's l. thigh. S.N.G. Von Aulock 4538 .. .. £350

5396   5398

5396 370-333 B.C. Æ stater (c. 10·9 gm.). Obv. Similar to 5392, but with KF between the
wrestlers. ℞. Slinger advancing r., about to discharge his sling; triskeles before,
ΕΣΤFΕΔΙΙVΣ behind; all in dotted square within incuse square. B.M.C. 19. 98, 44
£200

5397 — — Obv. Similar to 5390; between the wrestlers, ME. ℞. As last. S.N.G. Von
Aulock 4555 .. .. £200

5398 — — Similar, but with LΦ between the wrestlers, and without incuse square on rev.
B.M.C. 19. 98, 35-6 .. .. £200

The 4th century staters of Aspendos often bear countermarks, frequently three or four on one
coin. These normally take the form of animals or heads and are sometimes associated with
Aramaic letters.

5399   5401

Aspendos *continued*

5399 3rd cent. B.C. Æ *stater* (*c.* 10·5 gm.). Two naked athletes, wrestling, grasping each other by the arms; between them, E. ℞. Slinger stg. r., about to discharge his sling; before, triskeles above club; behind, EΣTFEΔIY; between slinger's legs, O; all within circle of dots. *B.M.C. 19.* 101, 63 ..   ..   £175

5400 — — Similar, but with ΠO between the wrestlers, and with legend ECTFEΔIIYC on *rev.*; no letter between slinger's legs. *B.M.C. 19.* 101, 67 ..   ..   £175

5401 Late 3rd-early 2nd cent. B.C. Æ *tetradrachm* (*c.* 16·75 gm.), restoring the types of Alexander the Great. Hd. of young Herakles r., clad in lion's skin. ℞. Zeus enthroned l., holding eagle and sceptre, AΛEΞANΔPOY behind; before, AΣ and H (= year 8). *Müller* (*Numismatique d'Alexandre le Grand*) 1202 ..   ..   £175

     This dated series runs from year 1 (A) *to* 29 (KΘ), *but the era is uncertain. See also no.* 5339, *of Phaselis, and* 5412, *of Perge.*

5402   5405   5408

5402 *Bronze Coinage.* 4th-3rd cent. B.C. Æ 18. Forepart of bridled horse galloping r. ℞. Δ — M either side of sling. *B.M.C. 19.* 102, 71   ..   ..   £15

5403 — Æ 14. Gorgoneion. ℞. Σ — K either side of caduceus. *Forrer/Weber* 7321   £14

5404 2nd-1st cent. B.C. Æ 15. Similar to 5402, but with AΣΠEN / ΔIΩN either side of sling on *rev.* *B.M.C. 19.* 102, 73   ..   ..   £12

5405 — — Horse galloping r. ℞. Slinger stg. r., about to discharge his sling; A — C in field. *B.M.C. 19.* 102, 74 ..   ..   £12

5406 — — *Obv.* Similar; above horse, star and crescent. ℞. Warrior stg. r., brandishing spear and holding shield; A — C in field. *B.M.C. 19.* 102, 75 ..   ..   ..   £12

5407 — Æ 11. Circular shield surrounded by dots. ℞. A — Σ either side of caduceus. *B.M.C. 19.* 103, 77 ..   ..   £11

5408 **Attaleia** (a coastal city, situated south-west of Perge, Attaleia was founded by Attalos II of Pergamon about the middle of the 2nd cent. B.C.). 2nd-1st cent. B.C. Æ 15. Hd. of Poseidon r., wearing tainia. ℞. Poseidon stg. l., dolphin beneath extended r. hand, holding trident in l.; to r., ATTAΛEΩN. *B.M.C. 19.* 110, 1-2   ..   ..   ..   £13

5409 — Æ 18. Two heads of Athena, jugate, each wearing crested Corinthian helmet. ℞. Nike advancing l., holding wreath; ATTA / ΛEΩN before. *B.M.C. 19.* 110, 5-6   £15

5410 — Æ 11. Hd. of Athena r., in crested Corinthian helmet. ℞. ATTA / ΛEΩN either side of Artemis stg. r., drawing arrow from quiver and holding bow. *B.M.C. 19.* 110, 4   £10

5411 — Æ 13. Dolphin l. ℞. ATTAΛEΩN. Rudder. *S.N.G. Von Aulock* 4613 ..   £12

5412 **Perge** (an important city situated between the rivers Kestros and Katarrhaktes, Perge was a centre for the worship of Artemis, a famous temple in whose honour stood nearby). 3rd cent. B.C. Æ *tetradrachm* (*c.* 16·75 gm.), restoring the types of Alexander the Great. Hd. of young Herakles r., clad in lion's skin. Ŗ. Zeus enthroned l., holding eagle and sceptre, ΑΛΕΞΑΝΔΡΟΥ behind; before, IH (= year 18). *Müller* (*Numismatique d'Alexandre le Grand*) 1235 .. .. £175

  This dated series runs from year 1 (A) to 33 (ΛΓ), but the era is uncertain. See also no. 5339, of Phaselis, and 5401, of Aspendos.

5413   5415

5413 — — Laur. hd. of Artemis r., quiver behind neck. Ŗ. Artemis stg. l., holding wreath and sceptre, stag at her feet; ΑΡΤΕΜΙΔΟΣ behind, ΠΕΡΓΑΙΑΣ before; in field to l., Sphinx seated r. *B.M.C. 19.* 119, 1 .. .. £500

5414 2nd cent. B.C. Æ *tetradrachm* (*c.* 15·2 gm.). Similar, but with I instead of Sphinx in *rev.* field to l. *S.N.G. Von Aulock* 4659 .. .. £450

5415 — Æ *drachm* (*c.* 3·7 gm.). Similar, but with B instead of I in *rev.* field to l. *B.M.C. 19.* 119, 2 .. .. £150

5416 — Æ *hemidrachm* (*c.* 1·8 gm.). Similar; no letter or symbol in *rev.* field. *B.M.C. 19.* 119, 3 .. .. £75

5417   5422

5417 *Bronze Coinage.* 3rd cent. B.C. Æ 17. Sphinx, wearing kalathos, seated r. Ŗ. ѴΑΝΑѰΑΣ / ΠΡΕΙΙΑΣ either side of Artemis stg. l., holding wreath and sceptre. *B.M.C. 19.* 122, 17 .. .. £14

5418 2nd-1st cent. B.C. Æ 18. As 5416. *B.M.C. 19.* 120, 5-7 .. .. .. £13

5419 — Æ 19. Laur. bust of Artemis r., bow and quiver behind neck. Ŗ. Nike advancing l., holding wreath; ΑΡΤΕΜΙΔΟΣ behind, ΠΕΡΓΑΙΑΣ before. *S.N.G. Von Aulock* 4662 £15

5420 — Æ 16. Laur. heads of Artemis and Apollo, jugate, r. Ŗ. Artemis stg. r., holding torch and bow; ΑΡΤΕΜΙΔΟΣ before, ΠΕΡΓΑΙΑΣ behind. *S.N.G. Von Aulock* 4663 £16

5421 — Æ 19. Cultus-statue of Artemis of Perge within distyle shrine. Ŗ. As last, but ΑΡΤΕΜΙΔΟΣ behind, ΠΕΡΓΑΙΑΣ before. *S.N.G. Von Aulock* 4664 .. .. £15

5422 — — *Obv.* Similar. Ŗ. ΑΡΤΕΜΙΔΟΣ / ΠΕΡΓΑΙΑΣ either side of bow and quiver. *B.M.C. 19.* 121, 10 .. .. £14

5423   5425

5423 **Side** (an important coastal city, south-east of Aspendos, Side was a place of great antiquity, resettled by colonists from Kyme in the 7th-6th cent. B.C. Its inhabitants, who abandoned Greek in favour of a curious local dialect, were reputed to be most dishonest, and the city was a centre for piracy in the 2nd and 1st centuries B.C.). 460-410 B.C. Æ *stater* (*c.* 11 gm.). Pomegranate; beneath, dolphin l. R. Hd. of Athena r., of archaic style, wearing crested helmet; all within incuse square. *B.M.C. 19.* 143, 1-3   £550

5424 — — Pomegranate, encircled by olive-wreath. R. Dolphin l., human eye beneath; all in linear square within incuse square. *B.M.C. 19.* 143, 5-6   £500

5425 — — Pomegranate, within guilloche border. R. Hd. of Athena r., in crested Corinthian helmet; all within incuse square. *B.M.C. 19.* 144, 8   £450

5426 — Æ *tetrobol* (*c.* 3·45 gm.). Similar, but dotted border on *obv.*, and Athena's helmet without crest on *rev. B.M.C. 19.* 144, 9   £300

5427 — Æ *obol* (*c.* 0·78 gm.). As last. *B.M.C. 19.* 144, 10   £125

5428   5430

5428 400-375 B.C. Æ *stater* (*c.* 10·7 gm.). Athena stg. l., holding owl and resting l. arm on shield behind which stands spear; pomegranate in field to l. R. Naked Apollo stg. l., holding laurel-branch and bow, altar at feet; raven on ground to r.; Pamphylian legend behind; all within incuse square. *B.M.C. 19.* 145, 14   £400

5429 — Æ *tetrobol* (*c.* 3·53 gm.). Similar, but without spear on *obv. S.N.G. Von Aulock* 4768 ..   £650

5430 375-333 B.C. Æ *stater* (*c.* 10·7 gm.). *Obv.* Similar to 5428, but Athena holds wreath-bearing Nike instead of owl; Pamphylian letters in field to r. R. Naked Apollo stg. l., pouring libation from patera on to lighted altar, and holding long laurel-branch; Pamphylian legend behind. *B.M.C. 19.* 146, 16   £350

5431 — Æ *obol* (*c.* 0·8 gm.). Lion's hd. r. R. Hd. of Athena r., in crested Corinthian helmet. *S.N.G. Von Aulock* 4774 ..   £110

5432   5435

5432 Late 3rd—early 2nd cent. B.C. Æ *tetradrachm* (*c.* 16·9 gm.). Hd. of Athena r., in crested Corinthian helmet. ℞. Nike advancing l., holding wreath; in field to l., pomegranate and AΘ. *B.M.C. 19.* 146, 21 .. .. £225

5433 — — Similar, but with ΔEI—NO in *rev.* field instead of AΘ. *S.N.G. Von Aulock* 4787 £225

5434 — — Similar to 5432, but with AP instead of AΘ on *rev.*, and also with crested helmet in field to l. *B.M.C. 19.* 146, 23 .. .. £225

These late silver issues of Side often bear countermarks.

5435 — Æ *drachm* (*c.* 3·9 gm.). Similar to 5432, but with S̄T̄H̄ instead of AΘ in *rev.* field to l. *B.M.C. 19.* 150, 54 .. .. £140

5436   5438

5436 2nd-1st cent. B.C. Æ *tetradrachm* (*c.* 16 gm.). Similar to 5432, but of poor style, and with KΛE—YX in *rev.* field instead of AΘ. *B.M.C. 19.* 148, 43 .. .. .. £200

See also no. 5693 issued in the name of Amyntas, king of Galatia.

5437 *Bronze Coinage.* 3rd-2nd cent. B.C. Æ 16. Hd. of Athena r., in crested Corinthian helmet. ℞. Pomegranate. *B.M.C. 19.* 150, 59-61 .. .. £12

5438 2nd-1st cent. B.C. Æ 18. Laur. hd. of Apollo r. ℞. Athena stg. r., holding spear and shield, snake l. in background; ΣΙΔH—TΩN across lower field. *B.M.C. 19.* 151, 62 £13

5439 — — Similar to 5437, but of inferior style, and with ΣΙ—ΔH across lower field. *S.N.G. Von Aulock* 4805 .. .. £10

5440   5443

5440 — Æ 16. Hd. of Athena r., in crested Corinthian helmet. ℞. Nike advancing l., holding wreath and palm; ΣΙ—ΔHTΩN before, pomegranate in field to l. *B.M.C. 19.* 151, 66-7 .. .. £9

5441 — Æ 12. Pomegranate. ℞. Hd. of Athena r., in crested Corinthian helmet. *S.N.G. Von Aulock* 4804 .. .. £11

5442 **Sillyon** (an inland town, situated midway between Perge and Aspendos). Late 3rd-early 2nd cent. B.C. Æ *tetradrachm* (*c.* 16·75 gm.), restoring the types of Alexander the Great. Hd. of young Herakles r., clad in lion's skin. ℞. Zeus enthroned l., holding eagle and sceptre, ΑΛΕΞΑΝΔΡΟΥ behind; before, ΣΙΛ and Γ (=year 3). *Müller (Numismatique d'Alexandre le Grand)* 1222 .. .. £225

5443 *Bronze Coinage.* 3rd cent. B.C. Æ 15. Bearded hd. of Ares (?) r., wearing crested Corinthian helmet. ℞. Naked male figure stg. l., r. hand raised, holding chlamys in l. hand; behind, ΣΕΛΥΙΙΥΣ; before, thunderbolt. *B.M.C. 19.* 165, 1 .. .. £20

5444 — Æ 11. Laur. hd. of Apollo r. ℞. ΣΕΛΥ / ΙΙΙΥΣ above and beneath thunderbolt. *Forrer/Weber* 7369 .. .. £15

5445   5447

5445 **PISIDIA. Adada** (situated on the upper waters of the Kestros, north-west of Selge). 1st cent. B.C. Æ 20. Laur. hd. of Zeus r. R. Nike stg. l., holding palm-branch and crowning trophy; ΑΔΑΔΕ between. *B.M.C. 19.* 171, 1 ..   ..   £16

5446 — Æ 15. Bucranium between two dolphins, star above. R. Triskeles of human legs l., Α—Δ—Α between. *S.N.G. Von Aulock* 4895 ..   ..   £15

5447 — Æ 13. Similar, but without dolphins and star on *obv.*, and without legend on *rev.* *B.M.C. 19.* 171, 2 ..   ..   £13

5448 **Keraitai** (possibly the inhabitants of Kretopolis/Panemoteichos, south-west of Kremna). 1st cent. B.C. Æ 16. Turreted female hd. r. R. Κ—Ε either side of caduceus; all within laurel-wreath. *S.N.G. Von Aulock* 5051-2. *B.M.C. 18.* 78, 4-5 (*mis-attributed to Keramos in Caria*) £14

5449 — Æ 14. *Obv.* Similar. R. Forepart of running boar r., ΚΕΡΑ beneath. *S.N.G. Von Aulock* 5053 ..   ..   £15

5450 — Æ 11. Laur. hd. of Artemis r., quiver behind neck. R. Club; Ⱶ above, ΚΕ beneath. *B.M.C. 19.* 210, 1-4   ..   ..   £11

       See also no. 5452 below.

5451   5452   5455

5451 **Komama** (situated south-west of Kremna). 1st cent. B.C. Æ 13. Two bearded and laur. heads, jugate, r. R. Lion bounding r., ΚΟ in ex. *Forrer/Weber* 7384 ..   £17

5452 **Kremna** (a strongly fortified town of central Pisidia). 1st cent. B.C. Æ *drachm* (*c.* 2·9 gm.). Turreted hd. of Tyche r. R. Double cornucopiae; ΚΡΗΜΝΕΩΝ to r., ΚΑΙ/ ΚΕΡΑΕΙΤΩΝ to l. *S.N.G. Von Aulock* 5075   ..   ..   £300

       Issued jointly in the names of Kremna and Keraitai.

5453 — Æ 18. Turreted hd. of Tyche r., spear-head behind. R. Forepart of lion r.; ΚΡΗ beneath, Γ above. *B.M.C. 19.* 215, 1 ..   ..   £14

5454 — Æ 16. Laur. hd. of Zeus r. R. Winged thunderbolt; ΚΡΗ beneath, Ζ above. *B.M.C. 19.* 215, 4 ..   ..   £10

5455 — (time of King Amyntas, 36-25 B.C.) Æ 11. Hd. of Hermes r., wearing petasos. R. ΚΡ—Η either side of caduceus. *B.M.C. 19.* 215, 2   ..   ..   ..   £12

5456 **Etenna** (exact site uncertain, but probably in the vicinity of Kotenna, north of Side). Mid-4th cent. B.C. Æ *stater* (*c.* 11 gm.). Two naked athletes, wrestling; τ in field. R. ΕΤΕΝΝΕΩΝ. Beardless male figure advancing r., l. hand extended, holding crooked knife in r.; triskeles in field. *Historia Numorum, p.* 708   ..   ..   ..   £2,000

5457 — Æ *obol* (*c.* 0·7 gm.). Gorgoneion. R. Crooked knife. *Historia Numorum, p.* 708   £175

5458   5459

5458 1st cent. B.C. Æ 18. Female figure advancing r., grappling with snake which attacks her; oinochoe on ground behind. R. ET—EN either side of crooked knife. *B.M.C. 19.* 220, 4-5   ..   ..   £11

5459 — Æ 13. Two male figures running l., side by side, brandishing crooked knives. R. Female figure and snake, as *obv.* of last; ET—EN in field. *B.M.C. 19.* 220, 2-3   £10

5460   5462

5460 **Isinda** (situated in the south-west of the country, about 10 miles west of Termessos). 1st cent. B.C. Æ 15. Hd. of Artemis r. R. IΣ—IN either side of quiver. *B.M.C. 19.* 223, 1   ..   ..   £13

5461 — Æ 16. *Obv.* Similar, but with quiver behind neck. R. Crested helmet r., IΣ—IN in lower field, Γ (=year 3) to r. *Forrer/Weber* 7396   ..   ..   ..   £15

5462 — Æ 13. *Obv.* Similar. R. IΣ—IN either side of ear of corn. *B.M.C. 19.* 223, 2   £13

5463 — Æ 15. Laur. hd. of Artemis r. R. IΣIN within wreath. *B.M.C. 19.* 223, 4   £13

5464 — Æ 20. Laur. hd. of Zeus r. R. Warrior, brandishing spear, on horseback galloping r.; IΣIN and snake beneath; Γ (=year 3) behind. *B.M.C. 19.* 223, 5   ..   £14

5465 — — Similar, but diad. bust of Zeus on *obv.;* ICIN instead of IΣIN, ZI (=year 17) instead of Γ on *rev.* *B.M.C. 19.* 224, 9   ..   ..   £15

5466   5467

5466 **Sagalassos** (situated north-west of Kremna, near the source of the river Kestros. Its coinage only commenced about the time of King Amyntas, 36-25 B.C.). Æ *didrachm* (c. 7·65 gm.). Laur. hd. of Zeus r. R. Nike advancing l., holding wreath; before, ΣΑΓΑΛΑΣ / ΣΕΩΝ. *S.N.G. Von Aulock* 5153   ..   ..   £750

5467 — Æ *drachm* (c. 3·72 gm.). *Obv.* Similar. R. ΣΑΓΑΛΑΣ / ΣΕΩΝ either side of cornucopiae, bound with fillet. *B.M.C. 19.* 240, 1   ..   ..   ..   £350

5468 — Æ 15. Hd. of Athena r., in crested Corinthian helmet. R. ΣΑΓΑ / ΛΑΣΣ either side of Nike advancing r., holding wreath and palm-branch. *B.M.C. 19.* 240, 3   £12

5469 — Æ 14. Laur. hd. of Zeus r. R. Two goats contending, stg. on their hind legs; between them, ΣΑ. *S.N.G. Von Aulock* 5156   ..   ..   £14

5470   5471

5470 **Selge** (the principal city of Pisidia, Selge was situated on the Eurymedon river about 25
miles north of Aspendos. Its wealth derived from the fertility of the surrounding country,
and its inhabitants, who claimed descent from the Lakedaimonians, were the most warlike
in Pisidia). 2nd half of 5th cent. B.C. Æ *trihemiobol*? (*c.* 1·05 gm.). Gorgoneion, with
protruding tongue. R. Hd. of Athena l., wearing crested helmet ornamented with olive-
leaves; all within incuse square. *B.M.C. 19*. 256, 2   ..   ..   £75

5471 370-360 B.C. Æ *stater* (*c.* 10·9 gm.). Two naked athletes, wrestling, grasping each
other by the arms. R. Slinger advancing r., about to discharge his sling; astragalos before,
ΣΤΛΕΛΙΙΥΣ behind; all in dotted square within incuse square. *Forrer/Weber* 7417
£250

The legend on rev. gives the Pisidian form of the name of Selge.

5472 — — Similar, but with EY between wrestlers on *obv.;* and on *rev.*, triskeles in field before
slinger, astragalos between his legs, ΣΤΛΕΓΕΥΣ behind. *S.N.G. Von Aulock* 5255-7
£250

Like the contemporary staters of Aspendos, these coins often bear countermarks.

5473   5475

5473 — Æ *trihemiobol*? (*c.* 1·05 gm.). Gorgoneion, with protruding tongue. R. Hd. of
Athena r., in crested helmet; before, astragalos and ΣΤ. *B.M.C. 19*. 256, 3   ..   £50

5474 2nd half of 4th cent. B.C. Æ *stater* (*c.* 10·35 gm.). *Obv.* As 5471/2, but with Σ between
wrestlers. R. Naked Herakles facing, looking r., wielding club in r. hand and holding
lion's skin in outstretched l.; circular shield before, ΣΕΛΓΕΩΝ behind. *S.N.G. Von
Aulock* 5269   ..   ..   £1,250

5475 — Æ *trihemiobol*? (*c.* 0·95 gm.). *Obv.* As 5473. R. Hd. of Athena l., in crested helmet.
B.M.C. 19. 257, 4-6   ..   ..   £45

5476 — — Similar, but on *rev.* hd. of Athena r., with astragalos behind. *B.M.C. 19*. 257,
10   ..   ..   £45

5477   5479   5481

5477 3rd cent. B.C. Æ *stater* (*c.* 9·5 gm.). Two naked athletes, wrestling, grasping each other
by the arms; between them, K. R. Slinger stg. r., about to discharge his sling; before,
triskeles above cornucopiae and club; behind, ΣΕΛΓΕΩΝ; all within circle of dots. *B.M.C.
19*. 258, 20   ..   ..   £225

5478 — Æ *trihemiobol*? (*c.* 0·95 gm.).   Gorgoneion with long hair, resembling Apollo or Helios (tongue not protruding).   R. Hd. of Athena r., in crested helmet; astragalos behind.   *B.M.C. 19.* 259, 23-5   ..   ..   £40

5479 — — Similar, but also with spear-head behind Athena's hd. on *rev.*   *B.M.C. 19.* 259, 28   ..   ..   £40

5480 — Æ ¾ *obol*? (*c.* 0·45 gm.).   *Obv.* As 5478.   R. Lion's hd. r.; astragalos beneath.   *B.M.C. 19.* 257, 14-15   ..   ..   £55

5481 — — Similar, but the astragalos is behind the lion's head on *rev.*   *B.M.C. 19.* 260, 33-4 ..   ..   £55

5482 Early 2nd cent. B.C.   Æ *drachm* (*c.* 4·6 gm.).   Hd. of bearded Herakles r., wreathed with styrax; behind, club.   R. Artemis advancing r., carrying long torch; ΣΕΛΓΕΩΝ behind, ΙΔ before.   *B.M.C. 19.* 260, 35   ..   ..   £550

5483 — Æ *triobol*? (*c.* 1·85 gm.).   Similar, but without club on *obv.*   *S.N.G. Von Aulock* 5283 ..   ..   £300

5484   5487   5489

5484 2nd-1st cent. B.C.   Æ *triobol* (*c.* 2·15 gm.).   Hd. of bearded Herakles three-quarter face to r., wreathed with styrax; club in field to l.   R. ΣΕΛΓΕΩΝ between club and styrax-plant in pot.   *B.M.C. 19.* 260, 37   ..   ..   £275

5485 — Æ *diobol* (*c.* 1·42 gm.).   Hd. of Artemis r., quiver behind neck.   R. Forepart of stag r., looking back.   *S.N.G. Von Aulock* 5285 ..   ..   £175

5486 *Bronze Coinage.*   3rd-2nd cent. B.C.   Æ 22.   Circular shield, on which ΠΟ monogram.   R. Triskeles of human legs l.   *B.M.C. 19.* 263, 57   ..   ..   ..   £24

5487 — Æ 18.   *Obv.* Similar.   R. Hd. of Athena r., in crested helmet.   *B.M.C. 19.* 262, 55   £17

5488 — Æ 14.   Circular shield, of Macedonian type.   R. Σ—Ε either side of spear-head.   *B.M.C. 19.* 263, 59 ..   ..   £14

5489 2nd-1st cent. B.C.   Æ 13.   *Obv.* Similar to 5484.   R. Forepart of stag r., looking back; ΣΕ—Λ in field.   *B.M.C. 19.* 261, 38-9   ..   ..   £10

5490 — — *Obv.* Similar, but the club is held in Herakles' r. hand and appears over his l. shoulder.   R. Stag lying r., looking back; ΣΕ—Λ in field, Κ beneath.   *B.M.C. 19.* 261, 43   ..   ..   £11

5491   5494

5491 — Æ 14.   Hd. of bearded Herakles r., club behind neck.   R. Winged thunderbolt and bow; Σ—Ε in field.   *B.M.C. 19.* 262, 47-8   ..   ..   £8

5492 — — Similar, but with C—Ε instead of Σ—Ε.   *B.M.C. 19.* 262, 50   ..   ..   £8

5493 — Æ 16.   Hd. of Athena r., in crested helmet.   R. Slinger advancing r., about to discharge his sling; Ο—Θ in field.   *B.M.C. 19.* 262, 53   ..   ..   ..   £10

5494 — Æ 14.   ΠΟ monogram on shield represented by circle of dots.   R. Triskeles of human legs l.   *B.M.C. 19.* 263, 58   ..   ..   £15

5495 Termessos Major (an important city of south-western Pisidia, high up in the Tauros mountains, Termessos at one time controlled a large area of territory extending into northern Lycia. Its position was given recognition by the Romans in 71 B.C. from which era its earliest coins date). 71-36 B.C. Æ 18. Laur. hd. of Zeus r. ℞. Free horse galloping l.; A (=year 1) above, TEP beneath. *B.M.C. 19.* 268, 3-4 .. .. .. £11

5496   5497   5500

5496 — — Similar, but with ΙΓ (=year 13) above horse on *rev. B.M.C. 19.* 268, 8-9 £11

5497 — Æ 22. Similar, but hd. of Zeus to l. on *obv.*, ΚΣ (=year 26) above horse on *rev.* and ΤЄΡ instead of TEP beneath. *B.M.C. 19.* 269, 16 .. .. £13

5498 — Æ 18. *Obv.* As 5495. ℞. Forepart of bridled horse galloping l.; ΚЄ(=year 25) above, TEP beneath, thunderbolt behind. *B.M.C. 19.* 269, 18 .. .. .. £12

5499 — — Similar, but with Λ (=year 30) above horse on *rev.*, and without thunderbolt behind. *S.N.G. Von Aulock* 5337 .. .. £12

5500 — Æ 14. Laur. hd. of Artemis r., quiver behind neck. ℞. Humped bull stg. l.; TEP in ex. *B.M.C. 19.* 268, 1-2 .. .. £13

5501 — — Laur. hd. of Zeus r. ℞. Forepart of humped bull butting l.; ΤЄΡΜΗ / CЄΩΝ above and in ex., Γ (=year 3) behind. *S.N.G. Von Aulock* 5338 .. .. £14

5502 — — Bare hd. of bearded Herakles r., club behind neck. ℞. ΤЄΡ / ΜΗ either side of Nike stg. l., holding wreath and palm. *Forrer/Weber* 7464 .. .. .. £14

5503 — Æ 13. Bust of Selene r., crescent behind shoulders. ℞. As last, but with legend ΤЄ/Ρ. *S.N.G. Von Aulock* 5340 .. .. £14

5504 LYCAONIA. Eikonion (=Iconium: the chief city of the district, Eikonion was an important road junction for routes in all directions. It lay about 55 miles to the east of Lake Karalis). 2nd half of 1st cent. B.C. Æ 21. Bust of Perseus r., in winged Phrygian helmet, harpe and Gorgoneion at l. shoulder. ℞. Zeus enthroned l., holding thunderbolt and sceptre; ЄΙΚΟΝΙЄΩΝ behind, ΜЄΝЄΔΗΜ / ΤΙΜΟΘЄΟΥ before. *S.N.G. Von Aulock* 5384 .. .. £26

5505 — Æ 15. Laur. hd. of Zeus r. ℞. Naked Perseus stg. l., holding harpe and Gorgon's hd.; ЄΙΚΟΝΙ / ЄωΝ in field. *B.M.C. 21.* 4, 1 .. .. £20

5506 Parlaïs (the exact site of this town has not been identified with certainty, but it is usually placed in the area south of Lake Karalis). 2nd half of 1st cent. B.C. Æ 16. Laur. hd. of Zeus r. ℞. Panther walking r., caps of the Dioskouroi above; ΠΑΡΛΑΙΤЄΩΝ / ΔΙΟΜΗΔΟΥ above and in ex. *Forrer/Weber* 7491 .. .. £20

5507 CILICIA. Adana (situated east of Tarsos, on the river Saros, Adana commenced issuing coins in the time of Antiochos IV of Syria, 175-164 B.C.). 2nd-1st cent. B.C. Æ 27. Veiled hd. of Demeter (?) r., eagle behind. ℞. Zeus seated l., holding Nike and sceptre; ΑΔΑΝЄΩΝ behind, two monograms before. *B.M.C. 21.* 15, 1 .. .. £22

5508   5509

5508 — Æ 23.   Laur. hd. of Apollo r.   R. Similar to last, but all within wreath.   *B.M.C. 21.* 16, 5 ..   ..   £18

5509 — Æ 24.   Bust of Athena r., wearing crested Corinthian helmet and aegis.   R. Nike advancing l., holding wreath and palm; ΑΔΑΝΕΩΝ before, ΛΥ / CAN / ϵΥ / ΜΑ in field to l. *B.M.C. 21.* 16, 7 ..   ..   £20

5510   5515

5510 — Æ 18.   Turreted hd. of Tyche r.   R. ΑΔΑΝΕΩΝ.   Eagle stg. l. on ear of corn; monogram in field to l.   *B.M.C. 21.* 16, 8   ..   ..   £14

5511 — Æ 17.   Veiled female hd. r.   R. ΑΔΑΝΕΩΝ.   Horse pacing l.; monograms before and beneath.   *S.N.G. Von Aulock* 5435   ..   ..   £15

5512 — Æ 20.   Laur. hd. of Zeus r.   R. Naked Hermes stg. l., holding purse and caduceus; ΑΔΑΝΕΩΝ behind; ΕΥΜΑ, monogram and ΝΙΚΑ in field to l.   *B.M.C. 21.* 16, 10. .   £16

5513 **Aigeai** (a town of eastern Cilicia, Aigeai was situated on the north-western shores of the Gulf of Issos).   2nd-1st cent. B.C.   Æ 20.   Turreted hd. of Tyche r.   R. Bridled horse's hd. l.; ΑΙΓΕΑΙΩΝ above, monogram behind.   *B.M.C. 21.* 20, 1 ..   ..   ..   £15

5514 — — Similar, but Tyche also wears veil on *obv.*, and forepart of horse l. on *rev.*   *S.N.G. Von Aulock* 5441   ..   ..   £16

5515 — Æ 22.   *Obv.* As last.   R. Similar to 5513, but with legend ΑΙΓΕΑΙΩΝ / ΤΗΣ ΙΕΡΑΣ above, ΚΑΙ / ΑΥΤΟΝΟΜΟΥ below.   *B.M.C. 21.* 20, 2   ..   ..   £14

5516 — — Laur. hd. of Zeus r.   R. Athena stg. l., holding Nike, spear and shield; ΑΙΓΕΑΙΩΝ behind, ΕΡ in field to l.   *B.M.C. 21.* 21, 12   ..   ..   £13

5517   5520

5517 — Æ 17.   Bust of Athena r., wearing crested Corinthian helmet.   R. Goat lying l.; above, ϵΡ; beneath, ΑΙΓΕΑΙΩΝ; in field to l., ΔΙ (=year 14 of the Caesarean era =34/3 B.C.). *B.M.C. 21.* 22, 15 ..   ..   £14

5518 — — Diad. hd. of Alexander the Great (?) r.   R. Nike advancing l., holding wreath and palm; to l., ΑΙΓϵ / ΑΙΩΝ and ΔΙ (=year 14, as last); to r., ΜΗ monogram.   *B.M.C. 21.* 22, 18 ..   ..   £20
    It is possible that this type was struck to commemorate the 300th anniversary of Alexander's famous victory at the battle of Issos, 333 B.C.

5519 — Æ 15.   Bare hd. of bearded Herakles r.   R. Club and bow in case; ΑΙΓΕΑΙΩΝ / ΤΗΣ ΙΕΡΑΣ above, ΚΑΙ ΑΥΤΟΝΟΜΟΥ below.   *B.M.C. 21.* 21, 10-11   ..   ..   ..   £11

5520 **Alexandreia ad Issum** (a city founded by Alexander the Great as a memorial to the battle of Issos, Alexandreia lay on the south-eastern shores of the Gulf of Issos, opposite Aigeai.   It was about 30 miles north of Antiocheia, the Syrian capital).   2nd-1st cent. B.C. Æ 20.   Hd. of Alexander as young Herakles r., clad in lion's skin.   R. Zeus stg. l., holding wreath; ΑΛΕΞΑΝΔΡΕΩΝ behind, monogram in field to l.; all within wreath.   *B.M.C. 21.* 29, 3-4   ..   ..   £20

5521   5523

5521 **Anazarbos** (an important inland city of eastern Cilicia, Anazarbos was situated on the left bank of the river Pyramos). 2nd-1st cent. B.C. Æ 22. Laur. hd. of Zeus r. ℞. Tyche stg. l., holding corn-ears (?) and cornucopiae; ΑΝΑΖΑΡΒΕΩΝ behind, monogram in field to l.; all within wreath. *B.M.C. 21.* 31, 1 .. .. £22

5522 — Æ 19. *Obv.* Similar. ℞. Zeus seated l., holding Nike and sceptre; ΑΝΑΖΑΡΒΕΩΝ behind, monogram in field to l. *S.N.G. Von Aulock* 5470 .. .. .. £20

5523 **Aphrodisias** (on the southern coastline of Cilicia, opposite Cyprus, Aphrodisias was built on the neck of the peninsula of Zephyrion). *Circa* 380 B.C. Æ *stater* (c. 9·9 gm.). Aphrodite seated l. on throne flanked by two Sphinxes, holding flower in raised r. hand. ℞. Athena Parthenos stg. facing; her r. hand, which is resting on tree-trunk, holds tainia-bearing Nike; her l. rests on shield. *B.M.C. 21.* 112, 15 (*attributed to Nagidos*) £1,250

The reverse type is inspired by Pheidias' masterpiece in the Parthenon.

5524   5527

5524 — Æ *obol* (c. 0·7 gm.). Gorgon's hd. facing, with curly hair, wearing ear-rings. ℞. Sphinx seated l., within incuse square. *B.M.C. 21.* 113, 16 (*attributed to Nagidos*) £175

5525 — Æ ³ *obol*? (c. 0·57 gm.). Hd. of Hermes l., wearing petasos. ℞. Similar to *obv.* of 5523. *Forrer/Weber* 7508 .. .. £150

5526 **Kelenderis** (an important coastal city of Cilicia, midway between Nagidos and Aphrodisias, Kelenderis was said to have been founded by Sandokos, father of Kinyras, and later colonized by Samians). Mid-5th cent. B.C. Æ *stater* (c. 10·8 gm.). Naked rider, with whip in l. hand, seated sideways on horse prancing l., from which he is about to dismount. ℞. Forepart of kneeling goat l.; all in circle of dots within circular incuse. *Kraay* (*Archaic and Classical Greek Coins*) *pl.* 58, 1008 .. .. (*Unique*)

5527 440-400 B.C. Æ *stater* (c. 10·8 gm.). *Obv.* Similar. ℞. Goat kneeling l., looking back; all within circular incuse. *B.M.C. 21.* 52, 5 .. .. £300

5528 — — Similar, but with ΚΕΛ in ex. on *obv.*, and astragalos above goat on *rev.* *B.M.C. 21.* 52, 7 .. .. £300

5529 — — Similar to 5527, but with Λ beneath horse on *obv.*, and ΚΕΛΕΝ with ivy-spray above goat on *rev.* *B.M.C. 21.* 52, 10 .. .. £300

5530 — Æ *tetrobol* (c. 3·5 gm.). Similar to 5527, but with ΚΕΛΕ and two ivy-leaves above goat on *rev.* *S.N.G. Von Aulock* 5634 .. .. £450

5531   5533

5531 — Æ *obol* (*c.* 0·8 gm.). Gorgoneion, with protruding tongue. R. Forepart of Pegasos r.; all in dotted square within incuse square. *B.M.C. 21.* 53, 13 .. .. £110

5532 — — Hd. of Athena l., in crested helmet. R. Forepart of Pegasos l., within incuse square. *B.M.C. 21.* 53, 15 .. .. £125

5533 400-350 B.C. Æ *stater* (*c.* 10·5 gm.). Naked rider, with whip in r. hand, seated sideways on horse prancing r., from which he is about to dismount; beneath, T. R. Goat kneeling r., looking back; above, KEΛEN and A within O; all within circular incuse. *B.M.C. 21.* 55, 22 .. .. £325

5534 — — Similar, but without letter on *obv.*, and with *rev.* legend KEΛENΔEPITIKON (partly retrograde); also, *rev.* type enclosed by incuse square instead of circle. *Kraay (Archaic and Classical Greek Coins) pl.* 58, 1011 .. .. £1,000

5535 — — *Obv.* As last. R. Goat kneeling l., looking back; KEΛ above, Π before. *B.M.C. 21.* 55, 26 .. .. £350

5536 5538

5536 — Æ *obol* (*c.* 0·8 gm.). Forepart of Pegasos l. R. Goat kneeling r., looking back; KEΛ above; all within circular incuse. *B.M.C. 21.* 56, 29 .. .. .. £75

5537 — Æ *hemiobol* (*c.* 0·44 gm.). Forepart of Pegasos r. R. Goat kneeling r., looking back; K — E (retrograde) in field, A in ex.; all within circular incuse. *B.M.C. 21.* 56, 33 £60

5538 350-333 B.C. Æ *stater* (*c.* 9·9 gm.). *Obv.* As 5534. R. Goat kneeling r., looking back; KEΛEN above, A within O in ex.; all within circular dotted border. *B.M.C. 21.* 56, 34-5 £325

5539 5543

5539 — Æ *obol* (*c.* 0·7 gm.). Horse prancing r. R. Goat kneeling l., looking back; KE above; all within circular incuse. *B.M.C. 21.* 57, 37 .. .. .. £100

5540 — — Similar, but star above horse on *obv.*, and goat kneeling r. on *rev.*; also, *rev.* type within circular dotted border. *S.N.G. Von Aulock* 5642 .. .. .. £110

5541 2nd cent. B.C. Æ 13. Gorgoneion. R. Goat kneeling r., looking back; KE above. *B.M.C. 21.* 57, 39 .. .. £14

5542 1st cent. B.C. Æ 16. Laur. hd. of hero r., beardless. R. KEΛENΔEPITΩN. Goat kneeling l., looking back; YΨ above. *S.N.G. Von Aulock* 5645.. .. .. £16

5543 — Æ 22. Veiled and turreted bust of Tyche r., IΣ behind. R. Naked Apollo stg. l., holding laurel-branch and resting l. elbow on column surmounted by tripod; KEΛENΔEPITΩN behind, ΛE in field to l. *B.M.C. 21.* 57, 40 .. .. £15

5544 **Kibyra Minor** (a town of western Cilicia. The exact site is not certainly known, but it appears to have been close to the coast east of Side and the Melas river). 2nd-1st cent. B.C. Æ 18. Conjoined hds. of the Dioskouroi r. R. Nike stg. l., crowning trophy. KIBYPATΩN in ex., EK in lower field to l. *S.N.G. Von Aulock* 5654 .. .. £22

5545 Korykos (a coastal town midway between the mouths of the rivers Lamos and Kalykadnos, Korykos was chiefly known for the nearby mountain grotto, called the Korykian
Cave, which was celebrated by the poets). 1st cent. B.C. Æ 22. Turreted hd. of Tyche
r., AN behind. ℞. Hermes stg. l., holding phiale (?) and caduceus; ΚΩΡΥΚΙΩΤΩΝ behind,
ΔI / NI / AN in field to l. *B.M.C. 21.* 66, 1-4 .. .. £12

5546 5549

5546 — — Similar, but with AK behind bust on *obv.*, and with EP / ПO / EP in *rev.* field to l.
B.M.C. 21. 66, 5 .. .. £12

5547 Hieropolis-Kastabala (a town of eastern Cilicia, situated on the river Pyramos east of
Anazarbos. It was the capital of the later kings of Cilicia). 2nd-1st cent. B.C. Æ 13.
Turreted hd. of Tyche r., monogram behind. ℞. ΙΕΡΟΠΟΛΙΤΩΝ — ΤΩΝ ΠΡΟΣ / ΤΩΙ
ΠΥΡΑ either side of palm-tree. *S.N.G. Von Aulock* 5566-7 .. .. .. £11

5548 — Æ 23. *Obv.* Similar. ℞. City-goddess enthroned l., holding sceptre, eagle beneath
seat; ΙΕΡΟΠΟΛΙΤΩΝ behind, ΤΩΝ ΠΡΟΣ ΤΩΙ / ΠΥΡΑΜΩΙ before. *B.M.C. 21.* 82, 1 £12

5549 — — Veiled and turreted hd. of Tyche r. ℞. River-god Pyramos swimming r., hd.
facing, eagle perched on his r. hand; ΙΕΡΟ / ΠΟΛΙΤΩΝ above, ΤΩΝ ΠΡΟC ΤΩ / ΠΥΡΑΜΩ
beneath. *B.M.C. 21.* 82, 3 .. .. £15

See also nos. 5682-3.

5550 5551

5550 Holmi (a coastal city, between Aphrodisias and Korykos, Holmi was abandoned early
in the 3rd cent. B.C. when Seleukos I transferred the population to his new foundation,
Seleukeia, a few miles to the north). *Circa* 380 B.C. Æ *stater* (*c.* 9·65 gm.). Athena stg.
l., holding Nike and shield, spear at side; dolphin in field to l. ℞. ΟΛΜΙ / ΤΙΚΟΝ either side
of Apollo Sarpedonios stg. l., holding phiale and long laurel-branch; A in upper field to l.
Babelon (Traité) pl. 139, 14, *var.* £1,750

5551 — Æ *obol* (*c.* 0·7 gm.). Hd. of Athena r., in crested helmet. ℞. Hd. of Apollo Sarpedonios r., hair bound with tainia; ΟΛΜ before. *B.M.C. 21.* 85, 1 .. .. £130

5552 — Æ 13. Similar, but with legend ΟΛ behind hd. of Apollo on *rev. S.N.G. Von Aulock*
5580 .. .. £18

5553 Issos (situated at the head of the Gulf of Issos, the city lost much of its importance after
the foundation of Alexandreia to the south). *Circa* 390 B.C. Æ *stater* (*c.* 10·4 gm.).
Apollo Apatorios stg. l., holding phiale and long laurel-branch; in upper field to l.,
ΑΠΑΤΟΡΙΟΣ (in minute letters); in lower field, ΙΣΣΙ. ℞. Naked Herakles stg. r., holding
club, bow and lion's skin; wreath behind, *ankh* symbol before. *Kraay (Archaic and
Classical Greek Coins) pl.* 59, 1028 .. .. £2,000

5554 5555

5554 386-380 B.C. (in the name of the satrap Tiribazos). Æ *stater* (*c.* 10·4 gm.). Zeus/Baal stg. l., holding eagle and sceptre; ΙΣΣΙΚΟΝ before, Aramaic legend (=*Teribazu*) behind. R. Ahura-Mazda (half bird, half man) facing, hd. r., holding wreath and lotus-flower; AMI in field to l. *B.M.C. 21.* 90, 3 .. .. £1,250

    In 386 B.C. Tiribazos, satrap of Sardeis, was placed in charge of the war against Evagoras of Salamis. To finance these operations coins were produced by a number of Cilician mints. See also nos. 5564, 5610 and 5638.

5555 *Circa* 380 B.C. Æ *stater* (*c.* 10·4 gm.). Hd. of Athena three-quarter face to l., wearing triple-crested helmet. R. Bare hd. of young Herakles r., ΙΣ before. *Kraay (Archaic and Classical Greek Coins) pl.* 59, 1029 .. .. £2,500

5556 333-328 B.C. (under Balakros, ruler of Cilicia for Alexander the Great). Æ *stater* (*c.* 10·9 gm.). Baal seated l., holding lotus-headed sceptre; ear of corn and bunch of grapes before; ı (=Issos) beneath seat; ʙ (=Balakros) behind. R. Dr. bust of Athena three-quarter face to l., wearing triple-crested helmet. *B.M.C. 21.* 174, 67 (*attributed to Tarsos*) £550

    Balakros was appointed by Alexander in succession to the satrap Arsames. See also nos. 5571, 5617 and 5654-5.

5557 **Mallos** (an important city of eastern Cilicia, on the lower course of the Pyramos, Mallos was a settlement of great antiquity traditionally founded by Mopsos and Amphilochos at the time of the Trojan War). *Circa* 420 B.C. Æ *stater* (*c.* 10·65 gm.). Bearded Hermes, holding caduceus, riding l. on ram; conical object before. R. Winged male figure in kneeling-running attitude l., looking back, holding disk with both hands; MAP behind; all in dotted square within incuse square. *S.N.G. Von Aulock* 5705 .. .. (*Unique*)

5558 420-375 B.C. Æ *stater* (*c.* 10·65 gm.). Janus-headed god, with four wings, holding disk with both hands; beneath, forepart of man-headed bull r. (river-god Pyramos). R. Swan stg. r.; MAP above; all within incuse square. *Kraay (Archaic and Classical Greek Coins) pl.* 59, 1021 .. .. £2,000

5559 — — Winged male figure in kneeling-running attitude r., holding disk with both hands. R. Swan walking l.; MAP above, dolphin before, *ankh* symbol behind; all in circle of dots within circular incuse. *B.M.C. 21.* 97, 13 .. .. £750

Mallos *continued*

5560 — Æ *obol* (*c.* 0·8 gm.). *Obv.* Similar. ℞. Swan stg. l., wings spread; MAP above, fish (?) before, *ankh* symbol behind. *S.N.G. Von Aulock* 5707   ..   ..   ..   £90

5561 — — Swan stg. l., wings spread. ℞. Astragalos, within circular incuse. *S.N.G. Von Aulock* 5711   ..   ..   £75

5562 — — Hd. of bearded Herakles r. ℞. Swan stg. l., wings spread; all within circular incuse. *Forrer/Weber* 7562   ..   ..   £75

5563 — Æ *hemiobol* (*c.* 0·4 gm.). Hd. of Athena l., in crested helmet. ℞. Swan stg. r., wings spread; *ankh* symbol before; all within incuse square. *Forrer/Weber* 7563
£65

5564 386-380 B.C. (in the name of the satrap Tiribazos). Æ *stater* (*c.* 10·6 gm.). *Obv.* Zeus/Baal stg., *rev.* Ahura-Mazda; as 5554, but with MAP instead of ΙΣΣΙΚΟΝ on *obv.*, and without legend in *rev.* field. *S.N.G. Von Aulock* 5712   ..   ..   ..   £1,250

5565 375-360 B.C. Æ *stater* (*c.* 10·3 gm.). Bare hd. of bearded Herakles r., lion's skin knotted round neck. ℞. Hd. of bearded satrap r., wearing Persian tiara; behind, MAΛ. *B.M.C. 21.* 100, 28 ..   ..   £550

5566   5567

5566 — — Hd. of bearded Kronos r., wearing ornamented tainia; behind, fish. ℞. Demeter stg. r., holding flaming torch and ears of corn; MAΛ before. *B.M.C. 21.* 99, 20   £1,800

5567 — — The Great King (of Persia) in kneeling-running attitude r., holding spear and bow; corn-grain behind. ℞. Naked Herakles stg. r., strangling the Nemean lion, club at feet to l.; behind, MAΛ. *B.M.C. 21.* 99, 24   ..   ..   £2,100

5568   5570

5568 — — Athena seated l., holding spear and resting l. arm on shield; behind, trunk of olive-tree with two branches. ℞. Hermes, naked but for chlamys, stg. facing, holding caduceus; to his l., Aphrodite stg. l., resting on column and placing her r. hand on Hermes' shoulder; to r., MAΛ. *B.M.C. 21.* 100, 26   ..   ..   £2,400

5569 — Æ ¾ *obol* ? (*c.* 0·5—0·6 gm.). *Obv.* Similar to 5567, but without corn-grain. ℞. Similar to 5565, but without legend. *B.M.C. 21.* 100, 25   ..   ..   ..   £125

5570 — — Veiled hd. of Demeter r., wearing stephane. ℞. Demeter stg. l., holding ear of corn and torch. *B.M.C. 21.* 99, 22   ..   ..   £110

5571 333-328 B.C. (under Balakros, ruler of Cilicia for Alexander the Great). Æ *stater* (*c.* 10·9 gm.). *Obv.* Baal seated, *rev.* bust of Athena; as 5556, but with M (=Mallos) instead of I beneath seat on *obv.* *B.M.C. 21.* 174, 69 (*attributed to Tarsos*) £450

5572 *Bronze Coinage.* 375-360 B.C. Æ 11. Youthful hd. of Triptolemos (?) r., wreathed with corn; ΠΥ behind. R. Gorgoneion, MAΛ beneath. *Forrer/Weber* 7569 .. £17

5573 1st cent. B.C. Æ 20. Veiled and turreted bust of Tyche r. R. Cultus-statue of Athena Magarsis facing, holding spear; fringe of serpents on either side of robe, star above each shoulder; MAΛΛΩΤΩΝ to r., ΔΗ monogram in field to l. *S.N.G. Von Aulock* 5722 £15

5574 — Æ 24. Hd. of Apollo r. R. Athena seated l., holding Nike and spear, shield at side; MAΛΛΩΤΩΝ behind, ME monogram (retrograde) in field to l. *B.M.C. 21.* 101, 29 £16

5575   5578

5575 **Mopsos** (situated on the river Pyramos, north-east of Mallos, the city was named after the brother of Amphilochos. During the reign of Antiochos IV of Syria, 175-164 B.C., it bore the name of Seleukeia). 2nd-1st cent. B.C. Æ 20. Laur. hd. of Zeus r. R. Lighted circular altar, with three legs; two monograms in field, on either side; MOΨEATΩN in ex. *B.M.C. 21.* 103, 2-3 .. .. £13

5576 — — Similar, but on *rev.* the two monograms are in ex., and the legend is either side of the altar, thus: MOΨEATΩN / THΣ IEPAΣ — KAI / AYTONOMOY. *B.M.C. 21.* 103-4, 5-6 £12

5577 — Æ 22. Veiled and turreted bust of Tyche r. R. Zeus enthroned l., holding Nike and sceptre; MOΨEATΩN / THΣ IEPAΣ behind, KAI / AYTONOMOY before; two monograms in ex. *S.N.G. Von Aulock* 5732 .. .. £14

5578 **Nagidos** (an important coastal town of western Cilicia, Nagidos lay about 20 miles to the west of Kelenderis). 420-390 B.C. Æ *stater* (*c.* 10·6 gm.). Aphrodite enthroned l., holding phiale; at her l. side, Eros stg. l. R. Dionysos, naked but for chlamys, stg. l., holding kantharos and thyrsos; behind, NAΓIΔEΩN; in field to l., vine-leaf and Σ; all within circular incuse. *B.M.C. 21.* 109, 1 .. .. £650

5579   5581

5579 — — Aphrodite enthroned l., holding phiale; before, Eros flying r. to crown her; astragalos in field to r. R. NAΓIΔ — IKON either side of Dionysos stg. l., holding vine-branch with grapes, and thyrsos; all within circular incuse. *B.M.C. 21.* 109, 2 £650

5580 390-380 B.C. Æ *stater* (*c.* 10·4 gm.). Hd. of bearded Dionysos r., wreathed with ivy. R. NAΓIΔEΩN. Hd. of Aphrodite r., hair in sphendone; all within circular incuse. *B.M.C. 21.* 110, 3 .. .. £800

5581 — — Similar, but with *rev.* legend NAΓIΔIKON. *B.M.C. 21.* 110, 4-5 .. £750

5582 — Æ *obol* (*c.* 0·8 gm.). Bearded hd. of Satyr (?) r. R. NAΓIΔIKON. Amphora. *S.N.G. Von Aulock* 5752 .. .. £140

Nagidos *continued*

5583   5585

5583 — —Hd. of Aphrodite r., hair tied in bunch at top. Ŗ. NAΓI. Hd. of bearded Dionysos
r. *B.M.C. 21.* 111, 9   ..   ..   £130

5584 379-374 B.C. (in the name of the satrap Pharnabazos). Æ *stater* (*c.* 10·5 gm.). Aphrodite seated r. on throne flanked by two Sphinxes, holding phiale and flower; NAΓIΔIKON
behind. Ŗ. Male hd. l., bearded, wearing crested helmet; before, Aramaic legend
(=*Pharnabazu*). *B.M.C. 21.*, *pl.* XL, 10   ..   ..   ..   £2,500
     In 379 B.C. Pharnabazos, satrap of Daskylion in Bithynia, was given the task of re-
conquering Egypt for the Persian Empire. To finance this undertaking large quantities of
silver staters were struck in Cilicia, mostly at Tarsos.

5585 374-356 B.C. Æ *stater* (*c.* 10·5 gm.). Aphrodite enthroned l., feet on stool, holding
phiale over circular altar before her; behind, Eros stg. l., holding up branch. Ŗ. Dionysos
stg. l., holding vine-branch with grapes, and thyrsos; behind, NAΓIΔEΩN. *B.M.C. 21.* 111,
12   ..   ..   £350

5586 — Æ *tetrobol* (*c.* 3·2 gm.). Aphrodite enthroned l., holding phiale; behind her, Eros
kneeling l., wings spread. Ŗ. Dionysos stg., as last; NAΓIΔ behind, o in upper field to l.
B.M.C. 21. 112, 14 ..   ..   £300

5587   5589

5587 356-333 B.C. Æ *stater* (*c.* 10·1 gm.). Aphrodite enthroned l., feet on stool, holding
phiale; before, Eros flying r. to crown her; at her feet, plant growing with flower; beneath
seat, mouse l. Ŗ. Dionysos stg. l., holding vine-branch with grapes, and thyrsos; behind,
NAΓIΔIKON; in field to l., ΠΥ / MO. *B.M.C. 21.* 114, 19 ..   ..   £275

5588 — — Similar, but with IΩ monogram and ΠOΛY in *rev.* field to l. *B.M.C. 21.* 114, 23
     £275

5589 — Æ 14. Hd. of Aphrodite r., hair rolled. Ŗ. Kantharos; NA / Γ — I in field. *B.M.C.*
21. 115, 27-8   ..   ..   £15

5590 — Æ 11. Bearded hd. of Satyr (?) r. Ŗ. Kantharos; N above. *S.N.G. Von Aulock*
5761   ..   ..   £13

5591 **Seleukeia** (founded by Seleukos I on the lower course of the river Kalykadnos, Seleukeia
absorbed the population of Holmi, a few miles to the south. It grew into a city of great
wealth and importance rivalling Tarsos). 2nd-1st cent. B.C. Æ 23. Hd. of Athena r., in
crested Corinthian helmet; EY behind. Ŗ. ΣΕΛΕΥΚΕΩΝ ΤΩΝ ΠΡΟΣ ΤΩΙ ΚΑΛΥΚΑΔΝΩΙ. Nike
advancing l., holding wreath; in field to l., two monograms. *B.M.C. 21.* 128, 2   £14

5592   5593

5592 — — Similar, but with ΣΑ behind hd. of Athena on *obv.*, and ΔΙΟΦ / ΗΡΑ in *rev.* field to l. instead of monograms. *B.M.C. 21.* 129, 7   ..   ..   £14

5593 — Æ 19.   Laur. hd. of Apollo r.; ΕΥ behind.   R. ΣΕΛΕΥΚΕΩΝ ΤΩΝ ΠΡΟΣ ΤΩΙ ΚΑΛΥΚΑΔΝΩΙ. Forepart of horse r.; ΑΘ above, ΛΑ beneath. *B.M.C. 21.* 130, 11   ..   ..   £12

5594 — Æ 22.   Veiled and turreted hd. of Tyche r.   R. Athena stg. l., holding Nike, shield and spear; CЄΛЄΥΚЄΩΝ behind, ΚΑΠΙ / ΤΩΝΟC before. *Forrer/Weber* 7589   ..   £15

5595 — Æ 24.   Laur. bust of Artemis r., bow and quiver at shoulder, branch before; behind, ΗΘΑ. R. Athena stg., as last; ΧΟΥ / ΠΟΛЄΜΑΡ behind, ΩΝ / CЄΛЄΥΚЄ before. *B.M.C. 21.* 130, 15   ..   ..   £16

5596 — Æ 18.   ΣЄΛЄΥΚЄΩΝ.   Hd. of Athena r., in crested Corinthian helmet.   R. ЄΠΙ ΚΥΝΤΙ. Rad. bust of Helios r. *S.N.G. Von Aulock* 5816   ..   ..   ..   £14

5597 — — CЄΛЄΥΚЄ.   Bust of Athena r., wearing crested Corinthian helmet and aegis.   R. ΔΙΟCΚΟΥΡΙ. Owl stg. l. on olive-branch, hd. facing. *S.N.G. Von Aulock* 5817   £15

5598 — Æ 17.   ΣЄΛЄΥΚЄΩΝ.   Club; all within oak-wreath.   R. ΔΙΟCΚΟΥΡΙ. Owl stg. l., hd. facing; all within olive-wreath. *S.N.G. Von Aulock* 5818 ..   ..   ..   £14

5599 — Æ 15.   Hd. of Aphrodite (?) r., wearing stephane; Ν—Ε in field.   R. Flower; ΔΗΜΕ in field to l., ΔΗ to r. *S.N.G. Von Aulock* 5815 ..   ..   £13

5600   5602

5600 **Soloi** (an important coastal town south-west of Zephyrion and Tarsos, Soloi seems to have been a Rhodian foundation, though its coin types suggest some connection with Athens also.   Early in the 1st cent. B.C. it was destroyed by Tigranes of Armenia, but in 66 B.C. Pompey the Great re-founded it under the name of **Pompeiopolis**).   430-390 B.C.   Æ *stater* (*c.* 10·7 gm.).   Amazon kneeling l., examining arrow held with both hands; quiver and bow in case at her l. side.   R. Bunch of grapes on stalk; Σ / Ο in field to r.; all in dotted square within incuse square. *B.M.C. 21.* 144, 1 ..   ..   ..   £600

5601 — — Amazon kneeling l., examining bow held with both hands; quiver and bow-case at her l. side; in field to r., facing hd. of Satyr (?).   R. Bunch of grapes on stalk with tendrils; ΣΟΛΕΩΝ to l., fly in lower field to r.; all in dotted square within incuse square. *B.M.C. 21.* 145, 3 ..   ..   £500

5602 — — *Obv.* Similar, but without symbol in field.   R. Bunch of grapes on stalk with tendrils; ΣΟΛΕΩΝ to l., ΝΙ above, *ankh* symbol in lower field to r.; all in dotted circle within circular incuse. *B.M.C. 21.* 145, 7 ..   ..   £550

5603 — Æ *tetrobol* (*c.* 3·5 gm.).   As last, but without ΝΙ above grapes on *rev.* *B.M.C. 21.* 146, 11 ..   ..   £350

5604   5606

Soloi *continued*

5604 — Æ *obol* (*c.* 0·8 gm.).   Hd. of Amazon l., wearing pointed cap ornamented with wing. Ŗ. Bunch of grapes on stalk; Σ — ο in field; all in dotted square within incuse square. *B.M.C. 21.* 146, 12 ..   ..   £110

5605 — Æ *hemiobol* ? (*c.* 0·32 gm.).   *Obv.* Similar.   Ŗ. Bunch of grapes on stalk with tendrils; all within circular incuse.   *S.N.G. Von Aulock* 5861 ..   ..   £65

5606 390-375 B.C.   Æ *stater* (*c.* 10·1 gm.).   Hd. of Athena r., in crested Athenian helmet ornamented with griffin.   Ŗ. Bunch of grapes on stalk with tendrils; ΣΟΛΙΟ beneath; the type placed diagonally in dotted square within incuse square. *B.M.C. 21.* 146, 15   £350

5607 — — *Obv.* Similar.   Ŗ. Bunch of grapes on stalk with leaves and tendrils; ΣΟΛΙΟΝ beneath, crescent in lower field to r.; all within circle of dots.   *B.M.C. 21.* 147, 19   £325

5608 — — (*c.* 10·6 gm.).   *Obv.* Similar.   Ŗ. Bunch of grapes on stalk; ΣΟΛΙΚΟΝ to l., ΣΑΤΥ to r.; all within circular incuse.   *S.N.G. Von Aulock* 5868 ..   ..   £450

5609 — Æ *obol* (*c.* 0·75 gm.).   *Obv.* Similar, but without griffin on helmet.   Ŗ. Bunch of grapes on stalk with tendril; ΣΟΛΕΩΝ to r.; all within circular incuse.   *B.M.C. 21.* 147, 21   £80

5610 386-380 B.C. (in the name of the satrap Tiribazos).   Æ *stater* (*c.* 10·3 gm.).   *Obv.* Zeus/ Baal stg., *rev.* Ahura-Mazda; as 5554, but with ΣΟ instead of ΙΣΣΙΚΟΝ on *obv.*, and without legend in *rev.* field.   *B.M.C. 21.* 148, 26 ..   ..   £1,250

5611   5613

5611 375-360 B.C.   Æ *stater* (*c.* 10 gm.).   Bare hd. of bearded Herakles r., lion's skin knotted round neck.   Ŗ. ΣΟΛΙΚΟΝ.   Hd. of bearded satrap r., wearing Persian tiara.   *B.M.C. 21.* 149, 27   ..   ..   £500

5612 — — (*c.* 10·5 gm.).   Similar, but with legend ΣΟΛΕΩΝ before satrap's hd. on *rev.* *S.N.G. Von Aulock* 5862   ..   ..   £550

5613 360-333 B.C.   Æ *stater* (*c.* 9·8 gm.).   Hd. of Athena r., in triple-crested Corinthian helmet.   Ŗ. Bunch of grapes on stalk with leaf and tendrils; above, ΣΟΛΕΩΝ; to l., ΑΠΟΛ-ΛΩΝΙ and star; to r., owl.   *B.M.C. 21.* 149, 30 ..   ..   £350

5614 — — Similar, but on *rev.* ΣΟΛΕΩ beneath bunch of grapes, and in field to l. kantharos and ΙΗΝΟΣ.   *B.M.C. 21.* 150, 31 ..   ..   £375

5615 — Æ *obol* (*c.* 0·75 gm.).   Hd. of Athena r., in crested Corinthian helmet.   Ŗ. Bunch of grapes on stalk with leaf and tendrils; Λ — Λ in lower field, ΣΟΛΕΩΝ beneath.   *Grose/ McClean* 9085   ..   ..   £90

5616   5617

5616 — Æ ¾ *obol*? (*c.* 0·6 gm.).   Similar, but with A — Π in *rev.* field.   *B.M.C. 21.* 150, 33
£75

5617 333-328 B.C. (under Balakros, ruler of Cilicia for Alexander the Great).   Æ *stater* (*c.*
10·9 gm.).   *Obv.* Baal seated, *rev.* bust of Athena; as 5556, but with Σ (= Soloi) instead
of I beneath seat on *obv.;* also, crested Corinthian helmet in *obv.* field to r., and I — Σ in
rev. field.   *B.M.C. 21.* 174, 72 (*attributed to Tarsos*) £350

5618 *Bronze Coinage.*   Mid-4th cent. B.C.   Æ 13.   Hd. of Athena r., in crested Athenian
helmet.   ℞. Similar to 5615, but with Δ — Θ in lower field.   *B.M.C. 21.* 150, 34
£14

5619   5621

5619 3rd-2nd cent. B.C.   Æ 26.   Aegis, with winged Gorgoneion at centre.   ℞. Aphrodite
riding on bull r.; monogram above, eagle behind, ΣΟΛΕΩΝ beneath.   *B.M.C. 21.* 150, 35
£20

5620 — Æ 24.   Rad. hd. of Helios r., monogram behind.   ℞. Athena enthroned l., holding
Nike and resting l. arm on shield; ΣΟΛΕΩΝ before, two monograms behind.   *S.N.G. Von
Aulock* 5883   ..   ..   £18

5621 — Æ 22.   Hd. of Artemis r., wearing stephane, bow and quiver at neck, monogram
behind.   ℞. Athena advancing r., brandishing thunderbolt and holding shield; ΣΟΛΕΩΝ
before, two monograms behind.   *B.M.C. 21.* 151, 39   ..   ..   £14

5622 — — Hd. of Athena r., in crested Corinthian helmet.   ℞. Owl stg. r., hd. facing;
AΘE in field, ΣΟΛΕΩΝ to r.   *B.M.C. 21.* 151, 41   ..   ..   £16

5623 — Æ 19.   *Obv.* Similar.   ℞. Horned Dionysos stg. facing, holding kantharos and thyrsos; two monograms in field to l., ΣΟΛΕΩΝ to r.   *B.M.C. 21.* 151, 37   ..   ..   £12

5624   5627

5624 — — Laur., turreted and veiled hd. of Tyche r.   ℞. Caps of the Dioskouroi; beneath,
ΣΟΛΕΩΝ / ΑΡΤ.   *B.M.C. 21.* 151, 42   ..   ..   £13

5625 — — Hd. of Artemis r., wearing stephane.   ℞. Double cornucopiae; ΣΟΛΕΩΝ to r.,
AΘE to l.   *S.N.G. Von Aulock* 5881   ..   ..   £13

5626 — Æ 18.   *Obv.* As 5622.   ℞. Eagle stg. r. on thunderbolt; ΣΟΛΕΩΝ before; two monograms in field, to l. and above.   *B.M.C. 21.* 152, 46   ..   ..   £11

5627 After 66 B.C. (under the name **Pompeiopolis**).   Æ 14.   Two bunches of grapes on a
stalk, X beneath.   ℞. Π — O — M — Π — H — I between the rays of a star.   *B.M.C. 21.*
152, 47   ..   ..   £14

Soloi *continued*

5628 — Æ 24.   Bare hd. of Pompey the Great r.; ewer(?) behind, star and lituus before.   ℞.
ΠΟΝΠΗΙΟΠΟΛΙΤΩΝ ΕΤΟΥΣ ΙΣ (=year 16 =51/50 B.C.).   Athena stg. l., holding Nike, spear
and shield; in field to r., AP*; to l., ΝΙ / ΘΕ / ΝΑ.   *B.M.C. 21.* 152, 48   ..   £100

5629 **Tarsos** (the first city of Cilicia and capital of the native rulers down to *circa* 400 B.C.,
Tarsos was situated in the fertile eastern plain on the river Kydnos, about 12 miles from
the sea.   In the 4th century, until the arrival of Alexander in 333 B.C., Tarsos was the
chief mint of the Persian satraps.   Eventually, in the 1st cent. B.C., it became the capital
of the Roman province of Cilicia).   430-400 B.C. (under the Syennesis line of native rulers).
Æ *stater* (*c.* 10·6 gm.).   Bellerophon on Pegasos prancing r., *ankh* symbol beneath.   ℞.
Similar to *obv.* but type to left; all in dotted square within incuse square.   *Kraay (Archaic
and Classical Greek Coins) pl.* 60, 1031   ..   ..   (*Unique*)

5630 — — King of Cilicia on horse pacing l.   ℞. Persian archer kneeling r., drawing his
bow; *ankh* symbol behind; all in dotted square within incuse square.   *Kraay, pl.* 60,
1032 ..   ..   £1,500

5631   5632

5631 — — Lion r. on the back of a bull kneeling l. which it attacks with teeth and claws.   ℞.
Ear of corn, and Aramaic legend (= *Tarz*); the type placed diagonally in linear square
within circular incuse.   *B.M.C. 21.* 164, 11   ..   ..   £700

5632 — — Melkart seated on hippocamp r., riding over waves.   ℞. Bearded deity advancing
l., holding trident downwards; before, large ear of corn; behind, Aramaic legend (=*Tarz*);
all in dotted square within incuse square.   *S.N.G. Von Aulock* 5908   ..   ..   £800

5633   5636

5633 — — King of Cilicia on horse pacing r.   ℞. The god Nergal stg. r., on the back of lion
crouching r., holding spear and bow; behind, branch; before, Aramaic legend (=*Nergal
Tarz*); all in dotted square within incuse square.   *Kraay (Archaic and Classical Greek
Coins) pl.* 60, 1035 ..   ..   £800

5634 — Æ *tetrobol* (*c.* 3·2 gm.).   Forepart of Pegasos l.; eagle's hd. above.   ℞. Similar to
5630, but with eagle's hd. in field to r.   *B.M.C. 21.* 163, 10   ..   ..   ..   £450

5635 — Æ *triobol* (*c.* 2·6 gm.).   Forepart of Pegasos r.   ℞. The god Nergal advancing r.,
holding spear and bow; behind, Aramaic legend (=*Nergal*); all in dotted square within
incuse square.   *S.N.G. Von Aulock* 5910   ..   ..   £350

5636 400-386 B.C.   Æ *stater* (*c.* 10·6 gm.).   Persian satrap on horse prancing r.   ℞. Greek
hoplite, naked, kneeling l. in defensive pose, wearing Corinthian helmet and holding spear
and large shield; behind, Aramaic legend (=*Tarz*); all within circular incuse.   *B.M.C. 22.*
163, 8   ..   ..   £1,750

5637 — Æ *tetrobol* (*c.* 3·3 gm.).   *Obv.* Similar.   ℞. Greek hoplite, naked, kneeling r. in
defensive pose, wearing Corinthian helmet and holding spear and large shield; before,
Aramaic legend (=*Tarz*); the type placed diagonally in dotted square within incuse
square.   *B.M.C. 21.* 162, 2   ..   ..   £500

5638   5640

5638 386-380 B.C. (in the name of the satrap Tiribazos). Æ *stater* (*c.* 10·1 gm.). *Obv.*
Zeus/Baal stg., *rev.* Ahura-Mazda; as 5554, but with T instead of ΙΣΣΙΚΟΝ on *obv.*, and
without legend in *rev.* field. *B.M.C. 21.* 164, 12 ..   ..   £1,000

5639 379-374 B.C. (in the name of the satrap Pharnabazos). Æ *stater* (*c.* 10·75 gm.). Female
hd., with streaming hair, three-quarter face to l., wearing sphendone and necklace (type
derived from Kimon's Arethusa on the coinage of Syracuse). R. Male hd. l., bearded,
wearing crested helmet; before, Aramaic legend (=*Pharnabazu khilik*). *B.M.C. 21.*
165, 15 ..   ..   £250

   In 379 B.C. Pharnabazos, satrap of Daskylion in Bithynia, was given the task of re-
conquering Egypt for the Persian Empire. Datames, satrap of Cappadocia, was later ap-
pointed to assist him. To finance this undertaking large quantities of silver staters were
struck in Cilicia, mostly at Tarsos.

5640 — — Similar, but the *rev.* type to right; the Aramaic legend behind, *ankh* symbol
before. *B.M.C. 21.* 165, 17 ..   ..   £250

5641   5642

5641 — — Baal of Tarsos enthroned l., holding sceptre; behind, Aramaic legend (=*Baal tarz*).
R. Similar to 5639, but the Aramaic legend is before and behind the helmeted hd. *B.M.C.*
21. 165, 21 ..   ..   £275

5642 — (time of Pharnabazos). Æ *stater* (*c.* 10·7 gm.). Hd. of young Herakles three-quarter
face to r., clad in lion's skin; in field to r., Aramaic legend (=*Khilik*). R. Male hd. l.,
bearded, wearing crested helmet; before, ΤΕΡΣΙΚΟΝ. *B.M.C. 21.* 166, 22 ..   £1,000

5643 — Æ *obol* (*c.* 0·8 gm.). Similar to 5639, but with two dolphins in *obv.* field, either side
of female hd.; and with Aramaic legend (=*Khilik*) before male hd. on *rev.* *B.M.C. 21.*
166, 25 ..   ..   £75

5644 378-362 B.C. (in the name of the satrap Datames). Æ *stater* (*c.* 10·75 gm.). Similar to
5639, but with Aramaic legend (=*Tadnmu*) on *rev.* *B.M.C. 21.* 167, 30 ..   £250

   Datames was left in sole command of the Egyptian campaign following the death of Pharna-
bazos in 374 B.C. A few years later he became involved in the revolt of the satraps against
the Persian king in the course of which he extended his territory as far as the shores of the
Black Sea—see no. 3693 of Sinope.

Tarsos *continued*

5645 — — Baal of Tarsos enthroned r., holding eagle-tipped sceptre and corn-ear with
bunch of grapes, thymiaterion at his side; behind, Aramaic legend (= *Baal tarz*); beneath
throne, flower; all within border representing the battlements of the city. R. Satrap
enthroned r., examining arrow; quiver on his lap, bow at his feet; in field above, winged
solar disk; behind, Aramaic legend (= *Tadnmu*). *B.M.C. 21.* 167, 32   ..   £400

5646 — — *Obv.* Similar, but hd. of Baal facing, and without symbol beneath throne. R.
The sky-god Ana, naked, stg. r., his r. hand pointing towards Datames stg. l., his r.
hand raised in gesture of veneration; between them, thymiaterion; behind the god,
Aramaic legend (= *Ana*); before the satrap, Aramaic legend (= *Tadnmu*); all within
shrine, represented by linear square bordered inside with dots along the top and two sides,
and outside with crescents along the top. *B.M.C. 21.* 168, 35-6   ..   ..   £275

5647   5648

5647 — (time of Datames). R *stater* (*c.* 10·15 gm.). Athena seated l., holding spear and
resting l. arm on shield; behind, trunk of olive-tree with two branches. R. Girl, naked to
waist, kneeling l., playing knuckle-bones; behind, flower growing; before, ΤΕΡΣΙΚΟΝ.
B.M.C. 21.,pl. XL, 11   ..   ..   £1,500

5648 — — Young Herakles, naked, kneeling l., strangling the Nemean lion; club beneath.
R. Hd. of Hera l., wearing ornamented stephane; ΤΕΡΣΙΚΟΝ before.   *B.M.C. 21., pl.*
XL, 12   ..   ..   £1,250

5649 361-334 B.C. (in the name of the satrap Mazaios). R *stater* (*c.* 10·85 gm.). Baal of
Tarsos enthroned l., holding corn-ear with bunch of grapes and lotus-headed sceptre;
behind, Aramaic legend (= *Baal tarz*); beneath throne, *ankh* symbol. R. Lion l. on the
back of stag kneeling l. which it attacks with teeth and claws; above, Aramaic legend
(= *Mazdai*); all within incuse square. *B.M.C. 21.* 169, 38   ..   ..   ..   £225

   *Mazaios ruled Cilicia for 27 years until just before the Macedonian conquest. Later,
under Alexander, he became governor of Babylonia.*

5650   5651

5650 — — Baal of Tarsos enthroned l., hd. facing, holding eagle, corn-ear and bunch of grapes in r. hand, lotus-headed sceptre in l.; behind, Aramaic legend (=*Baal tarz*); Aramaic letters in field to l.   ℞. Lion l. on the back of bull kneeling l. which it attacks with teeth and claws; above, Aramaic legend (=*Mazdai*); all within circle of dots. *B.M.C. 21*. 171, 52 ..   ..   £200

5651 — — Baal of Tarsos enthroned l., holding lotus-headed sceptre; behind, Aramaic legend (= *Baal tarz*); Aramaic letter, corn-ear and bunch of grapes in field to l., Aramaic letter beneath throne.   ℞. Two lines of fortifications, one above the other; the upper one surmounted by bull kneeling r., attacked by lion leaping l. onto his back; around, Aramaic legend (=*Mazdai zi al Ebernahara vu Khilik*); all within circle of dots.   *B.M.C. 21*. 170, 48 ..   ..   £300

The inscription on rev. describes Mazaios as "Governor of Trans-Euphratesia and Cilicia." He held this rank from 351 B.C.

5652   5653

5652 — — Baal of Tarsos enthroned l., holding lotus-headed sceptre; behind, Aramaic legend (= *Baal tarz*); uncertain symbol beneath throne.   ℞. Lion walking l.; above, large star and Aramaic legend (=*Mazdai*); beneath, large crescent; all within linear circle. *B.M.C. 21*. 172, 59-60 ..   ..   £275

This type may have been issued in Syria, 333-331 B.C., following Alexander's victory at the battle of Issos.   It served as the prototype for Mazaios' coinage of Attic tetradrachms struck at Babylon, 331-328 B.C. (see no. 6139).   For other coins of Mazaios see under Sidon (nos. 5946-8).

5653 334-333 B.C. (time of the satrap Arsames). Æ *stater* (c. 10·8 gm.).   Baal seated l., holding lotus-headed sceptre; ear of corn and bunch of grapes before, ivy-leaf behind; beneath seat, т (=Tarsos). ℞. Dr. bust of Athena three-quarter face to l., wearing triple-crested helmet. *B.M.C. 21*. 175, 74 ..   ..   £250

Arsames was satrap of Cilicia for the brief period between the withdrawal of Mazaios and the Macedonian conquest.

5654 333-328 B.C. (*under Balakros, ruler of Cilicia for Alexander the Great*). Æ *stater* (c. 10·9 gm.).   Similar, but with ΒΑΛΑΚΡΟΥ instead of ivy-leaf behind Baal on *obv*. *S.N.G. Von Aulock* 5963 ..   ..   (*Unique*)

5655 — — Similar to 5653, but with Β (=Balakros) beneath the ivy-leaf on *obv*.   *B.M.C. 21*. 175, 77 ..   ..   £250

Balakros was appointed by Alexander in succession to the satrap Arsames.   See also nos. 5556, 5571 and 5617.

5656   5657

5656 — Æ *obol* (c. 0·75 gm.).   Bust of Athena, as *rev*. of 5653. ℞. Oval shield, indented at sides, ornamented with thunderbolt; star in field. *B.M.C. 21*. 175, 79 ..   £120

5657 4th cent. B.C. ANONYMOUS CILICIAN SILVER OF MINOR DENOMINATIONS, PROBABLY MOSTLY OF TARSOS.   *Obol* (c. 0·8 gm.).   Baal seated l., holding corn-ear with bunch of grapes, and sceptre. ℞. Eagle, wings spread, stg. l. on plough-share; all within dotted square. *B.M.C. 21*. 176, 82-3 ..   ..   £65

5658   5660

Tarsos *continued*

5658 — — Male hd. r., bearded and with long hair, wearing stephane. R. Forepart of Pegasos
     r. *Forrer/Weber* 7648-9 ..   ..   £110

5659 — — Baal seated l., holding eagle. R. Herakles striding r., about to club lion before
     him; all in dotted square within incuse square. *Forrer/Weber* 7651 ..   ..   £90

5660 — ¾ *obol* (*c.* 0·6 gm.). *Obv.* As 5657. R. Forepart of wolf r., crescent in field to l.;
     all within dotted square. *B.M.C. 21.* 176, 86 ..   ..   £30

5661 — — Similar, but on *rev.* forepart of wolf l., with crescent in field to r. *Forrer/Weber*
     7637 ..   ..   £35

5662 — — Baal seated l., holding lotus-headed sceptre. R. Lion walking l., hd. facing; above,
     winged solar disk. *S.N.G. Von Aulock* 5420 ..   ..   £75

5663 — — Facing hd. of young Herakles, in lion's skin. R. Eagle stg. l. between antlers;
     all within dotted square. *S.N.G. Von Aulock* 5424 ..   ..   £90

5664 — *Hemiobol* (*c.* 0·4 gm.). Similar to 5662, but with thunderbolt above lion on *rev.*
     S.N.G. Von Aulock 5421 ..   ..   £60

5665 — — Hd. of young Herakles r., in lion's skin. R. Pegasos flying r. *S.N.G. Von Aulock*
     5430 ..   ..   £65

5666   5670

5666 After 164 B.C. Æ *drachm* (*c.* 3·8 gm.). Turreted hd. of Tyche r.; fillet border. R.
     Sandan stg. r. on winged and horned lion r.; he carries bow-case and sword, raises r.
     hand and holds axe in l.; ΤΑΡΣΕΩΝ before, two monograms behind. *B.M.C. 21.* 178, 94
                                                                             £200

5667 *Bronze Coinage.* 175-164 B.C. (time of Antiochos IV: Tarsos under the name of
     Antiocheia). Æ 23. Turreted hd. of Tyche r., monogram behind. R. ΑΝΤΙΟΧΕΩΝ ΤΩΝ
     ΠΡΟΣ ΤΩΙ ΚΥΔΝΩΙ. Zeus enthroned l., holding sceptre; Ε in field to l., Η to r. *B.M.C.*
     21. 177, 92-3 ..   ..   £20

5668 — Æ 17. Turreted hd. of Tyche r., Θ behind. R. ΑΝΤΙΟΧΕΩΝ ΤΩΝ ΠΡΟΣ ΤΩΙ ΚΥΔΝΩΙ.
     Naked Sandan-Herakles stg. r. on winged and horned lion r.; monograms in field to l. and
     to r. *Forrer/Weber* 7653 ..   ..   £17

5669 2nd-1st cent. B.C. Æ 18. Turreted hd. of Tyche r., within ivy-wreath. R. Pegasos
     flying l.; ΤΑΡΣΕΩΝ before, monogram beneath. *S.N.G. Von Aulock* 5967 ..   £14

5670 — Æ 21. Veiled and turreted hd. of Tyche r.; fillet border. R. Sandan on lion, similar
     to 5666, but branch held in r. hand; ΤΑΡΣΕΩΝ before, ΑΛΚ / ΓΛΥ behind. *B.M.C. 21.*
     179, 99 ..   ..   £14

5671 — Æ 18. *Obv.* Similar. R. Naked Sandan-Herakles stg. r. on winged and horned lion
     r., holding flower and bipennis; ΤΑΡΣΕ — ΩΝ before and behind, star in field to l. *B.M.C.*
     21. 179, 103-4 ..   ..   £12

5672 — Æ 22. *Obv.* Similar, but with dotted border. ℞. Pyre of Sandan, in the form of pyramidal structure, containing figure of Sandan on lion, surmounting square basis; eagle perched on apex; ΤΑΡΣΕΩΝ in field to r., monogram to l. *B.M.C. 21.* 180, 107
£14

5673 — Æ 20. Turreted hd. of Tyche r., Δ behind. ℞. Zeus enthroned l., holding eagle-tipped sceptre; ΤΑΡΣΕΩΝ before, two monograms behind. *B.M.C. 21.* 181, 115   £11

5674   5675

5674 — Æ 26. Tyche of the City seated r., holding ears of corn; river-god Kydnos swimming r. at her feet. ℞. Zeus enthroned l., holding Nike and sceptre; ΤΑΡΣΕΩΝ behind, monogram before. *B.M.C. 21.* 181, 118   ..   ..   £16

5675 — Æ 17. *Obv.* Similar to *rev.* of last, but star instead of monogram before. ℞. Club, ΛΥΣΙΑ beneath; all within oak-wreath. *B.M.C. 21.* 183, 126   ..   ..   ..   £10

5676 **Zephyrion** (a coastal town between Soloi and Tarsos). 1st cent. B.C. Æ 24. Two sticks (?) crossed, to form 'X'; all within laurel-wreath. ℞. ΙΕΦΥΡΙ / ΩΤΩΝ in two lines, two monograms beneath; all within laurel-wreath. *B.M.C. 21.* 232, 1   ..   £20

5677 — Æ 20. Turreted hd. of Tyche r., Α behind. ℞. ΖΕΦΥΡΙΩΤΩΝ. City-goddess (?), turreted, enthroned l., holding lotus-headed sceptre; two monograms in field to l. *B.M.C. 21.* 232, 6   ..   ..   £18

5678 — Æ 18. Turreted hd. of Tyche r. ℞. ΖΕΦΥΡΙΩΤΩΝ. Athena seated l., holding Nike and spear, shield at side; two monograms in field to l. *B.M.C. 21.* 232, 4   ..   £16

5679   5680

5679 **Elaiussa** (a short distance north-east of Korykos, Elaiussa was originally an island but is now joined to the mainland). 1st cent. B.C. Æ *tetradrachm* (c. 15·5 gm.). Turreted and veiled bust of Tyche r.; fillet border. ℞. Female figure stg. l., holding tiller (?); ΕΛΑΙΟΥΣΙΩΝ / ΤΗΣ ΙΕΡΑΣ behind, ΚΑΙ / ΑΥΤΟΝΟΜΟΥ before; aplustre and monograms in field to l.; all within wreath. *B.M.C. 21, pl.* XL, 14   ..   .. (*Unique*)

5680 — Æ 20. Hd. of Zeus r., hair bound with tainia; ΕΡ behind. ℞. Nike advancing l., holding wreath; ΕΛΑ — ΙΟΥΣΙΩΝ and two monograms before. *B.M.C. 21.* 234, 4   £12

Elaiussa *continued*

5681 — Æ 19. Turreted hd. of Tyche r., ΣΑ behind. ℞. Naked Hermes stg. l., holding
phiale (?) and caduceus; before, ΕΛΑΙΟVΣΣΙΩΝ, ΙΣΙ and monogram. *B.M.C. 21.* 235, 10-
11 .. .. £13

5682   5683

5682 **KINGDOM OF CILICIA** (coins struck at the capital, **Hieropolis-Kastabala**).
Tarkondimotos I, 39-31 B.C. (created dynast by Pompey the Great in 64 B.C., and made
king by Mark Antony 25 years later). Æ 22. Diad. hd. of Tarkondimotos r. ℞.
Zeus enthroned l., holding Nike and sceptre; ΒΑΣΙΛΕΩΣ behind, ΤΑΡΚΟΝΔΙΜΟ / ΤΟV before,
ΦΙΛΑΝΤΩΝΙΟV in ex. *B.M.C. 21.* 237, 1-2 .. .. £45

5683 **Philopator** (either a son or grandson of Tarkondimotos I. Little is known of this
ruler, though it is recorded that a King Philopator of Cilicia died early in Tiberius' reign,
circa A.D. 17). Æ 23. Veiled and turreted hd. of the Tyche of Hieropolis r. ℞. Athena
stg. l., holding Nike and shield; ΒΑCΙΛΕΩC and monogram behind, ΦΙΛΟΠΑ / ΤΟΡΟC before.
B.M.C. 21. 238, 1 .. .. £22

5684   5687

5684 **GALATIA. Pessinus** (an important town of western Galatia, about 25 miles north-
east of Amorion in Phrygia. Pessinus was the capital of the Tolistobogii and a centre
for the worship of Kybele, under the name of Agdistis). 1st cent. B.C. Æ 26. Conjoined busts r. of Attis, in Phrygian cap, and Kybele (Agdistis), wearing turreted crown.
℞. Lion seated l., r. paw on drum; caps of the Dioskouroi on either side, and monogram
in field to r.; ΜΗΤΡΟΣ behind, ΘΕΩΝ in ex., ΠΕΣΣΙΝΕΣ before. *S.N.G. Von Aulock* 6205
£30

5685 — Æ 23. Dr. and turreted bust of Kybele (Agdistis) r. ℞. Lion seated r., between
two monograms; ΜΗΤΡΟΣ before, ΘΕΩΝ in ex., ΠΕΣΣΙΝΕΑΣ behind. *B.M.C. 20.* 18, 1
£24

5686 — Æ 22. Bust of Attis r., in Phrygian cap, crescent behind shoulders. ℞. ΜΗΤΡΟΣ
ΘΕΩΝ ΠΕΣΣΙΝΕΑΣ. Humped bull butting l. *S.N.G. Von Aulock* 6207 .. £24

5687 **Tavion** (the capital of the Trocmi, in the east of the country, Tavion lay at the centre of a
good agricultural area and at an important road junction). 1st cent. B.C. Æ 22. Humped bull running r. ℞. Amphora between caps of the Dioskouroi; ΤΑVΙΩΝ in ex. *B.M.C.
20.* 24, 1-2 .. .. £22

5688 — — Laur. hd. of Zeus r. ℞. Eagle, wings spread, stg. r. on thunderbolt; caps of the
Dioskouroi in field on either side; ΤΑVΙΩΝ beneath. *S.N.G. Von Aulock* 6237 £20

5689   5690

5689 **KINGDOM OF GALATIA** (lasting for four decades from 64 B.C., when Pompey the
Great bestowed kingship on a number of the tetrarchs, until 25 B.C. when the country
became a Roman province following the death of the last king, Amyntas). **Deiotaros,**
circa 64-40 B.C. (ruler of the Tolistobogii). Æ 26. Hd. of Nike r., winged. R. Eagle,
wings spread, stg. r. on sword in sheath, looking back; caps of the Dioskouroi in field on
either side; ΒΑΣΙΛΕΩΣ above, ΔΗΙΟΤΑΡΟΥ beneath. *B.M.C. 20.* 1, 1 ..   ..   £65

5690 — Æ 17. Laur. hd. of Zeus r. R. Eagle, wings spread, stg. l. on thunderbolt, looking
back; monogram (of ΔΗΙΟΤΑΡ) in field to l. *S.N.G. Von Aulock* 6099-6100 ..   £20

5691 — Æ 16. *Obv.* Similar. R. Large monogram (of ΔΗΙΟΤΑΡ) and Galatian shield side by
side. *S.N.G. Von Aulock* 6101 ..   ..   £ 25

5692 **Brogitaros,** *circa* 58-53 B.C. (ruler of the Trocmi). Æ *tetradrachm.* Hd. of Zeus r.,
wreathed with oak. R. ΒΑΣΙΛΕΩΣ ΒΡΟΓΙΤΑΡΟΥ ΦΙΛΟΡΩΜΑΙΟΥ. Eagle stg. r. on thunderbolt,
standard behind; two monograms in field, c (=year 6?) in ex. *Historia Numorum, p.*
747 ..   .. (*Unique?*)

5693 **Amyntas,** 36-25 B.C. (originally the secretary of Deiotaros, Amyntas saw service as an
auxiliary commander in the Roman army of Brutus and Cassius. Having gained the
favour of Mark Antony he was granted an extensive kingdom comprising Galatia, Lycaonia
and parts of neighbouring countries. By a timely desertion before the battle of Actium
he secured the patronage of Augustus, but on his death, in battle, in 25 B.C. his kingdom
was annexed to form a Roman province). Æ *tetradrachm* (*c.* 16 gm.), issued at Side in
Pamphylia. Hd. of Athena r., in crested Corinthian helmet. R. Nike advancing l.,
holding sceptre twined with diadem; ΒΑΣΙ — ΛΕΩΣ / ΑΜΥΝ — ΤΟΥ in field. *B.M.C. 20.*
2, 5   ..   ..   £350

5694 — Æ 24. Hd. of bearded Herakles r., club at neck; monogram behind. R. Lion
prowling r.; ΒΑΣΙΛΕΩΣ / ΑΜΥΝΤΟΥ above and in ex. *B.M.C. 20.* 3, 9 ..   ..   £24

5695 — — *Obv.* Similar, but with ΙΙ / ϵ behind. R. Lion prowling r.; Β above, monogram
(of ΑΜΥΝΤΟΥ) in ex. *B.M.C. 20.* 3, 12 ..   ..   £25

5696 — Æ 21. Laur. hd. of Zeus r., monogram behind. R. As 5694. *S.N.G. Von Aulock*
6106 ..   ..   £28

5697   5698

Amyntas *continued*

5697 — Æ 20. Hd. of Artemis r., wearing stephane, bow and quiver behind neck; monogram before. R. Stag stg. r.; ΒΑΣΙΛΕ — ΩΣ / ΑΜΥΝΤΟΥ above and in ex. *B.M.C. 20.* 3, 14 £21

5698 — Æ 15. Dr. bust of Hermes r., wearing petasos, caduceus behind shoulder. R. Winged caduceus; ΒΑΣΙΛΕΩΣ above, ΑΜΥΝ — ΤΟΥ below. *B.M.C. 20.* 4, 16 .. £17

5699   5704

5699 **CAPPADOCIA. Eusebeia** (originally named Mazaca, this important town at the foot of Mount Argaios was the capital of the Cappadocian kings. Towards the end of the 1st century B.C. its name was again changed, in honour of Augustus, and it is by the name of **Caesarea** that the place is best known). Late 1st cent. B.C. (time of King Archelaos). Æ 22. Bust of Athena r., wearing crested helmet and aegis. R. Mount Argaios, with eagle perched on summit; ΕΥΣΕ / ΒΕΙΑ to r. and to l. *B.M.C. 20.* 45, 2 .. £16

5700 — — Laur. hd. of Zeus r. R. Cultus-statue of Asiatic goddess facing; ΕΥΣΕ / ΒΕΙΑΣ to r. and to l., monogram in field to l. *B.M.C. 20.* 45, 5-6 .. .. .. £15

5701 — Æ 20. Turreted hd. of Tyche r. R. ΕΥΣΕ / ΒΕΙΑΣ either side of cornucopiae. *B.M.C. 20.* 45, 7 .. .. £12

5702 — Æ 19. Laur. hd. of Zeus r. R. Mount Argaios; below, ΕΥΣΕΒΕΙΑΣ / ΙΔ (=year 14 of Archelaos = 23/22 B.C.). *S.N.G. Von Aulock* 6338 .. .. £14

5703 — Æ 18. Bare hd. of Herakles r., lion's skin round neck. R. ΕΥΣΕ / ΒΕΙΑΣ either side of club draped with lion's skin; monogram beneath. *S.N.G. Von Aulock* 6334 .. £13

5704 — Æ 17. *Obv.* As 5701. R. ΕΥΣΕ / ΒΕΙΑΣ either side of palm-branch; monogram in field to r. *B.M.C. 20.* 46, 9 .. .. £10

5705 — — Dr. bust of Athena r., wearing crested helmet. R. Eagle stg. r., wings spread; ΕΥΣΕΒΕΙΑΣ below, monogram in field to r. *S.N.G. Von Aulock* 6333 .. .. £11

5706 — Æ 14. Aegis, with Gorgon's hd. at centre. R. Mount Argaios; below, ΕΥΣΕΒΕΙΑ / Τ. *B.M.C. 20.* 45, 1 .. .. £14

5707 — Æ 23. Laur. bust of Herakles r., lion's skin round neck, club at shoulder. R. ΕΥΣΕ / ΒΕΙΑΣ either side of tetrastyle temple; beneath, ΚΕ (=year 25 of Archelaos =12/11 B.C.). *B.M.C. 20.* 45, 3-4 .. .. £16

5708 — Æ 22. Laur. hd. of Apollo r. (with features of Archelaos?), lyre behind. ℞. ΕΥΣΕ / ΒΕΙΑΣ either side of tripod; beneath, ιΘ (=year 19 =18/17 B.C.). *S.N.G. Von Aulock* 6339 ..   ..   £18

5709 **CYPRUS. Amathus** (on the south coast of the island, a few miles to the east of Limassol, Amathus was the centre of an important kingdom. The attribution of the following coins is, however, only conjectural). 460–400 B.C. Æ *stater* (c. 11·5 gm.). Lion lying r.; Cypriot letters (=*to la*?) beneath. ℞. Forepart of lion r.; all in dotted square within incuse square. *B.M.C. 24.* 1, 1 ..   ..   £2,500

5710 — — Lion lying r.; above, eagle flying r., and Cypriot letter (= *mo*). ℞. As last, but in dotted circle within circular incuse. *Forrer/Weber* 7683   ..   ..   ..   £2,000

5711 — Æ *sixth-stater* (c. 1·68 gm.). Lion lying r., star above. ℞. As 5709. *B.M.C. 24.* 2, 3 ..   ..   £175

5712 — Æ *twelfth* (c. 0·82 gm.). *Obv.* As 5710. ℞. As 5709. *B.M.C. 24.* 2, 4 ..   £130

5713 — Æ *twenty-fourth* (c. 0·45 gm.). Similar to 5709, but without letters beneath lion on *obv. B.M.C. 24.* 2, 5 ..   ..   £85

5714 400–350 B.C. Æ *stater* (c. 6·6 gm.). Lion lying r., eagle flying r. above; in ex., E (=Evagoras I of Salamis?). ℞. Forepart of lion r.; *ankh* symbol before, Cypriot letters (=*ba* . . .) beneath. *B.M.C. 24.* 3, 7 ..   ..   £750

5715   5718

5715 — — of King Zotimos? Lion and eagle, as last; in ex., Cypriot letters (= *zo vi ti mo*) on raised band. ℞. Forepart of lion r., Cypriot letters (=*zo ti mo*) before. *B.M.C. 24.* 4, 12 ..   ..   £750

5716 — — of King Lysandros? Lion and eagle, as last; in ex., Cypriot letters (=*lu sa to ro*). ℞. Forepart of lion r.; before, Cypriot letters, as *obv. B.M.C. 24.* 5, 14 ..   £750

5717 — — of King Epipalos? Lion and eagle, as last; in ex., Cypriot letter (=*lo*) and large crescent (?). ℞. Forepart of lion r.; before, Cypriot letters (= *e pi pa*). *B.M.C. 24.* 6, 17 .. ..   £750

5718 — Æ *third-stater* (c. 2·2 gm.) of King Rhoikos? Lion's hd. r. ℞. Forepart of lion r., hd. facing; before, Cypriot letter (=*ro*). *B.M.C. 24.* 6, 18–19 .. ..   ..   £225

5719 — — Similar, but with star instead of Cypriot letter on *rev. B.M.C. 24.* 7, 22 £200

5720   5723

5720 **Kition** (this ancient and important city, near modern Larnaka, was a stronghold of the Phoenician influence in Cyprus. Zeno, the founder of the Stoic school of philosophy, was born here). Baalmelek I, *c.* 479-449 B.C. Æ *stater* (*c.* 10·8 gm.). Naked Herakles, wearing lion's skin, advancing r., brandishing club and holding bow. ℞. Lion seated r.; above, king's name in Aramaic letters; before, ram's hd. r.; all in dotted square within incuse square. *B.M.C.* 24. 9, 6 .. .. £900

5721 — Æ *third-stater* (*c.* 3·6 gm.). Similar. *B.M.C.* 24. 9, 7 .. .. .. £275

5722 — Æ *twelfth* (*c.* 0·8 gm.). Hd. of bearded Herakles r., clad in lion's skin. ℞. Similar to 5720, but king's name is abbreviated, and without ram's hd. *B.M.C.* 24. 10, 8 £100

5723 Azbaal, *c.* 449-425 B.C. (son of Baalmelek). Æ *stater* (*c.* 10·9 gm.). *Obv.* As 5720. ℞. Stag kneeling r., attacked by lion r. on its back; above, king's name in Aramaic letters; all in dotted square within incuse square. *B.M.C.* 24. 11, 12 .. .. .. £550

5724 — Æ *third-stater* (*c.* 3·6 gm.). Similar. *B.M.C.* 24. 13, 26 .. .. .. £200

5725 Baalmelek II, *c.* 425-400 B.C. (son of Azbaal). Æ *stater* (*c.* 10·9 gm.). Similar to 5723, with king's name in Aramaic letters on *rev. B.M.C.* 24. 14, 33 .. .. £450

5726 — Æ *third-stater* (*c.* 3·6 gm.). Similar. *B.M.C.* 24. 15, 37 .. .. .. £175

5727   5730   5732

5727 — Æ *sixth-stater* (*c.* 1·8 gm.). Similar. *B.M.C.* 24. 16, 46 .. .. .. £120

5728 — Æ *twelfth* (*c.* 0·9 gm.). Hd. of bearded Herakles r., clad in lion's skin. ℞. Stag attacked by lion, similar to 5723, but king's name is abbreviated. *B.M.C.* 24. 17, 49 £85

5729 2nd half of 5th cent. B.C. (reigns of Azbaal and Baalmelek II). Æ *sixth-stater* (*c.* 1·8 gm.). Naked Herakles / stag attacked by lion, all as 5723, but without inscription. *B.M.C.* 24. 17, 50 .. .. £110

5730 — Æ *twelfth* (*c.* 0·9 gm.). Hd. of young Herakles r., clad in lion's skin. ℞. Stag kneeling r., attacked by lion r. on its back; all in dotted square within incuse square. *B.M.C.* 24. 18, 52-5 .. .. £80

5731 — Æ *twenty-fourth* (*c.* 0·4 gm.). Similar. *B.M.C.* 24. 18, 57 .. .. £65

5732 — Æ *forty-eighth* (*c.* 0·22 gm.). Similar. *B.M.C.* 24. 19, 67 .. .. £55

5733 — Æ *ninety-sixth* (*c.* 0·12 gm.). *Obv.* Similar. ℞. Lion's hd. r., in dotted square; all within incuse square. *B.M.C.* 24. 19, 70 .. .. £50

5734   5738   5739

5734 Baalram, *c.* 400-392 B.C. *Æ third-stater* (*c.* 3·5 gm.). Naked Herakles, wearing lion's skin, advancing r., brandishing club and holding bow; *ankh* symbol before. ℞. Stag kneeling r., attacked by lion r. on its back; above, king's name in Aramaic letters; all in dotted square within incuse square. *B.M.C. 24.* 20, 71 .. .. .. £450

5735 Melekiathon, 392-361 B.C. *N half-stater* (*c.* 4·15 gm.). Naked Herakles advancing r., lion's skin over extended l. arm, brandishing club and holding bow. ℞. Stag attacked by lion, all as last, with king's name in Aramaic letters above. *Babelon (Traité) pl.* 131, 16 .. .. £1,250

5736 — *Æ third-stater* (*c.* 3·35 gm.). Similar. *Grose/McClean* 9146 .. .. £375

5737 — *Æ* 14. *Obv.* As 5735; in field to l., Aramaic letter (=*m*). ℞. Hd. of Aphrodite l., wearing ornamented stephanos. *B.M.C. 24.* 20, 72-3 .. .. £20

5738 Pumiathon, *c.* 361-312 B.C. (son of Melekiathon. Executed on the orders of Ptolemy I of Egypt). *N half-stater* (*c.* 4·15 gm.). Similar to 5735, but with *ankh* symbol in *obv.* field to r.; and Phoenician numeral, representing the regnal year, in *rev.* field to r. *B.M.C. 24.* 21-2, 75-81 .. .. £750

The regnal dates on these coins range from 3 to 47.

5739 — *N tenth-stater* (*c.* 0·83 gm.). As 5730. *B.M.C. 24.* 23, 82.. .. .. £350

5740   5741

5740 **Idalion** (in the interior of the island, north-west of Kition, Idalion was a centre for the worship of Aphrodite. Its coinage commenced in the archaic period, *c.* 500 B.C.). 480-470 B.C. *Æ stater* (*c.* 11 gm.) of king Ki .... Sphinx seated r., l. foreleg raised; beneath, two palmettes; in field to r., Cypriot letters (=*pa si ki*). ℞. Lotus flower on two spiral tendrils; all within incuse following the shape of the type. *B.M.C. 24.* 26, 9 .. £2,000

5741 470-460 B.C. *Æ stater* (*c.* 11 gm.) of king Kara .... Sphinx seated l. on tendril with bud and flower, her r. foreleg raised; in field, Cypriot letters (=*pa ka ra*). ℞. Lotus flower on two spiral tendrils; in field to l., ivy-leaf; to r., astragalos; all within circular incuse. *B.M.C. 24.* 27, 13 .. .. £1,750

5742 460-445 B.C. (Idalion was captured by Azbaal of Kition early in the third quarter of the 5th cent.). *Æ third-stater* (*c.* 3·55 gm.) of king Stasikypros? Similar, but with Cypriot letter (=*sa*) in *obv.* field to l. *B.M.C. 24.* 28, 20-28 .. .. .. £400

5743 **Lapethos** (situated in the north of the island, near the coast, about 25 miles north-east of Soloi. Its coinage commenced in archaic times towards the close of the 6th cent.). Sidqmelek, *c.* 435 B.C. *Æ stater* (*c.* 11 gm.). Hd. of Athena l., in crested Corinthian helmet; Phoenician legend around (='king of Lapethos'). ℞. Hd. of Athena facing, wearing double-crested helmet with bull's horns and ears; Phoenician legend on either side (='Sidqmelek'); all within incuse square. *B.M.C. 24.* 30-31, 7-9 .. £3,500

Lapethos *continued*

5744 *Circa* 425 B.C. Æ *stater* (*c.* 11 gm.). *Obv.* Similar, but without legend. ℞. Hd. of bearded Herakles r., clad in lion's skin; all within incuse square. *Kraay* (*Archaic and Classical Greek Coins*) *pl.* 63, 1094 ..   ..   £4,000

5745 Demonikos II, *c.* 390 B.C. Æ *stater* (Persic standard, *c.* 11 gm.). Athena stg. facing, hd. l., holding spear and shield; *ankh* symbol in lower field to l. ℞. Naked Herakles advancing r., holding club and bow; before, king's name and title in Phoenician script; all within incuse square. *B.M.C. 24., pl.* XIX, 9   ..   ..   ..   £2,500

5746 — — (Rhodian standard, *c.* 7 gm.). Similar, but with legend BA — ΔH in *obv.* field to l. and to r.; and the *ankh* symbol is on *rev.*, in field to r.; no inscription on *rev.* *B.M.C. 24., pl.* XIX, 12   ..   ..   £2,000

       5747   5749

5747 — Æ *sixth-stater* (Persic standard, *c.* 1·6 gm.). Similar to 5745, but the *ankh* symbol in field to r. on *obv.*, and no inscription on *rev.* *B.M.C. 24.* 21, 74 (*attributed to Kition*) £300

5748 — Æ *third-stater* (Rhodian standard, *c.* 2·1 gm.). Athena stg. r., holding spear and shield; Phoenician letters (= *b d*) in field to r. ℞. Naked Herakles advancing r., lion's skin over l. arm, holding club and bow. *B.M.C. 24., pl.* XIX, 13   ..   £450

5749 Praxippos (deposed by Ptolemy I of Egypt, 312 B.C.). Æ 15. Laur. hd. of Apollo l., ΠΡ behind. ℞. Krater; BA in field to r. *B.M.C. 24., pl.* XX, 2   ..   £35

        5750   5752

5750 **Marion** (a coastal town in the north-west of the island). *Circa* 450 B.C. Æ *stater* (*c.* 10·8 gm.). Lion stg. r., its hd. lowered and turned back licking its forepaw; above, Cypriot legend and double-axe (?); in ex., floral ornament. ℞. Phrixos, naked, running l., his r. arm round a ram jumping l.; Cypriot legend before, double-axe (?) beneath; all within incuse square. *Kraay* (*Archaic and Classical Greek Coins*) *pl.* 64, 1108 £3,500

> *The reading of the Cypriot legends is not certain, but they are thought to mean* 'Sasamarios, son of Doxandros, of Marion'.

5751 Stasioikos I, late 5th cent. B.C. Æ *stater* (*c.* 10·8 gm.). Laur. hd. of Apollo r., hair short; before and behind, king's name in Cypriot letters. ℞. Aphrodite (?) riding on bull galloping r.; above and below, Cypriot legend, as on *obv.;* all within incuse square. *B.M.C. 24.* 32, 1   ..   ..   £3,000

5752 — Æ *third-stater* (*c.* 3·55 gm.). Similar. *B.M.C. 24.* 32, 2 ..   ..   £750

5753 Timocharis, early 4th cent. B.C. (son of Stasioikos). Æ *third-stater* (*c.* 3·3 gm.). Laur. hd. of Apollo r., hair short. ℞. Similar to 5751, but with Cypriot letters (= *pa ti*) in field above, and fish r. beneath bull. *Grose/McClean* 9152 ..   ..   £700

5754 — Æ *twelfth* (*c.* 0·9 gm.). *Obv.* Similar, but with Cypriot letters (= *pa ti*) in field. ℞. Aphrodite (?) riding on bull galloping l.; Cypriot legend, as on *obv.*, in field; all within incuse square. *Grose/McClean* 9153   ..   ..   £200

5755   5757

5755 Stasioikos II (deposed by Ptolemy I of Egypt in 312 B.C., after which Marion was destroyed and its population moved south to Paphos). *N half-stater* (*c.* 4·1 gm.). Hd. of Athena r., in triple-crested helmet; B — Σ in field. R. Bull walking r.; Cypriot letters (=*pa sa*) in upper field, M — A — P in lower field. *B.M.C. 24.* 33, 4 .. .. £2,500

5756 — *N triobol* ? (*c.* 1·92 gm.). Laur. hd. of Zeus l.; Cypriot letters (=*pa sa*) in field. R. Hd. of Aphrodite r.; M / A behind. *B.M.C. 24.,pl.* XX, 10 .. .. .. £1,100

5757 — *N diobol* (*c.* 1·45 gm.). Hd. of Athena l., in triple-crested helmet. R. Eagle stg. l.; Cypriot letters (=*pa sa o*) in field. *Forrer/Weber* 7698 .. .. £850

5758 — *N obol* (*c.* 0·7 gm.). Similar to 5756. *B.M.C. 24.,pl.* XX, 11 .. .. £550

5759 — *N hemiobol* ? (*c.* 0·42 gm.). Hd. of Athena l., in crested helmet. R. Bull walking r.; above, Cypriot letters (=*pa sa*). *B.M.C. 24.,pl.* XX, 8 .. .. .. £350

5760 — Æ *trihemidrachm* (*c.* 6·1 gm.). Laur. hd. of Zeus l. R. Hd. of Aphrodite r.; traces of Cypriot letters in field. *B.M.C. 24.,pl.* XX, 12 .. .. £1,250

5761 — Æ *tetrobol* (*c.* 2·8 gm.). Similar, but with king's name in Cypriot letters before hd. of Zeus on *obv.*, and ΜΑΡΙΕΥΣ before hd. of Aphrodite on *rev.* *B.M.C. 24., pl.* XX, 13 £500

5762 — Æ *diobol* (*c.* 1·4 gm.). Laur. hd. of Zeus r., myrtle-branch before. R. Hd. of Aphrodite r., between two myrtle-branches; Cypriot letters (=*pa sa ta*) before, ΜΑΡΙ behind. *B.M.C. 24.,pl.* XX, 15 .. .. £300

5763 — Æ *obol* (*c.* 0·68 gm.). Hd. of Aphrodite l. R. Hd. of Zeus r., ΜΑΡΙ before. *Forrer/Weber* 7699 .. .. £175

5764 — — Laur. hd. of Apollo l. R. *Ankh* symbol, with double cross-bar and v within the ring. *B.M.C. 24.,pl.* XX, 17 .. .. £200

  The double cross-bar on the ankh *symbol forms the Cypriot letter* 'pa' *whilst the* v *represents* 'sa'.

5765 — Æ 14. Hd. of Aphrodite r. R. Thunderbolt; above, ΒΑ and Cypriot letters (=*si*); beneath, ΜΑΡΙΕ. *B.M.C. 24.,pl.* XX, 18 .. .. £22

5766   5767

5766 — Æ 15. *Obv.* Similar. R. *Ankh* symbol, with pellet in ring; all within wreath. *B.M.C. 24.* 34, 6 .. .. £16

5767 **Paphos** (a coastal city in the south-west of the island, Paphos was of Phoenician origin and was the chief seat of the worship of Aphrodite in Cyprus. Although a long series of coins, commencing in the archaic period, is usually given to this mint, the attribution is, at best, doubtful until the reigns of Timarchos and Nikokles in the latter part of the 4th cent. In Ptolemaic times the city was refounded on a site 10 miles further west). Stasandros, *c.* 450 B.C. Æ *stater* (*c.* 11 gm.). Bull stg. l.; winged solar disk above, *ankh* symbol before, palmette ornament in ex. R. Eagle stg. l.; king's name in Cypriot letters before and behind; vase in field to l.; all in dotted square within incuse square. *B.M.C. 24.* 38, 17 .. .. £1,500

5768   5770

Paphos *continued*

5768 — Æ *sixth-stater* (*c.* 1·7 gm.). Bull stg. l.; winged solar disk above. R. Eagle stg. l.; vase before, ivy-leaf behind; all within incuse square. *B.M.C. 24*. 38, 18-23   £130

5769 — Æ *twelfth* (*c.* 0·82 gm.). Similar. *B.M.C. 24*. 39, 24-9 ..   ..   ..   £90

5770 — Æ *twenty-fourth* (*c.* 0·4 gm.). Similar. *B.M.C. 24*. 39, 30-31 ..   ..   £75

5771 Punu .... II (Pnytos II or Pnytagoras II ?), *c.* 425 B.C. Æ *quarter-stater* (*c.* 2·6 gm.). Laur. hd. of Zeus r. R. Eagle stg. l.; before, *ankh* symbol and Cypriot letters (= *pa pu*); behind, laurel-spray; all in dotted square within incuse square. *Forrer/Weber* 7708   £375

5772   5774

5772 — Æ *sixth-stater* (*c.* 1·6 gm.). Bull stg. l.; winged solar disk above. R. Eagle stg. l.; before, Cypriot letters (= *pa pu*); behind, olive-spray; all within incuse square. *B.M.C. 24*. 37, 14 ..   ..   £140

5773 — Æ *twelfth* (*c.* 0·8 gm.). Similar. *B.M.C. 24*. 37, 16 ..   ..   ..   £100

5774 Aristo ...., late 5th cent. B.C. Æ *stater* (*c.* 11 gm.). Bull stg. l.; winged solar disk above, *ankh* symbol before, Cypriot letters (= *a ri*) beneath. R. Eagle flying l., hd. and body in profile, wings and tail as seen from below; all within incuse square. *B.M.C. 24*. 40, 39 ..   ..   £1,000

5775   5776

5775 Moagetas, early 4th cent. B.C. Æ *stater* (*c.* 11 gm.). Similar, but on *obv.* Cypriot letters (= *mo a ke ta*) beneath and before bull, and without *ankh* symbol; on *rev.*, the type is within dotted square in the two l. hand corners of which are sprays. *B.M.C. 24*. 42, 43 ..   ..   £1,000

5776 Late 5th-early 4th cent. B.C. Æ *third-stater* (*c.* 3·4 gm.). *Obv.* As 5772. R. Eagle flying l., as 5774; all in dotted square within incuse square. *B.M.C. 24*. 42, 44   £300

5777 — Æ *sixth-stater* (*c.* 1·5 gm.). Similar to 5774, but without Cypriot letters on *obv.* *B.M.C. 24*. 41, 41 ..   ..   £150

5778 — Æ *twelfth* (*c.* 0·75 gm.). As last. *B.M.C. 24*. 41, 42 ..   ..   ..   £110

5779 Late 4th cent. B.C. (before 309). N *diobol* (*c.* 1·45 gm.). Hd. of Aphrodite facing, wearing stephanos and crowned with myrtle. R. Eagle stg. l., wings closed; bunch of grapes before. *B.M.C. 24., pl.* XXII, 7 ..   ..   £850

5780 — *N obol* (*c.* 0·8 gm.) of Timarchos. Hd. of Aphrodite l., wearing ornamented stephanos, hair rolled. R. Dove stg. r. on sceptre (?); ΠΑ beneath, Cypriot letters (=*ti ma ra ko pa si*) above and before. *Grose/McClean* 9158 .. .. £400

 Timarchos was king of Paphos circa 323 B.C.

5781 — R Attic *tetradrachm* (*c.* 17·2 gm.) of Nikokles. *Obv.* Similar; behind, ΠΒΑ. R. Apollo seated l. on omphalos, holding arrow and resting on bow; in field to l., ΝΙΚΟΚΛΓΟΥΣ / ΠΑΦΙΟΝ in two lines. *B.M.C. 24., pl.* XXII, 10 .. .. (*Unique ?*)

 Nikokles, son of Timarchos, took his own life in 309 B.C. following an unsuccessful revolt against Ptolemy of Egypt.

    5782   5784

5782 — R *stater* (*c.* 10·6 gm.). Similar to 5780, but on *rev.* ΠΑΦΙ beneath the dove, astragalos above (no Cypriot legend). *B.M.C.* 24. 44, 47 .. .. £3,000

5783 — R *third-stater* (*c.* 3·33 gm.) of Timarchos. Similar, but with Cypriot letters (= *ti ma ra ko*) instead of astragalos above the dove. *B.M.C.* 24., *pl.* XXII, 5 .. £650

5784 — R Attic *tetrobol* (*c.* 2·9 gm.). Bust of Aphrodite r., wearing ornamented stephanos with triangular projections, hair long. R. Dove flying r., uncertain Cypriot legend around. *B.M.C.* 24. 43, 46 .. .. £800

5785 — Æ 16. Diad. hd of Aphrodite l. R. Dove stg. r. on sceptre (?); Cypriot letter (=*e*) above. *B.M.C.* 24., *pl.* XXII, 6 .. .. £16

5786 — Æ 15. Hd. of Aphrodite l., wearing ornamented stephanos. R. Similar to last, but with star above, and Cypriot letter (= *pa*) before. *B.M.C.* 24., *pl.* XXII, 8 .. £16

5787 — Æ 9. *Obv.* Similar. R. Dove stg. r. on sceptre (?); ΠΑΦΙ above. *B.M.C.* 24., *pl.* XXII, 9 .. .. £14

    5788   5789

5788 — Æ 11. *Obv.* Similar. R. Rose; uncertain letters in field. *B.M.C.* 24. 44, 49 £15

5789 **Salamis** (the principal city of the island, Salamis was situated on the east coast close to an important Mycenaean settlement at Enkomi. It was one of the earliest Cypriot mints, commencing issues about 520 B.C. Evagoras I of Salamis brought almost the entire island under his rule in the early part of the 4th cent., but his power was eventually checked by the Persians). 5th cent. B.C. (before *c.* 430). R *stater* (*c.* 11 gm.). Ram lying l.; above and below, Cypriot letters (= *e u ve le to to se* = Euelthontos). R *Ankh* symbol, with Cypriot letter (= *ku*) in the ring; all within incuse square, with flowers in lower corners and sprays of leaves in upper. *B.M.C.* 24. 48, 14 .. .. £500

5790 — — Similar, but on *rev.* sprays of leaves in all four corners of the incuse square, and Cypriot letter (=*ki*) in field to r. *B.M.C.* 24. 49, 21 .. .. £550

5791 — — As last, but with Cypriot letter (=*ke*) in *rev.* field to r. *B.M.C.* 24. 49, 22 £550

5792

5794

Salamis *continued*

5792 — — Ram lying r., pellet within crescent in field above; Cypriot legend, similar to 5789, above and below. R. *Ankh* symbol containing letter, as 5789; in field to l. and to r. Cypriot letters (=*ko ru*); all within incuse square, with sprays in corners. *B.M.C. 24.* 50, 23   ..   ..   £600

5793 — — Ram lying l.; uncertain Cypriot legend above and beneath. R. *Ankh* symbol, with Cypriot letter (=*pa*) in the ring; in field to l. and to r., Cypriot letters (=*pa si le o*); all within incuse square. *B.M.C. 24.* 51, 28 ..   ..   £550

5794 — Æ *third-stater* (c. 3·97 gm.). Ram lying l.; above and below, Cypriot letters (=*e u ve le to ne* =Euelthon). R. *Ankh* symbol, within incuse square. *B.M.C. 24.* 48, 13   £200

5795 — — (c. 3·38 gm.) of Nikodamos. Ram lying l.; king's name and title, in Cypriot letters, above, before and below. R. *Ankh* symbol, with double bar (forming the Cypriot letter *pa*); in field to l. and to r., Cypriot letters (=*se la mi ni*); all within incuse square. *B.M.C. 24.* 52, 31 ..   ..   £350

Nikodamos, king of Salamis, is otherwise unknown to history.

5796

5801

5796 — Æ *sixth-stater* (c. 1·7 gm.) of Nikodamos. Ram lying l.; above, Cypriot letters (=*pa si ni*). R. *Ankh* symbol, containing Cypriot letter (=*ni*); all within incuse square. *Forrer/Weber 7724* £200

5797 — — (c. 1·75 gm.). *Obv.* As 5792. R. Similar to last, but with Cypriot letter *ku* in ring of *ankh*. *Forrer/Weber 7720* £140

5798 — Æ *twelfth* (c. 0·82 gm.). Ram's hd. r. R. *Ankh* symbol, containing Cypriot letter (=*ku*). *B.M.C. 24. pl.* XXIII, 9   ..   ..   £110

5799 *Circa* 430 B.C. Æ *stater* (c. 11·2 gm.) of Euanthes. Ram lying l.; above and below, Cypriot letters (=*e u va te o se* =Euantheos). R. Ram's hd. r.; Cypriot letter (=*pa*) beneath; all within circular incuse. *B.M.C. 24.* 53, 38 ..   ..   ..   £2,500

    This king is only known from his coinage.

5800 — Æ *sixth-stater* (c. 1·78 gm.) of Euanthes. Ram lying l.; above, Cypriot letters (=*e u va te*). R. Ram's hd. l.; ivy-branch beneath, Cypriot letters (=*pa si le vo se*) above. *Forrer/Weber 7725* £225

5801 — — (c. 1·45 gm.) of Euanthes. Similar, but with *obv.* legend *pa ku*, *rev.* legend *pa e*, and *rev.* type to r. *B.M.C. 24.* 54, 41   ..   ..   £200

5802 — Æ *twelfth* (c. 0·82 gm.). Ram's hd. l. R. Ram's hd. l.; above, Cypriot letters (=*pa si le*); beneath, *ankh* symbol and Cypriot letter (=*e*). *B.M.C. 24., pl.* XXIV, 3   £120

5803 Evagoras I, 411-373 B.C. (the most celebrated of the kings of Salamis, Evagoras was a close ally of the Athenians until his rapidly growing power was curtailed by Persia). N *quarter-stater* (c. 2·04 gm.). Hd. of young Herakles three-quarter face to l., clad in lion's skin; Cypriot letters (=*e u va ko ro*) on either side. R. Goat lying r.; Cypriot letters (= *pa si le o se*) before, above and beneath. *B.M.C. 24.* 56, 51 ..   ..   £1,250

5804   5805   5806

5804 — *N tenth* (*c.* 0·78 gm.).   Hd. of bearded Herakles r., clad in lion's skin.   R. Forepart
of goat lying r., club beneath.   *B.M.C. 24.* 56, 52   ..   ..   £440

5805 — *N twentieth* (*c.* 0·4 gm.).   *Obv.* Similar.   R. Goat's hd. r.   *B.M.C. 24.* 56, 54
£275

5806 — *R stater* (*c.* 11·1 gm.).   *Obv.* Similar, but with Cypriot letters (=*e u va ko ro*) before.
R. Goat lying r., corn-grain above; Cypriot letters (=*pa si le vo se*) before, above and in ex.;
EY — A in ex. and in field to r.   *B.M.C. 24.* 57, 55   ..   ..   ..   £2,250

5807 — *R third-stater* (*c.* 3·2 gm.).   Naked Herakles seated r. on rock, holding club and horn,
bow behind; Cypriot letters (=*e u va ko ro*) before and behind.   R. Goat lying r.; Cypriot
letters (=*pa si le o se*) before, above and in ex.; A in field to r.   *B.M.C. 24.* 57, 57   £175

5808   5811   5812

5808 Nikokles, 373-361 B.C. (son of Evagoras I).   *N* Attic *third-stater* (*c.* 2·78 gm.).   Hd. of
Aphrodite l., wearing richly ornamented stephanos.   R. Hd. of Athena l., wearing crested
Corinthian helmet; Cypriot letters (=*pa ni*) behind and before.   *B.M.C. 24.* 58, 61
£1,500

5809 — *N* Attic *twelfth* (*c.* 0·68 gm.).   Similar, but without inscription on *rev.*   *B.M.C. 24.*
59, 62-3   ..   ..   £450

5810 Evagoras II, 361-351 B.C. (son of Nikokles).   *N stater* (*c.* 8·3 gm.).   Lion stg. l., devouring prey, eagle perched on his back; star in upper field, before eagle.   R. Hd. of Aphrodite
l., wearing turreted crown; EYA behind.   *Babelon (Traité) pl.* 128, 5   ..   ..   £6,500

5811 — *N twelfth* (*c.* 0·68 gm.).   Hd. of Aphrodite l., wearing turreted crown; BA behind.
R. Hd. of Athena l., wearing crested Corinthian helmet; EYA behind.   *B.M.C. 24.* 59,
64   ..   ..   £500

5812 — *R Rhodian didrachm* (*c.* 6·9 gm.).   Hd. of Athena r., wearing crested Corinthian
helmet; EYA behind.   R. Hd. of Aphrodite r., wearing turreted crown; BA behind.
B.M.C. 24. 60, 66-7   ..   ..   £750

5813 — *R hemidrachm* (*c.* 1·6 gm.).   *Obv.* Similar to 5811, but with EYA behind.   R. Hd. of
Athena r., wearing crested Athenian helmet.   *Forrer/Weber* 7734   ..   ..   £200

5814 — *R obol* (*c.* 0·58 gm.).   Hd. of Athena l., wearing crested Athenian helmet.   R. Star
of eight rays.   *B.M.C. 24.* 60, 68   ..   ..   £90

5815   5817

Salamis *continued*

5815 Pnytagoras, 351-332 B.C. (this king is mentioned as having assisted Alexander the Great at the siege of Tyre in 332 B.C.). *N stater* (*c.* 8·3 gm.). Dr. bust of Aphrodite (?) l., wearing crown ornamented with semicircular plates; BA behind. R. Dr. bust of Aphrodite l., wearing turreted crown; ΠΝ behind. *B.M.C. 24.* 62, 76 .. .. .. £7,500

5816 — *N twelfth* (*c.* 0·7 gm.). *Obv.* Similar to *rev.* of last, but with Π behind. R. Similar to *obv.* of last, but with Cypriot letter (=*pa*) behind. *Babelon* (*Bibliothèque Nationale Catalogue, ii*) *pl.* XVII, 20-21 .. .. £600

5817 — *R didrachm* (*c.* 6·9 gm.). Dr. bust of Aphrodite l., wreathed with myrtle, hair long; ΠΝ behind. R. Dr. bust of Artemis l., hair rolled; bow and quiver at shoulder, BA behind. *B.M.C. 24.* 63, 77-8 .. .. £750

5818 — *R tetrobol* (*c.* 2·2 gm.). *Obv.* As last. R. As *obv.* of 5815. *B.M.C. 24.* 63, 79
£275

5819   5822

5819 — — Dr. bust of Aphrodite l., hair rolled and confined by fillet; ΠΝ behind. R. Dr. bust of Artemis r., hair rolled; bow and quiver (?) at shoulder, BA behind. *B.M.C. 24.* 63-4, 80-84 .. .. £225

5820 Nikokreon, 331-310 B.C. (son of Pnytagoras, Nikokreon supported Ptolemy against Antigonos in 315 B.C., in recognition of which he was rewarded by the King of Egypt with dominion over the whole of Cyprus). *N stater* (*c.* 8·3 gm.). Similar to 5815, but with ΝΙ instead of ΠΝ on *rev. Babelon* (*B. N. Catalogue, ii*) *pl.* XVII, 24 .. £7,500

5821 — — As last, but with N͞I͞K instead of ΝΙ. *B.M.C. 24., pl.* XXIV, 21.. .. £7,500

5822 — *R didrachm* (*c.* 6·25 gm.). Hd. of Aphrodite r., wearing turreted crown; N͞I͞K behind. R. Laur. hd. of Apollo l., bow behind neck; BA behind. *B.M.C. 24.* 64, 85 .. £900

5823 — *R tetrobol* (*c.* 2·05 gm.). Similar, but the N͞I͞K is on *rev.*, the BA on *obv. Babelon* (*B.N. Catalogue, ii*) *pl.* XVII, 26 .. .. £300

5824   5826

5824 Menelaus, 310-306 B.C. (brother of Ptolemy of Egypt, Menelaus surrendered Cyprus to Demetrios Poliorketes following the naval battle of Salamis). *N third-stater* (*c.* 2·75 gm.). Hd. of Aphrodite l., wearing turreted crown; MEN behind. R. As 5816. *B.M.C. 24., pl.* XXIV, 23 .. .. £2,500

5825 — *N twelfth* (*c.* 0·69 gm.). Similar, but with M instead of MEN on *obv. B.M.C. 24., pl.* XXIV, 24 .. .. £750

5826 *Bronze Coinage.* Evagoras II, 361-351 B.C. Æ 18. Lion stg. l.; above, ram's hd. l. R. Horse stg. l.; star above, *ankh* symbol before. *B.M.C. 24.* 60-61, 69-73 .. £15

5827   5830

5827 2nd half of 4th cent. B.C. Æ 15. Hd. of Athena l., in crested Athenian helmet. ℞.
Prow of galley l.; ΣΑΛ in field to l. *B.M.C. 24.* 61, 74 ..   ..   £16

5828 — Æ 13. *Obv.* Similar. ℞. Forepart of kneeling bull l.; Σ before. *B.M.C. 24.* 61,
75 ..   ..   £15

5829 *Circa* 300 B.C. (time of Demetrios Poliorketes ?). Æ 15. Hd. of young Herakles r.,
clad in lion's skin. ℞. ΑΛΕΞΑΝΔΡΟΥ between club and bow with case; ΣΑ above, Α beneath.
B.M.C. 24. 65, 86 ..   ..   £12

5830 **Soloi** (an important coastal city of north-western Cyprus, Soloi seems to have had close
connections with Athens. Little coinage can, with certainty, be attributed to this mint,
but it is possible that much of the 5th century coinage given to Paphos belongs to Soloi).
Pasikrates, *c.* 331 B.C. Æ *diobol* (*c.* 1·8 gm.). Laur. and dr. bust of Apollo three-quarter
face to l. ℞. Tripod; in field, Β — Α / Π — Α / Σ — I. *B.M.C. 24.* 66, 1 ..   £325

5831 Eunostos, *c.* 310 B.C. (son-in-law of Ptolemy of Egypt). N *third-stater* (*c.* 2·63 gm.).
Laur. and dr. bust of Apollo l.; ΕΥ behind. ℞. Hd. of Aphrodite r.; ΒΑ behind. *B.M.C.
24., pl.* XXV, 2 ..   ..   £2,250

5832 — N *twelfth* (*c.* 0·68 gm.). Similar, but with Cypriot letter (=*e*) on *obv.*, and Cypriot
letter (=*pa*) on *rev.* *B.M.C. 24., pl.* XXV, 3 ..   ..   £550

5833 **Uncertain mint.** Mid-4th cent. B.C. Æ *didrachm* (*c.* 6·3 gm.). Naked Herakles
stg. r., strangling lion, club behind. ℞. Athena seated l. on beak of prow, holding
aplustre and spear; *ankh* symbol before, Cypriot letters (=*pa si a ri*) in field. *B.M.C. 24.,
pl.* XXV, 7 ..   ..   £1,800

5834 — Æ *triobol* (*c.* 1·62 gm.). Similar. *B.M.C. 24.* 72, 1 ..   ..   ..   £300

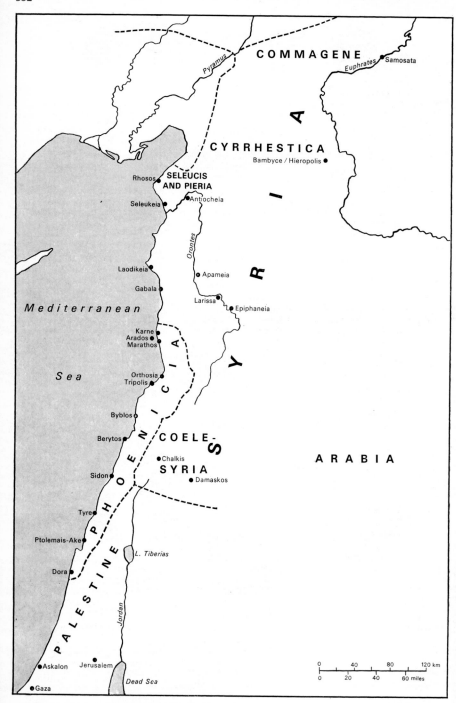

MAP 19   SYRIA, PHOENICIA AND PALESTINE

THE EAST

The lands at the eastern end of the Mediterranean—Syria, Phoenicia, Palestine, etc.—were under Persian rule down to the time of Alexander. No coinage was produced in the area during the Archaic period. Persian imperial currency sufficed for all monetary transactions until the mid-5th century B.C. when this was supplemented by issues from some of the Phoenician cities. From the time of the Macedonian conquest the area was under the rule of the two great Hellenistic kingdoms, the Ptolemaic of Egypt and the Seleukid of Syria. These two Greek dynasties vied with one another for control of Phoenicia and Palestine. Eventually, in the 1st century B.C., the power of the kingdoms crumbled before the might of Rome, by which time many of the city-states had regained a considerable degree of autonomy.

SYRIA

5837 **KINGDOM OF COMMAGENE** (the most northerly district of Syria, Commagene lay to the east of Cilicia). **Samos,** *c.* 140-130 B.C. (possibly the founder of Samosata on the Euphrates, capital of Commagene). Æ 16. Rad. and diad. hd. of Samos r. ℞. Nike advancing l., holding wreath; ΒΑΣΙΛΕΩΣ / ΣΑΜΟΥ behind, ΘΕΟΣΕΒΟΥΣ / ΚΑΙ ΔΙΚΑΙΟΥ before, ΓΛ in ex. *Babelon (Rois de Syrie) pl.* XXX, 1 .. .. .. £75

5838 **Mithradates I,** *c.* 96 B.C. (son of Samos, Mithradates married Laodike, daughter of Antiochos VIII of Syria). Æ 20. Hd. of Mithradates r., in pointed head-dress. ℞. Athena stg. l., holding Nike, spear and shield; ΒΑΣΙΛΕΩΣ behind, ΜΙΘΡΑΔΑΤΟΥ / ΚΑΛΛΙΝΙΚΟΥ before. *B.M.C. 20.* 104, 1-3 .. .. £65

5839 — Æ 18. Eagle stg. r., palm in background. ℞. ΒΑΣΙΛΕΩΣ — ΜΙΘΡΑΔΑΤΟΥ / ΚΑΛΛΙΝΙΚΟΥ either side of caduceus. *Babelon (Rois de Syrie) pl.* XXX, 3 .. .. .. £40

5840   5841

5840 — Æ 16. Similar, but palm instead of caduceus on *rev.*, and the legend is divided ΒΑΣΙΛΕΩΣ / ΜΙΘΡΑΔΑΤΟΥ — ΚΑΛΛΙΝΙΚΟΥ. *Babelon, pl.* XXX, 4 .. .. £35

5841 **Antiochos I,** *c.* 69-31 B.C. (son of Mithradates I and Laodike). Æ 20. Hd. of Antiochos r., wearing Armenian tiara ornamented with eagles and star. ℞. ΒΑΣΙΛΕΩΣ / ΑΝΤΙΟΧΟΥ above and beneath lion, prowling r. *B.M.C. 20.* 105, 1-2 .. .. .. £75

N.B. *Commagene became a Roman province under Tiberius, but the kingdom was restored in A.D. 38 by Caligula. The coinage of this later kingdom, lasting until A.D. 72, will be listed in a future catalogue covering the 'Greek Imperial' series and contemporary coinages.*

5842   5843

5842 **COMMAGENE. Samosata** (an important city on the right bank of the Euphrates, Samosata was the capital of the kings of Commagene. The period of issue of its autonomous bronze coinage is difficult to determine, but most specimens seem to belong to the 1st cent. B.C., perhaps to the time of Antiochos I). Æ 26. Lion stg. r. ℞. The Tyche of Samosata seated r. on rock, holding palm; ΣΑΜΟΣΑΤΩ behind, ΠΟΛΕΩΣ before. *B.M.C. 20.* 116, 4-5 .. .. £17

5843 — Æ 20. Laur. hd. of Zeus r. ℞. ΣΑΜΟ / ΣΑΤΩ above and beneath lion prowling r. *B.M.C. 20.* 116, 2-3 .. .. £15

Samosata *continued*

5844 — Æ 17. Eagle stg. r. R. самосатω. Zeus enthroned l., holding Nike and sceptre.
B.M.C. 20. 117, 16 ..   ..   £14

5845 **CYRRHESTICA** (this district lay to the south of Commagene, west of the Euphrates).
Bambyce (this important city of eastern Cyrrhestica, a centre for the worship of Atergatis,
was renamed **Hieropolis** by Seleukos I). *Circa* 332 B.C. Æ *didrachm* (*c.* 8·55 gm.).
Bust of Atergatis l., wearing ornamented head-dress, hair long; behind, ∩o (=30). R.
King of Persia in chariot driven l. by charioteer; above, Aramaic legend (=*Abd-Hadad*).
Babelon (*B.N. Catalogue, ii*) *pl.* VII, 16 ..   ..   £4,000

Abd-Hadad seems to have been a priest-king of Bambyce.

5846   5848

5846 — — *Obv.* Similar, but the bust of Atergatis is facing, with ∩o (=30) to l., and Aramaic
legend (=*Atergatis*) to r. R. Abd-Hadad, wearing conical hat, stg. l. before altar, holding
pine-cone; behind, Aramaic legend (=*Abd-Hadad*); all within distyle temple. *Babelon*,
pl. VII, 17 ..   ..   £4,000

5847 *Circa* 331 B.C. Æ *didrachm* (*c.* 8·4 gm.). Hd. of Atergatis r., hair short; Aramaic
legend (=*Ate*) behind, Δ above. R. Bull kneeling l., attacked by lion l. on his back;
above, Aramaic legend (=*Alexander*). *Babelon, pl.* VII, 18 ..   ..   ..   £4,500

*The name 'Alexander' on rev. refers, presumably, to the Macedonian conqueror who was,
at this time, engaged in the final stages of the destruction of the Persian Empire.*

5848 — — Warrior (Alexander ?), holding spear, on horse galloping l.; Aramaic legend
(=*Alexander*) before, м beneath, Aramaic letter (=*th*) behind. R. Lion walking l.;
above, Aramaic legend, as *obv.*, and letter (=*b*); before, bird perched on flower. *B.M.C.*
20. 138, 1 ..   ..   £4,500

5849 **SELEUKIS AND PIERIA** (a fertile district of north-western Syria, bounded by the
Mediterranean on the west and desert on the east, Seleukis included the valley of the lower
Orontes. The area was also known as Tetrapolis, after its four great cities, Antiocheia,
Seleukeia, Laodikeia and Apameia. **Tetrapolis of Seleukis** (a joint bronze coinage of
the four great cities of Seleukis). 149-147 B.C. Æ 26. Conjoined bearded heads r.
(Demoi of Antiocheia and Seleukeia ?), each bound with tainia. R. Zeus enthroned l.,
holding Nike and sceptre; ΑΔΕΛΦΩΝ / ΔΗΜΩΝ behind and before; εξρ (=year 165 of the
Seleukid era) and monogram in ex. *B.M.C. 20.* 152, 4 ..   ..   £24

5850   5851

5850 — Æ 23. *Obv.* Similar. R. City-goddess, turreted, stg. l., holding wreath and cornucopiae; ΑΔΕΛΦΩΝ / ΔΗΜΩΝ behind and before, monogram in field to l. *B.M.C. 20.* 152,
11 ..   ..   £20

5851 — Æ 20. Laur. hd. of Zeus r. R. ΑΔΕΛΦΩΝ / ΔΗΜΩΝ above and beneath thunderbolt;
in field above, εξρ (=year 165) and monogram; another monogram below; all within
laurel-wreath. *B.M.C. 20.* 152, 6 ..   ..   £15

5852 — Æ 18. Hd. of Apollo r., bow and quiver at shoulder. ℞. ΑΛΕΛΦΩΝ / ΛΗΜΩΝ either side of tripod; ΔΞΡ (=year 164) in field to r., two monograms to l.; all within laurel-wreath. *B.M.C. 20.* 151, 2 .. .. £13

5853   5854

5853 **Antiocheia** (one of the most celebrated cities of Antiquity, Antiocheia on the Orontes was founded by Seleukos I in 300 B.C. It was the royal capital of Seleukid Syria and in the 1st century B.C. became the capital of the Roman province of Syria). 1st cent. B.C. Æ 20. Laur. hd. of Zeus r. ℞. Zeus enthroned l., holding Nike and sceptre; ΑΝΤΙΟΧΕΩΝ / ΤΗΣ behind, ΜΗΤΡΟΠΟΛΕΩΣ before; Ε in field to l., ΑΚΣ (=year 221 of the Seleukid era =92/91 B.C.) in ex. *B.M.C. 20.* 153, 12 .. .. £8

Specimens of this type published in the B.M. Catalogue range in date from year 221 to 236 (=77/6 B.C.)

5854 — Æ 18. Veiled and turreted hd. of Tyche r. ℞. ΑΝΤΙΟΧΕΩΝ / ΤΗΣ — ΜΗΤΡΟΠΟΛΕΩΣ either side of tripod; Α and star in field to l., ΕΚΣ (=year 225) in ex. *B.M.C. 20.* 153, 19 £9

5855 — Æ 23. Laur. hd. of Zeus r. ℞. Zeus enthroned l., holding Nike and sceptre; ΑΝΤΙΟΧΕΩΝ ΤΗΣ / ΜΗΤΡΟΠΟΛΕΩΣ behind, ΙΕΡΑΣ ΚΑΙ ΑΣΥΛΟΥ / ΑΥΤΟΝΟΜΟΥ before; head-dress of Isis in field to l.; in ex., Γ (=year 3 of the Caesarian era =47/6 B.C.); all within laurel-wreath. *B.M.C. 20.* 154, 26 .. .. £9

5856   5858

5856 — Æ 27. Similar, but on *rev.* the legend is ΑΝΤΙΟΧΕΩΝ / ΤΗΣ ΜΗΤΡΟ — ΠΟΛΕΩΣ ΚΑΙ / ΑΥΤΟΝΟΜΟΥ; monogram in field to l., thunderbolt above Zeus, Η (=year 8) in ex. *B.M.C. 20.* 155, 29-30 .. .. £12

5857 — Æ 23. Similar, but on *rev.* the legend is ΑΝΤΙΟΧΕΩΝ / ΤΗΣ — ΜΗΤΡΟΠΟΛΕΩΣ; cornucopiae in field to l., ΘΙ (=year 19) in ex. *B.M.C. 20.* 155, 34 .. .. .. £10

5858 — Æ 18. *Obv.* As 5854. ℞. ΑΝΤΙΟΧΕΩΝ / ΜΗΤΡΟΠΟΛΕΩΣ — ΑΥΤΟΝΟΜΟΥ either side of tripod; Ε — Κ (=year 25) in field; all within laurel-wreath. *B.M.C. 20.* 156, 37 £9

5859 — — Laur. hd. of Zeus r. ℞. ΑΝΤΙΟΧΕΩΝ / ΤΗΣ — ΜΗΤΡΟΠΟΛΕΩΣ either side of Tyche of Antioch stg. l., holding staff (?) and cornucopiae. *B.M.C. 20.* 156, 40 .. £13

Antiocheia *continued*

5860 — Æ 20. *Obv.* Similar. ℞. Zeus enthroned l., holding Nike and sceptre; ΑΝΤΙΟΧΕΩΝ / ΜΗΤΡΟΠΟΛΕΩΣ behind, ΑΥΤΟΝΟΜΟΥ before; star in field to l.; all within laurel-wreath. *B.M.C. 20.* 157, 48 ..   ..   £7

5861 — Æ 26. Similar, but on *rev.* the legend is ΑΝΤΙΟΧΕΩΝ / ΤΗΣ — ΜΗΤΡΟΠΟΛΕΩΣ / ΚΑΙ ΑΥΤΟΝΟΜΟΥ; caps of the Dioskouroi in field to l. and r.; thunderbolt above Zeus. *B.M.C. 20.* 157, 49 ..   ..   £10

5862 — — As last, but with legend ΑΝΤΙΟΧΕΩΝ / ΤΗΣ ΜΗΤΡΟΠΟΛ — ΕΩΣ ΤΗΣ ΙΕΡΑ / Σ ΚΑΙ ΑΣΥΛΟΥ. *B.M.C. 20.* 157, 50 ..   ..   £10

5863 — — As last, but with legend ΑΝΤΙΟΧΕΩΝ ΤΗΣ / ΜΗΤΡΟΠΟΛΕΩΣ — ΙΕΡΑΣ ΚΑΙ ΑΣΥ / ΚΑΙ ΑΥΤΟΝ, and with palm in *rev.* field to l. *B.M.C. 20.* 157, 51 ..   ..   ..   £10

5864   5867

5864 **Apameia** (about 50 miles south of Antiocheia, Apameia was named after Apame, wife of Seleukos I). 2nd cent. B.C. Æ 17. Veiled and turreted hd. of Tyche r. ℞. Warrior advancing l., hd. r., r. hand raised, holding spear and shield in l.; ΑΠΑΜΕΩΝ behind; in field to l., ΓΞΡ (=year 163 of the Seleukid era =150/149 B.C.). *B.M.C. 20.* 233, 1   £13

5865 — — Bearded hd. of Poseidon (?) r. ℞. Poseidon stg. l., holding patera and trident, dolphin at feet; ΑΠΑΜΕΩΝ behind. *B.M.C. 20.* 233, 2 ..   ..   ..   £13

5866 1st cent. B.C. Æ 18. Veiled hd. of Demeter r., wreathed with corn. ℞. Ear of corn between poppy-heads; ΑΠΑΜΕΩΝ / ΤΗΣ ΙΕΡΑΣ to r., ΚΑΙ ΑΣΥΛΟΥ to l.; in field, ΘΛΣ (=year 239 =74/3 B.C.) and ΣΕ. *B.M.C. 20.* 233, 4 ..   ..   ..   £12

5867 — Æ 22. Laur. hd. of Zeus r. ℞. Elephant stg. r.; ΑΠΑΜΕΩΝ / ΤΗΣ ΙΕΡΑΣ above, ΚΑΙ ΑΣΥΛΟΥ / ΜΝΑ in ex.; in field to r., ΓΜΣ (=year 243). *B.M.C. 20.* 234, 5 ..   £14

5868 — Æ 20. Bust of Athena r., wearing crested Corinthian helmet. ℞. Nike advancing l., holding wreath and palm; ΑΠΑΜΕΩΝ / ΤΗΣ ΙΕΡΑΣ behind, ΚΑΙ ΑΥΤΟΝΟΜΟΥ before; in field to l., ΣΟΣ (=year 276); in ex., ΜΗ. *B.M.C. 20.* 234, 7 ..   ..   ..   £13

5869 — Æ 22. Hd. of young Dionysos r., wreathed with ivy. ℞. ΑΠΑΜΕΩΝ / ΤΗΣ ΙΕΡΑΣ — ΚΑΙ ΑΣΥΛΟΥ either side of cornucopiae; in field to l., ΓΤ (=year 303); beneath, ΜΑ. *B.M.C. 20.* 234, 11 ..   ..   £15

5870 — Æ 19. Similar, but with thyrsos instead of cornucopiae on *rev.*, and date ΔΤ (=year 304). *B.M.C. 20.* 234, 12-13 ..   ..   £14

5871 Epiphaneia (an important town on the Orontes, Epiphaneia received its name from Antiochos IV Epiphanes of Syria. In earlier times it had been known as Hamath under which name it receives frequent mention in the Old Testament). 2nd cent. B.C. Æ 18. Veiled and turreted hd. of Tyche r. ℞. Zeus enthroned l., holding Nike and sceptre; ΕΠΙΦΑΝΕΩΝ / ΤΗΣ ΙΕΡΑΣ behind, ΚΑΙ ΑΣΥΛΟΥ before; monogram beneath seat. *B.M.C. 20.* 242, 1 .. .. £22

5872   5873

5872 — Æ 17. Bust of Athena r., in crested Corinthian helmet. ℞. Naked Apollo stg. facing, resting on column and holding branch(?); ΕΠΙΦΑΝΕΩΝ / ΤΗΣ ΙΕϤΑΣ to r., ΚΑΙ ΑΣΥΛΟΥ to l. *B.M.C. 20.* 242, 2 .. .. £24

5873 Gabala (a coastal city about 18 miles south of Laodikeia). 1st cent. B.C. Æ 14. Rad. hd. of Helios r. ℞. ΓΑΒΑΛΕΩΝ beneath forepart of galley l., with superstructure. *B.M.C. 20.* 243, 1 .. .. £30

5874   5877

5874 Laodikeia (named in honour of Laodike, mother of Seleukos I, the important coastal city of Laodikeia replaced an earlier settlement, called Ramitha. It possessed the finest harbour in Syria and its prosperity was increased by the fertility of the surrounding countryside). Before 47 B.C. Æ tetradrachm (*c.* 14·9 gm.). Turreted and veiled bust of Tyche r.; bead and reel border. ℞. Zeus enthroned l., holding Nike and sceptre; ΛΑΟΔΙΚΕΩΝ / ΤΗΣ ΙΕΡΑΣ ΚΑΙ ΑΥΤΟΝΟΜΟΥ before; monogram beneath to l., ΣΕ in ex.; all within laurel-wreath. *B.M.C. 20.* 247, 6 .. .. £250

5875 After 47 B.C. Æ tetradrachm (*c.* 13·7 gm.). Similar, but on *rev.* the legend is ΙΟΥΛΙΕΩΝ / ΤΩΝ ΚΑΙ — ΛΑΟΔΙΚΕΩΝ; Λ and ΔΙ in field to l., ΘΕ beneath seat, and ΓΛ in ex. *B.M.C. 20.* 248, 8 .. .. £275

The inscription ΙΟΥΛΙΕΩΝ dates from the time of Julius Caesar's visit to Syria in 47 B.C. when he conferred honours on the principal cities of the province.

5876 *Bronze Coinage.* 2nd cent. B.C. Æ 18. Veiled and turreted hd. of Tyche r. ℞. Nike advancing l., holding wreath; ΛΑΟΔΙΚΕΩΝ / ΤΩΝ ΠΡΟΣ behind, ΘΑΛΑΣΣΗΙ before; א in field to l. *B.M.C. 20.* 247, 1-2 .. .. £13

5877 Before 47 B.C. Æ 24. Laur. hd. of Zeus r. ℞. ΛΑΟΔΙΚΕΩΝ / ΙΕΡΑΣ ΚΑΙ — ΑΥΤΟΝΟΜΟΥ either side of tripod-lebes; Β in field to l., ΕΙ in ex. *B.M.C. 20.* 248, 10 .. .. £15

5878   5879

Laodikeia *continued*

5878 — Æ 20. Rad. hd. of Helios r. ℞. Artemis stg. l., holding spear and bow; ΛΑΟΔΙΚΕ / ΤΗΣ ΙΕΡΑΣ behind, ΚΑΙ ΑΥΤΟΝΟΜ before; monogram in field to l. *B.M.C. 20.* 248, 12 £15

5879 After 47 B.C. Æ 22. Veiled and turreted hd. of Tyche r. ℞. Tyche stg. l., holding rudder and cornucopiae; ΙΟΥΛΙΕΩΝ / ΤΩΝ ΚΑΙ behind, ΛΑΟΔΙΚΕΩΝ before; ΔΜ (=44?) in field to l., ΖΜ in ex. *B.M.C. 20.* 249, 17 ..   ..   £12

5880 — — Tyche stg. l., holding rudder and cornucopiae; bead and reel border. ℞. Nike advancing l., holding wreath and akrostolion; ΙΟΥΛΙΕΩΝ / ΤΩΝ ΚΑΙ behind, ΛΑΟΔΙΚΕΩΝ before; Ε in field to l. *B.M.C. 20.* 249, 20   ..   ..   £16

5881 — Æ 20. Hd. of young Dionysos l., wreathed with ivy, thyrsos before. ℞. ΙΟΥΛΙΕΩΝ — ΤΩΝ ΚΑΙ ΛΑΟ / ΔΙΚΕΩΝ either side of pharos (lighthouse) surmounted by statue. *B.M.C. 20.* 250, 24 ..   ..   £35

5882 — Æ 18. Hd. of Artemis l., wearing stephane, quiver at shoulder. ℞. ΙΟΥΛΙΕΩΝ ΤΩΝ ΚΑΙ ΛΑΟΔΙΚΕΩΝ. Boar's hd. l. *B.M.C. 20.* 249, 21 ..   ..   £14

5883 — Æ 17. Laur. hd. of Zeus r. ℞. ΙΟΥΛΙΕΩΝ / ΤΩΝ ΚΑΙ — ΛΑΟΔΙΚΕΩΝ either side of tripod-lebes; ΝΗ in field to l., ΖΜ in ex. *B.M.C. 20.* 249, 13 ..   ..   ..   £11

5884   5886

5884 **Larissa** (called Sizara by the Syrians, Larissa was situated on the Orontes midway between Apameia and Epiphaneia). 1st cent. B.C. Æ 19. Laur. hd. of Zeus r. ℞. ΛΑΡΙΣΑΙΩΝ — ΤΗΣ ΙΕΡΑΣ either side of throne of Zeus, beneath which, monogram, Μ and ΙΚΣ (=year 227 of the Seleukid era =86/5 B.C.). *B.M.C. 20.* 264, 1 ..   £30

5885 **Rhosos** (on the gulf of Issos, north-west of Antiocheia, Rhosos was celebrated for its earthen-wares). 1st cent. B.C. Æ 20. Veiled and turreted hd. of Tyche r., palm over shoulder. ℞. Syrian divinity (Hadad?) stg. on pedestal between two recumbent bulls, holding thunderbolt and knife; caps of the Dioskouroi in field; ΡΟΣΕΩΝ / ΤΗΣ ΙΕΡΑΣ to r., ΚΑΙ / ΑΣΥΛΟΥ / ΑΥΤΟΝΟΜΟΥ to l. *Forrer/Weber* 7991 ..   ..   ..   £28

5886 — Æ 18. Laur. hd. of Zeus r. ℞. ΡΩΣΕΩΝ ΙΕΡΑΣ. Veiled and turreted bust of Tyche r. *B.M.C. 20.* 268, 1 ..   ..   £25

5887   5889

5887 Seleukeia (an important coastal city at the foot of Mt. Pieria, Seleukeia was founded by Seleukos I in 300 B.C., just a month before the foundation of nearby Antiocheia. The city was strongly fortified and possessed a fine harbour which also served the needs of Antiocheia). After 109/108 B.C. Æ *tetradrachm* (*c.* 14·9 gm.). Veiled and turreted bust of Tyche r.; bead and reel border. R. Thunderbolt, with fillet, on cushion placed on stool; above, ΣΕΛΕΥΚΕΩΝ / ΤΗΣ ΙΕΡΑΣ; beneath, ΚΑΙ / ΑΥΤΟΝΟΜΟΥ; between legs of stool, ΑΙ (=year 11=99/8 B.C.); in field to r., Γ; all within laurel-wreath. *B.M.C. 20.* 271, 18
£200

Seleukeia obtained its freedom from regal control in 109/08 *B.C.*

5888 — — Similar, but with ΖΙ (=year 17=93/2 B.C.) beneath stool on *rev.*, and Μ instead of Γ in field to r. *B.M.C. 20.* 271, 23 .. .. £200

5889 — Æ *drachm* (*c.* 3·5 gm.). *Obv.* Similar, but with border of dots. R. Winged thunderbolt; above, ΣΕΛΕΥΚΕΩΝ / ΤΗΣ ΙΕΡΑΣ; beneath, ΚΑΙ / ΑΥΤΟΝΟΜΟΥ; ΓΙ (=year 13=97/6 B.C.) in upper field, monogram in lower field to r.; all within laurel-wreath. *Forrer/Weber* 7996 .. .. £250

5890 *Bronze Coinage.* 2nd cent. B.C. Æ 23. Laur. hd. of Zeus r. R. Thunderbolt with large wings; ΣΕΛΕΥΚΕΩΝ above, monogram within circle beneath. *B.M.C. 20.* 269, 1
£15

5891 5892

5891 — Æ 22. Similar, but thunderbolt is without wings. *B.M.C. 20.* 269, 5 .. £14

5892 — Æ 20. *Obv.* Similar. R. Thunderbolt; above, ΣΕΛΕΥΚΕΩΝ / ΤΩΝ; beneath, ΕΜ ΠΙΕΡΙΑΙ, monogram and SΞP (=year 166 of the Seleukid era =147/6 B.C.); all within laurel-wreath. *B.M.C. 20.* 270, 11 .. .. £12

5893 — Æ 17. Hd. of Apollo r., quiver at neck. R. ΣΕΛΕΥΚΕΩΝ / ΤΩΝ — ΕΜ ΠΙΕΡΙΑΙ either side of tripod; monogram in field; all within laurel-wreath. *B.M.C. 20.* 270, 14
£13

5894 After 109/108 B.C. Æ 19. Laur. hd. of Zeus r. R. Thunderbolt; above, ΣΕΛΕΥΚΕΩΝ / ΤΗΣ ΙΕΡΑΣ; beneath, ΚΑΙ / ΑΥΤΟΝΟΜΟΥ; in field to r., Α (=year 1=109/08 B.C. ?). *B.M.C. 20.* 270, 15 .. .. £12

5895 — Æ 20. Similar to 5887, but with border of dots on *obv.*; on *rev.* ΘΚ (=year 29=81/80 B.C.) beneath stool, and Ν in field to r. *B.M.C. 20.* 271, 26 .. .. .. £12

5896 COELE-SYRIA (a district of southern Syria, bounded by Phoenicia in the west and Palestine to the south). **Chalkis** (situated at the foot of Mt. Antilibanon, Chalkis was, in the 1st cent. B.C., the centre of a small kingdom). Ptolemy, *c.* 85-40 B.C. Æ 22. Laur. hd. of Zeus r. R. Eagle flying r.; beneath, ΠΤΟΛΕΜΑΙΟΥ / ΤΕΤ. ΑΡΧ. *B.M.C. 20.* 279, 2 .. .. £30

5897   5898

Chalkis *continued*

5897 — Æ 19. *Obv.* Similar. ℞. ΠΤΟΛΕΜΑΙΟΥ ΤΕΤΡΑΡΧΟΥ ΚΑΙ ΑΡΧΙΙΕΡ. Two warriors stg. face to face, each holding spear; all within laurel-wreath. *B.M.C. 20.* 279-80, 3-4
£25

5898 Lysanias, 40-36 B.C. (the son of Ptolemy; he was put to death by Mark Antony who gave the kingdom of Chalkis to Cleopatra of Egypt). Æ 19. Diad. hd. of Lysanias r., ΠΤΟ monogram before. ℞. ΛΥΣΑΝΙΟΥ ΤΕΤΡΑΡΧΟΥ ΚΑΙ ΑΡΧΙΕΡΕΩΣ. Athena stg. l., holding Nike, spear and shield; ΦΛ monogram in field to r. *B.M.C. 20.* 280, 6 .. £100

5899 Zenodoros, 30-20 B.C. (following the death of Cleopatra, Zenodoros, son of Lysanias, was allowed to return to his father's kingdom. In 24 B.C. he lost part of his dominions when Augustus handed them over to Herod the Great). Æ 20. NE KAI. Bare hd. of Octavian r.; behind, L ΖΠ (=year 87 of an uncertain era). ℞. ΖΗΝΟΔΩΡΟΥ ΤΕΤΡΑΡΧΟΥ ΚΑΙ ΑΡΧΙΕΡΕΩΣ. Bare hd. of Zenodoros l. *B.M.C. 20.* 281, 7 .. .. £125

5900 **Damaskos** (situated on the river Chrysoroas, Damaskos was a city of great antiquity and receives mention in the Book of Genesis—xiv. 15. It fell into the hands of Alexander the Great in 333 B.C.). Early 3rd cent. B.C. Æ *tetradrachm* (*c.* 17 gm.) of the type of Alexander. Hd. of young Herakles r., clad in lion's skin. ℞. Zeus enthroned l., holding eagle and sceptre, ΑΛΕΞΑΝΔΡΟΥ behind; in field to l., forepart of ram r.; beneath throne, ΔΑ. *Müller (Numismatique d'Alexandre le Grand)* 1338 .. .. £140

5900A 1st cent. B.C. Æ 17. Bust of young Dionysos (?) l. ℞. Cornucopiae between cista and ear of corn; ΔΑΜΑC to l., ΖΟC (=year 277 of the Seleukid era =36/5 B.C.) to r. *B.M.C. 20.* 282, 1 .. .. £18

5901 — Æ 20 of Cleopatra VII, queen of Egypt. Her diad. bust r. ℞. ΔΑΜΑΣΚΗΝΩΝ. Tyche of Damaskos seated l. on rock, her r. arm extended, holding cornucopiae in l.; at her feet, river-god Chrysoroas swimming; in field to l., ΛΙΙΣ (=year 280=33/2 B.C.) and aphlaston; all within wreath. *Svoronos (Ta nomismata ton kratous ton Ptolemaion)* 1893
£150

5902   5903

5902 — Æ 26. Turreted hd. of Tyche r., Β behind. ℞. Tyche stg. l., holding rudder and cornucopiae; ΔΑΜΑΣΚΗ / ΝΩΝ to r., ΝΤ (=year 307 =6/5 B.C.) to l.; all within laurel-wreath. *B.M.C. 20.* 282, 2 .. .. £20

5903 Demetrias (the site of this city is not known, and it is possible that Damaskos temporarily bore the name Demetrias in honour of the Syrian king Demetrios III). *Circa* 95-85 B.C. Æ 20. Laur. hd. of Apollo r. R. Zeus (?) stg. l., holding sceptre; ΔΗΜΗΤΡΙ / ΕΩΝ to r., ΤΗΣ ΙΕΡ / ΑΣ to l.; all within laurel-wreath. *B.M.C. 20.* 289, 3-5 .. .. £20

5904 — Æ 17 Turreted hd. of Tyche r. R. Nike stg. l., holding wreath and palm; ΔΗΜΗ / ΤΡΙΕΩΝ to r., ΤΗΣ / ΙΕΡΑΣ to l. *B.M.C. 20.* 289, 2 .. .. £18

PHOENICIA

5905 Tyre (reputed to have been a colony of its rival city, Sidon, Tyre was one of the principal ports of the Phoenician coast and probably the first city in the area to issue its own coinage. It put up a stubborn resistance to the advance of Alexander the Great, in 332 B.C., but eventually fell after a famous siege. Despite this calamity it remained a place of great commercial importance in later Hellenistic and Roman times). *Circa* 450 B.C. Æ *dishekel* (*c.* 13·9 gm.). Dolphin leaping r. over waves; Phoenician legend = 'one-thirtieth' (of a mina) above. R. Owl stg. r., hd. facing, carrying crook and flail under l. wing; all within incuse square. *Kraay (Archaic and Classical Greek Coins) pl. 61, 1047 (Unique ?)*

5906   5909

5906 *Circa* 425 B.C. Æ *dishekel* (*c.* 13·9 gm.). Similar, but with murex shell beneath waves on *obv.*; and the *rev.* type is framed by an incuse impression following its contours. *B.M.C. 26.* 227, 1 .. .. £750

5907 — Æ ½ *shekel* (*c.* 3·4 gm.). As last, but the Phoenician legend on *obv.* = 'half of silver' (*i.e.* half-shekel). *Forrer/Weber* 8082 .. .. £500

5908 — Æ ¹⁄₁₂ *shekel* (*c.* 0·6 gm.). As 5906, but without legend on *obv.* *B.M.C. 26.* 227, 3 £125

5909 — — Dolphin r., within cable border. R. Owl stg. r., hd. facing, carrying crook and flail under l. wing; all within cable border. *B.M.C. 26.* 228, 5-7 .. .. £85

5910 — — Dolphin l.; murex shell beneath. R. Owl stg. l., hd. facing, carrying crook and flail under r. wing; border of dots. *B.M.C. 26.* 228, 9 .. .. .. £90

5911   5912

5911 Late 5th cent. B.C. Æ *dishekel* (*c.* 12·5—13·3 gm.) of thick fabric. Melqarth (?) riding r. on hippocamp, holding bow; beneath, waves and dolphin r.; cable border. R. Owl stg. r., hd. facing, carrying crook and flail under l. wing; Phoenician letters (=*m b*) in field; all within cable border. *B.M.C. 26.* 229, 13 .. .. £350

5912 400-360 B.C. Æ *dishekel* (*c.* 13—13·6 gm.) of flat fabric. Similar, but without letters in *rev.* field. *B.M.C. 26.* 230, 19 .. .. £450

Tyre *continued*

5913 — Æ $\frac{1}{12}$ shekel (c. 0·6 gm.). Hippocamp r., dolphin r. beneath; all within cable border. R. As last. *B.M.C. 26.* 230, 24 .. .. £95

5914 360-332 B.C. Æ Attic *didrachm* (c. 8·5—8·8 gm.). Melqarth (?) riding r. on hippocamp, all as 5911. R. Owl stg. r., hd. facing, carrying crook and flail under l. wing; in field to r., Phoenician letter (=*m*) and numeral 'II' (=2); all within cable border. *B.M.C. 26.* 231, 26 .. .. £140

  The numerals appearing on these later 4th century issues probably represent the regnal dates of various Tyrian dynasts. Although usually described as Attic didrachms these coins seem a little too heavy for this denomination Their weight indicates a value of 1⅓ shekels, though this seems an unlikely denomination.

5915 — — Similar, but in *rev.* field to r., Phoenician letter 'o' and numeral 'IIO' (=12). *B.M.C. 26.* 232, 37 .. .. £130

  This series has dates extending to year 17 (IIIIIIIꓴ).

5916 — Æ $\frac{1}{15}$ shekel ? (c. 0·45 gm.). Hippocamp l., above waves; border of dots. R As 5910. *B.M.C. 26.* 233, 43.. .. .. £60

5917 After 126/5 B.C. (in the centuries following the Macedonian conquest Tyre was subject first to the Ptolemaic Kingdom of Egypt then, at the end of the 3rd cent., to the Seleukids of Syria. In 126/5 B.C. the city regained its autonomy and commenced a remarkable issue of silver and bronze coins extending well into the Roman Imperial period. The famous silver tetradrachms ('shekels') of this series have achieved some notoriety as the most likely coinage with which Judas was paid his 'thirty pieces of silver' for the betrayal of Christ). N *octadrachm* (c. 28·35 gm.). Veiled and turreted hd. of Tyche r. R. ΤΥΡΟΥ ΙΕΡΑΣ ΚΑΙ ΑΣΥΛΟΥ. Double cornucopiae; in field to l., ΓΚ (=year 23 of the autonomy of Tyre =104/3 B.C.); to r., monogram. *B.M.C. 26, pl.* XLIV, 4 .. .. (*Unique*)

5918 — Æ *tetradrachm* (c. 14—14·5 gm.). Laur. hd. of beardless Melqarth r., lion's skin knotted round neck. R. ΤΥΡΟΥ ΙΕΡΑΣ ΚΑΙ ΑΣΥΛΟΥ. Eagle stg. l. on beak of ship, carrying palm under r. wing; in field to l., club and ΛΔ (=year 4 =123/2 B.C.); between eagle's legs, ΜΥ monogram and Phoenician letter (=*a*). *B.M.C. 26.* 234, 49 .. .. £130

5919

5919 — — Similar, but on *rev.* club and EΞ (=year 65 =62/1 B.C.) in field to l., Phoenician letter (=*b*) between eagle's legs, and Z in field to r. *B.M.C. 26.* 245, 159 .. £120

5920 — — Similar, but on *rev.* club and PE (=year 105 =22/1 B.C.) in field to l., Phoenician letter (=*b*) between eagle's legs, and BN in field to r. *B.M.C. 26.* 247, 182 .. £110

This dated series continues beyond the middle of the first century A.D. The later specimens are on small, thick flans generally lacking some of the details of the reverse design.

5921 — Æ *didrachm* (*c.* 6·5—7·2 gm.). Similar to 5918, but on *rev.* club and BΛ (=year 32 =95/4 B.C.) in field to l., Phoenician letter (=*a*) between eagle's legs, and monogram in field to r. *B.M.C. 26.* 251, 220 .. .. £100

The didrachms, though not produced in the same quantities as the larger denomination, were also in issue for almost two centuries.

5922   5924

5922 *Bronze Coinage.* After 126/5 B.C. Æ 15. Veiled and turreted hd. of Tyche r., palm behind. R. Galley l., surmounted by Astarte stg. l., holding aplustre (?) and standard; in field to l., TYP monogram; to r., LΔI (=year 14 =113/12 B.C.); beneath, Phoenician legend ='of Tyre'. *B.M.C. 26.* 254, 248 .. .. £14

5923 — Æ 22. *Obv.* Similar. R. Palm-tree, dividing IEPA — AΣ; in upper field to l., LΘI (=year 19 =108/7 B.C.); to r., TYP monogram; across lower field, Phoenician legend ='of Tyre'. *B.M.C. 26.* 254, 249 .. .. £15

5924 — Æ 15. Hd. of Melqarth, as 5918. R. Palm-tree; in field to l., HK (=year 28 =99/8 B.C.); to r., TYP monogram and Ιl. *B.M.C. 26.* 254, 251 .. .. .. £13

5925 — Æ 24. *Obv.* As 5922. R. Galley l.; above, LEM (=year 45 =82/1 B.C.), TYP monogram, and IEP AΣ; beneath, Phoenician legend ='of Tyre'. *B.M.C. 26.* 255, 252 £12

5926 — Æ 20. Hd. of Melqarth, as 5918. R. Club, surmounted by TYP monogram; in field to l., L५ (=year 90 =37/6 B.C.); to r., Phoenician legend ='of Tyre'; all within oak-wreath. *B.M.C. 26.* 257, 268 .. .. £12

5927   5931

5927 Sidon (about 20 miles north of Tyre, Sidon was a city of great antiquity and in early times the chief seat of the maritime power of the Phoenicians. Commercially it was important as the centre of a purple-dyeing industry and for the manufacture of glass—the art of glass-blowing having been discovered at Sidon in the 1st cent. B.C.). *Circa* 425 B.C. Æ *tetrashekel* (*c.* 27·5 gm.). War-galley l., under full sail; row of shields along bulwarks, naval standard at stern; zig-zag waves beneath. R. Bearded deity, his r. hand raised, stg. in horsedrawn car driven slowly l. by charioteer; all within incuse square. B.M.C. 26. 139, 1   ..   ..   £1,750

5928 — Æ *shekel* (*c* 6·8 gm.). *Obv.* Similar. R. Bearded deity, quiver at shoulder, stg. r., shooting with bow; all within incuse square. B.M.C. 26. 139, 2   ..   ..   £900

5929 — Æ ⅛ *shekel* (*c.* 0·85 gm.). As last. B.M.C. 26. 140, 3   ..   ..   ..   £100

5930 Late 5th cent. B.C. Æ *tetrashekel* (*c.* 27·5 gm.). War-galley l., lying before the walls of Sidon, represented by five towers connected by curtain-walls; beneath, two lions r. and l., back to back. R. Similar to 5927, but the horses are galloping; all in dotted circle within circular incuse. B.M.C. 26. 141, 6   ..   ..   £1,250

5931 — Æ *shekel* (*c.* 6·8 gm.). *Obv.* Similar, but only four towers of the walls of Sidon are shown. R. Bearded deity stg. r., about to slay, with dagger held in r. hand, a lion which he holds erect before him; all within incuse square. B.M.C. 26. 141, 10   £650

5932 — — Similar, but with Phoenician letters '90' above the walls on *obv.*, and between the god and lion on *rev.* B.M.C. 26. 142, 11   ..   ..   £700

5933 — Æ ⅛ *shekel* (*c.* 0·8 gm.). *Obv.* Similar to 5930, but only three towers of the walls of Sidon are shown, and with only one lion (to l.) beneath. R. Similar to 5928. B.M.C. 26. 142, 14-16 ..   ..   £75

These early issues of the Sidonian mint often have incuse symbols stamped in the rev. field (e.g. goat, goat's head, head of Bes).

5934 4th cent. B.C. (before 333). Æ *tetrashekel* (*c.* 28 gm.) of King Bodashtart (?), *c.* 384-370 B.C. War-galley travelling l., propelled by row of oars; shields along bulwarks, standard at stern; beneath, two lines of zig-zag waves; above, Phoenician letter '9'. R. Bearded deity in horsedrawn car, as 5927; behind, the King of Sidon walking l., holding animal-headed sceptre; cable border within circular incuse. B.M.C. 26. 143-4, 17-24   ..   £400

5935 — Æ *shekel* (*c.* 6·5 gm.). Similar, but without King of Sidon behind car on *rev.* B.M.C. 26. 144, 26-7   ..   ..   £250

5936 — Æ ⅛ *shekel* (*c.* 0·8 gm.). *Obv.* Similar. R. Bearded deity about to slay lion, as 5931; between them, Phoenician letter 'o'; all within incuse square. *B.M.C. 26.* 147, 37-44
£45

5937 — Æ *tetrashekel* (*c.* 25·75 gm.). of King Strato I (Abdashtart), *c.* 370-358 B.C. War-galley, as 5934; beneath, four lines of zig-zag waves; above, III (=regnal year 3). R. Similar to 5934, but the King of Sidon holds vase with flowers as well as sceptre; in field above, Phoenician letters '90'. *B.M.C. 26.* 145, 29 .. .. £550

5938 — Æ *shekel* (*c.* 6·35 gm.). Similar, but without King of Sidon behind car on *rev.* *B.M.C. 26.* 145, 31 .. .. £275

5939 — Æ ½ *shekel* (*c.* 3·2 gm.). As last, but with two lines of zig-zag waves beneath galley on *obv.*, and in field above, III III (=regnal year 6). *B.M.C. 26.* 146, 33 .. .. £200

5940   5941

5940 — Æ ⅛ *shekel* (*c.* 0·65 gm.). *Obv.* As last, but with III⁻ (=regnal year 13) above galley. R. Bearded deity about to slay lion, as 5931; between them, Phoenician letters '90'; all within incuse square. *B.M.C. 26.* 146, 35 .. .. £50

5941 — Æ *tetrashekel* (*c.* 25·75 gm.) of King Tennes, *c.* 354-348 B.C. War-galley, as 5934; beneath, four lines of zig-zag waves; above, III (=regnal year 3). R. Similar to 5934, but the King of Sidon holds vase with flowers as well as sceptre; in field above, Phoenician letters (=*te*); border of dots. *B.M.C. 26.* 150, 64 .. .. £650

5942 — — of King Evagoras (?), *c.* 345-342 B.C. Similar, but with II (=regnal year 2) above galley on *obv.*, and with star above poop; on *rev.*, Phoenician letters 'oo' in field above. *B.M.C. 26.* 151, 65 .. .. £650

5943 — Æ ⅛ *shekel* (*c.* 0·65 gm.). *Obv.* As last, but no star and with only two lines of zig-zag waves beneath galley. R. Bearded deity about to slay lion, as 5931; between them, Phoenician letters 'oo'; all within incuse square. *B.M.C. 26.* 151, 67 .. £55

5944 — Æ *tetrashekel* (*c.* 25·75 gm.) of King Strato II, *c.* 342-333 B.C. War-galley, as 5934; beneath, four lines of zig-zag waves; above, I (=regnal year 1). R. As 5937, but with border of dots instead of cable border. *B.M.C. 26.* 152, 71 .. .. .. £425

5945 — Æ *shekel* (*c.* 6·2 gm.). Similar to 5938, but with III III II (=regnal year 8) above galley on *obv.*, and with dotted instead of cable borders. *Forrer/Weber* 8058 .. £250

Sidon *continued*

5946 — Æ *tetrashekel* (*c.* 25·75 gm.) of the Persian satrap Mazaios, as commander-in-chief in Phoenicia, *c.* 343-335 B.C. War-galley, as 5934; beneath, four lines of zig-zag waves; above, Phoenician numerals (=regnal year 21). ℞. Bearded deity in horsedrawn car followed by King of Sidon holding animal-headed sceptre and vase, as 5941; in field above, Phoenician legend (= *m z d y*). *B.M.C. 26.* 153, 79 .. .. .. £950

The regnal date on obverse refers to Artaxerxes III, King of Persia.

5947 — — Similar, but with Phoenician numerals (=regnal year 3) above galley on *obv.*, and Phoenician legend (=*m z d z*) on *rev.* *B.M.C. 26.* 154, 82. .. .. £900

The regnal date in this case referes to Darius III.

5948 — Æ ⅛ *shekel* (*c.* 0·65 gm.). *Obv.* Similar, but with two lines of zig-zag waves beneath galley, and III III III⁻ (=regnal year 19 of Artaxerxes) above. ℞. Bearded deity about to slay lion, as 5931; between them, Phoenician legend (=*m z*); all within incuse square. *B.M.C. 26.* 154, 84 .. .. £70

For other issues of Mazaios see under Tarsos (nos. 5649-52) and Babylon (no. 6139).

5949 3rd cent. B.C. Æ *tetradrachm* (*c.* 16·75 gm.), restoring the types of Alexander the Great. Hd. of young Herakles r., clad in lion's skin. ℞. ΒΑΣΙΛΕΩΣ ΑΛΕΞΑΝΔΡΟΥ. Zeus enthroned l., holding eagle and sceptre; in field to l., ΣΙ and Α; beneath throne, two monograms. *Müller* (*Numismatique d'Alexandre le Grand*) 1421 .. .. £150

5950 After 111 B.C. (in which year Sidon became independent of Seleukid rule). Æ *tetra-drachm* (*c.* 13·5—14·25 gm.). Veiled, turreted and dr. bust of Tyche r. ℞. ΣΙΔΩΝΙΩΝ. Eagle stg. l. on beak of ship, carrying palm under r. wing; in field to l., ΛΕ (=year 5 =107/6 B.C.) and monogram. *B.M.C. 26.* 158, 100 .. .. £250

5951 — — Similar, but with *rev.* legend ΣΙΔΩΝΟΣ ΤΗΣ ΙΕΡΑΣ ΚΑΙ ΑΣΥΛΟΥ, and in field to l., ΛΛ (=year 30 =82/1 B.C.) and ΦΙ. *B.M.C. 26.* 158, 104 .. .. £225

5952 — — Similar, but with *rev.* legend ΣΙΔΩΝΙΩΝ ΤΗΣ ΙΕΡΑΣ ΚΑΙ ΑΣΥΛΟΥ; in field to l., Λ; to r., ΑΠ (=year 81 =31/30 B.C.) and monogram. *B.M.C. 26.* 159, 110 .. .. £225

5953 — Æ *didrachm* (*c.* 6—6·5 gm.). Similar to 5951, but in *rev.* field to l., ΛΘΝ (=year 59 =53/2 B.C.); to r., monogram. *B.M.C. 26.* 160, 111 .. .. £200

5954 — — Similar to 5952, but with monogram behind hd. on *obv.*, and in *rev.* field to l., ΣΤ; to r., ΛΓΞ (=year 66 =46/5 B.C.). *B.M.C. 26.* 160, 112 .. .. .. £200

5955   5957

5955 *Bronze Coinage.* 4th cent. B.C. Æ 18 of King Strato I (?), *c.* 370-358 B.C. War-galley travelling l. over two lines of waves. R. Bearded deity in horsedrawn car driven slowly l. by charioteer. *B.M.C. 26.* 148, 48 .. .. £20

5956 — Æ 15. *Obv.* Similar; above, III III III (=regnal year 9). R. Bearded deity in kneeling-running attitude r., holding spear and bow. *B.M.C. 26.* 149, 56 .. £16

5957 — Æ 14. Hd. of bearded deity r., wearing flat head-dress bound with diadem. R. War-galley travelling l.; above, I ⁻ (=regnal year 11). *B.M.C. 26.* 149, 60 .. £18

5958   5959

5958 *Circa* 174-150 B.C. Æ 18 (with bevelled edge). Turreted and dr. bust of Tyche r.; B behind. R. Rudder, placed horizontally; above and below, Phoenician legend in four lines ='belonging to (the city of) the Sidonians, the metropolis of Cambe, of Hippo, of Kition, of Tyre.' *B.M.C. 26.* 155, 87 .. .. £15

5959 — Æ 17 (with bevelled edge). *Obv.* Similar, but without letter behind. R. Europa seated facing on bull charging l.; beneath, Phoenician legend ='belonging to (the city of) the Sidonians.' *B.M.C. 26.* 156, 93 .. .. £14

5960 — Æ 14 (with bevelled edge). *Obv.* As last. R. ΣΙΔΩ above prow of galley l. *B.M.C. 26.* 157, 98 .. .. £9

5961 — Æ 13 (with bevelled edge). — R. Σ — I either side of aplustre. *B.M.C. 26.* 157, 97 £10

5962 After 111 B.C. Æ 23. Veiled, turreted and dr. bust of Tyche r.; B behind. R. War-galley l.; above, ΛΑΓ (=year 33 of the autonomy of Sidon =79/8 B.C.) and ΣΙΔΩΝΙΩΝ; beneath, Phoenician legend ='belonging to (the city of) the Sidonians'. *B.M.C. 26.* 162, 124 .. .. £12

5963 — Æ 19. *Obv.* As last. R. Astarte stg. l. on prow, holding aplustre and standard; before, ΣΙΔΩΝΙΩΝ; behind, Phoenician legend, as last; in field to r., ΛΕ (=year 5 =107/6 B.C.). *B.M.C. 26.* 163, 128 .. .. £11

5964 — Æ 20. *Obv.* Similar to 5962, but with MEN behind. R. Astarte stg. l. on war-galley, holding tiller and standard; in field to l., ΛΕΚ (=year 25 =87/6 B.C.); beneath, ΣΙΔΩΝΙΩΝ and Phoenician legend, as 5962. *B.M.C. 26.* 163, 130 .. .. .. £10

Sidon *continued*

5965 — Æ 22.   Jugate busts r. of Tyche, veiled and turreted, and Zeus; behind, monogram.
R. War-galley l.; above, ΛΕΑ (=year 35 =77/6 B.C.) / ΣΙΔΩΝΟΣ / ΘΕΑΣ; beneath, Phoenician
legend, as 5962.   *B.M.C. 26.* 165, 140   ..   ..   £15

5966 — Æ 26.   Laur. hd. of Zeus r.   R. Europa seated facing on bull charging l.; above, ΛΜ
(=year 40 =72/1 B.C.); beneath, ΣΙΔΩΝΙΩΝ and Phoenician legend, as 5962.   *B.M.C. 26.*
166, 143   ..   ..   £14

5967 — Æ 20.   Hd. of young Dionysos r., wreathed with ivy; Λ (?) behind.   R. Cista behind
which, thyrsos; across field, ΛΗ — Ξ (=year 68 =44/3 B.C.); beneath, ΣΙΔΩΝΟΣ and Phoenician legend, as 5962; all within ivy-wreath.   *B.M.C. 26.* 167, 149   ..   ..   £14

5968   5971

5968 **Arados** (an important city of northern Phoenicia, Arados itself occupied an island but it
controlled an extensive area on the mainland).   Late 5th cent. B.C.   Æ *third-stater* (*c.*
3·5 gm.).   Merman r., holding dolphin in each hand; above, Phoenician letters (=*m a*).
R. Galley r., row of shields along bulwarks; beneath, marine creature (hippocamp ?) r.; all
in dotted square within incuse square.   *B.M.C. 26.* 3, 7   ..   ..   ..   £200

5969 — Æ *sixth-stater* (*c.* 1·6 gm.).   Similar.   *B.M.C. 26.* 3, 11   ..   ..   ..   £125

5970 — Æ *twelfth* (*c.* 0·7 gm.).   Half-length figure of merman facing, holding dolphin in
each hand; Phoenician letters (=*m a*) in upper field.   R. Prow of galley r.; beneath,
dolphin r.; all in dotted square within incuse square.   *B.M.C. 26.* 3-4, 12-16..   £150

5971 *Circa* 400-350 B.C.   Æ *stater* (*c.* 10·6 gm.).   Laur. hd. of bearded deity r.   R. Galley r.,
on three lines of waves; above, Phoenician letters (=*m a*); beneath, incuse crescent; traces
of incuse square enclosing the type.   *B.M.C. 26.* 4-5, 18-26   ..   ..   ..   £175

5972 — Æ *third-stater* (*c.* 3·5 gm.).   Similar.   *B.M.C. 26.* 5-6, 27-36   ..   ..   £85

5973   5977

5973 — Æ *twelfth* (*c.* 0·8 gm.).   Similar, but only two lines of waves beneath galley on *rev.*
B.M.C. 26. 7-8, 45-53   ..   ..   £40

5974 — Æ *forty-eighth* (*c.* 0·15 gm.).   Male hd. r., with pointed beard.   R. Prow of galley r.;
beneath, dolphin r.; all within incuse square.   *B.M.C. 26.* 11, 69   ..   ..   £45

5975 — Æ *ninety-sixth* (*c.* 0·08 gm.).   *Obv.* Similar.   R. Tortoise, within incuse square.
B.M.C. 26. 12, 78   ..   ..   £50

5976 — — — Ꭱ. Hd. of Bes(?) facing, within incuse square. *B.M.C. 26.* 12, 79   £65

5977 350-332 B.C. Ꭱ *stater* (*c.* 10·6 gm.) of King Gerostratos(?). Similar to 5971, but with
numeral ᴵᴵᴵᴧ (=regnal year 13) in addition to the Phoenician letters above galley on *rev.*
B.M.C. 26. 11, 67 ..   ..   £150

5978 — — Similar, but with Phoenician letter (=s) instead of numeral. *B.M.C. 26.* 10,
59-60 ..   ..   £150

5979   5983   5986

5979 — Ꭱ *third-stater* (*c.* 3·4 gm.). Similar, but with o / z instead of Phoenician letter.
B.M.C. 26. 10, 64 ..   ..   £100

5980 — Ꭱ *twelfth* (*c.* 0·65 gm.). Similar to 5973, but with Phoenician letter (=p) in addition
to the other letters above galley on *rev.* *B.M.C. 26.* 10, 65 ..   ..   ..   £50

5981 1st half of 3rd cent. B.C. Ꭱ *tetrobol* (*c.* 2·7 gm.). Beardless male hd. r., laur. Ꭱ.
Prow of galley l.; above, Phoenician letters (=*m a*). *B.M.C. 26.*, *pl.* XXXVIII, 4
£250

5982 — — Laur. hd. of Zeus r. Ꭱ. Prow of galley l., with statue of fighting Athena as
figurehead; above, A͡P. *B.M.C. 26.* 13, 86 ..   ..   £175

5983 — Ꭱ *hemidrachm* (*c.* 1·8 gm.). Turreted hd. of Tyche r. Ꭱ. As last, but without figurehead. *B.M.C. 26.* 13, 87 ..   ..   £150

5984 After 259 B.C. (in which year Arados regained its freedom under Antiochos II). Ꭱ
tetradrachm (*c.* 17 gm.), restoring the types of Alexander the Great. Hd. of young
Herakles r., clad in lion's skin. Ꭱ. Zeus enthroned l., holding eagle and sceptre, ΑΛΕΞΑΝΔ-
POY behind; in field to l., palm-tree; beneath seat, A͡P; in ex., Phoenician date numeral
(=year 21 =239/8 B.C.). *Müller* (*Numismatique d'Alexandre le Grand*) 1381..   £150

5985 — — Similar, but in ex. Greek numeral ΞΑ (=year 61 =199/8 B.C.). *Müller* 1388
£175

5986 — Ꭱ *tetrobol* (*c.* 2·55 gm.). Similar to 5982, but with Phoenician date numeral (=year
27 =233/2 B.C.) beneath prow on *rev.* *B.M.C. 26.* 14, 93 ..   ..   ..   £150

5987 — Ꭱ *hemidrachm* (*c.* 1·95 gm.). Similar to 5983, but with Phoenician date numeral
(=year 44 =216/15 B.C.) beneath prow on *rev.* *B.M.C. 26.* 14, 96 ..   ..   £125

5988   5989

5988 2nd cent. B.C. Ꭱ *tetradrachm* (*c.* 16·1 gm.). Hd. of Poseidon r., wreathed with marine
plant, trident behind neck. Ꭱ. Zeus stg. l., holding thunderbolt and sceptre, palm-tree
at feet; behind, ΑΡΑΔΙΩΝ; in field to l., ιΝ / ΠϹ (=year 86 =174/3 B.C.). *B.M.C. 26.* 20,
146 ..   ..   £8,000

5989 — Ꭱ *drachm* (*c.* 4·1 gm.). Bee; in field to l., ρ (=year 100 =160/59 B.C.); to r., ΑΙ
monogram. Ꭱ. Stag stg. r., palm-tree in background; before, ΑΡΑΔΙΩΝ. *B.M.C. 26.*
21, 158 ..   ..   £75

Arados *continued*

5990 — — Similar, but in *obv.* field to l., MP (=year 140 =120/19 B.C.), to r., ЄN; beneath stag on *rev.*, Phoenician letter (=*a*). *B.M.C. 26.* 22, 169 .. .. .. £75

> This long series of Attic drachms, bearing dates from 174 to 110 B.C., would appear to be associated with a similar issue from Ephesos (see nos. 4387-8). Some form of monetary alliance between the two cities is perhaps indicated.

5991 2nd-1st cent. B.C. Æ *tetradrachm* (c. 15 gm.). Turreted, veiled and dr. bust of Tyche r. Ɍ. Nike stg. l., holding aplustre and palm, ΑΡΑΔΙΩΝ behind; in field to l., HKP (=year 128 =132/1 B.C.), Phoenician letter (=*g*) and ΔN; all in laurel-wreath. *B.M.C. 26.* 24, 180 £120

5992

5993

5992 — — Similar, but in *rev.* field to l., ΔΠΡ (=year 184 =76/5 B.C.), Phoenician letter (=*r*) and MΣ. *B.M.C. 26.* 31, 256-7 .. .. £100

> The dated coins of this series span almost a century, from 137 to 45 B.C.

5993 — Æ *tetrobol* (c. 2·4 gm.). Laur. hd. of Zeus r. Ɍ. Prow of galley l., with statue of fighting Athena as figurehead; above, ЄN; beneath, Phoenician date numeral (=year 130 =130/29 B.C.). *B.M.C. 26.* 38, 311 .. .. £90

5994 — Æ *hemidrachm* (c. 1·8 gm.). Turreted bust of Tyche r., palm-branch behind shoulder. Ɍ. Prow of galley l.; above, BC; beneath, NP (=year 150 =110/09 B.C.). *B.M.C. 26.* 39, 320-21 .. .. £80

5995

5996

5995 — Æ *diobol* (c. 1·2 gm.). Winged hd. of Medusa facing, serpents in hair. Ɍ. Aplustre; to l., ΘMP (=year 149 =111/10 B.C.); to r., Phoenician letter (=*g*) and BC. *B.M.C. 26.* 39, 322 .. .. £125

5996 *Bronze Coinage.* Mid-4th cent. B.C. Æ 14. Merman l., holding wreath and dolphin. Ɍ. Galley r., on two lines of waves; above, Phoenician letters (=*m a*). *B.M.C. 26.* 12, 83-5 £25

5997 1st half of 3rd cent. B.C. Æ 17. Turreted hd. of Tyche r. Ɍ. Prow of galley l., with statue of fighting Athena as figurehead; above, A͞P and club. *B.M.C. 26.* 13, 88 £13

5998 After 259 B.C. Æ 17. Similar, but without club above prow on *rev.*, and with Phoenician date numeral (=year 21 =239/8 B.C.) beneath. *B.M.C. 26.* 13, 91 .. £14

5999

6001

5999 — Æ 20. *Obv.* Similar. ℞. Prow of galley l.; above, A͞P between Phoenician letters (=*o r*); beneath, Phoenician date numeral (=year 45 =215/14 B.C.). *B.M.C. 26.* 15, 97 £14

6000 — Æ 17. *Obv.* As 5994. ℞. Stern of galley l.; above, A͞P between Phoenician letters (=*o t*); beneath, Phoenician date numeral (=year 74=186/5 B.C.). *B.M.C. 26.* 16, 103 .. .. £15

6001 2nd cent. B.C. Æ 17. Hd. of Zeus r. ℞. Triple-pointed ram of galley l.; above, Phoenician letters (=*a z*); beneath, Phoenician date numeral (=year 98 =162/1 B.C.). *B.M.C. 26.* 17, 111-12 .. .. £9

6002 — Æ 20. *Obv.* As 5994. ℞. Prow of galley l., with Athena figurehead, on which is Poseidon seated l., holding wreath and trident; above, Phoenician letters (=*a n*); beneath, Phoenician date numeral (=year 128 =132/1 B.C.) and letter (=*g*). *B.M.C. 26.* 37, 301-2 .. .. £11

6003 — Æ 14. *Obv.* Similar. ℞. Aplustre; to l., Phoenician letters (=*a n*); to r., Phoenician date numeral (= year 113 =147/6 B.C.). *B.M.C. 26.* 23, 175 .. .. .. £10

6004   6005

6004 2nd-1st cent. B.C. Æ 17. Conjoined hds. of Zeus and Hera r. ℞. Prow of galley l., with Athena figurehead; above, Phoenician letters (=*o n*); beneath, Phoenician date numeral (=year 133 =127/6 B.C.) and letter (=*r*). *B.M.C. 26.* 36, 298 .. £14

6005 — Æ 21. Veiled bust of Astarte r., wearing stephane. ℞. Humped bull galloping l.; above, BC / ΓC; beneath, ΡΞC (=year 166 =94/3 B.C.) and Phoenician letter (=*g*). *B.M.C. 26.* 40, 325-6 .. .. £12

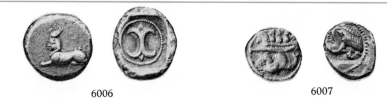

6006   6007

6006 **Byblos** (known also as **Gebal**. A coastal city of great antiquity, and a centre for the worship of Adonis, Byblos lay about 20 miles north of Berytos). Mid-5th cent. B.C. Æ *stater* (c. 9·4 gm.). Sphinx seated l., wearing the crown of Upper and Lower Egypt. ℞. Stylized lotus design within circle of dots; all within incuse square. *Kraay (Archaic and Classical Greek Coins)* pl. 61, 1051 .. .. £4,500

6007 Late 5th cent. B.C. Æ ½ *shekel* (c. 3·5 gm.). Galley l., containing three hoplites with round shields; beneath, hippocamp l. and murex shell. ℞. Vulture stg. l. on incuse ram; all in circle of dots within incuse square. *B.M.C. 26.* 94, 1 .. .. £450

6008 *Circa* 400 B.C. Æ *dishekel* (c. 14 gm.) of King Elpaal. *Obv.* Similar. ℞. Bull kneeling l., body incuse, hd. in relief, attacked by lion l. on his back; in field, Phoenician legend ='Elpaal, King of Gebal'. *Babelon (Bibliothèque Nationale Catalogue, ii)* pl. XXVI, 12 £750

6009 — Æ ½ *shekel* (c. 3·5 gm.) of King Elpaal. Similar. *B.M.C. 26.* 94, 2-3 .. £250

6010   6013

Byblos *continued*

6010 4th cent. B.C. (before *c.* 333). Æ ⅛ *shekel* (*c.* 0·75 gm.) of King Adramelek. Galley l., containing two hoplites with round shields; beneath, hippocamp l. and Phoenician letters (=*a k*). R. Bull kneeling l., attacked by lion l. on his back; in field, Phoenician legend ='Adramelek, King of Gebal'. *B.M.C. 26.* 96, 10   ..   ..   £75

6011 — Æ *dishekel* (*c.* 13·2 gm.) of King Azbaal. *Obv.* As 6007. R. Similar to last, but with Phoenician legend ='Azbaal, king of Gebal'. *B.M.C. 26.* 95, 4-5   ..   £750

6012 — Æ ⅛ *shekel* (*c.* 0·75 gm.) of King Azbaal. Similar to 6010, but with Phoenician letters (=*o z*) on *obv.*, and Phoenician legend, as last, on *rev.* *B.M.C. 26.* 95, 6-7   £75

6013 — Æ *dishekel* (*c.* 13·2 gm.) of King Ainel (mentioned, under the name of Enylos, by Arrian as being a contemporary of Alexander, *c.* 333 B.C.). *Obv.* As 6007. R. Similar to 6010, but with Phoenician legend ='Ainel, king of Gebal', and with *ankh* symbols in field beneath lion and bull. *Babelon (Bibliothèque Nationale Catalogue, ii) pl.* XXVI, 23   £750

6014 — Æ ⅛ *shekel* (*c* 0·75 gm.) of King Ainel. Similar to 6010, but without letters on *obv.*, and with Phoenician legend, as last, on *rev.* *B.M.C. 26.* 96, 9   ..   ..   £75

6015 1st cent. B.C. Æ 23. Turreted and veiled bust of Tyche r. R. Kronos, with three pairs of wings, stg. facing, hd. l., holding sceptre; Phoenician legend ='of Gebal the holy' on either side; above, ΛΑΛ ⊓ (=year 231 of the Seleukid era =82/1 B.C.). *B.M.C. 26.* 98, 17   ..   ..   £20

6016 — Æ 14. *Obv.* Similar. R. Harpokrates stg. l., r. hand raised to mouth, holding cornucopiae in l.; Phoenician legend, as last, on either side; BY monogram in field to r., Phoenician letter to l. *B.M.C. 26.* 97, 13   ..   ..   £16

6017   6019

6017 — Æ 15. Isis-Astarte stg. l., r. hand raised, holding sceptre in l. R. EI / ⊓I⊓ either side of crown of Isis. *B.M.C. 26.* 97, 14   ..   ..   £15

6018 **Berytos** (modern Beirut. This ancient Phoenician city, claiming Kronos as its founder, rose to commercial importance in Hellenistic times under the Ptolemies and, later, the Seleukids. The surrounding country produced wine and linen of the finest quality). 2nd cent. B.C. Æ 22. Turreted bust of Tyche r.; z behind, palm over shoulder. R. Poseidon, holding phiale and trident, stg. l. in car drawn by four hippocamps; around, on l., Phoenician legend ='of Laodikeia which is in Canaan'; in field to l., ΛΛ; to r., ΦΟΙ monogram. *B.M.C. 26.* 52, 5   ..   ..   £25

   Berytos bore the name Laodikeia at some time during the 2nd cent. B.C. in honour of a Seleukid queen, perhaps the mother of Antiochos IV.

6019 — — Similar, but without letter behind Tyche on *obv.*, and in *rev.* field, to r., BH and monogram of ΦΟΙ. *B.M.C. 26.* 51, 1   ..   ..   £15

6020   6022

6020 — Æ 17. Turreted bust of Tyche r. R. Astarte, holding aplustre, stg. l. on prow of galley; before, Phoenician legend =‘of Berit’; behind, ΛΛ and monogram of ΦΟΙ. *B.M.C. 26.* 52, 6   ..   ..   £14

6021 1st cent. B.C. Æ 19. Turreted and veiled bust of Tyche r. R. Dolphin entwined round trident, between caps of the Dioskouroi; across field, BH — PY / TI — ΩN and L — K (=year 20 of the era of Berytos =61/60 B.C.). *B.M.C. 26.* 53, 13   ..   ..   £14

6022 — Æ 22. Laur. hd. of Poseidon r., trident behind neck. R. Poseidon in car drawn l. by four hippocamps; across field, BHPY — TI; above LΓN (=year 53 =28/7 B.C.). *B.M.C. 26.* 54-5, 17-22   ..   ..   £15

6023 — Æ 19. *Obv.* As 6021. R. Nike, holding wreath and palm, stg. r. on prow of galley; before, aplustre; behind, BHPYTIωN; above, LΓN, as last. *B.M.C. 26.* 55, 25 ..   £13

6024 **Karne** (situated within Aradian territory on the Phoenician mainland, Karne served as a port for the island city eight miles to the south). 3rd cent. B.C. Æ *tetradrachm* (*c.* 17 gm.), restoring the types of Alexander the Great. Hd. of young Herakles r., clad in lion’s skin. R. Zeus enthroned l., holding eagle and sceptre, ΑΛΕΞΑΝΔΡΟΥ behind; in field to l., KAP above palm-tree and cornucopiae; beneath throne, Phoenician letter (=*b*); in ex., Phoenician date numeral (=year 35 of the era of Arados =225/4 B.C.). *B.M.C. 26, pl.* XXXVIII, 15   ..   ..   £500

6025 — Æ *tetrobol* (*c.* 2·65 gm.). Laur. hd. of Zeus r. R. Prow of galley l., with statue of fighting Athena as figurehead; above, KAP; beneath, Phoenician date numeral (=year 34 =226/5 B.C.). *B.M.C. 26., pl.* XXXVIII, 16   ..   ..   £300

6026 2nd cent. B.C. Æ *tetrobol* (*c.* 2·75 gm.). *Obv.* Similar. R. Cornucopiae, dividing two Phoenician letters (=*q r*); in field to r., Phoenician date numeral (=year 72 =188/7 B.C.). *B.M.C. 26., pl.* XXXVIII, 17   ..   ..   £250

6027   6029

6027 *Bronze Coinage.* 3rd cent. B.C. Æ 18. Turreted hd. of Tyche r. R. Prow of galley l., with statue of fighting Athena as figurehead; above, cornucopiae and Phoenician letters (=*q r n*); to r., Phoenician letter (=*r*); beneath, Phoenician date numeral (=year 37 =223/2 B.C.). *B.M.C. 26.* 111, 2 ..   ..   £16

6028 — Æ 20. *Obv.* Similar. R. Asklepios-Eshmun stg. r., holding serpent-staff; to r., column surmounted by Nike l.; in field to r., Phoenician letters (=*q r n*); to l., Phoenician date numeral (=year 39 =221/20 B.C.) and letter (=*g*). *B.M.C. 26.* 111, 3 ..   £18

6029 2nd cent. B.C. Æ 15. Turreted bust of Tyche r., wearing stephane. R. Cornucopiae; in field to l., Phoenician letters (=*q r n* and *g*); to r., Phoenician date numeral (=year 123 =137/6 B.C.) and letters (=*o q r*). *B.M.C. 26.* 112, 6 ..   ..   ..   £14

6030 **Dora** (a strongly fortified city in the far south of the country, Dora was traditionally founded by Doros, son of Poseidon). 1st cent. B.C. Æ 20. Turreted and veiled hd. of Tyche r. R. Tyche stg. l., holding rudder and cornucopiae; in field to l., ΛΑ (=year 1 of the Pompeian era =64/3 B.C.); to r., ΔΩ. *B.M.C. 26.* 113, 1 ..   ..   ..   £20

6031 — Æ 15. *Obv.* Similar. R. Ear of corn; across field, L — A / Δ — Ω. *B.M.C. 26.* 113, 2   £18

6032 **Marathos** (in the far north of Phoenicia, Marathos was a close neighbour and arch-rival of the island state of Arados. The Aradians eventually succeeded in destroying Marathos, *circa* 140 B.C., though the city appears to have been refounded as a colony of its conqueror). 3rd cent. B.C. Æ *tetradrachm* (*c.* 17 gm.), restoring the types of Alexander the Great. Hd. of young Herakles r., clad in lion's skin. Ŗ. Zeus enthroned l., holding eagle and sceptre, ΑΛΕΞΑΝΔΡΟΥ behind; in field to l., palm-tree and monogram of ΜΑΡΑΘ; in ex., Phoenician date numeral (=year 30 of the era of Arados =230/29 B.C.). *B.M.C. 26., pl.* XXXIX, 1 .. .. £450

6033   6034

6033 — Æ *tetradrachm* (*c.* 16·7 gm.). Turreted hd. of Tyche r. Ŗ. Marathos seated l. on pile of shields, holding aplustre and branch; behind, ΜΑΡΑΘΗΝΩΝ; before, Phoenician date numeral (=year 33 =227/6 B.C.). *B.M.C. 26.* 119, 1 .. .. £2,500

6034 — Æ *tetrobol* (*c.* 2·33 gm.). Veiled female hd. r. Ŗ. Marathos stg. l., holding aplustre and resting on column; behind, ΜΑΡΑΘΗΝΩΝ; before, Phoenician date numeral (=year 34 =226/5 B.C.). *B.M.C. 26.* 119, 2 .. .. £375

The head on obverse appears to be regal and may represent Berenike II, wife of Ptolemy III. The weight seems to conform to the Ptolemaic standard.

6035 — Æ 18. *Obv.* Similar. Ŗ. Asklepios-Eshmun stg. r., holding serpent-staff; before, Phoenician letters (=*m r th*); behind, Phoenician date numeral (=year 33 =227/6 B.C.). *B.M.C. 26., pl.* XXXIX, 3 .. .. £20

6036 — Æ 14. Laur. hd. of Zeus r. Ŗ. Trophy, between Phoenician letters (on r.) and Phoenician date numeral (on l.), as last. *B.M.C. 26., pl.* XXXIX, 4 .. .. £16

6037 2nd cent. B.C. Æ 23. Similar to 6034, but on *rev.* Phoenician letters (=*m r th*) behind Marathos; before, Phoenician date numeral (=year 103 =157/6 B.C.); other Phoenician letters in field to r. and to l. *B.M.C. 26.* 121, 9 .. .. £15

6038   6041

6038 — Æ 20. Laur. and dr. bust of Ptolemy VI, as Hermes, r., caduceus at shoulder. Ŗ. Marathos stg. l., holding aplustre; behind, Phoenician letters (=*m r th*); before, Phoenician date numeral (=year 91 =169/8 B.C.); other Phoenician letters in field to r. and to l. *B.M.C. 26.* 123, 23 .. .. £24

6039 — Æ 14. *Obv.* As 6034. Ŗ. Prow of galley l.; above, Phoenician letters; beneath, Phoenician date numeral (=year 73 =187/6 B.C.). *B.M.C. 26.* 122, 18 .. £13

6040 — Æ 11. Turreted bust of Tyche r. Ŗ. Nike stg. l., holding wreath; before, Phoenician letters (=*m r th*); behind, Phoenician date numeral (=year 70 =190/89 B.C.); Phoenician letter (=*g*) in field to l. *B.M.C. 26.* 121, 14 .. .. £11

6041 — Æ 17. *Obv.* Similar, but with palm at shoulder. R. Similar to 6038, but Marathos rests on column, and with Phoenician date numeral (=year 104 =156/5 B.C.) before. *B.M.C. 26.* 124, 28 ..   ..   £9

6042 — Æ 20. Laur. hd. of Zeus r. R. Double cornucopiae; to r., Phoenician date numeral (=year 147 =113/12 B.C.); in field to l., Phoenician letters (=*m a b*); other Phoenician letters (=*b n*) across lower field. *B.M.C. 26.* 125, 37 ..   ..   £12

6043 **Orthosia** (a coastal town about 8 miles north-east of Tripolis). 1st cent. B.C. Æ 20. Turreted bust of Tyche r. R. Kronos (?), holding harpe, in car drawn r. by two winged panthers(?); above, ΛΔΙΣ (=year 214 of the Seleukid era =99/8 B.C.); across field, ο — ο; in ex., ΟΡΘΩΣΙΕΩΝ. *B.M.C. 26.* 126, 1 ..   ..   £25

6044 — Æ 15. *Obv.* Similar. R. Nike advancing l., holding wreath and palm; before, ΛΑ (=year 1 of the Actian era =31/30 B.C.) and ΟΡΘΩΣΙΕΩΝ. *B.M.C. 26.* 126, 2 ..   £21

6045 **Ptolemais-Ake** (at the northern end of the bay of Haifa, Ake was renamed Ptolemais in the early part of the 3rd cent. B.C., probably by Ptolemy II. From the time of Antiochos IV of Syria, 175-164 B.C., it bore the additional name of Antiocheia). 2nd cent. B.C. Æ 19. Turreted bust of Tyche r. R. Nike stg. l., holding long palm-branch; behind, ΑΝΤΙΟΧΕΩΝ; before, ΤΩΝ / ΕΝ ΠΤΟΛΕΜΑΙΔΙ; ΚΡ monogram in field to l. *B.M.C. 26.* 129, 8
£14

6046   6048

6046 — Æ 15. Conjoined heads of the Dioskouroi r., laur. R. Cornucopiae; to r., ΑΝΤΙΟΧ-ΕΩΝ / ΤΩΝ; to l., ΕΝ ΠΤΟΛΕΜΑΙΔΙ; monogram in field to l. *B.M.C. 26.* 128, 7 ..   £15

6047 — — Similar, but on *rev.* ΑΝΤΙΟΧΕΩΝ / ΕΝ ΠΤΟΛΕΜΑΙ to r. of cornucopiae, ΙΕΡΑΣ ΑΣΥΛΟΥ to l.; and with date ΖΠΡ (=year 187 of the Seleukid era =126/5 B.C.) in field to r. *B.M.C. 26.* 129, 10   ..   ..   £16

6048 1st cent. B.C. Æ 23. Laur. hd. of Zeus r. R. Tyche stg. l., holding rudder and aplustre in r. hand, cornucopiae and branch in l.; in field to r., ΠΤΟΛΕ / ΜΑΕΩΝ; to l., ΛΕ (=year 5 of the Caesarean era =44/3 B.C.) above ΑΣΥ; ΚΑ — Ε (?) across lower field. *B.M.C. 26.* 130, 12   ..   ..   £18

6049 **Tripolis** (founded jointly by the three principal cities of Phoenicia, Tyre, Sidon and Arados—hence its name—Tripolis was a coastal town midway between Arados and Byblos). After 112/111 B.C. (in which year Tripolis became independent of Seleukid regal control). Æ *tetradrachm* (*c.* 15·1 gm.). Conjoined busts of the Dioskouroi r., laur. and dr., each surmounted by star; fillet border. R. Tyche stg. l., holding rudder and cornucopiae; behind, ΤΡΙΠΟΛΙΤΩΝ / ΤΗΣ ΙΕΡΑΣ ΚΑΙ; before, ΑΥΤΟΝΟΜΟΥ and ΑΝ monogram; in ex., ΑΣ (=year 201 of the Seleukid era =112/11 B.C.); all in laurel-wreath. *B.M.C. 26.* 200, 2 ..   ..   £350

Tripolis *continued*

6050 — — Similar, but with H / I instead of monogram in *rev.* field to l.; and in ex., HI
(=year 18 of the era of Tripolitan autonomy =95/4 B.C.). *B.M.C. 26.* 201, 5 £350

6051 *Bronze Coinage.* 2nd cent. B.C. Æ 16. Veiled female hd. r. (Cleopatra I of Egypt ?).
R. Caps of the Dioskouroi; Phoenician letters (=*a r t*) in field; above, ΔKP (=year 124 of
the Seleukid era =189/8 B.C.). *B.M.C. 26.*, *pl.* XLIII, 9 .. .. .. £25

6052 — Æ 18. Turreted bust of Tyche r. R. TPIΠOΛITΩN. The Dioskouroi galloping r.,
side by side. *B.M.C. 26.* 200, 1 .. .. £18

6053   6057

6053 After 112/111 B.C. Æ 19. Turreted and veiled bust of Tyche r. R. Nemesis stg. r.,
holding cubit-rule (?) and drawing out the breast-fold of her robe; behind, TPIΠOΛITΩN;
before, LA / Σ (=year 201 of the Seleukid era =112/11 B.C.); all in laurel-wreath. *B.M.C.*
26. 201, 8 .. .. £15

6054 — — *Obv.* Similar. R. The Dioskouroi galloping r., side by side; beneath, LH (=year
8 of the era of Tripolitan autonomy =105/4 B.C.); in ex., TPIΠOΛITΩN. *B.M.C. 26.* 202,
12-13 .. .. £17

6055 — — *Obv.* Similar to 6049, but with dotted border. R. Tyche stg. l., holding rudder
and cornucopiae; behind, TPIΠOΛITΩN; in field to l., LΘ (=year 9 =104/3 B.C.). *B.M.C.*
26. 202, 14 .. .. £16

6056 — Æ 17. *Obv.* Similar to 6053, but with palm behind shoulder. R. Prow of galley r.,
surmounted by caps of the Dioskouroi; behind, LΘK (=year 29 =84/3 B.C.); beneath,
TPIΠOΛITΩN. *B.M.C. 26.* 203, 17 .. .. £14

6057 50/49 B.C. Æ 23. Diad. bust of Cleopatra VII of Egypt r. R. Nike, holding wreath
and palm, stg. r. on prow of galley; behind, TPIΠOΛITΩN; in field to r., star and LB (=year
2 of Cleopatra). *B.M.C. 26.* 203, 19 .. .. £150

PALESTINE

6058 **'PHILISTO-ARABIAN' COINAGE** (much of this distinctive series, issued in the
first half of the 4th century B.C., seems to have been produced at **Gaza;** though doubtless
other mints, as yet unidentified, were also involved. Many of the designs were derived
from Athenian prototypes, the products of the Athenian mint being well-known in the
area, especially in neighbouring Egypt). 400-350 B.C. Æ *tetradrachm* (*c.* 17·15 gm.).
Hd. of Athena r., wearing crested helmet ornamented with olive-leaves and scroll. R.
Owl facing, wings closed, between two olive-sprays; across lower field, Aramaic letters
(=the initials of Gaza); all within incuse square. *Boston Museum Catalogue* 2203
(*Unique* ?)

The obverse of this coin is indistinguishable in style from the regular Athenian issues of the
second half of the 5th cent. B.C.

6059   6061

6059 — Æ *drachm* (c. 3·6—4 gm.). Female hd. r., hair bound with fillet. ℞. Owl stg. facing, wings spread; in upper field, Aramaic letters ($=a\,n$); all within incuse square. *B.M.C. 27.* 177, 8-9   .. .. £750
> *This obverse type may be derived from the Aphrodite head on the coinage of Knidos.*

6060 — — Janiform hd., with bearded face to l. and female face to r. ℞. Owl stg. r., hd. facing, between two ears of corn; in field to r., the name of Gaza in Aramaic letters; all within incuse square. *B.M.C. 27.* 176, 1-2   .. .. £1,250
> *The Janiform head may be derived from the coinage of Lampsakos.*

6061 — — *Obv.* Similar. ℞. Battlemented city-walls, represented by two towers with connecting curtain; in foreground, owl stg. r., hd. facing; all within incuse square. *B.M.C. 27.* 176, 3   .. .. £1,500
> *The city-walls type is reminiscent of the late-5th century coinage of Sidon.*

6062   6064

6062 — — Male hd. r., of oriental aspect, with pointed beard. ℞. Forepart of prancing horse r.; above, Aramaic letters, as 6058; all in dotted square within incuse square. *B.M.C. 27.* 178, 14 ..   .. £2,000
> *The reverse type would seem to be inspired by the coinages of the Thessalian cities.*

6063 — — Humped bull kneeling l., attacked by lion r. on its back. ℞. Similar to last. *B.M.C. 27.* 178, 15   .. .. £1,750
> *The obverse type may derive from the coinage of Akanthos in Macedon.*

6064 — — Female hd. r., wearing fillet, hair in bun behind. ℞. Mound surmounted by battlemented city-walls, represented by three towers with connecting curtains; two palm-trees between the towers; all within incuse square. *B.M.C. 27.* 179, 21   .. £1,750

6065 — — Beardless male hd. r., with short hair. ℞. Lion stg. l. on ram's hd. l.; all in dotted square within incuse square. *B.M.C. 27.* 180, 24   .. .. £1,750

6066 — — Bearded hd. of king (?) r., diad. and with hair in ringlets. ℞. Arab seated on camel r., holding bow and spear; ɣ in field to r.; all within incuse square. *B.M.C. 72.* 180, 25   .. .. £2,000

Gaza *continued*

6067 — — Horse pacing r.; above, Aramaic letters (=*k y*); all in dotted square. ℞. Winged man-headed lion seated r.; all in dotted square within incuse square. *B.M.C. 27.* 180, 26 .. .. £1,750

6068   6071

6068 — — (*c.* 3·29 gm.). Male hd. r., bearded, wearing crested Corinthian-type helmet. ℞. Bearded deity seated r. on winged wheel, holding falcon on extended l. hand; above, Aramaic legend ='Yehud'; in field to r., bald-headed and bearded mask l.; all in linear square within incuse square. *B.M.C. 27.* 181, 29 .. .. (*Unique ?*)

> *This remarkable type has been interpreted as being a representation of the God of the Jews as visualized by the Persian rulers of Judaea.*

6069 — Æ *obol* (*c.* 0·65-0·75 gm.). *Obv.* Similar to 6059. ℞. Owl stg. r., hd. facing; olive-spray in upper field to l.; to r., Aramaic letters (=*a n*); all within incuse square. *B.M.C. 27.* 177, 4 .. .. £125

6070 — — Forepart of lion r. ℞. As 6062. *B.M.C. 27.* 179, 16 .. .. .. £175

6071 — — Female hd. three-quarter face to l. ℞. Hd. of Bes facing, with crown of feathers. *B.M.C. 27.* 182, 1-2 .. .. £250

6072 — Æ *hemiobol* (*c.* 0·35 gm.). Falcon, with spread wings, hd. r.; in upper field to r., Hebrew legend ='Yehud'. ℞. Lily. *Meshorer* (*Jewish Coins*) *pl. I, X* .. (*Unique*)

6073   6076

6073 **LATER CITY COINAGES.** **Askalon** (a Philistine city on the Mediterranean coast about 12 miles north of Gaza). Before 104 B.C. Æ *diobol* (*c.* 1·1 gm.). Diad. hd. of Aphrodite r. ℞. Dove stg. l.; ΑΣ above, monogram before. *B.M.C. 27.* 104, 1 £130

6074 — Æ *triobol* (*c.* 1·7 gm.). Turreted and veiled bust of Tyche r. ℞. Prow of galley l.; ΑΣ above, monogram beneath. *B.M.C. 27.* 105, 5-6 .. .. £110

6075 — — *Obv.* Similar. ℞. War-galley l., with row of oars; above, ΑΣ and ΛΒΣ (=year 202 of the Seleukid era =111/10 B.C.); beneath, ΙΕΡΑΣ. *B.M.C. 27.* 106, 14 .. £150

6076 After 104 B.C. (in which year Askalon became independent of Seleukid rule). Æ *tetradrachm* (*c.* 13 gm.). Diad. and dr. bust of Ptolemy XII of Egypt r. ℞. ΑΣΚΑΛΩΝΙΤΩΝ ΙΕΡΑΣ ΑΣΥΛΟΥ. Eagle stg. l. on thunderbolt, palm-branch under r. wing; in field to l., dove and ΛΜΑ (=year 41 of the era of Askalon =64/3 B.C.); Ω / Δ between eagle's legs. *B.M.C. 27.* 107, 18 .. .. £450

6077   6079

6077 — · — Diad. and dr. bust of Cleopatra VII of Egypt r. Ɍ. Similar to previous, but with dove and ΠΑ monogram in field to l., and LNϹ (=year 55 =50/49 B.C.) in field to r.; no letters between eagle's legs. *B.M.C. 27.* 108, 20 .. .. £2,500

6078 *Bronze Coinage.* Before 104 B.C. Æ 13. *Obv.* Similar to 6073. Ɍ. Dove stg. r.; Α — Σ in field. *B.M.C. 27.* 104, 3 .. .. £15

6079 — Æ 14. Similar to 6074, but without monogram on *rev. B.M.C. 27.* 105, 9 £13

6080 After 104 B.C. Æ 22. *Obv.* As 6074. Ɍ. War-galley l., with row of oars, dove l. on the deck; above, ΑⴴΚΑ / ΙΕΡΑⴴ; beneath, LΙΛ (=year 37 of the era of Askalon =68/7 B.C.). *B.M.C. 27.* 106, 15 .. .. £17

6081   6084

6081 — Æ 23. Bare hd. of Zeus (?) r. Ɍ. Eagle stg. l., palm-branch under r. wing; in field to l., dove and ΑΣ; to r., ΛΟ (=year 74 =31/30 B.C.). *B.M.C. 27.* 106, 16 £20

6082 — Æ 24. *Obv.* As 6074. Ɍ. Tyche stg. l., holding rudder and sceptre (?); in field to l., dove and Αⴴ; to r., ΘΟ (=year 79 =26/5 B.C.). *B.M.C. 27.* 107, 17 .. .. £18

6083 **Gaza** (situated several miles inland from the Mediterranean coastline, Gaza was an important Philistine city in the extreme south-west of Palestine. It was, and remains today, a place of great strategic importance standing in the path of invading armies from Egypt. Its 4th century coinage forms a significant part of the 'Philisto-Arabian' series, listed above). 2nd-1st cent. B.C. Æ 18. Turreted hd. of Tyche r. Ɍ. Zeus stg. l., holding wreath in raised r. hand; behind, ΔΗΜΟΥ CϹ̆; before, ΤΩΝ ϵΝ / ΓΑΖΗ C (=year 200 of the Seleukid era =113/12 B.C.). *B.M.C. 27.* 143, 4-5 .. .. .. £17

6084 — — Laur. hd. of Zeus r. Ɍ. City-goddess stg. l., holding phiale and cornucopiae, ΔΗΜΟΥ ΓΑΖΑΙΩΝ around; ΙΕΡ — ΑΣ across field; to l., Phoenician letter (=*m*); to r., LΙⴴ (=year 210 =103/2 B.C.). *B.M.C. 27.* 144, 6 .. .. £18

6085 — — — Ɍ. ΔΗΜΟΥ ΓΑΙΑΙΩΝ. Double cornucopiae, springing from branch with two leaves. *B.M.C. 27.* 143, 2.. .. .. £16

6086   6087

6086 **JEWISH COINAGE** (Judaea was a province of the Persian Empire until 332 B.C. when Alexander the Great made himself master of the area. Thereafter the Jews came under the rule of the Ptolemies of Egypt, during the 3rd cent. B.C., and the Seleukids of Syria from 198 B.C. With the weakening of Seleukid power in the second half of the 2nd century Judaea achieved a measure of independence under the first rulers of the Hasmonaean dynasty. Before the end of the century the Jews had won full autonomy from their former Greek rulers. **Alexander Jannaeus**, 103-76 B.C. (son of John Hyrcanus I, Alexander Jannaeus was the first king of the Hasmonaean dynasty to produce a coinage). Æ *prutah* (*c.* 15mm. diameter). Lily; around, Hebrew legend =‘Yehonatan the King’. Ɍ. ΒΑΣΙΛΕΩΣ ΑΛΕΞΑΝΔΡΟΥ around circle containing anchor. *Meshorer* (*Jewish Coins of the Second Temple Period*) 5. *B.M.C. 27.* 198, 1-8 .. .. £16

Alexander Jannaeus *continued*

6087 — — ΒΑΣΙΛΕΩΣ ΑΛΕΞΑΝΔΡΟΥ around anchor. ℞. Wheel with eight ray-like spokes between which Hebrew legend = 'Yehonatan the King'. *Meshorer 8*. *B.M.C. 27*. 207-9, 61-86 .. .. £14

6088 — — *Obv.* As *rev.* of 6086. ℞. Star of eight rays within dotted circle around which uncertain Hebrew (?) legend. *Meshorer 9*. *B.M.C. 27*. 210, 1 .. .. £15

6089 6092

6089 — — Hebrew legend = 'Yonatan (*sic*) the high priest and the community of the Jews' within wreath. ℞. Double cornucopiae, with pomegranate between the horns. *Meshorer 17*. *B.M.C. 27*. 202-3, 30-38 .. .. £12

These were normally overstruck on prutahs of the type of 6086.

6090 — — Similar, but the ruler's name is rendered as 'Yehonatan' instead of 'Yonatan' in the Hebrew legend. *Meshorer 12*. *B.M.C. 27*. 204-7, 39-60 .. .. .. £11

6091 — Æ *half-prutah* ? (*c.* 12 mm.). Palm-branch; around, Hebrew legend = 'Yehonatan the King'. ℞. Lily. *Meshorer 6*. *B.M.C. 27*. 199, 9-10 .. .. .. £75

6092 — — Similar to 6088, but struck on a small, irregular flan with the types carelessly engraved; often there is little or no trace of the legends. *Meshorer 10*. *B.M.C. 27*. 211, 15 .. .. £8

The miserable coins of this type have sometimes been identified with the "widow's mite" of the Biblical story—see Mark 12, 42.

6093 6094 6096

6093 **Judah Aristobulus II,** 67-64 B.C. (on the death of Alexander Jannaeus' widow and successor, Alexandra Salome, in 67 B.C. the throne was inherited by their son, John Hyrcanus. However, Judah Aristobulus, brother of Hyrcanus, seized power and ruled Judaea until deposed by Pompey in 64 B.C.). Æ *prutah* (*c.* 14 mm.). Hebrew legend = 'Yehudah, high priest, and the community of the Jews' within wreath. ℞. Double cornucopiae, with pomegranate between the horns. *Meshorer 28*. *B.M.C. 27*. 197, 1-3 £25

6094 **John Hyrcanus II,** 67 and 63-40 B.C. (Hyrcanus was restored to the high-priesthood by Pompey in 63 B.C., and from this time the authority of Rome began to be imposed on the Jewish nation. After a troubled reign Hyrcanus was captured by the Parthians in 40 B.C. and eventually executed by Herod ten years later). Æ *double-prutah* ? (*c.* 17 mm.). Double cornucopiae; around, Hebrew legend = 'Yehohanan the high priest, head of the community of the Jews'. ℞. Crested helmet r. *Meshorer 25*. *B.M.C. 27*. 188, 1 £125

6095 — Æ *prutah* (*c.* 14 mm.). Hebrew legend = 'Yehohanan the high priest and the community of the Jews' within wreath. ℞. Double cornucopiae, with pomegranate between the horns. *Meshorer 18*. *B.M.C. 27*. 190-4, 15-44 .. .. £10

6096 — — Similar, but with Greek letter 'A' above the Hebrew legend on *obv*. *Meshorer 19*. *B.M.C. 27*. 188-90, 2-14 .. .. £15

6097 — — Similar to 6095, but with ΠΑ monogram in lower field to l. on *rev*. *Meshorer 20* £25

6098 — — Similar to 6095, but the Hebrew legend on *obv.* reads 'Yehohanan the high priest, head of the community of the Jews'. *Meshorer 22.* *B.M.C. 27.* 194-5, 45-7.. £20

6099 — — As last, but with A in lower field to r. on *rev.* *Meshorer 23* .. £25

6100 6103

6100 — Æ *half-prutah*? (*c.* 11 mm.). Palm-branch; on either side, Hebrew legend ='Yehohanan the high priest and the community of the Jews'. R. Lily. *Meshorer 21.* *B.M.C.* *27.* 195-6, 48-56 .. .. £30

6101 — — Similar, but with A in field to l. on *rev.* *Meshorer 21A* £40

6102 — — Similar to 6100, but the Hebrew legend on *obv.* reads 'Yehohanan the high priest, head of the community of the Jews'. *Meshorer 24* £45

6103 **Mattathias Antigonos,** 40-37 B.C. (the last of the Hasmonaean rulers, Mattathias was the son of Judah Aristobulus II. He was made king of Judaea by the Parthians in 40 B.C. but his position was contested by the Roman nominee for the throne, Herod. In 37 B.C. he was captured and executed by Mark Antony, leaving Herod as undisputed ruler of the Jews). Æ *8-prutah*? (*c.* 14-16 gm., 23-26 mm.). Double cornucopiae; in field, Hebrew legend ='Mattityah the high priest and the community of the Jews'. R. ΒΑCΙΛΕΩC ΑΝΤΙΓΟΝΟΥ around ivy-wreath. *Meshorer 30.* *B.M.C. 27.* 212-16, 1-34 £75

6104 6107

6104 — Æ *4-prutah*? (*c.* 7-8 gm., 19-21 mm.). Cornucopiae; around, Hebrew legend = 'Mattityah the high priest'. R. Greek legend — ΒΑCΙΛΕΩC ΑΝΤΙΓΟΝΟΥ or abbreviated form — in two, three or four lines within wreath. *Meshorer 31.* *B.M.C. 27.* 216-18, 35-55 .. .. £50

6105 — Æ *prutah* (*c.* 14 mm.). Hebrew legend ='Mattityah' within wreath. R. Double cornucopiae, with ear of barley between the horns. *Meshorer 33.* *B.M.C. 27.* 219, 57-8 £30

6106 — — Similar, but with pomegranate instead of ear of barley on *rev.* *Meshorer 35.* *B.M.C. 27.* 219, 59 .. .. £40

6107 — — ΒΑΣΙΛΕΩΣ ΑΝΤΙΓΟΝΟΥ around the menorah (seven-branched candlestick). R. Showbread table; around, Hebrew legend ='Mattityah the high priest'. *Meshorer 36.* *B.M.C. 27.* 219, 56 .. .. £100

N.B. *Herod the Great, founder of the Herodian dynasty, was, for much of his reign, the contemporary of Rome's first emperor, Augustus. The dynasty survived until the end of the 1st century A.D. and its coinage will, therefore, be listed in a future catalogue covering the 'Greek Imperial' series and contemporary coinages.*

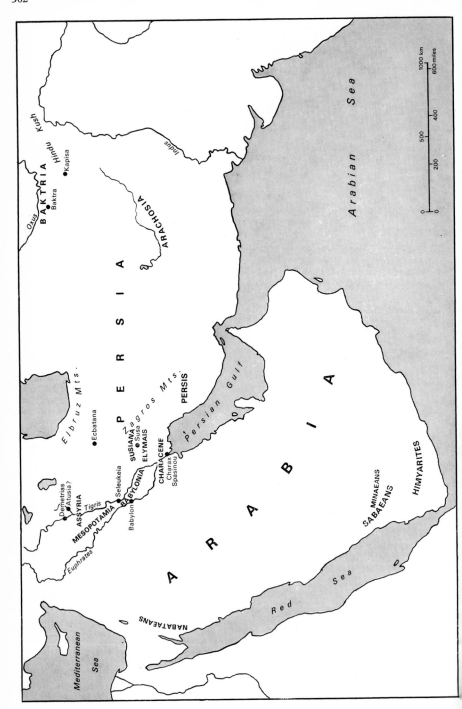

Arabian Sea

1000 km
600 miles

400

500

200

0

Hindu Kush

Indus

Oxus

Baktra BAKTRIA
●Kapisa

ARACHOSIA

P E R S I A

Elbruz Mts.

Persian Gulf

Zagros Mts.

PERSIS

A R A B I A

●Ecbatana

SUSIANA
●Susa
ELYMAIS

CHARACENE
Charax
Spasinou

Seleukeia
BABYLONIA

HIMYARITES

Demetrias
Atusia?
ASSYRIA
Tigris
MESOPOTAMIA
Babylon

Euphrates

MINAEANS
SABAEANS

NABATAEANS

Red Sea

Mediterranean Sea

ARABIA

6108 **KINGDOM OF NABATAEA** (the caravan-traders of northern Arabia, known as the Nabataeans, achieved great wealth through the transport of goods from southern Arabia to the Mediterranean coast. They remained independent of the Seleukid empire, but before the middle of the 1st century B.C. they had become subject to Roman overlordship. Their capital was the famous rock-hewn city of Petra). **Aretas III,** *c.* 87-62 B.C. (this energetic ruler captured Damaskos early in his reign, defeated the Jewish king Alexander Jannaeus, but was eventually compelled to leave Judaea by the Roman general Scaurus). Æ 20, struck at Damaskos. Diad. hd. of Aretas r. R. Turreted Nike stg. l., holding wreath and palm; behind, ΒΑΣΙΛΕΩΣ / ΑΡΕΤΟΥ; before, ΦΙΛΕΛΛΗΝΟΣ; ΑΡ in field to l. *B.M.C. 28.* 1, 1-2 ..   ..   £30

6109 — — *Obv.* Similar. R. City-goddess of Damaskos seated l. on rock, r. hand extended, holding cornucopiae in l.; river-god swimming at feet; legend behind and before, as last; ΑΡ in field to l. *B.M.C. 28.* 1-2, 3-6 ..   ..   £25

6110 **Obodas II,** *c.* 62-50 B.C. (son of Aretas III). Æ *didrachm* (*c.* 6·5 gm.). Diad. and dr. bust of Obodas r. R. Eagle stg. l., wings closed; Aramaic legend = 'King Obodas, King of Nabataea, year 3' around and across field. *B.M.C. 28.* 314, 1..   ..   £350

These silver issues appear to be modelled on the contemporary coinage of Tyre.

6111 **Malichus I,** *c.* 50-30 B.C. (son of Obodas II, he is mentioned in history as having given assistance to Julius Caesar in 47 B.C.). Æ *didrachm* (*c.* 6·5 gm.). Diad. hd. of Malichus r., hair in long curls. R. Eagle stg. l., wings closed; Aramaic legend ='King Malichus, King of Nabataea' around; Aramaic letters in field to l., ΙΚΗ to r. *B.M.C. 28.* 3, 1   £325

N.B. *The Nabataean kingdom survived until A.D. 106 when Trajan created the Roman province of Arabia. The issues subsequent to 30 B.C. (Obodas III—Rabbel II) will be listed in a future catalogue covering the 'Greek Imperial' series and contemporary coinages.*

6112   6116

6112 **SABAEANS AND HIMYARITES** (the relatively fertile lands of southern Arabia, bordering the Indian Ocean, were populated by powerful tribes foremost amongst which were the Sabaeans and, later, the Himyarites. The latter rose to pre-eminence about the middle of the 2nd century B.C. Trade with the Greek world, conducted mostly through the Mediterranean port of Gaza, made the ubiquitous Athenian tetradrachm familiar to the people of southern Arabia. It is scarcely surprising, therefore, that when they came to inaugurate a coinage of their own the types were, to begin with, closely copied from the 'owls'). 3rd-2nd cent. B.C. Æ *drachm* or *unit* (*c.* 5·3 gm.). Hd. of Athena r., wearing crested helmet ornamented with olive-leaves, etc.; on cheek, Sabaean letter (=*n*). R. Owl stg. r., hd. facing; olive-spray and crescent in upper field to l.; AΘE (carelessly engraved) before; traces of incuse square. *B.M.C. 28.* 45-6, 1-8 .. .. £125

    The weight of these units is not based on the Attic drachm but on the old Persian siglos.

6113 — Æ *half-unit* (*c.* 2·6 gm.). Similar, but with Γ on Athena's cheek on *obv.* *B.M.C. 28.* 46, 12-15 .. .. £85

6114 — Æ *quarter* (*c.* 1·3 gm.). Similar, but with X on Athena's cheek. *B.M.C. 28.* 47, 16-21 £65

6115 — Æ *eighth?* (*c.* 0·5 gm.). Similar, but with Σ on Athena's cheek. *B.M.C. 28.* 47, 22-3 £50

6116 2nd cent. B.C. Æ *drachm* or *unit* (*c.* 5·4 gm.). *Obv.* As 6112. R. Owl stg. r., hd. facing; olive-spray and crescent in upper field to l.; AΘE (carelessly engraved) before; Sabaean monogram in field to r. *B.M.C. 28.* 49, 41-3 .. .. £110

    Many different Sabaean letters and monograms have been recorded on the reverses of this series.

6117 — Æ *half-unit* (*c.* 2·6 gm.). *Obv.* As 6113. R. Similar to last. *B.M.C. 28.* 51, 63 £85

6118 — Æ *quarter* *c.* 1·3 gm.). *Obv.* As 6114. R. Similar to last. *B.M.C. 28.* 51, 66 £65

6119   6122

6119 Late 2nd cent. B.C. Æ *drachm* or *unit* (*c.* 5·4 gm.). *Obv.* As 6112. R. Owl stg. r., hd. facing; behind, monogram of Yanaf; above, uncertain Aramaic legend; before, AΘE (blundered) and Himyaritic signs. *B.M.C. 28.* 53, 73 .. .. £140

6120 — — Beardless male hd. r., with short curly hair. R. Owl stg. r., hd. facing, between two monograms. *B.M.C. 28.* 52, 70 .. .. £250

    This type, and the next, may have been issued by another tribe of Southern Arabia, the Katabanians.

6121 — Æ *third* (*c.* 1·78 gm.). *Obv.* Similar. R. Male hd. r., with short beard, between two monograms; below, mint name (=*Harb*). *B.M.C. 28.* 52, 72 .. .. £150

6122 100-24 B.C. N Phoenician *tetrobol?* (*c.* 2·48 gm.). Beardless male hd. r., laur., hair in ringlets; all within wreath. R. Owl stg. r., hd. facing, on handleless amphora; monogram of Yanaf behind, ribbon-like sign before; all within fillet border. *B.M.C. 28.* 54, 1 *(Unique?)*

6123   6125

6123 — Æ *drachm* or *unit* (c. 5·5 gm.). *Obv.* Similar. ℞. Owl stg. r., hd. facing, on handless amphora; above, Aramaic legend and monogram of Yanaf; before, AΘE (blundered) and Himyaritic signs; behind, Aramaic letter (=*n*); all within circular border composed of small handleless amphorae. *B.M.C. 28.* 55, 6 ..   ..   £90

6124 — — *Obv.* Similar, but hd. *left.* ℞. Owl stg. r., hd. facing, on amphora with handles; monograms in field, to l. and to r., small handleless amphora beneath the former; beneath, Sabaean letter (=*n*) and ribbon-like sign; border as last. *B.M.C. 28.* 57, 14-15   £100

6125 — — *Obv.* As 6122. ℞. Owl stg. r., hd. facing, on handleless amphora; monograms in field, to l. and to r., Aramaic letter (=*n*) beneath the former, ribbon-like sign beneath the latter; border as 6123. *B.M.C. 28.* 59, 23-6   ..   ..   £75

6126 — Æ *half-unit* (c. 2·7 gm.). Similar to 6123. *B.M.C. 28.* 56, 13   ..   £55

6127 — — *Obv.* Similar to 6122, but the laurel-wreath is ornamented with 'medallion' composed of pellet and crescent. ℞. Similar to 6125. *B.M.C. 28.* 58, 18-19   £45

N.B. *The coinage of the Himyarites continues with silver units and fractions bearing the head of Augustus and, later, other types extending down to the 2nd century A.D. These series will be listed in a future catalogue covering the 'Greek Imperial' coinage and contemporary issues.*

6128 **MINAEANS** (another important tribe of southern Arabia which, apparently, produced a limited coinage in the 2nd cent. B.C. based on the types of Alexander the Great). Æ *tetradrachm* (c. 16·72 gm.). Hd. of young Herakles r., clad in lion's skin. ℞. Zeus enthroned l., holding flower (?) and sceptre; behind, Himyarite legend (=*Abyatha*) to r. of which is another sceptre; in field to l., Himyarite letter (*Alif*). *B.M.C. 28., pl.* L, 5
                                            (*Unique* ?)

The name 'Abyada' is known to have been peculiar to the Minaean kings.

         6129   6130

6129 — Æ 18. *Obv.* Similar. ℞. Zeus enthroned l., holding eagle and sceptre. *B.M.C. 28.* 76, 1 ..   ..   £45

This piece, possibly originally a silver-plated drachm, is stylistically similar to the inscribed tetradrachm.

6130 **NORTHERN ARABIA FELIX** (within this area crude copies, in debased silver, of 5th century Athenian types seem to have been produced in the 4th-3rd cents. About two hundred years later another series was issued, this time small bronzes resembling in fabric the Jewish prutahs, though still retaining vestiges of the original Athenian types). 4th-3rd cent. B.C. *Tetradrachm* (debased silver, c. 14-15 gm.). Helmeted hd. of Athena r., eye depicted facing; large crescent on cheek. ℞. Owl stg. r., hd. facing; before, AΘE; behind, crescent and large olive-spray; traces of incuse square. *B.M.C. 28.* 77, 1-2 ..   £150

6131   6132

Northern Arabia Felix *continued*

6131 — — (of bronze, *c.* 10·87 gm.). Similar, but of cruder style: on *rev.* only ⊖E of the legend is represented, the olive-spray has become a stylised ornament, and no trace of the incuse square. *B.M.C. 28.* 77, 3 ..   .. (VF) £90

6132 1st cent. B.C. Æ 15. Vestiges of hd. of Athena, the only clearly recognizable [feature being the eye. ℞. Vestiges of owl stg. facing, and A⊖E. *B.M.C. 28.* 78-80, 1-29
£15

The examples of this type in the British Museum were acquired by the famous 19th century traveller Sir Richard Burton at Macna in the land of Midian.

MESOPOTAMIA

6133 **Seleukeia** (founded by Seleukos I about 312 B.C., Seleukeia was situated on the river Tigris close to the point where the Royal Canal from the Euphrates joined the eastern river.   It developed into one of the greatest cities of the ancient world and soon replaced Babylon as the emporium of the eastern empire.   From the mid-3rd cent. B.C. it came under Parthian rule and was the mint-place for the silver tetradrachms of that kingdom.   Nevertheless, there were occasional issues of autonomous bronze). 2nd-1st cent. B.C. Æ 18.   Turreted bust of Tyche r. ℞. Tripod; to r., ΣΕΛΕΥΚΕΩΝ; to l., ΤΩΝ ΠΡΟΣ ΤΩΙ / ΤΙΓΡΕΙ. *B.M.C. 28.* 140, 1-2   ..   .. £16

6134 — — *Obv.* Similar. ℞. City-goddess seated l., holding Nike and cornucopiae, thymiaterion (?) behind; to r., ΣΕΛΕΥΚΕΩΝ; to l., ΤΩΝ ΠΡΟΣ ΤΩΙ; in ex., ΤΙΓΡΕΙ. *B.M.C. 28.* 141, 4   ..   .. £16

6135   6137

6135 — Æ 13. *Obv.* Similar; behind, monogram. ℞. Cornucopiae; to r., ΣΕΛΕΥΚΕΩΝ / ΤΩΝ ΠΡΟΣ; to l., ΤΩΙ ΤΙΓΡΕΙ. *B.M.C. 28.* 140, 3   ..   .. £15

6136 1st cent. B.C. Æ 18. *Obv.* As 6133. ℞. City-goddess seated r., holding palm-branch; river-god Tigris swimming r. at her feet; around, ΣΕΛΕΥΚ . .... ΤΩΙ ΤΙΓΡΕΙ; in field to r., ΟΣ (=year 270 of the Seleukid era =43/2 B.C.). *B.M.C. 28.* 141, 6   ..   .. £17

6137 — Æ 13. Turreted hd. of Tyche r. ℞. ΔΚΣ / ΔΙΟΥ / A across field (=year 224 =89/8 B.C.). *B.M.C. 28.* 143-5, 19-40 ..   .. £10
The attribution of this and the following type to Seleukeia is not certain.

6138 — — *Obv.* Similar. ℞. City-goddess seated l. on rock, holding Nike; river-god swimming l. at her feet; before, ΠΟΛΙϹ; in field to r., A. *B.M.C. 28.* 142, 7-15   .. £12

BABYLONIA

6139   6142

6139 **Babylon** (this ancient and illustrious city, the capital of a great empire in the 7th-6th
cent. B.C., surrendered to Alexander the Great in 331 B.C. The Persian satrap Mazaios
was appointed governor of Babylon by the Macedonian conqueror and inaugurated a
distinctive series of Attic tetradrachms which continued in issue for the following half
century. Contemporary series, based on Athenian 'owls' and on the old Achaemenid
types, were also produced. Babylon was ultimately eclipsed by Seleukeia on the Tigris,
founded c. 312 B.C. by the first of the Seleukid monarchs, and during the Hellenistic age it
gradually declined). 331-328 B.C. (in the name of Mazaios). Æ tetradrachm (c. 17 gm.).
Baal seated l., holding sceptre; behind, Aramaic legend (=*Baal tarz*). R. Lion walking l.;
above, Aramaic legend (=*Mazdai*); in ex., wreath. *Mitchiner (Indo-Greek and Indo-
Scythian Coinage), type 5b. B.M.C. 28.* 180, 2 .. .. £450

6140 328-311 B.C. Æ tetradrachm (c. 17 gm.). *Obv.* Similar. R. Lion walking l. *Mitchiner,
type 6. B.M.C. 28.* 182, 7 .. .. £400

6141 — — Baal seated l., holding sceptre. R. Lion walking l.; above, spear-head l. *Mitchiner, type 7b. B.M.C. 28.* 181, 4 .. .. £200

6142 — — Similar, but with ΛY instead of spear-head above lion on *rev. Mitchiner, type 7e.
B.M.C. 28.* 185, 22-3 .. .. £200

6143 — Æ didrachm (c. 7·67 gm.). Baal seated l., holding sceptre. R. Lion walking l.;
above, Δ. *B.M.C. 28.* 184, 19 .. .. £200

6144   6147

6144 — Æ drachm (c. 4 gm.). Baal seated l., holding sceptre; M in field to l. R. Lion walking
l., looking back; in ex., AY monogram. *B.M.C. 28.* 185-6, 26-8 .. .. £140

6145 — Æ obol (c. 0·7 gm.). Baal seated l., holding sceptre. R. Lion walking r.; above,
spear-head r. *B.M.C. 28.* 182, 6 .. .. £75

6146 — Æ hemiobol (c. 0·35 gm.). Baal seated r., holding eagle (?). R. Lion walking r.
B.M.C. 28. 183, 13 .. .. £50

6147 311-280 B.C. Æ tetradrachm (c. 15·5-16·5 gm.). Baal seated l., holding sceptre. R.
Lion walking l.; above, pentalpha (five-pointed star). *Mitchiner, type 8a. B.M.C. 28.*
187-8, 39-41 .. .. £175

6148 — — — R. Lion walking l.; above, anchor l. *Mitchiner, type 8d. B.M.C. 28.* 188-9,
43-7 .. .. £175

6149 — — Similar, but in *obv.* field to l., horned horse's hd. r.; and in ex. on *rev.,* ΔI. *Mitchiner, type 8f. B.M.C. 28.* 189, 51 .. .. £250

6150 — — Baal seated l., holding sceptre. R. Lion walking l.; above, anchor l. and Π; in
ex., monogram and crescent. *Mitchiner, type 8h. B.M.C. 28.* 190, 55 .. £200

Babylon *continued*

6151 — Æ *trihemidrachm*? (*c.* 6·3 gm.). As 6149, but with monogram instead of ΔΙ on *rev.*
B.M.C. 28. 190, 52-3 .. .. £175

6152 — Æ *drachm* (*c.* 3·75 gm.). Baal seated l., holding sceptre. R. Lion walking l., looking
back; above, anchor l. *B.M.C. 28.* 189, 48 .. .. £130

6153 — Æ *hemidrachm* (*c.* 2 gm.). Similar, but lion walking r., looking back. *B.M.C. 28.*
189, 50 .. .. £90

6154 6155

6154 'OWL' TYPE COINAGE. Before 333 B.C.? (in the name of Mazakes, satrap of
Babylon). Æ *tetradrachm* (small, thick flans; *c.* 17 gm.). Hd. of Athena r., wearing
crested helmet ornamented with olive-leaves, etc. R. Owl stg. r., hd. facing; before,
Aramaic legend (=*Mazdaka*); behind, olive-spray and crescent; traces of incuse square.
Mitchiner, type 12d £350
For a similar coin of Mazakes, issued in Egypt, see no. 6233.

6155 Late 4th cent., before *c.* 305 B.C. Æ *tetradrachm* (*c.* 17 gm.). *Obv.* Similar; behind,
monogram. R. Owl stg. r., hd. facing; before, ΑΘΕ; behind, olive-spray and crescent,
and bunch of grapes. *Mitchiner, type* 13e. *B.M.C. 11.* (*Attica*) 25, 267-8 .. £250

6156 — — *Obv.* As 6154. R. Owl stg. r., hd. facing; before, ΑΘΕ and Ι/Δ; behind, olive-spray
and crescent; traces of incuse square. *Mitchiner, type* 13d. *B.M.C. 11.* 26, 270
£225

6157 6158

6157 'ACHAEMENID' TYPE COINAGE. 331-305 B.C. *N double daric* (*c.* 16·7 gm.).
Persian archer, in kneeling-running attitude r., holding dagger and bow. R. Oblong
incuse, containing irregular markings. *Mitchiner, type* 14. *B.M.C. 28.* 176, 1 £4,000

6158 — — Persian archer, in kneeling-running attitude r., holding spear and bow, quiver at
shoulder; behind, ΦΙ. R. Incuse impression, of elliptical form, containing wavy horizontal lines. *Mitchiner, type* 15d. *B.M.C. 28.* 177, 4 .. .. £3,000

6159 6162

Babylon *continued*

6159 — — Similar, but without quiver at archer's shoulder, and with ΣΤΑ behind, ΜΝΑ beneath, Φ / Λ before; on *rev.*, the markings within the incuse impression take the form of two large crescents, back to back, with other curves and lines in the field. *Mitchiner, type 15i. B.M.C. 28.* 179, 12 .. .. £4,500

    Stamenes was governor of Babylon in succession to Mazaios, 328-323 B.C.

6160 — — Similar to 6158, but with monogram behind archer; and on *rev.*, the markings take the form of two trapezoids, one divided into three segments, the other into four. *Mitchiner, type* 15n. *B.M.C. 28.* 177, 6 .. .. £3,000

6161 — *N daric* (c. 8·3 gm.). Similar to last, but on *obv.* Μ before archer, ΑΥ monogram behind. *Mitchiner, type* 16 .. .. (*Unique ?*)

6162 — Æ 2½ *sigloi*? (c. 14·5-15·5 gm.). Persian archer, in kneeling-running attitude r., holding spear and bow. Ŗ. Granulated incuse containing irregular markings. *Mitchiner, type* 17a. *B.M.C. 14.* (*Ionia*) 324, 3-6 .. .. £1,250

6163 — — Similar, but with ΠΥΘΑ — ΓΟΡΗΣ behind and before the archer on *obv.* *Mitchiner, type* 17b. *B.M.C. 14.* 323, 1 .. .. £2,000

    This may be the Pythagoras who impressed Alexander the Great by his powers of prophesy in 324-3 B.C.

ASSYRIA

6164 **Atusia** (exact site unknown, but situated on the river Kapros, a tributary of the Tigris). 1st cent. B.C. Æ 14. Turreted bust of Tyche l. Ŗ. ΑΤΟΥΣΙΕΩΝ Τ. ΠΡΟΣΤ· ΚΑΠΡΟΝ in square, enclosing palm-branch and arrow. *B.M.C. 28.* 147, 1 .. .. £35

6165 **Demetrias** (on the Tigris, in the vicinity of Arbela). 1st cent. B.C. Æ 17. Turreted bust of Tyche r. Ŗ. Tripod; ΔΗΜΗΤΡΙΕΩΝ to r., ΤΩΝ ΠΡΟΣ ΤΩΙ / ΤΙΓΡΕΙ to l. *Historia Numorum, p.* 817 .. .. £35

PERSIA

6166   6167

6166 **Ecbatana** (an important city on the Iranian plateau, Ecbatana was a royal residence of the Achaemenids and the summer capital of their empire. When Alexander captured the city in 330 B.C. he plundered a vast sum from the treasury which was housed there. In later times it became an important mint under the Parthian kings). *Circa* 315 B.C. *N stater* (c. 8·55 gm.). Diad. and dr. bust of Zeus r.; monogram behind. Ŗ. Armed figure in fast quadriga driven r. by Nike; in ex., ΑΝΔΡΑΓΟΡΟΥ. *Mitchiner, type* 19. *B.M.C. 28.* 193, 1 .. .. £12,500

    The Andragoras named on this type and the next may have been governor of Media in the period immediately preceding the first Seleukid issues from the Ecbatana mint.

6167 — *Æ tetradrachm* (c. 16·5 gm.). Turreted bust of Tyche r.; monogram behind. Ŗ. Athena stg. l., holding owl and resting l. hand on shield; spear, diagonally, in background; behind, ΑΝΔΡΑΓΟΡΟΥ. *Mitchiner, type* 20. *B.M.C. 28.* 193, 3 .. .. £2,500

SUSIANA

6168 **Susa** (the 'city of lilies', Susa was the capital of the Achaemenid Empire. It became an important mint under the Seleukids). *Circa* 320-315 B.C. *Æ tetradrachm* (c. 16·8 gm.). Laur. hd. of Zeus r. Ŗ. Elephant walking r., trunk raised; above, spear-head; in ex., Α. *Mitchiner, type* 18a. *B.M.C. 28.* 192, 64 .. .. £750

ELYMAIS

6169 **KINGDOM OF ELYMAIS** (little is known of the history and chronology of the Elymaid rulers. Although they maintained a quasi-independence they seem normally to have been subject to the Parthian Kings. The coinage commences about the middle of the 2nd cent. B.C. and extends to the third decade of the 3rd cent. A.D. when the Parthians were overthrown by the Sassanian Ardashir). **Kamnaskires I Nikephoros,** *circa* 163 B.C. Æ *tetradrachm* (*c.* 16·7 gm.). Diad. hd. of Kamnaskires r.; ЄA monogram behind; fillet border. Ŗ. Apollo seated l. on omphalos, holding two arrows and resting on bow; ΒΑΣΙΛΕΩΣ behind, ΚΑΜΝΙΣΚΙΡΟΥ before, ΝΙΚΗΦΟΡΟΥ in ex. *B.M.C.* 28., *pl.* LIII, 6
£3,500

6170 **Phraates II,** of Parthia, *circa* 138 B.C. (Elymais was conquered by the powerful Parthian monarch Mithradates I whose son and successor, Phraates II, issued a few tetradrachms of Elymaid type). Æ *tetradrachm* (*c.* 16·3 gm.). Diad. hd. of the young Phraates r.; fillet border. Ŗ. Apollo seated l. on omphalos, holding arrow and resting on bow; ΒΑΣΙΛΕΩΣ behind, ΑΡΣΑΚΟΥ before, ΒΑ in ex.; monogram in field to l. *Sellwood* (*Coinage of Parthia*), *type* 14/1. *De Morgan* (*Ancient Persian Numismatics, Elymais*) 2 .. £2,500

6171   6176

6171 **Kamnaskires II and Anzaze,** *circa* 82-80 B.C. Æ *tetradrachm* (*c.* 15·7 gm.). Conjoined busts l. of Kamnaskires, diad. and with long beard, and Queen Anzaze, diad.; behind, anchor-shaped symbol. Ŗ. Zeus enthroned l., holding Nike and sceptre; inscription, ΒΑCΙΛΕΩC ΚΑΜΝΑCΚΙΡΟΥ ΚΑΙ ΒΑCΙΛΙCCΗC ΑΝΖΑΖΗC, forms a square around the type; beneath, ΑΛΣ (=year 231 of the Seleukid era =82/1 B.C.). *B.M.C.* 28. 245, 1 £1,250
    The inscription is sometimes blundered.

6172 — Æ *drachm* (*c.* 3·9 gm.). Similar. *B.M.C.* 28. 246, 4   ..   ..   .. £250

6173 — Æ *hemidrachm* (*c.* 1·7 gm.). Similar. *De Morgan* 6   ..   ..   .. £150

6174 — Æ *obol* (*c.* 0·54 gm.). Similar. *De Morgan* 7   ..   ..   .. £90

6175 **Kamnaskires III,** *circa* 62/1 B.C. Æ *tetradrachm* (*c.* 15·5 gm.). Youthful diad. bust of Kamnaskires l., with short pointed beard. Ŗ. Zeus enthroned l., holding Nike and sceptre; ΚΡ monogram in field to l.; inscription, ΒΑCΙΛΕΩC ΚΑΜΝΑCΚΙΡΟΥ ΤΟΥ ΕΓ ΒΑCΙΛΕΩC ΚΑΜΝΑCΚΙΡΟΥ, forms a square around the type; beneath, traces of ΑΝΣ ? (=year 251 =62/1 B.C.). *B.M.C.* 28., *pl.* LIII, 8. *De Morgan* 3 ..   .. £1,500
    The inscription is sometimes blundered.

6176 — Æ *drachm* (*c.* 3·9 gm.). Similar. *B.M.C.* 28. 247, 2   ..   ..   .. £250

    N.B. *The later coinage of Elymais, mostly of debased silver and bronze, will be listed in a future catalogue covering the 'Greek Imperial' series and contemporary coinages.*

CHARACENE

6177 **KINGDOM OF CHARACENE** (situated at the head of the Persian Gulf, the small kingdom of Characene occupied the delta of the united Tigris and Euphrates. Its capital was Charax Spasinou, from which the kingdom took its name). **Hyspaosines,** *circa* 125/4 B.C. (son of Sagdodonakos). Æ *tetradrachm*. His diad. hd. r.; fillet border. ℞. Naked Herakles seated l., resting club on r. knee; behind, ΒΑΣΙΛΕΩΣ; before, ΥΣΠΑΟΣΙ-ΝΕΟΥ; in ex., ΗΠΡ (=year 188 of the Seleukid era =125/4 B.C.). *B.M.C. 28.*, *p.* cxcvi
£2,500

The rev. type would seem to be derived from the coinage of Euthydemos I of Baktria.

6178 **Apodakos,** *c.* 110-105 B.C. Æ *tetradrachm* (*c.* 15·66 gm.). His diad. hd. r.; fillet border. ℞. Naked Herakles, as last; behind, ΒΑΣΙΛΕΩΣ; before, ΑΠΟΔΑΚΟΥ; ΔΙ monogram in field to l.; in ex., ΖΣ (=year 207 of the Seleukid era =106/5 B.C.). *B.M.C. 28.* 289, 1, *variety* £1,500

6179 **Tiraios I,** *circa* 90/89 B.C. Æ *tetradrachm*. His diad. hd. r., with aged features; fillet border. ℞. Tyche seated l., holding Nike and cornucopiae; behind, ΒΑΣΙΛΕΩΣ / ΤΙΡΑΙΟΥ; before, ΕΥΕΡΓΕΤΟΥ; two monograms in field to l.; in ex., ΓΚΣ (=year 223=90/89 B.C.). *B.M.C. 28.*, *pl.* LIV, 3 .. .. £1,750

6180 **Tiraios II,** *c.* 61-48 B.C. Æ *tetradrachm* (*c.* 13·62 gm.). His diad. hd. r., with long beard; border of dots. ℞. Naked Herakles, as 6177; behind, ΒΑΣΙΛΕΩΣ / ΤΙΡΑΙΟΥ; before, ΣΩΤΗΡΟΣ / ΚΑΙ ΕΥΕΡΓΕΤΟΥ; monogram in upper field to l.; in ex., ΔΙΣ (=year 264 =49/8 B.C.). *B.M.C. 28.* 290, 1 .. .. £350

6181 — Æ 18. *Obv.* Similar. ℞. Nike stg. l., holding wreath; ΒΑΣΙΛΕ behind, ΤΙΡΑ before. *B.M.C. 28.* 290, 2 .. .. £30

6182

Kingdom of Characene *continued*

6182 Attambelos I, *c.* 44-40 B.C.   Æ *tetradrachm* (*c.* 10·5-13·7 gm.).   His diad. hd. r., with long beard.   ℞. Naked Herakles, as 6177; behind, ΒΑΣΙΛΕΩΣ / ΑΤΤΑΜΒΗΛΟΥ; before, ΣΩΤΗΡΟΣ / ΚΑΙ ΕΥΕΡΓΕΤΟΥ; monogram in upper field to l.; in ex., ΒΟΣ (=year 272 =41/40 B.C.).   *B.M.C. 28.* 291, 3 (*Illustrated on previous page*) £250

6183 Theonesios I, *circa* 40/39 B.C.   Æ *tetradrachm*.   His diad. hd. r., with long beard. ℞. Naked Herakles, as 6177; behind, ΒΑΣΙΛΕΩΣ / ΘΙΟΝΗΣΙΟΥ; before, ΣΩΤΗΡΟΣ / ΚΑΙ ΕΥΕΡΓΕΤΟΥ; monogram in upper field to l.; letter under Herakles' r. arm; in ex., ΓΟΣ (=year 273 =40/39 B.C.).   *B.M.C. 28., pl.* LIV, 4   ..   ..   £450

6184 Attambelos II, *c.* 30 B.C.—A.D. 6.   *Tetradrachm* (debased silver, *c.* 13·7-14·6 gm.). His diad. hd. r., with long beard.   ℞. Naked Herakles, as 6177; behind, ΒΑΣΙΛΕΩΣ / ΑΤΤΑΜΒΗΛΟΥ; before, ϹΩΤΗΡΟϹ / ΚΑΙ ΕΥΕΡΓΕΤΟΥ; monogram in upper field to l.; Aramaic letter (=*k*) under Herakles' r. arm; in ex., ΙΙΤ (=year 317 =A.D. 5/6).   *B.M.C. 28.* 293, 3   ..   ..   £150

N.B. *The coinage of the later kings of Characene will be listed in a future catalogue covering the 'Greek Imperial' series and contemporary coinages.*

PERSIS

6185   6187

6185 KINGDOM OF PERSIS (lying beyond the north-eastern shores of the Persian Gulf, the Kingdom of Persis issued an extensive series of silver coins over a period of more than four centuries.   Difficulty in interpreting some of the Aramaic legends has led to problems of attribution within this series, and the proposed chronology is only conjectural).   3rd cent. B.C.   **Bagadates I.**   Æ *tetradrachm* (*c.* 16·9 gm.).   His hd. r., with long moustache, wearing satrapal head-dress.   ℞. King enthroned l., holding sceptre and flower (?); standard in ground before him; Aramaic legends behind throne and to l. of standard. *B.M.C. 28.* 195, 1   ..   ..   £2,500

6186 — — *Obv.* Similar.   ℞. Fire-altar, between king stg. r. (on l.) and standard (on r.); Aramaic legends in field to r. and in ex.   *B.M.C. 28.* 196, 2   ..   ..   £1,500

6187 — **Vahuberz (Oborzos).**   Æ *drachm* (*c.* 3·9 gm.).   His hd. r., with moustache and beard, wearing satrapal head-dress.   ℞. Similar to last; Aramaic legends in field to l. and to r., and in ex.   *B.M.C. 28.* 197, 1   ..   ..   £140

6188 — — Æ *hemidrachm* (*c.* 1·75 gm.).   Similar.   *B.M.C. 28.* 197, 3   ..   ..   £110

6189   6191

6189 — **Artaxerxes I.** Ӕ *drachm* (*c.* 3·9 gm.). His hd. r., with moustache and beard, wearing satrapal head-dress. R. Fire-altar between stg. king and standard; Aramaic legends in field to l. and to r., and in ex. *B.M.C. 28.* 198, 2 ..   ..   ..   £130

6190 — — Ӕ *tetrobol* (*c.* 2·8 gm.). Similar. *B.M.C. 28.* 198, 3 ..   ..   ..   £120

6191 — **Autophradates I.** Ӕ *tetradrachm* (*c.* 16·8 gm.). His hd. r., with moustache and beard, wearing satrapal head-dress. R. Fire-altar surmounted by hovering half-length figure of Ahura-Mazda; on l., king stg. r.; on r., standard; Aramaic legends in field to l. and to r., and in ex. *B.M.C. 28.* 200, 1 ..   ..   £650

6192 — — Ӕ *drachm* (*c.* 4·2 gm.). Similar. *B.M.C. 28.* 201, 4 ..   ..   ..   £125

6193   6196

6193 2nd cent. B.C. **Darius I.** Ӕ *tetradrachm* (*c.* 16·5 gm.). His hd. r., with short beard, wearing satrapal head-dress surmounted by eagle. R. Fire-altar, with superstructure in the form of stepped battlements; Ahura-Mazda hovering above; on l., king stg. r.; on r., bird perched on standard. *B.M.C. 28.* 204, 1 ..   ..   £500

6194 — — Ӕ *drachm* (*c.* 4·1 gm.). Similar. *B.M.C. 28.* 204, 2 ..   ..   ..   £90

6195 — — — Similar, but of poorer style, and with crescent at the back of the satrapal head-dress on *obv.* *B.M.C. 28.* 207, 1-8 ..   ..   £75

6196 — — — *Obv.* Similar to 6193, but of poorer style, and the head-dress is surmounted by crescent instead of eagle. R. Fire-altar, etc., as 6193, but of poorer style—the standard is represented merely by an upright rectangle; Aramaic legend in ex. and on l. *B.M.C. 28.* 209, 2   ..   ..   £65

6197 — — Ӕ *hemidrachm* (*c.* 2·05 gm.). As 6193. *B.M.C. 28.* 206, 17-18   ..   £75

6198 — — — As 6195. *B.M.C. 28.* 208, 9 ..   ..   £55

6199 — — — As 6196. *B.M.C. 28.* 211, 14-15   ..   ..   £50

6200 — — Ӕ *obol* (*c.* 0·7 gm.). As 6193. *B.M.C. 28.* 206, 19   ..   ..   ..   £40

6201   6202

Kingdom of Persis *continued*

6201 — — —As 6196.   *B.M.C. 28.* 211, 17   .. ..   £35

6202 — **Autophradates II.**   Æ *drachm* (*c.* 4·1 gm.).   Hd. of Darius (?) r., similar to 6196.
Ɍ. Fire-altar between king stg. r. and bird perched on upright rectangle; Ahura-Mazda
hovering above; Aramaic legend in ex.   *B.M.C. 28.* 212, 1-5 ..   ..   ..   £75

6203 — — — Diad. and cuir. bust of Autophradates r., with long beard; crescent above hd.
Ɍ. As last.   *B.M.C. 28.* 213, 6   ..   ..   £90

6204 — — Æ *hemidrachm* (*c.* 2·1 gm.).   Similar.   *B.M.C. 28.* 214, 17   ..   ..   £65

6205 — — Æ *obol* (*c.* 0·6 gm.).   Similar.   *B.M.C. 28.* 215, 20   ..   ..   ..   £50

6206   6209

6206 1st cent. B.C.   **Darius II** (son of Autophradates II).   Æ *drachm* (*c.* 3·5 - 4·1 gm.).   His
cuir. bust l., with long beard, wearing Parthian tiara, ornamented with crescent, and diad.
Ɍ. King stg. l., holding sceptre, before lighted altar; Aramaic legend forming square
around the type.   *B.M.C. 28.* 216, 4   ..   ..   £75
*The obv. type resembles the contemporary Parthian coinage, especially that of Mithradates
II (123-88 B.C.).*

6207 — — Æ *hemidrachm* (*c.* 1·9 gm.).   Similar.   *B.M.C. 28.* 218, 16   ..   ..   £55

6208 — — Æ *obol* (*c.* 0·55-0·65 gm.).   Similar.   *B.M.C. 28.* 218, 19   ..   ..   £35

6209 — **Oxathres** (son of Darius II).   Æ *drachm* (*c.* 3·7 - 4 gm.).   His diad. and cuir. bust l.,
with short beard; monogram behind.   Ɍ. King stg. r., holding sceptre, before lighted
altar; Aramaic legend forming square around the type.   *B.M.C. 28.* 219, 1   ..   £90
The obv. type resembles the coinage of the Parthian monarch Gotarzes I (90-80 B.C.).

6210 — — — Similar, but on *rev.*, the king stands to l. before the altar.   *B.M.C. 28.* 219, 4
£90

6211 — — Æ *hemidrachm* (*c.* 1·9 gm.).   As 6209.   *B.M.C. 28.* 220, 6   ..   ..   £65

6212 — **Artaxerxes II** (son of Darius II).   Æ *drachm* (*c.* 3·5 - 4·1 gm.).   His dr. bust l.,
with pointed beard, wearing battlemented mural crown and diad.; monogram behind.
Ɍ. King stg. l., holding sceptre, before lighted altar; Aramaic legend forming square
around the type.   *B.M.C. 28.* 222, 1   ..   ..   £100

6213 — — — Similar, but with star above the monogram on *obv.*, and on *rev.* the king stands
to r. before the altar.   *B.M.C. 28.* 222, 5 ..   ..   £100

6214 — — Æ *hemidrachm* (*c.* 1·8 - 2 gm.).   As 6212.   *B.M.C. 28.* 223, 7 ..   ..   £65

6215 — — Æ *obol* (*c.* 0·65 gm.).   As 6212.   *B.M.C. 28.* 224, 19   ..   ..   ..   £50

N.B.   *The coinage of the later kings of Persis will be listed in a future catalogue covering
the 'Greek Imperial' series and contemporary coinages.*

BAKTRIA

6216 **Baktra** (an important city at the foot of Mt. Paropamisos, Baktra was of Persian foundation and was the capital of the Baktrian satrapy. Alexander the Great settled there some
of his Greek mercenaries and his disabled Macedonian troops). 329-323 B.C. Æ
dekadrachm (*c.* 42·3 gm.). Elephant walking r., carrying on his back two warriors, one of
whom aims spear at Macedonian horseman prancing r., behind, with lance couched. ℞.
Alexander, wearing Persian head-dress and cloak, stg. facing, hd. l., holding thunderbolt
and spear; he is crowned by Nike flying r. above; BA monogram in lower field to l. *Mitchiner* (*Indo-Greek and Indo-Scythian Coinage*), *type 21a*. *B.M.C. 28.* 191, 61 £25,000

6217   6219

6217 — Æ *tetradrachm* (*c.* 15·4 gm.). Archer, in Persian dress, advancing r., about to discharge arrow from large bow; BA monogram in lower field to l. ℞. Elephant stg. r.; Ξ in
ex. *Mitchiner, type 22* £7,500

6218 — Æ *didrachm* (*c.* 7 gm.), in imitation of Athenian types. Hd. of Athena r., wearing
crested helmet ornamented with olive-leaves, etc. ℞. Owl stg. r., hd. facing; AΘE before,
olive-spray and crescent behind. *Mitchiner, type 24. B.M.C. 11.* (*Attica*) 26, 272
£450

*These Baktrian 'owls' are to be distinguished by their neat and compact style, and by their
unusual weight standard.*

6219 — Æ *drachm* (*c.* 3·5 gm.). Similar, but also with o͞c behind owl on *rev*. *Mitchiner,
type 25b. B.M.C. 11.* 26, 273 .. .. £225

6220 323-315 B.C. Æ *drachm* (*c.* 3·5 gm.). *Obv.* Similar. ℞. Eagle stg. l., looking back,
wings closed. *Mitchiner, type 26a. B.M.C. 11.* 26, 274 .. .. .. £275

Baktra *continued*

6221 — Æ *diobol* (*c.* 1·17 gm.).   As last, but with two bunches of grapes behind eagle on *rev.*
Mitchiner, *type* 27 ..   ..   £110

6222 — — Diad. hd. of Zeus r.   ℞. As last.   *Mitchiner, type* 28 ..   ..   ..   £100

6223 315-311 B.C. (in the name of the satrap Sophytes).   Æ *drachm* (*c.* 3·75 gm.).   Hd. of
Sophytes r., wearing wreathed helmet with cheek-piece; Σ on neck.   ℞. Cock stg. r.;
ΣΩΦΥΤΟΥ before, caduceus behind.   *Mitchiner, type* 29a.   B.M.C. (*of Indian Coins, Greek
and Scythic Kings*) 2, 1   ..   ..   £750

6224 — Æ *hemidrachm* (*c.* 1·6 gm.).   Similar, but without Σ on *obv.   Mitchiner, type* 30
£300

6225 — Æ *diobol* (*c.* 1·2 gm.).   Hd. of Athena r., wearing Corinthian helmet.   ℞. As 6223.
Mitchiner, *type* 31 ..   ..   £175

6226 — Æ *obol* (*c.* 0·6 gm.).   As 6224.   *Mitchiner, type* 32   ..   ..   ..   £150

ARACHOSIA

6227 **Kapisa.**   325-323 B.C. (in the name of the satrap Vakhshuvar-Oxyartes).   *N* stater
(*c.* 8·6 gm.).   Hd. of Athena r., wearing crested Corinthian helmet; ΙΙΓ beneath.   ℞.
Nike stg. facing, hd. l., holding wreath and triple-headed sceptre; Aramaic legend (=*va
kh sh u va da*) on r.; Aramaic letter (=*b*) in field to l.   *Mitchiner, type* 35.   B.M.C. **28.**
194, 1   ..   ..   (*Extremely rare*)
*Vakhshuvar appears to be identical with Oxyartes, father of Roxana and thus father-in-
law of Alexander the Great.*

6228 — — (*c.* 8·8 gm.).   Bearded bust of Vakhshuvar r., wearing satrapal head-dress;
uncertain Aramaic legend behind.   ℞. Satrap driving fast quadriga r.; in ex., Aramaic
legend (=*va kh shu var*).   *Mitchiner, type* 34.   B.M.C. **28.** 194, 2   ..   ..   (*Unique*)

EGYPT AND NORTH AFRICA

MAP 21   EGYPT AND KYRENAICA

The ancient civilization of the land of the Pharaohs felt little need of coinage before the time of Alexander the Great.   However, demand for silver was high and large quantities of Greek coins, from all areas, found their way into Egypt from the closing decades of the 6th cent. B.C.   Once it had been imported this silver was treated merely as bullion and many Egyptian hoards of this time contain coins cut into halves, quarters, etc. for the purposes of individual transactions.   Large numbers of Athenian tetradrachms entered Egypt in the second half of the 5th century and these served as models for the insignificant Egyptian issues of the closing years of Persian rule.   After the time of Alexander Egypt once more became a powerful independent kingdom under the rule of the Greek Ptolemaic dynasty.

In North Africa there were two great commercial centres: Kyrene, founded from the Greek island of Thera about 630 B.C.; and Carthage, a Phoenician colony established by Tyrians in the 8th century.   The coinage of the former commenced in the archaic period, in the closing years of the 6th century.   Carthage, on the other hand, only began issuing currency in the 4th century and many of her coins were struck in Sicily to finance military operations against the Greek cities there.   After two protracted wars with the Romans Carthage eventually submitted in 201 B.C. and the once mighty city was razed to the ground half a century later.

EGYPT

6229 **Tachos,** *circa* 361 B.C. (this short-lived Pharaoh rebelled against Persian overlordship and enlisted the help of the Athenian Chabrias and Agesilaus, King of Sparta). *N stater* (*c.* 8·35 gm.).   Hd. of Athena r., wearing crested helmet ornamented with olive-leaves, etc. R. Owl stg. r., hd. facing; ΤΑΩΣ before, papyrus-stem behind; all within incuse square. *Kraay* (*Archaic and Classical Greek Coins*) *pl.* 12, 217   ..   ..   (*Unique*)

6230 **Nektanebo II,** *c.* 361-350 B.C. (nephew of the Pharaoh Tachos, Nektanebo gained the Egyptian throne with the assistance of Agesilaus.   For some years he successfully withstood Persian attempts to regain control, but he was finally defeated and fled to Ethiopia. Nektanebo was the last native ruler of Egypt).   *N stater* (*c.* 8·18 gm.).   Free horse galloping r.   R. Bead collar, heart and wind-pipe (hieroglyphic signs for *nefer nub* = 'fine gold'). *Principal Coins of the Greeks, pl.* 51, 12   ..   ..   £2,500

Egypt *continued*

6231 **Artaxerxes III** of Persia, died 338 B.C. Æ *tetradrachm* (*c.* 15·4 - 17 gm.). Hd. of Athena r., with facing eye, wearing crested helmet ornamented with olive-leaves, etc. R. Owl stg. r., hd. facing; before, inscription in Egyptian demotic = 'Artaxerxes Pharaoh'; behind, olive-spray and crescent; traces of incuse square. *Mitchiner* (*Indo-Greek and Indo-Scythian Coinage*), *type* 9 .. .. £1,500

6232 **Sabakes,** Persian satrap until 333 B.C. (killed at the Battle of Issos). Æ *tetradrachm* (*c.* 16-17·2 gm.). *Obv.* Similar, but Athena's eye is in profile. R. Owl stg. r., hd. facing; before, Aramaic legend (= *Savaka*) with thunderbolt and crescent; behind, olive-spray and crescent; traces of incuse square. *Mitchiner, type* 10*a*. *B.M.C. 11.* (*Attica*) 25, 263 .. .. £550

6233 **Mazakes,** Persian satrap 333-2 B.C. (appointed to the Egyptian satrapy on the death of Sabakes, Mazakes surrendered the country to Alexander the following year). Æ *tetradrachm* (broad, thin flans; *c.* 16·5 - 17 gm.). *Obv.* As last. R. Owl stg. r., hd. facing; before, Aramaic legend (= *Mazdaka*) and monogram; behind, olive-spray and crescent; traces of incuse square. *Mitchiner, type* 11 .. .. £650

 For a similar coin of Mazakes, issued at Babylon, see no. 6154.

N.B. *For the subsequent coinage of Egypt, see below under Hellenistic Monarchies—the Ptolemaic Kingdom of Egypt.*

NORTH AFRICA

    6234   6237

6234 **KYRENAICA** (this fertile coastal region of North Africa, directly south of the Peloponnesos, received its name from the principal city Kyrene). **Kyrene** (founded by colonists from Thera, *c.* 630 B.C., Kyrene grew to great commercial importance under the kings of the Battiad dynasty, the last of whom was deposed about 440 B.C. Kyrenaica was under Ptolemaic rule during the 3rd and 2nd cents. B.C., but early in the 1st cent. it was bequeathed to Rome). 510-470 B.C. (time of Battos IV). Æ *tetradrachm* (*c.* 17-17·5 gm.). Three silphium fruits. R. Two rectangular punches, side by side, each divided into three segments. *B.M.C. 29.* 1, 1 .. .. £3,500

 The silphium plant, which features so prominently on the coinage of the Kyrenaica, was of the umbelliferous variety and was peculiar to the area. The juice, extracted from the stalk and root, had medicinal properties whilst the stalk itself was eaten as a vegetable. The silphium appears to have become extinct in the 1st cent. A.D.

6235 — — Silphium plant between bird's hd., on l., and fruit. R. Oblong incuse divided into four compartments, the vertical lines of division double, the horizontal single. *B.M.C. 29., pl.* I, 11 .. .. £3,500

6236 — — Silphium plant between two fruits. R. Gorgon's hd. facing in square linear frame; all within incuse square. *B.M.C. 29.* 3, 10 .. .. £3,750

6237 — — Silphium plant; on r., large lion's hd. l., silphium fruit beneath jaws. R. Eagle's hd. r., holding serpent in its beak; floral pattern above; all in dotted square within incuse square. *B.M.C. 29.* 4, 13 .. .. £4,500

6238 — — Silphium plant between two fruits. ℞. Gazelle stg. l.; silphium plant before, fruit above; κ in field to l., and beneath gazelle; all within incuse square. *B.M.C. 29.* 4, 15 ..   ..   £3,750

6239 — — *Obv.* Similar; in field, κ — ʏ / ᴘ — ᴀ / ᴀ — ɴ. ℞. Silphium fruit between two dolphins, upwards; all within incuse square. *B.M.C. 29.,pl.* III, 12 ..   ..   £3,250

6240 — Æ *didrachm* (*c.* 8·5 gm.). Four silphium fruits, two large and two small. ℞. Incuse square, divided diagonally into four triangular segments. *B.M.C. 29.* 1, 3   ..   £750

6241 — — Silphium plant between two fruits. ℞. Two fruits placed diagonally within incuse square. *B.M.C. 29.,pl.* IV, 1   ..   ..   £900

6242   6246   6248

6242 — Æ *drachm* (*c.* 4 - 4·25 gm.). Two silphium fruits, side by side. ℞. Rectangular punch. *B.M.C. 29.* 2, 4   ..   ..   £350

6243 — — Hd. of man-faced bull l., bearded; behind, silphium fruit. ℞. Stellate floral pattern within incuse square. *B.M.C. 29.* 5, 19   ..   ..   ..   £550

6244 — Æ 'Asiatic' *drachm* (*c.* 3·25 - 3·5 gm.). Two silphium fruits, set base to base; flower (?) composed of pellets above and beneath. ℞. Lion's scalp facing, within incuse square. *B.M.C. 29.* 9, 38   ..   ..   £450

6245 — Æ *hemidrachm* (*c.* 2 gm.). Silphium fruit; above, lion's hd. l. ℞. Square punch. *B.M.C. 29.* 2, 8   ..   ..   £180

6246 — — Silphium fruit. ℞. Winged female figure stg. facing, hd. r., arms hanging at her sides; all in dotted square within incuse square. *B.M.C. 29.* 6, 24   ..   £240

6247 — — — ℞. Hd. of Kyrene r., her hair looped over fillet behind; two floral ornaments in field; all in square linear frame within incuse square. *B.M.C. 29.* 7, 25   £220

6248 — Æ 'Asiatic' *hemidrachm* (*c.* 1·65 gm.). Large silphium fruit, flanked by two smaller fruits. ℞. Scorpion, within incuse square. *B.M.C. 29.* 9, 41   ..   £200

6249 — Æ *trihemiobol* (*c.* 1 gm.). Silphium fruit. ℞. Gazelle's hd. facing, within incuse square. *B.M.C. 29.* 7, 31   ..   ..   £125

6250 — Æ *obol* (*c.* 0·65 gm.). Silphium fruit. ℞. As 6240. *B.M.C. 29., pl.* II, 16 £90

6251 — — — ℞. Stellate pattern within incuse square. *B.M.C. 29.* 8, 33   ..   £90

6252 — Æ *hemiobol* (*c.* 0·38 gm.). Silphium fruit. ℞. Quadripartite incuse square. *B.M.C. 29.* 3, 9   ..   ..   £65

6253 — — — ℞. As 6251. *B.M.C. 29.* 8, 34   ..   ..   £65

6254 *Circa* 470 B.C. Æ *tetradrachm* (*c.* 17·1 gm.). Hd. of Zeus-Ammon r., of magnificent late archaic style. ℞. Silphium plant; on r., forepart of bridled horse l., and silphium fruit; above, κʏᴘ; all within incuse square. *Kraay (Archaic and Classical Greek Coins), pl.* 62, 1070   ..   ..   (*Unique*)

6255 470-440 B.C. (time of Arkesilaus IV). N 'Asiatic' *drachm* (*c.* 3·43 gm.). Silphium plant. ℞. Hd. of Zeus-Ammon r., within circle of dots. *B.M.C. 29., pl.* VII, 20   (*Unique*)

6256 — Æ *tetradrachm* (*c.* 17 gm.). Silphium plant. ℞. Hd. of Zeus-Ammon r., of late archaic style, hair plaited; in field, κ — ᴠ / ᴘ — ᴀ; all within circle of dots. *B.M.C. 29.,pl.* V, 13 ..   ..   £4,500

6257 6258

Kyrene *continued*

6257 — — — R. Similar, but the hd. of Zeus-Ammon is of more developed style with hair crimped and plaited; KVPA before; all within heavy cable border. *B.M.C. 29.* 10, 42 .. £5,000

6258 — Æ 'Asiatic' *tetradrachm* (*c.* 13·25 gm.). Similar to 6256, but with legend K — VPA below and before the hd. of Zeus-Ammon. *B.M.C. 29.* 11, 45.. .. .. £4,000

6259 — Æ *didrachm* (*c.* 8·5 gm.). Similar to 6256, but with legend KVPA before the hd. of Zeus-Ammon. *B.M.C. 29.* 11, 44 .. .. £1,250

6260 6265

6260 — Æ 'Asiatic' *drachm* (*c.* 3·3 gm.). Silphium plant. R. Incuse square, with K — V — P — A in the corners, containing hd. of Kyrene r. within dotted circle. *B.M.C. 29.* 12, 47 £450

6261 — — Similar to 6256. *B.M.C. 29.* 12, 48 .. .. £375

6262 — — Similar to 6257, but with legend KV instead of KVPA. *B.M.C. 29.* 13, 53 £400

6263 — Æ 'Asiatic' *hemidrachm* (*c.* 1·65 gm.). Similar to 6256, but with KV before the hd. of Zeus-Ammon. *B.M.C. 29., pl.* VII, 4 .. .. £150

6264 — — As 6262. *B.M.C. 29.* 14, 58 .. .. £175

6265 — Æ *trihemiobol* (*c.* 0·95 gm.). Hd. of Kyrene r., within olive-wreath. R. Hd. of Zeus-Ammon r., hair crimped and plaited; all in dotted square within incuse square. *B.M.C. 29.* 14, 59 .. .. £125

6266 — Æ *obol* (*c.* 0·65 gm.). Silphium plant. R. As last. *B.M.C. 29.* 14, 60 .. £100

6267 — Æ 'Asiatic' *hemiobol* (*c.* 0·28 gm.). Similar. *B.M.C. 29., pl.* VII, 16 .. £75

6268 6270

6268 400–331 B.C. N *stater* (*c.* 8·6 gm.). Fast quadriga driven r. by male charioteer; in ex., KYPANAION. R. Zeus-Ammon stg. facing, hd. r., holding sceptre; owl at feet to l.; silphium plant in field to r.; around, ΧΑΙΡΕΦΟΝ. *Naville* (*Les monnaies d'or de la Cyrénaique*) 3. *B.M.C. 29.* 25, 105 .. .. £2,750

6269 — N *drachm* (*c.* 3·44 gm.). Hd. of Zeus-Ammon l. R. Silphium plant; in field, K — Y / P — A / N — A. *Naville* 4 .. .. £1,000

6270 — N *hemidrachm* (*c.* 1·7 gm.). Silphium plant. R. Hd. of Zeus-Ammon r., within circle of dots. *B.M.C. 29.* 15, 62 .. .. £550

6271 — *N trihemiobol* (*c.* 0·85 gm.). Hd. of Kyrene r., her ear covered by disk. ℞. As last. *B.M.C. 29.* 16, 65 ..   ..   £275

6272 — *N ¾ obol* (*c.* 0·42 gm.). Bow-case. ℞. Silphium plant, within circular incuse. *Naville* 15   ..   ..   £200

6273   6275

6273 — *Æ tetradrachm* (*c.* 13 - 13·5 gm.). Silphium plant; in field, κ — v / p — a / n — a. ℞. Hd. of Zeus-Ammon r., with short, shaggy hair. *B.M.C. 29.* 17, 69 ..   ..   £1,800

6274 — — Hd. of Zeus-Ammon l., with short, shaggy hair. ℞. Silphium plant. *B.M.C. 29.* 18, 75 ..   ..   £1,600

6275 — — Hd. of Zeus-Ammon three-quarter face to l., wearing laur. diadem with uraeus-shaped ornament; all within laurel-wreath. ℞. Silphium plant; in field, v — ɪ / p — a / a — ʌ. *B.M.C. 29.* 19, 77   ..   ..   £7,500

6276 — — Hd. of Zeus-Ammon r., laur.; ΝΙΚΙΟΣ before. ℞. Silphium plant; infield, y — ɪ / a — q; all within circular incuse. *B.M.C. 29.* 21, 85 ..   ..   ..   £2,000

6277 — *Æ drachm* (*c.* 3·3 gm.). Silphium plant; y — ɪ in lower field. ℞. Hd. of Zeus Ammon r., within square linear frame surrounded by dots. *B.M.C. 29.* 23, 97   £350

6278 — — Silphium plant. ℞. Hd. of Zeus-Ammon three-quarter face to r., within circle of dots. *B.M.C. 29., pl.* XII, 10   ..   ..   £1,000

6279 — — Hd. of Zeus-Ammon r., hair crimped and plaited. ℞. Silphium plant, within circular incuse. *B.M.C. 29., pl.* XVI, 3   ..   ..   £375

6280   6284

6280 — — Silphium plant. ℞. Hd. of Karneios l., ΚΥΔΙ before; all within circular incuse. *B.M.C. 29.* 24, 100 ..   ..   £400

6281 — *Æ hemidrachm* (*c.* 1·55 gm.). Silphium plant. ℞. Hd. of Karneios l., within circle of dots. *B.M.C. 29., pl.* XII, 13   ..   ..   £175

6282 — — — ℞. Hd. of Karneios r., ΚΥΔΙΟΣ (retrograde) before; all within circle of dots enclosed by linear circle. *B.M.C. 29., pl.* XII, 15   ..   ..   ..   £200

6283 — *Æ diobol?* (*c.* 0·9 gm.). Three silphium plants arranged star-wise. ℞. Hd. of Zeus-Ammon r. *B.M.C. 29.* 24, 102 ..   ..   £150

6284 — — *Obv.* Similar; across field, κy — pa (retrograde). ℞. Hd. of Kyrene three-quarter face to r., hair confined by fillet. *B.M.C. 29.* 24, 103 ..   ..   ..   £250

6285 — — Hd. of Kyrene l., hair confined by fillet; all within linear circle surrounded by dots. ℞. Three silphium plants arranged star-wise; around, κ — y — p (retrograde). *B.M.C. 29.* 24, 104 ..   ..   £175

Kyrene *continued*

6286 331-322 B.C. (in 331 Kyrenaica made a treaty with Alexander the Great, who had just
conquered Egypt, and from this time dates a huge output of gold staters, etc., from the
Kyrene mint). *N stater* (*c.* 8·6 gm.). Fast quadriga driven l. by charioteer; beneath,
ΚΥΡΑΝΑΙΟΝ on partially raised tablet. R. Zeus-Ammon enthroned r., r. foot on stool,
holding lotus-headed sceptre; before, ΙΑΣΩΝ. *Naville* 18. *B.M.C. 29.* 27, 109   £2,750

6287   6288

6287 — — Stationary quadriga facing, driven by winged Nike; ΚΥΡΑΝΑΙ — ΩΝ in ex. and to r.
R. Zeus-Ammon enthroned l., holding lotus-headed sceptre; eagle r. behind, ΙΑΣΟΝΟΣ
before. *Naville* 22. *B.M.C. 29.* 26, 108   ..   ..   £3,000

6288 — — Slow quadriga, driven by charioteer, three-quarter face to r.; above, ΚΥΡ —
ΑΝΑΙΟΝ divided by star. R. Zeus Lykaios enthroned l., feet on stool, holding eagle;
behind, ΚΥΔΙΟΣΘ. *Naville* 30. *B.M.C. 29.* 28, 114   ..   ..   £2,250

6289 — — Slow quadriga, driven by charioteer, three-quarter face to l.; in ex., ΑΡΙΣΤΑΓΟΡΑ.
R. Zeus-Ammon stg. facing, hd. r., holding sceptre; at his feet, in background, ram stg.
r.; behind, ΚΥΡΑΝΑΙΟΝ. *Naville* 73. *B.M.C. 29.* 25, 106   ..   ..   ..   £3,000

6290 — *N drachm* (*c.* 4·3 gm.). Youth mounted on horse pacing l.; Κ — Υ / Ρ — Α — Ν in
field; all within linear circle surrounded by dots. R. Silphium plant, dividing Θ — Ε at
base; border as on *obv. Naville* 36. *B.M.C. 29.* 31, 128   ..   ..   ..   £1,200

6291   6295

6291 — *N hemidrachm* (*c.* 2·15 gm.). Three silphium plants arranged star-wise. R. Hd. of
Athena l., in crested Corinthian helmet; ΚΥΡ above, ΙΑΣ behind. *Naville* 41. *B.M.C.
29.* 32, 134-5   ..   ..   £650

6292 — *N tenth-stater* (*c.* 0·86 gm.). Hd. of Karneios r., with ram's horn in front of ear. R.
Hd. of Kyrene r., her ear covered by disk; all in linear circle within circular incuse.
Naville 16. *B.M.C. 29.* 16, 68   ..   ..   £300

6293 — — *Obv.* Similar, but with ΑΡΙ — ΣΤΙΟΣ (retrograde) behind and before Karneios' hd.
R. Hd. of Kyrene l., her ear covered by disk; all within circular incuse. *Naville* 17.
B.M.C. 29. 33, 138 ..   ..   £300

6294 — — Hd. of Karneios l.; Θ — ΕΥ before and behind neck; all within linear circle. R.
Hd. of Kyrene r., hair rolled; border as 6292. *Naville* 48. *B.M.C. 29.* 35, 145   £250

6295 — — Diad. hd. of Zeus-Ammon r.; all within linear circle. R. Hd. of Kyrene r.,
hair rolled; ΚΥΘ before; all within linear circle. *Naville* 67. *B.M.C. 29.* 35, 153
£275

6296 — — Hd. of Zeus-Ammon r., ΑΡΙ behind. R. Hd. of Kyrene three-quarter face to r.,
hair rolled. *Naville* 77. *B.M.C. 29.* 34, 140   ..   ..   £325

6297   6300

6297 — Æ *tetradrachm* (*c.* 13 gm.). Laur. hd. of Karneios l.; ΙΑ — ΣΟΝΟΣ beneath and behind; all within linear circle. R. Silphium plant, within linear circle. *B.M.C. 29.* 37, 164 ... £3,500

6298 — — Hd. of Zeus-Ammon l., ΘΕΥΦΕΙ (retrograde) before. R. Silphium plant; Ρ — Α / Υ — Ν in field. *B.M.C. 29.* 37, 165 .. .. £3,000

6299 — Æ *drachm* (*c.* 3·2 gm.). Diad. hd. of Karneios l., ΘΕΥ behind. R. Silphium plant; Κ — Υ / Ρ — Α in field. *B.M.C. 29.* 38, 167 .. .. £550

6300 322-308 B.C. N *stater* (*c.* 8·6 gm.). Slow quadriga, driven by charioteer, three-quarter face to r.; ΚΥΡΑΝΑΙ — ΟΝ behind and above; rad. sun in upper field to r. R. Zeus Lykaios enthroned l., feet on stool, holding eagle; before, thymiaterion; behind, ΧΑΙΡΙΟΣ (retrograde). *Naville* 83. *B.M.C. 29.* 29, 116 .. .. £2,250

6301 — — Slow quadriga, driven by winged Nike, three-quarter face to r.; ΚΥΡΑΝΑΙΟΝ above. R. Zeus-Ammon stg. facing, hd. l., sacrificing from phiale over thymiaterion and holding lotus-headed sceptre; on r., ΠΟΛΙΑΝΘΕΥΣ. *Naville* 91. *B.M.C. 29.* 30, 120 .. £2,500

6302 — — Hd. of Athena r., in crested Corinthian helmet. R. Nike advancing l., holding wreath and mast of ship; on r., ΚΥΡΑΝΑΙΟΝ; on l., ΠΤΟΛ — ΕΜΑΙΩ; ΕΥ in lower field to l. *Naville* 127. *B.M.C. 29.* 39, 170 .. .. £2,500

6303   6304

6303 — N *drachm* (*c.* 4·3 gm.). Youth mounted on horse prancing r.; in upper field on l., ΧΑΙΡΙΟΣ. R. Silphium plant; Κ — Υ / Ρ — Α in field; cicada at base of plant on l. *Naville* 106. *B.M.C. 29.* 32, 131 .. .. £1,100

6304 — N *hemidrachm* (*c.* 2·15 gm.). Hd. of Athena r., in crested Corinthian helmet; ΠΟΛΙΑΝ (retrograde) before. R. Three silphium plants arranged star-wise; Κ — Υ — Ρ around. *Naville* 113. *B.M.C. 29.* 33, 136 .. .. £600

6305 — N *tenth-stater* (*c.* 0·86 gm.). Hd. of Zeus-Ammon l., ΠΟ behind. R. Hd. of Libya r., hair falling in spiral curls; ΚΥ (retrograde) behind. *Naville* 117. *B.M.C. 29.* 36, 156 £250

6306 — — (reduced weight, *c.* 0·78 gm.). Hd. of Karneios l.; Θ — Ε either side of neck. R. Hd. of Kyrene l., hair rolled. *Naville* 146. *B.M.C. 29.* 48, 212 .. .. £225

6307 — — — Hd. of Zeus-Ammon r. R. Hd. of Nike (?) r., hair gathered into knot on the crown. *Naville* 149. *B.M.C. 29.* 124, 214 *bis* £275

6308 — Æ *didrachm* (*c.* 8·4 gm.). Hd. of young Dionysos r., wreathed with ivy; thyrsos behind, ΘΕΥΦΕΙΔΕΥΣ before. R. Silphium plant; Κ — Υ / Ρ — Α in field; corn-ear at base of plant on r. *B.M.C. 29., pl.* XVII, 5 .. .. £1,400

6309 — — Hd. of Karneios l., ΠΟΛΙΑΝΘΕΥΣ before. R. Hermes, naked but for chlamys fastened at neck, stg. facing, hd. l., holding caduceus; ΔΑΜΩΚΥΡΑΖΑΣ on r. *B.M.C. 29.* 40, 172 .. .. £2,000

Kyrene *continued*

6310 — — Hd. of young Dionysos (?) r., wreathed with ivy; quiver behind, ΦΕΙΔΩΝΟΣ (retrograde) before. R. ΚΥΡΑΝΑ (retrograde) upwards between silphium plant, on l., and palm-tree. *B.M.C. 29.* 40, 173 .. .. £1,250

6311 — Æ *trihemiobol* (*c.* 1 gm.). Hd. of Karneios l., ΠΟΛΙ behind. R. Silphium plant; κ — γ / ρ — A in field. *B.M.C. 29., pl.* XVII, 14 .. .. £200

6312

6314

6312 308-277 B.C. (governorship of Magas, step-son of Ptolemy I of Egypt). *N tetrobol* (*c.* 2·83 gm.). Youth mounted on horse pacing l.; star in upper field to r. R. Silphium plant; κυρα on l. *Naville* 159. *B.M.C. 29.* 48, 210 .. .. £550

6313 — — Similar, but with monogram in *rev.* field to r. *Naville* 161. *B.M.C. 29.* 48, 211 £550

6314 — *N obol* (*c.* 0·72 gm.). Hd. of Zeus-Ammon r. R. Thunderbolt between two stars. *Naville* 183. *B.M.C. 29.* 49, 218 .. .. £200

6315 — — Hd. of Zeus-Ammon l. R. Thunderbolt between monogram, on l., and star. *Naville* 232. *B.M.C. 29.* 50, 224 .. .. £225

6316 — — Hd. of Zeus-Ammon r. R. Hd. of Kyrene r., hair rolled; ΕΠ monogram behind. *Naville* 233. *B.M.C. 29.* 49, 215 .. .. £225

6317

6319

6317 — Æ *tetradrachm* ('Rhodian' standard, *c.* 15 - 15·5 gm.). Hd. of Zeus-Ammon r. R. Silphium plant; κυ — ρα either side of base; cornucopiae in field to r. *B.M.C. 29.* 50, 225 .. .. £3,500

6318 — Æ *didrachm* (*c.* 7·75 gm.). Diad. hd. of Karneios r. R. Silphium plant; κ — γ / ρ — A in field. *B.M.C. 29.* 50, 227 .. .. £300

6319 — — Bare hd. of Karneios r. R. κυ — ρα either side of silphium plant; star in upper field to r. *B.M.C. 29.* 52, 234 .. .. £225

6320 — — Similar, but *obv.* type to l.; and monogram in *rev.* field to l. *B.M.C. 29.* 52, 238 £225

6321 — — Bare hd. of Karneios r., with thick, curly hair. R. Silphium plant; κυ — ρα across upper field; tripod to l., ΕΠ monogram to r. *B.M.C. 29.* 54, 252 .. £250

6322 — — (reduced weight, *c.* 6·8 gm.). Hd. of Apollo Myrtous l., wreathed with myrtle. R. Silphium plant; κ — γ / ρ — A in field; jerboa on l., ΣΩ on r. *B.M.C. 29.* 55, 261 £350

6323 — — — *Obv.* Similar, but hd. r. ℞. Silphium plant; KY — PA across upper field;
| 🪙 KAE monogram to l., crab to r. *B.M.C. 29.* 56, 264 .. .. £375

6324 — — (weight further reduced, *c.* 5·5 - 5·75 gm.). Diad. hd. of Karneios r., with uraeus
ornament above forehead. ℞. Silphium plant. *B.M.C. 29.* 56, 266-7 .. £275

6325 — Æ *tetrobol* (*c.* 2·65 gm.). Hd. of Isis (?) l., wreathed with corn. ℞. KY — PA either
side of silphium plant; star in upper field to l., monogram to r. *B.M.C. 29.* 57, 268
£250

6326 — Æ ¾ *obol*? (*c.* 0·4 - 0·5 gm.). Horse pacing l., star above. ℞. Lyre. *B.M.C. 29.*
57, 272 .. .. £75

6327 — — Young male hd. r., diad. ℞. Star. *B.M.C. 29., pl.* XXV, 8-9 .. £65

6328 — — Hd. of Zeus-Ammon three-quarter face to r. ℞. Hd. of Athena r., in crested
helmet. *B.M.C. 29.* 57, 273 .. .. £85

6329 — — *Obv.* Similar to 6325. ℞. Eagle stg. l., wings open, striking at serpent. *B.M.C.*
29. 58, 275 .. .. £75

6330 277-261 B.C. (Magas in revolt against his half-brother Ptolemy II of Egypt). Æ *di-*
drachm (*c.* 6·8 gm.). Diad. hd. of Ptolemy I r., wearing aegis. ℞. ΒΑΣΙΛΕ. ΠΤΟΛΕ.
Eagle stg. r. on thunderbolt; behind, ΜΑΓ monogram; before, two apples on branch.
B.M.C. 29. 75, 8 .. .. £300

6331 6332

6331 — — Diad. hd. r. of Berenike I of Egypt, mother of Magas and wife of Ptolemy I. ℞.
ΒΕΡΕΝΙΚΗΣ / ΒΑΣΙΛΙΣΣΗΣ either side of club, beneath which ΜΑΓ monogram; Π in field to l.,
trident to r.; all within wreath of apple. *B.M.C. 29.* 75, 9 .. .. .. £350

6332 Mid-3rd cent. B.C. (coinage of the Kyrenaic league organized by Demophanes and Ekde-
mos of Megalopolis). Æ *didrachm* (*c.* 7·6 gm.). Diad. hd. of Zeus-Ammon r. ℞.
ΚΟΙ — ΝΟΝ either side of silphium plant; in upper field to l., gazelle's horn. *B.M.C. 29.*
68, 1 .. .. £750

6333 *Bronze Coinage.* Before 308 B.C. Æ 22 (*unit*). Hd. of Karneios r.; A — ΝΑΡ beneath
and behind. ℞. Silphium plant; K — Y across field. *B.M.C. 29.* 41, 175 .. £20

6334 6336

Kyrene *continued*

6334 — — Hd. of Kyrene r., hair rolled; silphium fruit behind, KYPANA before. R. Three silphium plants arranged star-wise. *B.M.C. 29.* 41, 179 .. .. .. £20

6335 — — Laur. hd. of Zeus-Ammon r.; EY behind. R. Silphium plant; K — Y / P — A in field. *B.M.C. 29.* 42, 181 .. .. £18

6336 — — Laur. hd. of Apollo r.; THPEYΣ (retrograde) before. R. KYP / ANA either side of silphium plant. *B.M.C. 29.* 42, 183 .. .. £16

6337 — — Hd. of Zeus-Ammon r. R. Large six-spoked wheel, with hub, seen in perspective. *B.M.C. 29.* 43, 187 .. .. £20

6338 — — Horse's hd. r.; AΘ(?) above. R. As last. *B.M.C. 29.* 43, 188 .. £24

6339 — Æ 19 (*half-unit*). Horse prancing r., star above. R. Large wheel, as 6337; NIKΩNOΣ to r. *B.M.C. 29.* 43-4, 189-93 .. .. £20

6340   6343

6340 — — Youth mounted on horse prancing r., ΘA beneath. R. Large four-spoked wheel, with hub, seen in perspective; silphium plant between the spokes, on r. *B.M.C. 29.* 44, 194 .. .. £20

6341 — Æ 16 (*quarter-unit*). Hd. of Karneios r., THP behind. R. Three silphium plants arranged star-wise; K — Y — P around. *B.M.C. 29.* 45, 198 .. .. .. £13

6342 — — Diad. hd. of Karneios r.; AN — ΔP either side of neck. R. K — Y either side of silphium plant; all within linear circle. *B.M.C. 29.* 45, 200 .. .. .. £14

6343 — — Hd. of Athena r., in crested Corinthian helmet. R. Double silphium plant springing from a common base. *B.M.C. 29.* 46, 202-3 .. .. £13

6344   6347

6344 — Æ 13 (*eighth*). Horse pacing r. R. Wheel, as 6340, but without silphium plant; K — Y / P — A in field. *B.M.C. 29.* 46, 204-7 .. .. £15

6345 — Æ 10 (*sixteenth*). Hd. of Libya r., hair in spiral curls. R. Gazelle stg. r.; KYPA above, plectrum (?) before. *B.M.C. 29.* 47, 209 .. .. £12

6346 300-277 B.C. (governorship of Magas). Æ 22. Hd. of Zeus-Ammon r. R. Wheel, as 6337. *B.M.C. 29.* 58, 278.. .. .. £18

6347 — Æ 18. Gazelle stg. l.; ΣΩΣIOΣ above, bunch of grapes before. R. Silphium plant. *B.M.C. 29.* 59, 285 .. .. £16

6348 — Æ 15. Diad. hd. of Libya r., hair in spiral curls. R. Gazelle stg. r.; KY above, A before. *B.M.C. 29.* 60, 287 .. .. £15

6349   6351

6349 — Æ 11.   Hd. of Zeus-Ammon three-quarter face to r.   R. Hd. of Athena r., in crested helmet; cap (?) behind.   *B.M.C. 29.* 60, 288   ..   ..   £14

6350 — Æ 18.   *Obv.* As 6348.   R. Silphium plant; κ — Υ / P — A in field.   *B.M.C. 29.* 60, 290   ..   ..   £13

6351 — — Diad. hd. of Zeus-Ammon r.   R. Palm-tree with fruit; κ — Υ / PA in field; small silphium plant and crab at foot of tree on r.   *B.M.C. 29.* 61, 298   ..   £12

6352 — — Similar, but with κ — Υ / PA — ΔA in *rev.* field, and silphium plant only at foot of palm-tree.   *B.M.C. 29.* 62, 306 ..   ..   £12

6353 — — As last, but with Γ (=3) instead of ΔA in *rev.* field to r.   *B.M.C. 29.* 63, 311   £12

Other numerals, perhaps representing dates, are known for this series, e.g. A, B, Δ, E, H, I, K *and* M.

6354   6356

6354 — — Hd. of Apollo Myrtous r., wreathed with myrtle.   R. Lyre; κ — Υ / P — A in field.   *B.M.C. 29.* 64, 319 ..   ..   £12

6355 — — Similar, but also with star above lyre on *rev.*   *B.M.C. 29.* 66, 332   ..   £12

6356 — — *Obv.* Similar.   R. Horse prancing r.; ΚΥ and star above, crab beneath.   *B.M.C. 29.* 67, 343-6   ..   ..   £13

6357   6362

6357 277-261 B.C. (Magas in revolt).   Æ 22.   Diad. hd. of Ptolemy I of Egypt r.   R. Winged thunderbolt; above, ΠΤΟΛΕΜΑΙΟΥ and ΜΑΓ monogram; beneath, ΒΑΣΙΛΕΩΣ.   *B.M.C. 29.* 76, 14   ..   ..   £16

6358 — Æ 19.   *Obv.* Similar.   R. ΠΤΟΛΕΜΑΙΟΥ ΒΑΣΙΛΕΩΣ.   Eagle stg. l. on thunderbolt; ΜΑΓ monogram in field to l.   *B.M.C. 29.* 77, 20 ..   ..   £12

6359 — — — R. Prow of galley l.; ΠΤΟΛ above, ΒΑΣΙ beneath, ΜΑΓ monogram in field to l.   *B.M.C. 29.* 78, 25   ..   ..   £15

6360 — Æ 15.   *Obv.* Similar.   R. ΒΑΣΙΛ. ΠΤΟ.   Forepart of Pegasos r.; beneath, ΜΑΓ monogram and crab.   *B.M.C. 29.* 78, 26   ..   ..   £13

6361 — Æ 13.   *Obv.* Similar.   R. Horse galloping l.; ΜΑΓ monogram above.   *B.M.C. 29.* 79, 28   ..   ..   £11

Kyrene *continued*

6362 — Æ 20. Dr. and diad. bust of Berenike I of Egypt r. R. ΒΕΡΕΝΙΚΗΣ / ΒΑΣΙΛΙΣΣΗΣ either side of sling (?), beneath which ΜΑΓ monogram; all within olive-wreath. *B.M.C.* *29.* 79, 29 .. .. £20

6363   6368

6363 Mid-3rd cent. B.C. (coinage of the Kyrenaic league). Æ 23. Diad. hd. of Zeus-Ammon r. R. Silphium plant; K — O / I — N / O — N in field. *B.M.C. 29.* 69, 4-15 .. £17

6364 — — Similar, but with legend KOI — NON on either side of silphium plant. *B.M.C.* *29.* 70-71, 22-29 .. .. £18

6365 After 67 B.C. (under Roman rule). Æ 24. Hd. of Roma r., in crested Corinthian helmet. R. Bee. *B.M.C. 29.* 113, 1 .. .. £35

6366 — — Similar, but hd. of Roma to l., with ΡΩΜΙ (retrograde) above. *B.M.C. 29.*, *pl.* XXXIX, 1 .. .. £40

6367 — — Similar to 6365, but with KPHT above hd. of Roma, and K — Y / P — A in *rev.* field. *B.M.C. 29.*, *pl.* XXXIX, 2 .. .. £45

Kyrenaica and the island of Crete were united to form a single province in the first phase of Roman rule in the area.

6368 *Circa* 54 B.C. (?). Æ 18. P. LICINIVS P.F. PRO Q. Diad. and dr. bust of Libya r.; ΛΙ — ΒΥΗ across field. R. Legend as *obv.* Dr. bust of Creta-Artemis r., bow and quiver at shoulder; KPHTA beneath, Β in field to r. *B.M.C. 29.* 113, 2 .. .. .. £25

6369 *Circa* 35 B.C. Æ 32 (*sestertius*). Hd. of Zeus-Ammon r.; lotus-headed sceptre before, Я behind. R. Curule chair; ΛΟΛΛΙΟΥ above, Η between legs. *B.M.C. 29.* 116, 20 £75

6370 — Æ 28 (*dupondius*). Hd. of Apollo r., bow and quiver at shoulder; beneath chin, Β. R. Dromedary stg. r., Ε beneath; ΛΟΛ / Λ — Ι / Ο — Υ in field. *B.M.C. 29.* 116, 22 £50

6371 — Æ 18 (*as*). Diad. hd. of Libya r., hair in formal curls; beneath chin, Β. R. Caduceus between poppy and ear of corn; Λ — Ο / Λ — ΛΙ / ΟΥ in field, Β beneath corn-ear. *B.M.C.* *29.*, *pl.* XLII, 7 .. .. £25

6372 — Æ 15 (*semis*). Hd. of Libya, as last; K — P across field, A beneath (KPA = Crassus). R. Silphium plant; K — Y across field. *B.M.C. 29.* 117, 26 .. .. .. £18

This is the final appearance of the silphium plant as a coin type.

N.B. *For other coins struck at Kyrene see below under Hellenistic Monarchies—the Ptolemaic Kingdom of Egypt. The subsequent Roman Provincial bronze coinage of Kyrenaica will be listed in a future catalogue covering the 'Greek Imperial' series and contemporary coinages.*

6373 **Barke** (founded from Kyrene about 560 B.C., Barke was situated west of its mother-city and some distance inland from the Mediterranean coastline. In Ptolemaic times it was eclipsed by its port which, under the name of Ptolemais, became the principal city of western Kyrenaica). 485-475 B.C. Æ *tetradrachm* (*c.* 17-17·5 gm.). Silphium plant between two fruits; above, BAPKA. R. Silphium fruit between two dolphins, upwards; all within incuse square. *Price & Waggoner* (*The* "*Asyut*" *Hoard*) 845-55 .. £3,500

6374

6376

6374 — — *Obv.* Similar, but without legend. R. Bull stg. r., palm-tree in background; Ꙅ in lower field to r.; all within incuse square. *B.M.C. 29.* 91, 1 .. .. £4,000

6375 — Æ *didrachm* (*c.* 8·5 gm.). Forepart of bull l., silphium fruit before. R. Ram's hd. l., in dotted square; all within incuse square. *B.M.C. 29.* 91, 2 .. .. .. £1,400

6376 — Æ 'Asiatic' *drachm* (*c.* 3·25 - 3·5 gm.). Silphium plant. R. Ram's hd. l., BAP above; all within incuse square. *B.M.C. 29.* 92, 4 .. .. £550

6377 450-420 B.C. Æ *tetradrachm* (*c.* 17 gm.). Silphium plant. R. Hd. of Zeus-Ammon r., BAP before; all within heavy cable border. *B.M.C. 29.* 93, 7 .. .. .. £4,000

6378

6382

6378 — — Similar, but on *rev.* the hd. of Ammon is encircled by dots, around which BAPKAION; all within circular incuse. *B.M.C. 29.* 94, 9 .. .. £3,500

6379 — — Hd. of Zeus-Ammon r., with thick curly hair; BAP before; all within heavy cable border. R. Silphium plant, within incuse square. *B.M.C. 29., pl.* XXXIV, 6 £5,000

6380 — — (commemorating alliance with **Kyrene**). Silphium plant; K — Y either side of base, P in field to r. R. Hd. of Zeus-Ammon r., B / A / P before, encircled by dots; all within incuse square in the corners of which, B — A — P — K. *B.M.C. 29.* 107, 49 £6,000

6381 — — (commemorating alliance with **Teuchira**). Silphium plant; T — E either side of base. R. Hd. of Zeus-Ammon r., T before, encircled by heavy cable border; all within incuse square in the corners of which, B — A — P — K. *B.M.C. 29.* 107, 50 .. £6,500

6382 — Æ 'Asiatic' *drachm* (*c.* 3·3 gm.). Silphium plant. R. Hd. of Zeus-Ammon r. encircled by dots; all within incuse square in the corners of which, B — A — P — K. *B.M.C. 29.* 95, 11 .. .. £375

6383 — — — R. Hd. of Zeus-Ammon r., BAP before; all within circle of dots. *B.M.C. 29.* 96, 16 .. .. £400

6384 — Æ 'Asiatic' *hemidrachm* (*c.* 1·6 gm.). As 6382. *B.M.C. 29.* 96, 17 .. £200

6385 — — Silphium plant. R. Hd. of Zeus-Ammon r., surrounded by square dotted frame in the corners of which, B — A — P — K; all within incuse square. *B.M.C. 29.* 97, 18 £200

Barke *continued*

6386   6389

6386 400-331 B.C.   *N trihemiobol* (*c.* 0·84 gm.).   Hd. of Karneios r.   R. Ram's hd. r.   *Naville*
   (*Les monnaies d'or de la Cyrénaique*) 260.   *B.M.C. 29.* 98, 20 ..   ..   ..   £400
6387 — *N* ¾ *obol* (*c.* 0·42 gm.).   Horse's hd. r.   R. As last.   *Naville* 261-2   ..   £275
6388 — *Æ tetradrachm* (*c.* 13 - 13·5 gm.).   Silphium plant.   R. Diad. hd. of Zeus-Ammon r.,
   BAPKAI (retrograde) before.   *B.M.C. 29.* 98, 21 ..   ..   £2,750
6389 — — Silphium plant; ᗺ — A / ꟼ — K / A — I in field.   R. Hd. of Zeus-Ammon r.
   B.M.C. 29. 99, 25 ..   ..   £3,000
6390 — — Laur. hd. of Zeus-Ammon r., ear of corn behind.   R. Silphium plant, BAP on r.;
   all within linear circle surrounded by dots.   *B.M.C. 29.* 100, 29   ..   ..   £3,500

6394

6391   6397

6391 — — Three silphium plants arranged star-wise, BAPKAION (retrograde) around; in the
   angles, owl, chameleon and jerboa; heavy cable border.   R. Hd. of Zeus-Ammon facing,
   AKE — ΣΙΟΣ either side of neck; border as on *obv.*   *B.M.C. 29.* 101, 33 ..   ..   £10,000
6392 — *Æ drachm* (*c.* 3·3 gm.).   Silphium plant.   R. Hd. of Karneios l., BAP (retrograde)
   behind.   *B.M.C. 29.* 102, 35   ..   ..   £500
6393 — — Hd. of Zeus-Ammon r.   R. Silphium plant within incuse square, in the four
   corners of which B — A — P — K.   *B.M.C. 29.* 102, 36 ..   ..   £450
6394 — *Æ hemidrachm* (*c.* 1·65 gm.).   Silphium plant.   R. Hd. of Karneios r., BAP behind;
   all within linear circle.   *B.M.C. 29.* 103, 39-40 ..   ..   £275
6395 — — — R. Hd. of Zeus-Ammon r., KAINIΩ before.   *B.M.C. 29.* 103, 41   ..   £250
6396 — *Æ trihemiobol* (*c.* 0·82 gm.).   Female hd. r., ear covered by disk; BAPK behind.   R.
   Hd. of Zeus-Ammon r., within incuse square in the four corners of which, B — A (on r.)
   P — K (on l.).   *B.M.C. 29.* 104, 42   ..   ..   £175
6397 — — Three silphium plants arranged star-wise.   R. Hd. of Karneios r.; AΛA — I either
   side of neck.   *B.M.C. 29.* 105, 45   ..   ..   £175

6398 Late 4th-early 3rd cent. B.C.   Æ 19.   Horse prancing r.   R. Ram stg. r., BAP in ex.
   B.M.C. 29. 105, 47 ..   ..   £30

6399 — Æ 17. Diad. hd. of Zeus-Ammon r. R. Palm-tree between silphium plant (on l.) and ear of corn; in field to l., BAPK monogram; to r., ΔAP. *B.M.C. 29., pl.* XXXVII, 18
                                          £25

6400 — — Hd. of Apollo Myrtous r., wreathed with myrtle. R. Horse prancing r.; above, BAPK monogram and star; beneath, cornucopiae. *B.M.C. 29.* 106, 48   ..   £25

6401   6402

6401 **Euesperides** (the westernmost city of the Kyrenaica, Euesperides was subject to frequent attacks from the Libyans of the interior and had to be re-settled from Kyrene about 460 B.C. The name of the city was changed to Berenike by Ptolemy III of Egypt, *c.* 245 B.C.). 485-475 B.C. Æ 'Asiatic' *drachm* (*c.* 3·25-3·5 gm.). Silphium plant; Ε — Σ across lower field. R. Dolphin leaping l.; ΕΥ beneath, two pellets above; all within incuse square. *B.M.C. 29.* 109, 1   ..   ..   £600

6402 *Circa* 440 B.C. Æ 'Asiatic' *drachm* (*c.* 3·1 gm.). Silphium plant. R. Hd. of Zeus-Ammon r. encircled by dots; all within incuse square in the corners of which, Ε — Υ — Ε — Σ. *B.M.C. 29.* 110, 2   ..   ..   £500

6403 — Æ 'Asiatic' *hemidrachm* (*c.* 1·55 gm.). Similar. *B.M.C. 29.* 111, 5   ..   £250

6404 *Circa* 375 B.C. Æ *tetradrachm* (*c.* 12·5 gm.). Hd. of Zeus-Ammon r., within triple circle. R. Silphium plant; around, ΕΥΕΣΠΕΡΙΤΑΝ; heavy cable border. *B.M.C. 29., pl.* XXXVIII, 11   ..   ..   (*Unique*)

6405 313-308 B.C. Æ *didrachm* (*c.* 8·4 gm.). Hd. of young river-god Lethon (?) r., wearing wreath of water plants; behind, ΕΣΠΕΡ.... R. Gazelle (?) r., starting backwards at silphium plant before; another silphium, smaller, beneath; behind, ΤΙΜΑΓΟΡΑ. *B.M.C. 29., pl.* XXXVIII, 12   ..   ..   (*Unique*)

6406 Late 4th-early 3rd cent. B.C. Æ 20. Laur. hd. of Zeus-Ammon l. R. Trident; Ε — Υ either side of shaft. *B.M.C. 29.* 111, 6   ..   ..   £30

6407 — Æ 18. Hd. of young river-god Lethon r.; ΛΗΘΩΝ before. R. Silphium plant; Ε — Υ across field. *B.M.C. 29.* 112, 8   ..   ..   £30

6408   6409

6408 — Æ 15. Dolphin leaping r., ΕΥ beneath. R. Trident, within wreath. *B.M.C. 29.* 112, 11   ..   ..   £25

6409 — Æ 18. Hd. of Apollo Myrtous r., wreathed with myrtle. R. Horse prancing r.; above, Ε and star; beneath, apple-branch. *B.M.C. 29.* 112, 12-13   ..   ..   £25

Teuchira (situated between Ptolemais and Euesperides, Teuchira received the name Arsinoe in Ptolemaic times). See no. 6381 above.

6410 **Ptolemais** (originally the port of Barke, the city was greatly enlarged in Ptolemaic times and grew in importance at the expense of its inland neighbour). *Circa* 35 B.C. Æ 30. Turreted hd. of Tyche r.; Π — Τ / Ο — Λ / Ε — Μ / Α — Ι in field, reading from bottom to top. R. Crocodile stg. r.; above, ΚΡΑΣ (=Crassus). *B.M.C. 29., pl.* XLII, 10
                                          £90

MAP 22   SYRTICA TO NUMIDIA

6411   6413

6411 **SYRTICA** (the narrow coastal strip facing the great Mediterranean bay extending from
Syrtis Major in the east to Syrtis Minor in the west.   The land was, for the most part,
infertile comprising sand interspersed with salt marshes). **Leptis Magna** (a great
Phoenician emporium founded in the 7th cent. B.C. by colonists from Sidon).   1st cent.
B.C.   Æ *drachm* (*c.* 2·85 gm.).   Lion's skin draped over club; in field to l., bow; to r.,
cup and A.   R. Panther leaping l.; above, thyrsos; beneath, Punic legend (= *Lephki*).
Müller (Numismatique de l'ancienne Afrique) II, 5, 13   ..   ..   £350

6412 — Æ 27. Hd. of Dionysos l., wreathed with ivy; before, Punic legend (=*Lephki*).
R. Laur. hd. of bearded Herakles r.; before, legend as on *obv*. *Müller* II, 3, 3   £30

6413 — Æ 20. Turreted hd. of Tyche r. R. Club and thyrsos in saltire; in the angles,
Punic legend (=*Lephki*). *Müller* II, 4, 6   ..   ..   £15

6414 — — Cista mystica containing serpent; all within ivy-wreath. R. Wine-cup before
two thyrsoi in saltire; in the angles, Punic legend (=*Lephki*). *Müller* II, 4, 8   £20

6415 — Æ 15. Turreted hd. of Tyche r. R. Punic legend (=*Lephki*) either side of thyrsos;
all within wreath. *Müller* II, 5, 12   ..   ..   £15

6416 **Oea** (situated between Leptis Magna and Sabratha). 1st cent. B.C. Æ 30. Turreted
hd. of Tyche l.; behind, Punic legend (= *Oyath* ?). R. Laur. hd. of Apollo r.; uncertain
Punic legend before. *Müller* II, 15, 28 ..   ..   £45

6417 — Æ 18. Bow and quiver; in field, on either side, Punic legend (=*Oyath* ?). R. Two circular shields, with spear behind each. *Müller* II, 15, 31 .. .. .. £30

6418 — Æ 15. Crested helmet l. R. Tripod; in field, on either side, Punic legend (= *Oyath* ?). *Müller* II, 16, 33 .. .. £20

6419   6421

6419 **Sabratha** (the most westerly of the three chief cities of Syrtica which together formed the African Tripolis). 1st cent. B.C. Æ 33. Laur. hd. of bearded Herakles r.; x with four pellets beneath chin. R. Pentastyle temple; beneath, Punic legend (=*Tsabrathan*). *Müller* II, 26, 48 .. .. £65

6420 — Æ 26. Hd. of Serapis r., surmounted by kalathos. R. As last. *Müller* II, 27, 49 £45

6421 — Æ 16. Hd. of Hermes r., wearing winged petasos. R. Punic legend (=*Tsabran*) in two lines across field. *Müller* II, 27, 51 .. .. £20

6422 **BYZACIUM** (the area to the south of Zeugitana. The name more properly belongs to the Roman period). **Alipota** (also known as **Sullecti,** this town was situated between Achulla and Thapsus). 1st cent. B.C. Æ 30. Diad. hd. of Astarte l. R. Caduceus; in field, Punic legend (=*Alipota*). *Müller* II, 42, 5 .. .. £45

6423 **Hadrumetum** (a flourishing coastal city of Phoenician origin, Hadrumetum was in the northern part of Byzacium close to the border with Zeugitana). 1st cent. B.C. Æ 24. Dr. bust of Neptune r.; HADR behind, trident before. R. Veiled and diad. hd. of Astarte l.; behind, cruciform sceptre. *Müller* II, 51, 21.. .. .. £60

6424 **Thaena** (another Phoenician coastal town, Thaena was situated in the south-east of the country). 1st cent. B.C. Æ 30. Hd. of Serapis r., surmounted by kalathos; before, Punic legend (=*Thainath*). R. Diad. hd. of Astarte r.; before, Punic legend as on *obv*. *Müller* II, 40, 1 .. .. £65

6425 **Thysdrus** (an inland town lying on the road between Hadrumetum and Thaena, the site is today known as *el Djem*). 1st cent.B.C. Æ 22. Diad. and veiled hd. of Astarte r., cruciform sceptre behind. R. Lyre; on l., Punic legend (=*Stpsr*). *Müller* II, 58, 34 £45

6426   6428

6426 **ZEUGITANA** (the coastal region lying to the north of Byzacium and bordering Numidia in the west.   In addition to Carthage the region contained two other Phoenician colonies, Hippo and Utica, and a town of Greek foundation originally called Aspis, later Clypea). **Carthage** (the great maritime trading city of Carthage was founded by Phoenician colonists from Tyre in the 8th cent. B.C.   Through its favourable geographical position and the excellence of its harbour it gradually achieved economic and political importance and became independent of its mother city.   From the 6th to the 3rd cent. B.C. the Carthaginians dominated trade in the western Mediterranean area and established outposts in southern Spain, Sardinia and Sicily.   The first conflict with Rome (Punic Wars) came in 264 B.C.   The struggle continued, intermittently, for more than a century but finally resulted in the total destruction of Carthage, 146 B.C.   The Carthaginians felt no need of coinage until their large scale invasion of Sicily at the end of the 5th cent.   From this time, and throughout most of the following century, they minted large quantities of silver tetradrachms in the island for the payment of troops engaged in the wars against the Greek cities of Sicily.   This coinage is commonly called 'Siculo-Punic' and was largely derived from Greek prototypes, particularly the late 5th cent. issues of Syracuse.   Carthage itself, about the middle of the 4th cent., began issuing gold staters, and this important coinage remained in abundant production down to the time of the First Punic War. From about 320 B.C., however, the metal was progressively debased).   SICULO-PUNIC SERIES.   Late 5th cent. B.C.   *Æ tetradrachm* (*c.* 17 gm.).   Forepart of prancing horse r., crowned by Nike flying r. above; barleycorn in field to r.; beneath, Punic legend (='New city of Carthage').   ℞. Date-palm tree; across lower field, Punic legend (='the Camp').   *Kraay* (*Archaic and Classical Greek Coins*) *pl.* 51, 872.   *Müller* II, 74, 3   £1,250

6427 Early 4th cent. B.C.   *Æ tetradrachm* (*c.* 17 gm.).   Horse prancing l., crowned by Nike flying l. above; beneath, Punic legend, as last, but inscribed on tablet (?).   ℞. As last. *Principal Coins*, III. C. 40.   *Müller* II, 75, 7   .. .. £1,750

6428 — — Similar, but horse and Nike to r. on *obv.*, and without legends on either side. *Müller* II, 77, 33   .. .. £1,250

6429 Mid-4th cent. B.C.   *Æ tetradrachm* (*c.* 17 gm.).   Female hd. l., wreathed with corn; behind, Punic letter (=*m* ='the Camp'?).   ℞. Horse stg. l., palm-tree in background. *Müller* II, 76, 22   .. .. £1,600

The obv. type of this series is derived from the Persephone head by the artist Euainetos on the coinage of Syracuse.

6430   6433

6430 — — Female hd. r., wreathed with corn; before, thymiaterion. ℞. Horse stg. r., crowned by Nike flying l.; palm-tree in background; in field to r., caduceus; beneath horse, Punic letters (=*hb*). *Müller* II, 77, 28 .. .. £900

6431 — — *Obv.* Similar, but without thymiaterion. ℞. Horse prancing r.; palm-tree in background. *Müller* II, 78, 44 .. .. £1,750

6432 — — Female hd. l., wreathed with corn; around, four dolphins. ℞. Horse prancing l.; palm-tree in background. *Forrer/Weber* 1773. *Müller* II, 78, 40 .. .. £1,250

    This obv. type is a very close copy of the Syracusan original.

6433 — — Female hd. l. (Dido or Libya?), wearing tiara. ℞. Lion stg. l.; palm-tree in background; in ex., Punic legend (='the People of the Camp'). *Principal Coins*, III. C.41. *Müller* II, 75, 16 .. .. £3,000

6434 350-325 B.C. Æ *tetradrachm* (*c.* 17 gm.). *Obv.* Similar to 6432; beneath chin, pellet. ℞. Head and neck of horse l., palm-tree behind; beneath, Punic letter (=*m* ='the Camp'?). *Principal Coins*, IV.C.21. *Müller* II, 76, 24 .. .. .. £750

6435 — — Similar, but with scallop-shell instead of pellet on *obv.*, and with Punic legend (='the People of the Camp') beneath horse's hd. on *rev.* *Müller* II, 75, 14 .. £750

6436 325-300 B.C. Æ *tetradrachm* (*c.* 17 gm.). Hd. of young Herakles r., clad in lion's skin. ℞. As last. *Principal Coins*, IV.C.19. *Müller* II, 75, 8 .. .. .. £500

    This obv. type is clearly derived from the coinage of Alexander the Great.

6437 — — Similar, but on *rev.* the horse's hd. is turned to r., and with two corn-ears in field to r. *Müller* II, 75, 12 .. .. £750

6438 — — *Obv.* Similar. ℞. Head and neck of horse l., palm-tree behind; beneath, Punic legend (= 'the paymasters'). *Müller* II, 76, 18 .. .. £500

6439 — — Similar, but also with club in *rev.* field to l. *Müller* II, 76, 19 .. .. £550

N.B. *It is not possible to identify with certainty the Sicilian mint or mints involved in the production of this coinage (nos. 6426-39). It has recently been suggested, by G. Kenneth Jenkins, that* **Lilybaion** *was responsible for the majority of these issues.*

    For other 'Siculo-Punic' coins of the 5th-4th cent. B.C., see Volume I of this Catalogue (under Sicily), mints of Panormos (nos. 880-95), Kephaloidion (no. 775) and Motya (nos. 861-71).

6440 270-260 B.C. Electrum *triple-shekel* (*c.* 22·8 gm.). Hd. of Tanit l., wreathed with corn, wearing necklace and triple-drop ear-ring. ℞. Horse prancing r., palm-tree in background; beneath, Punic legend (='in the land'). *Jenkins & Lewis (Carthaginian Gold and Electrum Coins)* 368-76 (*Group* VIII). *Müller* II, 86, 76 .. .. .. £2,500

Siculo-Punic Series *continued*

6441 — Æ *dodekadrachm* (*c.* 45·6 gm.). *Obv.* Similar. ℞. Horse prancing l. *Principal Coins*, V. C.30. *Müller* II, 91, 125 .. .. £7,500

6442 — Æ *dekadrachm* (*c.* 38 gm.). *Obv.* Similar, but ear-ring has only single drop. ℞. Pegasos flying r.; beneath, Punic legend (='in the land'). *Principal Coins,* ℣V. C.29. *Müller* II, 91, 127 .. .. £3,000

6443 — Æ *hexadrachm* (*c.* 22 gm.). *Obv.* As 6440. ℞. Head and neck of horse r. *Principal Coins*, V. C.31. *Müller* II, 92, 129 .. .. £3,500

N.B. *The place of mintage of nos. 6440-43 is also uncertain, though Panormos has been suggested and the little evidence that is available would seem to support this view.*

6444 *Bronze Coinage.* Late 4th cent. B.C. Æ 16. Hd. of Tanit l., similar to 6440; behind, pellet. ℞. Horse stg. r., palm-tree in background; before, three pellets in triangular arrangement with a fourth pellet below. *Jenkins & Lewis, pl.* 26, 12. *Müller* II, 95, 168 .. .. £5

Many varieties of this type exist with different numbers of pellets variously disposed on *obv. and rev.*

6445

6445 MINT OF CARTHAGE. *Gold and electrum coinage.* 350-320 B.C. *N* 2½ *drachms* (*c.* 9·4 gm.). Hd. of Tanit l., wreathed with corn, wearing necklace and triple-drop ear-ring. R. Horse stg. r.; pattern resembling inscription in ex.; two pellets in lower field. *Jenkins & Lewis* 6. *Müller* II, 84, 46 .. .. £1,000

6446 — — Similar, but on *rev.* double exergual line, and three pellets in triangular arrangement at horse's feet; no pattern in ex. *Jenkins & Lewis* 14 .. .. .. £950

6447 — — As last, but also with circle in field above horse on *rev.* *Jenkins & Lewis* 18 £950

6448 — — *Obv.* Similar. R. Horse stg. r.; at feet, three pellets in triangular arrangement; in ex., eye (on l.) and goat's hd. (on r.). *Jenkins & Lewis* 22. *Müller (Supplement)*, 48, 45*A* £1,250

6449 — — As last, but without the symbols in ex. *Jenkins & Lewis* 36. *Müller* II, 84, 45 £800

6450 — — Similar, but also with fourth pellet, beneath horse. *Jenkins & Lewis* 25 £800

6451   6452

6451 — — *Obv.* Similar. R. Horse stg. r.; beneath, three pellets, two of them on the exergual line. *Jenkins & Lewis* 114. *Principal Coins*, IV. C.18 .. .. .. £800

6452 — *N half-stater* (*c.* 4·7 gm.). Hd. of Tanit l., as 6445. R. Horse stg. r., palm-tree in background. *Jenkins & Lewis* 52. *Müller* II, 84, 54 .. .. £750

6453 — *N quarter-stater* (*c.* 2·35 gm.). Hd. of Tanit l., wreathed with corn, wearing single-drop ear-ring. R. Palm-tree. *Jenkins & Lewis* 115. *Müller* II, 87, 78 .. £350

6454 — *N fifth-stater* or *hemidrachm* (*c.* 1·88 gm.). *Obv.* Similar. R. Horse stg. r., looking back. *Jenkins & Lewis* 120. *Müller* II, 85, 67 .. .. £275

6455 — *N tenth-stater* or *trihemiobol* (*c.* 0·94 gm.). Palm-tree. R. Head and neck of horse r. *Jenkins & Lewis* 138. *Müller* II, 87, 79 .. .. £200

6456   6458

6456 320-310 B.C. Electrum *shekel-didrachm* (*c.* 7·6 gm., 72% gold). Hd. of Tanit l., wreathed with corn, wearing necklace and triple-drop ear-ring. R. Horse stg. r., l. foreleg drawn slightly back; dotted pattern in ex. *Jenkins & Lewis* 177 .. £650

6457 — — *Obv.* Similar. R. Horse stg. r.; pellet on exergual line, between horse's hind-hooves. *Jenkins & Lewis* 190 .. .. £600

6458 — — — R. Horse stg. r. with hd. erect, giving the animal a somewhat haughty aspect. *Jenkins & Lewis* 209 .. .. £700

6459 — — — R. Horse stg. r.; beneath, two pellets on the exergual line. *Jenkins & Lewis* 226 .. .. £600

6460 — Electrum *fifth-stater* (*c.* 1·52 gm.). Hd. of Tanit l., wreathed with corn, wearing single-drop ear-ring. R. Horse stg. r., looking back; beneath, two pellets. *Jenkins & Lewis* 234 .. .. £275

6461

6462

Carthage continued

6461 — Electrum *tenth-stater* (c. 0·76 gm.). Palm-tree. ℞. Head and neck of horse r.; pellet in field to r. *Jenkins & Lewis* 243. *Müller* II, 87, 81 .. .. .. £200

6462 310-290 B.C. Electrum *shekel-didrachm* (c. 7·6 gm., 55-60% gold). Hd. of Tanit l., wreathed with corn and with prominent curl on top in place of the usual corn-ear; she wears necklace and triple-drop ear-ring; pellet in lower field before necklace. ℞. Horse stg. r. on double exergual line; pellet in lower field before horse's fore-hooves. *Jenkins & Lewis* 249 .. .. £500

6463 — — *Obv.* Similar. ℞. Horse stg. r., l. foreleg drawn slightly back. *Jenkins & Lewis* 256 .. .. £550

6464 — — — ℞. Horse stg. r.; two pellets beneath exergual line. *Jenkins & Lewis* 265. *Müller* II, 84, 51 .. .. £500

6465 290-280 B.C. Electrum *shekel-didrachm* (c. 7·6 gm., 43-47% gold). Hd. of Tanit l., wreathed with corn, wearing necklace and triple-drop ear-ring. ℞. Horse stg. r. *Jenkins & Lewis* 313 .. .. £450

6466

6469

6466 — — Similar, but with four pellets beneath horse on *rev.* *Jenkins & Lewis* 328 £450

6467 — — Similar, but with six pellets on *rev.*, three above and three below the exergual line. *Jenkins & Lewis* 336. *Müller (Supplement)*, 48, 53a £450

6468 — Electrum *half-stater* (c. 3·7 gm.). *Obv.* Similar, but Tanit wears simple necklace, without pendants. ℞. Horse stg. r., l. foreleg drawn slightly back; in background, palm-tree. *Jenkins & Lewis* 342. *Müller* II, 85, 56 .. .. £400

6469 280-270 B.C. Electrum *shekel-didrachm* (c. 7·5 gm., 43-47% gold). Hd. of Tanit l., large and somewhat stylized, wreathed with corn, and wearing necklace and triple-drop ear-ring. ℞. Horse stg. r. *Jenkins & Lewis* 362 .. .. £500

6470 270-264 B.C. Æ Attic *tridrachm*? (c. 12·5 gm.). Hd. of Tanit l., wreathed with corn, wearing necklace and triple-drop ear-ring. ℞. Horse stg. r., looking back. *Jenkins & Lewis* 377. *Principal Coins, pl.* 52, 34 .. .. £1,800

6471 — — Similar, but with four pellets on *rev.* along the exergual line. *Jenkins & Lewis* 398 .. .. £2,000

6472

6474

6472 — *N sixth-stater* or *hemidrachm* (*c.* 2·06 gm.).   Hd. of Tanit l., wreathed with corn, wearing necklace without pendants and single-drop ear-ring. R. Horse stg. r.; palm-tree in background. *Jenkins & Lewis* 401. *Müller* II, 85, 57   ..   ..   (*Unique*)

6473 *Circa* 264 B.C.   Electrum 2½ *drachms* (Phoenician standard, *c.* 9·25 gm.; 40-46% gold). As 6470. *Jenkins & Lewis* 402 ..   ..   (*Only two known*)

6474 264-241 B.C. (time of the First Punic War).   Electrum *tridrachm* (Phoenician standard, *c.* 10·9 gm.; 45-49% gold).   Hd. of Tanit l., wreathed with corn, wearing necklace and triple-drop ear-ring. R. Horse stg. r.; above, sun-disk between two uraeus-cobras. *Jenkins & Lewis* 405. *Müller* II, 85, 63 ..   ..   £1,400

6475 — — Similar, but with three pellets on *rev.* above the exergual line. *Jenkins & Lewis* 412. *Müller* II, 85, 65   ..   ..   £1,400

6476 — — (reduced weight and purity, *c.* 10·6 gm., 34-36% gold).   Similar, but with pellet on leaf of Tanit's wreath on *obv.*; and on *rev.* one pellet above the exergual line, behind horse's l. hind-hoof. *Jenkins & Lewis* 428. *Müller* II, 85, 64   ..   £1,200

6477 — Electrum *quarter-stater* (*c.* 2·7 gm.). *Obv.* Similar to 6474, but Tanit wears simple necklace, without pendants. R. Horse stg. r., l. foreleg drawn slightly back; beneath, pellet. *Jenkins & Lewis* 427   ..   ..   £350

6478   6479

6478 240-230 B.C.   Electrum *sixth-stater* (*c.* 1·7 gm., 14% gold).   Hd. of Tanit l., wreathed with corn, wearing single-drop ear-ring. R. Horse stg. r., looking back; sometimes with ⊖ above. *Jenkins & Lewis* 462-3. *Müller* II, 86, 69   ..   ..   ..   £175

The gold content of these coins is so low that they can easily be mistaken for silver.

6479 230-220 B.C.   *N quarter-shekel* (*c.* 1·9 gm.).   Hd. of Tanit l., wreathed with corn, wearing necklace without pendants and single-drop ear-ring. R. Horse stg. r., l. foreleg drawn slightly back. *Jenkins & Lewis* 465. *Müller* II, 85, 62   ..   ..   £300

6480 220-210 B.C. (time of the Second Punic War).   Electrum ⅜ *shekel* (*c.* 2·8 gm.).   Hd. of Tanit l., wreathed with corn, wearing necklace and ear-ring. R. Horse stg. r. *Jenkins & Lewis* 469   ..   ..   £350

6481 — — Similar, but on *rev.* the horse's l. hind-leg is raised. *Jenkins & Lewis* 468
£375

6482 — — *Obv.* Similar. R. Horse stg. r., l. foreleg drawn slightly back; in ex., bow. *Jenkins & Lewis* 470. *Grose/McClean* 9980   ..   ..   £400

6483   6485

6483 — — — R. As last, but without bow in ex. *Jenkins & Lewis* 473   ..   ..   £350

6484 — — Similar to 6480, but with A on Tanit's hd. at base of corn-ears. *Jenkins & Lewis* 480   ..   ..   £375

6485 — — *Obv.* As 6480. R. Horse stg. r., l. foreleg raised. *Jenkins & Lewis* 483   £375

6486 — — *Obv.* Similar, but before the face of Tanit the border is cut by the arc of another circle. R. Horse pacing r. *Jenkins & Lewis* 485-6 ..   ..   £400

6487 200-146 B.C.   *N ⅖ shekel* (*c.* 3 gm.).   Hd. of Tanit l., wreathed with corn, wearing necklace and ear-ring. R. Horse stg. r., l. foreleg raised. *Jenkins & Lewis* 496 ..   £450

6488 — — Similar, but with Punic letter *aleph* beneath horse on *rev. Jenkins & Lewis* 497
£450

6489   6491

Carthage *continued*

6489 — — (with serrated edge). Similar to 6487, but with pellet in *rev.* field, beneath
horse's raised foreleg. *Jenkins & Lewis* 506. *Müller* II, 86, 70 .. .. £425

6490 — *N* ⅕ *shekel* (*c.* 1·5 gm.). *Obv.* Similar. R. Head and neck of horse r. *Jenkins &
Lewis* 500. *Müller* II, 87, 77 .. .. £300

6491 *Silver and billon coinage.* 300-264 B.C. Æ *shekel-didrachm* (*c.* 7·5 gm.). Hd. of
Tanit l., wreathed with corn, wearing necklace and single-drop ear-ring. R. Horse stg.
r., looking back; in background, palm-tree; in field to r., star. *Müller* II, 89, 108
£175

6492 264-241 B.C. (time of the First Punic War). Æ *triple-shekel* or *hexadrachm* (debased
metal, *c.* 23 gm.). Hd. of Tanit l., wreathed with corn, wearing necklace and triple-drop
ear-ring. R. Horse stg. r.; above, sun-disk between two uraeus-cobras. *Müller* II, 88,
99 .. .. £2,500

6493 — Æ *double-shekel* or *tetradrachm* (debased metal, *c.* 15 gm.). Similar, but with large
star above horse instead of sun-disk and cobras. *Müller* II, 88, 94 .. .. £275

6493   6494

6494 — Æ 1½ *shekel* or *tridrachm* (debased metal, *c.* 11·8 gm.). *Obv.* Similar. R. Horse stg.
r.; in background, palm-tree. *Müller* II, 89, 103 .. .. £250

6495 — Æ *shekel-didrachm* (debased metal, *c.* 7·3 gm.). *Obv.* Similar, but with pellet on leaf
of Tanit's wreath. R. Horse stg. r., looking back. *Müller* II, 90, 112 .. £200

*The pellet on obv. connects this issue with the electrum tridrachms of the First Punic War
listed above (see no. 6476).*

6496 240-230 B.C. Æ *tridrachm* ? (debased metal, *c.* 9·8 gm.). Hd. of Tanit l., wreathed with
corn, wearing necklace and single-drop ear-ring. R. Horse stg. r.; in background, palm-
tree. *Müller* II, 89, 105 .. .. £300

6497 230-220 B.C. *Æ tridrachm*? (debased metal, *c.* 8·5 gm.). *Obv.* Similar. ℞. Horse stg.
r., looking back, r. foreleg raised. *Müller* II, 90, 115 .. .. £175

6498 220-210 B.C. (time of the Second Punic War). *Æ half-shekel* or *drachm* (*c.* 3·75 gm.).
Obv. Similar. ℞. Horse stg. r.; above, sun-disk between two uraeus-cobras. *Müller*
II, 87, 87 .. .. £125

6499   6500

6499 — *Æ quarter-shekel* or *hemidrachm* (*c.* 1·87 gm.). Similar, but without the sun-disk and
cobras in *rev.* field. *Müller* II, 88, 90 .. .. £75

6500 200-146 B.C. *Æ double-shekel* or *tetradrachm*? (with serrated edge, *c.* 13·1 gm.). Hd. of
Tanit l., wreathed with corn, wearing necklace and single-drop ear-ring. ℞. Horse stg.
r., l. foreleg raised; pellet in field to r. *Müller* II, 90, 116 .. .. .. £325

6501 — — Similar, but with Punic letters (=*go*) beneath horse on *rev.* (no pellet in field).
Müller II, 90, 121 .. .. £325

6502 — — Similar, but with star above horse on *rev.* (no inscription or pellet in field).
Müller II, 90, 122 .. .. £325

6503 — *Æ shekel-didrachm*? (*c.* 6·35 gm.). *Obv.* Similar. ℞. Horse stg. r., l. foreleg raised;
beneath, Punic letter *aleph*. *Müller* II, 91, 124, *var.* .. .ᵛ .. £250

6504 — — (with serrated edge). *Obv.* Similar. ℞. Horse stg. r.; before, two corn-ears;
beneath, pellet. *Müller* II, 88, 92 .. .. £250

Carthage *continued*

6505 *Bronze coinage* (the base-metal issues cannot be dated with the same degree of accuracy as the gold and silver. The bulk of the coinage is probably of the latter part of the 3rd cent. B.C., with more restricted issues after the Carthaginian defeat in the Second Punic War. Some types may have been struck at mints in Sicily or Sardinia rather than at Carthage itself). 2nd half of 3rd cent. B.C. Æ 32. Hd. of Tanit l., wreathed with corn, wearing necklace and ear-ring. R. Horse stg. r.; above, sun-disk between two uraeus-cobras; before, Punic letter (=*o*). *Müller* II, 93, 143 .. .. £25

6506 — Æ 29. *Obv.* Similar. R. Horse stg. r., palm-tree in background; before, Punic letter (=*h*). *Müller* II, 95, 171 .. .. £22

6507 — — Hd. of Tanit l., wreathed with corn, wearing ear-ring. R. Horse stg. r., palm-tree in background, on l.; beneath horse, Punic letter (=*th*). *Müller* II, 94, 154 £18

6508 — Æ 22. Similar to 6505, but with Punic letter (=*m*) beneath horse on *rev.* *Müller* II, 93, 142 .. .. £14

6509 — — Similar, but on *rev.* pellet within crescent above horse, and Punic letter (=*o*) in field to r. *Müller* II, 96, 184 .. .. £15

6510   6512

6510 — — *Obv.* As 6507. R. Horse stg. r.; beneath, Punic letter (=*g*). *Müller* II, 96, 192 £12

6511 — Æ 20. Similar to 6506, but without Punic letter on *rev.* *Müller* II, 94, 162 £13

6512 — Æ 22. Hd. of Tanit l., wreathed with corn. R. Horse stg. r., looking back. *Müller* II, 97, 201 .. .. £8

6513 — — Similar, but on *rev.* star above horse, Punic letter (=*b*) beneath. *Müller* II, 97, 216 .. .. £8

6514 — — Similar, but with standard behind horse, on l., and with Punic letter (=*h*) beneath. *Müller* II, 98, 220 .. .. £10

6515 — — Hd. of Tanit l., wreathed with corn; beneath, crescent and pellet. R. Horse stg. r., looking back; behind, on l., long caduceus; in field to r., Punic letter (=*b*). *Müller* II, 98, 223 .. .. £11

6516 — Æ 15. *Obv.* Similar. R. Horse stg. r., looking back; above, crescent and pellet. *Müller* II, 98, 226 .. .. £9

6517 — Æ 25. Hd of Tanit l., wreathed with corn, wearing ear-ring. ℞. Horse stg. r.,
looking back, r. foreleg raised; beneath, pellet. *Müller* II, 98, 231   ..   .. £9

6518 — Æ 20. *Obv.* Similar. ℞. Horse stg. r., looking back, l. foreleg raised; beneath,
Punic letter (=*a*). *Müller* II, 98, 237 ..   .. £9

6519 — Æ 15. Similar to 6517, but without pellet on *rev.* *Müller* II, 98, 232   .. £9

6520 — Æ 27. Hd. of Tanit l., wreathed with corn, wearing ear-ring. ℞. Head and neck of
horse r.; in field to r., star above, caduceus beneath. *Müller* II, 102, 299   .. £20

6521 — — Similar, but with crescent and pellet behind Tanit on *obv.*, and Punic letter (=*m*)
in *rev.* field to r. *Müller* II, 101, 284   ..   .. £18

6522 — Æ 24. Hd. of Tanit l., wreathed with corn, wearing plain necklace and ear-ring.
℞. Head and neck of horse r.; before, Punic letter (=*a*). *Müller* II, 100, 261   £15

6523 — Æ 18. *Obv.* Similar, but necklace with pendants. ℞. Head and neck of horse r.
Müller II, 101, 268 ..   .. £6

6524 — — As last, but with large pellet before horse's neck on *rev.* *Müller* II, 101, 276   £6

6525 — — As last, but with Punic letter (=*m*) before horse's neck. *Müller* II, 101, 285   £6

6526   6531

6526 — — As last, but with Punic letter (=*o*) in *rev.* field to r. *Müller* II, 102, 286   £6

6527 — — As last, but with star before horse's neck. *Müller* II, 102, 294 ..   .. £6

6528 — — As last, but with palm-tree before horse's neck. *Müller* II, 103, 304 .. £6

6529 — Æ 22. Horse stg. r.; in background, long caduceus. ℞. Palm-tree. *Müller* II, 103,
313 ..   .. £18

6530 — Æ 17. Horse stg. r., looking back. ℞. Palm-tree. *Müller* II, 104, 315 .. £9

6531 — Æ 18. Head and neck of horse r. ℞. Palm-tree. *Müller* II, 104, 317 .. £7

6532 Late 3rd cent. B.C. Æ 47. Hd. of Tanit l., wreathed with corn, wearing single-drop
ear-ring. ℞. Horse stg. r., l. foreleg raised; above, sun-disk between two uraeus-cobras.
Collection de Luynes, IV, 3782   ..   .. £100

Carthage *continued*

6533 — Æ 43. Similar, but horse's foreleg is not raised. *Müller* II, 92, 131 .. £90

6534 200-146 B.C. Æ 29. *Obv.* Similar. R. Horse trotting r.; beneath, pellet. *Müller* II, 99, 244 .. .. £18

6535 — — Similar, but with Punic letter (=*a*) beneath horse on *rev.* *Müller* II, 99, 245 £18

6536 LIBYAN REVOLT (following her defeat in the First Punic War, 241 B.C., Carthage was faced with a serious uprising of her former allies in North Africa. The struggle continued for about four years and although the Carthaginians eventually prevailed this episode contributed to the decline of Punic power. The rebels produced a coinage part of which was in imitation of Carthaginian types whilst the remainder was issued in the name of the Libyans). 241-238 B.C. N *half-shekel* or *drachm* (*c.* 3·4 - 3·9 gm.). Hd. of Tanit l., wreathed with corn, wearing necklace and ear-ring; above, detached tip of corn-ear. R. Horse stg. r. *Jenkins & Lewis* 452. *Robinson (in Numismatic Chronicle* 1953), *pl.* II, 4 £750

6537 — — Similar, but with H above horse on *rev.* *Jenkins and Lewis* 450. *Müller* II, 85, 58 £750

6538 — — Similar, but without detached tip of corn-ear on *obv.*; and on *rev.*, III above horse, Punic letter (=*m*) beneath. *Jenkins & Lewis* 451. *Robinson, pl.* II, 5 .. £750

6539 — R *shekel-didrachm* (debased metal, *c.* 7·3 gm.). Hd. of Tanit l., wreathed with corn, wearing necklace and ear-ring; pellet on leaf of wreath. R. Horse stg. r.; beneath, Punic letter (=*m*); three pellets in triangular arrangement between horse's hind-legs. *Robinson, pl.* II, 11. *Müller* II, 88, 97 .. .. £275

6540 6542

6540 — — Similar, but with A instead of pellets between horse's hind-legs. *Robinson, pl.* II, 15. *Müller* II, 88, 98 .. .. £275

6541 — R *double-shekel* or *tetradrachm* (debased metal, *c.* 12·5 gm.). Laur. hd. of Zeus l.; ΛΙΒΥΩΝ before, Punic letter (=*m*) behind. R. Bull butting r.; Punic letter (=*m*) above, ΛΙΒΥΩΝ in ex. *Robinson, pl.* III, 17-18 .. .. £450

6542 — — Similar, but hd. of Zeus to r. on *obv.*; and on *rev.*, A between bull's hind-legs. *Robinson, pl.* III, 20. *Müller* I, 130, 347 .. .. £450

Libyan Revolt *continued*

6543 — Æ *shekel-didrachm* (debased metal, *c.* 7·3 - 7·9 gm.). Hd. of young Herakles l., clad in lion's skin. ℞. Lion prowling r.; above, Punic letter (=*m*). *Robinson, pl.* III, 22. *Müller* I, 131, 351 .. .. £150

6544 — — Similar, but also with ΛΙΒΥΩΝ or ΛΙ8ΥΩΝ on *rev.,* in ex. *Robinson, pl.* III, 23-8. *Müller* I, 131, 349-50 .. .. £140

6545 — — As last, but also with M on *rev.,* beneath lion. *Müller* I, 130, 348 .. £160

6546 — Æ *quarter-shekel* or *hemidrachm?* (*c.* 2·17 gm.). Diad. hd. of young Herakles l., club before neck; behind, A. ℞. Lion prowling r.; club above, ΛΙΒΥΩΝ in ex. *Müller* I, 130, 345 .. .. £175

6547 THE BARCIDS IN SPAIN (following the suppression of the Libyan Revolt, Hamilcar Barca left for Spain to 'call a new world into existence to redress the balance of the old.' He and his successors greatly extended the area of Carthaginian territory in Spain, and in 228 B.C. Hasdrubal founded Carthago Nova (New Carthage). Ten years later Hannibal, son of Hamilcar Barca, left Spain for his historic invasion of Italy. The Romans, under Scipio, captured Carthago Nova in 209 B.C., and Hannibal's defeat at Zama in 202 brought the Second Punic War to an end). 237-234 B.C. Billon 1½ *shekel* or *tridrachm* (mint of Gades, *c.* 11 gm.). Female hd. l., wearing triple-crested head-dress. ℞. Horse stg. r. *Robinson (Punic Coins of Spain* in *Essays in Roman Coinage presented to Harold Mattingly)* 1 (*a*). *Müller* II, 146, 4 .. .. £250

6548 — Æ 20 (mint of Gades). *Obv.* Similar; beneath chin, Punic letter *yod.* ℞. Palm-tree. *Robinson* 1 (*e*). *Müller* II, 146, 5 .. .. £30

6549   6551

6549 234-228 B.C. *N shekel-didrachm* (mint of Gades, *c.* 7·6 gm.). Winged bust of Nike l., wearing bay-wreath. ℞. Horse prancing r.; pellet beneath. *Robinson* 2 (*b*). *Jenkins & Lewis* 457. *Müller* III, 16, 7 .. .. £1,500

6550 — *N quarter-shekel* or *hemidrachm* (mint of Gades, *c.* 1·9 gm.). Similar, but without pellet on *rev. Robinson* 2 (*e*). *Jenkins & Lewis* 459 .. .. £750

6551 — Æ *shekel-didrachm* (mint of Gades, *c.* 7·2 gm.). Hd. of Tanit l., wreathed with corn. ℞. Horse stg. r., looking back; in background, on l., palm-tree. *Robinson* 2 (*g*). *Müller* II, 89, 109 .. .. £500

6552 — Æ *half-shekel* or *drachm* (mint of Gades, *c.* 3·6 gm.). *Obv.* Similar. ℞. Horse stg. r., looking back; beneath, pellet. *Robinson* 2 (*i*). *Müller* II, 89, 110 .. .. £350

6553   6555

The Barcids in Spain *continued*

6553 — Æ 22 (mint of Gades). *Obv.* Similar; of crude style. ℞. Head and neck of horse r.; before, Punic letter *aleph*. *Robinson* 2 (*o*). *Müller* II, 103, J10   ..   ..   £20

6554 — — — Similar, but *obv.* of better style, and with Punic letter *yod* on *rev.* *Robinson* 2 (*m*). *Müller* II, 101, 267   ..   ..   £25

6555 230-228 B.C. Æ *shekel-didrachm* (mint of the White Cape, *c.* 7·37 gm.). Hd. of Tanit l., looking upwards, wreathed with corn. ℞. Horse prancing r.; above, large star. *Robinson* 3(*a*). *Müller* II, 91, 126   ..   ..   £750

6556 — Æ 21 (mint of the White Cape). Hd. of Tanit l., wreathed with corn. ℞. Horse prancing l. *Robinson* 3(*c*). *Müller* II, 100, 257   ..   ..   ..   £30

6557 *Circa* 228 B.C. (on the foundation of Carthago Nova). *N shekel-didrachm* (mint of Carthago Nova, *c.* 7·58 gm.). Diad. hd. of Hasdrubal (?) l., looking upwards. ℞. Prow of galley r.; a pennant flying from the forepost which terminates in a bird's hd. *Robinson* 4(*a*). *Jenkins & Lewis* 461   ..   ..   (*Unique*)

6558 — Æ *double-shekel* or *tetradrachm* (mint of Carthago Nova, *c.* 14·8 gm.). Similar, but also with sea-horse beneath prow on *rev.* *Robinson* 4(*b*). *Müller* (*Supplement*), 71, 4a £10,000

6559   6560

6559 — Æ *shekel-didrachm* (mint of Carthago Nova, *c.* 7·1 gm.). Similar, but with dolphin instead of sea-horse on *rev.* *Robinson* 4(*c*). *Müller* (*Supplement*), 71, 4b   £4,500

6560 — Æ 21 (mint of Carthago Nova). Beardless male hd. r., wearing crested Corinthian helmet ornamented with griffin. ℞. Palm-tree. *Robinson* 4(*d*). *Müller* II, 145, 3 £40

6561 228-221 B.C. (time of Hasdrubal). Æ *triple-shekel* or *hexadrachm* (mint of Carthago Nova, *c.* 22 gm.). Hd. of Eshmun-Apollo (?) l., wearing laur. diadem. ℞. Horse stg. r. *Robinson* 5(*a*)   ..   ..   (*Unique*)

6562 — Æ *shekel-didrachm* (mint of Carthago Nova, *c.* 7·3 gm.). Similar. *Robinson* 5(*b*). *Müller* (*Supplement*), 61, 12A £5,000

6563 — Æ *half-shekel* or *drachm* (mint of Carthago Nova, *c.* 3·8 gm.). Bearded hd. of Melqarth-Herakles r., clad in lion's skin. ℞. Horse stg. r. *Robinson* 5(*c*)   ..   £2,500

6564   6565

6564 221-218 B.C. (time of Hannibal). Æ *double-shekel* or *tetradrachm* (mint of Carthago Nova, *c.* 14·75 gm.). Laur. bust of bearded Melqarth-Herakles l., heavy knotted club behind neck. Ɍ. Elephant walking r., ridden by cloaked driver holding goad. *Robinson* 6(*a*). *Müller* III, 17, 16. *Principal Coins*, V. C.1 .. .. £12,500

    The features of Melqarth on obv. may be intended to represent Hannibal's father, Hamilcar Barca.

6565 — Æ 1½ *shekel* or *tridrachm* (mint of Carthago Nova, *c.* 11·16 gm.). Laur. bust of young Melqarth-Herakles l., heavy knotted club behind neck. Ɍ. Elephant walking r. *Robinson* 6(*c*). *Müller* III, 17, 17. *Principal Coins*, V. C.2 .. .. .. £7,500

    The younger Melqarth, on the obv. of this issue, may represent the features of Hannibal himself.

6566 — Æ *quarter-shekel* or *hemidrachm* (mint of Carthago Nova, *c.* 1·75 gm.). Similar. *Robinson* 6(*d*). *Müller* III, 17, 18.. .. .. £1,000

6567 218-209 B.C. (time of the Second Punic War). Æ *triple-shekel* or *hexadrachm* (mint of Carthago Nova, *c.* 22·05 - 23·4 gm.). Bare-headed and beardless bust of Hannibal (?) l. Ɍ. Horse stg. r.; in background, palm-tree. *Robinson* 7(*b*). *Müller* (*Supplement*), 61, 8*A*. *Principal Coins*, *pl.* 52, 35 .. .. £15,000

        6568   6571

6568 — Æ *shekel-didrachm* (mint of Carthago Nova, *c.* 6·75 - 7·5 gm.). Similar. *Robinson* 7(*c*). *Müller* III, 16, 8 .. .. £2,000

6569 — — Similar, but also with pellet beneath chin on *obv.*, and Punic letter *ayin* beneath horse on *rev.* *Robinson* 7(*e*). *Müller* (*Supplement*), 61, 9*a* .. £2,250

6570 — — Young male hd. l., beardless and bare-headed (Hasdrubal Barca, younger brother of Hannibal ?). Ɍ. Horse stg. r.; above, sun-disk between two uraeus-cobras; beneath, pellet. *Robinson* 7(*a*). *Müller* III, 17, 12 .. .. £3,000

6571 — Æ *half-shekel* or *drachm* (mint of Carthago Nova, *c.* 3·6 gm.). *Obv.* As 6567. Ɍ. Horse stg. r.; beneath, pellet. *Robinson* 7(*k*). *Müller* III, 17, 14 .. .. £1,750

6572 — Æ *quarter-shekel* or *hemidrachm* (mint of Carthago Nova, *c.* 1·8 gm.). Similar. *Robinson* 7(*o*). *Müller* III, 17, 15 .. .. £1,250

6573 After 209 B.C. (following the capture of Carthago Nova by the Romans). Æ *shekel-didrachm* (mint of Carthago Nova, *c.* 6·5-7·2 gm.). Young male hd. l., beardless and bare-headed, with short straight hair and Roman nose (the Roman general P. Scipio ?). Ɍ. Horse stg. r.; in background, palm-tree; in field to r., Punic letter *yod*. *Robinson* 7(*h*). *Müller* III, 13, 3 .. .. £1,250

6574 — Æ *half-shekel* or *drachm* (mint of Carthago Nova, *c.* 3·6 gm.). *Obv.* Similar, but hd. fo Scipio (?) of crude style. Ɍ. Horse stg. r. *Robinson* 7(*m*). *Müller* (*Supplement*), 61, 1*b* £750

The Barcids in Spain *continued*

6575 — Æ 24 (mint of Carthago Nova). *Obv.* As last. ℞. Horse stg. r.; in background, palm-tree. *Robinson 7(p). Müller III, 13, 4* £65

6576 — Æ *shekel-didrachm* (mint of Gades, *c.* 7 - 7·5 gm.). Beardless male hd. l., wearing laur. diadem (Mago, youngest brother of Hannibal?). ℞. Elephant walking r.; in ex., Punic letter *aleph. Robinson 8(a). Müller III, 34, 43* £750

6577 — Æ *half-shekel* or *drachm* (mint of Gades, *c.* 3·6 gm.). Similar. *Robinson 8(b). Müller III, 34, 44* £350

6578 — Æ *quarter-shekel* or *hemidrachm* (mint of Gades, *c.* 1·56 gm.). Similar. *Robinson 8(c)* £250

6579   6581

6579 **ISLANDS BETWEEN AFRICA AND SICILY. Cossura** (the modern Pantelleria, Cossura had a Phoenician population which was brought into subjection by Rome in 217 B.C.). Late 3rd cent. B.C. Æ 24. Female hd. r., with Egyptian head-dress. ℞. Punic legend (=*'irnm*) within laurel-wreath. *Grose/McClean 10007* £50

6580 — Æ 22. Similar, but on *obv.* the hd. is to left and crowned by Nike stg. r. before. *Forrer/Weber 8517* £45

6581 1st cent. B.C. Æ 27. *Obv.* As 6579, but crowned by Nike flying r. behind. ℞. cossvra across field, monogram above; all within laurel-wreath. *Grose/McClean 10010* £35

6582 — Æ 23. *Obv.* As 6580. ℞. cossvra within laurel-wreath. *Forrer/Weber 8518* *These are often countermarked on obv. with branch between D—D.* £25

6583   6584

6583 **Gaulos** (a small island north-west of Melita, Gaulos, now called Gozo, passed under Roman control at the beginning of the Second Punic War, 218 B.C.). 1st cent. B.C. Æ 18. Hd. of Astarte r., large crescent beneath. ℞. ΓΑΥΛΙΤΩΝ. Warrior advancing r., brandishing spear and holding shield; large star in lower field to r. *Forrer/Weber 8520* £50

6584 **Melita** (better known by its modern name, Malta, Melita achieved importance through its strategic position and the excellence of its harbours. Its Phoenician population came under Roman rule in 218 B.C.). Late 3rd cent. B.C. Æ 29. Veiled female hd. r., wearing stephane. R. Mummy of Osiris, holding flail and sceptre, between Isis and Nephthys, each with wings crossed in front; in field, Punic legend (=*'nn*). *Grose/McClean* 10012
£65

6585   6586

6585 — Æ 21. Archaistic hd. of bearded Herakles r.; caduceus before. R. Sacrificial cap and Punic legend (=*'nn*) within wreath. *Forrer/Weber* 8521 .. .. .. £40

6586 — Æ 17. *Obv.* As 6584. R. Ram's hd. r.; Punic legend (=*'nn*) beneath. *Forrer/Weber* 8522 .. .. £30

6587 — — — R. Tripod; Punic legend (=*'nn*) on either side. *Forrer/Weber* 8523 £25

6588 2nd-1st cent. B.C. Æ 26. ΜΕΛΙΤΑΙΩΝ. Hd. of Isis l., wearing uraeus crown; before, ear of corn. R. Four-winged figure (Osiris ?) kneeling l., holding flail and sceptre. *Forrer/Weber* 8525 .. .. £35

6589 — Æ 20. Veiled female hd. l. R. ΜΕΛΙ / ΤΑΙΩΝ either side of tripod. *Forrer/Weber* 8531 .. .. £20

6590 — Æ 18. Veiled female hd. r., wearing stephane. R. ΜΕΛΙ / ΤΑΙΩΝ either side of lyre. *Forrer/Weber* 8527 .. .. £20

6591 1st cent. B.C. Æ 21. Veiled female hd. r. R. ΜΕLΙ / ΤΑS either side of tripod. *Forrer/Weber* 8532 .. .. £20

6592 — Æ 20. Veiled female hd. l. R. C. ARRVNTANVS BALB. PRO PR. Curule chair. *Forrer/Weber* 8533-4 .. .. £30

6593 **NUMIDIA** (the area lying south-west of Carthaginian territory, Numidia originally had a nomad population. Contact with Punic civilization brought about the development of agriculture and urbanization. The country was under the rule of a native dynasty until 46 B.C. when it became the Roman province of Africa Nova). REGAL COINAGE. **Masinissa,** 202-148 B.C. (a friend of Scipio Africanus, Masinissa became ruler of Numidia following Hannibal's defeat at Zama. He remained a faithful ally of Rome until his death more than half a century later). Æ 35. Laur. and dr. bust of Masinissa (?) l., with pointed beard, lotus-headed sceptre over r. shoulder. R. Horse pacing l., lotus-headed sceptre in background; in ex., Punic legend (=*Masinisan hammamleket*). *Collection de Luynes* 3912. *Müller* III, 17, 19 .. .. £100

Masinissa *continued*

6594 — Æ 32. Laur. hd. of Masinissa (?) l., with pointed beard. R. Horse stg. l.; long
caduceus in background. *Müller* III, 18, 20   ..   ..   £90

6595 **Micipsa,** 148-118 B.C. (the eldest of Masinissa's three sons, Micipsa succeeded to the
Numidian throne jointly with his brothers in 148 B.C.   The latter, however, died after
only a short period of joint rule, leaving Micipsa sole master of the country for most of his
reign).   Æ 26.   Laur. hd. of Micipsa (?) l., with pointed beard; beneath, Punic letters
(=*m k*).   R. Horse galloping l.; beneath, Punic letters (= *e t*).   *Müller* III, 18, 23   £20

6596 — — Similar, but without inscription on *obv.*, and with Punic letters (=*m k*) beneath
horse on *rev.*   *Müller* III, 18, 25 ..   ..   £10
These are sometimes struck in lead instead of bronze (cf. Müller III, 19, 36).

6597 — — Similar, but without inscriptions on *obv.* or *rev.*, and with pellet beneath horse.
Müller III, 18, 32 ..   ..   £8

6598 — Æ 16.   *Obv.* As last.   R. Horse stg. l.; above, pellet and crescent.   *Müller* III, 19, 34
£18

6599 — Æ 14.   *Obv.* As last.   R. Horse galloping l.   *Collection de Luynes* 3936.   *Muller* III,
19, 35   ..   ..   £18

6600 **Gulussa,** 148-*circa* 140 B.C. (son of Masinissa and brother of Micipsa).   Æ 26.   Laur.
hd. of Gulussa (?) l., with pointed beard.   R. Horse galloping l.; beneath, Punic letters
(=*g n*).   *Müller* III, 18, 30   ..   ..   £45

6601 **Adherbal,** 118-112 B.C. (son of Micipsa).   Æ 26.   Laur. hd. of Adherbal (?) l., with
pointed beard.   R. Horse galloping l.; beneath, Punic letters (=*a l*); above, hd. of Zeus-
Ammon l.   *Müller* III, 18, 31   ..   ..   £45

6602   6605

6602 **Hiempsal II,** 106-60 B.C. (son of Gauda, king of eastern Numidia, Hiempsal was expelled from his kingdom by Iarbas, an ally of the Marian party, but restored in 81 B.C. by Pompey). Æ *denarius* (*c.* 4 gm.). Beardless hd. of Hiempsal (?) r., wreathed with corn. R. Horse galloping r., Punic letter (= *h*) beneath; all within laurel-wreath. *Müller* III, 38, 45 ..   ..   £350

6603 — Æ *quinarius* (*c.* 2 gm.). *Obv.* Similar. R. Horse galloping r.; beneath, Punic letters (= *h t*). *Müller* III, 38, 47   ..   ..   £140

6604 — Æ *sestertius* (*c.* 1 gm.). Similar to 6602, but without wreath on *rev.* *Müller* III, 38, 46
£175

6605 — Æ 20. Veiled hd. of Demeter r., wreathed with corn. R. Horse galloping r.; Punic letter (= *h*) beneath, palm-branch in background. *Müller* III, 38, 48 ..   £25

6606 — Æ 18. *Obv.* Similar. R. Horse galloping r.; Punic letter (= *h*) beneath, wreath above. *Müller* III, 38, 49..   ..   ..   £25

6607   6608

6607 **Juba I,** 60-46 B.C. (son of Hiempsal II, Juba was an ambitious ruler notorious for his cruelty and arrogance. He supported Pompey in the Civil War and committed suicide after Caesar's victory at Thapsus in 46 B.C. His son, Juba II, later became king of Mauretania under Augustus). Æ *denarius* (*c.* 4 gm.). Diad. and dr. bust of Juba r., with pointed beard and hair in formal curls, sceptre at shoulder; REX IVBA before. R. Octastyle temple; on either side, Neo- Punic legend (= *Yubai hammamleket*). *Müller* III, 42, 50   ..   ..   £50

6608 — Æ *quinarius* (*c.* 1·8 gm.). Winged bust of Victory r., REX IVBA before. R. Horse galloping r.; above, Neo-Punic legend, as last. *Müller* III, 42, 52   ..   £200

6609 — — *Obv.* As 6607, but without legend. R. Horse galloping r. *Müller* III, 42, 53
£175

6610 — Æ *sestertius* (*c.* 0·8 gm.). Bust of Numidia r., clad in elephant's skin; two spears behind. R Lion walking r., ? above. *Müller* III, 42, 54   ..   ..   £150

6611 — Æ 38. Hd. of Zeus-Ammon r. R. Elephant walking r.; above, Neo-Punic legend (= *Yubai hammamleket*). *Müller* III, 42, 55   ..   ..   ..   £125

6612 — Æ 35. Octastyle temple. R. Facade of two-storeyed building (the royal palace ?); in ex., Neo-Punic legend, as last. *Müller* III, 43, 57   ..   ..   £100

6613   6614

6613 — Æ 26. As 6611. *Müller* III, 43, 56   ..   ..   £20

6614 — Æ 22. Hd. of Numidia r., clad in elephant's skin. R. Lion walking r.; above, Neo-Punic legend, as 6611. *Müller* III, 43, 58   ..   ..   ..   £15

6615 **CIVIC COINAGE.** **Bulla Regia** (situated in the Bagradas valley, its modern name is Hammon Daradji). 1st cent. B.C. Æ 17. Eagle stg. r., wings spread. R. Punic legend ($=bb'l$) beneath large crescent. *Collection de Luynes* 3973. *Müller* III, 57, 66
£30

6616 **Cirta** (the modern Constantine, Cirta was the Numidian capital and principal residence of the kings. After 46 B.C. it became a Roman colony). Before 46 B.C. Æ 26. Turreted hd. of Tyche r.; behind, Punic legend ($=k r t n$). R. Horse pacing r.; above, Punic legend ($=b d m l k r t$). *Collection de Luynes* 3976. *Müller* III, 60, 71 .. £35

6617 — Æ 19. Turreted hd. of Tyche l.; before, Punic legend, as last. R. Horse galloping l., caduceus above; beneath, Punic legend ($='lbt$). *Collection de Luynes* 3974-5. *Müller* III, 60, 72 .. .. £25

6618   6619

6618 — — *Obv.* As 6616. R. Two upright ears of corn; uncertain Punic legend in field to r. *Müller* III, 60, 73 .. .. £25

6619 **Gadiauphala** (about 35 miles south-east of Cirta). 1st cent. B.C. Æ 26. Turreted hd. of Tyche l. R. Horse pacing l.; above, Punic letters xo. *Müller* III, 65, 75
£40

6620 — Æ 20. Similar. *Collection de Luynes* 3979. *Müller* III, 65, 76 .. .. £30

6621 **Hippo Regius** and **Tipasa** (these two cities appear to have produced a joint coinage. Hippo, near modern Bône, was a seaport near the mouth of the river Ubus, whilst Tipasa lay over forty miles to the south). 1st cent. B.C. Æ 26. Laur. hd. of Baal l., surmounted by star, sceptre behind; before, Punic legend ($='pon$). R. Veiled hd. of Astarte r., surmounted by globe and crescent; behind, Punic legnd ($=thp'tn$). *Müller* III, 53, 63 £40

6622 — Æ 22. Hd. of bearded Melqarth r., surmounted by star, club behind; before, Punic legend, as last. R. Hd. of Chusor-Phtah (?) l., wearing bonnet surmounted by star, axe behind; before, Punic legend, as last. *Müller* III, 53, 64 .. .. .. £35

6623 — Æ 18. Young male hd. l.; before, Punic legend ($=thp'tn$). R. Panther bounding r.; above, Punic legend ($='pon$). *Müller* III, 53, 65 .. .. £25

6624 **Macomades** (about 40 miles south-east of Cirta). 1st cent. B.C. Æ 21. Hd. of Chusor-Phtah (?) r., wearing bonnet with floating ribbons attached to top; star (?) behind; uncertain Punic legend before and above. R. Hog running r.; above, Punic legend ($=mqma$). *Müller* III, 66, 77 .. .. £45

6625 6626

6625 — Æ 17. Horse galloping l. R. Punic legend (=*mqma*) beneath large globe and crescent. *Müller* III, 66, 79 .. .. £35

6626 **Salviana** (situated south-west of Cirta, probably at the place now called Belesma). 1st cent. B.C. Æ 20. Veiled bust of Turo-Chusartis (?) r.; before, caduceus and Punic letter (=*g*). R. Horse galloping r., pellet and crescent above; beneath, Punic legend (=*aslbn*). *Collection de Luynes* 3982. *Müller* III, 68, 81 .. .. £35

6627 **Suthul** (a fortified town between Cirta and Hippo, Suthul is today called Guelma). 1st cent. B.C. Æ 23. Hd. of Sarapis r., wearing modius. R. Punic letters (=*st*) within wreath. *Müller* III, 59, 68 .. .. £45

6628 — Æ 19. Hd. of Hermes r., wearing petasos. R. As last. *Müller* III, 59, 69
£40

6629 **Thabraca** and **Tuniza** (like Hippo Regius and Tipasa, these two towns had a joint coinage. Both were situated on the coast to the east of Hippo). 1st cent. B.C. Æ 24. Diad. and veiled hd. of Astarte r.; before, Punic legend (=*tbrk'n*). R. Beardless hd. l., hair in ringlets; above, Punic legend (=*tnnsn*); behind, symbol of Baal. *Müller* III, 52, 62 .. .. £50

6630 **Thagura** (about 40 miles south-east of Hippo Regius). 1st cent. B.C. Æ 15. Bearded hd. l., laur. R. Horse prancing r., star above; beneath, Punic legend (=*tgrn*). *Müller* (*Supplement*), 67, 76a £35

6631 **Zarai** (situated in the south-west of the country). 1st cent. B.C. Æ 17. Hd. of Aphrodite-Astarte (?) r., wreathed with myrtle. R. Cornucopiae, dividing Punic legend (=*sra'a*); all within myrtle-wreath. *Müller* III, 69, 82 .. .. .. £45

6632 **MAURETANIA** (the land of the Moors, Mauretania extended from the Numidian border westwards to the Atlantic Ocean. By the late 3rd cent. B.C. the small Moorish tribes had formed a kingdom which, through many vicissitudes, survived until the reign of Claudius who made the country a Roman province in A.D. 42). **REGAL COINAGE. Syphax,** 213-203 B.C. (chief of the Masaesyles tribe, Syphax was a rival of Masinissa and gave his support to Carthage in the later stages of the Second Punic War. He was defeated and captured in 203 B.C. and spent the remainder of his life in captivity in Italy). Æ 24. Diad. hd. of Syphax l., bearded. R. Horseman galloping l.; beneath, pellet and Punic legend (=*spq hammamleket*) on tablet. *Müller* III, 90, 2 .. .. .. £75

6633 — Æ 26. Bare male hd. l., with short hair and pointed beard. R. Similar to last, but horseman galloping r. *Müller* III, 91, 3 .. .. £65

6634 — Æ 21. As last, but with three pellets instead of one on *rev*. *Müller* III, 91, 4
£50

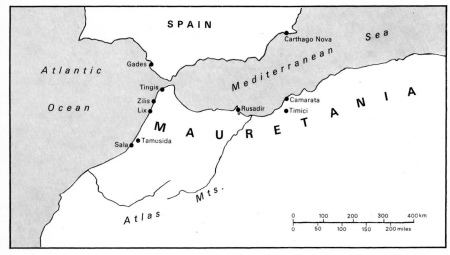

MAP 23   MAURETANIA AND SOUTHERN SPAIN

6635   6636

6635 **Vermina,** 203-202 B.C. (son of Syphax, Vermina was defeated by Scipio soon after the
battle of Zama). Æ *tetradrachm* (*c.* 14·75 gm.). Diad. and dr. bust of Vermina r.,
beardless. ℞. Horse galloping l.; beneath, Punic legend (=*urmnd hammamleket*) on
tablet. *Müller* III, 88, 1 ..   ..   £5,000

6636 **Bogud II,** *circa* 49-38 B.C. (King of western Mauretania, Bogud was an ally of Julius
Caesar. He lost his throne to his brother Bocchus in 38 B.C. and was killed seven years
later fighting for Mark Antony in the Peloponnese). Æ *denarius* (*c.* 3·5 - 4 gm.). Stag
kneeling l., attacked by griffin l. ℞. Griffin stg. l.; above, winged disk; beneath, REX
BOGVT. *Müller* III, 95, 7 ..   ..   £450

6637 — — (*c.* 3 gm.). Hd. of Africa l., clad in elephant's skin. ℞. REX / BOGVT before and
behind griffin stg. r.; above, winged disk; beneath, thunderbolt. *Müller* III, 95, 5
£550

6638 — Æ 24. Male hd. r., bearded. ℞. REX / BOGVT above and beneath prow of galley l.
Müller III, 95, 8 ..   ..   £65

6639   6641

6639 Bocchus III, *circa* 49-33 B.C. (King of eastern Mauretania until 38 B.C., when he took over the western portion of the kingdom after deposing his brother Bogud. On his death five years later Mauretania became, temporarily, a Roman province). Æ 22. Male hd. r., with pointed beard; before, Punic legend ($=bqs$). R. Bacchus, naked, stg. l., holding thyrsus and small bull by one of his horns; in field to l., bunch of grapes; to r., Punic legend ($=sigan$). *Müller III*, 97-8, 9 .. .. £50

This type and the next were struck at the coastal town of Siga.

6640 — Æ 15. Similar, but on *obv.* the legend is beneath the head; and on *rev.* the legend replaces the bunch of grapes in field to l. *Müller* III, 98, 11 .. .. .. £35

6641 — Æ 17. Male hd. r., with pointed beard; Punic legend, $=$'Bocchus the King', in semicircle below. R. Large star between bunch of grapes and ear of corn; above, Maeander symbol; beneath, Punic legend ($=sms$ $=$mint of Semes). *Müller* III, 98, 12 £25

N.B. *The Mauretanian Kingdom was restored in 25 B.C. by Augustus, who placed on the throne Juba II, son of Juba I of Numidia. The extensive coinage of Juba II and that of his son, Ptolemy, will be listed in a future catalogue covering the 'Greek Imperial' series and contemporary coinages.*

6642   6643

6642 CIVIC COINAGE. Camarata (on the Mediterranean coast at a place now called Oued-Rhaser). 1st cent. B.C. Æ 22. Male hd. r., beardless, of crude style. R. Bunch of grapes and ear of corn; above, pellet and crescent; on r., Punic legend ($=$ $km'a$). *Müller* III, 142-3, 214 .. .. £35

6643 Lix (an important town of western Mauretania, on the Atlantic coastline about 30 miles south of Tingis). 1st cent. B.C. Æ 26. Hd. of Chusor-Phtah(?) l., wearing conical bonnet with long tassel attached to top. R. Two bunches of grapes, between which Neo-Punic legend ($=lks$ above, *mbal* beneath). *Müller* III, 155, 234 .. .. £30

6644 — Æ 15. Similar, but with only one bunch of grapes on *rev.*, dividing the legend. *Müller* III, 156, 236 .. .. £20

6645 — Æ 18. *Obv.* Similar, but head to r. and with close beard. R. Two fishes r., one above the other; between them, Neo-Punic legend, as 6643, in one line. *Müller* III, 156, 238 £25

6646 — Æ 26. Two ears of corn, side by side; between them, below, LIXS. R. Two fishes, upright, side by side; between them, above and beneath, Neo-Punic legend, as 6643. *Müller* III, 156, 239 .. .. £35

6647 — — Large ornamented altar; LIX on l. R. Similar to 6643, but the Neo-Punic legend is reversed, with *mbal* above and *lks* beneath. *Müller* III, 156, 240 .. .. £35

6648 — Æ 21. Similar to 6643, but also with LIX in *obv.* field to l. *Müller* III, 156, 241 £25

6649 Rusadir (a coastal town on the Mediterranean, west of Siga). 1st cent. B.C. Æ 21. Male hd. l., beardless. R. Bee between two ears of corn; beneath, Neo-Punic legend ($=rs'dr$). *Müller (Supplement)*, 78, 215a .. .. (*Unique*)

6650   6653

6650 **Sala** (the southernmost town of Mauretania on the Atlantic coastline, Sala lay at the mouth of a river of the same name). 1st cent. B.C. Æ 15. Male hd. r., with pointed beard. R. Ear of corn and bunch of grapes; above, pellet within crescent; beneath, Neo-Punic legend (=*s'lt*). *Müller* III, 163, 243 .. .. £20

6651 **Semes** (named 'City of the Sun' on its coinage, the site of Semes remains undiscovered). 1st cent. B.C. Æ 19. Bearded hd. of Sun-god facing. R. Large star between bunch of grapes and ear of corn; Neo-Punic legend above (=*maqom*) and beneath (=*sms*). *Müller* III, 165, 248 .. .. £20

6652 — Æ 15. Male hd. r., with pointed beard; before, Neo-Punic legend (= *maqom sms*). R. As last. *Müller* III, 164, 246 .. .. £25
      See also no. 6641.

6653 **Tamusia** (about 30 miles north-east of Sala on the Atlantic coastline). 1st cent. B.C. Æ 15. Bearded male hd. r., with long hair; behind, Neo-Punic legend (=*tmd't*). R. Two ears of corn, with Maeander symbol and pellet between. *Müller* III, 161-2, 242 £25

6654 **Timici** (an inland town of eastern Mauretania near the modern village of Ain-Temouchent). 1st cent. B.C. Æ 22. Male hd. r., beardless. R. Bunch of grapes between two laurel-branches; beneath, Neo-Punic legend (=*tmki*). *Collection de Luynes* 4046. *Müller* III, 143, 215 .. .. £35

6655   6658

6655 **Tingis** (modern Tangiers, on the straits of Gibraltar, Tingis was founded by Phoenicians not later than the 5th cent. B.C.). 1st cent. B.C. Æ 25. Bearded hd. of Baal l., without neck; sceptre behind. R. Two ears of corn; between them, below, globe within crescent; Neo-Punic legend to l. (=*ting'*) and to r. (=*b'lt*). *Müller* III, 144, 216 .. £20

6656 — Æ 27. Hd. of Demeter r., wreathed with corn. R. Two ears of corn; between them, above, globe within crescent; Neo-Punic legend to l. (=*mb'l*) and to r. (=*ting'*). *Collection de Luynes* 4049. *Müller* III, 145, 223 .. .. £25

6657 — Æ 20. *Obv.* As 6655. R. Ear of corn, dividing Neo-Punic legend (=*tng'* on l., *b'lt* on r.). *Müller* III, 145, 222 .. .. £18

6658 — Æ 18. Male hd. r., with pointed beard. R. Three ears of corn; in lower field, Neo-Punic legend (=*tng'*). *Müller* III, 145, 224 .. .. £15

6659 — — Similar, but with only two ears of corn on *rev. Müller* III, 146, 229 .. £16

6660 **Zilis** (on the Atlantic coastline, between Tingis and Lix). 1st cent. B.C. Æ 17. Bare hd. of Hermes r., caduceus before. R. Two ears of corn; between them, Neo-Punic legend (=*'slit*). *Müller* III, 153, 233 .. .. £30

THE HELLENISTIC MONARCHIES

(The coins of the principal Kingdoms of the Hellenistic Period, 4th-1st cent. B.C.)

The accession of Philip II to the Macedonian throne in 359 B.C. marked the beginning of a new chapter in the history of the Greek World. Having made himself master of Greece, by a mixture of military skill and diplomacy, he was free to pursue his greatest ambition—the conquest of the Persian Empire. But the assassin's sword prevented Philip from realizing this dream (336 B.C.) and the invasion of Asia was undertaken instead by his son Alexander, known to posterity as 'the Great.' The total destruction of the two-hundred-year-old Persian Empire and its ultimate replacement by a number of independent Greek kingdoms represented the final triumph of autocracy over democracy in the Greek world. The city-states were now subject to an omnipotent regal authority which curtailed their individual freedoms including the issue of autonomous coinage. It is true that many of the city-states regained some of their lost liberty in the 2nd century B.C. with the weakening and gradual disintegration of the great Hellenistic Kingdoms. But it was merely a brief respite, for the power of the Greek kings was being replaced by an even mightier authority—that of Rome—which was destined to dominate the entire Mediterranean world for the following half-millennium.

Strictly speaking the Hellenistic period commences with Alexander the Great (336-323 B.C.) but numismatically it is difficult to separate the reigns of Philip II and his son. Coinage in the name of Philip remained in production in Macedon for more than forty years after his death. It was struck on the Thraco-Macedonian weight-standard (tetradrachm of *c.* 14·4 gm.) and served the needs of the northern lands, where Alexander's Attic tetradrachms of *c.* 17 gm. would not have been acceptable. Later, the Attic weight-standard became almost universal in the Hellenistic Kingdoms, except in Ptolemaic Egypt where a lighter standard, based on a tetradrachm of *c.* 14·2 gm., was ultimately adopted.

To list all the known types of the Hellenistic regal coinages would be quite beyond the scope of this work. What has been attempted is a catalogue of the major types for each reign with representative examples of each denomination. Mint attribution is a complex subject dependent, in the main, on criteria which would not be easily comprehensible to the majority of coin collectors (*e.g.* fabric, style and the interpretation of minor symbols and monograms). Accordingly, in the following lists little attempt has been made to assign coins to particular mints, except in the rare instances where the attribution is obvious by virtue of the types and inscriptions borne by the coins.

THE MACEDONIAN KINGDOM

(For the earlier kings of Macedon, Alexander I-Perdikkas III, see Vol. I of this catalogue, pages 150-153).

6661 **Philip II,** 359-336 B.C. (the Macedonian coinage in the name of Philip II was produced at two mints, Pella and Amphipolis. The change in the *rev.* type of the silver, from king on horseback to naked youth, was made *c.* 348 B.C., whilst the introduction of gold staters and fractions followed about three years later. As noted above, Philip's coinage continued to be struck long after his death—until *c.* 310 B.C. at Pella, and *c.* 294 B.C. at Amphipolis). *N* stater (*c.* 8·6 gm.). Laur. hd. of Apollo l., hair long. ℞. Galloping biga driven r. by charioteer holding goad; in field above, wreath; in ex., ΦΙΛΙΠΠΟΥ. *Le Rider* (*Le Monnayage d'Argent et d'Or de Philippe II*) 129, 1 .. .. £4,000

6662   6663

6662 — — Similar, but with *obv.* type laur. hd. of Apollo r., hair long. *Le Rider* 130, 4 £2,000

6663 — — Laur. hd. of Apollo r., hair short. ℞. Galloping biga, as 6661; in field beneath horses, trident; in ex., ΦΙΛΙΠΠΟΥ. *Le Rider* 155, 255 .. .. £750

Philip II *continued*

6664 — — Similar, but with club instead of trident beneath horses on *rev.* *Le Rider* 205, 37
£750

Many different sequence marks (symbols in reverse field) have been recorded for the gold staters of Philip.

6665 6667

6665 — *N half-stater* (*c.* 4·3 gm.). Hd. of young Herakles r., clad in lion's skin. ℞. Forepart of lion r.; ΦΙΛΙΠΠΟΥ above, kantharos beneath. *Le Rider* 248, 120 .. £900

6666 — — *Obv.* Similar. ℞. Forepart of lion l.; ΦΙΛΙΠΠ — ΟΥ beneath and above; trident in field to l. *Le Rider* 248, 121 .. .. £1,100

6667 — *N quarter-stater* (*c.* 2·15 gm.). *Obv.* Similar. ℞. ΦΙΛΙΠΠΟΥ across field, above club l. and bow; in field above, thunderbolt. *Le Rider* 239, 52 .. .. .. £350

6668 — — — ℞. ΦΙΛΙΠΠΟΥ beneath club l. and bow; in field above, kantharos. *Le Rider* 240, 61 .. .. £350

6669 — — — ℞. ΦΙΛΙΠΠΟΥ beneath club r. and bow; in field beneath, trident. *Le Rider* 241, 70 .. .. £350

6670 — — — ℞. Similar, but the trident is above ΦΙΛΙΠΠΟΥ. *Le Rider* 243, 86 .. £350

6671 — — — — ℞. ΦΙΛΙΠΠΟΥ between bow (above) and club l.; in field beneath, trident. *Le Rider* 249, 128 .. .. £350

6672 6673 6675

6672 — *N eighth-stater* (*c.* 1·08 gm.). Hd. of young Herakles r., clad in lion's skin. ℞. ΦΙΛΙ / ΠΠΟΥ above and beneath thunderbolt. *Le Rider* 244, 90.. .. .. £350

6673 — — *Obv.* Similar. ℞. ΦΙΛΙΠ / ΠΟΥ either side of kantharos. *Le Rider* 245, 98 £375

6674 — — — ℞. ΦΙΛΙ / ΠΠΟΥ either side of trident. *Le Rider* 246, 103 .. .. £325

6675 — — — ℞. Similar, but the inscription is in one line, to l. of trident, and with small lion's hd. facing in field to r. *Le Rider* 233, 3 .. .. £325

6676 — *N twelfth-stater* (*c.* 0·72 gm.). Laur. hd. of Apollo r., hair short. ℞. ΦΙΛΙΠΠΟΥ across field, between thunderbolt, above, and lion's hd. facing, beneath. *Le Rider* 236, 35
£300

6677 — *Æ tetradrachm* (*c.* 14·4 gm.). Laur. hd. of Zeus r. ℞. King, wearing kausia, riding horse pacing l.; his r. hand raised; above, ΦΙΛΙΠΠΟΥ; beneath, I / M. *Le Rider* 9, 31 £650

6678 6680

6678 — — Similar, but on *rev.* the legend ΦΙΛΙΠ — ΠΟΥ is behind and before the king on horseback; and with rad. hd. of Helios facing beneath horse's raised foreleg, and spearhead above exergual line.   *Le Rider* 18, 106   ..   ..   £650

6679 — — As last, but with M instead of Helios hd. and trident instead of spear-head on *rev.* *Le Rider* 76, 28   ..   ..   £650

6680 — — Laur. hd. of Zeus r.   ℞. Naked youth on horse pacing r., holding long palm-branch; ΦΙΛΙΠ — ΠΟΥ behind and before; thunderbolt beneath; N in ex.   *Le Rider* 37, 263 ..   ..   £375

6681   6684

6681 — — Laur. hd. of Zeus l.   ℞. As last, but with ϴ beneath horse's raised foreleg, nothing in ex.   *Le Rider* 57, 437   ..   ..   £1,500

6682 — — Laur. hd. of Zeus r.   ℞. As last, but with amphora instead of ϴ beneath horse's foreleg.   *Le Rider* 95, 230 ..   ..   £300

6683 — — — — ℞. As last, but with wreath beneath horse's belly, and TE monogram beneath foreleg.   *Le Rider, pl.* 45, 23   ..   ..   £250

6684 — — — — ℞. As last, but with ΗΓ monogram beneath horse's belly, and Λ / Τ / race-torch beneath foreleg.   *Le Rider, pl.* 47, 11   ..   ..   £225

Coins of this series, with race-torch symbol on rev., belong to the latest issues in the name of Philip from the Amphipolis mint, circa 315-294 B.C.   As in the case of the gold staters, many different sequence marks (symbols, letters, monograms) have been recorded for the silver tetradrachms of Philip.

6685 — Æ didrachm (c. 7·2 gm.).   Hd. of young Herakles r., clad in lion's skin.   ℞. King, wearing kausia, riding horse pacing l.; his r. hand raised; ΦΙΛΙΠ — ΠΟΥ behind and before; beneath horse's raised foreleg, rad. hd. of Helios facing.   *Le Rider* 19, 122   £700

6686   6687

6686 — — *Obv.* Similar.   ℞. Naked youth on horse stg. r., his r. hand raised to touch horse's mane; ΦΙΛΙΠ — ΠΟΥ behind and before; thunderbolt beneath, N in ex.   *Le Rider* 41, 313   ..   £650

6687 — Æ *drachm* (c. 3·6 gm.).   *Obv.* Similar.   ℞. King on horseback, as 6685; ΦΙΛΙΠΠΟΥ above; spear-head and Ι / M beneath.   *Le Rider* 10, 45 ..   ..   £300

6688 — — — ℞. Naked youth on horse pacing l., his r. hand raised, holding palm-branch in l.; ΦΙΛΙΠΠΟΥ above, thunderbolt beneath, ΔΗ in ex.   *Le Rider* 75, 22   ..   ..   £275

6689 — Æ *fifth-stater* (c. 2·4-2·9 gm.).   Hd. of Apollo (?) r., hair bound with tainia.   ℞. Naked youth on horse prancing r.; ΦΙΛΙΠΠΟΥ above, ϴ beneath.   *Le Rider* 59, 455   £75

6690 — — Similar, but with club instead of ϴ beneath horse on *rev.*   *Le Rider* 69, 538   £75

6691 — — Similar, but with star beneath horse on *rev.*   *Le Rider, pl.* 43, 4   ..   £75

Many different sequence marks have been recorded for this denomination, which is the commonest silver coin of Philip after the tetradrachm.

6692   6694

Philip II *continued*

6692 — — Laur. bust of Artemis three-quarter face to l., wearing ear-rings and necklace, quiver behind r. shoulder. ℞. Naked youth on horse pacing r., holding palm-branch; ΦΙΛΙΠ — ΠΟΥ behind and before; forepart of Pegasos r. beneath horse's raised foreleg. *Le Rider* 119, 504 .. .. £350

6693 — Æ *hemidrachm* (c. 1·8 gm.). *Obv.* As 6689. ℞. Similar to 6688, but with Δ / Ι monogram instead of thunderbolt beneath horse, nothing in ex. *Le Rider* 6, 6 .. £150

6694 — Æ *tenth-stater* (c. 1·1-1·3 gm.). *Obv.* As 6689. ℞. Hd. and neck of bridled horse r.; ΦΙΛΙΠΠ — ΟΥ behind and before; thunderbolt beneath. *Le Rider* 62, 482 .. £140

6695 — — — ℞. Forepart of prancing horse r.; ΦΙΛΙ — ΠΠ — ΟΥ above, before and beneath; ear of corn in lower field to l. *Le Rider, pl.* 46, 33 .. .. £140

6696 — Æ 18. Hd. of Apollo (?) r., hair bound with tainia. ℞. Naked youth on horse prancing r.; ΦΙΛΙΠΠΟΥ above, barleycorn beneath. *Forrer/Weber* 2067. *Müller (Numismatique d'Alexandre le Grand)* 178.. .. .. £10

6697 — — Similar, but with race-torch instead of barleycorn beneath horse on *rev.* *Müller* 30
                                                                          £10

6698   6699

6698 — — Similar, but with ΗΡ monogram beneath horse. *Müller* 129 .. .. £10

6699 — — Similar, but *obv.* type to left; and with forepart of bull butting r. beneath horse on *rev.* *Forrer/Weber* 2068 .. .. £15

Many different sequence marks have been recorded for the extensive bronze coinage issued in the name of Philip II.

6700   6702

6700 **Alexander III, the Great,** 336-323 B.C. (the immense issues of coinage made in the name of Alexander the Great form a topic which could occupy the pages of a large volume. Obviously it is not possible, in a work of this scope, to do justice to such a subject. All that is attempted here is a brief listing of representative examples; with notes, where appropriate, on mint attributions and chronology. As in the case of Philip II, coinage in the name of Alexander continued long after the king's death. No doubt this was largely due to the lack of an effective successor to the imperial throne. Almost two decades were to elapse before Alexander's generals, his true successors, felt sufficiently secure to take the title of 'king' and to issue coinage in their own names. Although he began his career as King of Macedon, Alexander spent only the first two years of his reign in his native kingdom, and by the time of his death, at the age of thirty-three, he ruled a vast empire stretching from Greece to India. Consequently, his coinage was on an imperial scale, unlike those of his predecessors, and was struck at a multitude of mints in many lands, often replacing an existing autonomous series. Nevertheless, the Macedonian mint of Amphipolis remained one of the principal sources of currency. In later ages (3rd-2nd cent. B.C.) the types of Alexander's silver coinage were revived by various cities as they regained a measure of autonomy from the declining Hellenistic Monarchies. These are civic issues, however, and many of them will be found listed in this catalogue under the mints concerned). *N distater* (*c.* 17·2 gm.). Hd. of Athena r., in crested Corinthian helmet ornamented with serpent. ℞. Nike stg. l., holding wreath and ship's mast; on r., ΑΛΕΞΑΝΔΡΟΥ; in field to l., kantharos. *Price* (*Coins of the Macedonians*) *pl.* XI, 60. *Müller* (*Numismatique d'Alexandre le Grand*) *192* £3,000

6701 — — Similar, but on *rev.* thunderbolt instead of kantharos in field to l., and with ΛΟ monogram at Nike's feet to l. *Principal Coins*, IV.B.4. *Müller* 5   ..   £3,000

6702 — *N stater* (*c.* 8·6 gm.). Hd. of Athena r., as 6700. ℞. Nike stg. l., as 6700; on r., ΑΛΕΞΑΝΔΡΟΥ; in field to l., coiled serpent. *Le Rider* (*Le Monnayage d'Argent et d'Or de Philippe II*) *pl.* 92, 36. *Müller* 529   ..   ..   £650

6703 — — Similar, but on *rev.* thunderbolt instead of serpent in field to l. *Le Rider, pl.* 91, 18. *Müller* 2   ..   ..   £650

6704 — — Similar, but on *rev.* ΜΗ monogram and pentagram in field to l., and with cornucopiae at Nike's feet to l. *Le Rider, pl.* 91, 25. *Müller* 381   ..   ..   £650

6705   6706

6705 — — Hd. of Athena r., in crested Corinthian helmet ornamented with sphinx. ℞. Nike stg. l., as 6700; on r., ΑΛΕΞΑΝΔΡΟΥ; in lower field to l., monogram above Μ. *Principal Coins*, IV.A.2   ..   ..   £800

6706 — — Hd. of Athena r., in crested Corinthian helmet ornamented with griffin. ℞. Nike stg. l., as 6700; on l., around, ΑΛΕΞΑΝΔΡΟΥ; in lower field to r., caduceus. *Le Rider, pl.* 91, 21. *Müller* 205   ..   ..   £750

6707 — — *Obv.* As 6700. ℞. Nike stg. l., as 6700; on r., ΑΛΕΞΑΝΔΡΟΥ; on l., ΒΑΣΙΛΕΩΣ; in lower field to r., monogram within wreath; to l., bald and bearded hd. of Satyr l. *Le Rider, pl.* 92, 44. *Müller* 729   ..   ..   £700

Many different sequence marks (symbols, letters, monograms in reverse field) have been recorded for the gold staters of Alexander.

6708   6710

6708 — *N half-stater* (*c.* 4·3 gm.). Hd. of Athena r., in crested Corinthian helmet ornamented with serpent. ℞. Nike stg. l., holding wreath and ship's mast; on r., ΑΛΕΞΑΝΔΡΟΥ; in field to l., hd. of griffin l. *Müller* 294 ..   ..   £1,250

6709 — *N quarter-stater* (*c.* 2·15 gm.). *Obv.* Similar; beneath, thunderbolt. ℞. As last, but king's name abbreviated to ΑΛΕΞΑΝ., and ΗΔ monogram instead of griffin's hd. in field to l. *Forrer/Weber* 2079. *Müller* 761, *var.* £900

6710 — — *Obv.* As 6708. ℞. ΑΛΕΞΑΝ / ΔΡΟΥ above and beneath bow and club l.; in field above, thunderbolt. *Jenkins* (*Ancient Greek Coins*) 513/14   ..   ..   £450

6711 — *N eighth-stater* (*c.* 1·08 gm.). *Obv.* As 6708. ℞. ΑΛΕΞΑ / ΝΔΡΟΥ above and beneath thunderbolt. *Jenkins* 515/16   ..   ..   £400

Alexander III *continued*

6712 — Æ *dekadrachm* (*c.* 42·4 gm.). Hd. of young Herakles r., clad in lion's skin. R. Zeus enthroned l., feet on stool, holding eagle and sceptre; on r., ΑΛΕΞΑΝΔΡΟΥ; beneath throne, monogram and м. *Müller* 669 .. .. £12,500

> *Early in his reign Alexander adopted the Attic weight standard for his silver coinage. The lighter Thraco-Macedonian denominations, based on a tetradrachm of circa 14·4 gm., continued to be struck in Macedon, for local use, but with the types and in the name of Alexander's father, Philip II.*

6713   6715

6713 — Æ *tetradrachm* (*c.* 17 gm.). Hd. of young Herakles r., clad in lion's skin. R. Zeus seated l. on backless throne, his legs parallel, holding eagle and sceptre; on r., ΑΛΕΞΑΝΔΡΟΥ; in field to l., prow of galley l. *Newell* (*Alexander Hoards: Demanhur,* 1905) 5-55. *Müller* 503 .. .. £140

6714 — — Similar, but on *rev.* cock l. instead of prow in field to l. *Newell* 792-894. *Müller* 392 .. .. £140

6715 — — *Obv.* Similar, but type to *left.* R. Zeus seated l. on throne with back, his legs parallel, holding eagle and sceptre; on r., ΑΛΕΞΑΝΔΡΟΥ; in field to l., bee. *Newell* 1599-1600. *Forrer/Weber* 2094 .. .. £650

6716 — — *Obv.* As 6713. R. As last, but in field to l., naked athlete l., both arms outstretched. *Newell* 1649-66. *Müller* 637. *Forrer/Weber* 2096 .. .. £175

6717   6718

6717 — — — R. Zeus seated l. on backless throne; his legs parallel, feet on stool, holding eagle and sceptre; protuberances on the legs of the throne; on r., ΑΛΕΞΑΝΔΡΟΥ; in field to l., plough. *Newell* 2232-64. *Muller* 1282. *Forrer/Weber* 2114 .. .. £150

6718 — — — R. Zeus seated, similar to last; on r., ΑΛΕΞΑΝΔΡΟΥ; in field to l., forepart of
ram r.; beneath throne, ΔΑ (=*Damaskos*) and pellet. *Newell* 2976-3050. *Müller*
1339 .. .. £140

6719 — — — R. Zeus seated l. on throne with back; his legs parallel, feet on stool, holding
eagle and sceptre; on r., ΑΛΕΞΑΝΔΡΟΥ; in field to l., wreath-bearing Nike flying l.; beneath
throne, monogram and Μ. *Newell* 4263-73. *Müller* 687. *Forrer/Weber* 2123 £175

6720 — — — R. Zeus seated, as last; on r., ΑΛΕΞΑΝΔΡΟΥ; in ex., ΒΑΣΙΛΕΩΣ; in field to l.,
thunderbolt and Μ; beneath throne, monogram. *Newell* 4466. *Forrer/Weber* 2125
£200

*The above varieties of the Attic tetradrachm (nos. 6713-20) were struck during Alexan-
der's lifetime. Those which follow are posthumous issues belonging, in the main, to the last
two decades of the 4th century and the first decade of the 3rd.*

6721   6723

6721 — — Hd. of young Herakles r., clad in lion's skin. R. Zeus seated l. on backless throne;
his r. leg drawn back, feet on stool, holding eagle and sceptre; on r., ΑΛΕΞΑΝΔΡΟΥ; in field
to l., Λ / Τ and race-torch; beneath throne, ΗΓ monogram. *Price (Coins of the Macedonians)*
pl. XI, 63. *Müller* 57 .. .. £125

6722 — — *Obv.* Similar. R. Zeus seated, similar to last, but throne with back; on r.,
ΑΛΕΞΑΝΔΡΟΥ; in field to l., Boeotian shield; in ex., thyrsos. *Müller* 755. *Forrer/Weber*
2095 .. .. £140

6723 — — — R. Zeus seated l. on throne with back; his r. leg drawn back, feet on stool,
holding eagle and sceptre; protuberances on the legs of the throne; on r., ΑΛΕΞΑΝΔΡΟΥ; in
field to l., ΥΟ (*i.e.* Phoenician letters '*ak*' =mint of *Ake*) and ΙΙΟ = (Phoenician numerals
=year 32 =315/14 B.C.). *Cf. Müller* 1430-48. *Forrer/Weber* 2121 .. .. £165

6724 — — — R. Zeus seated, similar to last, but no protuberances on the legs of throne; on r.,
ΑΛΕΞΑΝΔΡΟΥ; in ex., ΒΑΣΙΛΕΩΣ; in field to l., Μ; beneath throne, ΛΥ. *Newell* 4479-4525.
Müller 1272. *Forrer/Weber* 2127 .. .. £140

6725 — — — R. Zeus seated, as 6721; on r., ΑΛΕΞΑΝΔΡΟΥ; in field to l., rose; ΔΙ — ο beneath
and behind throne. *Newell* 4614-4747. *Müller* 124 .. .. £250

*The above selection of tetradrachms (nos. 6713-25) represents only a tiny proportion of the
many hundreds of varieties known to exist.*

6726   6727

Alexander III *continued*

6726 — Æ *tetradrachm* (Thraco-Macedonian standard, *c.* 14·4 gm.).   Laur. hd. of Zeus r.
R. ΑΛΕΞΑΝ — ΔΡΟΥ. Eagle stg. r. on thunderbolt, looking back; in field to l., spray of
olive; to r., satrapal head-dress. *Principal Coins*, IV. B.3.   ..   ..   .. £10,000
      *This very rare type seems to indicate that the decision to continue issuing Thraco-Mace-
donian coins in the name of Philip II was not taken immediately on the accession of Alexander.*

6727 — Æ *didrachm* (*c.* 8·5 gm.).   Hd. of young Herakles r., clad in lion's skin.   R. Zeus
seated l. on throne with back; his legs parallel, feet on stool, holding eagle and sceptre;
on r., ΑΛΕΞΑΝΔΡΟΥ; in field to l., M; beneath throne, monogram.   *Müller 674*   £500

.   6728   6730

6728 — Æ *drachm* (*c.* 4·25 gm.).   *Obv.* Similar.   R. ΑΛΕΞΑΝ — ΔΡΟΥ behind and before eagle
stg. r. on thunderbolt; in field to r., eagle's hd. l.   *Forrer/Weber 2083*   .. £250

6729 — — — R. Similar, but the legend is divided ΑΛΕΞΑ — ΝΔΡΟΥ, the eagle on thunderbolt
looks back, and with bucranium instead of eagle's hd. in field to r.   *Forrer/Weber 2090*
£275

6730 — — — R. Zeus enthroned l., holding eagle and sceptre; his r. leg drawn back and feet
resting on stool; on r., ΑΛΕΞΑΝΔΡΟΥ; in field to l., lion's hd. l. surmounted by crescent;
beneath throne, N.   *Müller 339.   Forrer/Weber 2100* £50

6731 — — — R. Zeus enthroned l., holding eagle and sceptre; his l. leg drawn back; on r.,
ΑΛΕΞΑΝΔΡΟΥ; in field to l., Hermes stg., holding caduceus; beneath throne, Ξ. *Müller*
907, *var.   Forrer/Weber 2104* £55
      *Many varieties of the drachm, with reverse type Zeus, have been recorded.   After the
tetradrachm it is the commonest silver denomination of Alexander's coinage.*

6732 — Æ *hemidrachm* (*c.* 2·1 gm.).   Similar to 6728, but with caduceus instead of eagle's
hd. in *rev.* field.   *Historia Numorum, p.* 225 ..   .. £175

6733   6734   6735

6733 — — Hd. of Herakles/Zeus enthroned, all as 6727.   *Müller 675* £120

6734 — Æ *diobol* (*c.* 1·4 gm.).   Hd. of young Herakles r., clad in lion's skin.   R. ΑΛΕΞΑΝΔΡΟΥ,
around, above two eagles stg. face to face on torch.   *Forrer/Weber 2086*   .. £90

6735 — Æ *obol* (*c.* 0·7 gm.).   *Obv.* Similar.   R. ΑΛΕΞΑ — ΝΔΡΟΥ either side of thunderbolt.
Forrer/Weber 2088 ..   .. £75

6736   6738   6739

6736 — — — ℞. Zeus enthroned l., holding eagle and sceptre; his legs parallel; on r., ΑΛΕΞΑΝ; in field to l., M; monogram beneath throne. *Forrer/Weber* 2135 .. £60

6737 — — — ℞. Similar, but Zeus' r. leg drawn back; on r., ΑΛΕΞΑΝΔΡΟΥ; in field to l., anchor and forepart of grazing horse l.; beneath throne, ΣΩ. *Forrer/Weber* 2131 £65

6738 — Æ *hemiobol* (*c*. 0·35 gm.). Hd. of young Herakles r., clad in lion's skin. ℞. ΑΛΕΞΑΝΔ across field; club l. above, bow and quiver beneath. *Forrer/Weber* 2138 .. £65

6739 — Æ 20. Hd. of young Herakles r., clad in lion's skin. ℞. ΑΛΕΞΑΝΔΡΟΥ across field; above, club r.; beneath, bow in case; in upper field, Π. *Forrer/Weber* 2140 .. £10

6740 — — Hd. of Apollo (?) r., hair bound with tainia. ℞. Horseman cantering r.; ΒΑΣΙΛΕΩΣ / ΑΛΕΞΑΝ above and beneath; bipennis and ΑΣ monogram in field to l.; M within O beneath horse. *Forrer/Weber* 2153 .. £14

6741 — Æ 18. Hd. of young Herakles r., clad in lion's skin. ℞. ΑΛΕΞΑΝΔΡΟΥ / ΒΑΣΙΛΕΩΣ above and beneath bow in case; above, club r. and monogram. *Forrer/Weber* 2187 £9

6742   6743   6744

6742 — — *Obv.* Similar. ℞. Large ΒΑ; above, bow in case and quiver; beneath, club r. and small thunderbolt. *Forrer/Weber* 2146 .. .. £8

6743 — — *Obv.* Similar. ℞. ΑΛΕΞΑΝ — ΔΡΟΥ. Eagle stg. r. on thunderbolt, looking back; leaf in upper field to l. *Forrer/Weber* 2142 .. .. .. £12

6744 — Æ 16. *Obv.* 6740. ℞. Horse prancing r.; ΑΛΕΞΑΝΔΡΟΥ above, thunderbolt beneath. *Forrer/Weber* 2150 .. .. £11

6745 — Æ 12. *Obv.* As 6741. ℞. ΑΛΕ / ΞΑΝΔΡΟΥ above and beneath club r., bow and quiver below; crescent in upper field to r. *Forrer/Weber* 2145 .. .. .. £8

Some of the above types of the bronze coinage (nos. 6739-45) were struck after Alexander's death. Those most likely to be posthumous are the ones bearing the title 'ΒΑΣΙΛΕΩΣ'.

6746 **Philip III, Arrhidaeus,** 323-317 B.C. (the sudden and unexpected death of Alexander at Babylon in June, 323 B.C., created a power vacuum which none of the great king's generals had sufficient authority to fill. Four decades of civil wars were to ensue, but

Philip III *continued*

for the time being a compromise settlement was reached.   Arrhidaeus, a feeble-minded half-brother of Alexander was to share the throne with Alexander IV, the infant son of the late king born soon after his father's death.   Thus the real power still lay with the generals—Perdikkas, Antigonos, Lysimachos, Seleukos, Ptolemy and others—who were merely biding their time.   After only six years of nominal rule Arrhidaeus was murdered by Olympias, mother of Alexander the Great).   *N stater* (*c.* 8·6 gm.).   Hd. of Athena r., in crested Corinthian helmet ornamented with serpent.   R. Nike stg. l., holding wreath and ship's mast; on r., ΦΙΛΙΠΠΟΥ; in field to l., MH monogram and pentagram; cornucopiae at Nike's feet to l.   *Le Rider* (*Le Monnayage d'Argent et d'Or de Philippe II*) *pl.* 91, 26.   *Müller* (*Numismatique d'Alexandre le Grand*) 63   ..   ..   ..   £750

6747 — — Obv. Similar.   R. Nike stg., as last; on r., ΦΙΛΙΠΠΟΥ; on l., ΒΑΣΙΛΕΩΣ; in field to l., wheel; monogram at Nike's feet to l.   *Le Rider, pl.* 92, 41.   *Müller* 23   ..   £700

6748 — Æ *tetradrachm* (*c.* 17 gm.).   Hd. of young Herakles r., clad in lion's skin.   R. Zeus enthroned l., holding eagle and sceptre; on r., ΦΙΛΙΠΠΟΥ; in field to l., N; beneath throne, ΣΙ (=*Sidon*).   *Newell* (*Alexander Hoards: Demanhur*, 1905) 3762-5.   *Müller* 106
£150

6749   6750

6749 — — Obv. Similar.   R. Zeus enthroned, as last; on r., ΦΙΛΙΠΠΟΥ; in ex., ΒΑΣΙΛΕΩΣ; in field to l., M; beneath throne, ΛΥ.   *Newell* 4526-94.   *Müller* 99.   *Forrer/Weber* 2155
£140

6750 — Æ *drachm* (*c.* 4·25 gm.).   Similar to 6748, but on *rev.* serpent in field to l., and ΑΩ monogram beneath throne.   *Müller* 79.   *Forrer/Weber* 2158 ..   ..   ..   £60

6751 — — Similar, but with ΠΑ monogram in *rev.* field to l., nothing beneath throne.   *Müller* 135.   *Forrer/Weber* 2159 ..   ..   £60

6752 — Æ *hemidrachm* (*c.* 2·1 gm.).   As last, but with M in *rev.* field to l.   *Müller* 104a
£120

Although the coinage in the name of Philip III is on a much smaller scale than that of Alexander there are, nevertheless, many recorded varieties.

6753   6754

6753 **Kassander,** 319-297 B.C. (the son of Antipater, Regent of Macedon appointed by Alexander, Kassander succeeded to the government of the country on his father's death in 319 B.C. He was notorious for his cruelty, and in 311 B.C. he executed Alexander's widow Roxana and her young son Alexander IV. In 305 B.C. he assumed the title of King). Æ 18. Hd. of young Herakles r., clad in lion's skin. ℞. ΚΑΣΣΑΝ / ΔΡΟΥ above and beneath lion seated r.; A in field to r. *Forrer/Weber* 2161 .. .. .. £13
  This type was issued before Kassander's assumption of the royal title in 305 B.C. The following types belong to the period 305-297.

6754 — Æ 20. *Obv.* Similar. ℞. ΒΑΣΙΛΕΩΣ / ΚΑΣΣΑΝΔΡΟΥ above and beneath naked youth on horse pacing r.; AP monogram before horse, ΚΑ monogram beneath. *Price (Coins of the Macedonians) pl.* XII, 65 .. .. £12

6755 — Æ 18. Laur. hd. of Apollo r. ℞. ΒΑΣΙΛΕΩΣ / ΚΑΣΣΑΝΔΡΟΥ either side of tripod; caduceus in field to r. *Forrer/Weber* 2162 .. .. £14

6756   6757

6756 — — Helmet. ℞. ΒΑΣΙΛΕΩΣ / ΚΑΣΣΑΝΔΡΟΥ above and beneath spear-head r. *Forrer/ Weber* 2166 .. .. £16
  The silver coinage of this reign was all struck in the name of Alexander.

6757 **Demetrios Poliorketes,** 294-288 B.C. (son of Antigonos the One-eyed, Demetrios Poliorketes (the 'Besieger') was a romantic character who pursued a most colourful career spanning more than three decades. In his earlier years he assisted his father, whose power was centred in Asia Minor, and in 306 he achieved a great naval victory over Ptolemy of Egypt in the battle of Salamis, off the coast of Cyprus. After many vicissitudes he seized the Macedonian throne in 294, and although he reigned for only six years the dynasty which he founded lasted until the end of the Macedonian Kingdom. He died as a captive in Syria in 283 B.C.). *N stater* (*c.* 8·6 gm.). Hd. of Athena r., wearing crested Corinthian helmet. ℞. Nike stg. l., holding wreath and ship's mast; on r., ΒΑΣΙΛΕΩΣ; on l., ΔΗΜΗΤΡΙΟΥ; ΑΝΤΙ monogram at Nike's feet to l. *Newell* (*The Coinages of Demetrius Poliorcetes*) 78 .. .. £1,750

6758 — — *Obv.* Similar. ℞. Nike stg. l., holding wreath and ship's mast; on r., ΔΗΜΗΤΡΙΟΥ; in field to l., ΙΩ monogram. *Newell* 65 .. .. £1,750

6759 — — Winged Nike stg. l. on prow of galley, blowing trumpet and holding mast. ℞. Athena Promachos advancing l., brandishing spear and holding shield; ΔΗΜΗΤΡΙΟΥ behind, ΒΑΣΙ — ΛΕΩΣ across lower field; monogram resembling double-axe in field to l. *Newell* 21 .. .. £7,500

6760 — — Diad. hd. of Demetrios r., with bull's horn. ℞. Macedonian horseman prancing r., holding spear couched; ΒΑΣΙΛΕΩΣ behind, ΔΗΜΗΤΡΙΟΥ beneath; ΕΡΥΚ monogram in field, below horse. *Newell* 88 .. .. £4,500

Demetrios Poliorketes *continued*

6761 — Æ *tetradrachm* (*c.* 17 gm.). Hd. of young Herakles r., clad in lion's skin. ℞. Zeus enthroned l., holding eagle and sceptre; on r., ΔHMHTPIOY; in field to l., club and E. *Newell* 26 .. .. £750

6762 — — Winged Nike stg. on prow, as 6759. ℞. Naked Poseidon, viewed from behind, striding l., brandishing trident and holding chlamys on outstretched l. arm; on r., ΔHMHTPIOY; beneath, BAΣ — IΛEΩ — Σ; in field to r., monogram resembling double-axe; to l., HP monogram. *Newell* 22 .. .. £1,400

6763 — — Diad. hd of Demetrios r., with bull's horn. ℞. Poseidon, naked to waist, seated l. on rock, holding aplustre and trident; on r., ΔHMHTPIOY; on l., BAΣIΛEΩΣ; in field to r., EY monogram; to l., APT monogram and Ι. *Forrer/Weber* 2175. *Newell* 105 .. £850

6764   6765

6764 — — *Obv.* Similar. ℞. Poseidon, naked, stg. l., r. foot set on rock; he rests his r. arm on thigh and holds trident in l.; on r., BAΣIΛEΩΣ; on l., ΔHMHTPIOY; in field to r., AP monogram; to l., EYΘ monogram. *Newell* 124 .. .. £650

6765 — Æ *drachm* (*c.* 4·25 gm.). Winged Nike stg. on prow, as 6759. ℞. Naked Poseidon brandishing trident, as 6762; on r., ΔHMHTPIOY; beneath, BAΣI — ΛEΩ — Σ; in field to l., A; to r., N within circle. *Forrer/Weber* 2171. *Newell* 44 .. .. .. £275

6766 — — Diad. hd. of Demetrios r., with bull's horn. ℞. Naked Poseidon brandishing trident, as 6762; on r., ΔHMHTPIOY; beneath, BAΣIΛ — EΩΣ; in field to l., monogram; to r., ivy-leaf. *Newell* 55 .. .. £550

6767 — — *Obv.* Similar. ℞. Naked Poseidon resting foot on rock, as 6764; on r., BAΣIΛEΩΣ; on l., ΔHMHTPIOY; in field to l., AΓ monogram. *Newell* 154 .. .. .. £550

6768 — Æ *hemidrachm* (*c.* 2·1 gm.). As 6765. *Newell* 45 .. .. £140

6769 — — Similar to 6766, but on *rev.* the monogram and ivy-leaf are both in field to r. *Newell* 56 .. .. £250

6770 — — Similar to 6767, but on *rev.* ΒΑΣΙΛΕΩΣ is on l., ΔΗΜΗΤΡΙΟΥ on r.; and with ΑΥ monogram within circle between feet of Poseidon.   *Newell* 140   ..   ..   £250

6771 — Æ 20. Hd. of Athena r., in crested helmet. R. Prow of galley l., ΒΑΣΙ above, ΔΗΜΗ beneath; on forecastle, ΚΙ. *Newell* 176   ..   ..   £17

6772 — Æ 19. *Obv.* Similar to *rev.* of last, but without inscription. R. Naked Poseidon brandishing trident, as 6762; on r., ΒΑΣΙ; beneath, ΔΗΜ; in field to l., caduceus. *Newell* 175 ..   ..   £18

6773   6774

6773 — Æ 18. Laur. hd. of Poseidon r. R. ΒΑΣΙΛΕΩΣ / ΔΗΜΗΤΡΙΟΥ before and behind Athena Promachos advancing r., brandishing spear and holding shield; in field to l., ΑΡ monogram; to r., double-axe. *Forrer/Weber* 2176. *Newell* 166   ..   £16

6774 — Æ 15. Macedonian shield, with monogram of Demetrios at centre. R. ΒΑ — ΣΙ either side of crested Macedonian helmet; in field to l., anchor. *Newell* 131 ..   £14

6775 — Æ 14. Hd. of Demetrios (?) r., wearing crested Corinthian helmet ornamented with bull's horn. R. Prow of galley r.; ΒΑ above, monogram beneath. *Newell* 20   £12

6776 — Æ 13. Youthful male hd. r., in crested Corinthian helmet. R. Β — Α either side of trident-head; in lower field to l., ΑΡ monogram; to r., double-axe. *Forrer/Weber* 2180. *Newell* 164 ..   ..   £10

6777   6779

6777 — Æ 12. Laur. hd. of Poseidon r. R. As last, but aplustre instead of trident-head. *Newell* 169 ..   ..   £10

6778 — Æ 10. Macedonian shield, with star at centre. R. ΒΑΣΙΛΕΩΣ ΔΗΜΗΤΡΙΟΥ. Crested Macedonian helmet; monogram in lower field to l. *Newell* 182   ..   ..   £11

6779 **Interregnum,** 288-277 B.C. (following Demetrios' overthrow by Lysimachos and Pyrrhos, Macedon underwent a decade during which no ruler was able to control the country for any length of time. Most of the bronze coins issued in this period were anonymous, though a few have the name of Pyrrhos in monogrammatic form. Lysimachos also struck some tetradrachms of his usual type at the Amphipolis mint). Æ 17. Macedonian shield, with monogram of **Pyrrhos** at centre. R. Helmet, beneath which ΒΑ — ΣΙ divided by monogram; all within oak-wreath. *Forrer/Weber* 2181   ..   ..   £15

6780 — Æ 20. Hd. of young Herakles r., clad in lion's skin. R. ΒΑΣΙΛΕΩΣ across field, between bow in case, above, and club r., beneath; race-torch in field below. *Forrer/Weber* 2185   ..   ..   £10

6781 — Æ 18. Macedonian shield, with Gorgon's hd. at centre. R. Macedonian helmet dividing Β — Α; in lower field to l., caduceus; to r., monogram. *Forrer/Weber* 2189   £9

6782 — Æ 16. Similar, but with thunderbolt instead of Gorgoneion on the shield, and without caduceus on *rev.* *Forrer/Weber* 2183 ..   ..   £10

6783 **Antigonos Gonatas,** 277-239 B.C. (son of Demetrios Poliorketes, Antigonos Gonatas claimed his father's throne after achieving a notable victory over the Gallic invaders in Thrace. The Macedonian kingdom prospered again under his long and enlightened rule). Æ *tetradrachm* (*c.* 17 gm.). Macedonian shield, at centre of which horned bust of Pan l., pedum at shoulder. Ŗ. Athena Alkidemos advancing l., brandishing thunderbolt and holding shield; on r., ΒΑΣΙΛΕΩΣ; on l., ΑΝΤΙΓΟΝΟΥ; in lower field to l., Macedonian helmet; to r., HP monogram. *Price (Coins of the Macedonians) pl.* XII, 70 ..   £300

    The god Pan is said to have intervened on behalf of the Macedonians in Antigonos' battle with the Gauls in 277 B.C.

6784 — — Hd. of young Herakles r., clad in lion's skin. Ŗ. Zeus enthroned l., holding eagle and sceptre; on r., ΒΑΣΙΛΕΩΣ; on l., ΑΝΤΙΓΟΝΟΥ; in field to l., monogram. *Historia Numorum, p.* 229 ..   ..   £750

        6785   6786

6785 — Æ *drachm*? (*c.* 3·43 gm.). Hd. of Poseidon r., hair bound with marine plant. Ŗ. Similar to 6783, but with TI instead of monogram in field to r. *Forrer/Weber* 2192, *var.*   £600

6786 — Æ 20. Hd. of Athena r., in crested Corinthian helmet. Ŗ. Pan advancing r., erecting trophy; B — A in upper field; ΑΝΤΙ monogram beneath Pan; Φ in field to l. *Price, pl.* XII, 71 ..   ..   £10

6787 — Æ 17. Hd. of young Herakles r., clad in lion's skin. Ŗ. Naked youth on horse pacing r.; B — A in upper field; ΑΝΤΙ monogram beneath horse; monogram in field to r. *Forrer/Weber* 2196 ..   ..   £12

6788 — — Macedonian shield, with monogram of Antigonos at centre. Ŗ. ΒΑ — ΣΙ either side of Macedonian helmet. *Historia Numorum, p.* 232 ..   ..   ..   £14

Demetrios II, 239-229 B.C. (son of Antigonos Gonatas, Demetrios ruled Macedon for ten troubled years before falling in battle against Dardanian invaders of his kingdom. No coins have been satisfactorily attributed to this reign).

                             6789

6789 **Antigonos Doson,** 229-221 B.C. (Demetrios' son, Philip, was too young to assume power on his father's death, so the government was carried on by a cousin of Demetrios, named Antigonos Doson. His short reign saw the re-establishment of Macedonian authority and paved the way for his remarkable successor, Philip V). Æ *tetradrachm* (*c.* 17 gm.). Hd. of Poseidon r., with luxuriant hair bound with marine plant. R. Naked Apollo, holding bow, seated l., at ease, on prow of galley inscribed ΒΑΣΙΛΕΩΣ / ΑΝΤΙΓΟΝΟΥ; monogram beneath. *Price, pl.* XIII, 72 .. .. £650

This type commemorates a naval victory of Antigonos Doson and Antiochos Hierax over the Ptolemaic fleet off the island of Andros.

6790 **Philip V,** 221-179 B.C. (son of Demetrios II, Philip V came to power in 221 B.C. on the death of Antigonos Doson. He was a vigorous ruler and maintained the power of the Macedonian kingdom in the earlier part of his reign. However, he made the mistake of arousing the enmity of the Romans, and in 197 B.C. his power was crushed at the battle of Kynoskephalai by the Roman general T. Quinctius Flamininus. After this his power and territory were severely curtailed by Rome, and the days of the Macedonian kingdom were numbered). Æ *tetradrachm* (*c.* 17 gm.). Diad. hd. of Philip r., with close beard. R. Athena Alkidemos advancing l., brandishing thunderbolt and holding shield; on r., ΒΑΣΙΛΕΩΣ; on l., ΦΙΛΙΠΠΟΥ; monograms in field to l. and to r. *Price, pl.* XIII, 73 £2,000

6791 — — Macedonian shield, at centre of which hd. of the hero Perseus l., wearing winged helmet terminating in forepart of griffin, harpa behind neck. R. ΒΑΣΙΛΕΩΣ / ΦΙΛΙΠΠΟΥ above and beneath club r.; three monograms in field, one above and two below; all within oak-wreath to l. of which, harpa. *Price, pl.* XIII, 74 .. .. £500

6792 — Æ *didrachm* (*c.* 8·5 gm.). *Obv.* As 6790. R. As last, but with trident-head instead of harpa outside wreath. *Boston Museum Catalogue* 718 .. .. £500

6793 — Æ *drachm* (*c.* 4·25 gm.). Similar, but with thunderbolt outside wreath on *rev.* *Boston Museum Catalogue* 719 .. .. £400

Philip V *continued*

6794 — Æ *hemidrachm* (*c.* 2·1 gm.).   Similar, but with caduceus outside wreath on *rev.*
Forrer/Weber 2201   ..   ..   £225

6795 — Æ 24.   Rad. hd. of Helios r.   R. ΒΑΣΙΛΕΩΣ / ΦΙΛΙΠΠΟΥ above and beneath thunderbolt; monogram in field above; all within oak-wreath.   *Forrer/Weber* 2203   ..   £20

6796 — Æ 23.   Hd. of Poseidon r., hair bound with marine plant.   R. ΒΑΣΙΛΕΩΣ / ΦΙΛΙΠΠΟΥ
behind and before naked Herakles advancing l., holding club over r. shoulder.   *Forrer/
Weber* 2202   ..   ..   £20

6797 — Æ 20.   Hd. of young Herakles r., clad in lion's skin.   R. ΒΑ / Φ above and beneath
two goats kneeling r., side by side; two monograms in lower field, another to r.   *Forrer/
Weber* 2204   ..   ..   £18

6798 — Æ 19.   Hd. of the hero Perseus r., in winged cap, harpa behind neck.   R. Eagle stg.
l. on thunderbolt, hd. r.; Β — Α / Φ — Ι in upper field, Α to l.   *Forrer/Weber* 2208
£16

6799 — Æ 15.   *Obv.* As 6797.   R. ΒΑ / Φ above and beneath horseman prancing r.   *Forrer/
Weber* 2206   ..   ..   £14

6800 — Æ 14.   Macedonian shield, with hd. of the hero Perseus r. at centre.   R. ΒΑΣΙΛΕΩΣ /
ΦΙΛΙΠΠΟΥ either side of Macedonian helmet.   *Forrer/Weber* 2209   ..   ..   £15

The bronze coinage of this reign is extensive and many other types are known.

6801 **T. Quinctius Flamininus** (the Roman general who defeated Philip V at Kynoskephalai
in 197 B.C. issued gold staters with his own portrait on obverse, and a reverse type remini-
scent of the coinage of Alexander.   These may not have been struck in Macedon, where
Philip continued to rule, but at Corinth where Flamininus proclaimed the 'Freedom of
Greece' at the Isthmian Games of 196 B.C.).   *N stater* (*c.* 8·43 gm.).   Bare hd. of Flamininus r., with close beard.   R. Nike stg. l., holding wreath and palm; on l., T. QVINCTI.
Price (*Coins of the Macedonians*) *pl.* XIII, 75   ..   ..   £25,000

6802 **Perseus,** 179-168 B.C. (the eldest son of Philip V, Perseus was the last king of Macedon.
He inherited a kingdom already largely dependent on Rome, but his policies aroused
Roman suspicions and armed conflict became inevitable.   At the battle of Pydna, in 168
B.C., Perseus lost his kingdom and he died two years later as an exile in Italy).   Æ *tetra-
drachm* (*c.* 17 gm.).   Diad. hd. of Perseus r., with close beard.   R. Eagle, wings open,
stg. r. on thunderbolt; ΒΑΣΙ — ΛΕΩΣ / ΠΕΡ — ΣΕΩΣ across field; monograms above, to r.
and between eagle's legs; all within oak-wreath beneath which, star.   *Jenkins* (*Ancient
Greek Coins*) 543/4 ..   ..   £500

6803 — — Similar, but with ΙΩΙΛΟΥ beneath Perseus' hd. on *obv.*, and with monogram and letter in *rev.* field to r. of eagle. *Principal Coins* VI. B.7 .. .. .. £1,000

> *Zoilos, whose name appears on the obv. of this type, was probably mint-master under Perseus.*

6804 — Æ *tetradrachm* (reduced weight, *c.* 15·5 gm.). Similar to 6802, but with plough instead of star beneath the wreath on *rev.* *Price, pl.* XIII, 76 .. .. .. £350

> *This weight reduction was made in 171 B.C. when the final conflict with Rome began.*

6805 — Æ *didrachm* (*c.* 8·5 gm.). *Obv.* As 6802. Ɍ. ΒΑΣΙΛΕΩΣ / ΠΕΡΣΕΩΣ above and beneath harpa; three monograms in field, one above and two below; all within oak-wreath to l. of which, star. *Historia Numorum, p.* 235 .. .. £1,000

6806   6807

6806 — Æ *drachm* (*c.* 4·25 gm.). *Obv.* As 6802. Ɍ. ΒΑΣΙΛΕΩΣ / ΠΕΡΣΕΩΣ above and beneath club r.; three monograms in field, one above and two below; all within oak-wreath to l. of which, star. *Boston Museum Catalogue* 723 .. .. £400

6807 — Æ 19. Hd. of the hero Perseus r., wearing winged cap terminating in bird's hd. Ɍ. Eagle, wings open, stg. l. on thunderbolt, hd. r.; ΒΑ above, ΠΕΡ monogram to l., ΙΩ monogram to r., two stars in ex. *Forrer/Weber* 2222, *var.* £16

6808 — Æ 16. Hd. of young Herakles r., clad in lion's skin. Ɍ. Horseman prancing r.; in field to r., ΒΑ and ΠΕΡ monogram. *Forrer/Weber* 2223 .. .. £14

6809 — Æ 14. Macedonian shield, with wheel-ornament at centre. Ɍ. ΒΑ — ΠΕ either side of harpa. *Historia Numorum, p.* 235 .. .. £15

KINGDOM OF THRACE

6810 Lysimachos, 323-281 B.C. (one of the most remarkable of the 'Successors' of Alexander, Lysimachos was of Thessalian stock and was a bodyguard of the great Macedonian King. In the confused period following Alexander's death he obtained the government of Thrace, and in 309 B.C. founded his capital city of Lysimacheia where many of his coins were struck. In 305 B.C. he took the title of King, and four years later extended his rule over much of Asia Minor following the defeat of Antigonos the One-eyed at Ipsos. His later years were marred by domestic tragedy and his harsh rule made him unpopular with his subjects. In 281 B.C. Lysimachos, now aged 80, was attacked by Seleukos of Syria who was only two years his junior. Lysimachos died fighting at the battle of Korupedion and his kingdom disappeared with him. But his memory lived on and generations later a number of mints in the Black Sea area restored his coin types for their autonomous issues—see Vol. 1 of this catalogue, *pp.* 160-169). ALEXANDRINE TYPES, 305-297 B.C. *N stater* (*c.* 8·5 gm.). Hd. of Athena r., in crested Corinthian helmet ornamented with serpent. R. Nike stg. l., holding wreath and ship's mast; on r., ΒΑΣΙΛΕΩΣ; in ex., ΛΥΣΙΜΑ-XOY; in field to l., forepart of lion and monogram; to r., M. *Müller (Die Münzen des thrakischen Königs Lysimachos)* 1 .. .. £1,750

6811 — *R tetradrachm* (*c.* 17 gm.). Hd. of young Herakles r., clad in lion's skin. R. Zeus enthroned l., holding eagle and sceptre; on r., ΒΑΣΙΛΕΩΣ; in ex., ΛΥΣΙΜΑΧΟΥ; in field to l., forepart of lion and monogram within wreath; another monogram beneath throne. *Müller* 2 .. .. £500

6812   6813

6812 — *R drachm* (*c.* 4·25 gm.). Similar, but on *rev.* ΒΑΣΙΛΕΩΣ is in ex., ΛΥΣΙΜΑΧΟΥ on r.; in field to l., forepart of lion and crescent; beneath throne, pentagram. *Forrer/Weber* 2721. *Müller* 20 .. .. £75

6813 LYSIMACHAN TYPES, 297-281 B.C. *N stater* (*c.* 8·5 gm.). Diad. hd. of Alexander the Great r., wearing horn of Ammon. R. Athena enthroned l., holding Nike and resting l. arm on shield; transverse spear resting against her r. side; on r., ΒΑΣΙΛΕΩΣ; on l., ΛΥΣΙΜΑ-XOY, crowned by the Nike; in field to l., star. *Principal Coins* IV. B.12. *Müller* 337 £1,250

6814 — Æ *tetradrachm* (*c.* 17 gm.). Similar, but on *rev.*, in field to l., monogram within wreath and Σ. *Principal Coins* IV. B.13. *Müller* 302 .. .. £275

6815 — — Similar, but with caduceus in *rev.* field to l., and monogram to r. *Boston Museum Catalogue* 826. *Müller* 106 .. .. £300

6816 — — Similar, but with κ beneath hd. on *obv.*; and on *rev.*, archaic xoanon and N in field to l., crescent in ex. *Jenkins (Ancient Greek Coins)* 534/5. *Müller* 290, *var.* .. £350

The tetradrachms of Lysimachos were struck in great quantity, attesting the wealth of his Kingdom, and many varieties have been recorded.

6817   6818

6817 — Æ *drachm* (*c.* 4·25 gm.). Similar to 6813, but with spear-head instead of star in rev. field to l., and A on Athena's throne. *Forrer/Weber* 2728. *Müller* 59 .. £100

6818 — Æ 22. Helmeted hd. of Athena (?) r. ℞. ΛΥΣΙΜΑΧΟΥ / ΒΑΣΙΛΕΩΣ either side of trophy. *Müller, pl.* II, 13 .. .. £18

6819   6822   6823

6819 — Æ 17. Young male hd. r., in crested Athenian helmet. ℞. ΒΑΣΙΛΕΩΣ / ΛΥΣΙΜΑΧΟΥ above and beneath lion leaping r.; in field above, ΔΙ; to l., race-torch; below, ΜΕ monogram and spear-head. *Forrer/Weber* 2734. *Müller, pl.* II, 10 .. .. £14

6820 — Æ 14. *Obv.* Similar. ℞. ΒΑΣΙΛΕΩΣ / ΛΥΣΙΜΑΧΟΥ above and beneath forepart of lion r.; in field to l., caduceus and Λ / Ο; beneath lion, spear-head. *Forrer/Weber* 2731. *Müller* 113 .. .. £12

6821 — Æ 12. *Obv.* Similar. ℞. ΒΑΣΙΛΕΩΣ ΛΥΣΙΜΑΧΟΥ around lion's hd. facing. *Müller, pl.* II, 12 .. .. £13

6822 — Æ 14. Hd. of young Herakles r., clad in lion's skin. ℞. ΒΑΣΙ / ΛΥΣΙ within corn-wreath. *Forrer/Weber* 2735. *Müller, pl.* II, 14 .. .. £13

6823 OTHER TYPES (the following do not bear the title ΒΑΣΙΛΕΩΣ and belong, therefore, to the period before Lysimachos' assumption of royal status in 305 B.C.). Æ *hemidrachm* (*c.* 2·04 gm.). Hd. of Apollo (?) r., hair bound with tainia. ℞. Naked youth on horse prancing r.; above, ΛΥ; beneath, forepart of lion r.; in ex., ear of corn. *Boston Museum Catalogue* 821. *Müller, pl.* I, 1, *var.* £150

This type is based on the coinage of Philip II of Macedon.

6824 — Æ 16. Laur. hd. of Apollo r. ℞. As last, but without the corn-ear in ex. *Müller, pl.* I, 2 .. .. £16

6825 — — *Obv.* As 6819. ℞. Lion leaping r.; above, ΛΥ; beneath, spear-head. *Müller, pl.* I, 3 .. .. £15

THE SELEUKID KINGDOM

(The territorial extent of this mighty realm varied greatly from period to period. At its zenith, under Seleukos I and Antiochos I, it comprised almost the whole of Alexander's conquests, except Egypt. In the mid-3rd century the easternmost provinces were lost when both Baktria and Parthia achieved independence. Antiochos III, the Great, attempted to regain the lost territories, but he was only partially successful and in 190 B.C. he was defeated by the Romans at the battle of Magnesia. This destroyed the Seleukid power in Asia Minor, their former possessions passing to Rome's ally, the Kingdom of Pergamon. The Seleukid Kingdom, now restricted to Syria and the surrounding area, maintained a precarious existence until 64 B.C. when it finally succumbed to Pompey the Great).

6826 **Seleukos I, Nikator,** 312-280 B.C. (destined to be the longest-surviving of the 'Successors' of Alexander, Seleukos had a difficult time establishing his power. Allotted the satrapy of Babylon in 321 B.C. he was ousted from this position five years later, by Antigonos the One-eyed, and fled to his friend Ptolemy in Egypt. In 312 B.C. he regained Babylon and it is from this event that the Seleukid Era is dated. Seleukos gradually consolidated his power and in 305 B.C. took the title of King. From 305-3 he campaigned in the east, extending his rule as far as India. With his defeat of Lysimachos in 281 he became master of the whole of Alexander's empire, except Egypt; but the following year he was assassinated by Ptolemy Keraunos, a renegade son of his late friend, the King of Egypt). N *double-daric* (*c.* 16·6 gm.). Hd. of Alexander the Great r., clad in elephant's skin. ℞. Nike stg. l., holding wreath and ship's mast; in field to l., ΔΙ and horse's hd. r., with horns. *Principal Coins* IV. A.7 .. .. £7,500

6826A — N *distater* (*c.* 17·2 gm.). Hd. of Athena r., in crested Corinthian helmet ornamented with serpent. ℞. Nike stg., as last; on l., ΒΑΣΙΛΕΩΣ; on r., ΣΕΛΕΥΚΟΥ; monogram in lower field to l. *Newell (Western Seleucid Mints)* 1334.. .. .. (*Unique*)

6827   6829

6827 — N *stater* (*c.* 8·5 gm.). Hd. of Athena r., in crested Corinthian helmet ornamented with serpent. ℞. Nike stg., as last; on r., ΒΑΣΙΛΕΩΣ; on l., ΣΕΛΕΥΚΟΥ; monograms in lower field, to l. and to r. *B.M.C.* 4. 1, 1 .. .. £1,750

6828 — — Laur. hd. of Apollo r. ℞. Artemis, with bow and arrow, stg. in chariot drawn r. by two horned elephants; in ex., ΒΑΣΙΛΕΩΣ / ΣΕΛΕΥΚΟΥ; monogram within circle in field above, another to r. *Principal Coins, pl.* 51, 9. *Newell (Eastern Seleucid Mints)* 331 £5,000

6829 — Æ *tetradrachm* (*c.* 17 gm.). Hd. of young Herakles r., clad in lion's skin. ℞. Zeus enthroned l., holding eagle and sceptre; on r., ΣΕΛΕΥΚΟΥ; in ex., ΒΑΣΙΛΕΩΣ; in field to l., monogram within wreath; beneath throne, ΔΙ monogram. *B.M.C.* 4. 2, 6 .. £175

6830 — — Similar, but on *rev.* Zeus holds wreath-bearing Nike instead of eagle; in field to l., ΕΠ monogram on shield; beneath throne, ΑΣ. *B.M.C.* 4. 2, 21 .. .. £250

6831   6833

6831 — — Laur. hd. of Zeus r. ℞. Athena, brandishing spear and holding shield, stg. in chariot drawn r. by four horned elephants; on l., ΒΑΣΙΛΕΩΣ; in ex., ΣΕΛΕΥΚΟΥ; in field above, two monograms and anchor. *B.M.C. 4.* 3, 25 .. .. £450

6832 — — Similar, but on *rev.* the chariot is drawn by only two horned elephants; in field above, spear-head; to r., Μ / Ω. *B.M.C. 4.* 3, 33.. .. .. £600

6833 — — Hd. of Alexander (?) r., wearing helmet covered with panther skin and ornamented with bull's horn and ear; lion's skin (?) knotted at neck. ℞. Nike stg. r., crowning trophy; on r., ΒΑΣΙΛΕΩΣ; on l., ΣΕΛΕΥΚΟΥ; in lower field to l., Μ; between Nike and trophy, ΑΧ. *Newell (E.S.M.)* 420 .. .. £2,500
The portrait head on obverse is sometimes described as that of Seleukos himself.

6834 — — Horned and bridled horse's hd. r. ℞. ΒΑΣΙΛΕΩΣ / ΣΕΛΕΥΚΟΥ above and beneath elephant walking r.; in field above, star; below, anchor. *Babelon (Rois de Syrie) pl. II,* 9. *Newell (Western Seleucid Mints)* 1529 .. .. £7,500
This remarkable type, issued at Pergamon, commemorates the victory of Seleukos over Lysimachos in 281 B.C.

6835 — Æ *drachm* (c. 4·25 gm.). Similar to 6829, but in *rev.* field to l. dolphin l. and monogram within circle; another monogram within circle beneath throne. *B.M.C. 4.* 2, 14 £90

6836 6838

6836 — — Similar to 6831, but on *rev.* ΒΑΣΙΛΕΩΣ / ΣΕΛΕΥΚΟΥ is in two lines in ex.; in field above, monogram and anchor; to r., monogram within circle. *B.M.C. 4.* 3, 32 £225

6837 — — Similar to 6833, but with Η — ΑΧ instead of Μ — ΑΧ in *rev.* field. *B.M.C. 4.* 4, 39 £500

6838 — — Horned and bridled horse's hd. r. ℞. ΒΑΣΙΛΕΩΣ / ΣΕΛΕΥΚΟΥ either side of anchor; in field to l., bunch of grapes. *B.M.C. 4.* 4, 41 .. .. £750

6839 — Æ *hemidrachm* (c. 2·1 gm.). Hd. of young Herakles r., clad in lion's skin. ℞. Zeus enthroned l., holding eagle and sceptre; on r., ΣΕΛΕΥΚΟΥ; in field to l., anchor and Θ; beneath throne, ΩΡ monogram. *Newell (E.S.M.)* 133 .. .. £125

6840 — — Laur. hd. of Zeus r. ℞. Fighting Athena in biga of elephants r., as 6832; on l., ΒΑΣΙΛΕΩΣ; in ex., ΣΕΛΕΥΚΟΥ; in field to l., Θ; above elephants, anchor; to r., ΑΒ monogram. *Newell (E.S.M.)* 98.. .. .. £175

6841 — — As 6837. *B.M.C. 4.* 4, 40 .. .. £300

6842 — Æ *obol* (c. 0·65 gm.). Similar to 6839, but on *rev.* ΑΒΤ monogram in field to l., and Θ beneath throne. *Newell (E.S.M.)* 99 .. .. £90

6843 — — Hd. of Athena r., in crested Corinthian helmet. ℞. Horned elephant's hd. r.; on l., ΒΑΣΙΛΕΩΣ; beneath, ΣΕΛΕΥΚΟΥ; in field above, anchor; below, Μ and bee. *Newell (E.S.M.)* 325 .. .. £150

6844 — — Similar to 6833, but with ΕΡ monogram — ΛΙ instead of Μ — ΑΧ in *rev.* field. *Newell (E.S.M.)* 416 .. .. £125

6845 — — Tripod-lebes with cover. ℞. ΒΑΣΙΛΕΩΣ / ΣΕΛΕΥΚΟΥ either side of anchor; Λ in field to l., monogram to r. *B.M.C. 4.* 4, 42 .. .. £100

Seleukos I *continued*

6846 — — — R. ΒΑΣΙΛΕΩΣ / ΣΕΛΕΥΚΟΥ either side of bow and quiver; ɪ in field to l., ɵ to r. *Newell (E.S.M.)* 61.. .. .. £110

6847 — Æ 26. Horned hd. of horse r. R. ΒΑΣΙΛΕΩΣ / ΣΕΛΕΥΚΟΥ either side of anchor; ΚΡ monogram in field to l. *Newell (E.S.M.)* 45 .. .. £25

6848 — Æ 22. Facing busts of the Dioskouroi, side by side. R. ΒΑΣΙΛΕΩΣ / ΣΕΛΕΥΚΟΥ either side of Nike advancing l., holding wreath and palm; two monograms in field to l. *Newell (W.S.M.)* 803 .. .. £28

6849   6850

6849 — Æ 20. Laur. hd. of Apollo r. R. ΒΑΣΙΛΕΩΣ / ΣΕΛΕΥΚΟΥ either side of Athena Alkidemos stg. r., brandishing thunderbolt and holding shield; ɵ in field to r. *B.M.C. 4.* 6, 59 .. .. £15

6850 — — Elephant stg. r. R. ΒΑΣΙΛΕΩΣ / ΣΕΛΕΥΚΟΥ either side of horned hd. of horse l., anchor beneath. *B.M.C. 4.* 5, 49-50 .. .. £18

6851 — Æ 19. Laur. hd. of Apollo r. R. ΒΑΣΙΛΕΩΣ / ΣΕΛΕΥΚΟΥ above and beneath humped bull butting r.; in field above, ɵ and pentagram. *B.M.C. 4.* 7, 71 .. .. £13

6852 — — Winged hd. of Medusa r., serpents in hair. R. As last, but nothing in field above, and with Ξ beneath king's name in ex. *B.M.C. 4.* 6, 62.. .. .. .. £14

6853 — — Hd. of Athena r., in crested Corinthian helmet. R. ΒΑΣΙΛΕΩΣ / ΣΕΛΕΥΚΟΥ either side of Nike stg. l., holding palm and crowning the king's name; anchor in field to l. *B.M.C. 4.* 5, 44-5 .. .. £12

6854 — Æ 17. As 6847. *B.M.C. 4.* 5, 47 .. .. £15

6855 — Æ 15. Hd. of young Herakles r., clad in lion's skin. R. ΒΑΣΙΛΕΩΣ ΣΕΛΕΥΚΟΥ. Horned hd. of elephant r., monograms beneath. *Newell (E.S.M.)* 336 .. £15

The bronze coinage of Seleukos I is extensive and the above listing is no more than a selection from the known types.

6856

6857

6856 **Antiochos I, Soter,** 280-261 B.C. (Seleukos was succeeded by his son, Antiochos, who had already been ruler of the eastern satrapies from 293 B.C. Little is known of his reign other than his victory over the Gallic invaders of Asia Minor, *c.* 273 B.C., which earned him the title of *Soter*—'Saviour'). JOINT REIGN IN THE EAST WITH SELEUKOS I, 293-280 B.C. Æ *tetradrachm* (Aryandic standard, *c.* 13·9 gm.). Laur. hd. of Zeus r. Ɍ. Armed Athena in quadriga of horned elephants r.; ΒΑΣΙΛΕΩΣ above, ΣΕΛΕΥΚΟΥ / ΑΝΤΙΟΧΟΥ in ex.; monogram within circle in field above. *Newell (E.S.M.)* 665 £1,250

6857 — Æ *drachm* (*c.* 3·45 gm.). *Obv.* Similar; behind, AP monogram. Ɍ. Armed Athena in biga of horned elephants r.; ΒΑΣΙΛΕΩΝ above; ΣΕΛΕΥΚΟΥ / ΚΑΙ ΑΝΤΙΟΧΟΥ in ex.; monogram within circle in field above. *Newell (E.S.M.)* 664 .. .. .. £400

6858 — Æ *hemidrachm* (*c.* 1·7 gm.). Similar to 6856, but Athena is in *biga* of elephants on *rev. Newell (E.S.M.)* 667.. .. .. £250

6859 — Æ *obol* (*c.* 0·55 gm.). As last, but without inscription on *rev. Newell (E.S.M.)* 671 £90

6860 SOLE REIGN, 280-261 B.C. Ꞥ *stater* (*c.* 8·5 gm.). Hd. of Athena r., in crested Corinthian helmet ornamented with serpent. Ɍ. Nike stg. l., holding wreath and ship's mast; on r., ΑΝΤΙΟΧΟΥ; on l., ΒΑΣΙΛΕΩΣ; monograms in lower field, to l. and to r. *Newell (E.S.M.)* 353 .. .. £2,000

6861

6862

6861 — — Diad. hd. of Seleukos I r., with bull's horn. Ɍ. Horned and bridled horse's hd. r.; ΒΑΣΙΛΕΩΣ behind, ΣΕΛΕΥΚΟΥ beneath; monograms in field, to r. and below. *Newell (W.S.M.)* 784. *B.M.C.* 4. 3, 24 .. .. £6,000
Issued by Antiochos in honour of his father, whose divinity is indicated by the bull's horn above the ear. See also no. 6869.

6862 — — Diad. hd. of Antiochos r. Ɍ. Horned and bridled horse's hd. r.; ΒΑΣΙΛΕΩΣ behind, ΑΝΤΙΟΧΟΥ beneath; monogram within circle in upper field to r. *Newell (E.S.M.)* 676 .. .. £4,500

6863 — — *Obv.* Similar, but with more elderly features. Ɍ. Apollo seated l. on omphalos, holding arrow and resting on bow; on r., ΒΑΣΙΛΕΩΣ; on l., ΑΝΤΙΟΧΟΥ; Δ in field to l. *Newell (E.S.M.)* 704 .. .. £2,500

6864 — Æ *tetradrachm* (*c.* 17 gm.). Hd. of young Herakles r., clad in lion's skin. Ɍ. Zeus enthroned l., holding wreath-bearing Nike and sceptre; on r., ΑΝΤΙΟΧΟΥ; in ex., ΒΑΣΙΛΕΩΣ; in field to l., H; beneath throne, monogram. *B.M.C.* 4. 8, 1 .. .. .. £600

Antiochos I *continued*

6865 — — Diad. hd. of Antiochos r., with comparatively youthful features. ℞. Apollo
seated l. on omphalos, holding two arrows and resting on bow; on r., ΒΑΣΙΛΕΩΣ; on l.,
ΑΝΤΙΟΧΟΥ; monograms in field, to l. and to r.   *B.M.C. 4.* 8, 3 ..   ..   ..   £350
Antiochos was already forty-four years old at the time of his accession.

6866 — — *Obv.* Similar, but Antiochos' features are middle-aged.   ℞. Similar to last, but
Apollo holds only one arrow.   *B.M.C. 4.* 9, 10 ..   ..   £275

                    6867   6869

6867 — — *Obv.* Similar, but Antiochos' features are elderly.   ℞. Apollo seated l. on omphalos,
holding three arrows and resting on bow; at his feet, horse grazing l.; on r., ΒΑΣΙΛΕΩΣ; on l.,
ΑΝΤΙΟΧΟΥ; two monograms in field to l.   *B.M.C. 4.* 9, 20   ..   ..   ..   £400

6868 — — *Obv.* As last.   ℞. Apollo seated l. on omphalos, holding arrow and resting on bow;
on r., ΣΩΤΗΡΟΣ; on l., ΑΝΤΙΟΧΟΥ.   *B.M.C. 4.* 10, 22   ..   ..   ..   £450

6869 — — Diad. hd. of Seleukos I r., with bull's horn.   ℞. Apollo seated l. on omphalos,
holding bow and resting l. hand on the omphalos; on r., ΒΑΣΙΛΕΩΣ; on l., ΑΝΤΙΟΧΟΥ;
monograms in field, to l. and below.   *Newell (W.S.M.)* 1367 ..   ..   ..   £2,000

            6870   6873

6870 — — *Obv.* As 6866. ℞. Horned and bridled horse's hd. r.; ΒΑΣΙΛΕΩΣ behind, ΑΝΤΙΟΧΟΥ beneath; in field to r., Δ within Ο.   *Newell (E.S.M.)* 677   ..   ..   ..   £1,500

6871 — Æ *drachm* (c. 4·15 gm.).   Laur. hd. of Zeus r. ℞. Fighting Athena in quadriga of horned elephants r.; on l., ΑΝΤΙΟΧΟΥ; in ex., ΒΑΣΙΛΕΩΣ; in field above, anchor, monogram and Δ.   *Newell (E.S.M.)* 134   ..   ..   £275

6872 — — *Obv.* As 6866. ℞. Apollo seated l. on omphalos, holding arrow and resting on bow; on r., ΒΑΣΙΛΕΩΣ; on l., ΑΝΤΙΟΧΟΥ; in field to l., Δ within Ο; in ex., ΑΝΔΡ monogram. *Newell (E.S.M.)* 701   ..   ..   £175

6873 — — Similar to 6870, but without monogram in *rev.* field.   *Newell (E.S.M.)* 678
£450

6874 — Æ *hemidrachm* (c. 2 gm.).   As 6870.   *Newell (E.S.M.)* 681   ..   ..   £250

6875 — Æ *obol* (c. 0·65 gm.).   As 6873.   *Mitchiner (Indo-Greek and Indo-Scythian Coinage)*, *type* 57   ..   ..   £90

6876 — Æ 23.   Laur. hd. of Apollo r. ℞. ΒΑΣΙΛΕΩΣ / ΑΝΤΙΟΧΟΥ either side of Athena Alkidemos stg. r., brandishing thunderbolt and holding shield; monograms in field to l. and to r.   *B.M.C. 4.* 12, 50   ..   ..   £17

6877 — Æ 22.   Bust of Athena, in crested helmet, three-quarter face to l. ℞. ΒΑΣΙΛΕΩΣ / ΑΝΤΙΟΧΟΥ either side of Apollo seated r. on omphalos, playing lyre; tripod behind; monogram in field to r.   *B.M.C. 4.* 13, 56   ..   ..   £24

6878   6879

6878 — Æ 18.   *Obv.* As 6867. ℞. ΒΑΣΙΛΕΩΣ / ΑΝΤΙΟΧΟΥ either side of Apollo seated l. on omphalos, holding arrow and resting on bow; monograms in field to l. and to r.   *B.M.C. 4.* 10, 27   ..   ..   £14

6879 — — Laur. hd. of Apollo r. ℞. ΒΑΣΙΛΕΩΣ / ΑΝΤΙΟΧΟΥ either side of tripod; in field to l., bow; to r., club and monogram.   *B.M.C. 4.* 12, 47   ..   ..   £12

6880 — — Laur. hd. of Zeus r. ℞. ΒΑΣΙΛΕΩΣ / ΑΝΤΙΟΧΟΥ above and beneath thunderbolt; in field above, club and monogram; below, jaw-bone of boar.   *B.M.C. 4.* 11, 41   £12

6881   6883

6881 — — Macedonian shield, with anchor at centre. ℞. ΒΑΣΙΛΕΩΣ / ΑΝΤΙΟΧΟΥ above and beneath elephant walking r.; monogram and symbols above and below, as last.   *B.M.C. 4.* 11, 37   ..   ..   £14

6882 — Æ 17.   Laur. bust of Apollo three-quarter face to r. ℞. ΒΑΣΙΛΕΩΣ / ΑΝΤΙΟΧΟΥ either side of Nike stg. r., erecting trophy; monograms in field to l. and to r.   *B.M.C. 4.* 12, 53
£15

6883 — Æ 14.   Bust of Athena facing, in triple-crested helmet. ℞. ΒΑΣΙΛΕΩΣ / ΑΝΤΙΟΧΟΥ either side of Nike stg. l., holding wreath and palm; monogram within circle in field to l   *B.M.C. 4.* 13, 58   ..   ..   £14

6884 Antiochos II, Theos, 261-246 B.C. (son of Antiochos I, the new king was of weak character, addicted to alcohol and under the influence of favourites. His kingdom was at war
with Ptolemaic Egypt for much of his reign, and Parthia and Baktria both asserted their
independence at this time). *N stater* (*c.* 8·5 gm.). His diad. hd. r. ℞. Athena stg. l.,
holding Nike and palm, large shield leaning against her r. leg; on r., ΒΑΣΙΛΕΩΣ; on l.,
ΑΝΤΙΟΧΟΥ; in field to r., Φ, and monogram above Σ. *Newell* (*W.S.M.*) 1497 (*Unique*)

6885   6886

6885 — — *Obv.* Similar. ℞. Apollo seated l. on omphalos, holding arrow and resting on
bow; on r., ΒΑΣΙΛΕΩΣ; on l., ΑΝΤΙΟΧΟΥ; in field to l., Δ. *Newell* (*E.S.M.*) 706 .. £2,500

6886 — *Æ tetradrachm* (*c.* 17 gm.). *Obv.* Similar. ℞. As last, but with monograms in field
to l. and to r. *Newell* (*W.S.M.*) 980. *B.M.C. 4.* 20, 9 .. .. £400

6887 — — Diad. hd. of Antiochos I r., with wing above ear. ℞. Similar to 6885, but with
monogram and female hd. in field to l., and horse grazing l. in ex. *Newell* (*W.S.M.*)
1561 .. .. £650

6888   6890

6888 — — *Obv.* Similar, but without wing. ℞. Naked Herakles seated l. on rock, his r. hand
resting on club, his l. on the rock; on r., ΒΑΣΙΛΕΩΣ; on l., ΑΝΤΙΟΧΟΥ; kantharos in field to l.,
monogram in ex. *Newell* (*W.S.M.*) 1510. *B.M.C. 4.* 15, 10 .. .. .. £1,250
*This reverse served as the prototype for the coinage of Euthydemos I of Baktria, 230-
190 B.C.*

6889 — *Æ drachm* (*c.* 4·15 gm.). Similar to 6885, but in *rev.* field to l., ΡΟ; to r., ΑΠ monogram. *Newell* (*W.S.M.*) 973. *B.M.C. 4.* 21, 16 .. .. £225

6890 — Æ 20. The Dioskouroi on horseback prancing r., holding spears. ℞. ΒΑΣΙΛΕΩΣ /
ΑΝΤΙΟΧΟΥ either side of Athena stg. r. on anchor, brandishing spear and holding shield;
monogram in field to l. *Newell* (*W.S.M.*) 1312 .. .. £22

6891 — Æ 19. Laur. hd. of Apollo r. ℞. ΒΑΣΙΛΕΩΣ / ΑΝΤΙΟΧΟΥ either side of tripod-lebes;
in field to r., Δ within Ο; to l., ΔΗ; in ex., anchor. *Newell* (*W.S.M.*) 982. *B.M.C. 4.*
15, 11 .. .. £12

6892   6895

6892 — Æ 17. Diad. hd. of Antiochos II r. ℞. ΒΑΣΙΛΕΩΣ / ΑΝΤΙΟΧΟΥ either side of Apollo stg. l., r. foot on omphalos, holding arrow and bow; monogram in field to l. *Newell* (*E.S.M.*) 538 .. .. £16

6893 — Æ 12. Conjoined busts of the Dioskouroi; the one on r. three-quarter face to l., the other to l. ℞. ΒΑΣΙ / ΑΝΤΙ above and beneath elephant's hd. r.; Φ in field to r. *Newell* (*W.S.M.*) 806 .. .. £15

6894 — Æ 11. Laur. and dr. bust of Apollo r., quiver at shoulder. ℞. ΒΑΣΙΛΕΩΣ / ΑΝΤΙΟΧΟΥ above and beneath bull butting r.; in field to l., ΑΧ monogram; beneath bull, anchor. *Newell* (*W.S.M.*) 1482 .. .. £11

N.B. *For other coins in the name of Antiochos II see below under Diodotos of Baktria.*

6895 **Seleukos II, Kallinikos,** 246-226 B.C. (the elder son of Antiochos II and Laodike, Seleukos spent much of his reign in conflict with his younger brother, Antiochos Hierax, who ruled independently in Asia Minor. Seleukos was killed by a fall from his horse after a troubled reign of twenty years). *N stater* (*c.* 8·5 gm.). His diad. hd. r. ℞. Naked Apollo stg. l., holding arrow and resting on bow; on r., ΒΑΣΙΛΕΩΣ; on l., ΣΕΛΕΥΚΟΥ; monogram in field to l., Β to r. *Newell* (*W.S.M.*) 997 .. .. £4,000

6896 — Æ *tetradrachm* (*c.* 17 gm.). His diad. hd. r. ℞. Naked Apollo stg. l., holding arrow and resting l. arm on tripod; on r., ΒΑΣΙΛΕΩΣ; on l., ΣΕΛΕΥΚΟΥ; monograms in field to l. and to r. *Newell* (*W.S.M.*) 991. *B.M.C. 4.* 16, 1 .. .. £400

6897 — — His diad. hd. r., bearded. ℞. Similar to last, but both monograms are in field to l. *Newell* (*W.S.M.*) 819 .. .. £750

6898 — — His diad. and dr. bust r., bearded. ℞. Similar to 6896. *Newell* (*W.S.M.*) 1322. *B.M.C. 4.* 19, 35 .. .. £2,000

6899 — Æ *drachm* (*c.* 4·2 gm.). Similar to 6896, but monogram only in field to l. on *rev.* *Newell* (*W.S.M.*) 1423. *B.M.C. 4.* 16, 10 .. .. £200

6900 — — Hd. of Athena r., in crested helmet. ℞. Similar to 6895, but with monograms in field to l. and to r. *Newell* (*W.S.M.*) 1014 .. .. £300

6901 — Æ *obol* (*c.* 0·7 gm.). *Obv.* As 6897. ℞. Similar to 6896, but without monograms in field. *Newell* (*W.S.M.*) 824 .. .. £125

6902 — Æ 33. Dr. bust of Dionysos three-quarter face to r., wreathed with ivy. ℞. ΒΑΣΙΛΕΩΣ / ΣΕΛΕΥΚΟΥ above and beneath elephant advancing l.; monograms in field to r. and in ex. *Newell* (*E.S.M.*) 557 .. .. £65

Seleukos II *continued*

6903 — Æ 28. *Obv.* As 6895. ℞. ΒΑΣΙΛΕΩΣ / ΣΕΛΕΥΚΟΥ above and beneath king on horse-back prancing l., holding couched spear; monogram in field below horse. *Newell (W.S.M.)* 1162 .. .. £45

6904 — Æ 25. Diad. and dr. bust of Seleukos r. ℞. ΒΑΣΙΛΕΩΣ / ΣΕΛΕΥΚΟΥ either side of Nike stg. l., holding wreath and palm; monograms in field to l. and to r. *Newell (E.S.M.)* 370 .. .. £20

6905   6907

6905 — Æ 24. Laur. and dr. bust of Apollo three-quarter face to l. ℞. ΒΑΣΙΛΕΩΣ / ΣΕΛΕΥΚΟΥ above and beneath humped bull stg. r.; monograms in field to l. and to r. *Newell (E.S.M.)* 205 .. .. £35

6906 — Æ 22. Diad. hd. of Seleukos r., bearded. ℞. ΒΑΣΙΛΕΩΣ / ΣΕΛΕΥΚΟΥ either side of bow in case and quiver; monograms in field to l. and to r. *Newell (E.S.M.)* 563. *B.M.C. 4*. 19, 36-7 .. .. £22

6907 — Æ 21. Laur. and dr. bust of Apollo r., bow and quiver at shoulder. ℞. ΒΑΣΙΛΕΩΣ / ΣΕΛΕΥΚΟΥ above and beneath humped bull butting l.; monogram in upper field to l. *Newell (W.S.M.)* 1156. *B.M.C. 4*. 18, 32 .. .. £13

6908 — — Laur. hd. of Apollo r. ℞. ΒΑΣΙΛΕΩΣ / ΣΕΛΕΥΚΟΥ either side of tripod; ΕΥ in field to l., monogram to r. *Newell (W.S.M.)* 1017. *B.M.C. 4*. 23, 11-12 .. .. £12

6909 — Æ 19. Conjoined busts of the Dioskouroi, as 6893. ℞. ΒΑΣΙΛΕΩΣ / ΣΕΛΕΥΚΟΥ above and beneath elephant's hd. r.; Φ in field to r. *Newell (W.S.M.)* 807. *B.M.C. 4*. 6, 53-4 .. .. £15

6910 — — Hd. of Athena r., in crested Corinthian helmet. ℞. ΒΑΣΙΛΕΩΣ / ΣΕΛΕΥΚΟΥ either side of Nike stg. l., holding palm and crowning large anchor before her; ΕΥ in field to l., monogram to r. *Newell (W.S.M.)* 1015 .. .. £14

6911 — — *Obv.* Similar to 6905, but also with lyre above Apollo's l. shoulder. ℞. King stg. facing, holding spear, crowned by Nike stg. l., on r.; on l., ΒΑΣΙΛΕΩΣ; between the figures, ΣΕΛΕΥΚΟΥ; monograms above and in field to r. *Newell* (*E.S.M.*) 208 .. .. £18

6912 — Æ 17. Laur. hd. of Apollo r. ℞. ΒΑΣΙΛΕΩΣ / ΣΕΛΕΥΚΟΥ above and beneath bull's hd. facing, with fillets; monograms in field to l. and to r. *Newell* (*E.S.M.*) 207. *B.M.C. 4.* 18, 31 .. .. £16

6913 — — Similar to 6895, but with monograms in *rev.* field to l. and to r. *Newell* (*E.S.M.*) 212. *B.M.C. 4.* 16, 13 .. .. £13

6914 — — Hd. of young Herakles r., clad in lion's skin. ℞. ΒΑΣΙΛΕΩΣ / ΣΕΛΕΥΚΟΥ either side of Apollo seated l. on omphalos, holding arrow and resting on bow; monogram in field to l., ε to r. *Newell* (*W.S.M.*) 1427. *B.M.C. 4.* 5, 46 .. .. £14

6915   6916

6915 — Æ 15. Conjoined heads of the Dioskouroi r. ℞. ΒΑΣΙΛΕΩΣ / ΣΕΛΕΥΚΟΥ either side of anchor flanked by Φ, on l., and horse's hd. r. *Newell* (*W.S.M.*) 816. *B.M.C. 4.* 5, 51 .. .. £14

6916 — — Diad. hd. of Seleukos r. ℞. ΒΑΣΙΛΕΩΣ / ΣΕΛΕΥΚΟΥ above and beneath horse trotting l.; two stars above, monogram below. *Newell* (*W.S.M.*) 1163. *B.M.C. 4.* 17, 16 .. .. £14

6917 — Æ 10. Hd. of Athena r., in crested helmet. ℞. ΒΑΣΙΛΕΩΣ / ΣΕΛΕΥΚΟΥ either side of anchor; monogram in field to l., two others to r. *Newell* (*W.S.M.*) 1663 .. £10

6918 **Antiochos Hierax**, 246-227 B.C. (the younger son of Antiochos II and Laodike, Hierax, with his mother's support, maintained an independent regime in Asia Minor for most of the reign of his brother, Seleukos II. In 228 B.C. he attacked Seleukos' territory but was defeated, and the following year he was murdered by a band of marauding Gauls). Æ *tetradrachm* (*c.* 17 gm.). His diad. and dr. bust r., with slight beard. ℞. Naked Apollo seated l. on omphalos, holding arrow and resting on bow; on r., ΒΑΣΙΛΕΩΣ; on l., ΑΝΤΙΟΧΟΥ; monograms in field to r. and in ex. *Newell* (*W.S.M.*) 1319 .. £750

6919 — — Youthful diad. hd. of Antiochos I r., with wing above ear. ℞. Similar to last, but with two monograms in field to l., and in ex. horse grazing r. *Newell* (*W.S.M.*) 1572. *B.M.C. 4.* 14, 6 .. .. £650

Antiochos Hierax *continued*

6920 — — His diad. hd. r. ℞. Similar to 6918, but both monograms are in ex. *Newell* (*W.S.M.*) 1460 .. .. £450

6921 — Æ *drachm* (*c.* 4·2 gm.). *Obv.* Similar. ℞. Similar to 6918, but without monograms. *Newell* (*W.S.M.*) 1675 .. .. £250

6922   6926

6922 **Seleukos III, Keraunos,** 226-223 B.C. (the elder son of Seleukos II, most of his brief reign was spent in attempting to check the growing power of Attalos I of Pergamon. His invasion of Pergamene territory was a dismal failure and soon after he was murdered by his own officers). Æ *tetradrachm* (*c.* 17 gm.). His diad. hd. r. ℞. Naked Apollo seated l. on omphalos, holding arrow and resting on bow; on r., ΒΑΣΙΛΕΩΣ; on l., ΣΕΛΕΥΚΟΥ; monograms in field to l. and to r. *Newell* (*W.S.M.*) 1029. *B.M.C. 4.* 22, 1 .. £350

6923 — — *Obv.* Similar. ℞. Apollo seated l. on omphalos, holding arrow and resting l. arm on tripod; on r., ΒΑΣΙΛΕΩΣ; on l., ΣΕΛΕΥΚΟΥ; monograms in field to l. and to r.; in ex., elephant l. *Newell* (*W.S.M.*) 1028. *B.M.C. 4.* 22, 5 .. .. £750

6924 — Æ *drachm* (*c.* 4 gm.). Similar to 6922, but on *rev.* monogram in field to l. only. *Forrer/Weber* 7867. *Newell* (*W.S.M.*) 1327 .. .. £250

6925 — Æ 21. His diad. hd. r. ℞. ΒΑΣΙΛΕΩΣ / ΣΕΛΕΥΚΟΥ either side of Apollo stg. facing, holding plectrum and lyre; monograms in field to l. and to r. *Newell* (*E.S.M.*) 218 £14

6926 — Æ 19. Laur. hd. of Apollo r. ℞. ΒΑΣΙΛΕΩΣ / ΣΕΛΕΥΚΟΥ above and beneath the Dioskouroi on horseback pacing r.; monograms in field to l. and to r. *Newell* (*W.S.M.*) 829. *B.M.C. 4.* 18, 28 .. .. £14

6927 — Æ 16. Laur. hd. of Apollo r., hair in formal curls. ℞. ΒΑΣΙΛΕΩΣ / ΣΕΛΕΥΚΟΥ either side of tripod before which, at base, horse's hd. r.; Π in field to r. *Newell* (*E.S.M.*) 572. *B.M.C. 4.* 32, 16 .. .. £10

6928 — Æ 15. Hd. of Athena r., in crested Corinthian helmet. ℞. ΒΑΣΙΛΕΩΣ / ΣΕΛΕΥΚΟΥ either side of Apollo stg. facing, holding plectrum and lyre. *Newell* (*E.S.M.*) 378 £11

6929 — — Hd. of Artemis r., quiver behind neck. ℞. ΒΑΣΙΛΕΩΣ / ΣΕΛΕΥΚΟΥ either side of Apollo seated l. on omphalos, holding arrow and resting on bow; ΣΕ / Λ in field to l., ΑΡ monogram in ex. *Newell* (*W.S.M.*) 1036. *B.M.C. 4.* 22, 8 .. .. .. £10

6930   6931

6930 **Antiochos III, the Great,** 223-187 B.C. (the younger brother of Seleukos III, Antiochos III was one of the most celebrated of the Seleukid monarchs. Only in his late teens at the time of his accession it took several years for him to establish his authority. But he soon showed himself to be a soldier of great ability, and between 212 and 205 B.C. he was in the east attempting to emulate the campaigns of Alexander and Seleukos I, and to re-establish Seleukid authority in Parthia and Baktria. In the first decade of the 2nd century B.C. he turned his attention to Europe, which brought him into conflict with the Romans who had just defeated Philip V of Macedon (197 B.C.). Defeated twice, at Thermopylai and at Magnesia in western Asia Minor, Antiochos had to accept humiliating peace terms by which he lost his possessions in Asia Minor to Rome's ally, the Kingdom of Pergamon. Antiochos, broken in spirit, marched eastward again, and in 187 B.C. he was murdered in Elymais). *N oktadrachm* (c. 34 gm.). His diad. hd. r. ℞. Naked Apollo seated l. on omphalos, holding arrow and resting on bow; on r., ΒΑΣΙΛΕΩΣ; on l., ΑΝΤΙΟΧΟΥ; monogram in field to l. *Newell (W.S.M.)* 1074. *B.M.C. 4.* 25, 2   £15,000

These were probably 'presentation pieces' and may have been struck from gold which Antiochos looted from the great temple of Aene at Ecbatana in 209 B.C.

6931 — *N stater* (c. 8·5 gm.). Similar, but with monograms in field to l. and to r. on *rev.* *Newell (E.S.M.)* 242. *B.M.C. 4.* 25, 3 .. .. £4,500

6932 — — *Obv.* Similar. ℞. Elephant walking r.; on l., ΒΑΣΙΛΕΩΣ; above, ΑΝΤΙΟΧΟΥ; monograms in lower field to r. and in ex. *Newell (E.S.M.)* 397. *Babelon (Rois de Syrie) pl.* X, 1 .. .. £6,000

6933 — *Æ tetradrachm* (c. 17 gm.). His diad. hd. r., with very youthful features. ℞. Naked Apollo seated l. on omphalos, holding arrow and resting on bow; on r., ΒΑΣΙΛΕΩΣ; on l., ΑΝΤΙΟΧΟΥ; monograms in fields to l. and to r. *Newell (E.S.M.)* 221 .. .. £300

6934 — — *Obv.* Similar, but with the features of a young man, and all within fillet border. ℞. As last, but with monogram only in field to l. *Newell (W.S.M.)* 1051. *B.M.C. 4.* 26, 25 .. .. £250

6935 — — As last, but the king's features are middle-aged, and with bow in case instead of monogram in *rev.* field to l. *Newell (W.S.M.)* 1116. *B.M.C. 4.* 26, 27 .. £250

Antiochos III *continued*

6936 — — His diad. hd. r., with idealized features; normal dotted border. ℞. Similar to
6933, but with monogram and race-torch in field to l., another monogram to r., and club
r. in ex. *Newell (W.S.M.)* 1263. *B.M.C. 4.* 25, 7 ..   ..   £250

6937 — — His diad. hd. r., with features suggesting early middle-age. ℞. Indian elephant
stg. l.; on r., ΒΑΣΙΛΕΩΣ; on l., ΑΝΤΙΟΧΟΥ; monogram in ex. *Newell (E.S.M.)* 252
                                                                                £3,000

6938 — — *Obv.* Similar, but with fillet border. ℞. Indian elephant walking r.;
ΒΑΣΙΛΕΩΣ; beneath, ΑΝΤΙΟΧΟΥ; monograms in field to l. and to r. *Newell (E.S.M.)* 628.
B.M.C. 4. 26, 28 ..   ..   £2,500

6939 — ℞ *drachm* (*c.* 4·2 gm.). *Obv.* As 6937. ℞. Naked Apollo seated l. on omphalos,
holding arrow and resting on bow; on r., ΒΑΣΙΛΕΩΣ; on l., ΑΝΤΙΟΧΟΥ; monogram in field to
l., Φ in ex. *Newell (W.S.M.)* 1099. *B.M.C. 4.* 26, 15 ..   ..   £90

6940   6945

6940 — — — ℞. Similar to 6938, but with monogram only in field to r. *Newell (E.S.M.)*
631. *B.M.C. 4.* 26, 31-2 ..   ..   £250

6941 — ℞ *hemidrachm* (*c.* 2 gm.). His diad. hd. r. ℞. ΑΝΤΙΟΧΟΥ / ΒΑΣΙΛΕΩΣ either side of
horse's hd. r.; monogram beneath. *Newell (E.S.M.)* 589   ..   ..   ..   £200

6942 — ℞ *obol* (*c.* 0·65 gm.). Similar. *Newell (E.S.M.)* 590   ..   ..   ..   £125

6943 — Æ 31. His diad. hd. r. ℞. ΒΑΣΙΛΕΩΣ / ΑΝΤΙΟΧΟΥ above and beneath horseman
prancing r., holding spear couched; monograms in field to l. and to r. *Newell (E.S.M.)*
614. *B.M.C. 4.* 28, 45   ..   ..   £30

6944 — Æ 26. *Obv.* Similar. ℞. ΒΑΣΙΛΕΩΣ / ΑΝΤΙΟΧΟΥ above and beneath elephant stg. r.,
bell around neck; anchor in field to l., monogram below elephant. *Newell (E.S.M.)* 648.
B.M.C. 4. 27, 36 ..   ..   £20

6945 — — — ℞. ΒΑΣΙΛΕΩΣ / ΑΝΤΙΟΧΟΥ either side of Nike advancing l., holding wreath and
palm; horse's hd. and monogram in field to l., another monogram to r. *Newell (E.S.M.)*
611. *B.M.C. 4.* 27, 43-4 ..   ..   £15

6946 — Æ 24. Laur. hd. of Apollo r., with features of Antiochos. ℞. ΒΑΣΙΛΕΩΣ / ΑΝΤΙΟΧΟΥ
either side of naked Apollo seated l. on omphalos, holding arrow and resting on bow; in
field to l., monogram above r. *Newell (W.S.M.)* 1060. *B.M.C. 4.* 28, 50 ..   £15

6947   6949

6947 — — His diad. hd. r. ℞. ΒΑΣΙΛΕΩΣ / ΑΝΤΙΟΧΟΥ either side of naked Apollo stg. r., holding arrow and bow; monogram above anchor in field to r., another monogram to l. *Newell* (*E.S.M.*) 591   ..   ..   £16

6948 — — *Obv.* Similar. ℞. ΒΑΣΙΛΕΩΣ / ΑΝΤΙΟΧΟΥ above and beneath mare stg. l., her hd. turned back to lick suckling foal; monogram in field to l. *Newell* (*E.S.M.*) 623   £17

6949 — Æ 22. His diad. hd. r., with middle-aged features. ℞. ΒΑΣΙΛΕΩΣ / ΑΝΤΙΟΧΟΥ above and beneath stern of galley l.; in field above, ΡΙϹ (=year 116 of the Seleukid era =197/6 B.C.). *Newell* (*W.S.M.*) 1272   ..   ..   £16

6950 — — *Obv.* As 6933. ℞. ΒΑΣΙΛΕΩΣ / ΑΝΤΙΟΧΟΥ either side of Apollo stg. facing, holding plectrum and lyre; monograms in field to l. and to r. *Newell* (*E.S.M.*) 223   ..   £15

6951 — Æ 16. Laur. hd. of Apollo three-quarter face to r. ℞. ΒΑΣΙΛΕΩΣ / ΑΝΤΙΟΧΟΥ either side of tall tripod; monogram in field to l. *Newell* (*E.S.M.*) 250   ..   ..   £14

6952 — — Hd. of Zeus three-quarter face to r., sceptre over r. shoulder. ℞. ΒΑΣΙΛΕΩΣ / ΑΝΤΙΟΧΟΥ either side of naked Apollo stg. r. before tripod; monogram in field to l. *Newell* (*E.S.M.*) 251   ..   ..   £15

6953 — Æ 15. His diad. hd. r. ℞. ΒΑΣΙΛΕΩΣ / ΑΝΤΙΟΧΟΥ either side of tripod; monogram in field to l. *Newell* (*E.S.M.*) 603 ..   ..   £10

6954 — Æ 14. Laur. hd. of Apollo r. ℞. ΒΑΣΙΛΕΩΣ / ΑΝΤΙΟΧΟΥ either side of Artemis advancing l., holding torch; monograms in field to l. and to r. *Newell* (*E.S.M.*) 407
    £9

6955 — — *Obv.* Similar. ℞. ΒΑΣΙΛΕΩΣ / ΑΝΤΙΟΧΟΥ either side of Athena-Nike, winged and helmeted, stg. l., holding wreath and palm; monograms in field to l. and to r. *Newell* (*E.S.M.*) 408   ..   ..   £9

6956 — Æ 13. *Obv.* As 6949. ℞. ΒΑΣΙΛΕΩΣ / ΑΝΤΙΟΧΟΥ either side of palm-tree. *Newell* (*W.S.M.*) 1279. *B.M.C. 4.* 28, 48   ..   ..   £9

6957 — Æ 10. Similar, but with *rev.* type club instead of palm-tree. *Newell* (*W.S.M.*) 1280 ..   ..   £7

6958 **Molon,** 222-220 B.C. (satrap of Media, Molon rebelled against Seleukid rule soon after the accession of the young Antiochos III. After initial successes the usurper was ultimately defeated in battle and took his own life). Æ 22. Laur. hd. of Zeus r. ℞. ΒΑΣΙΛΕΩΣ / ΜΟΛΩΝΟΣ either side of Apollo advancing r., holding plectrum and lyre; monogram in field to l. *Newell* (*E.S.M.*) 228. *B.M.C. 4.* 30, 1   ..   ..   £45

Molon *continued*

6959 — Æ 18. Laur. hd. of Apollo r. ℞. ΒΑΣΙΛΕΩΣ / ΜΟΛΩΝΟΣ either side of Nike stg. l., holding palm and crowning king's name; monograms in field to l. and to r. *Newell* (*E.S.M.*) 574. *B.M.C. 4.* 30, 2 .. .. £40

6960 **Achaios,** 220-214 B.C. (uncle of Antiochos III, Achaios was appointed commander-in-chief in Asia Minor. He restored Seleukid authority in the area but then rebelled against his young nephew and proclaimed himself king. In 216 B.C. Antiochos moved against the rebel, many of whose troops then deserted him. After a two-year siege of his capital city of Sardeis, in Lydia, Achaios was captured and beheaded). *N stater* (*c.* 8·5 gm.). His diad. and dr. bust r., bearded. ℞. Athena advancing l., brandishing spear and holding shield; on r., ΒΑΣΙΛΕΩΣ; on l., ΑΧΑΙΟΥ, Θ Ε above horse's hd. in field to l., ΑΡ monogram to r. *Newell* (*W.S.M.*) 1439 .. .. (*Unique*)

6961 — Æ *tetradrachm* (*c.* 15·48 gm.). Similar, but with horse's hd. in *rev.* field to l., Π / Υ to r. *Newell* (*W.S.M.*) 1440 .. .. £12,500

6962 — Æ 19. Laur. hd. of Apollo r., hair in formal curls. ℞. ΒΑΣΙΛΕΩΣ / ΑΧΑΙΟΥ either side of eagle stg. r., palm-branch in background. *Newell* (*W.S.M.*) 1441. *B.M.C. 4.* 30, 1 £30

6963 — Æ 17. Similar, but on *rev.* the eagle stands on wreath, and without the palm-branch; Ι in field to r. *Newell* (*W.S.M.*) 1450. *B.M.C. 4.* 30, 4 .. .. £30

6964 — Æ 11. *Obv.* Similar. ℞. ΒΑΣΙΛΕΩΣ / ΑΧΑΙΟΥ either side of tripod; Δ in field to r. *Newell* (*W.S.M.*) 1447. *B.M.C. 4.* 30, 5 .. .. £18

6965 — Æ 9. *Obv.* Similar. ℞. ΒΑΣΙ / ΑΧΑΙ either side of horse's hd. r. *Newell* (*W.S.M.*) 1444 .. .. £17

6966   6968

6966 **Seleukos IV, Philopator,** 187-175 B.C. (the kingdom bequeathed by Antiochos the Great to his son, Seleukos IV, was very different from the one which he himself had ruled just a few years before. Asia Minor was lost to the kings of Pergamon, the eastern provinces of Parthia and Baktria were now firmly established as independent kingdoms, and in addition Seleukos had to pay a heavy annual war-indemnity to the Romans. What was left of the Seleukid realm he seems to have governed wisely and well until 175 B.C. when he was murdered by his minister Heliodoros). Æ *tetradrachm* (*c.* 17 gm.). His diad. hd. r.; fillet border. ℞. Naked Apollo seated l. on omphalos, holding arrow and resting on bow; on r., ΒΑΣΙΛΕΩΣ; on l., ΣΕΛΕΥΚΟΥ; in field to l., wreath and palm-branch; in ex., ΔΙ monogram. *Newell* (*Seleucid Mint of Antioch*) 39. *B.M.C. 4.* 31, 12-13 £300

6967 — Æ *drachm* (*c.* 4·15 gm.). His diad. hd. r. ℞. Similar to last, but with two monograms in field to l., nothing in ex. *B.M.C. 4.* 31, 3-5 .. .. £100

6968 — Æ 23 (serrated edge). Laur. hd. of Apollo r., ΜΕ monogram behind. ℞. ΒΑΣΙΛΕΩΣ / ΣΕΛΕΥΚΟΥ either side of naked Apollo stg. l., holding arrow and resting l. arm on tripod; ΝΒ monogram in field to l. *B.M.C. 4.* 32, 22 .. .. £12

6969 — Æ 21. His diad. hd. r. ℞. ΒΑΣΙΛΕΩΣ / ΣΕΛΕΥΚΟΥ above and beneath stern of galley l.; in field above, ΡΛΙ (=year 137 of the Seleukid era=176/5 B.C.). *Babelon* (*Rois de Syrie*) *pl.* XI, 20 .. .. £15

6970   6972

6970 — Æ 20 (serrated edge). Bust of young Dionysos r., wreathed with ivy, thyrsos at shoulder; behind, ME monogram. ℞. ΒΑΣΙΛΕΩΣ / ΣΕΛΕΥΚΟΥ above and beneath prow of galley l.; in field above, ΑΠ. *B.M.C. 4.* 32, 26 ..   ..   £12

6971 — Æ 17 (serrated edge). Diad. bust of Artemis r., quiver at shoulder. ℞. ΒΑΣΙΛΕΩΣ / ΣΕΛΕΥΚΟΥ either side of Artemis stg. l., holding spear; deer l. at her side. *B.M.C. 4.* 33, 27-8 ..   ..   £9

6972 — Æ 15 (serrated edge). Veiled and daid. bust of Queen Laodike (?) r. ℞. ΒΑΣΙΛΕΩΣ / ΣΕΛΕΥΚΟΥ above and beneath elephant's hd. l.; ΑΤ in lower field to r. *B.M.C. 4.* 33, 29
                                                         £9

6973 **Antiochos,** son of Seleukos IV, *c.* 175-170 B.C. (on the assassination of Seleukos IV, Heliodoros seized power as regent for the late king's five-year-old son, Antiochos. But Seleukos' brother, also named Antiochos, invaded Syria and made himself master of the kingdom, reigning as Antiochos IV. His young nephew disappears from history after several years of nominal joint rule, but a few coins were struck with his portrait). Æ *tetradrachm* (*c.* 17 gm.). Diad. hd. of the child-king r.; fillet border. ℞. Naked Apollo seated l. on omphalos, holding arrow and resting on bow; on r., ΒΑΣΙΛΕΩΣ; on l., ΑΝΤΙΟΧΟΥ; in field to l., tripod; in ex., Β. *B.M.C. 4.* 24, 3 ..   ..   £750

6974 — Æ *drachm* (*c.* 4 gm.). Similar, but without the symbol or letter on *rev.* *B.M.C. 4.* 24, 4 ..   ..   £250

6975 **Antiochos IV, Epiphanes,** 175-164 B.C. (younger son of Antiochos the Great, Antiochos IV seized the Seleukid throne in 175 B.C. after having spent the previous twelve years as a hostage in Rome. He was a vigorous ruler and attempted to extend Seleukid influence by invading Egypt, though he was obliged to withdraw because of Roman opposition. He also aroused the hatred of the Jews by despoiling the Temple in Jerusalem and later tearing down the city walls. Antiochos died on campaign in the east in 164 B.C.). *N stater* (*c.* 8·6 gm.). His diad. hd. r. ℞. Zeus enthroned l., holding Nike and sceptre; on r., ΒΑΣΙΛΕΩΣ / ΑΝΤΙΟΧΟΥ; on l., ΘΕΟΥ / ΕΠΙΦΑΝΟΥΣ; in ex., ΝΙΚΗΦΟΡΟΥ. *Newell* (*S.M.A.*) 62
                                                  £8,000

Antiochos IV *continued*

6976 — Æ *tetradrachm* (*c.* 17 gm.). His diad. hd. r.; fillet border. ℞. Naked Apollo seated l. on omphalos, holding arrow and resting on bow; on r., ΒΑΣΙΛΕΩΣ; on l., ΑΝΤΙΟΧΟΥ; in field to l., tripod; to r., lyre; ΔΙ monogram in ex. *Newell* (*S.M.A.*) 44. *B.M.C. 4.* 34, 3-4 .. .. £350

6977 — — *Obv.* Similar. ℞. Similar to 6975, but with ΔΙ monogram in ex., instead of ΝΙΚΗΦΟΡΟΥ. *Newell* (*S.M.A.*) 54. *B.M.C. 4.* 35, 13-15 .. .. .. £300

6978 — — — ℞. As 6975, but also with ΙΣ in field to l. *Newell* (*S.M.A.*) 68. *B.M.C. 4.* 35, 16 .. .. £275

6979 — — Laur. hd. of Zeus r.; fillet border. ℞. As 6975. *Newell* (*S.M.A.*) 63. *B.M.C. 4.* 36, 22 .. .. £3,000

6980 — — Laur. hd. of Apollo r.; fillet border. ℞. Apollo advancing r., holding phiale and lyre; on r., ΒΑΣΙΛΕΩΣ / ΑΝΤΙΟΧΟΥ / ΘΕΟΥ; on l., ΕΠΙΦΑΝΟΥΣ / ΝΙΚΗΦΟΡΟΥ. *Newell* (*S.M.A.*) 64 .. .. £5,000

6981 — Æ *drachm* (*c.* 4 gm.). His diad. hd. r. ℞. Naked Apollo seated l. on omphalos, holding arrow and resting on bow; on r., ΒΑΣΙΛΕΩΣ; on l., ΑΝΤΙΟΧΟΥ / ΕΠΙΦΑΝΟΥΣ; ΑΠ monogram in ex. *B.M.C.4.* 34, 9 .. .. £120

6982 — — *Obv.* Similar. ℞. Eagle stg. r. on thunderbolt; on r., ΒΑΣΙΛΕΩΣ / ΑΝΤΙΟΧΟΥ; on l., ΘΕΟΥ / ΕΠΙΦΑΝΟΥΣ. *Newell* (*S.M.A.*) 57 .. .. (*Unique*)

This, and the bronzes listed below (*nos.* 6985-7) *were issued in connection with Antiochos'* *invasion of Egypt.*

6983 — Æ *hemidrachm* (*c.* 1·9 gm.). His radiate hd. r. ℞. Aegis; on r., ΒΑΣΙΛΕΩΣ /ΑΝΤΙΟΧΟΥ; on l., ΘΕΟΥ / ΕΠΙΦΑΝΟΥΣ. *Newell* (*S.M.A.*) 65 .. .. £200

6984 — Æ *diobol* (*c.* 1·2 gm.). Similar, but with *rev.* type tripod instead of aegis. *Newell* (*S.M.A.*) 66. *B.M.C. 4.* 35, 10 .. .. £140

6985

6985 — Æ 32. Laur. hd. of Zeus-Sarapis r. ℞. Eagle stg. r. on thunderbolt; on r., ΒΑΣΙΛΕΩΣ / ΑΝΤΙΟΧΟΥ; on l., ΘΕΟΥ / ΕΠΙΦΑΝΟΥΣ. *Newell* (*S.M.A.*) 59. *B.M.C. 4.* 38, 42
£25

6986 6987

6986 — Æ 27. Hd. of Isis r., wreathed with corn. ℞. As last. *Newell* (*S.M.A.*) 60. *B.M.C. 4.* 38, 46 .. .. £24

6987 — Æ 22. His rad. hd. r. ℞. As last. Newell (*S.M.A.*) 61. *B.M.C. 4.* 38, 48 £22

6988 — Æ 4-*chalkoi* (diam. *c.* 25 mm.). His rad. hd. r.; Δ / x behind. ℞. ΒΑΣΙΛΕΩΣ / ΑΝΤΙΟΧΟΥ either side of Tyche enthroned l., holding Nike; bird at her feet. *B.M.C. 4.* 36, 23 £24

6989 — Æ *dichalkon* (*c.* 20 mm.). Similar, but with B / x behind hd. on *obv*. *B.M.C. 4.* 36, 25
£14

6990 — Æ *chalkos* (*c.* 16 mm.). Similar, but with A / x behind hd. on *obv*. *B.M.C. 4.* 36, 29
£12

6991 — Æ 19. His rad. hd. r. ℞. Zeus stg. l., holding thunderbolt and sceptre, eagle at feet; on r., ΒΑΣΙΛΕΩΣ / ΑΝΤΙΟΧΟΥ; on l., ΘΕΟΥ / ΕΠΙΦΑΝΟΥΣ. *B.M.C. 4.* 37, 32.. £16

6992 — Æ 18. As 6983. *B.M.C. 4.* 37, 39 .. .. £15

6993 — Æ 17. His rad. hd. r. ℞. Naked Apollo advancing r., holding bow and drawing arrow from quiver; legend as 6991. *B.M.C. 4.* 37, 36 .. .. £13

6994 — Æ 15 (serrated edge). His rad. hd. r.; fillet border. ℞. ΒΑΣΙΛΕΩΣ / ΑΝΤΙΟΧΟΥ either side of Hera (?) stg. facing, holding sceptre. *B.M.C. 4.* 38, 41.. .. .. £11

6995 — Æ 22 of *Sidon*. His rad. hd. r., M behind. ℞. Galley l.; above, ΒΑΣΙΛΕΩΣ / ΑΝΤΙΟΧΟΥ; beneath, ΣΙΔΩΝΙΩΝ and Phoenician legend. *B.M.C. 4.* 39, 50 .. .. .. £15

6996 — Æ 18 of *Sidon*. ΒΑΣΙΛΕΩΣ ΑΝΤΙΟΧΟΥ. His rad. hd. r. ℞. ΣΙΔΩΝΙΩΝ and Phoenician legend. Europa seated on bull galloping l. *B.M.C. 4.* 39, 53-4 .. .. £15

6997 — Æ 20 of *Antiocheia ad Daphnen*. His rad. hd. r. ℞. Zeus stg. facing, hd. l., holding wreath; on r., ΑΝΤΙΟΧΕΩΝ; on l., ΤΩΝ / ΠΡΟΣ ΔΑΦΝΗΙ; monograms in field to l. and to r. *B.M.C. 4.* 40, 64 .. .. £14

6998   7001

Antiochos IV *continued*

6998 — — of *Seleukeia in Pieria*. His rad. hd. r. ℞. ΣΕΛΕΥΚΕΩΝ / ΤΩΝ — ΕΜ ΠΙΕΡΙΑΙ either
side of winged thunderbolt; monograms in field to l. and to r. *B.M.C. 4.* 42, 83   £14

6999 — Æ 19 of *Antiocheia ad Kallirhoen* (=*Edessa*). His rad. hd. r. ℞. Zeus stg. l., holding
eagle and sceptre; on r., ΑΝΤΙΟΧΕΩΝ; on l., ΤΩΝ / ΕΠΙ ΚΑΛΛΙΡΟΗΙ; monogram in field to l.
B.M.C. 4. 41, 77-8   ..   ..   £15

7000 — Æ 17 of *Laodikeia ad Mare*. His diad. bust r., monogram behind. ℞. Poseidon stg.
l., holding dolphin and trident; on r., ΛΑΟΔΙΚΕΩΝ; on l., ΠΡΟΣ ΘΑΛΑΣΣΗΙ. *B.M.C. 4.* 41, 82
£15

7001 — Æ *dichalkon* of *Antiocheia in Mygdonia* (=*Nisibis*), *c.* 17 mm. His rad. hd. r.;
Β / Χ behind. ℞. Nike advancing l., holding wreath and palm; on r., ΑΝΤΙΟΧΕΩΝ; on l.,
ΤΩΝ / ΕΝ ΜΥΓΔΟΝΙΑΙ; monograms in field to l. and to r., and in ex. *B.M.C. 4.* 42, 88
£16

7002 — Æ 15 of *Mopsos*. His diad. hd. r. ℞. Artemis stg. facing, holding bow and drawing
arrow from quiver; on r., ΜΟΨΕΑΤΩΝ; in field to l., Μ / Π. *B.M.C. 4.* 40, 58 ..   £16

> *The bronze coinage of this reign is remarkably varied, and the above listing is only a
> selection of the types which have been recorded. An interesting feature is the issue of coinage
> in the name of the mint city, with the royal name often omitted.*

7003 **Antiochos V, Eupator,** 164-162 B.C. (son of Antiochos IV, the new king was only nine
years old, and his position was soon challenged by his cousin Demetrios who escaped from
captivity in Rome. Demetrios was received with enthusiasm in Syria and the unfortunate
boy-king was murdered). Æ *tetradrachm* (*c.* 16·75 gm.). His young diad. hd. r. ℞.
Naked Apollo seated l. on omphalos, holding arrow and resting on bow; on r., ΒΑΣΙΛΕΩΣ;
on l., ΑΝΤΙΟΧΟΥ; in ex., ΕΥΠΑΤΟΡΟΣ; monogram and wreath (?) in field to l., monogram
and club to r. *B.M.C. 4.* 44, 1 ..   ..   £650

7004   7005

7004 — — His young diad. hd. r.; fillet border. ℞. Zeus enthroned l., holding Nike and
sceptre; legend as last; ΠΤ monogram in field to l. *Newell (S.M.A.)* 75. *B.M.C. 4.* 44,
5-6 ..   ..   £400

7005 — Æ *drachm* (*c.* 4·05 gm.). His young diad. hd. r.; ΑΒ behind. ℞. Similar to 7003, but
with ΑΣΚ in field to l., nothing to r. *B.M.C. 4.* 44, 2 ..   ..   £250

7006 — Æ 18. His young diad. hd. r. ℞. Thunderbolt; ΒΑΣΙΛΕΩΣ / ΑΝΤΙΟΧΟΥ above,
ΕΥΠΑΤΟΡΟΣ beneath. *Babelon (Rois de Syrie) pl.* XV, 11 ..   ..   ..   £18

7007 **Timarchos,** 162 B.C. (satrap of Babylon, appointed by Antiochos IV, Timarchos refused
to acknowledge Demetrios and proclaimed himself king of Media. Demetrios advanced
against the usurper and the revolt quickly collapsed). *N stater* (*c.* 8·5 gm.). His diad.
hd. r.; fillet border. ℞. Nike in galloping quadriga r.; above, ΒΑΣΙΛΕΩΣ / ΜΕΓΑΛΟΥ;
in ex., ΤΙΜΑΡΧΟΥ. *Babelon, p.* cxv ..   ..   (*Unique*)

7008 — Æ *tetradrachm* (*c.* 16·75 gm.). His helmeted and dr. bust r.; fillet border. ℞. ΒΑΣΙΛΕΩΣ ΜΕΓΑΛΟΥ ΤΙΜΑΡΧΟΥ. The Dioskouroi galloping r.; fillet border. *B.M.C. 4., p.* 50 .. .. £10,000

7009   7010

7009 — Æ *drachm* (*c.* 4 gm.). His diad. hd. r. ℞. Artemis stg. r., holding bow and drawing arrow from quiver; on r., ΒΑΣΙΛΕΩΣ; on l., ΜΕΓΑΛΟΥ / ΤΙΜΑΡΧΟΥ. *B.M.C. 4.* 50, 2 £3,000

7010 — Æ 34. His diad. hd. r. ℞. Nike advancing l., holding palm and crowning king's name; on r., ΒΑΣΙΛΕΩΣ / ΜΕΓΑΛΟΥ; on l., ΤΙΜΑΡΧΟΥ. *B.M.C. 4.* 50, 3 .. .. £150

7011 — Æ 26. Similar, but on *rev.* the legend is divided ΒΑΣΙΛΕΩΣ on r., ΜΕΓΑΛΟΥ / ΤΙΜΑΡΧΟΥ on l. *Babelon, pl.* XV, 16 .. .. £75

7012 **Demetrios I, Soter,** 162-150 B.C. (son of Seleukos IV, Demetrios was a hostage in Rome at the time of his father's death and thus unable to take up his inheritance. His uncle, Antiochos IV, seized power in Syria, as related above, and Demetrios had to wait thirteen years in Rome before his chance came to ascend the Seleukid throne. He became something of a recluse in the latter part of his reign, and in 150 B.C. he lost his life in battle against Alexander Balas, who claimed to be a son of Antiochos IV). *N pentadrachm* (*c.* 21·48 gm.). Tyche enthroned l., holding baton and cornucopiae; in field to l., B⊢. ℞. Cornucopiae, with diadem attached; on r., ΒΑΣΙΛΕΩΣ / ΔΗΜΗΤΡΙΟΥ; on l., ΣΩΤΗΡΟΣ; in field to l., monogram above ΣΑ; to r., ΒΞΡ (=year 162 of the Seleukid era=151/50 B.C.). *Babelon, pl.* XVII, 1 .. .. £12,500

7012A — *N stater* (*c.* 8·3 gm.). His diad. hd. r.; fillet border. ℞. Naked Apollo seated l. on omphalos, holding arrow and resting on bow; on r., ΒΑΣΙΛΕΩΣ; on l., ΔΗΜΗΤΡΙΟΥ; in ex., ΣΩΤΗΡΟΣ; in upper field to l., ΚΑ. *Leu auction, April* 1978, *lot* 164 .. .. (*Unique*)

7013 — Æ *tetradrachm* (*c.* 16·75 gm.). His diad. hd. r.; fillet border. ℞. Naked Apollo seated l. on omphalos, holding arrow and resting on bow; on r., ΒΑΣΙΛΕΩΣ; on l., ΔΗΜΗΤΡΙΟΥ; monograms in field to l. and to r. *Babelon, pl.* XVI, 1 .. .. £450

7014 — — His diad. hd. r., within laurel-wreath. ℞. Tyche seated l., on throne supported by winged monster, holding baton and cornucopiae; on r., ΒΑΣΙΛΕΩΣ; on l., ΔΗΜΗΤΡΙΟΥ; ΠΤ monogram in field to l. *Newell (S.M.A.)* 81. *B.M.C. 4.* 47, 33 .. .. £225

7015 — — *Obv.* Similar. ℞. Tyche enthroned, as last; on r., ΒΑΣΙΛΕΩΣ; on l., ΔΗΜΗΤΡΙΟΥ / ΣΩΤΗΡΟΣ; in field to l., two monograms; in ex., Seleukid date ΑΞΡ (=161=152/1 B.C.). *B.M.C. 4.* 46, 17 .. .. £200

Demetrios I *continued*

7016 — — Conjoined hds. r. of Demetrios, diad., and his wife Laodike, wearing stephane; fillet border. ℝ. Tyche enthroned, as 7014; on r., ΒΑΣΙΛΕΩΣ; on l., ΔΗΜΗΤΡΙΟΥ; in ex., ΣΩΤΗΡΟΣ; in field to l., ΗΡ monogram and palm. *B.M.C. 4.* 50, 1 .. .. £3,500

Laodike, sister and wife of Demetrios, was the widow of King Perseus of Macedon.

7017 — Æ *drachm* (*c.* 4·15 gm.). His diad. hd. r.; fillet border. ℝ. Apollo seated, as 7013; on r., ΒΑΣΙΛΕΩΣ; on l., ΔΗΜΗΤΡΙΟΥ; in ex., ΣΩΤΗΡΟΣ; in field to l., Seleukid date ΑΞΡ, as 7015, and ΘΕΟ; to r., ΦΙΛΙΠ. *B.M.C. 4.* 45, 2 .. .. £60

7018 — — *Obv.* Similar. ℝ. Similar to 7014, but with monograms in field to l. and to r., and with club in ex. *Newell* (*Seleucid Coinages of Tyre*) 46a £75

7019   7020

7019 — — — ℝ. Cornucopiae; on r., ΒΑΣΙΛΕΩΣ; on l., ΔΗΜΗΤΡΙΟΥ / ΣΩΤΗΡΟΣ; beneath, two monograms and Seleukid date ΘΝΡ (=159=154/3 B.C.). *Newell* (*S.M.A.*) 110. *B.M.C. 4.* 47, 36 .. .. £50

7020 — Æ 25. Lion's hd. l.; fillet border. ℝ. Boar's hd. r.; ΒΑΣΙΛΕΩΣ above, ΔΗΜΗΤΡΙΟΥ / ΣΩΤΗΡΟΣ beneath; monogram in field to l. *B.M.C. 4.* 49, 57 .. .. .. £20

7021 — Æ 20 of *Tyre*. His diad. hd. r. ℝ. Stern of galley l.; above, ΒΑΣΙΛΕΩΣ / ΔΗΜΗΤΡΙΟΥ and Seleukid date L ΗΝΡ (=158=155/4 B.C.); beneath, ΤΥΡΙΩΝ and Phoenician legend. *B.M.C. 4.* 48, 45-6 .. .. £14

7022 — Æ 19 of *Sidon*. ΒΑΣΙΛΕΩΣ ΔΗΜΗΤΡΙΟΥ ΣΙΔΩΝΙΩΝ. His diad. hd. r., ΜΙ behind. ℝ. Rudder l.; Phoenician legend above and beneath. *B.M.C. 4.* 48, 50 .. .. £16

7023 — Æ 17. Griffin's hd. l. ℝ. Similar to 7020, but with hd. of stag instead of boar. *B.M.C. 4.* 49, 58 .. .. £15

7024 — Æ 15. His diad. hd. r.; before, small horse's hd. r. ℝ. ΒΑΣΙΛΕΩΣ ΔΗΜΗΤΡΙΟΥ ΣΩΤΗΡΟΣ. Caps of the Dioskouroi on two thrones. *B.M.C. 4.* 49, 55.. .. £15

7025 — Æ 17. Conjoined hds. of Demetrios and Laodike, as 7016. ℝ. ΒΑΣΙΛΕΩΣ / ΔΗΜΗΤΡΙΟΥ either side of Nike advancing l., crowning the king's name and holding palm. *Babelon,* *pl.* XVII, 7 .. .. £20

7026   7027

7026 — Æ 25 (serrated edge). Laur. hd. of Apollo r., bow and quiver at shoulder. ℞.
ΒΑΣΙΛΕΩΣ / ΔΗΜΗΤΡΙΟΥ either side of tripod. *B.M.C. 4.* 80, 2 .. .. .. £10

7027 — Æ 20 (serrated edge). Bust of Artemis r., wearing stephane, bow and quiver at shoulder.
℞. ΒΑΣΙΛΕΩΣ / ΔΗΜΗΤΡΙΟΥ either side of bow and quiver. *B.M.C. 4.* 80, 4 .. £8

7028 — Æ 17 (serrated edge). Horse's hd. l. ℞. ΒΑΣΙΛΕΩΣ / ΔΗΜΗΤΡΙΟΥ above and beneath
elephant's hd. r. *B.M.C. 4.* 49, 60-61 .. .. £9

7029 **Alexander I (Balas)**, 150-145 B.C. (claiming to be a son of Antiochos IV, Alexander
Balas swept to power in Syria in 150 B.C. with the support of Attalos of Pergamon and
Ptolemy of Egypt. However, his dissolute life-style soon made him unpopular, and he
was overthrown after a reign of only five years). *Ả stater* (c. 8·45 gm.). His diad. hd. r.
℞. Zeus enthroned l., holding Nike and sceptre; on r., ΒΑΣΙΛΕΩΣ / ΑΛΕΞΑΝΔΡΟΥ; on l.,
ΘΕΟΠΑΤΟΡΟΣ / ΕΥΕΡΓΕΤΟΥ. *Babelon, pl.* XVII, 9 .. .. £7,500

7030   7032

7030 — Ꭱ *tetradrachm* (c. 16·75 gm.). His diad. hd. r.; fillet border. ℞. Similar to last,
but also in field to l., cornucopiae; and in ex., Seleukid date ΓΞΡ (=163=150/49 B.C.) and
monogram. *Newell (S.M.A.)* 135. *B.M.C. 4.* 52, 8 .. .. £250

7031 — — *Obv.* Similar. ℞. Athena stg. l., holding Nike, spear and shield; legend as 7029;
in field to l., two monograms; in ex., Seleukid date ΔΞΡ (=164=149/8 B.C.). *Newell
(S.M.A.)* 150. *B.M.C. 4.* 52, 15 .. .. £1,500

7031A — — Conjoined busts r. of Alexander, diad., and his wife Cleopatra, veiled and diad.
and wearing polos, cornucopiae at shoulder; A behind. ℞. Similar to 7029. *Jenkins
(Ancient Greek Coins)* 657 .. .. £10,000

7032 — — Laur. hd. of Zeus r. ℞. ΒΑΣΙΛΕΩΣ / ΑΛΕΞΑΝΔΡΟΥ above and beneath thunderbolt;
in field above, Seleukid date ΣΞΡ (=166=147/6 B.C.) and monogram; two more monograms below; all within wreath. *B.M.C. 4.* 52, 16 .. .. £7,500

7033 — — (Phoenician standard, c. 14·25 gm.), mint of *Tyre*. His diad. and dr. bust r.
℞. ΑΛΕΞΑΝΔΡΟΥ ΒΑΣΙΛΕΩΣ. Eagle stg. l. on beak of galley, palm-branch in background;
in field to l., ΤΥΡ monogram above club; to r., Seleukid date ΓΞΡ (=163=150/49 B.C.)
and ΗΡ monogram. *B.M.C. 4.* 51, 1 .. .. £200

7034 — — — of *Sidon*. Similar, but in *rev.* field to l., Seleukid date ΒΞΡ (=162=150 B.C.);
and to r., ΣΙΔΩ and aplustre. *B.M.C. 4.* 51, 6 .. .. £225

7035 — Ꭱ *drachm* (c. 4·1 gm.). His diad. hd. r. ℞. Naked Apollo seated l. on omphalos,
holding arrow and resting on bow; legend as 7029; in ex., Seleukid date ΓΞΡ (=163=150/49
B.C.). *Newell (S.M.A.)* 138. *B.M.C. 4.* 52, 17 . .. . £50

Alexander I (Balas) *continued*

7036 — Æ *hemidrachm* (*c.* 2 gm.).   His rad. hd. r.   ℞. ΒΑΣΙΛΕΩΣ / ΑΛΕΞΑΝΔΡΟΥ either side of
naked Apollo stg. l., holding arrow and resting on bow; Φ in field to l.   *Newell* (*S.M.A.*)
192. *B.M.C. 4.* 53, 30   ..   ..   £75

7037 — Æ *diobol* (*c.* 1·25 gm.).   His diad. hd. r.   ℞. ΒΑΣΙΛΕΩΣ / ΑΛΕΞΑΝΔΡΟΥ either side of
tripod. *Babelon, pl.* XVII, 13   ..   ..   £65

7038 — Æ 24.   Laur. hd. of Zeus r.   ℞. ΒΑΣΙΛΕΩΣ / ΑΛΕΞΑΝΔΡΟΥ either side of Athena stg. l.,
holding owl, spear and shield; all within wreath.   *B.M.C. 4.* 56, 55   ..   ..   £15

7039   7040

7039 — Æ 20.   His hd. r., clad in lion's skin.   ℞. Similar to 7036, but with palm in field to l.,
monogram to r.   *B.M.C. 4.* 55, 44-5   ..   ..   £9

7040 — Æ 19.   His hd. r., in crested helmet.   ℞. ΒΑΣΙΛΕΩΣ / ΑΛΕΞΑΝΔΡΟΥ either side of Nike
stg. l., crowning the king's name and holding palm; in field to l., corn-ear and monogram.
B.M.C. 4. 55, 51-2   ..   ..   £10

7041 — Æ 14.   Hd. of young Dionysos r., wreathed with ivy.   ℞. ΒΑΣΙΛΕΩΣ / ΑΛΕΞΑΝΔΡΟΥ
above and beneath elephant stg. l.; monogram in field to r.   *B.M.C. 4.* 56, 57-8   £10

7042   7045

7042 — Æ 21.   Conjoined busts r. of his wife Cleopatra, veiled and diad., and Alexander
himself, diad.   ℞. ΑΛΕΞΑΝΔΡΟΥ ΒΑΣΙΛΕΩΣ.   Cornucopiae, with diadem attached.   *B.M.C.
4.* 57, 1   ..   ..   £24

7043 — Æ 20 (serrated edge).   His diad. hd. r.   ℞. ΒΑΣΙΛΕΩΣ / ΑΛΕΞΑΝΔΡΟΥ either side of
Zeus enthroned l., holding Nike and sceptre, anchor beneath.   *B.M.C. 4.* 54, 35   £13

7044 — — — *Obv.* Similar.   ℞. Legend, as last, either side of Athena stg. l., holding Nike,
spear and shield; monograms in field to l. and in ex.   *B.M.C. 4.* 54, 36   ..   £12

7045 — Æ 17 (serrated edge).   *Obv.* Similar.   ℞. Legend, as last, either side of owl stg. r.,
hd. facing; ΚΛΕ in ex.   *B.M.C. 4.* 55, 41 ..   ..   £9

7046 — Æ 19 of *Sidon*.   His diad. hd. r.   ℞. Galley l.; above, ΒΑΣΙΛΕΩΣ / ΑΛΕΞΑΝΔΡΟΥ;
beneath, ΣΙΔΩΝΙΩΝ and Phoenician legend.   *B.M.C. 4.* 53, 31   ..   ..   £14

7047 — Æ 20 of *Antioch*.   His diad. hd. r.   ℞. Zeus stg. facing, hd. l., holding wreath; on l.,
ΑΝΤΙΟΧΕΩΝ; monogram in field to l., Γ Ι to r.   *B.M.C. 4.* 56, 63 ..   ..   ..   £14

7048 — — of *Laodikeia*.   His diad. hd. r.   ℞. Poseidon enthroned l., holding dolphin and
trident; on r., ΛΑΟΔΙΚΕΩΝ; on l., ΤΩΝ / ΠΡΟΣ ΘΑΛΑΣΣΗΙ; monogram in field to l.   *B.M.C. 4.*
57, 66   ..   ..   £15

7049 — Æ 15 of *Kyrrhos*.   His diad. hd. r.   ℞. Athena stg. l., holding Nike, spear and
shield; on l., ΚΥΡΡΗΣΤΩΝ; in field to l., monogram; to r., Seleukid date ΔΞΡ (=164 =149/8
B.C.).   *B.M.C. 4.* 56, 62   ..   ..   £13

*Despite the brevity of his reign, Alexander produced an extensive bronze coinage in the
tradition of his supposed father, Antiochos IV.   The above listing is merely a selection of the
known types.*

7050 **Demetrios II, Nikator,** first reign, 145-140 B.C. (the elder son of Demetrios I, he managed to overthrow Alexander Balas with the assistance of Ptolemy of Egypt. His hold on the throne was, however, precarious and his rule was mostly confined to the cities of the Phoenician coast. In 140 B.C. he marched against the Parthians, but was captured by them and remained in honourable captivity at the Arsacid court for the following decade). Æ *tetradrachm* (*c.* 16·75 gm.). His young diad. hd. r.; fillet border. ℞. Naked Apollo seated l. on omphalos, holding arrow and resting on bow; on r., ΒΑΣΙΛΕΩΣ / ΔΗΜΗΤΡΙΟΥ; on l., ΘΕΟΥ / ΦΙΛΑΔΕΛΦΟΥ / ΝΙΚΑΤΟΡΟΣ; in field to l., monogram; in ex., Seleukid date ΙΞΡ (=167=145 B.C.) and monogram. *Newell* (*S.M.A.*) 198. *B.M.C. 4.* 58, 8-9   ..   ..   £250

7051 — — *Obv.* Similar. ℞. Zeus enthroned l., holding Nike and sceptre; on r., ΒΑΣΙΛΕΩΣ / ΔΗΜΗΤΡΙΟΥ; on l., ΘΕΟΥ / ΝΙΚΑΤΟΡΟΣ; monogram in ex. *B.M.C. 4.* 59, 14   ..   £400

7052 — — *Obv.* Similar, but border of dots. ℞. Athena stg. l., holding Nike, spear and shield; on r., ΒΑΣΙΛΕΩΣ / ΔΗΜΗΤΡΙΟΥ; on l., ΦΙΛΑΔΕΛΦΟΥ / ΝΙΚΑΤΟΡΟΣ; in field to l., branch; in ex., two monograms and ΙΣΙ. *B.M.C. 4.* 59, 16   ..   ..   £400

7053 — — *Obv.* As 7050. ℞. Tyche seated l., on throne supported by winged monster, holding baton and cornucopiae; on r., ΒΑΣΙΛΕΩΣ / ΔΗΜΗΤΡΙΟΥ; on l., ΦΙΛΑΔΕΛΦΟΥ / ΝΙΚΑΤΟΡΟΣ; monogram in ex. *B.M.C. 4.* 60, 18..   ..   ..   £300

7054   7055

7054 — — *Obv.* As 7052, but with Μ behind hd. ℞. Cultus-statue of Athena Magarsis facing, holding spear, star either side of neck; legend as last; monograms in lower field to l. and to r. *B.M.C. 4.* 59, 17   ..   ..   £1,500

7055 — — (Phoenician standard, *c.* 14·1 gm.), mint of *Sidon.* His young diad. and dr. bust r. ℞. ΔΗΜΗΤΡΙΟΥ ΒΑΣΙΛΕΩΣ. Eagle stg. l., palm-branch in background; in field to l., Seleukid date ΗΞΡ (=168=145/4 B.C.) and monogram; to r., ΣΙΔΩ and aplustre. *B.M.C. 4.* 58, 1   £200

Demetrios II *continued*

7056 — Æ *didrachm* (Phoenician standard, *c.* 6·55 gm.), mint of *Tyre*. Similar, but on *rev.* the eagle stands on beak of galley; in field to l., TYP monogram above club; to r., Seleukid date ΘΞΡ (=169=144/3 B.C.) and monogram. *Babelon, pl.* XX, 1 .. .. £250

7057 — Æ *drachm* (*c.* 4 gm.). Similar to 7050, but with dotted border on *obv.*; and on *rev.* star and two monograms in field to l., Seleukid date ΗΞΡ (=168=145/4 B.C.) in ex. *Newell* (*S.M.A.*) 213. *B.M.C. 4.* 59, 13 .. .. £75

7058 — — His young diad. hd. r., monogram behind; fillet border. Ɍ. Zeus enthroned l., holding eagle and sceptre; legend as 7053. *B.M.C. 4.* 60, 19 .. .. .. £125

7059 7061

7059 — — *Obv.* As 7057. Ɍ. Cornucopiae; on r., ΒΑΣΙΛΕΩΣ; on l., ΔΗΜΗΤΡΙΟΥ / ΝΙΚΑΤΟΡΟΣ. *Babelon, pl.* XIX, 4 .. .. £100

7060 — — — Ɍ. Anchor; on r., ΒΑΣΙΛΕΩΣ / ΔΗΜΗΤΡΙΟΥ; on l., ΝΙΚΑΤΟΡΟΣ; flower in field to l. *Babelon, pl.* XIX, 6 .. .. £150

7061 — Æ *hemidrachm* (*c.* 2 gm.). *Obv.* As 7057. Ɍ. Naked Apollo stg. l., holding arrow and resting on bow; on r., ΒΑΣΙΛΕΩΣ; on l., ΔΗΜΗΤΡΙΟΥ; two monograms in field to l. *Newell* (*S.M.A.*) 215 .. .. £110

7062 — Æ *diobol* (*c.* 1·25 gm.). *Obv.* As 7057. Ɍ. Ear of corn; legend as last; two monograms in lower field, to l. and to r. *Babelon, pl.* XIX, 5 .. .. £95

7063 — Æ 25. His young diad. hd. r. Ɍ. Artemis stg. l., holding long torch; legend as 7050. *B.M.C. 4.* 60, 23 .. .. £18

7064 — Æ 24. Laur. hd. of Zeus r. Ɍ. Similar to 7050, but nothing in field to l., monogram and star in ex. *B.M.C. 4.* 61, 30 .. .. £14

7065 — — *Obv.* Similar. Ɍ. Athena-Nike, winged, stg. l., holding Nike, spear and shield; legend as 7050; star in field to l. *B.M.C. 4.* 62, 37 .. .. £13

7066 — Æ 19. Laur. hd. of Apollo r. Ɍ. Tripod; legend as 7053; two monograms in ex. *B.M.C. 4.* 62, 40 .. .. £10

7067 — Æ 16. His hd. r., clad in elephant's skin. ℞. Athena stg. l., holding spear and resting on shield; legend as 7053. *B.M.C. 4.* 61, 27 .. .. £11

7068 — — His diad. hd. r. ℞. Similar to 7060, but without flower in field. *B.M.C. 4.* 61, 25 £12

7069 — Æ 15 (serrated edge). His diad. hd. r. ℞. ΒΑΣΙΛΕΩΣ / ΔΗΜΗΤΡΙΟΥ either side of Demeter stg. facing, holding long torch. *B.M.C. 4.* 61, 28 .. .. .. £9

7070 — Æ 20 of *Tyre.* His diad. hd. r. ℞. Stern of galley l.; above, ΒΑΣΙΛΕΩΣ / ΔΗΜΗΤΡΙΟΥ; beneath, ΤΥΡΙΩΝ and Phoenician legend; in field, above galley, Seleukid date Λ ΗΞΡ (=168=145/4 B.C.). *B.M.C. 4.* 60, 20-22 .. .. £13

7071 **Antiochos VI, Dionysos, 145-142 B.C.** (the infant son of Alexander Balas, Antiochos VI was proclaimed king, in opposition to Demetrios II, by the general Diodotos. Antioch soon fell to the rebels, and Syria had two kings until Antiochos was murdered by Diodotos, who now aspired to the throne himself). Æ *tetradrachm* (*c.* 16·75 gm.). Diad. hd. of the child-king r.; fillet border. ℞. Zeus enthroned l., holding Nike and sceptre; on r., ΒΑΣΙΛΕΩΣ; on l., ΑΝΤΙΟΧΟΥ / ΕΠΙΦΑΝΟΥΣ; in ex., Seleukid date ΙΞΡ (=167=145 B.C.) and monogram. *Babelon, pl.* XX, 6 .. .. £650

7072 — — Rad. hd. of the child-king r.; fillet border. ℞. The Dioskouroi on horseback charging l.; above, ΒΑΣΙΛΕΩΣ / ΑΝΤΙΟΧΟΥ; beneath, ΕΠΙΦΑΝΟΥΣ / ΔΙΟΝΥΣΟΥ; beneath horses, Seleukid date ΟΡ (=170=143/2 B.C.); in field to r., ΤΡΥ / Φ / ΣΤΑ; all within wreath. *Newell (S.M.A.)* 244. *B.M.C. 4.* 63, 6 .. .. £600

7073   7074

7073 — Æ *drachm* (*c.* 4 gm.). *Obv.* Similar, but with dotted border. ℞. Naked Apollo seated l. on omphalos, holding arrow and resting on bow; on r., ΒΑΣΙΛΕΩΣ / ΑΝΤΙΟΧΟΥ; on l., ΕΠΙΦΑΝΟΥΣ / ΔΙΟΝΥΣΟΥ; monogram between Apollo's feet; in ex., Seleukid date ΟΡ, as last, and ΣΤΑ. *Newell (S.M.A.)* 248. *B.M.C. 4.* 64, 11 .. .. £75

7074 — — *Obv.* As last. ℞. Spiked Macedonian helmet r., ornamented with ibex-horn; legend as last; in field above, ΤΡΥ; beneath, monogram. *Newell (S.M.A.)* 259. *B.M.C. 4.* 65, 20 .. .. £125

7075 — Æ *hemidrachm* (*c.* 2 gm.). *Obv.* As last. ℞. ΒΑΣΙΛΕΩΣ / ΑΝΤΙΟΧΟΥ either side of naked Apollo stg. l., holding arrow and resting on bow. *Newell (S.M.A.)* 251. *B.M.C. 4.* 64, 15 .. .. £100

7076 — — — — ℞. Panther l., holding palm-branch; legend as 7072; in field above, ΣΤΑ. *Newell (S.M.A.)* 255. *B.M.C. 4.* 64, 16-18 .. .. £125

7077 — Æ *diobol* (*c.* 1·25 gm.). *Obv.* As 7073. ℞. Thyrsos; legend as 7073; in field, ΣΤΑ. *Newell (S.M.A.)* 256. *B.M.C. 4.* 64, 19 .. .. £95

Antiochos VI *continued*

7078 — Æ 21. Rad. hd. of the child-king r. ℞. Dionysos stg. l., holding kantharos and thyrsos; legend as 7073; in ex., ΔΙ. *B.M.C. 4.* 65, 24 .. .. £15

7079 — Æ 19. *Obv.* Similar. ℞. Amphora; legend as 7073; palm in field to r., ΑΒ monogram below. *B.M.C. 4.* 65, 25 .. .. £10

7080   7081

7080 — Æ 17. Forepart of panther leaping r. ℞. ΒΑΣΙΛΕΩΣ / ΑΝΤΙΟΧΟΥ / ΕΠΙΦΑΝΟΥΣ / ΔΙΟΝΥΣΟΥ in four lines within ivy-wreath. *B.M.C. 4.* 67, 50 .. .. .. £15

7081 — Æ 21 (serrated edge). Hd. of Antiochos, as Dionysos, r., rad. and wreathed with ivy. ℞. Elephant advancing l., holding torch with his trunk; legend as 7072; in field to r., ΣΤΑ and cornucopiae. *B.M.C. 4.* 67, 45 .. .. £12

7082 — Æ 20 (serrated edge). *Obv.* As 7078. ℞. Naked Apollo stg. l., holding arrow and resting l. arm on tripod; legend as 7073. *B.M.C. 4.* 66, 39 .. .. .. £14

7083 — Æ 18 (serrated edge). *Obv.* As 7078. ℞. Panther l., holding palm-branch; legend as 7072; in field to r., ΣΤΑ above cornucopiae. *B.M.C. 4.* 66, 35-7 .. .. £13

7084 — Æ 17 (serrated edge). *Obv.* As 7078. ℞. Nike stg. l., holding wreath and palm; legend as 7073. *B.M.C. 4.* 66, 41.. .. .. £12

7085 **Tryphon,** 142-138 B.C. (having disposed of the child Antiochos VI, Diodotos proclaimed himself king under the name of Tryphon and with the remarkable title 'Autokrator'. After a reign of four years he was overthrown by Antiochos VII, younger brother of Demetrios II). Æ *tetradrachm* (*c.* 16·75 gm.). His diad. hd. r.; fillet border. ℞. Spiked Macedonian helmet l., ornamented with ibex-horn; on r., ΒΑΣΙΛΕΩΣ / ΤΡΥΦΩΝΟΣ; on l., ΑΥΤΟΚΡΑΤΟΡΟΣ; all within oak-wreath. *Newell (S.M.A.)* 263. *B.M.C. 4.* 68, 2
£2,000

7086 — — (Phoenician standard, *c.* 13.5 gm.), mint of *Ptolemais.* His diad. hd. r. ℞. Eagle stg. l. on thunderbolt, ear of corn in background; behind, ΒΑΣΙΛΕΩΣ; before, ΤΡΥΦΩΝΟΣ / ΑΥΤΟΚΡΑΤΟΡΟΣ; in field to r., ΠΤΟ monogram and ΛΓ (=regnal year 3=140/39 B.C.); ΜΕ monogram between eagle's legs. *Babelon, pl.* XXI, 4 .. .. £1,500

7087 — Æ *didrachm* (Phoenician standard, *c.* 6·25 gm.), mint of *Askalon.* Similar, but on *rev.* no ear of corn; in field to r., regnal date ΛΓ, as last, and ΑΣ; to l., aplustre and ΣΩ monogram; nothing between eagle's legs. *B.M.C. 4.* 68, 1 .. .. .. £1,250

7088 — Æ *drachm* (*c.* 4 gm.). Similar to 7085, but dotted border on *obv.* and without oak-wreath on *rev.*; in *rev.* field to l., ΧΑΡ monogram. *B.M.C. 4.* 68, 4 .. .. £450

7089 — Æ 18. As last, but with star instead of monogram in *rev.* field to l. *B.M.C. 4.* 69, 12
£14

7090 — Æ 20 of *Askalon.* His diad. hd. r. ℞. Zeus stg. facing, hd. l., r. hand raised; on r.ʾ
ΒΑΣΙΛΕΩΣ; on l., ΤΡΥΦΩΝΟΣ / ΑΥΤΟΚΡΑΤΟΡΟΣ; in field to l., regnal date ΛΔ (=year 4=139/8
B.C.) and ΑΣΚ. *B.M.C. 4.* 69, 16 ..   ..   £20

7091 **Antiochos VII, Euergetes (Sidetes),** 138-129 B.C. (almost alone amongst the later
Seleukid monarchs, Antiochos VII ruled with competence and integrity. He was the
younger brother of Demetrios II, and following the latter's capture by the Parthians he
seized power and quickly disposed of the usurper Tryphon. He campaigned with success
in Palestine and Babylonia, but in 129 B.C. he was killed in battle against the Parthians).
Æ *tetradrachm* (*c.* 16·75 gm.). His diad. hd. r.; fillet border. ℞. Athena stg. l., holding
Nike, spear and shield; on r., ΒΑΣΙΛΕΩΣ / ΑΝΤΙΟΧΟΥ; on l., ΕΥΕΡΓΕΤΟΥ; in field to l., ΛΕ
and monogram; in ex., Seleukid date ΣΟΡ (=176=137/6 B.C.); all within laurel-wreath.
B.M.C. 4. 71, 13 ..   ..   £165

7092 — — Similar, but on *rev.* ΔΙ monogram and Α in field to l., ΜΔ monogram to r., nothing
in ex. *Newell* (*S.M.A.*) 283. *B.M.C. 4.* 71, 22..   ..   ..   ..   £150

7093   7094

7093 — — *Obv.* Similar. ℞. Pyre of Sandan, in the form of pyramidal structure, containing
figure of Sandan on lion, surmounting garlanded square basis; eagle perched on apex;
legend as 7091; in field to l., ΛΥ / ΜΕ. *B.M.C. 4.* 72, 37 ..   ..   ..   £650

7094 — — (Phoenician standard, *c.* 14.1 gm.), mint of *Tyre.* His diad. and dr. bust r. ℞.
ΑΝΤΙΟΧΟΥ ΒΑΣΙΛΕΩΣ. Eagle stg. l. on beak of galley, palm-branch in background; in field
to l., Α/ ΡΕ and ΤΥΡ monogram above club; to r., Α and ΣΥ monogram above Seleukid date
ΣΟΡ (=176=137/6 B.C.); ΓΗΡ monogram between eagle's legs. *B.M.C. 4.* 70, 5   £130

Antiochos VII *continued*

7095 — Æ *didrachm* (Phoenician standard, *c.* 7·05 gm.), mint of *Tyre*.   Similar, but with Seleukid date SOP, as 7091, on *rev.*   *B.M.C. 4.* 70, 6   ..   ..   £150

7096   7098

7096 — Æ *drachm* (*c.* 4·1 gm.).   *Obv.* As 7091.   R. Nike advancing l., holding wreath and supporting fold of dress; legend as 7091; in field to l., HP monogram above Δ.   *B.M.C. 4.* 73, 44   ..   ..   £50

7097 — Æ 22.   Prow of galley r.   R. Trident; on r., ΒΑΣΙΛΕΩΣ / ΑΝΤΙΟΧΟΥ; on l., ΕΥΕΡΓΕΤΟΥ; MH monogram in field to l.; Seleukid date ΔΟΡ (=174=138 B.C.) beneath.   *B.M.C. 4.* 73, 46   ..   ..   £15

7098 — Æ 18.   Winged bust of Eros r., wreathed with myrtle.   R. Head-dress of Isis; legend as last; beneath, crescent and Seleukid date ΔΟΡ, as last.   *B.M.C. 4.* 73, 49   £8

7099 — — Hd. of Athena r., in crested Corinthian helmet.   R. Tripod; legend as 7097; beneath, Seleukid date ΒΠΡ, as 7094.   *B.M.C. 4.* 74, 63..   ..   ..   ..   £10

7100   7101

7100 — Æ 15.   Lion's hd. r.   R. Club; legend as 7097; in field to l., ΔΙ monogram and aplustre; beneath, Seleukid date ΕΟΡ (=175=138/7 B.C.).   *B.M.C. 4.* 75, 67 ..   £10

7101 — Æ 14 of *Jerusalem*.   Lily.   R. Anchor; legend as 7097.   *B.M.C. 4.* 75, 69   £15

These were issued in connection with Antiochos' campaign in Judaea during which he captured Jerusalem, circa 132 B.C.   The first coins of the Hasmonaean dynasty, issued by Alexander Jannaeus (103-76 B.C.) were based on this coinage of Antiochos VII — see no. 6086.

7102 **Demetrios II, Nikator,** second reign, 129-125 B.C. (Antiochos VII's elder brother, Demetrios II, was released from captivity by the Parthians in 129 B.C.   His arrival at Antioch coincided with the death of Antiochos in battle, and he resumed his former place as King of Syria.   Following an abortive attack on Ptolemaic Egypt he lost the northern part of his Kingdom to the usurper Alexander Zebina, and in 125 B.C. he was murdered at Tyre).   Æ *tetradrachm* (*c.* 16·5 gm.).   His diad. hd. r., bearded; fillet border.   R. Zeus enthroned l., holding Nike and sceptre; on r., ΒΑΣΙΛΕΩΣ / ΔΗΜΗΤΡΙΟΥ; on l., ΘΕΟΥ / ΝΙΚΑΤΟΡΟΣ; in field to l., Ξ; beneath throne, Δ.   *Newell* (*S.M.A.*) 321.   *B.M.C. 4.* 77, 18   £350

7103 — — Similar, but on *rev.*   Δ Ω beneath throne, and Seleukid date SΠΡ (=186=127/6 B.C.) in ex.; nothing in field to l.   *B.M.C. 4.* 77, 15   ..   ..   £375

7104 — — *Obv.* Similar. ℞. Pyre of Sandan, as 7093; legend as 7102; two monograms in field to l. *B.M.C. 4.* 78, 22   ..   ..   £900

7105   7108

7105 — — (Phoenician standard, *c.* 14·2 gm.), mint of *Tyre.* His diad. and dr. bust r., beardless. ℞. ΔΗΜΗΤΡΙΟΥ ΒΑΣΙΛΕΩΣ. Eagle stg. l. on beak of galley, palm-branch in background; in field to l., A / PE and TYP monogram above club; to r., A and ΣΥ monogram above Seleukid date ΕΠΡ (=185=128/7 B.C.); ΓΗΡ monogram between eagle's legs. *B.M.C. 4.* 76, 6   ..   ..   £120

7106 — Æ *didrachm* (Phoenician standard, *c.* 7 gm.), mint of *Tyre.* Similar, but with Seleukid date ΓΠΡ (=183=129 B.C.) on *rev.* *B.M.C. 4.* 76, 2   ..   ..   £140

7107 — Æ *drachm* (*c.* 3·9 gm.). Similar to 7102, but without letters in field and beneath throne. *Newell (S.M.A.)* 324. *B.M.C. 4.* 77, 19-20 ..   ..   £120

7108 — — *Obv.* As 7102. ℞. Sandan stg. r. on horned lion, r. hand raised, holding double-axe in l.; legend as 7102; two monograms in field to l. *B.M.C. 4.* 78, 23   ..   £250

7109 — — — ℞. Cultus-statue of Athena Magarsis facing, holding spear, star either side of neck; legend as 7102; in lower field to l., ΕΡ; to r., ΕΤ monogram. *B.M.C. 4.* 77, 21   £300

7110 — Æ 20. His diad. hd. r., beardless. ℞. Male figure in Parthian attire stg. r., holding cornucopiae and clasping hands with City-goddess stg. l., also holding cornucopiae; on r., ΔΗΜΗΤΡΙΟΥ; on l., ΝΙΚΑΤΟΡΟΣ; in field, ΗΓ / ΕΥ. *B.M.C. 4.* 78, 25   ..   ..   £18

7111 — Æ 18. *Obv.* Similar, but bearded. ℞. Naked Apollo stg. l., holding arrow and bow, quiver at shoulder; on r., ΔΗΜΗΤΡΙΟΥ; on l., ΘΕΟΥ / ΝΙΚΑΤΟΡΟΣ. *B.M.C. 4.* 78, 26   £15

7112 — — Laur. hd. of Zeus r. ℞. Nike advancing l., holding wreath and palm; legend as 7102; in field to l., bunch of grapes and Ξ. *B.M.C. 4.* 79, 2-3 ..   ..   ..   £12

7113   7114

7113 — Æ 19 of *Sidon.* His diad. and dr. bust r., beardless. ℞. City-goddess of Sidon stg. l. on prow of galley, holding aplustre and stylis; on l., ΣΙΔΩΝΟΣ / ΘΕΑΣ; on r., Phoenician legend; in field to r., Seleukid date ΔΠΡ (=184=129/8 B.C.). *B.M.C. 4.* 79, 28   £14

7114 **Alexander II (Zebina),** 128-123 B.C. (claiming to be an adopted son of Alexander Balas, Zebina rebelled against Demetrios II with the backing of Ptolemy VIII of Egypt. Five years later he was defeated by the forces of Cleopatra and her son Antiochos VIII). Æ *stater* (*c.* 8·66 gm.). His diad. hd. r.; fillet border. ℞. Zeus enthroned l., holding Nike and sceptre; on r., ΒΑΣΙΛΕΩΣ / ΑΛΕΞΑΝΔΡΟΥ; on l., ΘΕΟΥ / ΕΠΙΦΑΝΟΥΣ; in ex., ΝΙΚΗΦΟΡΟΥ. *Newell (S.M.A.)* 358   ..   ..   (*Unique*)

This remarkable issue was probably struck from the metal obtained by the melting-down of the gold Nike held by the statue of Zeus at Daphne.

Alexander II (Zebina) *continued*

7115 — Æ *tetradrachm* (*c.* 16·75 gm.). Similar, but on *rev.* the legend is ΒΑΣΙΛΕΩΣ, on r., ΑΛΕΞΑΝΔΡΟΥ, on l.; in field to l., ΗΡΔ monogram; beneath throne, Δ. *Newell* (*S.M.A.*) 339. *B.M.C.* 4. 81, 4　　..　　..　　..　　..　　..　　..　　..　£200

7116 — — *Obv.* Similar. ℞. Pyre of Sandan, in the form of pyramidal structure, containing figure of Sandan on lion, surmounting garlanded square basis; eagle perched on apex; on r., ΒΑΣΙΛΕΩΣ; on l., ΑΛΕΞΑΝΔΡΟΥ; two monograms in field to l. *Historia Numorum, p.* 769
　　　　£750

7117 — Æ *didrachm* (Phoenician standard, *c.* 6·82 gm.), mint of *Askalon*. His diad. hd. r. ℞. ΑΛΕΞΑΝΔΡΟΥ ΒΑΣΙΛΕΩΣ. Eagle stg. l. on thunderbolt, palm-branch in background; in field to l., ΑΣ and dove; to r., Seleukid date ΣΠΡ (= 187 = 126/5 B.C.). *Babelon, p.* cl, *fig.* 35
　　　　£250

7118　　　　　　　　　　　7119

7118 — Æ *drachm* (*c.* 4 gm.). *Obv.* As 7114. ℞. Athena stg. l., holding Nike, spear and shield; on r., ΒΑΣΙΛΕΩΣ; on l., ΑΛΕΞΑΝΔΡΟΥ; in field to l., ΠΑΡ monogram above Α. *Newell* (*S.M.A.*) 336. *B.M.C.* 4. 81, 5　..　　..　　..　　..　　..　　..　£90

7119 — — His diad. hd r.; dotted border. ℞. Double-cornucopiae, bound with diadem; legend as last; in field to l., Ξ above ΑΦ. *Newell* (*S.M.A.*) 351. *B.M.C.* 4. 82, 7　£75

7120 — — His diad. hd. r. ℞. Sandan stg. r. on horned lion, r. hand raised, holding double-axe in l.; legend as 7118; ΝΕ monogram in field to l., club to r. *Babelon, pl.* XXIII, 6
　　　　£250

7121 — — (Phoenician standard, *c.* 3·4 gm.), mint of *Askalon*. Similar to 7117, but with Seleukid date ΘΠΡ (= 189 = 124/3 B.C.) on *rev.* *B.M.C.* 4. 81, 1　..　　..　£150

7122 — Æ *hemidrachm* (*c.* 2 gm.). His diad. hd. r. ℞. Nike advancing l., holding wreath and palm; on r., ΒΑΣΙΛΕΩΣ; on l., ΑΛΕΞΑΝΔΡΟΥ; in field to l., Ξ above ΑΦ. *Newell* (*S.M.A.*) 352. *B.M.C.* 4. 82, 10-11　　..　　..　　..　　..　　..　　..　£100

7123 — — *Obv.* Similar. ℞. Single cornucopiae; legend as last; in field to l., ΠΑ monogram above Σ. *Newell* (*S.M.A.*) 337　..　　..　　..　　..　　..　　..　£110

7124 — Æ *diobol* (*c.* 1·25 gm.). *Obv.* Similar. ℞. ΒΑΣΙΛΕΩΣ / ΑΛΕΞΑΝΔΡΟΥ either side of anchor. *Newell* (*S.M.A.*) 338　..　　..　　..　　..　　..　　..　£90

7125　　　　　　　　　　　7127

7125 — Æ 21. His diad. hd. r. R. ΒΑΣΙΛΕΩΣ / ΑΛΕΞΑΝΔΡΟΥ either side of young Dionysos stg. l., holding kantharos and thyrsos; in field to l., Σ and Seleukid date ΕΠΡ (= 185 = 128/7 B.C.). *B.M.C. 4.* 82, 16 .. .. £12

7126 — — His rad. hd. r. R. ΒΑΣΙΛΕΩΣ / ΑΛΕΞΑΝΔΡΟΥ either side of Athena stg. l., holding Nike, spear and shield; in field to l., ΕΥ monogram and aplustre. *B.M.C. 4.* 83, 17 £10

7127 — — — R. Same legend, either side of double-cornucopiae bound with diadem; in field to l., Α above palm; to r., Π. *B.M.C. 4.* 83, 22 .. .. £11

7128 — — His hd. r., clad in lion's skin. R. Same legend, either side of Nike advancing l., holding wreath and palm; in field to l., ΗΡΔ monogram above wreath. *B.M.C. 4.* 83, 27 £6

7129 — Æ 18. Prow of galley r., surmounted by caps of the Dioskouroi. R. Same legend, either side of tripod; in field to l., Α above quiver; to r., Π. *B.M.C. 4.* 84, 31.. £13

7130 — Æ 17. His hd. r., clad in elephant's skin. R. Same legend, either side of aplustre; in field to l., monogram above ear of corn. *B.M.C. 4.* 83, 28 .. .. .. £14

7131 — — His hd. r., in Corinthian helmet. R. Same legend, either side of tripod; star in ex. *B.M.C. 4.* 84, 29 .. .. £11

7132 — Æ 15. Winged bust of Eros r., wreathed with myrtle. R. As 7124; in field to l., Σ and Seleukid date ΔΠΡ (= 184 = 128 B.C.). *B.M.C. 4.* 84, 30 .. .. .. £10

7133 — Æ 19 (serrated edge). Hd. of young Dionysos r., wreathed with ivy. R. ΒΑΣΙΛΕΩΣ / ΑΛΕΞΑΝΔΡΟΥ either side of Tyche stg. l., holding rudder and cornucopiae; in field to l., monogram and aplustre. *B.M.C. 4.* 84, 34 .. .. £8

Seleukos V, 125 B.C. (on the death of Demetrios II his elder son, Seleukos, claimed the throne. However, his mother, Cleopatra, wanted the supreme power for herself and the unfortunate young man was murdered. It is doubtful if any coins were struck bearing his name).

7134 **Cleopatra,** 125 B.C. (this extraordinary woman was the daughter of Ptolemy VI of Egypt. She married, in succession, three of the Seleukid monarchs — Alexander Balas, Demetrios II and Antiochos VII — bearing a total of eight children by them. Having disposed of her son Seleukos V she reigned alone for a short while until public opinion forced her to acknowledge Seleukos' younger brother, Antiochos, as her colleague in the government). Æ *tetradrachm* (c. 16·65 gm.). Her veiled and diad. bust r.; fillet border. R. Double-cornucopiae, bound with diadem; on r., ΒΑΣΙΛΙΣΣΗΣ / ΚΛΕΟΠΑΤΡΑΣ; on l., ΘΕΑΣ / ΕΥΕΤΗΡΙΑΣ; in field to r., ΣΥ monogram; beneath, on l., Seleukid date ΙΠΡ (= 187 = 125 B.C.). *B.M.C. 4.* 85, 1 .. .. £10,000

7135 **Cleopatra and Antiochos VIII,** 125-121 B.C. (the uneasy joint reign of mother and son lasted just four years, until Cleopatra was obliged to drink a cup of poisoned wine which she had prepared for the king). AR *tetradrachm* (*c.* 16·65 gm.). Their conjoined hds. r., Cleopatra veiled and diad., her son diad.; fillet border. ℞. Zeus enthroned l., holding Nike and sceptre; on r., ΒΑΣΙΛΙΣΣΗΣ / ΚΛΕΟΠΑΤΡΑΣ / ΘΕΑΣ; on l., ΚΑΙ / ΒΑΣΙΛΕΩΣ / ΑΝΤΙΟΧΟΥ; monograms in field to l. and beneath throne; in ex., Seleukid date ΑϘΡ (=191= 122/1 B.C.). *B.M.C. 4.* 86, 3, *var.* £350

7136 — — Similar, but with border of dots on *obv.* and without ΘΕΑΣ on *rev.*; in *rev.* field to l., ΙΕ; beneath throne, Δ; nothing in ex. *Newell* (*S.M.A.*) 360. *B.M.C. 4.* 86, 5 £375

7137

7139

7137 — — (Phoenician standard, *c.* 14 gm.). *Obv.* As last. ℞. Eagle stg. l. on thunderbolt; behind, ΒΑΣΙΛΙΣΣΗΣ / ΚΛΕΟΠΑΤΡΑΣ; before, ΒΑΣΙΛΕΩΣ / ΑΝΤΙΟΧΟΥ; in field to l., ΣΥ monogram; to r., Seleukid date ΒϘΡ (=192=121 B.C.). *B.M.C. 4.* 85, 1 .. .. £500

7138 — Æ 21. *Obv.* As last. ℞. Nike advancing l., holding wreath; legend as 7135; in field to l., Η; beneath, star. *B.M.C. 4.* 86, 7 .. .. £18

7139 — Æ 19. Rad. hd. of Antiochos r. ℞. Owl stg. r., hd. facing, on prostrate amphora; on r., ΒΑΣΙΛΙΣΣΗΣ / ΚΛΕΟΠΑΤΡΑΣ; on l., ΚΑΙ / ΒΑΣΙΛΕΩΣ / ΑΝΤΙΟΧΟΥ; in field to r., ΙΕ; in ex., Seleukid date ϘΡ (=190=123/2 B.C.) and palm. *B.M.C. 4.* 87, 10 .. .. £10

7140 — Æ 18. *Obv.* Similar. ℞. Head-dress of Isis; legend as last; in field to r., ΣΥ monogram; beneath, Seleukid date ΘΠΡ (=189=124/3 B.C.). *B.M.C. 4.* 86, 9 .. £14

7141 — Æ 17. Hd. of Artemis (?) r., surmounted by kalathos. ℞. Handle of rudder; legend as last; in field to l., Seleukid date ΑϘΡ (=year 191=122/1 B.C.); beneath, aplustre. *B.M.C. 4.* 87, 16 .. .. £12

7142

7142 **Antiochos VIII (Grypos),** 121-96 B.C. (this undistinguished son of Demetrios II, having disposed of his mother in 121 B.C. embarked on an inglorious reign of a quarter of a century. For much of this time he was at war with his half-brother, Antiochos IX, and this disastrous period witnessed the final decline of the once-mighty Seleukid realm into a minor east Mediterranean state). Æ *tetradrachm* (*c.* 16·5 gm.). His diad. hd. r.; fillet border. R. Athena stg. l., holding Nike, spear and shield; on r., ΒΑΣΙΛΕΩΣ / ΑΝΤΙΟΧΟΥ; on l., ΕΠΙΦΑΝΟΥΣ; in field to l., ΙΕ / Θ; all within laurel-wreath. *Newell* (*S.M.A.*) 362. *B.M.C. 4.* 89, 17 .. .. £300

7143 — — *Obv.* Similar. R. Zeus stg. l., crescent on hd., holding star and sceptre; legend as last; in field to l., ΙΕ / Α; to r., ΑΙ; in ex., Κ; all within laurel-wreath. *Newell* (*S.M.A.*) 371. *B.M.C. 4.* 88, 9 .. .. £140

7144 — — mint of *Sidon.* As last, but in *rev.* field to l., ΣΙΔΩ / ΙΕΡ / ΑΣΥ and monogram; and in ex., Seleukid date ϚϘΡ (=116/15 B.C.); nothing to r. *B.M.C. 4.* 88, 8 .. £175

7145 7149

7145 — — *Obv.* As 7142. R. Zeus enthroned l., holding Nike and sceptre; legend as 7142; in field to l., ΕΡ monogram above Α; beneath throne, ΔΙ monogram; all within laurel-wreath. *Newell* (*S.M.A.*) 405. *B.M.C. 4.* 98, 2 .. .. £115

7146 — — — R. Pyre of Sandan, in the form of pyramidal structure, containing figure of Sandan on lion, surmounting garlanded square basis; eagle perched on apex; legend as 7142; two monograms in field to l. *B.M.C. 4.* 89, 22 .. .. £450

7147 — — (Phoenician standard, *c.* 14 gm.), mint of *Askalon.* His diad. and dr. bust r. R. ΑΝΤΙΟΧΟΥ ΒΑΣΙΛΕΩΣ. Eagle stg. l. on thunderbolt, palm-branch in background; in field to l., ΑΣ and dove; to r., Seleukid date ΓϚΡ (=193=120/19 B.C.); between eagle's legs, ΠΤΟ monogram. *B.M.C. 4.* 88, 1 .. .. £350

7148 — Æ *didrachm* (Phoenician standard, *c.* 6·85 gm.). Similar, but without palm-branch on *rev.*; and in field to l., ΜΥ monogram; to r., Seleukid date ϚϘΡ (=197=116/15 B.C.); nothing between eagle's legs. *Babelon, pl.* XXIV, 14 .. .. £250

7149 — Æ *drachm* (*c.* 4 gm.). His diad. hd. r.; dotted border. R. Tripod-lebes, surmounted by holmos and laurel-twigs; on r., ΒΑΣΙΛΕΩΣ / ΑΝΤΙΟΧΟΥ; on l., ΕΠΙΦΑΝΟΥΣ; in field to l., ΕΡ monogram above Α. *Newell* (*S.M.A.*) 409. *B.M.C. 4.* 98, 6 .. .. £75

7150 — — *Obv.* Similar, but fillet border. R. Sandan stg. r. on horned lion, r. hand raised, holding double-axe in l.; on r., ΒΑΣΙΛΕΩΣ; on l., ΑΝΤΙΟΧΟΥ; ΠΑ monogram in field to l. *Babelon, pl.* XXV, 6 .. .. £250

Antiochos VIII *continued*

7151 — Æ *hemidrachm* (*c.* 2 gm.). *Obv.* As 7149. ℞. Nike advancing l., holding wreath; legend as 7149; in field to l., ΦΙΛ monogram above Γ. *Newell* (*S.M.A.*) 393. *B.M.C. 4.* 98, 9 .. .. £100

7152 — Æ *diobol* (*c.* 1·25 gm.). *Obv.* As 7149. ℞. Ear of corn on stalk; legend as 7149; in field to l., ΦΙΛ monogram above Α. *Newell* (*S.M.A.*) 395 .. .. .. £90

7153   7154

7153 — Æ 21. His diad. hd. r. ℞. Double cornucopiae, bound with diadem; on r., ΒΑΣΙΛΕΩΣ/ ΑΝΤΙΟΧΟΥ; on l., ΕΠΙΦΑΝΟΥΣ; in field to l., ΕΡ monogram above star. *B.M.C. 4.* 99, 11 £14

7154 — Æ 19. His rad. hd. r. ℞. Eagle stg. l., sceptre in background; legend as last; in field to l., ΙΕ; in ex., Seleukid date ΒϞΡ (=192=121/20 B.C.) and palm. *B.M.C. 4.* 90, 27 £9

7155 — — Similar, but on *rev.* the king's title is ΦΙΛΟΜΗΤΟΡΟΣ instead of ΕΠΙΦΑΝΟΥΣ; monogram in field to l.; in ex., Seleukid date ΒΣ (=202=111/10 B.C.). *Hunter Catalogue, pl.* LXX, 2 .. .. £18

7156 — — His diad. hd. r. ℞. Tripod surmounted by thunderbolt; legend as 7153; in field to l., ΦΙΛ monogram. *B.M.C. 4.* 99, 14 .. .. £12

7157 — Æ 16. *Obv.* Similar. ℞. Tyche stg. l., holding rudder and cornucopiae; legend as 7153; in field to l., ΕΡ monogram. *Babelon, pl.* XXV, 14 .. .. .. £10

7158 — Æ 15. Bust of Artemis r., bow and quiver at shoulder. ℞. Naked Apollo stg. l., holding arrow and resting on bow; legend as 7153; in field to l., ΙΕ; in ex., Seleukid date ΣϞΡ (=196=117/16 B.C.) and star. *Babelon, pl.* XXIV, 13 .. .. .. £11

7159 — Æ 13. His diad. hd. r. ℞. Rose; legend as 7153; in field to l., ΕΡ monogram. *Babelon, pl.* XXV, 15 .. .. £10

7160 **Antiochos IX (Kyzikenos),** 113-95 B.C. (son of Antiochos VII and Cleopatra, Antiochos Kyzikenos claimed a share of his half-brother's kingdom, and captured Antioch in 113 B.C. The struggle continued for many years, gravely weakening the Seleukid state, and was only finally resolved by the murder of Antiochos VIII in 96 B.C. Antiochos IX perished the following year at the hands of his nephew, Seleukos VI). Æ *tetradrachm* (*c.* 16·5 gm.). His diad. hd. r.; fillet border. ℞. Athena stg. l., holding Nike, spear and shield; on r., ΒΑΣΙΛΕΩΣ / ΑΝΤΙΟΧΟΥ; on l., ΦΙΛΟΠΑΤΟΡΟΣ; in field to l., ΔΙΟ monogram above Α; to r., Ο; all within laurel-wreath. *Newell* (*S.M.A.*) 396. *B.M.C. 4.* 92, 11 .. .. £150

7161 — — mint of *Sidon.* Similar, but in *rev.* field to l., ΣΙΔΩ / ΙΕΡ / ΑΣΥ and ΣΕ monogram; in ex., Seleukid date Σ (=200=113/12 B.C.); nothing to r. *B.M.C. 4.* 92, 6 .. £175

7162 — — *Obv.* Similar. ℞. Zeus enthroned l., holding Nike and sceptre; legend as 7160; in field to l., Ε / Λ / Α and Η; beneath throne, ΔΙ monogram; all within laurel-wreath. *Newell* (*S.M.A.*) 415. *B.M.C. 4.* 91, 5 .. .. £300

7163 — — — R. Pyre of Sandan, as 7146; legend as 7160; two monograms in field to l. *Babelon, pl.* XXVI, 12 .. .. £500

7164 — — (Phoenician standard, *c.* 13·9 gm.), mint of *Sidon*. His diad. and dr. bust r. R. ANTIOXOY BAΣIΛEΩΣ. Eagle stg. l. on beak of galley, palm-branch in background; in field to l., Seleukid date Σ, as 7161, ΣE monogram and aplustre; to r., ΣIΛΩ / IEP / AΣ̄Y *B.M.C.* 4. 91, 1 .. .. £350

7165 — Æ *didrachm* (Phoenician standard, *c.* 6·9 gm.), mint of *Askalon*. Similar, but on *rev.* eagle stands on thunderbolt; in field to l., AΣ / IEP and dove; to r., AΣY and Seleukid date LΛΣ(= 204 = 109/8 B.C.); between eagle's legs, MY monogram. *B.M.C.* 4. 91, 3 £250

7166 — Æ *drachm* (*c.* 4 gm.). His diad. hd. r. R. Tyche stg. l., holding rudder and cornucopiae; legend as 7160; in field to l., Ξ / A / Π. *B.M.C.* 4. 92, 15 .. .. £150

7167 — — *Obv.* As 7160. R. Sandan stg. r. on horned lion, r. hand raised, holding double-axe in l.; legend as 7160; two monograms in field to l. *Babelon, pl.* XXVI, 13 £250

7168 — Æ *hemidrachm* (*c.* 2 gm.). His diad. hd. r. R. Nike advancing l., holding wreath; legend as 7160; in field to l., EA monogram. *Newell* (*S.M.A.*) 420. *Babelon, pl.* XXVI, 11 £100

7169 7170

7169 — Æ 22. His diad. hd. r. R. Dionysos stg. l., holding kantharos and thyrsos; on r., BAΣIΛEΩΣ / ANTIOXOY; on l., ΦIΛOΠATOPOΣ; in field to l., E and NIK monogram. *B.M.C.* 4. 93, 22 .. .. £12

7170 — Æ 19. *Obv.* Similar. R. Winged thunderbolt; above, BAΣIΛEΩΣ / ANTIOXOY; beneath, ΦIΛOΠATOPOΣ; in field to l., ΠY monogram, aplustre and Seleukid date Θ4P (= 199 = 113 B.C.). *B.M.C.* 4. 92, 16 .. .. £10

7171 — — — R. Zeus enthroned l., holding Nike and sceptre; legend as 7169; in field to l., EA monogram and star. *B.M.C.* 4. 93, 20 .. .. £11

7172 — — Laur. hd. of bearded Herakles r. R. Athena stg. l., holding Nike, spear and shield; legend as 7169; in field to l., ΔIO monogram and aplustre; in ex., Seleukid date EΣ (= 205 = 108/7 B.C.). *B.M.C.* 4. 93, 25 .. .. £13

7173　　　　　　　　　　　　　　7176

Antiochos IX *continued*

7173 — — Winged bust of Eros r. ℞. Nike advancing l., holding wreath; legend as 7169; in field to l., Seleukid date ΑΣ (=201 = 112/11 B.C.). *B.M.C. 4.* 94, 27　　..　　£12

7174 — Æ 17. Diad. hd. of Zeus r. ℞. Tyche stg. l., holding rudder and cornucopiae; legend as 7169. *B.M.C. 4.* 93, 26..　..　　..　　..　　..　　..　　£11

7175 — Æ 15. Hd. of Athena r., in crested helmet. ℞. Prow of galley r.; legend as 7170. *B.M.C. 4.* 94, 32-4 ..　　..　　..　　..　　..　　..　　..　　£11

7176 **Seleukos VI, Epiphanes Nikator,** 95-94 B.C. (eldest son of Antiochos VIII, Seleukos attacked and defeated his uncle Antiochos IX in 95 B.C., but was himself driven from Antioch the following year by his cousin Antiochos X). *Æ tetradrachm* (*c.* 16·2 gm.). His diad. hd. r.; fillet border. ℞. Zeus enthroned l., holding Nike and sceptre; on r., ΒΑΣΙΛΕΩΣ / ΣΕΛΕΥΚΟΥ; on l., ΕΠΙΦΑΝΟΥΣ / ΝΙΚΑΤΟΡΟΣ; in field to l., ΚΡ monogram above Α; beneath throne, C; all within laurel-wreath. *Newell* (*S.M.A.*) 424　　..　　..　　£200

7177　　　　　　　　　　　　7179

7177 — — *Obv.* Similar. ℞. Athena stg. l., holding Nike, spear and shield; legend as last; in field to l., palm-branch, monogram and ΖΗ. *B.M.C. 4.* 95, 4　　..　　..　　£450

7178 — *Æ drachm* (*c.* 3·85 gm.). ℞. Nike advancing l., holding wreath; on r., ΒΑΣΙΛΕΩΣ / ΣΕΛΕΥΚΟΥ; on l., ΝΙΚΑΤΟΡΟΣ; in field to l., ΚΡ monogram above Α, and C. *Newell* (*S.M.A.*) 427. *Babelon, pl.* XXVII, 3 ..　　..　　..　　£150

7179 — *Æ hemidrachm* (*c.* 1·95 gm.). *Obv.* Similar. ℞. Double cornucopiae, bound with diadem; legend as 7176; in field to l., ΚΡ monogram; beneath, C. *Newell* (*S.M.A.*) 428. *B.M.C. 4.* 95, 5-6 ..　　..　　..　　..　　..　　..　　£120

7180 — Æ 22. *Obv.* Similar. ℞. Naked Apollo stg. l., holding lyre (?) and resting on column; legend as 7176; in field to l., ΚΡ monogram and Α. *B.M.C. 4.* 96, 7 ..　　£16

7181 — Æ 15. His diad. hd. r. ℞. Tripod; legend as 7176; in field to l., ΚΡ monogram and Α; in ex., star. *B.M.C. 4.* 96, 8　　..　　..　　..　　..　　..　　..　　£12

7182　　　　　　　　　　　　　7185

7182 **Antiochos X, Eusebes Philopator,** 94-83 B.C. (son of Antiochos IX, he avenged his father by defeating Seleukos VI in 94 B.C. The rest of his troubled reign was spent in almost continuous warfare with Seleukos' brothers and for a while he had to seek refuge in Parthia). Æ *tetradrachm* (*c.* 15·5 - 16 gm.). His diad. hd. r.; fillet border. ℞. Zeus enthroned l., holding Nike and sceptre; on r., ΒΑΣΙΛΕΩΣ / ΑΝΤΙΟΧΟΥ; on l., ΕΥΣΕΒΟΥΣ / ΦΙΛΟΠΑΤΟΡΟΣ; in field to l., ΣΩ monogram above A; beneath throne, ΔΙ monogram; all within laurel-wreath. *Newell* (*S.M.A.*) 430. *B.M.C. 4.* 97, 2 .. .. £140

7183 — Æ *drachm* (*c.* 3·9 gm.). *Obv.* Similar, but with dotted border. ℞. Tyche stg. l., holding rudder and cornucopiae; legend as last; in field to l., ΣΩ monogram above A. *Newell* (*S.M.A.*) 431. *Babelon, pl.* XXVII, 8 .. .. £140

7184 — Æ *hemidrachm* (*c.* 1·95 gm.). *Obv.* As last. ℞. Nike stg. l., holding wreath and palm; legend as 7182; in field to l., ΣΩ monogram above A. *Newell* (*S.M.A.*) 432 .. £100

7185 — Æ 21. His diad. hd. r., bearded. ℞. Caps of the Dioskouroi; legend as 7182; in field to l., ΣΩ monogram. *B.M.C. 4.* 97, 3-4 .. .. £15

7186 — Æ 16. *Obv.* Similar. ℞. Nike advancing l., holding wreath; legend as 7182; in field to l., ΣΩ monogram. *Babelon, pl.* XXVII, 10 .. .. £12

7187 **Antiochos XI, Epiphanes Philadelphos,** 93 B.C. (son of Antiochos VIII, Antiochos XI and his brother Philip made war on their cousin, Antiochos X, to avenge their elder brother, Seleukos VI. Antiochos XI lost his life in battle but Philip survived to fight another day). Æ *tetradrachm* (*c.* 15·5 gm.). Conjoined diad. heads of Antiochos and his brother Philip r.; fillet border. ℞. Zeus enthroned l., holding Nike and sceptre; on r., ΒΑΣΙΛΕΩΣ / ΑΝΤΙΟΧΟΥ; on l., ΚΑΙ ΒΑΣΙΛΕΩΣ / ΦΙΛΙΠΠΟΥ; in field to l., C / Φ / ΙΕ / A; beneath throne, A; all within wreath. *Babelon, pl.* XXVII, 13 .. .. £2,500

7188 — — His diad. hd. r.; fillet border. ℞. Zeus enthroned, as last; on r., ΒΑΣΙΛΕΩΣ / ΑΝΤΙΟΧΟΥ; on l., ΕΠΙΦΑΝΟΥΣ / ΦΙΛΑΔΕΛΦΟΥ; in field to l., ΙΩ monogram above A; beneath throne, ΔΙ monogram; all within wreath. *Newell* (*S.M.A.*) 433 .. .. £1,250

7189 — Æ 20. *Obv.* Similar, but with dotted border. ℞. Athena stg. l., holding Nike, spear and shield; legend as last; in field to l., ΕΡ monogram. *B.M.C. 4.* 99, 15 £25

7190 **Demetrios III, Philopator,** 95-88 B.C. (another son of Antiochos VIII, Demetrios joined forces with his brother Philip to drive their cousin, Antiochos X, out of Syria. Later, the two brothers quarrelled and Demetrios was defeated, leaving Philip master of Antioch). Æ *tetradrachm* (*c.* 15·8 gm.). His diad. hd. r., bearded; fillet border. ℞. Zeus enthroned l., holding Nike and sceptre; on r., ΒΑΣΙΛΕΩΣ / ΔΗΜΗΤΡΙΟΥ / ΘΕΟΥ; on l., ΦΙΛΟΠΑΤΟΡΟΣ / ΣΩΤΗΡΟΣ; in field to l., N / A; beneath throne, ΔΙ monogram; all within wreath. *Newell* (*S.M.A.*) 435. *Babelon, pl.* XXVIII, 4 .. .. .. £350

7191   7192

Demetrios III *continued*

7191 — — *Obv.* Similar. ℞. Cultus-statue of Atargatis facing, holding flower in l. hand, ear of corn either side of hd.; legend as last; in field to l., N / Δ; in lower field to r., ΔH monogram; in ex., Seleukid date ΓΚΕ (=223=90/89 B.C.); all within wreath. *B.M.C. 4.* 101, 4
£600

This type was issued at Damaskos which, during this reign, bore the name of Demetrias in the king's honour.

7192 — Æ 20. His diad. hd. r., bearded. ℞. Thunderbolt; above, ΒΑΣΙΛΕΩΣ / ΔΗΜΗΤΡΙΟΥ / ΦΙΛΟΜΗΤΟΡΟΣ; beneath, ΕΥΕΡΓΕΤΟΥ / ΚΑΛΛΙΝΙΚΟΥ; Κ in lower field to r. *B.M.C. 4.* 101, 7
£15

7193 — — His rad. hd. r., bearded. ℞. Nike advancing l., holding wreath and palm; legend as 7190; in field to l., Δ and Σ; in ex., Seleukid date ΗΙΣ (=218=95/4 B.C.). *Babelon, pl.* XXVIII, 1 ..   ..   £16

7194 — Æ 18. *Obv.* Similar. ℞. Statue of naked Hermes stg. l. on pedestal, holding caduceus and palm; legend as 7190; monogram in field to l. *B.M.C. 4.* 101, 5 ..   £14

7195 — Æ 22 of *Demetrias (Damaskos).* His diad. hd. r., bearded. ℞. City-goddess seated l. on rock, river-god swimming at her feet; behind, ΔΗΜΗΤ / ΡΙΕΩΝ; before, ΤΗΣ / ΙΕΡΑΣ. *B.M.C. 20.* 289, 1 ..   ..   £22

7196   7197

7196 **Philip, Philadelphos,** 93-83 B.C. (son of Antiochos VIII, Philip gained possession of the capital in 88 B.C., as related above. After a troubled reign, during most of which he was at war with one or other of his relatives, he was eventually driven out of Syria by Tigranes, king of Armenia). Æ *tetradrachm* (*c.* 15·8 gm.). His diad. hd. r.; fillet border. ℞. Zeus enthroned l., holding Nike and sceptre; on r., ΒΑΣΙΛΕΩΣ / ΦΙΛΙΠΠΟΥ; on l., ΕΠΙΦΑΝΟΥΣ / ΦΙΛΑΔΕΛΦΟΥ; in field to l., Φ / Α and Ν; beneath throne, ΔΙ monogram; all within wreath. *Newell (S.M.A.)* 441. *B.M.C. 4.* 100, 10 ..   ..   £80

For similar coins in the name of this ruler, but struck posthumously after the constitution of the Roman province of Syria, see nos. 7214-15 *below. See also no.* 7187 *above.*

7197 **Antiochos XII, Dionysos,** 88-84 B.C. (the youngest of the five sons of Antiochos VIII, he succeeded his brother Demetrios III as ruler of Damaskos and the surrounding territory. He fought with his brother Philip, the ruler of Antioch, but eventually fell in battle against the Nabataean Arabs). Æ *tetradrachm* (*c.* 15·2 - 15·7 gm.). His diad. hd. r.; fillet border. ℞. Bearded statue of Hadad stg. facing on double basis, holding ear of corn, foreparts of two bulls at his feet; on r., ΒΑΣΙΛΕΩΣ / ΑΝΤΙΟΧΟΥ / ΕΠΙΦΑΝΟΥΣ; on l., ΦΙΛΟΠΑΤΟΡΟΣ / ΚΑΛΛΙΝΙΚΟΥ; in ex., ΠΤΟ monogram and Seleukid date ΣΚΕ (=226=87/6 B.C.); all within wreath. *Newell (Late Seleucid Mints in Ake-Ptolemais and Damascus)* 132 ..   £2,500

7198 — Æ 22. His diad. and dr. bust r. ℞. Zeus stg. l., holding Nike and sceptre; on r.,
ΒΑΣΙΛΕΩΣ / ΑΝΤΙΟΧΟΥ / ΔΙΟΝΥΣΟΥ; on l., ΕΠΙΦΑΝΟΥΣ / ΦΙΛΟΠΑΤΟΡΟΣ / ΚΑΛΛΙΝΙΚΟΥ; ΠΤΟ
monogram in ex. B.M.C. 4. 102, 5 .. ..   £22
7199 — Æ 21. Obv. Similar. ℞. Tyche stg. l., holding palm and cornucopiae; legend as
7197; monogram in field to l. B.M.C. 4. 102, 4 .. ..   £22

7200   7202

7200 — Æ 20. His diad. hd. r. ℞. Naked Apollo stg. l., holding palm and resting on tripod;
legend as 7197; monogram in field to l. B.M.C. 4. 102, 1 .. .. ..   £20
7201 — Æ 16. Obv. Similar. ℞. Nike advancing r., holding wreath and palm; legend as
7197. Babelon, pl. XXVIII, 14 .. ..   £18
7202 **Tigranes II of Armenia,** 83-69 B.C. (in 83 B.C. the Syrians, wearied by the endless
fratricidal wars of the Seleukids, called upon the King of Armenia to restore order in their
country. He defeated Philip and ruled the Syrian kingdom for the following fourteen
years, issuing coinage on the Seleukid pattern. Eventually he was driven out of Syria by
the Roman general Lucullus). Æ tetradrachm (c. 15·4 - 16·4 gm.). His dr. bust r.,
wearing Armenian tiara ornamented with star between eagles; fillet border. ℞. The
Tyche of Antioch seated r. on rock, holding palm, river-god Orontes swimming at her
feet; on r., ΒΑΣΙΛΕΩΣ; on l., ΤΙΓΡΑΝΟΥ; in field to l., Δ / Μ; to r., Η; all within wreath.
B.M.C. 4. 103, 2 .. ..   £450
7203 — — Similar, but on rev. pellet in field to r., ΣΩ monogram on rock (nothing in field to l.).
B.M.C. 4. 103, 7-8 .. ..   £400
7204 — — Obv. Similar. ℞. The Tyche of Antioch and river-god Orontes, as last; on r.,
ΒΑΣΙΛΕΩΣ; on l., ΒΑΣΙΛΕΩΝ / ΤΙΓΡΑΝΟΥ; in field above, ΗΛ; in ex., ΞΚ; all within wreath.
Babelon, pl. XXIX, 15 .. ..   £750

7205 — — — ℞. The Tyche of Damaskos seated l. on rock, r. hand extended, holding cornucopiae in l.; at her feet, river-god Chrysoras swimming; legend as 7202; in field to l.,
ΔΗ monogram / ΘΕ / ΟΣ and Α; in ex., Seleukid date ΒΜΣ (=242=71 / 70 B.C.); all within
wreath. B.M.C. 4. 103, 1 .. ..   £1,500
7206 — Æ drachm (c. 4·1 gm.). Obv. Similar, but with dotted border. ℞. As 7204, b ΕΛυτ
instead of ΗΛ in field above, and with Θ in field to r. (nothing in ex.). B.M.C. 4. 104, 13
£500

Tigranes II of Armenia *continued*

7207 — Æ 23. His dr. bust r., wearing Armenian tiara. ℞. As 7205, but in field to l., ΘЄ / οι (nothing in ex.). *B.M.C. 4*. 104, 10 .. .. £45

7208 — Æ 22. *Obv.* Similar. ℞. As 7204, but without letters in field or in ex. *B.M.C. 4*. 105, 17 .. .. £35

7209 — Æ 19. *Obv.* Similar. ℞. Naked Herakles stg. l., holding club and lion's skin; legend as 7204. *B.M.C. 4*. 105, 18 .. .. £30

7210 — Æ 18. *Obv.* Similar. ℞. Palm-branch between ΒΑΣΙΛΕΩΣ (on r.) and ΤΙΓΡΑΝΟΥ; in lower field to l., ΔΗ monogram; to r., ΛΦ / ꟼ. *Babelon, pl.* XXIX, 13 .. £30

7211 — Æ 17. *Obv.* Similar; behind, Α. ℞. Nike advancing l., holding wreath; legend as last. *B.M.C. 4*. 104, 12 .. .. £28

7212 — Æ 15. *Obv.* As 7207. ℞. Tyche stg. l., holding rudder and cornucopiae; legend as 7210. *Babelon, pl.* XXIX, 14 .. .. £26

7213   7214

7213 **Antiochos XIII (Asiatikos)**, 69–64 B.C. (the last of the Seleukid kings of Syria, Antiochos XIII was the son of Antiochos X and spent his youth in Asia Minor and then in Rome. Following the withdrawal of Tigranes from Syria, Antiochos was placed on the Seleukid throne by the Romans. His brief reign was very troubled and eventually he was murdered by the Arab chieftain Sampsigeramus. Syria was made a Roman province by Pompey and the line of Seleukos was ended). Æ *tetradrachm* (*c.* 15 gm.). His diad. hd. r.; fillet border. ℞. Zeus enthroned l., holding Nike and sceptre; on r., ΒΑΣΙΛΕΩΣ / ΑΝΤΙΟΧΟΥ; on l., ΦΙΛΑΔΕΛΦΟΥ; in field to l., ΜΑ monogram; all within wreath. *Newell* (*S.M.A.*) 460. *Babelon, pl.* XXVII, 11 .. .. £500

7214 **Roman Province of Syria,** after 64 B.C. (after deposing the last of the Seleukid kings Pompey the Great created Roman provinces out of Syria and Cilicia. For about three decades Seleukid-type tetradrachms were issued by the new rulers. These were in the name of Philip Philadelphos, the last legitimate Seleukid king before the usurpation of Tigranes. They closely resemble the type listed as no. 7196 above, but have the monograms ΧΑΒ or ΧΑΤ in the reverse field, and date numerals in the exergue). Æ *tetradrachm* (*c.* 14·5 - 15·5 gm.). Diad. hd. of Philip r.; fillet border. ℞. Zeus enthroned l., holding Nike and sceptre; on r., ΒΑΣΙΛΕΩΣ / ΦΙΛΙΠΠΟΥ; on l., ΕΠΙΦΑΝΟΥΣ / ΦΙΛΑΔΕΛΦΟΥ; in field to l., Φ / Α and ΧΑΤ monogram; beneath throne, ΔΙ monogram; in ex., ΘΙ (=year 19 of the era of the province of Syria=46/5 B.C.); all within wreath. *B.M.C. 4*. 100, 6 .. £100

7215 — — Similar, but with date ΚΔ (=year 24=41/40 B.C.) in ex. on *rev. Babelon* 1545 £100

Many other dates have been recorded, from year 3 (Γ) to year 29 (ΘΚ).

THE PERGAMENE KINGDOM

7216   7217

7216 **Philetairos,** 282-263 B.C. (the founder of the Attalid dynasty, Philetairos was appointed by Lysimachos of Thrace to guard the royal treasure of 9000 talents which had been deposited at the fortress city of Pergamon in western Asia Minor. After many years of loyalty to Lysimachos, Philetairos transferred his allegiance to Seleukos. Following the latter's assassination in 280 B.C. he became independent ruler of Pergamon, retaining control of the royal treasury which formed the basis of the future prosperity of the Pergamene Kingdom). Æ *tetradrachm* (*c.* 17 gm.). Hd. of deified Seleukos Nikator r., wearing tainia. R. Athena enthroned l., her r. hand resting on shield, holding spear in l.; on r., ΦΙΛΕΤΑΙΡΟΥ and bow; in field to l., ivy-leaf. *Newell* (*the Pergamene Mint under Philetaerus*) 14. *B.M.C. 15.* 114, 29 .. .. £2,500

7217 **Eumenes I,** 263-241 B.C. (nephew of Philetairos, Eumenes consolidated the power of his kingdom and defeated an attempt by Antiochos I to reimpose Seleukid authority over Pergamon). Æ *tetradrachm* (*c.* 17 gm.). Diad. hd. of Philetairos r. R. Athena enthroned, as last; on r., ΦΙΛΕΤΑΙΡΟΥ and bow; beneath Athena's r. arm, ivy-leaf; on seat of throne, AΘ monogram. *Westermark* (*Das Bildnis des Philetairos von Pergamon*) V.V. / R.2. *B.M.C. 15.* 115, 30 .. .. £450

7218 — — Similar, but on *obv.* Philetairos wears laurel-wreath and diadem entwined. *Westermark* V.XXII. / R.1. *B.M.C. 15.* 115, 31 .. .. £400

7219 **Attalos I, Soter,** 241-197 B.C. (nephew or cousin of Eumenes, Attalos extended the influence of Pergamon in successful wars against Antiochos Hierax and against the Gaulish barbarians. Towards the end of his reign Pergamon was threatened by Philip V of Macedon, and Attalos sought the help of Rome). Æ *tetradrachm* (*c.* 17 gm.). *Obv.* As last. R. Athena enthroned l., holding spear and resting l. arm on shield; on r., ΦΙΛΕΤΑΙΡΟΥ and bow; in field to l., ivy-leaf and AΘ monogram. *Westermark* V.XXIX. / R.4 £500

7220 — — — R. Athena enthroned l., crowning ΦΙΛΕΤΑΙΡΟΥ, before her, and resting l. arm on shield; in field to l., ivy-leaf and AΘ monogram; to r., bow. *Westermark* V.LIII / R.1. *B M.C. 15.* 116, 35 .. .. £350

7221 — — Similar, but with bunch of grapes instead of ivy-leaf in *rev.* field to l. *Westermark* V.LXXVI. / R.1. *B.M.C. 15.* 116, 37 .. .. £350

7222 — — Similar, but in *rev.* field to l., cornucopiae and EYMO monogram. *Westermark* V.CIII.A. / R.2. *B.M.C. 15.* 117, 42 .. .. £350

7223 — — Similar, but in *rev.* field to l., ANAPX monogram only. *Westermark* V.CXX. / R.2. *B.M.C. 15.* 117, 45 .. .. £350

7224 **Eumenes II,** 197-160 B.C. (the eldest son of Attalos I, Eumenes was a wise and gifted ruler and a loyal ally of the Romans, whom he assisted at the battle of Magnesia, 190 B.C., when the power of Antiochos the Great was broken.   Eumenes was rewarded with large areas of former Seleukid territory making Pergamon the richest and most powerful state in Asia Minor). Æ *tetradrachm* (*c.* 16·75 gm.). Diad. bust of Eumenes r. ℟. The Dioskouroi, naked, stg. facing, each holding spear; on r., ΒΑΣΙΛΕΩΣ; on l., ΕΥΜΕΝΟΥ; in ex., ΔΙΛ; all within laurel-wreath. *B.M.C. 15.* 117, 47   ..   ..   ..   (*Unique*)
This is the only portrait coin of a reigning monarch in the entire Pergamene series.

7225 — — Hd. of Philetairos r., wearing laurel-wreath and diadem entwined. ℟. Athena enthroned l., crowning ΦΙΛΕΤΑΙΡΟΥ, before her, and resting l. arm on shield; in field to l., small cornucopiae and ΗΜ; to r., bow. *Westermark* V.CXXXIII. / R.2. *B.M.C. 15.* 118, 48   ..   ..   £300
7226 — — Similar, but in *rev.* field to l., thyrsos and tablet inscribed ΑΣ. *Westermark* V.CLII. / R.1. *B.M.C. 15.* 118, 53   ..   ..   £350

N.B.   *The series of Attic-weight tetradrachms issued by the Pergamene kings seems to have ceased about 190 B.C., when the kingdom was greatly extended as a result of the battle of Magnesia.   The silver coins of the remainder of Eumenes' reign, and of his successors* **Attalos II** *and* **Attalos III,** *were cistophoric tetradrachms lacking the royal name but bearing the mint marks of many of the cities of the Pergamene realm.   These coins will be found in this catalogue listed under the mints of issue, e.g. nos. 3943-5 of Pergamon.   In weight they appear to have been the equivalent of three Roman denarii.   The last of the Attalid kings, Attalos III, bequeathed his kingdom to Rome in 133 B.C. and Pergamon became the capital of the Roman province of Asia.   For coins issued by the usurper Aristonikos (Eumenes III) see nos. 4686 and 4739-40.*

7227   7230

7227 **Regal Bronze Coinage of Pergamon,** 282-133 B.C. (these are all inscribed with the name of the dynasty's founder, Philetairos, and firm attributions to particular reigns are not yet possible). Æ 18. Hd. of Athena r., in crested helmet ornamented with griffin. ℟. Asklepios seated l., feeding coiled serpent, before him, and holding sceptre; on r., ΦΙΛΕΤΑΙΡΟΥ. *B.M.C. 15.* 121, 73 ..   ..   £14

7228 — Æ 16. *Obv.* Similar. ℞. Coiled serpent r.; on r., ΦΙΛΕΤΑΙΡΟΥ; in field to l , ΛΙ monogram. *B.M.C. 15.* 121, 76-7 .. .. £12

7229 — Æ 15. *Obv.* Similar. ℞. Thyrsos; on r., ΦΙΛΕΤΑΙΡΟΥ. *B.M.C. 15.* 121, 70 £10

7230 — — Laur. hd. of Asklepios r. ℞. Temple-key; on r., ΦΙΛΕΤΑΙΡΟΥ; on l., serpent. *B.M.C. 15.* 122, 84 .. .. £16

7231 — Æ 13. *Obv.* As 7227. ℞. ΦΙΛΕ / ΤΑΙΡΟΥ either side of ivy-leaf. *B.M.C. 15.* 120, 60 £10

7232 — Æ 11. Laur. hd. of Apollo r. ℞. ΦΙΛΕ / ΤΑΙΡΟΥ either side of tripod. *B.M.C. 15.* 120, 66 .. .. £8

7233 7236

7233 — — *Obv.* As 7227. ℞. ΦΙΛΕ / ΤΑΙΡΟΥ above and beneath bow; in field to r., bee. *B.M.C. 15.* 119, 55 .. .. £9

7234 — Æ 10. Laur. hd. of Apollo r. ℞. ΦΙΛΕ / ΤΑΙΡΟΥ either side of thyrsos. *B.M.C. 15.* 120, 67 .. .. £7

7235 — — — ℞. ΦΙΛΕ / ΤΑΙΡΟΥ either side of bee; ΛΙ beneath. *B.M.C. 15.* 120, 65 £8

7236 — — *Obv.* As 7227. ℞. ΦΙΛΕ / ΤΑΙΡΟΥ above and beneath star of eight rays. *B.M.C. 15.* 120, 63 .. .. £8

7237 — Æ 8. Laur. hd. of Apollo r. ℞. ΦΙΛΕ / ΤΑΙΡΟΥ above and beneath bow in case. *B.M.C. 15.* 121, 68-9 .. .. £7

THE PONTIC KINGDOM

7238 **Mithradates II,** *c.* 255-220 B.C. (at the time of Alexander's invasion of Asia Minor the district of Pontos, on the southern shores of the Black Sea, was a satrapy of the Persian Empire. Subsequently it became a quasi-independent territory under the rule of the Mithradatic dynasty who claimed descent from Darius I of Persia. The first two kings, **Mithradates I** (*c.* 302-265 B.C.) and **Ariobarzanes** (*c.* 265-255 B.C.), do not appear to have issued any coinage, and the series commences with gold staters in the name of Mithradates II, son of Ariobarzanes). *N stater* (*c.* 8·52 gm.). Hd. of Athena r., in crested Corinthian helmet ornamented with serpent. ℞. Nike stg. l., holding wreath and ship's mast; on r., ΜΙΘΡΑΔΑΤΟΥ; on l., ΒΑΣΙΛΕΩΣ; in lower field, Σ — Κ / Π. *S.N.G. Von Aulock 1* £5,000

7239 **Mithradates III,** *c.* 220-185 B.C. (son of Mithradates II). *Æ tetradrachm* (*c.* 17 gm.). His diad. and dr. bust r., with close beard. ℞. Zeus enthroned l., holding eagle and sceptre; on r., ΒΑΣΙΛΕΩΣ; on l., ΜΙΘΡΑΔΑΤΟΥ; in field to l., star and crescent; to r., two monograms; another beneath throne. *B.M.C. 13.* 42, 1 .. .. .. £7,500

Mithradates III *continued*

7240 — Æ *drachm* (*c.* 4 gm.).   Similar.   *Historia Numorum, p.* 500   . .   . .   £1,500

7241 **Pharnakes I,** *c.* 185-159 B.C. (son of Mithradates III, Pharnakes pursued an aggressive foreign policy and captured the important Black Sea port of Sinope, which became the capital of the Kingdom). *N stater* (*c.* 8·47 gm.). His diad. hd. r., with close beard. R. Male deity (Men—Pharnakou?) stg. facing, holding vine-branch, cornucopiae and caduceus; doe at his feet to l.; on r., ΒΑΣΙΛΕΩΣ; on l., ΦΑΡΝΑΚΟΥ; in field to l., star and crescent; to r., monogram. *Leu auction, May* 1979, *lot* 116   . .   . .   . .   (*Unique*)

7242 — Æ *tetradrachm* (*c.* 17 gm.).   Similar, but with three monograms in *rev.* field to r. *B.M.C. 13.* 43, 1   . .   . .   £7,500

7242A — Æ *drachm* (*c.* 4 gm.).   As 7241.   *S.N.G. Von Aulock* 2   . .   . .   . .   £1,500

7243 **Mithradates IV,** *c.* 159-150 B.C. (brother of Pharnakes, Mithradates IV made an alliance with Rome and supported Attalos II of Pergamon against Prusias II of Bithynia. He was married to his own sister, Laodike). *N stater* (*c.* 8·53 gm.). His laur. hd. r. R. Hera stg. facing, holding sceptre; on r., ΒΑΣΙΛΕΩΣ; on l., ΜΙΘΡΑΔΑΤΟΥ; in field to l., star and crescent. *S.N.G. Von Aulock* 4 . .   . .   (*Unique*)

7244 — Æ *tetradrachm* (*c.* 17 gm.).   His diad. hd. r.   R. Naked Perseus stg. facing, holding head of Medusa and harpe; on r., ΒΑΣΙΛΕΩΣ / ΜΙΘΡΑΔΑΤΟΥ; on l., ΦΙΛΟΠΑΤΟΡΟΣ / ΚΑΙ ΦΙΛΑΔΕΛΦΟΥ; above, star and crescent; in lower field to l., monogram. *Boston Museum Catalogue* 1354   . .   . .   £7,500

7245 — — Diad. and dr. busts of Mithradates and Queen Laodike r., conjoined. R. Zeus, on r., and Hera stg. facing, side by side, each holding sceptre; on r., ΒΑΣΙΛΕΩΣ / ΜΙΘΡΑΔΑΤΟΥ ΚΑΙ; on l., ΒΑΣΙΛΙΣΣΗΣ / ΛΑΟΔΙΚΗΣ / ΦΙΛΑΔΕΛΦΩΝ.   *Davis & Kraay* (*The Hellenistic Kingdoms*) 204-5   . .   . .   £12,500

7246 **Mithradates VI, Eupator, the 'Great',** 120-63 B.C. (Mithradates IV was succeeded by his nephew **Mithradates V** who seems not to have issued any coinage.   On his death, in 120 B.C., the Pontic throne passed to his eleven-year-old son, Mithradates VI, who was destined to be one of the most remarkable monarchs of the Hellenistic Age.   He added to his realm by conquering Bosporos and Kolchis, to the north and east of the Black Sea, and also adopted an aggressive policy towards his neighbours in Asia Minor.   This inevitably brought him into conflict with Rome and he came to regard himself as the champion of the Greeks against their Roman masters.   Like Hannibal, a hundred years before, he tried valiantly to stem the relentless advance of Roman power. But after three wars he was eventually defeated by Pompey the Great and later committed suicide, in his sixty-ninth year).   *N stater* (*c.* 8·5 gm.).   His diad. hd. r.   R. ΒΑΣΙΛΕΩΣ / ΕΥΠΑΤΟΡΟΣ above and beneath ivy-wreath containing star and crescent.   *S.N.G. Von Aulock* 5   . .   £7,500

7247

7247 — — *Obv.* Similar, but with flowing hair. R. Stag stg. l., grazing; above, ΒΑΣΙΛΕΩΣ; beneath, ΜΙΘΡΑΔΑΤΟΥ / ΕΥΠΑΤΟΡΟΣ; in field to l., star and crescent; to r., Δ (=year 4 = 85/4 B.C.) and mint-monogram of Pergamon; another monogram in ex.; all within ivy-wreath. *B.M.C. 13.* 43, 1.. .. .. £3,000

   Dated according to an era commencing in 88/7 B.C. when Mithradates first went to war with the Romans.

   N.B. *For another gold stater, issued at Athens in the name of Mithradates VI, see no. 2552 in Volume 1 of this Catalogue.*

7248 — Æ *tetradrachm* (*c.* 16·75 gm.). His diad. hd. r. R. Pegasos stg. l., drinking, r. foreleg raised; legend as last; in field to l., star and crescent; to r., ΗΣ (=year 208 = 90/89 B.C.) and monogram; in ex., Θ; all within ivy-wreath. *Forrer /Weber* 4788, *var.* £650

   Dated according to an era commencing in October, 297 B.C.

7249 — — *Obv.* Similar, but with flowing hair. R. Stag stg. l., grazing; legend as 7247; in field to l., star and crescent, and monogram; to r., ΓΚΣ (=year 223 = 75/4 B.C.) and monogram; in ex., ΙΑ; all within ivy-wreath. *B.M.C. 13.* 44, 6 .. .. .. £600

7250 — Æ *drachm* (*c.* 4 gm.). Similar to last. *Historia Numorum, p.* 502.. .. £450

7251 — Æ 20. Lion leaping r., star above. R. Large monogram of ΒΑ Ε (=ΒΑΣΙΛΕΩΣ ΕΥΠΑΤΟΡΟΣ). *B.M.C. 13.* 45, 10 .. .. £22

7252 — — Hd. of Zeus Ammon r., within border of dots between two linear circles. R. Serpent r.; behind, monogram of ΒΑ Ε. *B.M.C. 13.* 44, 9 .. .. .. £24

7253 — — Laur. hd. of Apollo r., within laurel-wreath. R. Tripod; in field to l., ΒΑ Ε mono-gram; to r., laurel-branch and Δ. *B.M.C. 13.* 45, 12 .. .. £20

7254 — — Winged hd. of Perseus l., harpe before. R. Bearded term r., filleted palm-branch before; in field to l., ΒΑ Ε monogram; to r., Ζ. *B.M.C. 13.* 45, 14 .. £24

   N.B. *The issues of the later kings of Pontos and of Bosporos will be listed in a future catalogue covering the 'Greek Imperial' series and contemporary coinages.*

THE BITHYNIAN KINGDOM

7255 **Nikomedes I,** *c.* 279-255 B.C. (the Kingdom of Bithynia was founded in the early years of the 3rd cent. B.C. by Zipoetes, a chieftain of the Bithyni. This tribe had, in early times, migrated from Thrace to north-western Asia Minor where they eventually came under Persian suzerainty. Zipoetes, who issued no coinage, was succeeded by his son Niko-medes who extended his kingdom with the help of the Gauls. The famous city of Nikomedia was founded by this king about 265 B.C.). Æ *tetradrachm* (*c.* 17 gm.). His diad. hd. r. R. Warrior goddess (the Thracian Bendis ?) seated l. on rock, holding two spears and sword in sheath; circular shield at her side, tree-stump in background; on r., ΒΑΣΙΛΕΩΣ; on l., ΝΙΚΟΜΗΔΟΥ; in field to l., small Nike and ΔΙ monogram.   *Davis & Kraay* (*The Hellenistic Kingdoms*) 186-7   ..   ..   £4,500

7256 — Æ *drachm* (*c.* 4·17 gm.).   *Obv.* Similar. R. Naked male figure (Ares ?) seated l. on rock, holding two spears and sword in sheath; legend as last; in field to l., ΔΙ monogram. *B.M.C. 13.* 208, 1   ..   ..   £900

7257 — Æ 22.   Hd. of Apollo (?) r., hair bound with tainia. R. ΒΑΣΙΛΕ / ΝΙΚΟΜΗ above and beneath horse pacing r.; spear-head in lower field to r.   *S.N.G. Von Aulock* 242   £35

7258 **Ziaelas,** *c.* 255-228 B.C. (son of Nikomedes; little is known of his reign during which very few coins were struck, and those only in bronze). Æ 21. His diad. hd. r. R. ΒΑΣΙΛΕΩΣ / ΖΙΑΗΛΑ either side of trophy.   *S.N.G. Von Aulock* 243   ..   ..   £75

7259 **Prusias I,** *c.* 228-185 B.C. (under Ziaelas' son, Prusias, the Bithynian Kingdom reached its zenith. He was an enlightened and courageous ruler who managed to maintain the prosperity of his realm at a time of great political turmoil in Asia Minor. The celebrated Carthaginian leader, Hannibal, was given refuge at Prusias' court when being pursued by the victorious Romans). Æ *tetradrachm* (*c.* 17 gm.). His diad. hd. r., with whisker. R. Zeus stg. l., holding sceptre and crowning the king's name ΠΡΟΥΣΙΟΥ on l.; on r., ΒΑΣΙΛΕΩΣ; thunderbolt and two monograms in field to l.   *B.M.C. 13.* 209, 1   ..   £650

7260 — Æ 28.   Laur. hd. of Apollo l. R. Winged Athena stg. l., crowning the king's name ΠΡΟΥΣΙΟΥ, on l., and resting on shield; on r., ΒΑΣΙΛΕΩΣ; monogram in field to l.   *B.M.C. 13.* 209, 3   ..   ..   £18

7261 — Æ 20. Diad. hd. of Zeus r. R. ΒΑΣΙΛΕΩΣ / ΠΡΟΥΣΙΟΥ either side of thunderbolt; all within oak-wreath. *S.N.G. Von Aulock* 245 .. .. £16

7262 — Æ 19. Laur. hd. of Zeus l. R. ΒΑΣΙΛΕΩΣ / ΠΡΟΥΣΙΟΥ either side of trophy. *S.N.G. Von Aulock* 246 .. .. £15

7263 — — Laur. hd. of Apollo r. R. ΒΑΣΙΛΕΩΣ / ΠΡΟΥΣΙΟΥ either side of quiver and bow. *B.M.C. 13.* 209, 9 .. .. £14

7264 — Æ 18. *Obv.* Similar. R. ΒΑΣΙΛΕΩΣ / ΠΡΟΥΣΙΟΥ either side of lyre. *B.M.C. 13.* 209, 8 .. .. £14

7265 **Prusias II,** *c.* 185-149 B.C. (Prusias II inherited his father's name but not his character or abilities. His cringing subservience to the Romans earned him the hatred of his subjects, and few mourned his passing when he was murdered in the temple of Zeus at Nikomedia). Æ *tetradrachm* (*c.* 16·85 gm.). His hd. r., wearing winged diadem. R. Zeus stg. l., holding sceptre and crowning the king's name ΠΡΟΥΣΙΟΥ on l.; on r., ΒΑΣΙΛΕΩΣ; in field to l., eagle on thunderbolt above monogram. *B.M.C. 13.* 210, 2 .. £500

7266					7268

7266 — Æ 22. Hd. of young Dionysos r., wreathed with ivy. R. ΒΑΣΙΛΕΩΣ / ΠΡΟΥΣΙΟΥ before and behind the Centaur Cheiron stg. r., playing lyre; monogram in lower field to r. *B.M.C. 13.* 211, 10 .. .. £12

7267 — Æ 19. Eagle stg. r., wings spread. R. ΒΑΣΙΛΕΩΣ / ΠΡΟΥΣΙΟΥ above and beneath thunderbolt; monogram in field below. *B.M.C. 13.* 211, 18 .. .. .. £14

7268 — Æ 18. *Obv.* As 7265. R. ΒΑΣΙΛΕΩΣ / ΠΡΟΥΣΙΟΥ either side of naked Herakles stg. l., holding club and lion's skin; monogram in lower field to r. *B.M.C. 13.* 210, 3 £13

7269 — Æ 14. Hd. of Hermes r., wearing petasos. R. ΒΑΣΙΛΕΩΣ / ΠΡΟΥΣΙΟΥ either side of caduceus. *B.M.C. 13.* 211, 19 .. .. £10

7270 — Æ 13. Hd. of king (?) r. R. ΒΑΣΙΛΕΩΣ / ΠΡΟΥΣΙΟΥ either side of simulacrum; K in field to r. *B.M.C. 13.* 212, 21 .. .. £11

7271 — Æ 9. Helmeted hd. of Athena r. R. ΒΑΣΙΛΕΩΣ / ΠΡΟΥΣΙΟΥ either side of trophy. *B.M.C. 13.* 212, 20 .. .. £8

7272 **Nikomedes II, Epiphanes,** 149-128 B.C. (the unpopular Prusias II was overthrown by his son Nikomedes, who took possession of the Kingdom with the help of Attalos II of Pergamon. He was a popular ruler, but during his reign Bithynia sank to the status of a client-kingdom of Rome. The portrait of this king was retained unchanged on the coinages of his successors). N *stater* (*c.* 8·5 gm.). His diad. hd. r. R. Horseman galloping l., holding large circular shield; ΒΑΣΙΛΕΩΣ above, ΝΙΚΟΜΗΔΟΥ / ΕΠΙΦΑΝΟΥΣ beneath; monogram in lower field to l. *Grose/McClean* 7541 .. .. £7,500

Nikomedes II, Epiphanes *continued*

7273 — Æ *tetradrachm* (*c.* 16·85 gm.). His diad. hd. r. ℞. Zeus stg. l., holding wreath and sceptre; on r., ΒΑΣΙΛΕΩΣ; on l., ΕΠΙΦΑΝΟΥΣ / ΝΙΚΟΜΗΔΟΥ; in field to l., eagle on thunderbolt, magistrate's monogram and dynastic date Ν̅Ρ (=year 150 = 149/8 B.C.). *B.M.C.* *13.* 213, 1 .. .. £400

From the reign of Nikomedes II all regal tetradrachms of Bithynia bear dates according to an era commencing in 298 B.C.   Those of this reign range from year 150-170.

7274 **Nikomedes III, Euergetes,** 128-94 B.C. (son of Nikomedes II, he gained the title of Euergetes through his gifts to various Greek cities.   His coinage continued in the pattern set by his father, only the dates indicating the change of ruler).   Æ *tetradrachm* (*c.* 16·6 gm.).   Diad. hd. of Nikomedes II r.   ℞. Similar to last, but with date ΑΟΡ (=year 171 =128/7 B.C.) in field to l.   *B.M.C. 13.* 213, 4 .. .. £350

The dates of this reign range from year 171-204.

7275 — — Similar, but with date ΖϞΡ (=year 197 =102/1 B.C.) on *rev.*   *B.M.C. 13.* 214, 14 £350

7276 **Nikomedes IV, Philopator,** 94-74 B.C. (the son of Nikomedes III was the last king of Bithynia.   He was merely the puppet of his more powerful neighbours, the Romans and Mithradates VI of Pontos.   After a troubled reign lasting two decades he died in 74 B.C., bequeathing his kingdom to Rome.   The territory was quickly organized as a Roman province, with Nikomedia as its capital).   Æ *tetradrachm* (*c.* 15·5 - 16·6 gm.).   Diad. hd. of Nikomedes II r.   ℞. Similar to 7273, but with date ΖΣ (=year 207 =92/1 B.C.) in field to l.   *B.M.C. 13.* 215, 3 .. .. £350

The dates of this reign range from year 205-224.

7277 — — Similar, but with date ΔΚΣ (= year 224 =75/4 B.C.) on *rev.*   *B.M.C. 13.* 215, 8 £350

THE CAPPADOCIAN KINGDOM

Ariarathes I, *c.* 330-322 B.C. (the founder of the Cappadocian dynasty, Ariarathes was born about 404 B.C. At the time of Alexander's conquest of the Persian Empire he made himself independent satrap of Cappadocia, a position which he maintained until 322 B.C. when he was put to death by Perdikkas and Eumenes. His coinage was issued at Gaziura and Sinope and is listed in this catalogue as nos. 3658 and 3699).

7278 **Ariaramnes,** *c.* 280-230 B.C. (after the death of Ariarathes I Cappadocia was under Greek rule until the end of the century, when the late satrap's son, **Ariarathes II,** recovered the country. About 280 B.C. he was succeeded by his son, Ariaramnes, who achieved recognition of the independence of Cappadocia from the Seleukid kings). Æ 17. His bearded hd. r., wearing leather helmet with flat top. ℞. Horseman, brandishing spear, prancing r.; ΑΡΙΑΡΑΜΝΟΥ above, around; monogram and Ι beneath. *S.N.G. Von Aulock* 6257, *var.* £65

7279 **Ariarathes III,** *c.* 250-220 B.C. (son of Ariaramnes, he was made co-ruler by his father about the middle of the 3rd century. He married Stratonike, the daughter of the Seleukid king Antiochos II). Æ 18. His hd. r., wearing pointed Cappadocian tiara. ℞. Upper-part of male deity stg. facing between two sphinxes seated back to back; he wears lotus head-dress and holds lotus-flower in r. hand; on r., ΒΑΣΙΛΕΩΣ; on l., ΑΡΙΑΡΑΘΟΥ; in upper field, Τ — Υ (= mint of **Tyana**). *S.N.G. Von Aulock* 6258 .. .. .. £85

7280 — Æ 17. *Obv.* Similar. ℞. Horseman galloping r., brandishing spear, palm-tree before; above, ΑΡΙΑΡΑΘ; beneath, ΔΣ / ΤΥΑΝΑ. *S.N.G. Von Aulock* 6259 .. £65

7281 **Ariarathes IV, Eusebes,** 220-163 B.C. (son of Ariarathes III, he came to the throne at a very early age and reigned for more than half a century. His second wife was Antiochis, a daughter of Antiochos the Great of Syria. After his father-in-law's defeat at Magnesia in 190 B.C. Ariarathes became an ally of Rome and Pergamon). Æ *tetradrachm* (*c.* 16·7 gm.). His diad. and dr. bust r. ℞. ΒΑΣΙΛΕΩΣ / ΑΡΙΑΡΑΘΟΥ either side of Athena seated l., holding Nike, spear and shield; in field to l., owl on bunch of grapes, and mono-gram; to r., Δ. *B.M.C. 20. p.* xxvi, i .. .. (*Unique ?*)

7282   7286

7282 — Æ 18. His dr. bust r., wearing domed tiara; monogram behind. ℞. Similar to last, but without symbol, monogram and letter in field. *S.N.G. Von Aulock* 6261 .. £65

7283 — Æ 16. *Obv.* As last. ℞. ΒΑΣΙΛΕΩΣ / ΑΡΙΑΡΑΘΟΥ either side of bow in case. *S.N.G. Von Aulock* 6262. *B.M.C. 20.* 43, 3 .. .. £50

7284 **Ariarathes V, Eusebes Philopator,** 163-130 B.C. (son of Ariarathes IV and Antiochis, he was temporarily expelled from his kingdom in 158 B.C. by the pretender Orophernes. A man of culture, he ruled his kingdom wisely until 130 B.C. when he was killed fighting for the Romans against the Pergamene pretender Aristonikos). Æ *tetradrachm* (*c.* 16·7 gm.). His middle-aged diad. hd. r. ℞. Athena stg. l., holding Nike l. (crowning king's name), spear and shield; on r., ΒΑΣΙΛΕΩΣ; on l., ΑΡΙΑΡΑΘΟΥ; in ex., ΕΥΣΕΒΟΥΣ / Λ (= regnal year 30 = 134/3 B.C.); three monograms in field. *S.N.G. Von Aulock* 6263 .. £2,500

7285 — Æ *drachm* (*c.* 4·2 gm.). Similar, but with youthful portrait of king on *obv.*, and on *rev.* only two monograms in field, and regnal date Ε (= year 5 = 159/8 B.C.) in ex. *S.N.G. Von Aulock* 6264 .. .. £40

7286 — — As 7284, but with regnal date ΓΛ (= year 33 = 131/30 B.C.) in ex. on *rev.* *B.M.C. 20.* 31, 6-7 .. .. £25

7287 Orophernes, 158-157 B.C. (with the help of Demetrios I of Syria Orophernes managed to usurp the throne of Ariarathes V. His success was, however, short-lived and the legitimate king was restored following Roman intervention. Specimens of Orophernes' very rare tetradrachms have been found at Priene, in Ionia, where the pretender deposited his treasure). Æ *tetradrachm* (*c.* 16·4 gm.). His diad. hd. r., of fine style. ℞. Nike stg. l., crowning the king's name and holding palm; on r., ΒΑΣΙΛΕΩΣ; on l., ΟΡΟΦΕΡΝΟΥ; beneath, ΝΙΚΗΦΟΡΟΥ; in field to l., owl on basis above monogram. *B.M.C. 20.* 34, 1
£12,500

7288 Ariarathes VI, Epiphanes Philopator, 130-116 B.C. (the son of Ariarathes V was only a child at the time of his father's death and the government was, for a time, in the hands of Queen Nysa, the king's mother. Later, Ariarathes married Laodike, daughter of Mithradates V, by whom he had two sons. He was assassinated about 116 B.C. by a Cappadocian noble). Æ *drachm* (*c.* 4·1 gm.). Conjoined hds. r. of Queen Nysa and the young Ariarathes VI. ℞. ΒΑΣΙΛΙΣΣΗΣ ΝΥΣΗΣ ΚΑΙ ΒΑΣΙΛΕΩΣ ΑΡΙΑΡΑΘΟΥ ΕΠΙΦΑΝΟΥΣ ΤΟΥ ΥΙΟΥ. Athena seated l., holding Nike, spear and shield. *Historia Numorum, p.* 751 .. (*Unique*)

7289   7290   7291

7289 — — His young diad. hd. r. ℞. Athena stg. l., holding Nike l. (crowning king's name), spear and shield; on r., ΒΑΣΙΛΕΩΣ; on l., ΑΡΙΑΡΑΘΟΥ; in ex., ΕΠΙΦΑΝΟΥΣ / Δ (=regnal year 4 =127/6 B.C.); monogram in field to l., A to r. *B.M.C. 20.* 35, 6   ..   ..   £30

7290 — — Similar, but the king's features are more mature, and with regnal date ΕΙ (=year 15 =116 B.C.) in ex. on *rev.;* in field to l., A; to r., Δ. *B.M.C. 20.* 35, 7-8   ..   £30

7290A Ariarathes VII, Philometor, 116-101 B.C. (son of Ariarathes VI, this young monarch had a most troubled reign during which his kingdom was dominated by the neighbouring states of Bithynia and Pontos. Eventually he was murdered by Mithradates VI of Pontos who placed his own son on the Cappadocian throne). Æ *tetradrachm* (*c.* 16·23 gm.). His young diad. hd. r.; fillet border. ℞. Athena stg. l., holding Nike r., spear and shield; on r., ΒΑΣΙΛΕΩΣ / ΑΡΙΑΡΑΘΟΥ; on l., ΦΙΛΟΜΗΤΟΡΟΣ; monogram above Λ in field to l., ο — Λ either side of Athena; all within wreath. *Leu auction, April,* 1978, *lot* 154   .. (*Unique*)

7291 — Æ *drachm* (*c.* 4·1 gm.). *Obv.* Similar, but without fillet border. ℞. Athena stg., as last; on r., ΒΑΣΙΛΕΩΣ; on l., ΑΡΙΑΡΑΘΟΥ; in ex., ΦΙΛΟΜΗΤΟΡΟΣ / Θ (=regnal year 9 =108/7 B.C.); monogram in field to l., Λ to r. *B.M.C. 20.* 36, 2 ..   ..   ..   £30

7292 — — Similar, but with regnal date IB (=year 12 =105/4 B.C.) in ex. on *rev.*; and in field to l., M; to r., K. *B.M.C. 20.* 36, 6 .. .. £30

7293 **Ariarathes VIII, Epiphanes,** 101-100 B.C. (the younger brother of Ariarathes VII, he was placed on the throne by the Cappadocian nobles in opposition to the son of Mithradates of Pontos. However, the powerful Pontic king soon had him removed, and his death brought the dynasty to an end). Æ *drachm* (*c.* 4·1 gm.). His young diad. hd. r. ℞. Athena stg. l., holding Nike r., spear and shield; on r., ΒΑΣΙΛΕΩΣ; on l., ΑΡΙΑΡΑΘΟΥ; in field, M — K; in ex., regnal date A (=year 1). *S.N.G. Von Aulock* 6297 .. £75

7294   7295

7294 — — Similar, but with ΕΠΙΦΑΝΟΥΣ / A in ex. on *rev.*, and with T in field to l., nothing to r. *B.M.C. 20.* 35, 2 .. .. £75

7295 **Ariarathes IX, Eusebes Philopator,** 101-87 B.C. (son of Mithradates VI of Pontos, he was only eight years of age when his father placed him on the Cappadocian throne. His elevation was opposed both by the Cappadocians themselves and by the Romans, who eventually succeeded in having him deposed in 89 B.C. Two years later he died in Thessaly during the First Mithradatic War). Æ *tetradrachm* (*c.* 16 - 16·3 gm.). His young diad. hd. r. ℞. Athena stg. l., holding Nike r., spear and shield; on r., ΒΑΣΙΛΕΩΣ / ΑΡΙΑΡΑΘΟΥ; on l., ΕΥΣΕΒΟΥΣ; in ex., ΦΙΛΟΠΑΤΟΡΟΣ / A (=regnal year 1 =101/100 B.C.). *B.M.C. 20.* 33, 1 .. .. £2,500

7296   7297

7296 — — (*c.* 16·5 - 16·7 gm.). His diad. hd. r., with more mature features resembling his father Mithradates VI of Pontos. ℞. Pegasos stg. l., drinking; above, ΒΑΣΙΛΕΩΣ / ΑΡΙΑΡΑΘΟΥ; beneath, ΕΥΣΕΒΟΥΣ / ΦΙΛΟΠΑΤΟΡΟΣ; in field to l., star and crescent; to r., monogram (of Amphipolis ?); all within vine-wreath. *B.M.C. 20.* 38, 1 .. .. £2,000

Ariarathes, acting as his father's general in Macedonia during the First Mithradatic War, captured Amphipolis in 87 B.C. and probably issued these tetradrachms from the mint there.

7297 — Æ *drachm* (*c.* 4·1 gm.). His young diad. hd. r. ℞. Athena stg., as 7295; on r., ΒΑΣΙΛΕΩΣ; on l., ΑΡΙΑΡΑΘΟΥ; in ex., ΕΥΣΕΒΟΥΣ / A (=regnal year 1 =101/100 B.C.); monogram in field to l., T to r. *B.M.C. 20.* 33, 2 .. .. £35

7298   7299

Ariarathes IX, Eusebes Philopator *continued*

7298 — — Similar, but with slightly older portrait with features resembling his father Mithradates VI of Pontos; and on *rev.* regnal date Δ (=year 4 =98/7 B.C.) in ex., monogram
in field to l.   *B.M.C. 20.* 38, 3   ..   ..   £30

7299 — — Obv. As 7296.   ℞. As last, but with regnal date ιΓ (=year 13 =89 B.C.) in ex.
B.M.C. 20. 38, 6   ..   ..   £30

7300   7301

7300 **Ariobarzanes I, Philoromaios,** 95-63 B.C. (the line of Ariarathes now being extinct,
the Cappadocians chose as their king a noble called Ariobarzanes.   His long reign was
much troubled by attacks from Tigranes of Armenia, and several times he was driven from
his kingdom, though always restored by his allies the Romans.   In 63 B.C. he abdicated
in favour of his son).   Æ *drachm* (*c.* 4·2 gm.).   His young diad. hd. r.   ℞. Athena stg. l.,
holding Nike r., spear and shield; on r., ΒΑΣΙΛΕΩΣ; on l., ΑΡΙΟΒΑΡΖΑΝΟΥ; in ex., ΦΙΛΟΡΩ-
ΜΑΙΟΥ / Γ (=regnal year 3 =93/2 B.C.); in field to l., Θ / Μ; to r., Ε.   *B.M.C. 20.* 39, 1-2
£26

7301 — — Similar, but the king's features are middle-aged; and on *rev.* regnal date ιΓ
(=year 13 =83/2 B.C.) in ex., monogram in field to l., Μ to r.; also, the small Nike held by
Athena is turned to l. and is crowning the king's name.   *B.M.C. 20.* 39, 5   ..   £25

7302   7303

7302 — — Similar to 7300, but the king's features are elderly; and on *rev.* regnal date Λ
(=year 30 =66/5 B.C.) in ex., monogram in field to l., Α to r.   *B.M.C. 20.* 40, 20
£24

7303 **Ariobarzanes II, Philopator,** 63-52 B.C. (son of Ariobarzanes I, he married Athenais,
a daughter of Mithradates VI of Pontos.   After a troubled reign of little more than a
decade he was assassinated by members of a pro-Parthian faction).   Æ *drachm* (*c.* 3·75
gm.).   His diad. hd. r.   ℞. Athena stg. l., holding Nike r., spear and shield; on r.,
ΒΑΣΙΛΕΩΣ; on l., ΑΡΙΟΒΑΡΖΑΝΟΥ; in ex., ΦΙΛΟΠΑΤΟΡΟΣ / Ζ (=regal year 7 =57/6 B.C.).
B.M.C. 20. 41, 1   ..   ..   £40

7304   7305   7306

7304 Ariobarzanes III, Eusebes Philoromaios, 52-42 B.C. (son of Ariobarzanes II and Athenais, his already difficult position was made worse by involvement in the civil wars which afflicted the Roman world at this time. In 42 B.C. he refused to aid Cassius, one of Caesar's assassins, in consequence of which he was murdered). Æ *drachm* (*c.* 3·85 gm.). His diad. hd. r., bearded. ℞. Athena stg. l., holding Nike r., spear and shield; above, ΒΑΣΙΛΕΩΣ; on r., ΑΡΙΟΒΑΡΖΑΝΟΥ; on l., ΕΥΣΕΒΟΥΣ; in ex., ΚΑΙ ΦΙΛΟΡΩΜΑΙΟΥ / ΙΑ (=regnal year 11 =42 B.C.); in field to l., star and crescent; to r., monogram. *B.M.C. 20.* 42, 3 £30

7305 Ariarathes X, Eusebes Philadelphos, 42-36 B.C. (younger brother of Ariobarzanes III, he was executed by Mark Antony after a reign of only six years). Æ *drachm* (*c.* 3·5 - 3·9 gm.). His diad. hd. r., bearded. ℞. Athena stg., as last; above, ΒΑΣΙΛΕΩΣ; on r., ΑΡΙΑΡΑΘΟΥ; on l., ΕΥΣΕΒΟΥΣ ΚΑΙ; in ex., ΦΙΛΑΔΕΛΦΟΥ; in field to l., trophy; to r., monogram above Є (=regnal year 5 =38/7 B.C.). *B.M.C. 20.* 43, 1 .. .. .. £45

7306 Archelaus, Philopatris Ktistes, 36 B.C.-A.D. 17 (placed on the Cappadocian throne by Mark Antony, Archelaus' position was later confirmed by Augustus who added to his territories. After ruling for more than half a century he died at Rome early in the reign of Tiberius whereupon Cappadocia became a Roman province). Æ *drachm* (*c.* 3·75 gm.). His diad. hd. r. ℞. ΒΑΣΙΛΕΩΣ ΑΡΧΕΛΑΟΥ ΦΙΛΟΠΑΤΡΙΔΟΣ ΤΟΥ ΚΤΙΣΤΟΥ around club, dividing Κ — Β (=regnal year 22 =15/14 B.C.). *B.M.C. 20.* 44, 2 .. .. .. £140

7307 — — Similar, but with fillet border on *obv.*, and with regnal date Μ — Β (=year 42 =A.D. 6/7) on *rev. B.M.C. 20.* 44, 4 .. .. £125

KINGS OF ARMENIA

7308 Charaspes (a king unknown to history). Æ 24. Conjoined hds. of the Dioskouroi r. ℞. ΒΑΣΙΛΕΩΣ / ΧΑΡΑΣΠΟΥ before and behind eagle stg. r. on thunderbolt; ΜΕ monogram beneath. *Babelon* (*Rois de Syrie, d'Arménie et de Commagène*) 1 .. .. £100

7309 Arsames, *c.* 230 B.C. Æ 20. His bust r., wearing conical tiara bound with diadem. ℞. Horseman galloping r., holding spear; above, ΒΑΣΙΛΕΩΣ / ΑΡΣΑΜΟΥ. *Babelon* 2 £75

7310   7313   7314

7310 Abdissares, *c.* 200 B.C. Æ 17. His dr. bust r., bearded, and wearing Armenian tiara. ℞. ΒΑΣΙΛΕΩΣ / ΑΒΔΙΣΣΑΡΟΥ before and behind eagle stg. r. *Babelon* 3 .. .. £75

7311 — Æ 12. *Obv.* Similar. ℞. Same legend above and beneath horse's hd. r. *Babelon* 5 .. .. £55

7312 Xerxes, *c.* 170 B.C. Æ 21. His dr. bust r., bearded, and wearing Armenian tiara; monogram behind. ℞. ΒΑΣΙΛΕΩΣ / ΞΕΡΞΟΥ behind and before Nike advancing l., crowning king's name; monogram in lower field to l. *Babelon* 6 .. .. £70

7313 — Æ 14. *Obv.* Similar. ℞. Similar to last, but with Athena, instead of Nike, stg. l., crowning king's name and holding spear and shield. *B.M.C. 20.* 100, 1 .. £50

Tigranes II, the Great, *c.* 97-56 B.C. (for the coinage of this king, see above under the Seleukid Kingdom, nos. 7202-12).

7314 Artavasdes II, *c.* 56-31 B.C. (son of Tigranes II, he quarrelled with Mark Antony and was imprisoned in Alexandria where Cleopatra put him to death just before the battle of Actium). Æ *drachm* (*c.* 3·65 gm.). His dr. bust r., wearing ornamented Armenian tiara. ℞. King in galloping quadriga l., holding Nike; above, ΒΑΣΙΛΕΩΣ / Ζ; beneath, ΒΑΣΙΛΕΩΝ / ΑΡΤΑΥΑΖΔΟΥ; monogram in field to l. *B.M.C. 20.* 101, 1. *Bedoukian* (*Coinage of the Artaxiads of Armenia*) 131 .. .. £400

7315 — Æ 20. *Obv.* Similar; behind, Α. ℞. Nike advancing l., holding wreath; on r., ΒΑΣΙΛΕΩΣ; on l., ΒΑΣΙΛΕΩΝ / ΑΡΤΑΥΑΖΔΟΥ. *Babelon* 25. *Bedoukian* 132 .. £60

7316 **Tigranes III,** c. 20-8 B.C. (son of Artavasdes II, he was placed on the Armenian throne in 20 B.C. with the support of a Roman army under the command of Tiberius). Æ 17. His hd. r., wearing Armenian tiara. ℞. Dove stg. l., holding olive-branch in beak; on l., ΒΑΣΙΛΕΩΣ / ΜΕΓΑΛΟΥ; on r., ΤΙΓΡΑΝΟΥ. *Bedoukian* 138 .. .. .. £50

7317 **Tigranes IV,** c. 8-5 B.C. and 2 B.C.-A.D. 1 (with the support of the pro-Parthian faction in Armenia Tigranes IV came to power following his father's death. During his second reign he shared the throne with his sister-consort **Erato**). Æ 18. His hd. r., with long beard, wearing Armenian tiara. ℞. Nike stg. r., holding wreath and cornucopiae; on r., ΒΑΣΙΛΕΩΣ / ΤΙΓΡΑΝΟΥ; on l., ΜΕΓΑΛΟΥ. *Bedoukian* 148 .. .. £55

7318 — Æ 19. Conjoined hds. r. of Tigranes and Queen Erato. ℞. Tyche enthroned l., holding cornucopiae; on r., ΒΑΣΙΛΕΩΣ / ΤΙΓΡΑΝΟΥ; on l., ΜΕΓΑΛΟΥ. *Bedoukian* 161 £75

7319 **Artavasdes III,** c. 5-2 B.C. (a brother of Tigranes III, Artavasdes was placed on the Armenian throne by the Romans to replace the deposed Tigranes IV). Æ 21. His hd. r., wearing Armenian tiara. ℞. Minerva (?) stg. facing, hd. l., holding spear and resting on shield; on r., ΒΑΣΙΛΕΩΣ / ΜΕΓΑΛΟΥ; on l., ΑΡΤΑΥΑΖΔΟΥ. *Bedoukian* 160 £70

7320 **Artavasdes IV,** c. A.D. 4-6 (the son of Ariobarzanes II of Media, Artavasdes was placed on the Armenian throne by Augustus). Æ *denarius* (c. 3·55 gm.). ΘΕΟΥ ΚΑΙΣΑΡΟΣ ΕΥΕΡΓΕΤΟΥ. Laur. hd. of Augustus r. ℞. ΒΑΣΙΛΕΩΣ ΜΕΓΑΛΟΥ ΑΡΤΑΝΑΞΔΟΥ. Diad. hd. of Artavasdes r. *B.M.C. 20.* 101, 1. *Bedoukian* 163 .. .. £500

7321 **Tigranes V,** circa A.D. 6 (distantly related to the Armenian royal house, Tigranes V was another Roman nominee, elevated to the throne to replace the murdered Artavasdes IV. With his death the Artaxiad line became extinct). Æ 22. ΒΑCΙΛΕΥC ΜΕΓΑC ΝΕΟC ΤΙΓΡΑΝΗC. His dr. bust r., wearing Armenian tiara. ℞. ΕΡΑΤω ΒΑCΙΛΕωC ΤΙΓΡΑΝΟΥ ΑΔΕΛΦΗ. Dr. bust of Queen Erato l. *Bedoukian* 166 .. .. (*Unique*)

THE PARTHIAN KINGDOM

(From small beginnings this kingdom eventually rose to become a world power, rivalling even the Empire of Rome. The Parthian coinage extends down to the third century of the Christian era, and only the first half of it is dealt with here. The remainder will be listed in a future catalogue covering the 'Greek Imperial' coinage and contemporary issues).

7322 **Arsakes I,** c. 238-211 B.C. (a nomad leader in north-east Iran, Arsakes led a successful rebellion of the Parthian satrapy against Seleukid rule. He became the first king of Parthia and established a royal line that was destined to rule the area for nearly five hundred years). Æ *drachm* (the main denomination of the Parthian coinage, normally weighing c. 3·75 - 4·25 gm.). His hd. r., wearing bashlik (felt cap of the nomads). ℞. Archer seated l. on stool, holding bow; on r., ΑΡΣΑΚΟΥ; on l., ΑΥΤΟΚΡΑΤΟΡΟΣ. *Sellwood (Coinage of Parthia)* 1/1. *B.M.C. 23., p. 5,* vi £200

7323 — — *Obv.* Similar, but hd. to l. ℞. Archer seated r. on stool, holding bow; on l., ΑΡΣΑΚΟΥ; on r., Aramaic legend (=*k r n y*); ΜΤ monogram beneath stool. *Sellwood* 4/1 £125

7324   7325

7324 **Arsakes II,** *c.* 211-191 B.C. (son of Arsakes I; early in his reign he was obliged to submit to the reimposition of Seleukid authority when Antiochos the Great invaded Parthia. This led to a temporary cessation of Parthian coinage). Æ *drachm.* His hd. l., wearing bashlik. ℞. Archer seated r. on stool, holding bow; on l., ΑΡΣΑΚΟΥ; eagle at archer's feet. *Sellwood* 6/1 . .   ..   £90

7325 **Mithradates I,** *c.* 171-138 B.C. (with the defeat of Antiochos the Great by the Romans in 190 B.C., and the consequent general weakening of Seleukid power, the Parthians gradually began to recover their autonomy. However, it seems unlikely that the following two kings, **Phriapatios** and **Phraates I,** resumed the issue of coinage. This probably took place under the next king, Mithradates, whose great military exploits added considerably to the territory of the Parthian kingdom). Æ *tetradrachm* (*c.* 15·5 gm.). His diad. hd. r., bearded; fillet border. ℞. Naked Herakles stg. l., holding wine-cup and club; on r., ΒΑΣΙΛΕΩΣ / ΜΕΓΑΛΟΥ; on l., ΑΡΣΑΚΟΥ / ΦΙΛΕΛΛΗΝΟΣ; monogram in field to l.; in ex., Seleukid date ΓΟΡ (=year 173 =140/39 B.C.). *Sellwood* 13/2. *B.M.C. 23.* 14, 56   £650

     This, and almost all other tetradrachms of the Parthian series, was struck at the mint of Seleukeia-on-the-Tigris.

7326   — Æ *drachm.* His bust l., wearing bashlik. ℞. Archer seated r. on omphalos, holding bow; on l., ΑΡΣΑΚΟΥ. *Sellwood* 8/1. *B.M.C. 23.* 1, 1 ..   ..   ..   £100

7327 — — — ℞. As last, but with legend ΒΑΣΙΛΕΩΣ on l., ΑΡΣΑΚΟΥ on r. *Sellwood* 9/1. *B.M.C. 23.* 2, 3   ..   ..   £80

7328   7330

7328 — — — ℞. As last, but with legend ΒΑΣΙΛΕΩΣ on l., ΜΕΓΑΛΟΥ above, ΑΡΣΑΚΟΥ on r. *Sellwood* 10/1. *B.M.C. 23.* 3, 13 ..   ..   £75

7329 — — — ℞. As last, but with legend ΒΑΣΙΛΕΩΣ on l., ΜΕΓΑΛΟΥ above, ΑΡΣΑΚΟΥ / ΘΕΟΠΑΤΟΡ on r. *Sellwood* 10/14. *B.M.C. 23.* 5, 30   ..   ..   £90

7330 — — His diad. and dr. bust l., with long beard; fillet border. ℞. As 7328. *Sellwood* 11/1. *B.M.C. 23.* 10, 31 ..   ..   £75

7331 — — His diad. and dr. bust r., with long beard. ℞. Archer seated r. on omphalos, holding bow; on r., ΒΑΣΙΛΕΩΣ / ΜΕΓΑΛΟΥ; on l., ΑΡΣΑΚΟΥ; monogram in field to l. *Sellwood* 12/2. *B.M.C. 23.* 6, 1   ..   ..   £100

7332 — — *Obv.* As 7325. ℞. Zeus enthroned l., holding eagle and sceptre; legend as last; in ex., ΧΑΡ monogram. *Sellwood* 13/5. *B.M.C. 23.* 13, 51 ..   ..   ..   £125

Mithradates I *continued*

7333 — Æ *diobol* (*c.* 1·3 gm.). As 7328. *Sellwood* 10/15. *B.M.C. 23.* 4, 27 .. £100

7334 — Æ *obol* (*c.* 0·65 gm.). As 7328. *Sellwood* 10/16. *B.M.C. 23.* 4, 28 .. £75

7335 — — *Obv.* As 7331. R. Bust r., with long pointed beard, wearing bashlik; on l., ΒΑΣΙΛΕΩΣ; above, ΜΕΓΑΛΟΥ; on r., ΑΡΣΑΚΟΥ. *Sellwood* 12/4. *B.M.C. 23.* 7, 3 £65

7336 — Æ 14. *Obv.* As 7326. R. Elephant walking r., ΑΡΣΑΚΟΥ above. *Sellwood* 8/3, *B.M.C. 23.* 2, 2 .. .. £25

7337 — Æ 15. *Obv.* As 7330. R. Horse pacing r.; on l., ΒΑΣΙΛΕΩΣ; above, ΜΕΓΑΛΟΥ; on r.. ΑΡΣΑΚΟΥ. *Sellwood* 11/5. *B.M.C. 23.* 12, 43 .. .. £14

7338 — Æ 27. His diad. and dr. bust r., bearded. R. Elephant stg. r.; ΒΑΣΙΛΕΩΣ ΜΕΓΑΛΟΥ in circle above, ΑΡΣΑΚΟΥ beneath. *Sellwood* 12/5. *B.M.C. 23.* 9, 21 .. .. £35

7339   7340

7339 — — — R. The Dioskouroi on horseback prancing r.; ΒΑΣΙΛΕΩΣ in circle above, ΑΡΣΑΚΟΥ beneath. *Sellwood* 12/8. *B.M.C. 23.* 8, 15 .. .. £40

7340 — Æ 23. *Obv.* Similar. R. Horse's hd. r.; legend as 7337. *Sellwood* 12/12. *B.M.C. 23.* 9, 25 .. .. £20

7341 — Æ 20. *Obv.* Similar. R. Bow in case; legend as 7338. *Sellwood* 12/13. *B.M.C. 23.* 9, 27 .. .. £18

7342 — — — R. Nike in biga r.; ΒΑΣΙΛΕΩΣ above, ΑΡΣΑΚΟΥ beneath. *Sellwood* 12/10. *B.M.C. 23.* 8, 16 .. .. £24

7343 — Æ 15. His diad. and dr. bust r., bearded. R. As 7335. *Sellwood* 12/18. *B.M.C. 23.* 7, 10 .. .. £15

7344 — — R. Bee; ΒΑΣΙΛΕΩΣ on l., ΜΕΓΑΛΟΥ above, ΑΡΣΑΚΟΥ on r. *Sellwood* 12/20. *B.M.C. 23.* 8, 19 .. .. £16

7345 — Æ 13. *Obv.* Similar. R. Nike advancing r., holding wreath and palm; legend as last. *Sellwood* 12/27. *B.M.C. 23.* 8, 17 .. .. £13

7346 **Phraates II,** *c.* 138-127 B.C. (son of Mithradates I, his short reign was troubled by a Seleukid invasion from the west, and incursions of nomadic Scythian tribes on the eastern frontier. Antiochos VII was defeated, but Phraates died in battle against the nomads in 127 B.C.). Æ *tetradrachm* (*c.* 15·5 gm.). His diad. and dr. bust l., with short beard. R. Archer seated r. on omphalos, holding bow; on l., ΒΑΣΙΛΕΩΣ; above, ΜΕΓΑΛΟΥ; on r., ΑΡΣΑΚΟΥ. *Sellwood* 15/1 .. .. £1,250

7347 — — *Obv.* Similar, but hd. to r.; fillet border. ℞. Male deity enthroned l., holding Nike and cornucopiae; on r., ΒΑΣΙΛΕΩΣ / ΜΕΓΑΛΟΥ; on l., ΑΡΣΑΚΟΥ / ΝΙΚΗΦΟΡΟΥ; two monograms in ex. *Sellwood* 17/1 .. .. £2,000

7348 — Æ *drachm*. As 7346. *Sellwood* 15/2 .. .. £100

7349 — — His diad. hd. l., with short beard. ℞. Archer seated r. on omphalos, holding bow; on r., ΒΑΣΙΛΕΩΣ / ΜΕΓΑΛΟΥ; on l., ΑΡΣΑΚΟΥ / ΘΕΟΠΑΤΟΡΟΣ. *Sellwood* 16/1. *B.M.C. 23.* 16, 5 .. .. £65

7350 — — Similar, but with Α behind hd. on *obv.* *Sellwood* 16/2. *B.M.C. 23.* 17, 6 £70

7351   7354

7351 — — Similar, but with ΤΑΜ (=mint of Tambrax) behind hd. on *obv.*, and with a dividing line between the inscription on either side of *rev.* type. *Sellwood* 16/6. *B.M.C. 23.* 17, 15 .. .. £75

7352 — — As last, but with ΝΙΚΑΙΑ (=mint of Nisa) behind hd. on *obv.* *Sellwood* 16/9. *B.M.C. 23.* 17, 12 .. .. £75

7353 — — As 7349, but with *rev.* legend ΒΑΣΙΛΕΩΣ on l., ΜΕΓΑΛΟΥ above, ΑΡΣΑΚΟΥ / ΘΕΟΠΑΤΟ-ΡΟΣ (with dividing line between) on r. *Sellwood* 16/19. *B.M.C. 23.* 16, 1 .. £70

7354 — — His diad. hd. r., with short beard; fillet border. ℞. Nike stg. l., holding wreath and palm; legend as 7347; Ξ in field to l., monogram in ex. *Sellwood* 17/3. *B.M.C. 23.* 23, 2 .. .. £300

7355 — Æ *obol* (*c* 0·55 gm.). As 7349. *Sellwood* 16/20. *B.M.C. 23.* 18, 21 .. £75

7356 — Æ 15. *Obv.* As 7349. ℞. Horse pacing r.; on l., ΒΑΣΙΛΕ / ΜΕΓΑΛΟΥ; on r., ΑΡΣΑΚΟΥ / ΘΕΟΠΑΤ. *Sellwood* 16/22. *B.M.C. 23.* 18, 27 .. .. £15

7357 — — — ℞. Elephant walking r.; legend as 7349. *Sellwood* 16/21. *B.M.C. 23.* 18, 22 .. .. £16

7358 **Artabanos I,** *c.* 127-123 B.C. (brother of Mithradates I, Artabanos succeeded his nephew at a time of national crisis, and spent much of his brief reign in conflict with the Scythian nomads). Æ *tetradrachm* (*c.* 15·5 gm.). His diad. and cuir. bust r., with pointed beard; fillet border. ℞. Tyche enthroned l., holding Nike and cornucopiae; on r., ΒΑΣΙΛΕΩΣ; on l., ΑΡΣΑΚΟΥ; in field to l., monogram and ΘΕ; in ex., Seleukid date ΗΠΡ (=year 188 =125/4 B.C.). *Sellwood* 21/2. *B.M.C. 23.* 20, 2 .. .. £650

7359 — Æ *drachm*. His diad. and cuir. bust l., with pointed beard. ℞. Archer seated r. on omphalos, holding bow; on r., ΒΑΣΙΛΕΩΣ / ΜΕΓΑΛΟΥ; on l., ΑΡΣΑΚΟΥ / ΘΕΟΠΑΤΟΡΟΣ (each with dividing line between). *Sellwood* 19/1. *B.M.C. 23.* 20, 3 .. .. £100

Artabanos I *continued*

7360 — — *Obv*. Similar. ℞. Archer seated r. on omphalos, holding bow; on r., ΒΑΣΙΛΕΩΣ / ΜΕΓΑΛΟΥ; on l., ΑΡΣΑΚΟΥ / ΦΙΛΑΔΕΛΦΟΥ. *Sellwood* 20/1. *B.M.C. 23.* 21, 4 .. £85

7361 — — As last, but with ΡΑ (=mint of Rhagae) behind hd. on *obv*. *Sellwood* 20/3. *B.M.C. 23.* 21, 8-9 .. .. £90

7362 — — *Obv*. Similar, but with ΑΙ monogram behind hd. ℞. Archer seated r. on omphalos, holding bow; on r., ΒΑΣΙΛΕΩΣ / ΜΕΓΑΛΟΥ; on l., ΑΡΣΑΚΟΥ / ΦΙΛΑΔΕΛΦΟΥ / ΦΙΛΕΛΛΗΝΟΣ; in ex., ΕΚΡ (= year 125 of the Arsakid era =124/3 B.C.). *Sellwood* 22/2. *B.M.C. 23.* 21, 10 .. .. £125

7363 — Æ 18. *Obv*. As 7359. ℞. Horse pacing r.; legend as 7360. *Sellwood* 20/5. *B.M.C. 23.* 22, 11 .. .. £16

7364 **Mithradates II,** *c.* 123-88 B.C. (son of Artabanos I, he was one of the most celebrated of the Parthian monarchs. During his long reign he succeeded in stemming the advance of the Scythian tribes, and his intervention in the affairs of Armenia led to the elevation of Tigranes to the throne of that country. His last years were troubled by the rebellion of Gotarzes). Æ *tetradrachm* (*c.* 15·5 gm.). His diad. and cuir. bust r., with short beard; fillet border. ℞. Tyche enthroned l., holding Nike and cornucopiae; on r., ΒΑΣΙΛΕΩΣ / ΑΡΣΑΚΟΥ; on l., ΕΠΙΦΑΝΟΥΣ / ΦΙΛΕΛΛΗΝΟΣ; in ex., ΤΥ and monogram. *Sellwood* 23/2. *B.M.C. 23.* 23, 1 .. .. £1,250

7365　　　　　　　　　　7367

7365 — — His diad. and cuir. bust l., with long beard. ℞. Archer seated r. on omphalos, holding bow; on l., ΒΑΣΙΛΕΩΣ; above, ΜΕΓΑΛΟΥ; on r., ΑΡΣΑΚΟΥ; in ex., ΕΠΙΦΑΝΟΥΣ; in field to r., palm-branch. *Sellwood* 24/1. *B.M.C. 23.* 24, 3 .. .. .. £350

7366 — Æ *drachm*. *Obv*. Similar; behind hd., ᴈ. ℞. Archer seated r. on omphalos, holding bow; on r., ΒΑΣΙΛΕΩΣ / ΑΡΣΑΚΟΥ; on l., ΕΠΙΦΑΝΟΥΣ / ΦΙΛΕΛΛΗΝΟΣ. *Sellwood* 23/3 £125

7367 — — *Obv*. As 7365. ℞. Archer seated r. on omphalos, holding bow; legend as 7365. *Sellwood* 24/7. *B.M.C. 23.* 26, 12 .. .. £45

7368 — — Similar, but with ΑΡ behind hd. on *obv*., and with Α behind archer on *rev*. *Sellwood* 24/16. *B.M.C. 23.* 25, 6-7 .. .. £45

7369 — — *Obv*. As 7365. ℞. Archer seated r. on omphalos, holding bow; on l., ΒΑΣΙΛΕΩΣ; above, ΜΕΓΑΛΟΥ; on r., ΑΡΣΑΚΟΥ; in ex., ΣΩΤΗΡΟΣ. *Sellwood* 25/1 .. .. £75

7370　　　　　　　　　　7372

7370 — — His diad. and cuir. bust l., with long pointed beard. ℞. Archer seated r. on *throne*, holding bow; legend as 7365; behind archer, A. *Sellwood* 26/6. *B.M.C. 23.* 26, 21
£40
The archer's seat is here changed from an omphalos to a throne, a modification which was adopted on all subsequent issues.

7371 — — *Obv.* Similar. ℞. Archer seated r. on throne, holding bow; above, ΒΑΣΙΛΕΩΣ; on r., ΒΑΣΙΛΕΩΝ; in ex., ΜΕΓΑΛΟΥ; on l., ΑΡΣΑΚΟΥ / ΕΠΙΦΑΝΟΥΣ. *Sellwood* 27/1. *B.M.C. 23.* 30, 66 ..   ..   £40

7372 — — His cuir. bust l., with long pointed beard, wearing tiara ornamented with star device. ℞. Archer seated r. on throne, holding bow; legend as last. *Sellwood* 28/3. *B.M.C. 23.* 34, 106   ..   ..   £40

7373 — — Similar, but with *rev.* legend ΒΑΣΙΛΕΩΣ above, ΒΑΣΙΛΕΩΝ / ΑΡΣΑΚΟΥ on r., ΔΙΚΑΙΟΥ in ex., ΕΥΕΡΓΕΤΟΥ / ΚΑΙ ΦΙΛΕΛΛΗΝ on l. *Sellwood* 29/1. *B.M.C. 23.* 35, 117 ..   £50

7374 — Æ 18. His diad. hd. r., with long beard. ℞. Cornucopiae; on r., ΒΑΣΙΛΕΩΣ; on l., ΑΡΣΑΚΟΥ; beneath, Seleukid date AϘΡ (=year 191 =122/1 B.C.). *Sellwood* 23/4   £18

7375   7378

7375 — Æ 20. His diad. and cuir. bust l., with long pointed beard; ΜΙ behind. ℞. Horse pacing r.; on l., ΒΑΣΙΛΕΩΣ; above, ΜΕΓΑΛΟΥ; on r., ΑΡΣΑΚΟΥ; in ex., ΕΠΙΦΑΝΟΥΣ; above horse, ΜΙ. *Sellwood* 26/15. *B.M.C. 23.* 28, 40   ..   ..   £14

7376 — Æ 19. *Obv.* Similar, but with monogram beneath the ΜΙ. ℞. Horse's hd. r.; legend as 7371. *Sellwood* 27/7. *B.M.C. 23.* 32, 83   ..   ..   £13

7377 — Æ 18. *Obv.* Similar, but without letters or monogram behind. ℞. Pegasos flying r.; legend as 7375. *Sellwood* 26/14. *B.M.C. 23.* 29, 57   ..   ..   ..   £13

7378 — Æ 15. *Obv.* As 7376. ℞. Bow in case; legend as 7371. *Sellwood* 27/9. *B.M.C. 23.* 33, 94   ..   ..   £11

7379 — Æ 13. *Obv.* As 7372. ℞. Nike advancing r., holding wreath and palm; legend as 7371. *Sellwood* 28/9. *B.M.C. 23.* 36, 124   ..   ..   £9

7380 — — — ℞. Club; legend as 7371. *Sellwood* 28/11. *B.M.C. 23.* 37, 136..   £9

7381 **Gotarzes I,** *c.* 90-80 B.C. (this king seems to have rebelled against Mithradates II about 90 B.C. and to have obtained full control of the kingdom on the latter's death two years later. He seems not to have been in the direct line of descent from Arsakes, and was attacked by Mithradates' former ally, Tigranes of Armenia, who seized large areas of Parthian territory). Æ *tetradrachm* (*c.* 15·5 gm.). His diad. and cuir. bust l., with short beard. ℞. Archer enthroned r., holding bow; above, ΒΑΣΙΛΕΩΣ; on r., ΜΕΓΑΛΟΥ / ΑΡΣΑΚΟΥ; in ex., ΘΕΟΠΑΤΟΡΟΣ / ΕΥΕΡΓΕΤΟΥ; on l., ΕΠΙΦΑΝΟΥΣ / ΦΙΛΕΛΛΗΝΟΣ; Κ within ο above bow. *Sellwood* 30/6. *B.M.C. 23.* 38, 2 ..   ..   £350

N.B. *David Sellwood now attributes coins of his Type 30 to an 'Unknown King', reigning circa 80-70 B.C.*

Gotarzes I *continued*

7382 — Æ *drachm*. *Obv*. Similar. ℞. Archer enthroned r., holding bow; above, ΒΑΣΙΛΕΩΣ; on r., ΜΕΓΑΛΟΥ; in ex., ΑΡΣΑΚΟΥ; on l., ΘΕΟΠΑΤΟΡΟΣ / ΕΥΕΡΓΕΤΟΥ. *Sellwood* 30/11. *B.M.C. 23*. 39, 8 ..   ..   £35

7383 — — Similar, but with additional line of legend ΚΑΤΑΣΤΡΑΤΕΙΑ (=travelling court mint ?) to r. of ΜΕΓΑΛΟΥ. *Sellwood* 30/12. *B.M.C. 23*. 40, 23 ..   ..   ..   £75

7384 — — Similar, but the additional legend reads ΜΑΡΓΙΑΝΗ (= mint of Margiane). *Sellwood* 30/17 ..   ..   £65

7385 — Æ 18. *Obv*. Similar. ℞. Horse pacing r.; legend as 7382. *Sellwood* 30/23. *B.M.C. 23*. 41, 26 ..   ..   £12

      7386   7388

7386 — Æ 14. Similar, but with *rev*. type elephant walking r. *Sellwood* 30/24. *B.M.C. 23*. 41, 32 ..   ..   £10

7387 — — Similar, but with *rev*. type horse's hd. r. *Sellwood* 30/35. *B.M.C. 23*. 41, 31 £9

7388 **Orodes I,** *c.* 80-77 B.C. (little is known of this confused period of Parthian history. Orodes may have been a son of Mithradates II). Æ *tetradrachm* (*c.* 15·5 gm.). His cuir. bust l., with medium-length beard, wearing tiara ornamented with star device. ℞. Archer enthroned r., holding bow; above, ΒΑΣΙΛΕΩΣ / ΜΕΓΑΛΟΥ; on r., ΑΡΣΑΚΟΥ; in ex., ΑΥΤΟΚ-ΡΑΤΟΡΟΣ / ΦΙΛΟΠΑΤΟΡΟΣ; on l., ΕΠΙΦΑΝΟΥΣ / ΦΙΛΕΛΛΗΝΟΣ; Α in field to r. *Sellwood* 31/1. *B.M.C. 23.*, *pl. X*, 1 ..   ..   £500

N.B. *David Sellwood now dates the rule of Orodes I to circa 90-80 B.C.*

     7389   7392   7394

7389 — Æ *drachm*. Similar, but without letter in *rev*. field. *Sellwood* 31/5. *B.M.C. 23*. 42, 4 ..   ..   £35

7390 — — As last, but the tiara is ornamented with trefoil device. *Sellwood* 31/6   £50

7391 — Æ 18. *Obv.* As 7388. ℞. Horse prancing r.; legend as 7388. *Sellwood* 31/9.
B.M.C. 23. 43, 16 .. .. £12

7392 — Æ 14. Similar, but with *rev.* type horse's hd. r. *Sellwood* 31/10. B.M.C. 23.
44, 21 .. .. £10

7393 — — Similar, but with *rev.* type bow in case. *Sellwood* 31/11. B.M.C. 23. 44, 31
£10

7394 **Sinatruces,** *c.* 77-70 B.C. (this ruler had, for many years, lived in exile amongst the
Scythian nomads. He was already eighty years of age when he returned to Parthia to
ascend the throne). Æ *drachm.* His cuir. bust l., with pointed beard, wearing tiara
ornamented with horn, on side, and foreparts of stags around the crest. ℞. Archer
enthroned r., holding bow; above, ΒΑΣΙΛΕΩΣ; on r., ΜΕΓΑΛΟΥ; in ex., ΑΡΣΑΚΟΥ; on l.,
ΘΕΟΠΑΤΟΡΟΣ / ΝΙΚΑΤΟΡΟΣ. *Sellwood* 33/2. B.M.C. 23. 51, 55 .. .. £40

N.B. *David Sellwood now attributes coins of his Type 33 to Gotarzes I, whose reign he dates
to circa 95-85 B.C.*

7395 — Æ 17. *Obv.* Similar. ℞. Pegasos flying r.; legend as last. *Sellwood* 33/7. B.M.C.
23. 54, 88 .. .. £12

7396 — Æ 15. Similar, but with *rev.* type Nike advancing r., holding wreath and palm.
Sellwood 33/9. B.M.C. 23. 53, 81 .. .. £11

7397 — Æ 11. Similar, but with *rev.* type club. *Sellwood* 33/11. B.M.C. 23. 54, 89
£9

7398 **Phraates III,** *c.* 70-57 B.C. (son of Sinatruces. Early in his reign he was driven from
his kingdom by a usurper named Darius. But he succeeded in regaining his throne only
to fall victim to the ambitions of his own sons, Mithradates and Orodes). Æ *tetradrachm*
(*c.* 15·5 gm.). His diad. and cuir. bust l., with long beard. ℞. Archer enthroned r.,
holding bow; above, ΒΑΣΙΛΕΩΣ; on r., ΜΕΓΑΛΟΥ / ΑΡΣΑΚΟΥ; in ex., ΕΥΕΡΓΕΤΟΥ; on l.,
ΕΠΙΦΑΝΟΥΣ / ΚΑΙ ΦΙΛΕΛΛΗΝΟΣ; ΧΡΔ monogram above bow. *Sellwood* 38/1. B.M.C. 23.
45, 1 .. .. £900

7399   7400

7399 — — His cuir. bust l., with long pointed beard, wearing tiara ornamented with horn
and foreparts of stags, as 7394. ℞. The king enthroned l., holding eagle and sceptre,
crowned by Tyche stg. l. behind him, also holding sceptre; above, ΒΑΣΙΛΕΩΣ; on r.,
ΜΕΓΑΛΟΥ / ΑΡΣΑΚΟΥ; in ex., ΘΕΟΥ / ΕΥΕΡΓΕΤΟΥ; on l., ΕΠΙΦΑΝΟΥΣ / ΦΙΛΕΛΛΗΝΟΣ. *Sellwood*
39/1. B.M.C. 23. 48, 25 .. .. £800

7400 — Æ *drachm.* His cuir. bust l., with pointed beard, wearing tiara ornamented with
trefoil device, on side, and spiked appendages around the crest; behind, anchor-like
symbol. ℞. Archer enthroned r., holding bow; legend as 7398, but without ΚΑΙ. *Sellwood* 34/1. B.M.C. 23. 54, 90 .. .. £75

N.B. *David Sellwood now attributes coins of his Type 34 to Sinatruces, whose reign he
dates to circa 75 B.C. Specimens exist on which the anchor symbol and tiara appendages have
been intentionally erased from the die.*

7401   7403   7407

Phraates III *continued*

7401 — — His diad. and cuir. bust l., with long pointed beard. Ɍ. Archer enthroned r.;
holding bow beneath which, ΑΓΤ monogram; above, ΒΑΣΙΛΕΩΣ / ΜΕΓΑΛΟΥ; on r., ΑΡΣΑΚΟΥ;
in ex., ΕΥΕΡΓΕΤΟΥ; on l., ΕΠΙΦΑΝΟΥΣ / ΦΙΛΕΛΛΗΝΟΣ. *Sellwood 38/5. B.M.C. 23.* 45,
2 .. .. £45

7402 — — Similar, but with ΜΤ monogram / Θ beneath bow on *rev.* *Sellwood 38/7.* *B.M.C*
23. 46, 8 .. .. £45

7403 — — *Obv.* As 7399. Ɍ. As 7401. *Sellwood 39/4. B.M.C. 23.* 48, 27 .. £45

7404 — — — Ɍ. As 7401, but with κ beneath bow. *Sellwood 39/8. B.M.C. 23.* 49, 33
£45

7405 — Ɍ *hemidrachm* (*c.* 2 gm.). *Obv.* As 7401. Ɍ. Archer seated r., holding bow
which, pellet; above, ΒΑΣΙΛΕΩΣ / ΜΕΓΑΛΟΥ; on r., ΑΡΣΑΚ; in ex., ΕΥΕΡΓΕΤ; on l., ΕΠΙΦΑΝΟ /
ΦΙΛΕ. *Sellwood 38/12* £125

7406 — Æ 17. *Obv.* As 7401. Ɍ. Horse prancing r., ΑΓΤ monogram above; legend as 7401.
Sellwood 38/14. B.M.C. 23. 47, 18 .. .. £13

7407 — Æ 14. Similar, but with *rev.* type horse's hd. r., the monogram behind. *Sellwood*
38/15. *B.M.C. 23.* 47, 15 .. .. £11

7408 — Æ 12. Similar, but with *rev.* type bow in case, the monogram above. *Sellwood*
38/16. *B.M.C. 23.* 47, 24 .. .. £10

7409 — Æ 17. *Obv.* As 7399. Ɍ. Horse prancing r.; legend as 7401, but partly blundered.
Sellwood 39/19. B.M.C. 23. 51, 49 .. .. £13

7410 — Æ 13. Similar, but with *rev.* type horse's hd. r. *Sellwood 39/21. B.M.C. 23.* 51,
53 .. .. £11

7411 **Darius,** *c.* 70 B.C. (a prince of Arsakid blood and the ruler of Media Atropatene, Darius
seized the Parthian throne soon after the accession of Phraates III. His success was short-
lived, however, and Phraates managed to regain his inheritance. The attribution of the
following coins is not certain, but seems likely on the evidence available). Ɍ *tetradrachm*
(*c.* 15·5 gm.). His diad. and cuir. bust l., with short beard. Ɍ. Archer enthroned r.,
holding bow beneath which, ΗΡ monogram; above, ΒΑΣΙΛΕΩΣ; on r., ΜΕΓΑΛΟΥ / ΑΡΣΑΚΟΥ;
in ex., ΦΙΛΟΠΑΤΟΡΟΣ / ΕΥΕΡΓΕΤΟΥ; on l., ΕΠΙΦΑΝΟΥΣ / ΦΙΛΕΛΛΗΝΟΣ. *Sellwood 36/1*
£450

7412 — — His cuir. bust l., with short beard, wearing tiara ornamented with horn. Ɍ.
As last, but with Β beneath bow. *Sellwood 37/1* £900

7413   7416

7413 — Ɍ *drachm.* His diad. and cuir. bust facing, with short beard. Ɍ. Archer enthroned
r., holding bow beneath which, ΑΓΤ monogram; above, ΒΑΣΙΛΕΩΣ / ΜΕΓΑΛΟΥ; on r.,
ΑΡΣΑΚΟΥ; in ex., ΘΕΟΠΑΤΟΡΟΣ / ΕΥΕΡΓΕΤΟΥ; on l., ΕΠΙΦΑΝΟΥΣ / ΦΙΛΕΛΛΗΝΟΣ. *Sellwood*
35/3. *B.M.C. 23.* 56, 1 .. .. £150

7414 — — Similar, but on *rev.* ΡΓ monogram beneath bow, and legend ΒΑΣΙΛΕΩΣ / ΜΕΓΑΛΟΥ above, ΑΡΣΑΚΟΥ on r., ΘΕΟΠΑΤΟΡΟΣ / ΕΥΕΡΓΕΤΟΥ on l., ΕΠΙΦΑΝΟΥΣ / ΚΑΙ ΦΙΛΕΛΛΗΝΟΣ in ex. *Sellwood* 35/1.   *B.M.C. 23.* 56, 6 .. .. £150

7415 — — *Obv.* As 7411. ℞. As last, but with ΦΙΛΟΠΑΤΟΡΟΣ instead of ΘΕΟΠΑΤΟΡΟΣ, and ΑΓ monogram beneath bow.   *Sellwood* 36/4.   *B.M.C. 23.* 59, 27 .. .. £50

7416 — — — ℞. Similar, but with ΜΤ monogram / Θ beneath bow.   *Sellwood* 36/7.   *B.M.C. 23.* 59, 29 .. .. £50

7417 — Æ 18. *Obv.* As 7413. ℞. Horse stg. r.; legend as 7413.   *Sellwood* 35/12.   *B.M.C. 23.* 58, 20 .. .. £22

7418 — Æ 15. Similar, but with *rev.* type Nike advancing r., holding wreath and palm. *Sellwood* 35/14.   *B.M.C. 23.* 57, 8 .. .. £20

7419 — Æ 14. Similar, but with *rev.* type elephant stg. r.   *Sellwood* 35/15.   *B.M.C. 23.* 57, 13 .. .. £18

7420   7422

7420 — Æ 18. His diad. and cuir. bust l., with short beard; crowned by small Nike flying l. behind. ℞. Horse pacing r.; above, ΒΑΣΙΛΕΩΣ / ΜΕΓΑΛΟΥ; on r., ΑΡΣΑΚΟΥ; on l., ΦΙΛΟΠΑΤΟΡΟΣ / ΕΥΕΡΓΕΤΟΥ; in ex., ΕΠΙΦΑΝΟΥΣ / ΚΑΙ ΦΙΛΕΛΛΗΝΟΣ.   *Sellwood* 36/13. *B.M.C. 23.* 60, 40 .. .. £14

7421 — Æ 14. Similar, but with *rev.* type Nike advancing r., holding wreath and palm. *Sellwood* 36/14.   *B.M.C. 23.* 60, 35 .. .. £12

7422 **Mithradates III,** *c.* 57-54 B.C. (son of Phraates III, he conspired with his brother, Orodes, to remove their father from the throne of Parthia.   Soon after the murder the two brothers quarrelled, and in the ensuing power struggle Mithradates was defeated and executed by Orodes).   Æ *drachm.* His diad. and cuir. bust l., with short beard. ℞. Archer enthroned r., holding bow beneath which, ΑΓΤ monogram; behind archer, Β; above, ΒΑΣΙΛΕΩΣ / ΜΕΓΑΛΟΥ; on r., ΑΡΣΑΚΟΥ; in ex., ΔΙΚΑΙΟΥ / ΕΠΙΦΑΝΟΥΣ; on l., ΘΕΟΥ ΕΥΠΑΤΟΡΟΣ / ΦΙΛΕΛΛΗΝΟΣ.   *Sellwood* 40/1.   *B.M.C. 23.* 61, 1 .. .. .. £40

N.B.   *Tetradrachms of this reign are known to have been issued as a number of specimens exist which have been overstruck with the types of Orodes II.   However, no example has yet been found in its original state.   The inscription on reverse was exceptional in that it included the king's personal name* ΜΙΘΡΑΔΑΤΟΥ — *see Sellwood* 41/1.

7423 — — *Obv.* Similar. ℞. Archer enthroned r., holding bow above which, ΡΓ monogram; legend similar to last, but ΕΠΙΦΑΝΟΥΣ / ΔΙΚΑΙΟΥ in ex., and ΚΑΙ before ΦΙΛΕΛΛΗΝΟΣ on l. *Sellwood* 40/4.   *B.M.C. 23.* 62, 10 .. .. £40

7424 — — — ℞. Archer enthroned r., holding bow beneath which, ΑΓΤ monogram; above, ΒΑΣΙΛΕΩΣ / ΒΑΣΙΛΕΩΝ; on r., ΑΡΣΑΚΟΥ / ΜΕΓΑΛΟΥ; in ex., ΔΙΚΑΙΟΥ / ΕΠΙΦΑΝΟΥΣ; on l., ΘΕΟΥ ΕΥΠΑΤΟΡΟΣ / ΦΙΛΕΛΛΗΝΟΣ.   *Sellwood* 41/2.   *B.M.C. 23.* 64, 25 .. .. £50

7425 — — — ℞. Archer enthroned r., holding bow beneath which, ΣΥΡΓ monogram; above, ΒΑΣΙΛΕΥΟΝΤΟΣ / ΒΑΣΙΛΕΩΝ; on r., ΑΡΣΑΚΟΥ ΘΕΟΥ / ΕΥΠΑΤΟΡΟΣ; in ex., ΔΙΚΑΙΟΥ / ΕΠΙΦΑΝΟΥΣ; on l., ΚΑΙ ΦΙΛΕΑ / ΛΗΝΟΣ.   *Sellwood* 41/10.   *B.M.C. 23.* 64, 28 .. .. £50

Mithradates III *continued*

7426 — — *Obv.* Similar; behind, star. R. Archer and monogram, as last; legend as 7424, but with και before ΦΙΛΕΛΛΗΝΟΣ on l. *Sellwood* 41/11. *B.M.C. 23.* 66, 39 .. £50

7427 7432

7427 — — *Obv.* Similar; behind, star and crescent. R. Archer and monogram, as last; above, ΒΑΣΙΛΕΩΣ / ΒΑΣΙΛΕΩΝ; on r., ΑΡΣΑΚΟΥ ΔΙΟ • / ΕΥΕΡΓΕΤΟΥ; in ex., ΦΡΑΑΤΟΥ / ΕΠΙΦΑΝΟΥΣ; on l., ΕΠΙΚΑΛΟΥΜΕΝΟΥ / ΦΙΛΕΛΛΗΝΟΣ ΓΟΣ. *Sellwood* 41/12. *B.M.C. 23.* 66, 41 £100

7428 — Æ 18. *Obv.* As 7422. R. Horse stg. r.; legend as 7422. *Sellwood* 40/15. *B.M.C. 23.* 63, 17 .. .. £14

7429 — Æ 14. Similar, but with *rev.* type horse's hd. r. *Sellwood* 40/16. *B.M.C. 23.* 63, 21 .. .. £12

7430 — Æ 17. *Obv.* As 7422. R. Pegasos prancing r.; legend as 7424. *Sellwood* 41/13 £13

7431 — — *Obv.* As 7426. R. Elephant stg. r.; legend as 7424. *Sellwood* 41/16. *B.M.C. 23.* 67, 42 .. .. £15

7432 — Æ 14. Similar, but with *rev.* type elephant's hd. r. *Sellwood* 41/17. *B.M.C. 23.* 67, 50 .. .. £14

7433 **Orodes II,** *c.* 57-38 B.C. (having disposed of his brother Mithradates III, as described above, Orodes was left in undisputed possession of the Parthian throne. The following year his army gained an historic victory over the Roman legions under the command of Crassus, an achievement which greatly enhanced the prestige of the Parthian monarchy. Orodes, like his father before him, eventually fell victim to his own son, who despatched him by means of suffocation). Æ *tetradrachm* (*c.* 15·5 gm.). His diad. and cuir. bust l., with short beard. R. Archer enthroned r., holding bow; on l., ΒΑΣΙΛΕΩΣ; above, ΒΑΣΙΛΕΩΝ; on r., ΜΕΓΑΛΟΥ / ΑΡΣΑΚΟΥ; in ex., ΚΑΙ ΚΤΙΣΤΟΥ. *Sellwood* 44/1. *B.M.C. 23.* 68, 1 £450

7434 — — *Obv.* Similar. R. The king enthroned r., raising figure of Tyche who kneels l. before him, holding sceptre; above, ΒΑΣΙΛΕΩΣ / ΒΑΣΙΛΕΩΝ; on r., ΑΡΣΑΚΟΥ / ΕΥΕΡΓΕΤΟΥ; beneath, ΔΙΚΑΙΟΥ; on l., ΕΠΙΦΑΝΟΥΣ / ΦΙΛΕΛΛΗΝΟΣ; in field above type, ΠΟ monogram; in ex., ΠΕ (=month of Peritios = January). *Sellwood* 45/3. *B.M.C. 23.* 72, 31 £175

7435 — — — R. The king enthroned r., receiving palm-branch from Tyche who stands l. before him, holding sceptre; legend as last; in ex., ΞΑΝ (=month of Xandikos = March) and monogram. *Sellwood* 46/6. *B.M.C. 23.* 73, 33 .. .. £175

7436 — — — R. As last, but Tyche holds cornucopiae instead of sceptre; legend as 7434; in ex., ΔΥΣ (=month of Dystros = February) and ΖΗΜ. *Sellwood* 47/2 .. .. £200

7437 7438

7437 — — — R. The king enthroned l., holding Nike and sceptre; legend as 7434; in ex., Seleukid date ΓΟΣ (=year 273 = 40/39 B.C.). *Sellwood* 48/5. *B.M.C. 23.* 73, 37 £200

N.B. *The portraits of this king frequently show a wart on the forehead, a feature which was adopted by many of his successors as a sign of true Arsakid descent.*

7438 — Æ *drachm.* His diad. and cuir. bust l., with short beard, crowned by Nike flying l. behind. ℞. Archer enthroned r., holding bow beneath which, ΑΓΤ monogram; above, ΒΑΣΙΛΕΩΣ / ΒΑΣΙΛΕΩΝ; on ʀ., ΑΡΣΑΚΟΥ; in ex., ΦΙΛΟΠΑΤΟΡΟΣ / ΔΙΚΑΙΟΥ; on l., ΕΠΙΦΑΝΟΥΣ / ΦΙΛΕΛΛΗΝΟΣ. *Sellwood* 42/1. *B.M.C. 23.* 69, 3 .. .. £75

7439 — — Similar, but without Nike on *obv.* *Sellwood* 43/3. *B.M.C. 23.* 70, 10-11 £40

7440 — — As last, but on *rev.* ΜΤ monogram / Θ beneath bow, and with ΚΑΙ before ΦΙΛΕΛΛΗΝΟΣ on l. *Sellwood* 43/9. *B.M.C. 23.* 70, 15 .. .. £45

7441   7442

7441 — — His diad. and cuir. bust l., with short beard. ℞. Archer enthroned r., holding bow beneath which, ΑΓΤ monogram; above, ΒΑΣΙΛΕΩΣ / ΒΑΣΙΛΕΩΝ; on ʀ., ΑΡΣΑΚΟΥ; in ex., ΕΥΕΡΓΕΤΟΥ / ΔΙΚΑΙΟΥ; on l., ΕΠΙΦΑΝΟΥΣ / ΦΙΛΕΛΛΗΝΟΣ. *Sellwood* 45/9. *B.M.C. 23.* 74, 39 £25

N.B. *This form of reverse inscription was adopted as the norm by nearly all the successors of Orodes right down to the end of the dynasty. However, mechanical copying and ignorance of Greek on the part of the later die engravers led to the deterioration of the legend into an almost unrecognizable form.*

7442 — — Similar, but with crescent behind hd. of Orodes on *obv.* *Sellwood* 46/10. *B.M.C. 23.* 79, 93 .. .. £25

7443 — — Similar, but with crescent behind hd. of Orodes, star before. *Sellwood* 47/16. *B.M.C. 23.* 82, 123 .. .. £25

7444 — — *Obv.* As last. ℞. Similar to 7441, but with ΜΤ monogram / Θ beneath bow, and with anchor behind throne; legend blundered. *Sellwood* 47/25. *B.M.C. 23.* 89, 179 £30

7445 — — Similar to 7441, but with crescent and star behind hd. of Orodes, and star before; and on *rev.,* anchor behind throne. *Sellwood* 48/6. *B.M.C. 23.* 90, 189 .. £25

7446 — Æ *hemidrachm* (*c.* 2 gm.). *Obv.* As last. ℞. Archer enthroned r., holding bow beneath which, ΑΓΤ monogram; above, ΒΑΣΙΛΕΩΣ; on ʀ., ΒΑΣΙΛΕΩΝ; beneath, ΑΡΣΑΚΟΥ; on l., ΔΙΚΑΙΟΥ. *Sellwood* 48/11 .. .. £120

7447   7450

7447 — Æ *diobol* (*c.* 1·25 gm.). His diad. and cuir. bust l., with short beard, palm-branch before. ℞. As last. *Sellwood* 48/12. *B.M.C. 23.* 95, 237 .. .. .. £90

7448 — Æ *obol* (*c.* 0·6 gm.). Similar, but without palm-branch on *obv.* *Sellwood* 48/13. *B.M.C. 23.* 96, 240 .. .. £75

7449 — Æ 17. *Obv.* As 7438. ℞. Eagle stg. r., ΑΓΤ monogram before; legend as 7438. *Sellwood* 42/3. *B.M.C. 23.* 69, 5 .. .. £14

7450 — Æ 18. *Obv.* As 7441. ℞. Pegasos prancing r., ΑΓΤ monogram beneath; legend as 7438. *Sellwood* 43/12. *B.M.C. 23.* 71, 24 .. .. £13

7451 — — — ℞. Stag stg. r.; ΑΓΤ monogram before, ΟΔ monogram above; legend as 7441. *Sellwood* 45/22. *B.M.C. 23.* 77, 72 .. .. £12

7452 — Æ 17. *Obv.* As 7441. ℞. Stag's hd. r.; ΑΓΤ monogram before, ΟΔ monogram behind; legend as 7441. *Sellwood* 45/24. *B.M.C. 23.* 78, 76 .. .. .. £12

Orodes II *continued*

7453 — Æ 14. Similar, but with *rev.* type fort with four towers, and without monograms in field. *Sellwood* 45/21. *B.M.C. 23.* 78, 78   ..   ..   £11

7454 — Æ 11. Similar, but with *rev.* type star above crescent, ΑΓΤ monogram in field to r. *Sellwood* 45/29. *B.M.C. 23.* 79, 91   ..   ..   £8

7455 — Æ 18. *Obv.* As 7442. R. Tyche stg. r., holding wreath in outstretched r. hand; ΑΓΤ monogram before; legend as 7441. *Sellwood* 46/23. *B.M.C. 23.* 81, 113   £11

7456 — Æ 13. Similar, but with *rev.* type hd. of Tyche, turreted, r. *Sellwood* 46/26. *B.M.C. 23.* 82, 116 ..   ..   £9

7457 — — *Obv.* As 7443. R. Nike advancing r., holding wreath and palm; ΑΓΤ monogram before; legend as 7441. *Sellwood* 47/30. *B.M.C. 23.* 85, 146   ..   ..   £8

       7458   7461   7462

7458 — Æ 11. Similar, but with *rev.* type bow in case. *Sellwood* 47/28. *B.M.C. 23.* 86, 162   ..   ..   £8

7459 — — *Obv.* As 7445. R. Anchor; to r., crescent above ΑΓΤ monogram; legend as 7441. *Sellwood* 48/18. *B.M.C. 23.* 94, 224   ..   ..   £7

7460 — Æ 13. Similar, but *rev.* type ear of corn, with Ψ above ΑΓΤ monogram to r. *Sellwood* 48/20. *B.M.C. 23.* 95, 233   ..   ..   £8

7461 — — Similar, but *rev.* type star, with Λ to r. *Sellwood* 48/19. *B.M.C. 23.* 95, 236   £8

7462 **Pakoros I,** *c.* 39 B.C. (the eldest son of Orodes II, he was placed in command of the offensive against Roman possessions in the east following the great victory over Crassus. Later, he was made co-ruler by his father, but was killed in battle leading another invasion of Asia Minor). *R drachm.* His youthful beardless bust l., diad. and cuir., crowned by small Nike flying l. behind. R. Archer enthroned r., holding bow beneath which, ΑΓΤ monogram; behind throne, crescent; above, ΒΑΣΙΛΕΩΣ / ΒΑΣΙΛΕΩΝ; on r., ΑΡΣΑΚΟΥ; in ex., ΕΥΕΡΓΕΤΟΥ / ΔΙΚΑΙΟΥ; on l., ΕΠΙΦΑΝΟΥΣ / ΦΙΛΕΛΛΗΝΟΣ. *Sellwood* 49/1. *B.M.C. 23.* 97, 1   £350

7463 — Æ 10. *Obv.* Similar. R. Bust of one of the Dioskouroi (?) r., wearing pileus, ΑΓΤ monogram before; legend as last. *Sellwood* 49/2. *B.M.C. 23.* 97, 3 ..   ..   £35

7464 — — — R. Fort with five towers; legend as last. *Sellwood* 49/3. *B.M.C. 23.* 98, 5   £35

7465 **Phraates IV,** *c.* 38-2 B.C. (another son of Orodes II, Phraates became heir to the Parthian throne on the death of his brother Pakoros, and hastened his father's end in his eagerness for power. Early in his reign he successfully repulsed an invasion of Media by Mark Antony, and later established friendly relations with Augustus to whom he eventually restored the legionary standards captured from Crassus. This event was much commemorated on the contemporary Roman coinage. Phraates, like his father and grandfather before him, finally fell victim to his own son). *R tetradrachm* (*c.* 13-14·5 gm.). His diad. and cuir. bust l., with short beard. R. The king enthroned r., being presented with diadem by Tyche stg. l. before him, holding cornucopiae; above, ΒΑΣΙΛΕΩΣ / ΒΑΣΙΛΕΩΝ; on r., ΑΡΣΑΚΟΥ / ΕΥΕΡΓΕΤΟΥ; below, ΔΙΚΑΙΟΥ; on l., ΕΠΙΦΑΝΟΥΣ / ΦΙΛΕΛΛΗΝΟΣ; beneath throne, Seleukid date ΕΟΣ (=year 275 =38/7 B.C.); in ex., ΟΛΩ (=month of Lous =July). *Sellwood* 50/4. *B.M.C. 23.* 99, 1 ..   ..   £100

7466 — — *Obv.* Similar, but with short pointed beard. ℞. Similar, but Tyche presents palm-branch instead of diadem; Seleukid date ΗΟΣ (=year 278 =35/4 B.C.), and month ΠΑΝΗ (=Panemos=June); crescent in upper field. *Sellwood* 51/3. *B.M.C. 23.* 99, 2 .. .. £75

7467 — — *Obv.* As last. ℞. The king enthroned l., holding Nike and sceptre; legend as 7465; beneath throne, Seleukid date ΠΣ (=year 280 =33/2 B.C.); in ex., ΔΑΙΣΙ (=month of Daisios=May). *Sellwood* 54/3. *B.M.C. 23.* 100, 8 .. .. .. £100

7468 — — — ℞. The king enthroned r., raising figure of Tyche who kneels l. before him, holding sceptre; legend as 7465; beneath throne, pellet and Seleukid date ΓΠΣ (=year 283 = 30/29 B.C.); in ex., ΑΡΤΕ (=month of Artemisios=April); ΠΟ monogram in upper field. *Sellwood* 53/1. *B.M.C. 23.* 101, 12 .. .. £125

7469 — — *Obv.* Similar, but with longer pointed beard. ℞. The king enthroned r., receiving diadem from Athena stg. l. before him, holding spear; legend as 7465; in ex., Seleukid date ΗΠΣ (=year 288 = 25/4 B.C.) and month ΔΑΙ (=Daisios=May); pellet beneath throne. *Sellwood* 52/1. *B.M.C. 23.* 105, 34 .. .. £125

7470 — — — ℞. The king seated l. on throne without back, holding bow and sceptre; legend as 7465; in ex., month ΑΡΤΕΜΙ (=Artemisios=April); monogram above bow, Λ beneath throne, Α between king's feet. *Sellwood* 54/11. *B.M.C. 23.* 108, 52 .. .. £100

7471 — — — ℞. The king enthroned r., receiving palm-branch from Tyche stg. l. before him, holding sceptre; legend as 7465; in ex., month ΑΡΤΕΜ (as last); monogram in upper field, Χ̣ beneath throne, Α between king's feet. *Sellwood* 51/37. *B.M.C. 23.* 109, 55 £75

7472   7474

Phraates IV *continued*

7472 — Æ *drachm.* His diad. and cuir. bust l., with pointed beard; behind, eagle l. with wreath in beak. ℞. Archer enthroned r., holding bow beneath which, ΑΓΤ monogram; above, ΒΑΣΙΛΕΩΣ / ΒΑΣΙΛΕΩΝ; on r., ΑΡΣΑΚΟΥ; in ex., ΕΥΕΡΓΕΤΟΥ / ΔΙΚΑΙΟΥ; on l., ΕΠΙΦΑΝΟΥΣ / ΦΙΛΕΛΛΗΝΟΣ. *Sellwood* 52/7. *B.M.C. 23.* 110, 57   ..   ..   ..   £25

7473 — — Similar, but also with star before Phraates' hd. on *obv.*, and with star behind throne on *rev. Sellwood* 53/4. *B.M.C. 23.* 122, 191   ..   ..   ..   £25

7474 — — Similar, but with star and crescent before Phraates' hd. on *obv.*, and without star on *rev. Sellwood* 54/12. *B.M.C. 23.* 126, 219   ..   ..   ..   £25

7475 — — Similar, but with crescent before Phraates' hd. on *obv.*, and with ΜΤ monogram / Θ beneath bow on *rev.;* legend badly blundered. *Sellwood* 54/14. *B.M.C. 23.* 125, 217 £30

7476 — — Similar, but with star and crescent before Phraates' hd., and another star above the eagle behind; on *rev.*, ΜΤ monogram / Θ beneath bow, crescent behind throne; legend badly blundered. *Sellwood* 54/15. *B.M.C. 23.* 127, 230   ..   ..   ..   £30

7477   7482   7484

7477 — — His diad. and cuir. bust l., with pointed beard, crowned by Nike flying l. behind. ℞. Archer enthroned r., holding bow beneath which, ΡΓ monogram; legend as 7472, but badly blundered. *Sellwood* 50/16. *R.M.C. 23.* 131, 255   ..   ..   £50

7478 — — His diad. and cuir. bust l., with pointed beard. ℞. As 7472. *Sellwood* 51/38 £40

7479 — Æ 10. *Obv.* As 7472. ℞. Athena stg. l. at altar, holding palm-branch, spear and shield; legend only fragmentary, but probably as 7472. *Sellwood* 52/25. *B.M.C. 23.* 115, 103   ..   ..   £6

7480 — — Similar, but with *rev.* type Dikaiosyne stg. l., holding scales; ΑΓΤ monogram in field to l. *Sellwood* 52/26. *B.M.C. 23.* 115, 106   ..   ..   £6

7481 — — Similar, but with *rev.* type rad. hd. of Helios facing, between crescent, on l., and ΑΓΤ monogram. *Sellwood* 52/27. *B.M.C. 23.* 116, 111   ..   ..   £6

7482 — — Similar, but with *rev.* type triform hd. of Hekate, ΑΓΤ monogram in field to r. *Sellwood* 52/28. *B.M.C. 23.* 116, 116   ..   ..   ..   £8

7483 — — Similar, but with *rev.* type archer enthroned r., holding bow beneath which, ΑΓΤ monogram. *Sellwood—. B.M.C. 23.* 117, 129   ..   ..   ..   £7

7484 — — Similar, but with *rev.* type humped bull stg. r., ΑΓΤ monogram above. *Sellwood* 52/32. *B.M.C. 23.* 118, 141   ..   ..   £6

7485 — — Similar, but with *rev.* type large ΑΓΤ monogram. *Sellwood* 52/36. *B.M.C. 23.* 119, 156   ..   ..   £7

7486 — — Similar, but with *rev.* type winged caduceus, ΑΓΤ monogram in field to r. *Sellwood* 52/37. *B.M.C. 23.* 120, 161   ..   ..   ..   £6

7487 — — Similar, but with *rev.* type two cornuacopiae, monogram as last. *Sellwood* 52/39. *B.M.C. 23.* 121, 173   ..   ..   £6

7488 — — Similar, but with *rev.* type terminal figure between caduceus, on l., and ΑΓΤ monogram. *Sellwood* 52/42. *B.M.C. 23.* 122, 185 .. .. £7

7489 — — *Obv.* As 7473. ℞. Winged Eros, naked, stg. l. at altar; ΑΓΤ monogram in field to l.; legend only fragmentary, but probably as 7472. *Sellwood* 53/14. *B.M.C. 23.* 124, 201 .. .. £7

7490 — — Similar, but with *rev.* type Sphinx r., ΑΓΤ monogram before. *Sellwood* 53/17. *B.M.C. 23.* 124, 207 .. .. £7

7491 — — Similar, but with *rev.* type fish r., ΑΓΤ monogram above. *Sellwood* 53/18. *B.M.C. 23.* 125, 213 .. .. £7

7492 — Æ 13. His diad. and cuir. bust l., with pointed beard. ℞. Eagle stg. r., ΠΟΛΙΣ behind. *Sellwood* 51/42. *B.M.C. 23.* 134, 276 .. .. £9

7493   7494   7496

7493 — — *Obv.* Similar, but Phraates is crowned by Nike flying l. behind. ℞. Turreted bust of Tyche r., Α behind. *Sellwood* 50/17. *B.M.C. 23.* 131, 259 .. .. £10

7494 — — *Obv.* As 7492; star before. ℞. Bull's hd. facing, and corn-ear (to l.). *Sellwood* 54/19. *B.M.C. 23.* 130, 252 .. .. £9

7495 — — *Obv.* As 7492; star and crescent before. ℞. Turreted bust of Tyche r.; behind, Seleukid date ΠΣ (=year 280 = 33/2 B.C.). *Sellwood* 54/18. *B.M.C. 23.* 128, 231 £10

7496 **Tiridates I,** 26 B.C. (from the few coins which he has left behind it would seem that this usurper held power in Mesopotamia for a few months in 26 B.C., with Roman backing). Æ *tetradrachm* (c. 11·7 gm.). His diad. and cuir. bust l., with long pointed beard. ℞. The king enthroned r., receiving palm-branch from Tyche stg. l. before him, holding sceptre; above, ΒΑΣΙΛΕΩΣ / ΒΑΣΙΛΕΩΝ; on r., ΑΡΣΑΚΟΥ / ΕΥΕΡΓΕΤΟΥ; in ex , ΑΥΤΟΚΡΑΤΩΡ / ΦΙΛΟΡΩΜΑΙΟΥ; on l., ΕΠΙΦΑΝΟΥΣ / ΦΙΛΕΛΛΗΝΟΣ; in field above, ΞΑ (=month of Xandikos =March); behind Tyche, Seleukid date ϹΠΣ (=year 286 = 27/6 B.C.). *Sellwood* 55/1. *B.M.C. 23.* 135, 1 .. .. £650

N.B. *The coins of the later Parthian kings, extending down to the 3rd century A.D., will be listed in a future catalogue covering the 'Greek Imperial' coinage and contemporary issues.*

THE BAKTRIAN AND INDO-GREEK KINGDOMS

(The ancient authors have furnished us with very little information concerning this easternmost of all the Greek realms. Accordingly, the numismatic evidence is of more than usual importance in the attempt to piece together the history of the kings who ruled in Baktria and, later, in the area south of the Hindu Kush. The kingdom was created from the Seleukid province of Baktro-Sogdiana when the satrap Diodotos declared himself independent of Antiochos II about 256 B.C. Antiochos III, at the end of the century, tried unsuccessfully to reimpose Seleukid authority in the area, and early in the 2nd cent. B.C. King Demetrios of Baktria extended his rule southwards to include former provinces of the Mauryan Empire. The first bilingual coins, with inscriptions in Greek and Karosthi and struck on a new 'Indo-Greek' weight standard, date from this time of Greek expansion. Much of Baktria was lost to Scythian invaders about 130 B.C., and before the end of the century what was left of the Indo-Greek kingdom split into eastern and western divisions. By the end of the 1st cent. B.C. the last traces of Greek rule had disappeared, submerged beneath the tide of Kushan conquest. The following lists and historical notes are based on Michael Mitchiner's excellent work 'Indo-Greek and Indo-Scythian Coinage', Hawkins Publications, 1975).

7497 **Diodotos I,** *c.* 256-239 B.C. (originally the Seleukid satrap of Baktro-Sogdiana, he rebelled against Antiochos II *circa* 256 B.C. to become the region's first independent king). AS SATRAP, before *c.* 256 B.C. *N stater* (*c.* 8·3 gm.). Diad. hd. of Diodotos r. ℞. Naked Zeus striding l., brandishing thunderbolt and holding aegis, eagle at feet; ΒΑΣΙΛΕΩΣ on r., ΑΝΤΙΟΧΟΥ on l.; N in field to l. *Mitchiner (Indo-Greek and Indo-Scythian Coinage)* 63 .. .. £4,500

The Antiochos named on rev. is the Seleukid monarch Antiochos II, 261-246 B.C.

7498 — *Æ tetradrachm* (*c.* 16·65 gm.). Similar. *Mitchiner* 64*b*. *B.M.C.* 4. (*Seleucid Kings*) 15, 18 .. .. £750

7499 — *Æ drachm* (*c.* 4 gm.). Similar, but with ΠΡ monogram in *rev.* field to r., nothing to l. *Mitchiner* 65*a*. *B.M.C.* 4. 15, 22 .. .. £200

7500 — Æ 22. Bust of Hermes r., wearing petasos. ℞. ΒΑΣΙΛΕΩΣ / ΑΝΤΙΟΧΟΥ either side of caduceus; Δ within Ο in field to l. *Mitchiner* 78 .. .. £30

7501 AS KING, after *c.* 256 B.C. *N stater* (*c.* 8·3 gm.). His diad. hd. r. ℞. Naked Zeus, as 7497, with eagle at feet; ΒΑΣΙΛΕΩΣ on r., ΔΙΟΔΟΤΟΥ on l.; wreath in field to l. *Mitchiner* 70*a* £4,500

7502   7504

7502 — *Æ tetradrachm* (*c.* 16·65 gm.). As last, but with crescent instead of wreath in *rev.* field to l. *Mitchiner* 71*a* £1,250

7503 — — As 7501, but with *rev.* legend ΔΙΟΔΟΤΟΥ on r., ΣΩΤΗΡΟΣ on l.; and in *rev.* field, wreath to l., monogram to r. *Mitchiner* 72 .. .. £2,000

7504 — Æ 22. Laur. hd. of Zeus r. ℞. ΒΑΣΙΛΕΩΣ / ΔΙΟΔΟΤΟΥ either side of Artemis advancing r., holding torch, hound at feet. *Mitchiner* 82. *B.M.C. India* (=*Catalogue of Indian Coins in the British Museum: Greek and Scythic Kings of Bactria and India*) 3, 7 £25

7505 — Æ 14. *Obv.* As 7500. ℞. ΒΑΣΙΛΕΩΣ / ΔΙΟΔΟΤΟΥ either side of Athena stg. facing, holding spear and resting on shield. *Mitchiner* 80 .. .. £16

The bronze coins (nos. 7500, 7504-5), being without royal portrait, could equally well be in the name of Diodotos II.

7506   7511

7506 **Diodotos II,** *c.* 256-230 B.C. (son of Diodotos I, he appears to have ruled jointly with his father until the latter's death, *c.* 239 B.C., and then to have been sole ruler for about a decade until he was overthrown by Euthydemos). AS SATRAP, before *c.* 256 B.C. *N stater* (*c.* 8·3 gm.). Youthful hd. of Diodotos II, diad., r. ℞. Naked Zeus striding l., brandishing thunderbolt and holding aegis, eagle at feet; ΒΑΣΙΛΕΩΣ on r., ΑΝΤΙΟΧΟΥ on l.; N in field to l. *Mitchiner 66b* £4,000

7507 — Æ *tetradrachm* (*c.* 16·65 gm.). Similar, but with monogram instead of N in *rev.* field to l., and Ξ within Ο between Zeus' feet. *Mitchiner 67d. B.M.C. 4.* (*Seleucid Kings*) 15, 20 .. .. £750

7508 — Æ *drachm* (*c.* 4 gm.). As 7506. *Mitchiner 68b* £200

7509 — Æ *hemidrachm* (*c.* 2 gm.). Similar, but with ΔT monogram in *rev.* field to r., nothing to l. *Mitchiner 69a* £140

7510 AS KING, after *c.* 256 B.C. *N stater* (*c.* 8·4 gm.). His young diad. hd. r. ℞. Naked Zeus, as 7506, with eagle at feet; ΒΑΣΙΛΕΩΣ on r., ΔΙΟΔΟΤΟΥ on l.; wreath in field to l. *Mitchiner 73. B.M.C. India 3,* 1 .. .. £3,500

7511 — Æ *tetradrachm* (*c.* 16·65 gm.). Similar. *Mitchiner 74a. B.M.C. India 3,* 3 £1,250

7512 — Æ *drachm* (*c.* 4 gm.). Similar, but with MY monogram instead of wreath in *rev.* field to l. *Mitchiner 75b. B.M.C. India 3,* 6 .. .. £250

7513   7516

7513 **Euthydemos I,** *c.* 230-190 B.C. (this king obtained the Baktrian throne by force, deposing Diodotos II about 230 B.C. He was defeated in 208 B.C. by Antiochos III of Syria, but successfully withstood a two-year seige in his capital at Balkh as a result of which the Seleukid king was obliged to acknowledge his independence. Towards the end of Euthydemos' reign the northern province of Sogdiana broke away from the Baktrian kingdom). *N stater* (*c.* 8·25 gm.). His diad. hd. r. ℞. Naked Herakles seated l. on rock, holding club set on pile of stones; ΒΑΣΙΛΕΩΣ on r., ΕΥΘΥΔΕΜΟΥ on l., monogram in field to l. *Mitchiner 84a. B.M.C. India 4,* 1 .. .. £4,000

7514 — *N oktadrachm* (*c.* 32·73 gm.). Similar, but on *rev.* Herakles rests his club on his r. knee, and with monogram in field to r. instead of l. *Mitchiner 89i* .. .. (*Unique*)

7515 — Æ *tetradrachm* (*c.* 16·65 gm.). As 7513, but with monogram in *rev.* field to r. instead of l. *Mitchiner 85a. B.M.C. India 4,* 6-8 .. .. £500

7516 — — As 7514, but the king's features are elderly. *Mitchiner 94. B.M.C. India 5,* 13 .. .. £600

7517 — — (Persic standard, *c.* 11-13 gm.). As 7514. *Mitchiner 96. B.M.C. India 5,* 12 £750

This was adopted as the prototype for the coinage of the independent Kingdom of Sogdiana in the 2nd cent. B.C.

7518 — Æ *drachm* (*c.* 4 gm.). As 7513. *Mitchiner 86a* £250

7519 — — As 7514, but the king's features are elderly. *Mitchiner 95. B.M.C. India 5,* 14 .. .. £300

7520 — Æ *hemidrachm* (*c.* 2 gm.). As 7513, but with monogram in *rev.* field to r. instead of l. *Mitchiner 91a* £150

Euthydemos I *continued*

7521 — Æ *obol* (*c.* 0·65 gm.).   As 7514, but without monogram in *rev.* field.   *Mitchiner* 92
                                                                                                £100
7522 — Æ *hemiobol* (*c.* 0·3 gm.).   Similar.   *Mitchiner* 93 ..   ..   £85

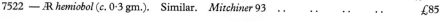

7523   7525

7523 — Æ 23.   Bare hd. of bearded Herakles r.   R. ΒΑΣΙΛΕΩΣ / ΕΥΘΥΔΗΜΟΥ above and
beneath horse prancing r.   *Mitchiner* 97a.   *B.M.C. India* 8, 6   ..   ..   £25

7524 — Æ 10.   Similar, but with *rev.* type horse's hd. r.   *Mitchiner* 88   ..   ..   £14

7525 **Demetrios,** *c.* 205-171 B.C. (son of Euthydemos I, Demetrios was made co-ruler by his
father *circa* 205 B.C. and succeeded to the supreme power about fifteen years later.   His
reign was notable for the expansion of Greek power southwards into the Kabul valley and
beyond.   For this achievement he became known to posterity as 'Demetrios, King of the
Indians.'   He eventually fell victim to a rebellion led by Eukratides).   Æ *tetradrachm*
(*c.* 16·8 gm.).   His diad. and dr. bust r.   R. Athena stg. facing, holding spear and resting
on shield; ΒΑΣΙΛΕΩΣ on r., ΔΗΜΗΤΡΙΟΥ on l.; ΠΑ monogram in lower field to l., Δ in upper
field to r.   *Mitchiner* 101h £500
This type probably belongs to the period of joint reign with his father, 205-190 B.C.

7526   7527

7526 — — His diad. and dr. bust r., wearing elephant's scalp head-dress.   R. Young naked
Herakles stg. facing, crowning himself, and holding club and lion's skin; legend as last;
ΚΡ monogram in field to l.   *Mitchiner* 103d.   *B.M.C. India* 6, 1-2   ..   ..   £850

7527 — — (Indo-Greek standard, *c.* 9 gm.).   ΒΑΣΙΛΕΩΣ ΑΝΙΚΗΤΟΥ ΔΗΜΗΤΡΙΟΥ.   His diad.
and dr. bust r., wearing kausia.   R. Zeus stg. facing, holding thunderbolt and sceptre;
Karosthi legend around; monogram in field to r.   *Mitchiner* 111   ..   .. (*Unique ?*)

7528 — Æ *drachm* (*c.* 3·9 gm.).   As 7525, but without the Δ in *rev.* field.   *Mitchiner* 102
                                                                                                £150

7529 — — As 7526.   *Mitchiner* 104d.   *B.M.C. India* 6, 6 ..   ..   £225

7530 — — (Indo-Greek standard, *c.* 2·25 gm.).   As 7527, but the king does not wear a
kausia.   *Mitchiner* 110   ..   .. (*Unique ?*)

7531 — Æ *obol* (*c.* 0·65 gm.).   As 7526.   *Mitchiner* 105e.   *B.M.C. India* 6, 10-11   £75

7532 — Æ 34.   Circular shield, ornamented with Gorgon's hd.   R. ΒΑΣΙΛΕΩΣ / ΔΗΜΗΤΡΙΟΥ
either side of trident; Ξ / Α in field to l.   *Mitchiner* 107b.   *B.M.C. India* 7, 15 ..   £75

7533   7534

7533 — Æ 29. Hd. of elephant r., bell hanging from neck. ℞. ΒΑΣΙΛΕΩΣ / ΔΗΜΗΤΡΙΟΥ either side of caduceus; monogram in field to l. *Mitchiner* 108b. *B.M.C. India* 7, 16   £40

7534 — Æ 25. Bearded bust of Herakles r., lion's skin knotted at neck, club over shoulder. ℞. ΒΑΣΙΛΕΩΣ / ΔΗΜΗΤΡΙΟΥ either side of Artemis, rad., stg. facing, drawing arrow from quiver, and holding bow; in field to l., ο / Ξ. *Mitchiner* 109e. *B.M.C. India* 7, 13-14 £25

7535 — Square Æ 18. His bust r., clad in elephant's scalp, as 7526; ΒΑΣΙΛΕΩΣ behind, ΑΝΙΚΗΤΟΥ above, ΔΗΜΗΤΡΙΟΥ before. ℞. Thunderbolt, Karosthi legend around; monogram in field to r. *Mitchiner* 112 .. .. £35

7536 **Euthydemos II,** *c.* 190-171 B.C. (son of Demetrios, Euthydemos was associated with his father as co-ruler throughout the latter's reign, and shared his fate in the revolt of Eukratides). Æ *tetradrachm* (*c.* 16·8 gm.). His young diad. and dr. bust r. ℞. Young naked Herakles, crowned with ivy, stg. facing, holding wreath, club and lion's skin; ΒΑΣΙΛΕΩΣ on r., ΕΥΘΥΔΗΜΟΥ on l.; monogram in field to l. *Mitchiner* 113b £1,500

7537 — Æ *drachm* (*c.* 4·2 gm.). Similar. *Mitchiner* 114b £300

7538 — Æ *hemidrachm* (*c.* 2 gm.). Similar. *Mitchiner* 115 .. .. .. £175

7539 — Æ *obol* (*c.* 0·65 gm.). Similar. *Mitchiner* 116c £90

7540 — Nickel *didrachm* (*c.* 8 gm.) Laur. hd. of Apollo r. ℞. ΒΑΣΙΛΕΩΣ / ΕΥΘΥΔΗΜΟΥ either side of tripod; monogram in field to l. *Mitchiner* 118a. *B.M.C. India* 8, 4 £350

7541 — Æ 27. Similar. *Mitchiner* 121. *B.M.C. India* 8, 5 .. .. .. £30

7542 Antimachos, *c.* 171-160 B.C. (when Demetrios and Euthydemos II were overthrown by the rebel Eukratides, the dynastic cause was taken up by Antimachos who seems to have been a brother of Demetrios. Antimachos promoted his nephews, Agathokles and Pantaleon, to the rank of co-rulers, and the three kings jointly opposed Eukratides. However, the usurper was more than a match for his adversaries and by *circa* 160 B.C. the entire kingdom was under his control). Æ *tetradrachm* (*c.* 16·8 gm.). His diad. and dr. bust r., wearing kausia. R. Poseidon stg. facing, holding trident and palm-branch; ΒΑΣΙΛΕΩΣ ΘΕΟΥ on r., ΑΝΤΙΜΑΧΟΥ on l.; N within O in field to r. *Mitchiner* 124*b. B.M.C. India* 12, 1-2 .. .. £900

7543 — — Diad. hd. of Diodotos I, founder of the kingdom, r.; ΔΙΟΔΟΤΟΥ before, ΣΩΤΗΡΟΣ behind. R. Naked Zeus striding l., brandishing thunderbolt and holding aegis, eagle at feet; ΒΑΣΙΛΕΥΟΝΤΟΣ on r., ΘΕΟΥ in ex., ΑΝΤΙΜΑΧΟΥ on l.; ΑΝ monogram in field to r., wreath to l. *Mitchiner* 128 .. .. £6,000

This type and the next were issued to emphasize the legitimacy of Antimachos' claim to the throne, in the face of the rebellion of Eukratides. Other 'pedigree' types were issued by Agathokles and by Eukratides himself.

7544 — — Diad. hd. of Euthydemos I r.; ΕΥΘΥΔΗΜΟΥ before, ΘΕΟΥ behind. R. Naked Herakles seated l. on rock, holding club resting on rock; legend as last; ΑΝ monogram in field to r. *Mitchiner* 129 .. .. £5,000

7545 — Æ *drachm* (*c.* 4 gm.). As 7542. *Mitchiner* 125*a. B.M.C. India* 12, 4 .. £225

7546   7551

7546 — — (Indo-Greek standard, *c.* 2·45 gm.). ΒΑΣΙΛΕΩΣ ΝΙΚΗΦΟΡΟΥ ΑΝΤΙΜΑΧΟΥ. Nike advancing l., holding palm and wreath; monogram in field to l. R. The king on horseback prancing r.; Karosthi legend around. *Mitchiner* 135*b. B.M.C. India* 55, 1-2 £35

7547 — Æ *hemidrachm* (*c.* 2 gm.). As 7542, but with ΗΑ monogram in *rev.* field to r. *Mitchiner* 126. *B.M.C. India* 12, 5 .. .. £175

7548 — Æ *obol* (*c.* 0·7 gm.). As 7542, but with ΚΡ monogram in *rev.* field to r. *Mitchiner* 127*c. B.M.C. India* 12, 6 .. .. £80

7549 — Æ 24. Elephant walking r. R. Nike advancing l., holding wreath and palm; ΒΑΣΙΛΕΩΣ on r., ΑΝΤΙΜΑΧΟΥ on l., ΚΡ monogram in field to r. *Mitchiner* 130*b* .. £30

7550 — Square Æ 20×14. *Obv.* Similar. R. ΒΑΣΙΛΕΩΣ / ΑΝΤΙΜΑΧΟΥ above and beneath winged thunderbolt. *Mitchiner* 133 .. .. £25

7551 — Square Æ 19. Aegis; ΒΑΣΙΛΕΩΣ on l., ΝΙΚΗΦΟΡΟΥ above, ΑΝΤΙΜΑΧΟΥ on r. R. Wreath and palm; Karosthi legend around, monogram beneath. *Mitchiner* 136*a. B.M.C. India* 55, 10 .. .. £20

7552 **Agathokles,** *c.* 171-160 B.C. (probably a son of Demetrios and nephew of Antimachos, Agathokles was co-ruler with his uncle and brother, Pantaleon, until their defeat by Eukratides). *Æ tetradrachm* (*c.* 16·8 gm.). His diad. and dr. bust r. ℞. Zeus stg. facing, holding torch-bearing figure of Hekate, and sceptre; ΒΑΣΙΛΕΩΣ on r., ΑΓΑΘΟΚΛΕΟΥΣ on l.; ΦΛΩ monogram in field to l. *Mitchiner* 137. *B.M.C. India* 10, 4 .. .. £2,000

7553 — — Hd. of young Herakles r., clad in lion's skin; ΑΛΕΞΑΝΔΡΟΥ before, ΤΟΥ ΦΙΛΙΠΠΟΥ behind. ℞. Zeus enthroned l., holding eagle and sceptre; ΒΑΣΙΛΕΥΟΝΤΟΣ on r , ΔΙΚΑΙΟΥ in ex., ΑΓΑΘΟΚΛΕΟΥΣ on l.; ΚΡ monogram in field to l. *Mitchiner* 142. *B.M.C. India* 10, 1 £7,500

7554 — — Diad. and dr. bust of Demetrios r., clad in elephant's skin; ΔΗΜΗΤΡΙΟΥ before, ΑΝΙΚΗΤΟΥ behind. ℞. Naked Herakles stg. facing, crowning himself and holding club and lion's skin; legend and monogram as last. *Mitchiner* 146 .. .. £6,000

In addition to the two examples listed above, Agathokles issued other 'pedigree' tetradrachms in the names of Antiochos I, Diodotos I and Euthydemos I.

7555 — Æ *drachm* (*c.* 4 gm.). As 7552. *Mitchiner* 138. *B.M.C. India* 10, 5 .. £400

7556 — Square Æ *drachm* (Indo-Greek standard, *c.* 2·3 - 3·3 gm.). ΒΑΣΙΛΕΩΣ / ΑΓΑΘΟΚΛΕΟΥΣ either side of male deity, with elaborate head-dress, stg. facing, holding sword and ankus. ℞. Similar deity to *obv.*, but holding vase and wheel; Brahmi legend on either side. *Mitchiner* 149 .. .. £500

7557   7559

7557 — Nickel *didrachm* (*c.* 8 gm.). Dr. bust of young Dionysos r., wreathed with ivy, thyrsos at shoulder. ℞. ΒΑΣΙΛΕΩΣ / ΑΓΑΘΟΚΛΕΟΥΣ above and beneath panther stg. r., one paw raised to touch vine before; ΦΛΩ monogram in field to l. *Mitchiner* 147a. *B.M.C. India* 11, 6 .. .. £250

7558 — Square Æ 26 × 20. Female deity walking l., holding flower; Brahmi legend on either side. ℞. ΒΑΣΙΛΕΩΣ / ΑΓΑΘΟΚΛΕΟΥΣ above and beneath maneless lion stg. r. *Mitchiner* 151. *B.M.C. India* 11, 12 .. .. £20

7559 — Square Æ 19 × 16. Six-arched buddhist stupa, surmounted by star; Karosthi legend beneath. ℞. Tree within rectangular railing; Karosthi legend beneath. *Mitchiner* 156. *B.M.C. India* 12, 15 .. .. £22

These often have one curved edge, indicating that the flan has been cut from a larger coin.

7560 **Pantaleon,** *c.* 171-160 B.C. (co-ruler with his uncle, Antimachos, and brother, Agathokles). *Æ tetradrachm* (*c.* 16·8 gm.). His diad. and dr. bust r. ℞. Zeus enthroned l., holding torch-bearing figure of Hekate, and sceptre; ΒΑΣΙΛΕΩΣ on r., ΠΑΝΤΑΛΕΟΝΤΟΣ on l.; ΦΛΩ monogram in field to l. *Mitchiner* 157 .. .. £5,000

Pantaleon *continued*

7561 — Æ *drachm* (*c.* 4⅛gm.). Similar. *Mitchiner* 158 .. .. £1,000

7562 — Æ *obol* (*c.* 0·65 gm.). Similar, but without monogram on *rev.* *Mitchiner* 159
£250

7563 — Nickel *didrachm* (*c.* 8 gm.). Types as the nickel *didrachm* of Agathokles, 7557, but with legend ΒΑΣΙΛΕΩΣ / ΠΑΝΤΑΛΕΟΝΤΟΣ on *rev.* *Mitchiner* 160a £550

7564 — Square Æ 23×20. Female deity walking l., holding flower; Brahmi legend on either side. ℞. ΒΑΣΙΛΕΩΣ / ΠΑΝΤΑΛΕΟΝΤΟΣ above and beneath maneless lion stg. r. *Mitchiner* 161. *B.M.C. India* 9, 3 .. .. £30

7565 **Eukratides**, *c.* 171-135 B.C. (one of the most celebrated of the Indo-Greek monarchs, Eukratides first rose to power in revolt against Demetrios and Euthydemos II. By *circa* 160 B.C. he had disposed of all his rivals and the following three decades were probably the most settled and prosperous period in the history of the kingdom. Eukratides appointed a number of sub-kings, with special local responsibilities, and each of these issued coinage in his own name. Menander was, perhaps, the best-known of these local rulers. Eukratides was murdered by his own son, Heliokles). N 20-*stater* (*c.* 168 gm.). His diad. and dr. bust r., wearing crested helmet ornamented with bull's horn and ear. ℞. ΒΑΣΙΛΕΩΣ ΜΕΓΑΛΟΥ ΕΥΚΡΑΤΙΔΟΥ. The Dioskouroi on horseback prancing r., each holding spear and palm; monogram in lower field to r. *Mitchiner* 175 .. .. .. (*Unique*)

7566 — N *stater* (*c.* 8·15 gm.). Similar. *Mitchiner* 176b £12,500

7567 — Æ *tetradrachm* (*c.* 16·8 gm.). His diad. and dr. bust r.; fillet border. ℞. Apollo stg. facing, hd. l., holding arrow and resting on bow; ΒΑΣΙΛΕΩΣ on r., ΕΥΚΡΑΤΙΔΟΥ on l.; ΗΛ monogram in field to l. *Mitchiner* 164 m. *B.M.C. India* 13, 3 .. .. £300

7568 — — *Obv.* Similar. ℞. The Dioskouroi on horseback, as 7565; ΒΑΣΙΛΕΩΣ above, ΕΥΚΡΑΤΙΔΟΥ in ex.; ΚΡ monogram in lower field to r. *Mitchiner* 168f. *B.M.C. India* 13, 6 .. .. £350

7569 — — — ℞. Apollo stg., as 7567; around, ΒΑΣΙΛΕΩΣ ΣΩΤΗΡΟΣ ΕΥΚΡΑΤΙΔΟΥ; ΠΚ monogram in field to l. *Mitchiner* 173a £450

7570 — — As 7565, but with fillet border on *obv.* *Mitchiner* 177i. *B.M.C. India* 14, 9 £375

7571 — — Heroic bust of king, viewed from behind, hd. turned to l., wearing diad. and crested helmet, and thrusting with spear held in r. hand; fillet border. ℞. As 7565. *Mitchiner* 179a £3,000

7572 — — ΒΑΣΙΛΕΥΣ ΜΕΓΑΣ ΕΥΚΡΑΤΙΔΗΣ. His helmeted bust r., as 7565; fillet border. ℞. Conjoined busts r. of Heliokles and Laodike, father and mother of Eukratides; ΗΛΙΟΚΛΕΟΥΣ above, ΚΑΙ ΛΑΟΔΙΚΗΣ beneath; monogram in field to l.; fillet border. *Mitchiner* 182a £2,500

7573 — Æ *drachm* (*c.* 4 gm.). As 7565. *Mitchiner* 178a. *B.M.C. India* 14, 16 .. £80

7574 — — As 7572, but with dotted borders on both sides. *Mitchiner* 183. *B.M.C. India* 19, 2 .. .. £500

7575   7578

Eukratides *continued*

7575 — — (Indo-Greek standard, *c.* 2·4 gm.). ΒΑΣΙΛΕΩΣ ΜΕΓΑΛΟΥ ΕΥΚΡΑΤΙΛΟΥ. His helmeted bust r., as 7565. ℞. The Dioskouroi stg. facing, side by side, each holding spear; Karosthi legend around; ΜΤ monogram in field to l. *Mitchiner* 188a £250

7576 — Æ *obol* (*c.* 0·65 gm.). *Obv.* As 7565. ℞. Naked Herakles stg. facing, crowning himself and holding club and lion's skin; ΒΑΣΙΛΕΩΣ on r., ΕΥΚΡΑΤΙΛΟΥ on l. *Mitchiner* 166 .. .. £50

7577 — — His diad. and dr. bust r. ℞. Caps of the Dioskouroi and two palm-branches; legend as last; monogram beneath. *Mitchiner* 180c. *B.M.C. India* 15, 22 .. £30

7578 — — Similar, but with helmeted bust on *obv.*, as 7565. *Mitchiner* 181a. *B.M.C. India* 15, 28 .. .. £30

7579 — Æ *hemiobol* (*c.* 0·35 gm.). As 7576. *Mitchiner* 167 .. .. .. £50

7580 — Æ 28. As 7565, but with fillet border on *obv.* *Mitchiner* 185 .. .. £35

7581 — Æ 15. Similar, but with only one of the Dioskouroi on *rev.*, prancing r. holding spear. *Mitchiner* 187. *B.M.C. India* 16, 35 .. .. £18

7582   7585

7582 — Square Æ 22. His helmeted bust r., as 7565; ΒΑΣΙΛΕΩΣ behind, ΜΕΓΑΛΟΥ above, ΕΥΚΡΑΤΙΛΟΥ beneath. ℞. The Dioskouroi on horseback prancing r., each holding spear and palm; Karosthi legend above and beneath; monogram in field to l., E to r. *Mitchiner* 190k. *B.M.C. India* 16, 36 .. .. £12

7583 — Square Æ 22 × 20. Heroic bust of the king, as 7571; legend as last. ℞. Nike advancing r., holding wreath and palm; Karosthi legend before and behind; monogram in field to r. *Mitchiner* 189. *B.M.C. India* 18, 62.. .. .. £20

7584 — Square Æ 19 × 17. *Obv.* As 7582, but ΕΥΚΡΑΤΙΛΟΥ before instead of beneath. ℞. Linear square containing Nike stg. l. with wreath and palm, monogram to l.; Karosthi legend around. *Mitchiner* 193a. *B.M.C. India* 18, 59 .. .. £14

7585 — Square Æ 18 × 16. *Obv.* As last. ℞. Tyche of Kapisa enthroned l., holding palm-branch; forepart of elephant to l., mountain and monogram to r.; all within linear square around which Karosthi legend. *Mitchiner* 194b. *B.M.C. India* 19, 63 .. £15

7586 — Square Æ 13. His diad. and dr. bust r.; legend as 7582. ℞. Caps of the Dioskouroi and two palm-branches; Karosthi legend on r. and l. *Mitchiner* 195. *B.M.C. India* 18, 56-7 .. .. £10

7587 **Plato,** c. 150 B.C. (appointed by Eukratides as co-ruler in Baktria). Æ tetradrachm (c. 16·8 gm.). His diad. and dr. bust r.; fillet border. Ɍ. ΒΑΣΙΛΕΩΣ ΕΠΙΦΑΝΟΥΣ ΠΛΑΤΩΝΟΣ. Rad. Helios in galloping quadriga three-quarter face to r.; monogram in lower field to r., ΜΗ in ex. Mitchiner 196c £2,500

7588 — — Similar, but on obv. the king wears crested helmet ornamented with bull's horn and ear; and on rev. the monogram is in upper field to r., ΜΖ in ex. Mitchiner 197. B.M.C. India 20, 1 .. .. £2,750

7589 — — Obv. As 7587. Ɍ. Rad. Helios stg. facing, r. hand raised, holding sceptre in l.; legend as 7587; ΜΤ monogram in field to l. Mitchiner 199 .. .. .. (Unique?)

7590 **Apollodotos I,** c. 160-150 B.C. (following the final defeat of Antimachos, Agathokles and Pantaleon, Eukratides appointed two sub-kings, Apollodotos and Menander, to administer the southern provinces of his realm). Æ drachm (Indo-Greek standard, c. 2 gm.). ΒΑΣΙΛΕΩΣ ΑΠΟΛΛΟΔΟΤΟΥ ΣΩΤΗΡΟΣ. Elephant stg. r. Ɍ. Humped bull stg. r., Karosthi legend around. Mitchiner 203. B.M.C. India 34, 1-2 .. .. £45

7591   7594

7591 — Square Æ drachm (Indo-Greek standard, c. 2·45 gm.). Elephant stg. r.; ΒΑΣΙΛΕΩΣ behind, ΑΠΟΛΛΟΔΟΤΟΥ above, ΣΩΤΗΡΟΣ before; ΚΡ monogram beneath. Ɍ. Humped bull stg. r., Karosthi legend around; ΔΑ monogram beneath. Mitchiner 207a. B.M.C. India 34, 3 .. .. £40

7592 — Square Æ hemidrachm (c. 1·2 gm.). Similar, but with ΞΕ beneath elephant on obv., and without monogram on rev. Mitchiner 208a. B.M.C. India 34, 12 .. £75

7593 — Square Æ 21 × 18. Apollo enthroned r., holding bow; ΒΑΣΙΛΕΩΣ behind, ΣΩΤΗΡΟΣ above, ΑΠΟΛΛΟΔΟΤΟΥ before. Ɍ. Tripod; Karosthi legend around; monogram in field to r. Mitchiner 204a £18

7594 — Square Æ 22 × 21. Naked Apollo, rad., stg. facing, holding arrow and resting on bow; ΒΑΣΙΛΕΩΣ on l., ΑΠΟΛΛΟΔΟΤΟΥ above, ΣΩΤΗΡΟΣ on r. Ɍ. Tripod on stand, within dotted square; Karosthi legend around. Mitchiner 209a. B.M.C. India 35, 13 £12

7595 Menander, c. 160-145 B.C. (perhaps the best-known of the Indo-Greek kings, Menander was appointed by Eukratides to rule the areas south of the Hindu Kush. His colleagues in this task were Apollodotos and, later, Zoilos. According to Buddhist tradition, in which he is named Milinda, Menander was a just and powerful ruler and a convert to Buddhism). Æ *tetradrachm* (Attic standard, c. 16·8 gm.). His diad. and dr. bust r.; fillet border. ℞. Athena advancing l., brandishing thunderbolt and holding shield; ΒΑΣΙΛΕΩΣ ΣΩΤΗΡΟΣ on r., ΜΕΝΑΝΔΡΟΥ on l.; ΜΤ monogram in field to l. *Mitchiner* 212b £7,500

7596 — — (Indo-Greek standard, c. 9·7 gm.). ΒΑΣΙΛΕΩΣ ΣΩΤΗΡΟΣ ΜΕΝΑΝΔΡΟΥ. His diad. and dr. bust r. ℞. Athena l., as last; Karosthi legend around; monogram in field to l. *Mitchiner* 214f. *B.M.C. India* 44, 3 .. .. £175

7597   7599

7597 — — — Similar, but the king wears crested helmet on *obv.*; and in *rev.* field, Σ to l., monogram to r. *Mitchiner* 217f. *B.M.C. India* 44, 5 .. .. £200

7598 — — — As last, but with *obv.* type heroic bust of the king, viewed from behind, hd. turned to l., wearing diad. and aegis, and thrusting with spear held in r. hand. *Mitchiner* 219c £350

7599 — Æ *drachm* (c. 2·45 gm.). ΒΑΣΙΛΕΩΣ ΣΩΤΗΡΟΣ ΜΕΝΑΝΔΡΟΥ around bust of Athena r., wearing crested helmet. ℞. Owl stg. r., hd. facing; Karosthi legend around; monogram in field to r. *Mitchiner* 213a £125

7600   7604

7600 — — As 7596. *Mitchiner* 215t. *B.M.C. India* 45, 15 .. .. .. £30

7601 — — As 7597. *Mitchiner* 218h £35

7602 — — *Obv.* As 7598. ℞. Athena l., as 7595; Karosthi legend around; monogram in field to r. *Mitchiner* 224b. *B.M.C. India* 46, 34 .. .. £35

7603 — — Similar, but the king also wears crested helmet on *obv. Mitchiner* 226a £40

7604 — — *Obv.* As 7598. ℞. Athena stg. r., brandishing thunderbolt and holding aegis; Karosthi legend around; monogram in field to l. *Mitchiner* 221b. *B.M.C. India* 47, 36-7 .. .. £35

7605 — — ΒΑΣΙΛΕΩΣ ΔΙΚΑΙΟΥ ΜΕΝΑΝΔΡΟΥ. His dr. bust r., wearing crested helmet. ℞. Nike stg. r., holding wreath and palm; Karosthi legend around; monogram in field to l. *Mitchiner* 229a £100

7606 — — *Obv.* Similar. ℞. The king on horseback prancing r.; Karosthi legend around; monogram beneath. *Mitchiner* 230 .. .. £150

7607 — Square Æ 28. Bust of Athena r., wearing crested helmet; ΒΑΣΙΛΕΩΣ on l., ΣΩΤΗΡΟΣ above, ΜΕΝΑΝΔΡΟΥ on r. ℞. Horse prancing r.; Karosthi legend around; monogram beneath. *Mitchiner* 231. *B.M.C. India* 48, 47 .. .. £50

7608   7611

7608 — Square Æ 26. Diad. and dr. bust of king r.; legend as last. ℞. Dolphin r.; Karosthi legend around; monogram and H beneath. *Mitchiner* 232 .. .. .. £35

7609 — Square Æ 23. Hd. of ox facing; legend as 7607. ℞. Tripod; Karosthi legend around; ΚΡΑ monogram in field to l. *Mitchiner* 233a. *B.M.C. India* 49, 64-5 £20

7610 — Square Æ 22. Elephant stg. l.; legend as 7607. ℞. Elephant goad; Karosthi legend around; Δ in field to l., monogram to r. *Mitchiner* 236 .. .. .. £22

7611 — Square Æ 22. Heroic bust of king, as 7598; ΒΑΣΙΛΕΩΣ above, ΣΩΤΗΡΟΣ on r., ΜΕΝΑΝΔΡΟΥ beneath. ℞. As 7604, but the monogram is in field to r. *Mitchiner* 237b. *B.M.C. India* 47, 44 .. .. £16

7612   7616

7612 — Square Æ 20. *Obv.* As 7607. ℞. Nike stg. r., holding wreath and palm; Karosthi legend around; monogram in field to r. *Mitchiner* 243b. *B.M.C. India* 48, 52 £12

7613 — Square Æ 21. *Obv.* As 7607. ℞. Circular shield, ornamented with Gorgon's hd.; Karosthi legend around; monogram beneath. *Mitchiner* 246d. *B.M.C. India* 49, 59 £14

7614 — Square Æ 20. Athena stg. l., holding spear, shield at feet; ΒΑΣΙΛΕΩΣ on l., ΔΙΚΑΙΟΥ above, ΜΕΝΑΝΔΡΟΥ on r. ℞. Maneless lion stg. l.; Karosthi legend around; monogram beneath. *Mitchiner* 252a. *B.M.C. India* 50, 74 .. .. £15

7615 — Square Æ 18. Hd. of boar r.; legend as 7607. ℞. Palm-branch; Karosthi legend around; monogram in field to l. *Mitchiner* 249a £16

7616 — Square Æ 14. Hd. of elephant r., bell round neck; legend as 7607. ℞. Club upwards; Karosthi legend around; monogram — A in lower field. *Mitchiner* 240a. *B.M.C. India* 50, 68 .. .. £10

7617 — Square Æ 12. Wheel; legend as 7607. ℞. As 7615, but the monogram is in field to r. *Mitchiner* 241. *B.M.C. India* 50, 73 .. .. £14

7618 Zoilos I, *c.* 150-145 B.C. (on the death of Apollodotos I, Zoilos became the colleague of Menander in the government of the southern provinces). Æ tetradrachm (*c.* 9·7 gm.). ΒΑΣΙΛΕΩΣ ΔΙΚΑΙΟΥ ΙΩΙΛΟΥ. His diad. and dr. bust r. ℞. Naked Herakles stg. facing, holding wreath, club and lion's skin; Karosthi legend around; monogram in field to l. *Mitchiner* 255 .. .. £1,250

7619   7622

7619 — Æ drachm (*c.* 2·45 gm.). Similar. *Mitchiner* 256*e*. *B.M.C. India* 52, 1   £70

7620 — — Similar, but with small figure of Nike on Herakles l. shoulder on *rev.* *Mitchiner* 257*a* £75

7621 — Square Æ 23. Bust of Herakles, bearded, r.; ΒΑΣΙΛΕΩΣ on l., ΔΙΚΑΙΟΥ above, ΙΩΙΛΟΥ beneath. ℞. Club and bow in case within wreath; Karosthi legend around; monogram in field to r. *Mitchiner* 258*b* £30

7622 Lysias, *c.* 145-135 B.C. (on the death of Menander, *circa* 145 B.C., Eukratides appointed a new pair of sub-kings, Lysias and Antialkidas, to rule the southern provinces of the Indo-Greek realm. Lysias may have been a son of King Demetrios). Æ *tetradrachm* (Attic standard, *c.* 16 - 16·9 gm.). His diad. and dr. bust r., wearing elephant's scalp head-dress; fillet border. ℞. ΒΑΣΙΛΕΩΣ ΑΝΙΚΗΤΟΥ ΛΥΣΙΟΥ. Naked Herakles stg. facing, crowning himself and holding club, palm and lion's skin; monogram in field to l. *Mitchiner* 259*c* £4,000

7623 — Æ drachm (Indo-Greek standard, *c.* 2·4 gm.). ΒΑΣΙΛΕΩΣ ΑΝΙΚΗΤΟΥ ΛΥΣΙΟΥ. Type as last. ℞. Naked Herakles, as last; Karosthi legend around; monogram — Σ in field. *Mitchiner* 262*b*. *B.M.C. India* 29, 3 .. .. £90

7619   7622

7624 — — Similar, but king wears crested helmet instead of elephant's scalp, and with monogram only in *rev.* field to l. *Mitchiner* 264*b*. *B.M.C. India* 29, 7 .. £85

7625 — Æ 24. ΒΑΣΙΛΕΩΣ ΑΝΙΚΗΤΟΥ ΛΥΣΙΟΥ. Bust of bearded Herakles r., club and palm over shoulder. ℞. Elephant walking r.; Karosthi legend around; monogram beneath. *Mitchiner* 267*a*. *B.M.C. India* 29, 8 .. .. £22

7626 — Square Æ 19 × 17. Bust of bearded Herakles r., club over shoulder; ΒΑΣΙΛΕΩΣ behind, ΑΝΙΚΗΤΟΥ above, ΛΥΣΙΟΥ before. ℞. As last, but with monogram and Σ beneath. *Mitchiner* 266*e*. *B.M.C. India* 30, 9 .. .. £18

7627 **Antialkidas,** *c.* 145-135 B.C. (colleague of Lysias in the government of the southern provinces, Antialkidas may have been a son of King Antimachos). Æ *tetradrachm* (Attic standard, *c.* 16 - 16·75 gm.). His diad. and dr. bust r.; fillet border. ℞. ΒΑΣΙΛΕΩΣ ΝΙΚΗΦΟΡΟΥ ΑΝΤΙΑΛΚΙΔΟΥ. Zeus enthroned three-quarter face to l., holding Nike and sceptre, forepart of elephant r. at his feet; monogram in field to r. *Mitchiner* 269. *B.M.C. India* 25, 1 .. .. £4,000

7628 — — (Indo-Greek standard, *c.* 9·6 gm.). ΒΑΣΙΛΕΩΣ ΝΙΚΗΦΟΡΟΥ ΑΝΤΙΑΛΚΙΔΟΥ. His diad. and dr. bust r. ℞. Zeus, holding sceptre, stg. three-quarter face to l. beside elephant walking l., small Nike on its hd.; Karosthi legend around; monogram in field to l. *Mitchiner* 273a £500

7629 — Æ *drachm* (*c.* 2·45 gm.). *Obv.* Similar, but king wears kausia. ℞. Type as 7627; Karosthi legend around; monogram beneath throne. *Mitchiner* 277e. *B.M.C. India* 25, 5 .. .. £50

7630 — — As last, but on *obv.* king wears crested helmet. *Mitchiner* 279d. *B.M.C. India* 26, 7 .. .. £50

7631 — — *Obv.* As 7628. ℞. Zeus enthroned three-quarter face to l., holding wreath and palm in r. hand, sceptre in l.; at his feet, elephant facing; Karosthi legend around; monogram beneath throne. *Mitchiner* 276 .. .. £60

7632 — Æ 21. ΒΑΣΙΛΕΩΣ ΝΙΚΗΦΟΡΟΥ ΑΝΤΙΑΛΚΙΔΟΥ. Bust of Zeus r., hurling thunderbolt with r. hand. ℞. Two palm-branches between caps of the Dioskouroi; Karosthi legend around; monogram beneath. *Mitchiner* 282a. *B.M.C. India* 27, 17 .. .. £20

7633 — Square Æ 19 × 17. Bust of Zeus r., thunderbolt over l. shoulder; ΒΑΣΙΛΕΩΣ behind, ΝΙΚΗΦΟΡΟΥ above, ΑΝΤΙΑΛΚΙΔΟΥ before. ℞. As last; monogram — Σ in lower field. *Mitchiner* 280d. *B.M.C. India* 27, 19 .. .. £16

7634 Heliokles, *c.* 135-110 B.C. (the son of Eukratides, Heliokles became supreme king after murdering his father. Within a few years of his accession a large part of Baktria was conquered by the Scythian nomads who now settled in this newly acquired territory. Heliokles ruled over his reduced realm until *circa* 110 B.C. when he appears to have been overthrown by Philoxenos and Diomedes). Æ *tetradrachm* (Attic standard, *c.* 16·8 gm.). His diad. and dr. bust r.; fillet border. ℞. Zeus stg. facing, holding thunderbolt and sceptre; ΒΑΣΙΛΕΩΣ on r., ΔΙΚΑΙΟΥ in ex., ΗΛΙΟΚΛΕΟΥΣ on l.; monogram in field to l. *Mitchiner* 284o. *B.M.C. India* 21, 1-2 .. .. £225

7635 — — — His helmeted, dr. and cuir. bust r.; fillet border. ℞. Zeus enthroned l., holding Nike and sceptre; legend as last; M in field to l. *Mitchiner* 286.. .. .. £400

7636   7637

7636 — — (Indo-Greek standard, *c.* 9·4 gm.). ΒΑΣΙΛΕΩΣ ΔΙΚΑΙΟΥ ΗΛΙΟΚΛΕΟΥΣ. His diad. and dr. bust r. ℞. Zeus stg. facing, holding thunderbolt and sceptre; Karosthi legend around; monogram in field to l. *Mitchiner* 288b. *B.M.C. India* 23, 22 .. £325

7637 — — — Similar, but with *obv.* type heroic bust of the king, viewed from behind, hd. turned to l., wearing crested helmet and aegis, and thrusting with spear held in r. hand. *Mitchiner* 292a £450

7638 — Æ *drachm* (Attic standard, *c.* 4 gm.). As 7634, but without monogram in *rev.* field, and with ΠΓ in ex. *Mitchiner* 285d. *B.M.C. India* 21, 8 .. .. .. £75

7639 — — — As 7635. *Mitchiner* 287 .. .. £125

7640 — — (Indo-Greek standard, *c.* 2·35 gm.). As 7636. *Mitchiner* 289c. *B.M.C. India* 23, 25 .. .. £65

7641   7643

7641 — Square Æ 21. Diad. bust of the king (?) r., bearded; ΒΑΣΙΛΕΩΣ on l., ΔΙΚΑΙΟΥ above, ΗΛΙΟΚΛΕΟΥΣ on r. ℞. Elephant stg. l.; Karosthi legend around; monogram above. *Mitchiner* 294a. *B.M.C. India* 24, 29 .. .. £14

7642 — Square Æ 24×22. Elephant stg. r.; legend as last. ℞. Humped bull stg. r.; Karosthi legend around; monogram and Σ beneath. *Mitchiner* 296a. *B.M.C. India* 24, 31 £16

7643 **Polyxenos,** *c.* 135-130 B.C. (when Heliokles came to power in *circa* 135 B.C. he appointed two new sub-kings to rule the southern provinces — Polyxenos and Epander. These were replaced by his own son, Strato, after the disastrous nomad invasion of *circa* 130 B.C.). *Æ tetradrachm* (*c.* 9·33 gm.). ΒΑΣΙΛΕΩΣ ΕΠΙΦΑΝΟΥΣ ΣΩΤΗΡΟΣ ΠΟΛΥΞΕΝΟΥ. His diad. and dr. bust r. ℞. Athena advancing l., brandishing thunderbolt and holding shield; Karosthi legend around; monogram in field to l. *Mitchiner* 298 .. £1,500

7644 — *Æ drachm* (*c.* 2·4 gm.). Similar. *Mitchiner* 299 .. .. £300

7645 — Square Æ 22. Bust of Athena r., in crested helmet; ΒΑΣΙΛΕΩΣ ΕΠΙΦΑ on l., ΝΟΥΣ ΣΩΤΗΡΟΣ above, ΠΟΛΥΞΕΝΟΥ on r. ℞. Aegis; Karosthi legend around; monogram beneath. *Mitchiner* 300b £35

7646 **Epander,** *c.* 135-130 B.C. (appointed by Heliokles as the colleague of Polyxenos in the government of the southern provinces). *Æ drachm* (*c.* 2·4 gm.). ΒΑΣΙΛΕΩΣ ΝΙΚΗΦΟΡΟΥ ΕΠΑΝΔΡΟΥ. His diad. and dr. bust r. ℞. Athena advancing, as 7643; Karosthi legend around; monogram in field to r. *Mitchiner* 301 .. .. £300

7647   7648

7647 — Square Æ 22×20. Nike advancing r., holding wreath and palm; ΒΑΣΙΛΕΩΣ on l., ΝΙΚΗΦΟΡΟΥ above, ΕΠΑΝΔΡΟΥ on r. ℞. Humped bull stg. r.; Karosthi legend around; two monograms beneath. *Mitchiner* 302a. *B.M.C. India* 51, 1 .. .. £30

7648 **Strato I,** *c.* 130-110 B.C. (following the nomad conquest of much of Baktria, *circa* 130 B.C., Heliokles replaced the two sub-kings, Polyxenos and Epander, with his own young son, Strato. Doubtless, this was to ensure dynastic continuity in a period of political upheaval, and for the first few years of Strato's reign the regency was in the hands of his mother, **Agathokleia.** Strato appears to have perished in the same revolution which removed his father from power). REGENCY OF AGATHOKLEIA. *Æ tetradrachm* (*c.* 9·3 gm.). ΒΑΣΙΛΕΩΣ ΣΩΤΗΡΟΣ ΣΤΡΑΤΩΝΟΣ ΚΑΙ ΑΓΑΘΟΚΛΕΙΑΣ. Their conjoined diad. and dr. busts r. ℞. Athena advancing l., brandishing thunderbolt and holding shield; Karosthi legend around; monogram in field to l. *Mitchiner* 306 .. .. £750

7649 — *Æ drachm* (*c.* 2·4 gm.). ΒΑΣΙΛΙΣΣΗΣ ΘΕΟΤΡΟΠΟΥ ΑΓΑΘΟΚΛΕΙΑΣ. Her diad. and dr. bust r. ℞. Warrior advancing r., r. hand raised, holding spear in l.; Karosthi legend around; monogram in field to r. *Mitchiner* 303a £350

7650 — Square Æ 20. Bust of Athena r., in crested helmet; ΒΑΣΙΛΙΣΣΗΣ on l., ΘΕΟΤΡΟΠΟΥ above, ΑΓΑΘΟΚΛΕΙΑΣ on r. ℞. Herakles seated l. on rock, holding club; Karosthi legend around; monogram in field to l. *Mitchiner* 307. *B.M.C. India* 43, 1-2 .. £35

7651 STRATO ALONE. *Æ tetradrachm* (*c.* 9·3 gm.). ΒΑΣΙΛΕΩΣ ΣΩΤΗΡΟΣ ΚΑΙ ΔΙΚΑΙΟΥ ΣΤΡΑΤΩΝΟΣ. His young diad. and dr. bust r. ℞. Athena stg. l., holding Nike, spear and shield; Karosthi legend around; monogram in field to l. *Mitchiner* 316 .. £325

7652   7653

Strato I *continued*

7652 — — *Obv.* Similar, but without ΚΑΙ in legend, and portrait more mature. R. Athena advancing l., brandishing thunderbolt and holding shield; Karosthi legend around; monogram in field to l.   *Mitchiner 320a* £300

7653 — — *Obv.* As last, but the king has short beard. R. Athena stg. facing, brandishing thunderbolt and holding shield; Karosthi legend around; monogram in field to l. *Mitchiner 329* £400

7654 — — ΒΑΣΙΛΕΩΣ ΕΠΙΦΑΝΟΥΣ ΣΩΤΗΡΟΣ ΣΤΡΑΤΩΝΟΣ. His mature helmeted and dr. bust r. R. As 7652.   *Mitchiner 332a* £300

7655 — Æ *drachm* (*c.* 2·3 gm.). ΒΑΣΙΛΕΩΣ ΣΩΤΗΡΟΣ ΣΤΡΑΤΩΝΟΣ. Type as 7651. R. Similar to 7652.   *Mitchiner 308c* £55

7656 — — *Obv.* Legend as last. Type as 7652. R. Similar to 7653. *Mitchiner 312*   £75

7657 — — Similar to 7652, but king wears crested helmet. *Mitchiner 326*   ..   £65

7658   7660

7658 — — Similar to 7654, but king wears diadem, without helmet. *Mitchiner 331a.* *B.M.C. India* 40, 3-4   ..   ..   £50

7659 — Æ 26. Legend as 7654. Laur. bust of Apollo r., hair in queue. R. Bow and quiver; Karosthi legend around; monogram in field to l. *Mitchiner 335a.* *B.M.C. India* 41, 12   £22

7660 — Square Æ 23 × 21. Naked Apollo stg. facing, holding arrow and resting on bow; ΒΑΣΙΛΕΩΣ ΕΠΙΦΑ on l., ΝΟΥΣ ΣΩΤΗΡΟΣ above, ΣΤΡΑΤΩΝΟΣ on r. R. Tripod on stand, between two monograms; all in dotted square, around which Karosthi legend. *Mitchiner 336b.* *B.M.C. India* 41, 13   ..   ..   £16

7661 — Square Æ 20. Bust of bearded Herakles r., club over shoulder; ΒΑΣΙΛΕΩΣ on l., ΣΩΤΗΡΟΣ above, ΣΤΡΑΤΩΝΟΣ on r. R. Nike advancing r., holding wreath and palm; Karosthi legend around; monogram in field to r. *Mitchiner 333a.* *B.M.C. India* 42, 17   £14

7662 **Philoxenos,** *c.* 110-80 B.C. (with the downfall of Heliokles and Strato I, *circa* 110 B.C., what remained of the Indo-Greek realm split into two independent kingdoms, divided approximately by the river Indus. The western kingdom was ruled by the joint kings Philoxenos and Diomedes; the eastern by Apollodotos II). Æ *tetradrachm* (Attic standard, *c.* 16·75 gm.). His diad. and dr. bust r.; fillet border. R. ΒΑΣΙΛΕΩΣ ΑΝΙΚΗΤΟΥ ΦΙΛΟΞΕΝΟΥ. King on horseback prancing r.; monogram beneath. *Mitchiner 337a*   £4,500

7663   7664

7663 — — (Indo-Greek standard, *c*. 9·75 gm.). His diad. and dr. bust r.; legend as on *rev.* of last. ℞. King on horseback prancing r.; Karosthi legend around; monogram beneath. *Mitchiner* 338*d*. *B.M.C. India* 56, 2 .. .. £275

7664 — Square Æ *drachm* (*c*. 2·4 gm.). His helmeted and dr. bust r.; ΒΑΣΙΛΕΩΣ on l., ΑΝΙΚΗΤΟΥ above, ΦΙΛΟΞΕΝΟΥ on r. ℞. Similar to last. *Mitchiner* 341*a*. *B.M.C. India* 56, 7 £65

7665 — Square Æ 24 × 21. Helios, rad., stg. facing, r. hand raised, holding sceptre in l.; legend as last. ℞. Nike stg. r., holding wreath and palm; Karosthi legend around; monogram in field to r. *Mitchiner* 346. *B.M.C. India* 57, 10 .. .. £18

7666 — Square Æ 19. Tyche stg. l., r. hand raised, holding cornucopiae in l.; legend as 7664; monogram in field to l. ℞. Humped bull stg. r.; Karosthi legend around; 1 beneath. *Mitchiner* 344*d*. *B.M.C. India* 57, 13 .. .. £15

7667   7671

7667 **Diomedes,** *c*. 110-80 B.C. (colleague of Philoxenos in the government of the western Indo-Greek Kingdom). Æ *tetradrachm* (*c*. 9·5 - 9·8 gm.). ΒΑΣΙΛΕΩΣ ΣΩΤΗΡΟΣ ΔΙΟΜΗΔΟΥ. His diad. and dr. bust r. ℞. The Dioskouroi on horseback prancing r., each holding spear and palm; Karosthi legend around; monogram beneath. *Mitchiner* 347*a* £400

7668 — Æ *drachm* (*c*. 2·3 gm.). Similar. *Mitchiner* 348*b*. *B.M.C. India* 31, 3 .. £95

7669 — — *Obv.* Similar, but king wears crested helmet. ℞. The Dioskouroi stg. facing, side by side, each holding spear; Karosthi legend around; monogram in field to l. *Mitchiner* 353. *B.M.C. India* 31, 2 .. .. £120

7670 — Square Æ 20 × 18. The Dioskouroi facing, as on *rev.* of last; ΒΑΣΙΛΕΩΣ on l., ΣΩΤΗΡΟΣ above, ΔΙΟΜΗΔΟΥ on r. ℞. Humped bull stg. r.; Karosthi legend around; monogram beneath. *Mitchiner* 354*a*. *B.M.C. India* 31, 5 .. .. £22

7671 **Apollodotos II,** *c*. 110-80 B.C. (founder of the independent eastern Indo-Greek Kingdom, Apollodotos was the contemporary of Philoxenos and Diomedes in the west). Æ *tetradrachm* (*c*. 9·2 - 9·6 gm.). ΒΑΣΙΛΕΩΣ ΜΕΓΑΛΟΥ ΣΩΤΗΡΟΣ ΚΑΙ ΦΙΛΟΠΑΤΟΡΟΣ ΑΠΟΛΛΟΔΟΤΟΥ. His diad. and dr. bust r. ℞. Athena advancing l., brandishing thunderbolt and holding shield; Karosthi legend around; monograms in field to l. and to r. *Mitchiner* 423*b* £250

7672   7674

Apollodotos II *continued*

7672 — Æ *drachm* (*c.* 2·4 gm.). Similar, but without ΜΕΓΑΛΟΥ in *obv.* legend. *Mitchiner* 424*b*. *B.M.C. India* 37, 3 .. ..   £35

7673 — — Similar, but with *obv.* legend ΒΑΣΙΛΕΩΣ ΣΩΤΗΡΟΣ ΑΠΟΛΛΟΔΟΤΟΥ. *Mitchiner* 425*k*. *B.M.C. India* 37, 7 .. ..   £40

7674 — Æ 27. Apollo stg. r., stringing arrow in bow; large monogram behind; legend as last. ℞. Tripod; Karosthi legend around; letters in field to l. and to r. *Mitchiner* 432*e*. *B.M.C. India* 38, 10 .. ..   £10

7675 — Square Æ 25. Apollo stg. facing, resting on arrow and holding bow; ΒΑΣΙΛΕΩΣ on l., ΣΩΤΗΡΟΣ above, ΑΠΟΛΛΟΔΟΤΟΥ on r. ℞. Tripod; Karosthi legend around; monograms in field to l. and to r. *Mitchiner* 433. *B.M.C. India* 38, 11 .. .. ..   £20

7676 — Square Æ 20. Apollo stg. r., as 7674; legend as last. ℞. Tripod, between two monograms; all within dotted square, around which Karosthi legend. *Mitchiner* 429*a*. *B.M.C. India* 38, 14 .. ..   £15

7677 — Square Æ 19. Apollo stg. r., as 7674; ΒΑΣΙΛΕΩΣ ΣΩ on l., ΤΗΡΟΣ ΚΑΙ above, ΦΙΛΟΠΑΤΟΡΟΣ on r., ΑΠΟΛΛΟΔΟΤΟΥ beneath. ℞. Tripod; Karosthi legend around; monogram in field to r. *Mitchiner* 427. *B.M.C. India* 39, 17.. .. ..   £10

7678 **Archebios,** *c.* 80-60 B.C. (one of the four co-rulers who succeeded Philoxenos and Diomedes in the western division of the kingdom about 80 B.C. His three colleagues were Peukolaus, Theophilos and Nikias). Æ *tetradrachm* (Attic standard, *c.* 16·8 gm.). Heroic bust of the king, viewed from behind, hd. turned to l., wearing crested helmet and aegis, and thrusting with spear held in r. hand; fillet border. ℞. ΒΑΣΙΛΕΩΣ ΔΙΚΑΙΟΥ ΝΙΚΗΦΟΡΟΥ ΑΡΧΕΒΙΟΥ. Zeus advancing to front, brandishing thunderbolt and holding sceptre; monogram in field to l. *Mitchiner* 355 ..   ..   £4,500

7679   7682

7679 — — (Indo-Greek standard, c. 9·6 gm.). ΒΑΣΙΛΕΩΣ ΔΙΚΑΙΟΥ ΝΙΚΗΦΟΡΟΥ ΑΡΧΕΒΙΟΥ. His diad. and dr. bust r. R. Zeus to front, as last; Karosthi legend around; monogram in field to l. *Mitchiner 356e. B.M.C. India* 32, 1 .. .. £350

7680 — — — Similar, but king wears crested helmet, and on *rev.* Zeus holds aegis instead of sceptre. *Mitchiner 364* £400

7681 — Æ *drachm* (c. 2·35 gm.). *Obv.* As last. R. As 7679, but the monogram is in field to r. *Mitchiner 359. B.M.C. India* 32, 3 .. .. £75

7682 — Æ 26. Nike advancing l., holding wreath and palm; legend as 7679. R. Owl stg. r., hd. facing; Karosthi legend around; monogram in field to r. *Mitchiner 367. B.M.C. India* 32, 6 .. .. £24

7683 — Square Æ 23. Elephant stg. r.; ΒΑΣΙΛΕΩΣ ΔΙ on l., ΚΑΙΟΥ ΝΙΚΗΦΟ above, ΡΟΥ ΑΡΧΕΒΙΟΥ on r. R. As last, but the monogram is beneath owl. *Mitchiner 368a. B.M.C. India* 33, 8 .. .. £22

7684 — Square Æ 22. Diad. and dr. bust of Zeus r., sceptre over shoulder; legend as last. R. Two palm-branches between caps of the Dioskouroi; Karosthi legend around; monogram beneath. *Mitchiner 365c* £20

7685 **Peukolaus,** c. 80-60 B.C. (junior colleague of Archebios in the government of part of the western division of the Indo-Greek kingdom). Æ *tetradrachm* (c. 9·6 gm.). ΒΑΣΙΛΕΩΣ ΔΙΚΑΙΟΥ ΚΑΙ ΣΩΤΗΡΟΣ ΠΕΥΚΟΛΑΟΥ. His diad. and dr. bust r. R. Zeus stg. l., r. hand raised, holding sceptre in l.; Karosthi legend around; monograms in field to l. and r. *Mitchiner 369* £1,500

7686 — Square Æ 21 × 19. Artemis stg. facing, drawing arrow from quiver and holding bow; legend, as last, on l., above and on r. R. City-goddess stg. l., holding flower and palm-branch; Karosthi legend around; monogram in field to l. *Mitchiner 370a* £35

7687 **Theophilos,** c. 80-60 B.C. (one of the four co-rulers who succeeded Philoxenos and Diomedes in the western kingdom about 80 B.C. His junior colleague was Nikias). Æ *tetradrachm* (Attic standard, c. 16·75 gm.). His diad. and dr. bust r.; fillet border. R. ΒΑΣΙΛΕΩΣ ΑΥΤΟΚΡΑΤΟΡΟΣ ΘΕΟΦΙΛΟΥ. Athena enthroned l., holding Nike, spear and shield; monogram in field to l. *Mitchiner 371* £3,500

7688 — — (Indo-Greek standard, c. 9·6 gm.). ΒΑΣΙΛΕΩΣ ΔΙΚΑΙΟΥ ΘΕΟΦΙΛΟΥ. His diad. and dr. bust r. R. Naked Herakles stg. facing, holding club and lion's skin; Karosthi legend around; monogram in field to r. *Mitchiner 372* £1,250

7689   7693

Theophilos *continued*

7689 — Æ *drachm* (*c.* 2·35 gm.). *Obv.* Similar. R. Naked Herakles stg. facing, crowning himself, and holding club and lion's skin in l. hand; Karosthi legend around; monogram in field to l. *Mitchiner* 374 .. .. £150

7690 — Square Æ 20. Bust of young Herakles r., clad in lion's skin; ΒΑΣΙΛΕΩΣ on l., ΔΙΚΑΙΟΥ above, ΘΕΟΦΙΛΟΥ on r. R. Club; Karosthi legend around; monogram in field to r. *Mitchiner* 376 .. .. £30

7691 — Square Æ 20 × 18. Diad. bust of bearded Herakles r., club over shoulder; legend as last. R. Cornucopiae; Karosthi legend around; monogram in field to l. *Mitchiner* 375a £30

7692 **Nikias,** *c.* 80-60 B.C. (junior colleague of Theophilos in the government of part of the western division of the Indo-Greek Kingdom). Æ *tetradrachm* (*c.* 9·6 gm.). ΒΑΣΙΛΕΩΣ ΣΩΤΗΡΟΣ ΝΙΚΙΟΥ. His diad. and dr. bust r. R. Athena advancing to front, brandishing thunderbolt and holding shield; Karosthi legend around; monogram in field to l. *Mitchiner* 377 .. .. £1,400

7693 — Æ *drachm* (*c.* 2·4 gm.). *Obv.* Similar, but king wears crested helmet. R. The king, in military dress, stg. l., r. hand raised, holding palm-branch in l.; Karosthi legend around; monogram in field to r. *Mitchiner* 379 .. .. £175

7694 — Square Æ 22 × 20. Bust of Poseidon r., trident over shoulder; ΒΑΣΙΛΕΩΣ on l., ΣΩΤΗΡΟΣ above, ΝΙΚΙΟΥ on r. R. Dolphin entwined round anchor; Karosthi legend around; monogram beneath. *Mitchiner* 380b. *B.M.C. India* 58, 2 .. .. £30

7695 — Square Æ 20 × 18. His diad. and dr. bust r.; ΒΑCΙΛΕωC on l., CωΤΗΡΟC above; ΝΙΚΙΟΥ on r. R. King on horseback prancing r.; Karosthi legend around. *Mitchiner* 384. *B.M.C. India* 58, 1 .. .. £25

7696   7698

7696 **Hippostratos,** *c.* 80-60 B.C. (on the death of Apollodotos II, *circa* 80 B.C., the eastern division of the Indo-Greek Kingdom passed to Hippostratos, who appointed two sub-kings Telephos and Dionysios). Æ *tetradrachm* (*c.* 9·5 gm.). ΒΑΣΙΛΕΩΣ ΣΩΤΗΡΟΣ ΙΠΠΟΣΤΡΑΤΟΥ. His diad. and dr. bust r. R. City-goddess stg. l., r. hand extended, holding cornucopiae in l.; Karosthi legend around; monogram in field to l., letter to r. *Mitchiner* 439. *B.M.C. India* 59, 1-2 .. .. £250

7697 — — *Obv.* Similar, but with additional title ΜΕΓΑΛΟΥ after ΒΑΣΙΛΕΩΣ. R. King on horse-back prancing r.; Karosthi legend around; monogram beneath. *Mitchiner* 443a. *B.M.C. India* 59, 3 .. .. £200

7698 — — — R. King on horseback stg. r.; Karosthi legend around; letters in field to l. and in ex.; Greek monogram in field to r. *Mitchiner* 445. *B.M.C. India* 59, 7 £225

7699 — Æ *drachm* (*c.* 2·35 gm.). As 7696. *Mitchiner* 440 .. .. £55

7700 — — Similar to 7697, but also with Karosthi letters in field to l. and in ex. on *rev*. *Mitchiner* 444. *B.M.C. India* 59, 6 .. .. £50

7701 — Æ 29. Apollo stg. r., stringing arrow in bow; legend as 7696. Ŗ. Tripod; Karosthi legend around; monogram in field to l. *Mitchiner* 447a £18

7702 — Square Æ 27 × 29. Triton facing, holding dolphin and rudder; ΒΑΣΙΛΕΩΣ on l., ΣΩΤΗΡΟΣ above, ΙΠΠΟΣΤΡΑΤΟΥ on r. Ŗ. City-goddess stg. l., r. hand extended, holding palm-branch in l.; Karosthi legend around; monogram in field to l., letter to r. *Mitchiner* 446. *B.M.C. India* 60, 13 .. .. £30

7703 — Square Æ 21 × 18. Deity enthroned three-quarter face to l., r. hand extended, holding sceptre in l.; legend as last. Ŗ. Horse stg. l., monogram before; all within square of fillet-pattern around which, Karosthi legend. *Mitchiner* 450c. *B.M.C. India* 60, 16 £22

7704 **Telephos,** *c*. 80-75 B.C. (junior colleague of Hippostratos in the eastern division of the Indo-Greek Kingdom, Telephos was defeated by the Scythian King Maues after only a brief reign). Æ *drachm* (*c*. 2·35 gm.). ΒΑΣΙΛΕΩΣ ΕΥΕΡΓΕΤΟΥ ΤΗΛΕΦΟΥ. Snake-god facing, his body terminating in three serpents, two of which he holds aloft. Ŗ. Helios (on l.), holding sceptre, and male attendant stg. facing side by side; Karosthi legend around; monogram in field to r. *Mitchiner* 451 .. .. £450

7705   7706

7705 — Square Æ 21 × 23. Zeus enthroned three-quarter face to l., r. hand raised, holding sceptre in l.; ΒΑΣΙΛΕΩΣ on l., ΕΥΕΡΓΕΤΟΥ above, ΤΗΛΕΦΟΥ on r. Ŗ. The king advancing r., r. hand extended, holding spear in l.; Karosthi legend around; monogram in field to r. *Mitchiner* 452 .. .. £40

7706 **Dionysios,** *c*. 80-75 B.C. (another junior colleague of Hippostratos in the eastern Indo-Greek Kingdom, Dionysios was succeeded by Ziolos II after only a brief reign). Æ *drachm* (*c*. 2·45 gm.). ΒΑΣΙΛΕΩΣ ΣΩΤΗΡΟΣ ΔΙΟΝΥΣΙΟΥ. His diad. and dr. bust r. Ŗ. Athena advancing l., brandishing thunderbolt and holding shield; Karosthi legend around; monogram in field to r. *Mitchiner* 454. *B.M.C. India* 51, 1 .. £125

7707 — Square Æ 21. Apollo stg. r., stringing arrow in bow; ΒΑΣΙΛΕΩΣ on l., ΣΩΤΗΡΟΣ above, ΔΙΟΝΥΣΙΟΥ on r. Ŗ. Tripod; Karosthi legend around; letters in field to l. and r. *Mitchiner* 455a. *B.M.C. India* 51, 2 .. .. £30

7708 **Zoilos II,** *c*. 75-50 B.C. (this king succeeded Dionysios about 75 B.C. as a junior colleague of Hippostratos in the government of the eastern Indo-Greek Kingdom. He later became sole ruler, and in *circa* 50 B.C. was succeeded by Apollophanes). Æ *drachm* (*c*. 2·4 gm.). ΒΑΣΙΛΕΩΣ ΣΩΤΗΡΟΣ ΙΩΙΛΟΥ. His diad. and dr. bust r. Ŗ. Athena advancing l., brandishing thunderbolt and holding shield; Karosthi legend around; monogram in field to r. *Mitchiner* 458a £35

7709   7710

Zoilos II *continued*

7709 — — Similar, but the king's name is spelt ΙΩΙΛΟΥ, and also with Karosthi letter in *rev.* field to l. *Mitchiner* 459r. *B.M.C. India* 52, 3 .. .. £30

7710 — Æ 28. Apollo stg. r., stringing arrow in bow; small elephant in field to l.; legend as 7708. ℞. Tripod; Karosthi legend around; letters in field to l. and to r. *Mitchiner* 462a. *B.M.C. India* 53, 9 .. .. £18

7711 — Square Æ 22 × 25. Apollo stg. r., stringing arrow in bow; ΒΑΣΙΛΕΩΣ on l., ΣΩΤΗΡΟΣ above, ΙΩΙΛΟΥ on r.; monogram in field to l. ℞. As last. *Mitchiner* 460. *B.M.C. India* 53, 11 .. .. £24

7712 **Amyntas,** *c.* 60-40 B.C. (following the joint reign of the four kings Archebios, Peukolaus, Theophilos and Nikias, the western Indo-Greek Kingdom was ruled by Amyntas, with Artemidoros as his junior colleague). Æ *double dekadrachm* (*c.* 85 gm.). His diad., dr. and cuir. bust r., wearing crested helmet; fillet border. ℞. ΒΑΣΙΛΕΩΣ ΝΙΚΑΤΟΡΟΣ ΑΜΥΝΤΟΥ. Zeus enthroned three-quarter face to l., holding statuette of Athena, sceptre and palm-branch; monogram in field to l. *Mitchiner* 385 .. .. .. (*Only two known*)

These extraordinary coins, the largest Greek silver denomination ever issued, may have been struck in celebration of some great military victory of Amyntas; but few details of this king's exploits have come down to us.

7713 — — Similar, but with *rev.* type Tyche enthroned l., r. hand extended, holding cornucopiae in l. *Mitchiner* 386 .. ..(*Only three known*)

7714 — Æ *tetradrachm* (*c.* 9·4 gm.). ΒΑΣΙΛΕΩΣ ΝΙΚΑΤΟΡΟΣ ΑΜΥΝΤΟΥ. Heroic bust of the king, viewed from behind, hd. turned to l., wearing crested helmet and aegis, and thrusting with spear held in r. hand. ℞. Zeus enthroned, as 7712; Karosthi legend around; monogram in field to l. *Mitchiner* 393a £500

7715   7718

7715 — — His helmeted, dr. and cuir. bust r.; legend as last. ℞. Athena advancing l., brandishing thunderbolt and holding shield; Karosthi legend around; monogram in field to l. *Mitchiner* 395. *B.M.C. India* 61, 1 .. .. £500

7716 — Æ *drachm* (*c.* 2·4 gm.). As 7714, but with *obv.* type diad. and dr. bust of king r. *Mitchiner* 388a. *B.M.C. India* 61, 2 .. .. £90

7717 — — Similar, but king also wears kausia. *Mitchiner* 391a £90

7718 — Square Æ 22 × 19. Bearded bust of king (?) r., dr. and wearing rad. Phrygian cap; ΒΑΣΙΛΕΩΣ on l., ΝΙΚΑΤΟΡΟΣ above, ΑΜΥΝΤΟΥ on r. ℞. Athena stg. l., r. hand extended, holding spear and shield in l.; Karosthi legend around; monogram in field to l. *Mitchiner* 397c £22

7719 **Artemidoros,** c. 60-40 B.C. (junior colleague of Amyntas in the government of the western division of the Indo-Greek Kingdom). Æ *tetradrachm* (c. 9·4 gm.). ΒΑΣΙΛΕΩΣ ΑΝΙΚΗΤΟΥ ΑΡΤΕΜΙΔΟΡΟΥ. His diad. and dr. bust r. ℞. Artemis advancing l., about to discharge arrow from bow; Karosthi legend around; monogram in field to l. *Mitchiner* 398
£750

7720 — — *Obv.* Similar. ℞. Nike stg. r., holding wreath and palm; Karosthi legend around; monogram in field to l. *Mitchiner* 402b £900

7721 — Æ *drachm* (c. 2·4 gm.). As 7719, but the king also wears crested helmet on *obv.* *Mitchiner* 401 .. .. £125

7722 — — As 7720, but on *rev.* the monogram is in field to r. *Mitchiner* 403c .. £150

7723 — Square Æ 21. Artemis stg. facing, drawing arrow from quiver and holding bow; ΒΑΣΙΛΕΩΣ Α on l., ΝΙΚΗΤΟΥ ΑΡ above, ΤΕΜΙΔΟΡΟΥ on r. ℞. Humped bull stg. r.; Karosthi legend around; two monograms beneath. *Mitchiner* 404c £24

7724 — Square Æ 15. *Obv.* As last. ℞. Panther walking l.; Karosthi legend around; monogram beneath. *Mitchiner* 406 .. .. £18

7725	7726	7728

7725 **Apollophanes,** c. 50-40 B.C. (successor of Zoilos II as king of what remained of the eastern division of the Indo-Greek Kingdom). Æ *drachm* (c. 2·4 gm.). ΒΑΣΙΛΕΩΣ ΣΩΤΗΡΟΣ ΑΠΟΛΛΟΦΑΝΟΥ. His dr. bust r., wearing helmet bound with diad. ℞. Athena advancing l., brandishing thunderbolt and holding shield; Karosthi legend around; letters in field on either side, monogram to r. *Mitchiner* 467b. *B.M.C. India* 54, 1-2 .. £50

7726 **Strato II,** c. 40-15 B.C. (the last of the Indo-Greek rulers in the eastern kingdom, Strato succeeded Apollophanes about 40 B.C. For the final decade of his reign his grandson, **Strato III,** was elevated to the rank of co-ruler. After their deaths the former Indo-Greek territory was ruled by a native king named Bhadryasa. The western kingdom, under Hermaios, survived a few years longer). Æ *drachm* (c. 2·35 gm.). ΒΑΣΙΛΕΩΣ ΣΩΤΗΡΟΣ ΣΤΡΑΤΩΝΟΣ. Diad. and dr. bust of Strato II r., with middle-aged features. ℞. Athena advancing l., as last; Karosthi legend around; letters in field to l. and to r. *Mitchiner* 468a £45

7727 — — Similar, but the king's features are elderly, with protruding chin. *Mitchiner* 469b £45

7728 — — As last, but with *obv.* legend ΒΑΣΙΛΕΩΣ ΣΩΤΗΡΟΣ ΣΤΡΑΤΩΝΟΣ ΚΑΙ ΦΙΛ ΣΤΡΑΤΩΝΟΣ, and with letter in *rev.* field to r. only. *Mitchiner* 473b £40

7729 — Lead 18. ΒΑΣΙΛΕΩΣ ΣΩΤΗΡΟΣ ΣΤΡΑΤΩΝΟΣ. Apollo stg. r., stringing arrow in bow. ℞. Tripod; Karosthi legend around; letter in field to l. *Mitchiner* 470a £14

7730 — Lead 22. Similar, but with *obv.* legend ΒΑΣΙΛΕΩΣ ΣΩΤΗΡΟΣ ΣΤΡΑΤΩΝΟΣ ΚΑΙ ΦΙΛ ΣΤΡΑΤΩΝΟΣ, and also with letter in *rev.* field to r. *Mitchiner* 474c £16

7731 Hermaios, *c.* 40-1 B.C. (the last king of the western Indo-Greek realm, Hermaios had a long and eventful reign in the course of which his fortunes fluctuated considerably. In the early stages, when his wife **Kalliope** seems to have shared his throne, Hermaios pursued an aggressive foreign policy and re-conquered some territories which his predecessors had lost. However, his success was only transitory and the Indo-Greeks found themselves surrounded by powerful enemies. Eventually Hermaios was defeated by the Kushan ruler Kujula Kadphises, bringing to an end more than three centuries of Greek dominion in the area). Æ *tetradrachm* (Attic standard, *c.* 16·54 gm.). His diad. and dr. bust r.; fillet border. ℞. ΒΑΣΙΛΕΩΣ ΣΩΤΗΡΟΣ ΕΡΜΑΙΟΥ. Zeus enthroned three-quarter face to l., r. hand extended, holding sceptre in l.; monogram in field to l. *Mitchiner* 409 .. .. *(Unique)*

7732   7733

7732 — — (Indo-Greek standard, *c.* 9·6 gm.: silver of good quality). ΒΑΣΙΛΕΩΣ ΣΩΤΗΡΟΣ ΕΡΜΑΙΟΥ ΚΑΙ ΚΑΛΛΙΟΠΗΣ. Conjoined busts r. of king and queen, diad. and dr. ℞. King on horseback prancing r.; Karosthi legend around; monogram beneath. *Mitchiner* 407*b*
               £650

7733 — — — ΒΑΣΙΛΕΩΣ ΣΩΤΗΡΟΣ ΕΡΜΑΙΟΥ. His diad. and dr. bust r. ℞. Zeus enthroned, as 7731; Karosthi legend around; monogram in field to r. *Mitchiner* 414*g*. *B.M.C. India* 62, 1 .. .. £75

7734 — — — Similar, but the king wears crested helmet, and on *rev.* the monogram is in field to l. *Mitchiner* 412*a* £150

7735 — — — ΒΑΣΙΛΕΩΣ ΣΩΤΗΡΟΣ ΕΡΜΑΙΟΥ. King on horseback prancing r. ℞. As 7733. *Mitchiner* 410 .. .. *(Unique ?)*

7736   7738

7736 — — Similar to 7733, but on *obv.* the Greek letters *omicron* and *rho* are of 'square' form; and on *rev.*, monogram in field to l., Karosthi letter to r. *Mitchiner* 418*d*. *B.M.C. India* 63, 21 .. .. £85

7737 — Billon *tetradrachm* (*c.* 9·3 gm.). As last. *Mitchiner* 420*b* £50

7738 — Æ *tetradrachm* (*c.* 9·3 gm.). As last. *Mitchiner* 421*a*. *B.M.C. India* 64, 35 (VF) £25

In the latter part of his reign Hermaios was obliged to debase his silver coinage and, finally, to issue bronze only. These latest Indo-Greek issues doubtless continued in production for some years after Hermaios' death, and served as prototypes for the coinage of Kujula Kadphises.

7739 — Æ *drachm* (*c.* 2·4 gm.). As 7732. *Mitchiner* 408*b*. *B.M.C. India* 66, 1-2 £130

7740   7745

7740 — — As 7733. *Mitchiner* 415*g*.. .. .. £30
7741 — — As 7736. *Mitchiner* 419*d*.. .. .. £35
7742 — Billon *drachm* (*c*. 2 - 2·4 gm.). As 7736. *Mitchiner* 420*i* £35
7743 — Æ *drachm* (*c*. 2 - 2·4 gm.). As 7736. *Mitchiner* 422*a*. *B.M.C. India* 65, 43 (VF) £25
7744 — Square Æ 19. Bearded bust of king (?) r., dr. and wearing Phrygian cap; ΒΑΣΙΛΕΩΣ
        on l., ΣΩΤΗΡΟΣ above, ΕΡΜΑΙΟΥ on r. ℞. Horse pacing r.; Karosthi legend around;
        monogram beneath. *Mitchiner* 416*b*. *B.M.C. India* 66, 51-2.. .. .. £15
7745 — — Similar, but the bust on *obv.* also wears rad. crown with long rays. *Mitchiner*
        417*a*. *B.M.C. India* 66, 55 .. .. £16

THE PTOLEMAIC KINGDOM OF EGYPT

Egypt had been part of the Persian Empire from 525 B.C., but in 332 Alexander the Great was crowned as Pharaoh at Memphis and three centuries of Greek rule were inaugurated. The great coastal city of Alexandreia was founded the following year and soon replaced Memphis as the seat of government. Ptolemy, one of Alexander's generals, was appointed satrap of Egypt in 323 B.C. and quickly set about consolidating his position. Eventually, in 305 B.C., he took the title of 'king' and became the founder of a royal dynasty which was destined to endure for 275 years, until the suicide of Cleopatra VII. During the 3rd century the Ptolemaic realm included many possessions outside Egypt—Phoenicia and Palestine, Cyprus, and various territories in Asia Minor and in the Aegean area. However, under the weak rule of the young Ptolemy V (204-180 B.C.) many of these outposts were lost to the rival kingdoms of Macedon and Syria. Egypt's rather isolated position, outside the main stream of Mediterranean politics, helped to preserve the autonomy of her kingdom long after most of the other great Hellenistic monarchies had fallen. It was not until 48 B.C. that Rome first intervened directly in Egyptian affairs, but within two decades the country had become just another province of the Roman Empire. The Ptolemies had tried to introduce Greek culture to their Egyptian subjects, but the native civilization was too deep-rooted to be much influenced by foreign ideas, and in the end it was the Greeks who became Egyptianized. The country had generally prospered under the benign administration of the Ptolemaic kings, in marked contrast to the economic disasters which overtook the Egyptians under Roman rule.

7746 **Ptolemy I, Soter,** 305-283 B.C. (a close boyhood friend of Alexander, Ptolemy, son of the Macedonian Lagus, became one of the conqueror's most trusted generals and distinguished himself in the destruction of the Persian Empire. After Alexander's death he

Ptolemy I, Soter *continued*

received Egypt as his share of the inheritance and over the following four decades he
created a stable and prosperous kingdom.   For the first eighteen years of his rule he was
officially only 'satrap' of Egypt, but in 305 B.C. he took the title of 'king' along with several
other 'successors' of Alexander.   Twenty years later he associated his son, Ptolemy II,
with him as co-ruler, and in 283 B.C. he died peacefully in his bed, the only one of the
Diadochi to do so.   Most of our knowledge of the life of Alexander is derived from a history written by Ptolemy.   The work itself is now lost, but it was the main source for the
Roman historian Arrian's *History of Alexander* and the *Indike*, an account of India).   AS
SATRAP, 323-305 B.C.   Æ *tetradrachm* (Attic standard, *c.* 17 gm.).   Hd. of Alexander
the Great r., with horn of Ammon, clad in elephant's skin and aegis.   R̶. Zeus enthroned
l., holding eagle and sceptre; ΑΛΕΞΑΝΔΡΟΥ on r.; thunderbolt in field to l., ΟΡ beneath
throne.   *Svoronos (Ta nomismata tou kratous ton Ptolemaion)* 24.⚓*B.M.C. 6.* 1, 1
£2,000

7747 — — *Obv.* Similar.   R̶. Athena Alkidemos advancing r., brandishing spear and holding
shield; ΑΛΕΞΑΝΔΡΕΙΟΝ on l., ΠΤΟΛΕΜΑΙΟΥ on r.; ΔΙ in field to l., small eagle on thunderbolt
to r.   *Svoronos 32.   Forrer/Weber* 8213 .. .. £1,000

7748 — — — R̶. Athena Alkidemos, as last; ΑΛΕΞΑΝΔΡΟΥ on l.; in field to l., ΑΠ monogram;
to r., ΕΥ and small eagle on thunderbolt.   *Svoronos 44.   B.M.C. 6.* 2, 6 .. £325

7749 — Æ *tetradrachm* (reduced weight, *c.* 15·5 gm.).   As last, but in *rev.* field to l., ΗΔΙ
monogram; to r., ΚΔΕ monogram and eagle on thunderbolt.   *Svoronos 139.   B.M.C. 6.*
6, 46 .. .. £275

7750 — — As last, but nothing in *rev.* field to l.; to r., ΗΡ monogram, Corinthian helmet, and
eagle on thunderbolt.   *Svoronos 170.   B.M.C. 6.* 4, 29-30 .. .. .. £275
Sometimes the letter Δ is visible on the aegis on the obv. of these reduced weight tetradrachms.

7751 — — *Obv.* As 7746.   R̶. Athena Alkidemos, as 7747; ΠΤΟΛΕΜΑΙΟΥ on l.; in field to l.,
caduceus; to r., small eagle on thunderbolt.   *Svoronos 96* £1,500

7752   7755   7758

7752 — Æ *drachm* (*c.* 3·75 gm.). As 7748, but without the monogram in *rev.* field to l.
Svoronos 43. *B.M.C. 6.* 3, 16 ..   ..   £175

7753 — Æ *hemidrachm* (*c.* 1·75 gm.). As 7748, but without the monogram in *rev.* field to l.,
and with ΔI instead of EY to r.   *Svoronos* 35   ..   ..   £140

7754 — Æ 18. Diad. hd. of Alexander r., with horn of Ammon. ℞. Eagle stg. l. on thunderbolt, wings open; ΑΛΕ on l.; EY in field to l., ΑΠ monogram to r.   *Svoronos* 46.   *B.M.C. 6.*
3, 17 ..   ..   £20

7755 — Æ 22. Hd. of Aphrodite r., wearing ornamented stephanos. ℞. Eagle stg. l. on
thunderbolt; ΠΤΟΛΕΜΑΙΟΥ on r.; wreaths in field to l. and in ex.   *Svoronos* 78.   *B.M.C. 6.*
7, 56 ..   ..   £22

7756 — Æ 17. Hd. of Aphrodite r., wearing tainia ornamented with leaves. ℞. Eagle stg. l·
on thunderbolt, wings open; ΠΤΟΛΕ on l.; wreath in field to l.   *Svoronos* 80.   *B.M.C. 6·*
7, 59 ..   ..   £18

7757 AS KING, 305-283 B.C. *N pentadrachm* (*c.* 17·8 gm.). Diad. hd. of Ptolemy I r.,
wearing aegis. ℞. ΠΤΟΛΕΜΑΙΟΥ ΒΑΣΙΛΕΩΣ. Eagle stg. l. on thunderbolt; ΠΑΜ monogram
in field to l.   *Svoronos* 204   ..   ..   £2,000

7758 — *N stater* (*c.* 7·1 gm.). *Obv.* Similar. ℞. Alexander, holding thunderbolt, in chariot
drawn l. by four elephants; above, ΠΤΟΛΕΜΑΙΟΥ / ΒΑΣΙΛΕΩΣ; in ex., Φ, ΤΙ and ΑΝΓ monogram.   *Svoronos* 150.   *Jenkins* (*Ancient Greek Coins*) 562/3   ..   ..   £2,500

7759 — *N hemidrachm* (*c.* 1·78 gm.). As 7757, but on *rev.* the eagle's wings are open, and
with A instead of monogram in field to l.   *Svoronos* 182.   *B.M.C. 6.* 23, 80-81   £350

7760 — Æ *oktadrachm* (*c.* 28·4 gm.). As 7757, but with MI monogram in *rev.* field to l.
Svoronos 198   ..   ..   £4,000

7761 — Æ *tetradrachm* (*c.* 14·2 gm.). As 7757, but with ΑΔ monogram in *rev.* field to l.
Svoronos 190.   *B.M.C. 6.* 23, 85 ..   ..   £150

Ptolemy I, Soter *continued*

7762 — — Similar, but with P / ΠAP monogram in *rev.* field to l.   *Svoronos* 255.   *B.M.C. 6.*
20, 59   .. ..   £150

7763

7765

7763 — Æ 27.   Laur. hd. of Zeus r.   R. ΠΤΟΛΕΜΑΙΟΥ ΒΑΣΙΛΕΩΣ.   Eagle stg. l. on thunderbolt,
wings open; A / ΠP in field to l.   *Svoronos* 285.   *B.M.C. 6.* 20, 61   .. ..   £15

7764 — Æ 31.   Diad. hd. of Ptolemy I r., wearing aegis.   R. As last, but with ΙΠ in field to l.
Svoronos 192.   *B.M.C. 6.* 12, 98 ..   ..   £50

7765 — Æ 22.   Hd. of Alexander r., wearing elephant's skin and aegis.   R. As 7763, but with
ΠY monogram in field to l.   *Svoronos* 220.   *B.M.C. 6.* 21, 66 ..   .. ..   £12

7766 — Æ 18.   Diad. hd. of Alexander r., with horn of Ammon, hair long.   R. As 7763, but
with HP monogram in field to l.   *Svoronos* 238.   *B.M.C. 6.* 8, 71   .. ..   £16

7767 — Æ 13.   As 7764, but with dolphin instead of letters in *rev.* field to l.   *Svoronos* 217.
B.M.C. 6. 39, 31   .. ..   £11

7767A **Ptolemy II, Philadelphos,** 285-246 B.C. (son of Ptolemy I, he was made co-ruler by
his father two years before the latter's death, thus ensuring a smooth succession.   His long
reign was a period of growing prosperity for his kingdom, and the capital city of Alexandreia was embellished with many splendid new buildings—the Pharos, the Museum and
the Library being foremost.   He was twice married: in *circa* 288 B.C. to Arsinoe I,
daughter of Lysimachos of Thrace; and about twelve years later to his own sister, **Arsinoe
II**).   *N double-oktadrachm* (c. 55·55 gm.).   Veiled hd. of Arsinoe II r., wearing stephane,
sceptre behind head visible above; behind, A.   R. ΑΡΣΙΝΟΗΣ ΦΙΛΑΔΕΛΦΟΥ.   Double
cornucopiae, bound with fillet, between caps of the Dioskouroi surmounted by stars.
Leu auction, April, 1978, *lot* 174   .. ..(*Only two known*)

 The *sister-wife of Ptolemy II was deified on her death in 270 B.C., and a remarkable
series of commemorative coins was instituted in high-value precious metal denominations.   The
letters on obverse appear as annual sequence marks.*

7768 — *N oktadrachm* (c. 27·8 gm.).   Similar, but with K instead of A behind hd. on *obv.*, and
without caps of the Dioskouroi on *rev.*   *Svoronos* 475.   *B.M.C. 6.* 43, 10   ..   £2,500

7769 — *N pentadrachm* (c. 17·8 gm.).   Diad. hd. of Ptolemy I r., wearing aegis.   R. ΠΤΟΛΕ-
ΜΑΙΟΥ ΒΑΣΙΛΕΩΣ.   Eagle stg. l. on thunderbolt; in field to l., ΣΩ monogram above shield;
between eagle's legs, Y.   *Svoronos* 595.   *B.M.C. 6.* 24, 6   .. .. ..   £2,000

7770 — Æ *dekadrachm* (*c.* 35 gm.). As 7768, but with Λ behind queen's hd. on *obv.* *Svoronos* 477. *B.M.C. 6.* 43, 15 .. .. £1,250

7771 — Æ *tetradrachm* (*c.* 14·2 gm.). Diad. hd. of Ptolemy I r., wearing aegis. ℞. ΠΤΟΛΕ-ΜΑΙΟΥ ΒΑΣΙΛΕΩΣ. Eagle stg. l. on thunderbolt; in field to l., ΠΤ / ΑΣΚ monogram; to r., shield. *Svoronos* 524. *B.M.C. 6.* 36, 156 .. .. £125

7772 — — of *Sidon.* Diad. hd. of Ptolemy I r., wearing aegis. ℞. ΠΤΟΛΕΜΑΙΟΥ ΣΩΤΗΡΟΣ. Eagle stg. l. on thunderbolt; in field to l., ΣΙ / ΜΤ monogram; to r., regnal date ΛΒ (=year 32 =254/3 B.C.). *Svoronos* 739. *B.M.C. 6.* 30, 68-9 .. .. £150

7773 — — of *Tyre.* Similar, but in *rev.* field to l., ΤΥΡ monogram above club; and to r., regnal date ΚΕ in monogram form (=year 25 =261/60 B.C.). *Svoronos* 650. *B.M.C. 6.* 31, 78 .. .. £150

7774   7777

7774 — — of *Ptolemais.* Similar, but in *rev.* field to l., ΠΤ monogram / ΜΕ monogram; and to r., regnal date ΛΓ (=year 33=253/2 B.C.) above Θ. *Svoronos* 777. *B.M.C. 6.* 33, 117-18 .. .. £175

7775 — — of *Joppa.* Similar, but in *rev.* field to l., ΙΟΠΙ; and to r., regnal date ΚΙ in mono-gram form (=year 27 =259/8 B.C.). *Svoronos* 796. *B.M.C. 6.* 34, 126-7 .. £250

7776 — — of *Gaza.* Similar, but in *rev.* field to l., ΓΑ monogram; and to r., regnal date ΚΕ as 7773. *Svoronos* 822. *B.M.C. 6.* 35, 135 .. .. £250

7777 — — Veiled hd. of Arsinoe II r., wearing stephane, sceptre behind head visible above. ℞. ΑΡΣΙΝΟΗΣ ΦΙΛΑΔΕΛΦΟΥ. Eagle stg. l. on thunderbolt; Χ between legs. *Svoronos* 410. *B.M.C. 6.* 43, 7 .. .. £750

Ptolemy II, Philadelphos *continued*

7778 — Æ *drachm* (*c.* 3·5 gm.).   As 7769, but on *rev.* the eagle's wings are open, and with Θ instead of Y between its legs.   *Svoronos* 570   ..   ..   £140

7779 — Æ 28.   Laur. hd. of Zeus r.   R. ΠΤΟΛΕΜΑΙΟΥ ΒΑΣΙΛΕΩΣ.   Eagle stg. l. on thunderbolt, wings open; in field to l., ΣΩ monogram above shield; between eagle's legs, ι.   *Svoronos* 576.   *B.M.C. 6.* 25, 15-16   ..   ..   £18

7780 — Æ 22.   Hd. of Alexander r., clad in elephant's skin and aegis.   R. ΠΤΟΛΕΜΑΙΟΥ ΒΑΣΙΛΕΩΣ.   Eagle stg. l. on thunderbolt; in field to l., ΔΙ above ear of corn.   *Svoronos* 382.   *B.M.C. 6.* 52, 54   ..   ..   £14

7781 — Æ 17.   Veiled hd. of Arsinoe II r., wearing stephane.   R. ΠΤΟΛΕΜΑΙΟΥ ΒΑΣΙΛΕΩΣ.   Eagle stg. l. on thunderbolt, wings open; in field to l., ΧΑ monogram.   *Svoronos* 346.   *B.M.C. 6.* 61, 20   ..   ..   £20

7782 — Æ 46.   Diad. hd. of Zeus Ammon r.   R. ΒΑΣΙΛΕΩΣ ΠΤΟΛΕΜΑΙΟΥ.   Eagle stg. l. on thunderbolt, looking back, wings open.   *Svoronos* 412.   *B.M.C. 6.* 37, 159-63   £26

7783 — Æ 42.   *Obv.* Similar.   R. ΠΤΟΛΕΜΑΙΟΥ ΒΑΣΙΛΕΩΣ.   Two eagles stg. l. on thunderbolt; Θ between the legs of eagle on l.   *Svoronos* 463.   *B.M.C. 6.* 49, 29-30..   ..   £30

7784 — — As last, but with double cornucopiae projecting behind hd. of the eagle on r., and without the Θ.   *Svoronos* 758   ..   ..   £32

7785 — Æ 36.   Diad. hd. of Zeus Ammon r.   R. ΠΤΟΛΕΜΑΙΟΥ ΒΑΣΙΛΕΩΣ.   Eagle stg. l. on thunderbolt, wings open; between legs, Y.   *Svoronos* 509.   *B.M.C. 6.* 32, 105   £20

7786 — Æ 29.   *Obv.* Similar.   R. ΠΤΟΛΕΜΑΙΟΥ ΒΑΣΙΛΕΩΣ.   Eagle stg. l. on thunderbolt; in field to l., club.   *Svoronos* 707.   *B.M.C. 6.* 53, 67   ..   ..   £17

7787 — Æ 23. As last, but with tripod instead of club in *rev.* field to l. *Svoronos* 791.
B.M.C. 6. 54, 75-6 .. .. £13

7787A — Æ 22. Diad. hd. of Ptolemy I r., wearing aegis. Ŗ. ΒΑΣΙΛΕΩΣ ΠΤΟΛΕΜΑΙΟΥ.
Hd. of Libya r., hair bound with tainia; beneath chin, small double cornucopiae. *Svoronos* 855. B.M.C. 6. 39, 17-18 .. .. £15
This, and no. 7788A *below, were struck in Kyrenaica.*

7788 — Æ 16. As 7785, but with Δ instead of Y between eagle's legs. *Svoronos* 442. B.M.C. 6. 57, 122 .. .. £8

7788A — Æ 14. As 7787A. *Svoronos* 867. B.M.C. 6. 39, 19 .. .. .. £9

7789   7790

7789 **Ptolemy III, Euergetes,** 246-221 B.C. (son of Ptolemy II by his first wife, Euergetes was an energetic ruler under whom the Ptolemaic kingdom reached its apogee as an international power. Early in his reign he invaded the Seleukid empire to avenge the murder of his sister Berenike, widow of Antiochos II. After penetrating as far as Media he was obliged to withdraw because of trouble in Egypt, where his wife **Berenike II** was ruling in his absence. He was also active in the Aegean area and on his death, in 221 B.C., he bequeathed to his successor a strong, secure and peaceful realm which had now prospered for more than a century under the wise rule of three generations of the Ptolemaic family). *N oktadrachm* (*c.* 27·8 gm.). Conjoined busts r. of Ptolemy II, diad. and dr., and Arsinoe II, diad. and veiled; above, ΑΔΕΛΦΩΝ; behind, shield. Ŗ. Conjoined busts r. of Ptolemy I, diad. and wearing aegis, and Berenike I, diad. and veiled; above, ΘΕΩΝ. *Svoronos* 603. *Principal Coins,* V.A.21 .. .. £2,750
The introduction of this remarkable type has sometimes been attributed to Ptolemy II. Most, if not all, specimens would seem to belong to the reign of Ptolemy III, though a few may be later.

7790 — *N tetradrachm* (*c.* 13·9 gm.). Similar. *Svoronos* 604. B.M.C. 6. 40, 4-5 £1,400

7791 — *N didrachm* (*c.* 6·95 gm.). Similar. *Svoronos* 605 .. .. .. £900

7792 — *N drachm* (*c.* 3·45 gm.). Similar. *Svoronos* 606 .. .. .. £600

7793 — *N dekadrachm* (Attic standard, *c.* 42·8 gm.). Veiled and diad. bust of Berenike II r. Ŗ. ΒΕΡΕΝΙΚΗΣ ΒΑΣΙΛΙΣΣΗΣ. Cornucopiae, bound with fillet, between two stars; in lower field, Ε. *Svoronos* 972 .. .. £10,000
The extensive issues in the name of Berenike II belong probably to the period of her husband's absence on campaign in Seleukid territory, 246-241 B.C.

7794 — *N pentadrachm* (Attic standard, *c.* 21·4 gm.). Similar. *Svoronos* 973 .. £6,000

7795 — *N* 2½ *drachm* (Attic standard, 10·7 gm.). Similar, but without the Ε in *rev.* field. *Svoronos* 979. B.M.C. 6. 59, 3 .. .. £3,000

7796 — *N drachm* (Attic standard, *c.* 4·3 gm.). As last. *Svoronos* 980 .. .. £1,600

Ptolemy III, Euergetes *continued*

7797 — *N hemidrachm* (Attic standard, *c.* 2·15 gm.).   As 7795.   *Svoronos* 981.   *B.M.C.* 6.
59, 4   ..   ..   £750

7798 — *N trihemiobol* (Attic standard, *c.* 1·07 gm.).   As 7795.   *Svoronos* 982.   *B.M.C.* 6.
60, 5-6   ..   ..   £350

7799 — *N oktadrachm* (*c.* 27·75 gm.) of *Ephesos.*   Similar to 7793, but without the two stars
and the E on *rev.*, and with bee in field to l.   *Svoronos* 899.   *B.M.C. 6.* 59, 1   ..   £7,500

7800 — Æ *dodekadrachm* (Attic standard, *c.* 51·6 gm.).   Veiled and diad. bust of Berenike II
r.   ℞. ΒΕΡΕΝΙΚΗΣ ΒΑΣΙΛΙΣΣΗΣ.   Cornucopiae, bound with fillet, between caps of the
Dioskouroi.   *Svoronos* 988   ..   ..   £9,000

7801 — Æ *pentadrachm* (Attic standard, *c.* 21 gm.).   Similar.   *Svoronos* 989.   *B.M.C.* 6.
60, 7   ..   ..   £3,500
7802 — Æ 2½ *drachm* (Attic standard, *c.* 10·2 gm.).   Similar.   *Svoronos* 990   ..   £1,400

7803 — Æ *dekadrachm* (*c.* 35 gm.).   Veiled hd. of Arsinoe II r., wearing stephane, sceptre
behind head visible above; behind, ΘΘ.   ℞. ΑΡΣΙΝΟΗΣ ΦΙΛΑΔΕΛΦΟΥ.   Double cornucopiae, bound with fillet.   *Svoronos* 943.   *B.M.C. 6.* 44, 23   ..   ..   ..   £1,000
    This is a continuation of the series inaugurated by Ptolemy II (see no. 7770 above).
According to Svoronos the specimens with double letters on obverse were struck under Ptolemy
III, the letters again representing annual sequence marks.

7804 — Æ *tetradrachm* (*c.* 14·2 gm.). Youthful bust of Ptolemy III r., diad. and wearing lion's skin knotted at neck. ℞. ΠΤΟΛΕΜΑΙΟΥ ΒΑΣΙΛΕΩΣ. Eagle stg. l. on thunderbolt. *Svoronos* 916. *B.M.C. 6.* 47, 14 .. .. £600

7805 — — Diad. and dr. bust of Ptolemy III r., with mature features. ℞. As last. *Svoronos* 996 .. .. £600

7806 — — Diad. hd. of Ptolemy I r., wearing aegis. ℞. ΠΤΟΛΕΜΑΙΟΥ ΣΩΤΗΡΟΣ. Eagle stg. l. on thunderbolt; in field to l., cornucopiae. *Svoronos* 1001. *B.M.C. 6.* 54, 83 £150

7807 7812

7807 — — Similar, but without cornucopiae on *rev.*, and with date numeral ΠΒ (=year 82= 230/29 B.C.) in ex. *Svoronos* 1103. *B.M.C. 6.* 101, 12 .. .. .. £175
The coins of this series appear to be dated according to an era of Ptolemy I commencing in 311 *B.C.*

7808 — — As last, but the date numeral ΠΗ (=year 88=224/3 B.C.) is in *rev.* field to l. *Svoronos* 1110. *B.M.C. 6.* 102, 16 .. .. £175

7809 — — of *Tyre*. Diad. hd. of Ptolemy I r., wearing aegis. ℞. ΠΤΟΛΕΜΑΙΟΥ ΣΩΤΗΡΟΣ. Eagle stg. l. on thunderbolt; in field to l., ΤΥΡ monogram above club; to r., regnal date Γ (=year 3=244/3 B.C.) above I; between eagle's legs, Θ. *Svoronos* 1016. *B.M.C. 6.* 48, 22 .. .. £175

7810 — — of *Sidon*. Similar, but in *rev.* field to l., ΣΙ / ΙΗ; and to r., regnal date Δ (=year 4=243/2 B.C.) above ΗΛ monogram; nothing between eagle's legs. *Svoronos* 1029. *B.M.C. 6.* 48, 20 .. .. £175

7811 — — of *Ptolemais*. As last, but in *rev.* field to l., ΠΤ monogram / ΜΕ monogram; and to r., regnal date Β (=year 2 = 245/4 B.C.) above Α. *Svoronos* 1035. *B.M.C. 6.* 49, 25 £200

7812 — — of *Joppa*. As last, but in *rev.* field to l., ΙΟΠ / ΗΡ monogram; and to r., regnal date Ε (=year 5 =242/1 B.C.) above Θ. *Svoronos* 1043. *B.M.C. 6.* 49, 27 .. £250

7813 — — of *Gaza*. As last, but in *rev.* field to l., ΓΑ monogram / ΑΓΝ monogram; and to r., regnal date Β (as 7811) above I. *Svoronos* 1045. *B.M.C. 6.* 49, 28 .. .. £250

7814 — Æ 42. Diad. hd. of Zeus Ammon r. ℞. ΠΤΟΛΕΜΑΙΟΥ ΒΑΣΙΛΕΩΣ. Eagle stg. l. on thunderbolt; in field to l., cornucopiae; between eagle's legs, ΧΡ monogram. *Svoronos* 964. *B.M.C. 6.* 55, 87-8 .. .. £25

Ptolemy III, Euergetes *continued*

7815 — Æ 38. *Obv.* Similar. ℞. ΠΤΟΛΕΜΑΙΟΥ ΒΑΣΙΛΕΩΣ. Eagle stg. l. on thunderbolt, looking back at cornucopiae on l. wing; between eagle's legs, ε. *Svoronos* 974. *B.M.C. 6.* 66, 38 .. .. £22

7816 — Æ 35. *Obv.* Similar. ℞. ΠΤΟΛΕΜΑΙΟΥ ΒΑΣΙΛΕΩΣ. Eagle stg. l. on thunderbolt, cornucopiae on l. wing; in field to l., large club; between eagle's legs, Π. *Svoronos* 1059. *B.M.C. 6.* 73, 59 .. .. £24

7817 — — As 7814. *Svoronos* 965. *B.M.C. 6.* 55, 89 .. .. £20

7818 — Æ 28. Diad. hd. of Zeus Ammon r. ℞. ΠΤΟΛΕΜΑΙΟΥ ΒΑΣΙΛΕΩΣ. Club, bound with fillet. *Svoronos* 1046 .. .. £35

7819 — Æ 25. Hd. of Alexander r., clad in elephant's skin and aegis. ℞. As 7815. *Svoronos* 976. *B.M.C. 6.* 66, 41-2 .. .. £14

7820   7823

7820 — Æ 23. Diad. hd. of Zeus Ammon r. ℞. ΠΤΟΛΕΜΑΙΟΥ ΒΑΣΙΛΕΩΣ. Cultus-statue of Aphrodite stg. facing on prow. *Svoronos* 1006. *B.M.C. 6.* 52, 59 .. .. £24

7821 — Æ 21. ΒΕΡΕΝΙΚΗΣ ΒΑΣΙΛΙΣΣΗΣ. Diad. bust of Berenike II r. ℞. ΒΑΣΙΛΕΩΣ ΠΤΟΛΕ-ΜΑΙΟΥ. Cornucopiae, bound with fillet; on l., club; on r., eagle stg. l. *Svoronos* 1047. *B.M.C. 6.* 61, 16 .. .. £30

7822 — — *Obv.* Similar. ℞. ΠΤΟΛΕΜΑΙΟΥ ΒΑΣΙΛΕΩΣ. Eagle stg. l. on thunderbolt. *Svoronos* 1055. *B.M.C. 6.* 61, 17-18 .. .. £26

7823 — Æ 20. Laur. bust of Ptolemy III r., wearing aegis. ℞. As last; in field to r., cornu-copiae. *Svoronos* 1000. *B.M.C. 6.* 56, 101 .. .. £20

7824 — Æ 17. As 7820. *Svoronos* 1008. *B.M.C. 6.* 52, 61 .. .. .. £12

7825 **Ptolemy IV, Philopator,** 221-204 B.C. (son of Ptolemy III and Berenike II, Ptolemy IV lacked his father's strength of character and was content to leave affairs of state in the hands of the unscrupulous minister Sosibios. Most of the king's time was spent in wild self-indulgences and drunken orgies, though he did achieve one remarkable victory over the invading army of Antiochos III of Syria. He died at the age of forty, leaving only an infant son to succeed him, the child of his sister-wife **Arsinoe III**). *N oktadrachm* (*c.* 27·8 gm.). Rad. bust of Ptolemy III r., wearing aegis, trident over l. shoulder. ℞. ΠΤΟΛΕΜΑΙΟΥ ΒΑΣΙΛΕΩΣ. Radiate cornucopiae, bound with fillet; beneath, ΔΙ. *Svoronos* 1117. *B.M.C. 6.* 56, 103-4 .. .. £3,500

7826 — — Veiled and diad. bust of Berenike II r. ℞. ΒΕΡΕΝΙΚΗΣ ΒΑΣΙΛΙΣΣΗΣ. Cornu-copiae, bound with fillet. *Svoronos* 1113 .. .. £5,000

7827   7828

7827 — — Diad. and dr. bust of Ptolemy IV r. Ŗ. ΠΤΟΛΕΜΑΙΟΥ ΦΙΛΟΠΑΤΟΡΟΣ. Eagle stg.
r. on thunderbolt; in field to r., ΠΥΡΕ monogram. *Svoronos* 1139. *B.M.C. 6.* 65, 33-4
£7,500

7828 — — Dr. bust of Arsinoe III r., wearing stephane, sceptre behind head visible above.
Ŗ. ΦΙΛΟΠΑΤΟΡΟΣ ΑΡΣΙΝΟΗΣ. Cornucopiae, bound with fillet; above, star. *Svoronos*
1159. *B.M.C. 6.* 67, 1-2 .. .. £10,000

7829 — Ņ *tetradrachm* (*c.* 13·9 gm.). As 7825. *Svoronos* 1118. *B.M.C. 6.* 56, 105
£1,750

7830 — Ņ *drachm* (*c.* 3·1 gm.). As 7825. *Svoronos* 1119 .. .. £750

7831 — Ņ *hemidrachm* (*c.* 1·55 gm.). As 7826, but the legend on *rev.* reads ΒΑΣΙΛΙΣΣΗΣ
ΒΕΡΕΝΙΚΗΣ. *Svoronos* 983. *B.M.C. 6.* 60, 15 .. .. £550

7832 — Ŗ *dekadrachm* (*c.* 35·5 gm.). As 7826. *Svoronos* 1114. *B.M.C. 6.* 59, 2 £6,500

7833 — Ŗ *tetradrachm* (*c.* 14·2 gm.). As 7826. *Svoronos* 1115 .. .. .. £1,250

7834   7837

7834 — — Conjoined dr. busts r. of Sarapis, laur., and Isis, wreathed with corn; the god is
surmounted by small cap of Osiris, the goddess by globe and horns. Ŗ. ΠΤΟΛΕΜΑΙΟΥ
ΒΑΣΙΛΕΩΣ. Eagle stg. l. on thunderbolt, looking back at cornucopiae on r. wing; between
eagle's legs, ΔΙ. *Svoronos* 1124. *B.M.C. 6.* 79, 7-8 .. .. £450
Ptolemy IV is known to have been closely associated with the worship of Sarapis and Isis.

7835 — — Diad. hd. of Ptolemy I r., wearing aegis. Ŗ. ΠΤΟΛΕΜΑΙΟΥ ΣΩΤΗΡΟΣ. Eagle stg. l.
on thunderbolt; in field to l., ΔΙ. *Svoronos* 1121. *B.M.C. 6.* 65, 26 .. .. £175

7836 — — Similar, but in *rev.* field to l., date numeral ꟻΒ (=year 92 =220/19 B.C.). *Svoronos*
1208 .. .. £175
*This is a continuation of the series inaugurated by Ptolemy III, with dates according to an
era of Ptolemy I commencing in 311 B.C. See nos. 7807-8 above.*

7837 — — of *Tyre*. Similar, but in *rev.* field to l., ΤΥΡ monogram above club; and to r.,
Ω / Σ. *Svoronos* 1180. *B.M.C. 6.* 64, 25 .. .. £225
*The ΣΩ appearing on this, and other coins of Phoenician and Palestinian mintage, probably
refers to Sosibios, the chief minister of Ptolemy IV.*

7838   7840

Ptolemy IV, Philopator *continued*

7838 — — — Diad. and dr. bust of Ptolemy IV r. ℞. ΠΤΟΛΕΜΑΙΟΥ ΦΙΛΟΠΑΤΟΡΟΣ. As last; between eagle's legs, ΛΣ monogram. *Svoronos* 1178. *B.M.C. 6.* 64, 24 .. £600

7839 — — of *Sidon. Obv.* As last. ℞. ΠΤΟΛΕΜΑΙΟΥ ΒΑΣΙΛΕΩΣ. Eagle stg. l. on thunderbolt; in field to l., ΣΩ; between eagle's legs, ΣΙ. *Svoronos* 1185. *B.M.C. 6.* 64, 23 .. £600

7840 — Æ didrachm (*c.* 7 gm.). Diad. hd. of Ptolemy I r., wearing aegis. ℞. ΠΤΟΛΕΜΑΙΟΥ ΒΑΣΙΛΕΩΣ. Eagle stg. l. on thunderbolt inscribed ΡΒ (=year 102 =210/09 B.C.). *Svoronos* 1210. *B.M.C. 6.* 102, 20 .. .. £90

These are dated according to an era commencing in 311 *B.C.*, like the tetradrachms above (*see no.* 7836) which they eventually superseded. The series of didrachms extended into the next reign—*see no.* 7873 below.

7841 — Æ 42. Diad. hd. of Zeus Ammon r. ℞. ΠΤΟΛΕΜΑΙΟΥ ΒΑΣΙΛΕΩΣ. Eagle stg. l. on thunderbolt, ΔΙ between its legs; in field to l., cornucopiae. *Svoronos* 1125. *B.M.C. 6.* 57, 108 .. .. £25

7842 — Æ 38. *Obv.* Similar. ℞. ΠΤΟΛΕΜΑΙΟΥ ΒΑΣΙΛΕΩΣ. Eagle stg. l. on thunderbolt, looking back, wings open; between legs, ΣΕ. *Svoronos* 1148. *B.M.C. 6.* 75, 73 £20

7843 — Æ 36. *Obv.* Similar. ℞. ΠΤΟΛΕΜΑΙΟΥ ΒΑΣΙΛΕΩΣ. Eagle stg. l. on thunderbolt, wings open, cornucopiae on l. wing; between legs, Λ. *Svoronos* 1167. *B.M.C. 6.* 66, 43 £20

7844 — Æ 33. Laur. hd. of Zeus r. ℞. ΠΤΟΛΕΜΑΙΟΥ ΒΑΣΙΛΕΩΣ. Eagle stg. l. on thunderbolt, looking back at cornucopiae on l. wing; between legs, Λ. *Svoronos* 1168. *B.M.C. 6.* 66, 39 .. .. £18

7845 — Æ 30. *Obv.* As 7841. ℞. ΠΤΟΛΕΜΑΙΟΥ ΦΙΛΟΠΑΤΟΡΟΣ. Eagle stg. l. on thunderbolt; in field to l., ΠΑΡ monogram; to r., ΤΥΡ (=mint of *Tyre*). *Svoronos* 1182 .. £35

7846 — Æ 26. Diad. hd. of Ptolemy I r., wearing aegis. ℞. ΒΑΣΙΛΕΩΣ ΠΤΟΛΕΜΑΙΟΥ. Hd. of Libya r., hair bound with tainia; behind, branch; before, double cornucopiae; beneath, ΣΕ. *Svoronos* 1152. *B.M.C. 6.* 76, 89 .. .. £16

Struck in Kyrenaica.

7847 — — Conjoined dr. busts r. of Apollo, laur., and Artemis, wearing stephane; bow and quiver behind Apollo's shoulder. ℞. ΒΑΣΙΛΕΩΣ ΠΤΟΛΕΜΑΙΟΥ. Diad. hd. of Ptolemy I r., wearing aegis. *Svoronos* 1137. *B.M.C. 6.* 79, 13 .. .. £30

7848   7851

7848 — Æ 23. Hd. of Isis r., hair in formal curls and bound with corn. ℞. ΠΤΟΛΕΜΑΙΟΥ ΒΑΣΙΛΕΩΣ. Eagle stg. l. on thunderbolt, looking back at cornucopiae on r. wing. *Svoronos* 1154. *B.M.C. 6.* 79, 9 ..   ..   £18

7849 — Æ 18. Young male bust r., helmeted and dr. ℞. ΠΤΟΛΕΜΑΙΟΥ ΒΑΣΙΛΕΩΣ. Eagle stg. l. on thunderbolt; cornucopiae on l. wing. *Svoronos* 1155. *B.M.C. 6.* 69, 11 £16

7850 — Æ 14. Hd. of Arsinoe III r., wearing stephane. ℞. ΠΤΟΛΕΜΑΙΟΥ ΒΑΣΙΛΕΩΣ. Double cornucopiae, bound with fillet. *Svoronos* 1160. *B.M.C. 6.* 67, 3 ..   ..   £15

7851 **Ptolemy V, Epiphanes,** 204-180 B.C. (son of Ptolemy IV and Arsinoe III, Ptolemy V was only five years old when his father died. For many years the government was in the hands of unscrupulous and incompetent ministers, and much of the Egyptian overseas empire was lost at this time. The young king was crowned at Memphis in 197 B.C. The famous Rosetta Stone, which provided the key to the decipherment of Egyptian hieroglyphics, was inscribed at the time of this coronation. In 193 B.C. Ptolemy married **Cleopatra I,** daughter of Antiochos III of Syria, and thirteen years later he died at the age of twenty-nine). N *oktadrachm* (c. 27·8 gm.). Rad. and dr. bust of Ptolemy V r., spear over l. shoulder. ℞. ΠΤΟΛΕΜΑΙΟΥ ΒΑΣΙΛΕΩΣ. Radiate cornucopiae, bound with fillet, between two stars; in lower field, ΠΑΚ monogram. *Svoronos* 1257. *B.M.C. 6.* 72, 50 ..   ..   £7,500

7852   7856

7852 — — Diad. and dr. bust of Ptolemy V r. ℞. ΠΤΟΛΕΜΑΙΟΥ ΒΑΣΙΛΕΩΣ. Eagle stg. l. on thunderbolt; in field to l., Θ; between eagle's legs, ΝΙ. *Svoronos* 1281. *B.M.C. 6.* 74, 62 £5,000

7853 — — Dr. bust of Arsinoe III r., wearing stephane, sceptre over l. shoulder. ℞. ΦΙΛΟΠΑΤΟΡΟΣ ΑΡΣΙΝΟΗΣ. Cornucopiae, bound with fillet; above, star; in field to l., ΝΙ. *Svoronos* 1269 ..   ..   £10,000

7854 — of *Paphos.* Veiled bust of Arsinoe II r., wearing stephane, sceptre behind head visible above. ℞. ΑΡΣΙΝΟΗΣ ΦΙΛΑΔΕΛΦΟΥ. Double cornucopiae, bound with fillet; beneath, Π; in field to r., regnal date ΛΙΓ (= year 13 = 192/1 B.C.). *Svoronos* 1319 £3,500

7855 — Æ *oktadrachm* (c. 28·75 gm.). Diad. hd. of Ptolemy I r., wearing aegis. ℞. ΠΤΟΛΕΜΑΙΟΥ ΒΑΣΙΛΕΩΣ. Eagle stg. l. on thunderbolt; in field to l., star. *Svoronos* 1230 £4,000

7856 — Æ *tetradrachm* (c. 14·2 gm.). Similar, but without the star in *rev.* field. *Svoronos* 1231. *B.M.C. 6.* 100, 9 ..   ..   £125

7857 — — *Obv.* Similar. ℞. ΠΤΟΛΕΜΑΙΟΥ ΣΩΤΗΡΟΣ. Eagle stg. l. on thunderbolt; in field to l., ΜΑΡΚ monogram; to r., spear-head. *Svoronos* 1250. *B.M.C. 6.* 73, 53 £200

Ptolemy V, Epiphanes *continued*

7858 — — As 7855, but with ΔH monogram instead of star in *rev.* field to l.   *Svoronos* 1261
B.M.C. 6. 73, 61 .. .. £175

7859 — — Similar, but with club instead of monogram in *rev.* field to l.   *Svoronos* 1267
£175

7860   7866

7860 — — of *Cyprus*. Diad. hd. of Ptolemy I r., wearing aegis. ℞. ΠΤΟΛΕΜΑΙΟΥ ΒΑΣΙΛΕΩΣ.
Eagle stg. l. on thunderbolt; in field to l., ΠΟ / ΑΡ; to r., ΑΠ. *Svoronos* 1305. B.M.C. 6.
68, 2 .. .. £150
    *The letters in reverse field to left probably refer to Polykrates of Argos, who was viceroy
of Cyprus in the early part of the reign. Later, he was recalled to Egypt to take command of
the army, and eventually became chief minister of Ptolemy V.*

7861 — — of *Paphos*. Similar, but in *rev.* field to l., regnal date LE (=year 5 = 200/199 B.C.);
and to r., Π. *Svoronos* 1310. B.M.C. 6. 68, 5 .. .. £125

7862 — — of *Salamis*. Similar, but in *rev.* field to l., regnal date LIΘ (=year 19 = 186/5 B.C.);
and to r., ΣΑ. *Svoronos* 1342. B.M.C. 6. 70, 26 .. .. £125

7863 — — of *Kition*. Similar, but in *rev.* field to l., regnal date LI (=year 7 = 198/7 B.C.);
and to r., ΚΙ. *Svoronos* 1355. B.M.C. 6. 71, 43 .. .. £140

7864 — — of *Amathus*. Similar, but in *rev.* field to l., head-dress of Isis and regnal date LΑ
(=year 1 = 204/3 B.C.); and to r., ΑΜΑΘ monogram. *Svoronos* 1372. B.M.C. 6. 71, 37
£160

7865 — — Diad. and dr. bust of Ptolemy V r. ℞. ΠΤΟΛΕΜΑΙΟΥ ΕΠΙΦΑΝΟΥΣ. Winged
thunderbolt, between two stars in upper field; in lower field to l., ΜΑΡ monogram; to r.,
spear-head. *Svoronos* 1249 .. .. £1,250

7866 — — — ℞. As 7858. *Svoronos* 1260. B.M.C. 6. 73, 60 .. .. .. £450

7867 — — — ℞. As 7852. *Svoronos* 1282 .. .. £450

7868 — — of *Berytos*. Diad. and dr. bust of Ptolemy V r. ℞. ΠΤΟΛΕΜΑΙΟΥ ΒΑΣΙΛΕΩΣ.
Eagle stg. l. on thunderbolt; in field to l., ΒΗ monogram and trident combined; between
eagle's legs, ΝΙ. *Svoronos* 1285. B.M.C. 6. 72, 49 .. .. .. £500

7869 — — of *Sidon*. Similar, but in *rev.* field to l., Σ. *Svoronos* 1292 .. .. £500

7870 — — of *Tyre*. Similar, but in *rev.* field to l., ΤΥΡ monogram above club; the ΝΙ is in
field to r.; ΔΙ between eagle's legs. *Svoronos* 1297 .. .. .. £500

7871   7873

7871 — — of *Tripolis*. As 7868, but in *rev.* field to l., ΤΡ monogram and branch combined.
Svoronos 1296. B.M.C. 6. 72, 52.. .. .. £500

7872 — — of *Joppa*. *Obv*. As 7868. ℞. ΠΤΟΛΕΜΑΙΟΥ ΒΑΣΙΛΕΩΣ. Eagle stg. l. on thunderbolt; in field to l., ΙΟΠ monogram; to r., regnal date ΛϹ (=year 5 =200 B.C.). *Svoronos* 1291. *B.M.C. 6.* 68, 1 .. .. £550

7873 — Æ *didrachm* (*c.* 7 gm.). Diad. hd. of Ptolemy I r., wearing aegis. ℞. ΠΤΟΛΕΜΑΙΟΥ ΒΑΣΙΛΕΩΣ. Eagle stg. l. on winged thunderbolt; in field, Ρ — ΙΖ (=year 117=195/4 B.C.). *Svoronos* 1227. *B.M.C. 6.* 103, 35 .. .. £90

These are dated according to an era commencing in 311 B.C., and are in continuation of the series of didrachms issued under Ptolemy IV—see no. 7840 above.

7874 — — of *Cyprus*. Dr. bust of Ptolemy V, as Dionysos, r., diad. and wreathed with ivy, thyrsos over shoulder. ℞. ΠΤΟΛΕΜΑΙΟΥ ΒΑΣΙΛΕΩΣ. Eagle stg. l. on thunderbolt, wings open; in field to l., aplustre. *Svoronos* 1795. *B.M.C. 6.* 99, 134 .. £225

7875 — Æ *drachm* (*c.* 3·5 gm.) of *Cyprus*. Similar, but without the aplustre in *rev.* field. *Svoronos* 1794 .. .. £140

7876 — Æ *hemidrachm* (*c.* 1·6 gm.) of *Cyprus*. As last. *Svoronos* 1787 .. .. £80

7877 — — Diad. and dr. bust of Ptolemy V r. ℞. No legend. Eagle stg. l. on thunderbolt. *Svoronos* 1301 *and* 1788 .. .. £90

7878 — Æ 36. Diad. hd. of Zeus Ammon r. ℞. ΠΤΟΛΕΜΑΙΟΥ ΒΑΣΙΛΕΩΣ. Eagle stg. l. on thunderbolt, cornucopiae on l. wing; in field to l., club; between eagle's legs, ΜΑΡ monogram. *Svoronos* 1251. *B.M.C. 6.* 73, 56-8 .. .. £25

7879 — Æ 33. Hd. of Cleopatra I, as Isis, r.; hair in formal curls and wreathed with corn. ℞. ΠΤΟΛΕΜΑΙΟΥ ΒΑΣΙΛΕΩΣ. Eagle stg. l. on thunderbolt, wings open. *Svoronos* 1233. *B.M.C. 6.* 93, 67-8 .. .. £28

7880 — Æ 26. Similar. *Svoronos* 1235. *B.M.C. 6.* 94, 72 .. .. .. £20

7881 — — of *Kyrenaica*. Diad. hd. of Ptolemy I r., wearing aegis. ℞. ΒΑΣΙΛΕΩΣ ΠΤΟΛΕΜΑΙΟΥ. Hd. of Libya r., hair in formal curls and bound with tainia; behind, branch; before, double cornucopiae; beneath, ΜΕ monogram. *Svoronos* 1266. *B.M.C. 6.* 76, 93 £14

7882   7883

7882 — Æ 23 of *Kyrenaica*. Similar, but with club behind hd. of Ptolemy on *obv.*; and without the branch and the monogram on *rev.* *Svoronos* 1268. *B.M.C. 6.* 77, 95 £15

7883 — — Hd. r., clad in elephant's skin. ℞. As 7879. *Svoronos* 1236. *B.M.C. 6.* 98, 128 £17

The head on obv. is probably that of Alexander, though the features are somewhat effeminate and a portrait of Cleopatra I could be intended.

Ptolemy V, Epiphanes *continued*

7884 — Æ 18. Ram stg. r. ℞. ΠΤΟΛΕΜΑΙΟΥ ΒΑΣΙΛΕΩΣ. Eagle stg. l. on thunderbolt; in field to l., star. *Svoronos* 1243 .. .. £20

7885 — Æ 17. *Obv.* As 7879. ℞. ΠΤΟΛΕΜΑΙΟΥ ΒΑΣΙΛΕΩΣ. Eagle stg. l. on thunderbolt, looking back at cornucopiae on l. wing. *Svoronos* 1238 .. .. .. £15

7886 **Ptolemy VI, Philometor,** 180-145 B.C. (the elder of the two sons of Ptolemy V and **Cleopatra I,** Ptolemy VI was only about five years of age at the time of his father's death. Cleopatra acted as regent until her death, in 176 B.C., after which the government was in the hands of two incompetent palace officials, Eulaios and Lenaios, who provoked a conflict with Antiochos IV of Syria. Later, Ptolemy VI was forced to share the throne with his younger brother, but after Roman diplomatic intervention the latter withdrew to rule Kyrenaica. Ptolemy VI married his own sister, **Cleopatra II,** by whom he had a son and two daughters. He died in 145 B.C. of wounds received in battle against Alexander Balas of Syria). *N oktadrachm* (*c.* 27·8 gm.) of *Paphos*. Veiled hd. of Arsinoe II r., wearing stephane, sceptre behind head visible above. ℞. ΑΡΣΙΝΟΗΣ ΦΙΛΑΔΕΛΦΟΥ. Double cornucopiae, bound with fillet; in field to l., regnal date ΛΛΑ (=year 31 = 150/49 B.C.); to r., ΠΑ above dove stg. r. *Svoronos* 1444 .. .. £3,500

7887 — — of *Salamis*. Similar, but in *rev.* field to l., regnal date ΛΙΓ (=year 13 =168/7 B.C.); ΣΑ beneath cornucopiae, nothing in field to r. *Svoronos* 1452 .. .. .. £3,500

7888 — — of *Kition*. As last, but with regnal date ΛΙΔ (=year 14 = 167/6 B.C.); and ΚΙ instead of ΣΑ beneath cornucopiae. *Svoronos* 1470 .. .. £3,500

7888A — — As 7886, but with Κ behind hd. of Arsinoe on *obv.*, and nothing in *rev.* field. *Svoronos* 1498 .. .. £1,750

7888B — — ΚΛΕΟΠΑΤΡΑΣ ΒΑΣΙΛΙΣΣΗΣ. Veiled and diad. bust of Cleopatra I r., sceptre over l. shoulder. ℞. ΠΤΟΛΕΜΑΙΟΥ ΒΑΣΙΛΕΩΣ. Diad. and dr. bust of young Ptolemy VI r., ΠΑ monogram behind. *Leu auction, April*, 1978, *lot* 180 .. .. .. (*Unique*)

7889 — Æ *tetradrachm* (*c.* 14·2 gm.) of *Ptolemais*. Diad. hd. of Ptolemy VI r. ℞. Eagle stg. l. on thunderbolt, corn-stalk in background; on l., ΠΤΟΛΕΜΑΙΟΥ / ΦΙΛΟΜΗΤΟΡΟΣ; on r., ΘΕΟΥ; in field to r., ΠΤΟ monogram; beneath eagle's tail, Α; between legs, regnal date ΛΑΓ retrograde (=year 33=148/7 B.C.). *Svoronos* 1485 .. .. .. £5,000
 This remarkable type is evidence of the authority wielded by Ptolemy VI in Seleukid territory during the closing years of his reign.

7890 — — Diad. hd. of Ptolemy I r., wearing aegis. ℞. ΠΤΟΛΕΜΑΙΟΥ ΒΑΣΙΛΕΩΣ. Eagle stg. l. on thunderbolt; in field to l., Ε. *Svoronos* 1394 .. .. £140
 The letter in rev. field may represent Eulaios, the regent with Lenaios during the early part of the reign. There are also bronzes inscribed ΕΥΛ — *see no.* 7899 *below.*

7891 7893

7891 — — of *Paphos*. Similar, but in *rev.* field to l., regnal date ΛΖ (=year 7 =174/3 B.C.); and to r., ΠΑ. *Svoronos* 1389. *B.M.C.* 6. 80, 14-15 .. .. £120

7892 — — — As last, but with regnal date ΛΚΘ (=year 29 =152/1 B.C.). *Svoronos* 1441. *B.M.C.* 6. 93, 57 .. .. £90

7893 — — of *Salamis*. As 7890, but in *rev.* field to l., regnal date ΛΚΕ (=year 25 =156/5 B.C.); and to r., ΣΑ. *Svoronos* 1457. *B.M.C.* 6. 90, 13 .. .. £100

7894 — — of *Kition*. As 7890, but in *rev.* field to l., regnal date LKΘ (as 7892); and to r., KI. *Svoronos* 1477. *B.M.C. 6.* 85, 52. . .. . £100

7895 — — As 7890, but nothing in *rev.* field. *Svoronos* 1489. *B.M.C. 6.* 100, 3 £125

7896 — Æ *didrachm* (*c.* 7 gm.). As last. *Svoronos* 1490. *B.M.C. 6.* 100, 5 .. £150

7897 — — of *Cyprus*. Dr. bust of Ptolemy VI, as Dionysos, r., diad. and wreathed with ivy, thyrsos over shoulder. ℞. ΠΤΟΛΕΜΑΙΟΥ ΒΑΣΙΛΕΩΣ. Eagle stg. l. on thunderbolt, wings open. *Svoronos* 1798. *B.M.C. 6.* 63, 18 .. .. £200

7898 — Æ 44. Diad. hd. of Zeus Ammon r. ℞. ΠΤΟΛΕΜΑΙΟΥ ΒΑΣΙΛΕΩΣ. Eagle stg. l. on thunderbolt; in field to l., lotus. *Svoronos* 1403. *B.M.C. 6.* 85, 59 .. .. £35

7899 — Æ 31. Similar, but on *rev.* the eagle has a transverse sceptre under its l. wing, and ΕΥΛ between its legs. *Svoronos* 1396. *B.M.C. 6.* 80, 16 .. .. .. £28

The letters beneath eagle represent the name of Eulaios, regent with Lenaios during part of the minority of Ptolemy VI.

7900 — Æ 29. Diad. hd. of Zeus Ammon r. ℞. ΠΤΟΛΕΜΑΙΟΥ ΒΑΣΙΛΕΩΣ. Two eagles stg. l. on thunderbolt, side by side; in field to l., double cornucopiae. *Svoronos* 1424. *B.M.C. 6.* 106, 29 .. .. £14

The two eagles on rev. may be symbolic of the joint rule of Ptolemy VI and his younger brother, 170-164 *B.C.*

7901 — Æ 21. Similar, but with *single* cornucopiae in *rev.* field to l. *Svoronos* 1426. *B.M.C. 6.* 106, 32-4 .. .. £8

7902 — Æ 31 of *Paphos*. As 7900, but with inscription ΒΑΣΙΛΙΣΣΗΣ ΚΛΕΟΠΑΤΡΑΣ around hd. of Zeus Ammon on *obv.*; and with ΠΑ monogram between legs of nearer eagle on *rev.* *Svoronos* 1380. *B.M.C. 6.* 106, 20 .. .. £26

The queen named on the obv. of this, and no. 7904 *below, could be Cleopatra I, regent for Ptolemy VI from* 180 *to* 176 *B.C., or her daughter Cleopatra II, sister-wife of Ptolemy VI.*

Ptolemy VI, Philometor *continued*

7903 — Æ 28 of *Paphos*. Hd. of Cleopatra I, as Isis, r., hair in formal curls and wreathed with corn. ℞. ΠΤΟΛΕΜΑΙΟΥ ΒΑΣΙΛΕΩΣ. Eagle stg. l. on thunderbolt, wings open; in field to l., ΠΑ monogram. *Svoronos* 1384. *B.M.C. 6.* 89, 6 .. .. .. £20

7904   7906

7904 — Æ 21 of *Paphos*. ΒΑΣΙΛΙΣΣΗΣ ΚΛΕΟΠΑΤΡΑΣ. Hd. r., clad in elephant's skin. ℞. As last. *Svoronos* 1381. *B.M.C. 6.* 96, 94 .. .. £17

    The head on obv. may be that of Alexander, though the features are effeminate, and the portrait of a queen could be intended. See also the note following no. 7902 above.

7905 — Æ 24. Hd. of bearded Herakles r., clad in lion's skin. ℞. ΠΤΟΛΕΜΑΙΟΥ ΒΑΣΙΛΕΩΣ. Eagle stg. l. on thunderbolt. *Svoronos* 1494. *B.M.C. 6.* 69, 9-10 .. .. £22

7906 — Æ 19. Diad. hd. of Ptolemy VI r. ℞. ΠΤΟΛΕΜΑΙΟΥ ΒΑΣΙΛΕΩΣ. Eagle stg. l. on thunderbolt, wings open; in field to l., dolphin. *Svoronos* 1488. *B.M.C. 6.* 86, 70 £30

    These are usually countermarked with a ΚΡΑ *monogram on obv.*

7907 **Ptolemy VII, Neos Philopator,** 145-144 B.C. (son of Ptolemy VI and Cleopatra II, Ptolemy VII was made joint-ruler by his father shortly before the latter's death in 145 B.C. However, the late king's younger brother, the ruler of Kyrenaica, was determined to claim the succession, and he invaded Egypt forcing his young nephew to share the throne. The following year the unfortunate Ptolemy VII was murdered). Æ *tetradrachm* (*c.* 14·2 gm.) of *Paphos*. Diad. hd. of Ptolemy I r., wearing aegis. ℞. ΠΤΟΛΕΜΑΙΟΥ ΒΑΣΙΛΕΩΣ. Eagle stg. l. on thunderbolt; in field, ΛΑϹ — ΚΑΙ / Α — ΠΑ; *i.e.* regnal year 36 (of Ptolemy VI) and regnal year 1 (of Ptolemy VII)=145 B.C., and mint mark of Paphos. *Svoronos* 1509. *B.M.C. 6., pp.* lxvii-lxviii, *and pl.* XXXII, 9 .. .. £1,250

7908 **Ptolemy VIII, Euergetes,** 145-116 B.C. (the younger brother of Ptolemy VI, with whom he was joint-ruler of Egypt from 170 to 164 B.C. The brothers then quarrelled, and the younger was eventually obliged to withdraw to the Kyrenaica which he ruled until the death of Ptolemy VI in 145 B.C. He then claimed the throne of Egypt, married his sister Cleopatra II, who was also his brother's widow, and did away with the legitimate successor

Ptolemy VII. As Ptolemy VIII he reigned for the following three decades, though he was once temporarily driven from Egypt by Cleopatra II. In 142 B.C. he had taken a second wife—**Cleopatra III,** daughter of Cleopatra II and Ptolemy VI—after which his relations with his first wife were always very strained. He was an unpopular ruler and the Alexandrians nicknamed him 'Physkon'—pot belly). Æ *tetradrachm* (*c.* 14·2 gm.) of *Paphos.* Diad. hd. of Ptolemy I r., wearing aegis. ℞. ΠΤΟΛΕΜΑΙΟΥ ΒΑΣΙΛΕΩΣ. Eagle stg. l. on thunderbolt; in field to l., regnal date ΛΛΘ (=year 39 =132/1 B.C.); to r., ΠΑ. *Svoronos* 1513. *B.M.C. 6.* 93, 66 .. .. £80

Ptolemy VIII reckoned his regnal years from his original proclamation in 170 B.C. In the case of tetradrachms bearing regnal dates from 26 (ΚϹ) to 36 (ΛϹ) it is, therefore, impossible to differentiate between the issues of the two brothers Ptolemy VI and Ptolemy VIII.

7909 — — — Similar, but with regnal date ΛΝΔ (=year 54 =117/16 B.C.). *Svoronos* 1531. *B.M.C. 6.* 98, 126 .. .. £80

7910   7911

7910 — — of *Salamis.* Similar, but in *rev.* field to l., regnal date ΛΜΔ (=year 44 =127/6 B.C.); and to r., ΣΑ. *Svoronos* 1557. *B.M.C. 6.* 96, 101 .. .. .. £90

7911 — — of *Kition.* Similar, but with thyrsos under eagle's l. wing; and in *rev.* field to l., regnal date ΛΛΖ (=year 37 = 134/3 B.C.); to r., ΚΙ. *Svoronos* 1595. *B.M.C. 6.* 92, 50 £100

7912 — — — As last, but without the thyrsos, and with regnal date ΛΝ (=year 50 = 121/20 B.C.) beneath which, star. *Svoronos* 1612 .. .. £100

7913 — Æ *didrachm* (*c.* 6 gm.) of *Paphos.* Rad. and dr. bust of Ptolemy VIII r. ℞. ΠΤΟΛ-ΕΜΑΙΟΥ ΒΑΣΙΛΕΩΣ. Eagle stg. l. on thunderbolt, sceptre under l. wing; in field to l., ΛΛΓ (=regnal year 33 =138/7 B.C.); to r., ΠΑ. *Svoronos* 1507 .. .. .. £600

7914 — Æ 46. Diad. hd. of Zeus Ammon r. ℞. ΕΥΕΡΓΕΤΟΥ ΒΑΣΙΛΕΩΣ ΠΤΟΛΕΜΑΙΟΥ. Two cornuacopiae, joined at base and bound with fillet; in field to l., Φ. *Svoronos* 1640. *B.M.C. 6.* 98, 132-3 .. .. £100

7915 — Æ 33. *Obv.* Similar. ℞. ΕΥΕΡΓΕΤΟΥ ΒΑΣΙΛΕΩΣ ΠΤΟΛΕΜΑΙΟΥ. Eagle stg. r. on thunderbolt, wings open; in field to r., Κ. *Svoronos* 1649. *B.M.C. 6.* 95, 86 .. £35

7916 — Æ 28. *Obv.* Similar. ℞. ΒΑΣΙΛΕΩΣ ΠΤΟΛΕΜΑΙΟΥ ΕΥΕΡΓΕΤΟΥ. Eagle stg. l. on thunderbolt, wings open; in field to l., Φ. *Svoronos* 1642. *B.M.C. 6.* 94, 80-81 .. £30

7917 — Æ 36. *Obv.* Similar. ℞. ΠΤΟΛΕΜΑΙΟΥ ΒΑΣΙΛΕΩΣ. Eagle stg. l. on thunderbolt, sceptre under l. wing; in field to l., lotus. *Svoronos* 1636. *B.M.C. 6.* 82, 26-7 £26

Ptolemy VIII, Euergetes *continued*

7918 — Æ 30. As last, but without sceptre under eagle's wing, and with crested helmet instead of lotus in *rev.* field to l. *Svoronos* 1635. *B.M.C. 6.* 82, 23-4 .. £24

7919 — Æ 23. Diad. hd. of Zeus Ammon r. ℞. ΠΤΟΛΕΜΑΙΟΥ ΒΑΣΙΛΕΩΣ. Eagle stg. l. on thunderbolt; in field to l., regnal date ΛΚΖ (=year 27 =144/3 B.C.) above lotus. *Svoronos* 1622. *B.M.C. 6.* 85, 61 .. .. £22

7920 — Æ 18 of *Kyrenaica.* Diad. hd. of Ptolemy I r., wearing aegis. ℞. ΒΑΣΙΛΕΩΣ ΠΤΟΛ-ΕΜΑΙΟΥ. Hd. of Libya r., hair in formal curls and bound with tainia; beneath, monogram of ΕΥΕΡΓΕΤΟΥ, and cornucopiae. *Svoronos* 1658 .. .. £16

7921   7923

7921 **Ptolemy IX, Soter,** 116-106 *and* 88-80 B.C. (the elder son of Ptolemy VIII and Cleopatra III, Ptolemy IX was born about 141 B.C. and succeeded his father in 116. His mother favoured her younger son, Alexander, and after a decade of rule Ptolemy IX fled to Cyprus, his place on the Egyptian throne being taken by his brother who reigned as Ptolemy X. Eighteen years later, following the death of Ptolemy X, Ptolemy IX returned to Egypt and occupied his former throne for the last eight years of his life). FIRST REIGN, 116-106 B.C. Æ *tetradrachm* (*c.* 14·2 gm.) of *Paphos.* Diad. hd. of Ptolemy I r., wearing aegis. ℞. ΠΤΟΛΕΜΑΙΟΥ ΒΑΣΙΛΕΩΣ. Eagle stg. l. on thunderbolt; in field to l., regnal date ΛΑ (=year 1 =116/1⁵ B.C.); to r., ΠΑ. *Svoronos* 1659. *B.M.C. 6.* 105, 7 .. .. £75

7922 — — — Similar, but with regnal date ΛΙ (=year 10 = 107/6 B.C.). *Svoronos* 1671. *B.M.C. 6.* 108, 63-4 .. .. £75

7923 — — of *Salamis.* As 7921, but in *rev.* field to l., regnal date ΛΕ (=year 5 = 112/11 B.C.) above club; and to r., ΣΑ. *Svoronos* 1780. *B.M.C. 6.* 111, 10 .. .. £85

7924 — — of *Kition.* As 7921, but in *rev.* field to l., regnal date ΛΒ (=year 2 =115/14 B.C.) above club; and to r., ΚΙ. *Svoronos* 1759. *B.M.C. 6.* 104, 3 .. .. .. £90

7925 — Æ *didrachm* (*c.* 7 gm.) of *Paphos.* As 7921, but with regnal date ΛΓ (=year 3 =114/13 B.C.). *Svoronos* 1664 .. .. £140

7926   7929

7926 — Æ *drachm* (*c.* 3·5 gm.) of *Paphos.* As 7921, but with regnal date ΛΒ (=year 2 =115/14 B.C.). *Svoronos* 1661. *B.M.C. 6.* 105, 11 .. .. £110

7927 — Æ *hemidrachm* (*c.* 1·85 gm.) of *Paphos.* As last. *Svoronos* 1662. *B.M.C. 6.* 105, 12 .. .. £100

7928 — Æ 34. Diad. hd. of Zeus Ammon r. ℞. ΠΤΟΛΕΜΑΙΟΥ ΒΑΣΙΛΕΩΣ. Two eagles stg. l. on thunderbolt, side by side; in field to l., winged thunderbolt. *Svoronos* 1694. *B.M.C. 6.* 114, 68 .. .. £32

7929 — Æ 27. *Obv.* Similar. ℞. ΠΤΟΛΕΜΑΙΟΥ ΒΑΣΙΛΕΩΣ. Eagle stg. l. on thunderbolt; in field to l., star above Δ. *Svoronos* 1706. *B.M.C. 6.* 120, 47 .. .. .. £26

7930 — Æ 18. *Obv.* Similar. ℞. ΠΤΟΛΕΜΑΙΟΥ ΒΑΣΙΛΕΩΣ. Double cornucopiae, bound with fillet, surmounted by two stars; in field, Σ — Ω / Θ — E. *Svoronos* 1718. *B.M.C. 6.* 107, 44 .. .. £17

7931 — Æ 15. *Obv.* Similar. ℞. ΣΩΤΗΡΟΣ ΒΑΣΙΛΕΩΣ ΠΤΟΛ. Eagle stg. l. on thunderbolt, wings open. *Svoronos* 1717 .. .. £15

7932 — Æ 14. *Obv.* Similar. ℞. ΠΤΟΛ. ΒΑΣΙΛ. (or similar abbreviated form). Head-dress of Isis; beneath, ΣΩ. *Svoronos* 1722. *B.M.C. 6.* 107, 49-50 .. .. £15

7933 — Æ 15 of *Kyrenaica.* Diad. hd. of Ptolemy I r., wearing aegis. ℞. ΒΑΣΙΛΕΩΣ ΠΤΟΛ-ΕΜΑΙΟΥ. Hd. of Libya r., hair in formal curls and bound with tainia; beneath, ΣΩ mono-gram. *Svoronos* 1725 .. .. £14

7934   7936

7934 AS KING OF CYPRUS, 101-88 B.C. Æ *tetradrachm* (c. 13·75 gm.) of *Paphos.* Diad. hd. of Ptolemy I r., wearing aegis. ℞. ΠΤΟΛΕΜΑΙΟΥ ΒΑΣΙΛΕΩΣ. Eagle stg. l. on thunder-bolt; in field to l., regnal date ΛΙΗ (=year 18 = 99/8 B.C.); to r., ΠΑ. *Svoronos* 1689. *B.M.C. 6.* 109, 65 .. .. £75

     Ptolemy IX was acknowledged as king of Cyprus by his younger brother in 101 B.C.

7935 — — of *Salamis.* Similar, but in *rev.* field to l., regnal date ΛΚΑ (=year 21 = 96/5 B.C.); and to r., ΣΑ. *Svoronos* 1691. *B.M.C. 6.* 109, 66 .. .. .. £85

7936 SECOND REIGN, 88-80 B.C. Æ *tetradrachm* (c. 14·2 gm.) of *Alexandria.* Diad. hd. of Ptolemy I r., wearing aegis. ℞. ΠΤΟΛΕΜΑΙΟΥ ΒΑΣΙΛΕΩΣ. Eagle stg. l. on thunderbolt; in field to l., regnal date ΛΚΘ (=year 29 =88/7 B.C.); to r., ΠΑ. *Svoronos* 1687. *B.M.C. 6.* 114, 70 .. .. £65

7937 — — — Similar, but with regnal date ΛΛϹ (=year 36 = 81/80 B.C.). *Svoronos* 1688
                                      £65

7938 **Ptolemy X, Alexander,** 106-88 B.C. (the younger son of Ptolemy VIII, and favourite of his mother Cleopatra III, Alexander was appointed governor of Cyprus in 113 B.C., the date from which he later reckoned his regnal years. In 106 B.C. he ousted his elder brother from the throne of Egypt and ruled jointly with his mother until her death five years later. An unpopular king, he was eventually driven from Egypt by his subjects and murdered at sea, in 88 B.C.). JOINT REIGN WITH CLEOPATRA III, 106-101 B.C. Æ *tetradrachm* (c. 14·2 gm.) of *Alexandria.* Diad. hd. of Ptolemy I r., wearing aegis. ℞. ΠΤΟΛΕΜΑΙΟΥ ΒΑΣΙΛΕΩΣ. Eagle stg. l. on thunderbolt; in field to l., regnal dates ΛΙΑ / Η (=year 11 of Cleopatra III, and year 8 of Ptolemy X =106/5 B.C.); to r., ΠΑ. *Svoronos* 1727. *B.M.C. 6.* 112, 18-19 .. .. £65

Ptolemy X, Alexander *continued*

7939 — — — Similar, but with regnal dates LIC / Ir (=years 16 and 13 =101 B.C.).   *Svoronos*
1731. *B.M.C. 6.* 112, 27-8   ..   ..   £65

7940 SOLE REIGN, 101-88 B.C.   Æ *tetradrachm* (*c.* 14·2 gm.) of *Alexandria.* Diad. hd. of
Ptolemy I r., wearing aegis. ℞. ΠΤΟΛΕΜΑΙΟΥ ΒΑΣΙΛΕΩΣ. Eagle stg. l. on thunderbolt;
in field to l., regnal date LIΔ (=year 14 =100/99 B.C.); to r., ΠΑ. *Svoronos* 1674. *B.M.C.*
6. 113, 29   ..   ..   £60

7941 — — — Similar, but with regnal date LIΖ (=year 17 = 97/6 B.C.).   *Svoronos* 1677·
B.M.C. 6. 113, 32   ..   ..   £60

7942 — — — Similar, but with regnal date LKE (=year 25 = 89/8 B.C.).   *Svoronos* 1686
£60

7943 — Æ *drachm* ? (*c.* 2·75 gm.) of *Alexandria.* Similar, but with regnal date LKB (=year
22 =92/1 B.C.).   *Svoronos* 1683   ..   ..   £100

Ptolemy XI, Alexander, 80 B.C. (son of Ptolemy X by his unknown first wife, Ptolemy
XI claimed the Egyptian throne on the death of his uncle in 80 B.C. He was obliged to
marry his stepmother Cleopatra Berenike, daughter of Ptolemy IX, but when he murdered
her just nineteen days after the wedding the Alexandrians were so enraged that they broke
into the palace and killed him. No coinage can be safely attributed to this brief reign).

7944 **Ptolemy XII, Neos Dionysos,** 80-58 *and* 55-51 B.C. (son of Ptolemy IX by an Alexan-
drian Greek concubine, Ptolemy XII had fled to the court of Mithradates VI of Pontos on
his father's death. Having disposed of Ptolemy XI the Alexandrians recalled the illegi-
timate son of their previous king and he ascended the throne as Ptolemy XII. A weak and
dissolute ruler, who displayed a fawning subservience to the Romans, he was given the
derisory title of 'Auletes'—the flute player. In 58 B.C. he was deposed by his subjects,
but managed to regain his throne three years later with Roman assistance. He died in
51 B.C. and was succeeded by his ambitious daughter Cleopatra VII, destined to be the
last of the Ptolemaic rulers of Egypt). FIRST REIGN, 80-58 B.C. Æ *tetradrachm* (*c.*
14·2—11·5 gm., declining as the series progresses), mint of *Alexandria.* Diad. hd. of
Ptolemy I r., wearing aegis. ℞. ΠΤΟΛΕΜΑΙΟΥ ΒΑΣΙΛΕΩΣ. Eagle stg. l. on thunderbolt; in
field to l., regnal date LA (=year 1 = 80/79 B.C.); to r., ΠΑ. *Svoronos* 1847. *B.M.C. 6.*
118, 1   ..   ..   £55

7945   7947

7945 — — Similar, but with regnal date LH (=year 8 =73/2 B.C.).   *Svoronos* 1855. *B.M.C.*
6. 118, 13-14   ..   ..   £50

7946 — — Similar, but with regnal date LKΓ (= year 23 =58 B.C.).   *Svorcnos* 1870. *B.M.C*
6. 120, 45-6 ..   ..   £45

N.B. *For another tetradrachm of Ptolemy XII, with his portrait, see no. 6076 of Askalon.*

7947 SECOND REIGN, 55-51 B.C. *Æ tetradrachm* (*c.* 14·2 gm.) of *Alexandria.* Diad. hd. of
Ptolemy I r., wearing aegis. R. ΠΤΟΛΕΜΑΙΟΥ ΒΑΣΙΛΕΩΣ. Eagle stg. l. on thunderbolt,
palm-branch in background; in field to l., regnal date LKI (=year 27 = 54/3 B.C.) above
head-dress of Isis; to r., ΠΑ. *Svoronos* 1836. *B.M.C. 6.* 116, 27 .. .. £50

7948 — — Similar, but with regnal date LΛ (=year 30 = 51 B.C.). *Svoronos* 1840. *B.M.C.*
6. 117, 37 .. .. £50

7949 — *Æ drachm* (*c.* 3·5 gm.) of *Alexandria.* Diad. hd. of Ptolemy XII r. R. As 7947,
but with regnal date LKH (=year 28 = 53/2 B.C.). *Svoronos* 1838. *B.M.C. 6.* 117, 34
£250

7950 — Æ 24. Diad. hd. of Zeus Ammon r. R. ΠΤΟΛΕΜΑΙΟΥ ΒΑΣΙΛΕΩΣ. Two eagles stg. l.
on thunderbolt, side by side; in field to l., head-dress of Isis above ΔΡ monogram. *Svoronos* 1842. *B.M.C. 6.* 121, 1 .. .. £24

7951 **Cleopatra VII,** 51-30 B.C. (daughter of Ptolemy XII and Cleopatra VI, and the last of
the Ptolemaic dynasty to rule in Egypt. In the early part of her reign she shared her
throne with her brothers **Ptolemy XIII,** 51-47 B.C., and **Ptolemy XIV,** 47-44 B.C. For
the last fourteen years of her reign the co-ruler was Caesarion (**Ptolemy XV**), her own
son by Julius Caesar. The story of her association with Mark Antony is well known
and need not be recounted here. Her suicide in 30 B.C. brought the Ptolemaic dynasty to
an end in Egypt. The country was incorporated into the Roman Empire and was henceforth administered as a private estate of the emperor). *Æ tetradrachm* (*c.* 13 - 14·2 gm.),
mint of *Alexandria.* Diad. hd. of Ptolemy I r., wearing aegis. R. ΠΤΟΛΕΜΑΙΟΥ ΒΑΣΙΛΕΩΣ.
Eagle stg. l. on thunderbolt, palm-branch in background; in field to l., regnal date LB
(=year 2 = 50/49 B.C.) above head-dress of Isis; to r., ΠΑ. *Svoronos* 1817. *B.M.C. 6.*
115, 2 .. .. £50

The metal of these tetradrachms becomes increasingly debased as the series progresses.

7952 7954

7952 — — Similar, but with regnal date LΘ (=year 9 = 43/2 B.C.). *Svoronos* 1823. *B.M.C.*
6. 115, 9 .. .. £45

7953 — — Similar, but with regnal date LKB (=year 22 = 30 B.C.). *Svoronos* 1835. *B.M.C.*
6. 116, 26 .. .. £40

N.B. *For another tetradrachm of Cleopatra, with her portrait, see no. 6077 of Askalon.*

7954 — *Æ drachm* (*c.* 3 gm.) of *Alexandria.* Diad. and dr. bust of Cleopatra VII r. R.
ΚΛΕΟΠΑΤΡΑΣ ΒΑΣΙΛΙΣΣΗΣ. Type as 7951, but with regnal date LS (=year 6 = 46/5 B.C.).
Svoronos 1853. *B.M.C. 6.* 122, 1 .. .. £1,500

Cleopatra VII *continued*

7955   7956

7955 — Æ *80 drachmai* of *Alexandria.*   *Obv.* As last.   ℞. ΚΛΕΟΠΑΤΡΑΣ ΒΑΣΙΛΙΣΣΗΣ.   Eagle
stg. l. on thunderbolt; in field to l., double cornucopiae; to r., mark of value π (=80).
Svoronos 1871.   *B.M.C. 6.* 123, 4-5   ..   ..   £140

     As 480 *bronze drachms were the equivalent of one silver drachm at this time, the* 80
drachmai piece would have circulated as an obol, and the 40 *drachmai as a hemiobol.*

7956 — Æ *40 drachmai* of *Alexandria.*   Similar, but with mark of value M (=40) instead of π
Svoronos 1872.   *B.M.C. 6.* 123, 6-11   ..   ..   £120

7957 — Æ 28 of *Cyprus.*   Diad. and dr. bust of Cleopatra, as Aphrodite, r., sceptre behind
shoulder, holding infant Ptolemy XV, as Eros, in her arms.   ℞. ΚΛΕΟΠΑΤΡΑΣ ΒΑΣΙΛΙΣΣΗΣ.
Two cornuacopiae, joined at base and bound with fillet; ΚΥΠΡ monogram in lower field to
r.   *B.M.C. 6.* 122, 2-3   ..   ..   £300

INDEX

This alphabetical listing includes geographical names (kingdoms, countries, districts, cities, etc.) as well as the personal names of rulers which are shown in italic type for ease of recognition. Names of gods and goddesses, also in italics, are included; the page references in this case being to the detailed notes on deities at the beginning of the Catalogue, not to their appearances on the listed coins.

Where more than one page reference is given the entries are further differentiated thus:

(*A*) following a page number indicates the separate listing of *Archaic* issues for that mint.

A page reference in italic type refers to the *map* on which the exact position of the town may be located.

is. = island.